MUSIC REFERENCE AND RESEARCH MATERIALS

An Annotated Bibliography

Fourth Edition

Vincent H. Duckles
Michael A. Keller

SCHIRMER BOOKS
A Division of Macmillan, Inc.
New York

Collier Macmillan Publishers
London

Schirmer Books
A Division of Macmillan, Inc.
866 Third Avenue, New York, N. Y. 10022

Collier Macmillan Canada, Inc.

Library of Congress Catalog Card Number: 88-18530

Printed in the United States of America

printing number
    4 5 6 7 8 9 10

Library of Congress Cataloging-in-Publication Data
Duckles, Vincent H. (Vincent Harris), 1913–
    Music reference and research materials : an annotated bibliography
/ Vincent H. Duckles, Michael A. Keller.—4th ed.
        p.   cm.
    Includes indexes.
    ISBN 0-02-870390-1
    1. Music—Bibliography.   2. Music—History and criticism—
–Bibliography.   3. Bibliography—Bibliography—Music.   I. Keller,
Michael A.   II. Title.
ML113.D83   1988
016.78—dc19   88-18530
                                                                              CIP
                                                                              MN

Contents

Contents

Introduction to the Fourth Edition

During the long interval between the third and fourth editions of this book, Vincent H. Duckles gathered and evaluated new titles, and wrote annotations for inclusion in the fourth edition. In 1984 he recognized that his declining health would not permit him to complete this edition without assistance and he called upon me, his succesor as Music Librarian at the University of California at Berkeley, to become his coauthor. Duckles died in mid-July of 1985, but had continued to work on *Music Reference and Research Materials* until he was hospitalized a few months before his death. In the short time we worked together, we agreed on some modest innovations, although this edition was completed on the basis of the previous editions, albeit with the substantial mechanical assistance of computers.

Music Reference and Research Materials continues to be a select, not comprehensive, and annotated bibliography of published reference works and research tools concerned with musical topics. It is intended that this work serve the scholar as a bibliogrpahic handbook, a repertory of sources for information covering the broadest expanse of the art of music. Music librarians and general reference librarians should find this classified bibliography helpful in pursuing their dual responsibilities of building and interpreting library collections. However, it is the students of music for whom this book principally was compiled. Long tested in introductory courses in musicology at Berkeley, this edition has benefited also from experiences in similar courses I taught at Cornell and Stanford.

The bibliography itself is an accumulation and synthesis of information, but in the selection of works to be included, it is a critical work. The theoretical basis for the work is evident in part by its organization of the repertory of titles into genres and subjects. The annotations are as much analytical as they are descriptive. The subject index is an interpretation of the contents, item by item.

If the decade of the 1970s was the era of reprinters, the decade of the 1980s has been the era of the makers of reference works. As computers and especially microcomputers become commonplace tools used by more and more of our colleagues, we should expect to see more reference works and research tools compiled and available solely on high technology equipment. None of the several "music processing" systems in some ways analogous to word processing systems were included, because they have not been tested sufficiently in support of musical research. Data base managers abound and these have already begun to assist musicologists in their work, but as these programs are not specifically musical in themselves, they have not been cited. Thousands of traditionally published works with potential for inclusion in this book were examined. Many works cited in earlier editions have been weeded from this one. Because of the great number of new books and articles potentially relevant, those printed after 1986 were not included; works published after this year will be included in the fifth edition. The section "Music for Instruction and Performance" has been reorganized to bring works for like or similar instruments together under their own headings. There is a new section on "Women in Music," although many of the works cited there are duplicated elsewhere in the bibliography. In the chapters "Bibliographies of Music" and "Discographies," jazz and popular music have been separated. There is a new popular music section in the chapter "Bibliographies of Music Literature." Many more names and titles are indexed than in previous editions and there is a new scheme for subject indexing. The divided indexes have been retained in the belief that most readers were best served by them.

As in the previous editions, people too numerous to name individually have provided assistance. A few persons have been so diligent and have contributed so much that we must acknowledge them in this introduction. The fourth edition would not have appeared without the persistence and forbearance of Madeline Duckles and Carol A. Lawrence. Ruth Siebenmorgen, Eva Einstein, and the indefatigable Harriet Nicewonger were of great assistance to Vincent H. Duckles. As the responsibility for completion fell entirely on me, my knowledgeable and energetic assistant at Berkeley, Keith Stetson, became a key figure in the work. Jeffrey Dean and Cynthia Underhill were instrumental in the Berkeley phase of my efforts. Once in New Haven, the Jackson Music Library of Yale University became my principal resource; its staff under Harold Samuel was supportive and helpful. Conrad Jacoby, a Yale student, provided some much-needed assistance at a crucial stage. Again and again the bibliographic resources of the Research Libraries Information Network (or RLIN) came to the rescue. Research for this edition has been based primarily on the collections of the Berkeley and the Yale music libraries, but it became apparent that even these great research collections did not have everything of interest. Inter-library loan and recourse to colleagues helped bring in the needed works. Among the most assiduous of the "foreign correspondents" was Kären Nagy, Music Librarian at Stanford University, but thanks to electronic mail and BITNET, colleagues from North America and Europe assisted me in gathering information for the book as well. Hideo Kaneko, Curator of Yale's East Asia Collection, and Anthony Marr, his colleague, provided substantial assistance with titles in Japanese and Chinese. Diane Perushek, Curator of the Gest Oriental Library and East Asia Collections at Princeton, provided assistance with some Chinese and Japanese titles as well. I am indebted to these and many other kind and generous people who have contributed to the completion of this edition.

Every book, particularly every bibliography, involves compromises of some sort. As in the past, readers with suggestions and criticisms of *Music Reference and Research Materials* are urged to send their comments to me. Assistance of this sort has made each edition a better book, and it is anticipated that the fifth edition will benefit in a comparable way.

Michael A. Keller
Yale University Library
New Haven, Connecticut
Spring, 1988

Introduction to
the Third Edition

Since the second edition of this work appeared in 1967, there have been substantial gains in the area of music reference and research materials, both in quantity and in quality. Quantity is indicated by the fact that this third edition incorporates more than 600 new entries; quality is represented in a number of distinguished new works that have come into existence during the past five years—for example, Barry Brook's *Thematic catalogues in music;* Rita Benton's *Directory of music research libraries,* volumes 2 and 3; and several important additions to the series issued under the auspices of the International Inventory of Musical Sources. The reprint publishers have been increasingly active during the past few years, and their work has restored a great many valuable music reference books to the shelves. A special effort has been made to call these titles to the attention of our readers.

No significant changes have been made in the organization of the work. A new section covering *Music History in Pictures* has been added. New categories treating *Individual Composers* and *Music of Individual Composers* have also been introduced. These sections are far from comprehensive; however, they are intended to call attention to useful types of reference tools that might otherwise be overlooked by the student. In spite of the increased size and scope of this volume, selectivity has remained the rule. Those who look for complete or comprehensive coverage in any category will be disappointed. In some cases the selection has been involuntary, based as it is upon the resources of a particular music research library here at Berkeley. But more often than not the selection has been deliberate, intended to highlight the kinds of questions raised by graduate students in music and to suggest approaches to the solution of their research problems. Over the years I have accumulated an increasing debt to those generous users who have both called my attention to errors and omissions in the text and suggested improvements. They are too numerous to mention individually, but their collective impact on this new edition of *Music Reference and Research Materials* has been considerable.

Vincent Duckles
Berkeley, California
1974

Introduction to
the Second Edition

The plea for corrections and additions that concluded the *Introduction* to the first edition of this work has not gone unheeded. Responses have come from a wide group of music students, teachers, and librarians. The chagrin at having one's oversights pointed out has been more than balanced by the pleasure at finding that this bibliography has been extensively and searchingly used. I am particularly grateful for suggestions made by my own students at the University of California, and to my colleague Daniel Heartz. John Davies, Music Librarian of the British Broadcasting Corporation, London, made many helpful comments, as did Jan La Rue, New York University, Frederick Crane, Louisiana State University, and George Skapski of San Fernando Valley State College. For assistance in the preparation of the manuscript of this edition, I am indebted to Lee Rosen.

Apart from the corrections of old entries and the addition of new, no major changes have been introduced in this edition. A few minor revisions in organization should be noted, however. These include (1) an added section on *Jazz and Popular Music* under *Bibliographies of Music;* (2) the printed and manuscript sources of early music have been combined under one alphabet rather than two; and (3) *Catalogs of Private Collections* have been extracted from the general list of music library catalogs and entered in a section of their own. A substantial number of new book reviews have been added, and much attention has been given to making the *Index* more usable from a subject point of view.

The bibliography of music is an actively growing field. This is reflected not only in the fact that more than 200 new entries have been added to this edition, but also in the high quality of the work that is being done. The International Inventory of Musical Sources has been progressing slowly but surely toward its goal. The publication of the catalogs of major Italian music libraries has been moving ahead under the direction of Claudio Sartori in the series Bibliotheca Musicae. In this country we have the exemplary bibliography of *Instrumental music printed before 1600* by Howard Brown and the long-awaited *Index of Festschriften* by Walter Gerboth. Our control over the materials of popular song has been greatly enhanced by the appearance of Richard Wolfe's bibliography of *Secular music in America, 1801–25* and by the work of James Fudd and Nat. Shapiro. Two new series devoted exclusively to music bibliography are off to a promising start: the Detroit Studies in Music Bibliography and the Music Library Association Index Series.

Vincent Duckles
1966

Introduction to the First Edition

A bibliography can be regarded as the relatively inert by-product of scholarly activity, or it can be treated as an active ingredient in the learning process. The latter perspective has been adopted in this guide to *Music Reference and Research Materials*. While no one but a professional bibliographer may be expected to come for his leisure reading to a list of books, most of us can respond with interest to an organized survey of the literature of a particular field. A bibliography, in fact, offers one of the best means of gaining an over-all impression of a subject area. It throws the essential patterns of a discipline into relief, casting light on what has been accomplished and drawing attention to the shadows where work still needs to be done. This guide has been designed to illuminate the bibliographical resources for musical scholarship. It is, above all, intended to serve a teaching purpose. Implicit in its organization is the concept that bibliography is an approach to knowledge, a way in which the student can progress toward mastery in his chosen field of specialization within the larger dimensions of the field of music. The guide was developed, through a series of editions beginning in 1949, as a text for a graduate seminar entitled "An Introduction to Musical Scholarship" given in the Music Department of the University of California at Berkeley. If its pattern has been determined to some extent by the way in which music bibliography is taught in a specific institution, its structure is still flexible enough to permit other teachers to use it in their own way.

The work is actually intended to fulfill the requirements of two groups: graduate students who need to become acquainted with the resources of musical research, and music reference librarians whose job it is to help others find the information they want. While the needs of the two have much in common, there are points at which their interests diverge. Much more is listed here than will be required for reference services in any but a large music research library, and there is material included which the scholar would rarely need to consult unless he moved outside of the traditional framework of historical musicology.

The present volume is much larger than any of its predecessors, yet it remains a selective list. One limitation in coverage, strictly enforced, is the selection of titles that pertain directly or exclusively to music. This criterion eliminates a great deal of valuable reference material, particularly important in areas that lie on the borderline between musicology and other disciplines: liturgics, the theater arts, literature, the dance, etc. No musicologist can afford to neglect such general reference tools as the *Encyclopedia of Religion and Ethics,* or Cabrol's *Dictionnaire d'archéologie chrétienne et de liturgie,* or, in another area, the *Census of Medieval and Renaissance Manuscripts in the U.S. and Canada,* by Seymour de Ricci, or Paul O. Kristeller's valuable survey of the catalogs of *Latin Manuscript Books before 1600.* The fact that these tools are indispensable only serves to demonstrate that musicology is far from being a self-sufficient and self-contained discipline. But an attempt to list all of the peripheral resources would inflate the present work and destroy its focus. There are excellent bibliographies of general reference works currently available. Perhaps the best service to be offered to the young musicologist here is to direct him to Constance M. Winchell's *Guide to Reference Books* (7th ed., 1951, and later supplements) or to Theodore Besterman's *World Bibliography of Bibliographies* (3rd ed., 1955–56). If all else fails, he should be urged to rely on that universal repository of fact and resource, *the reference librarian,* who sits behind a desk in every large library, prepared to guide the inquiring student through the complex paths of information retrieval. But there is a distinct advantage to be gained in approaching the general reference tools from the musician's point of view. Recently Keith E. Mixter has furnished such an approach in his manual on *General Bibliography for Music Research* (1962), published as Number 4 in the Detroit Studies in Music Bibliography. It is a pleasure to be able to point to that work as a useful complement to this one.

A few further statements should be added to make clear what ground this guide is, and is not, intended to cover. It does not represent the well-rounded library of musical literature; it contains no entries for biography, no local histories, no monographs or studies devoted to most of the subject areas into which the field of music can be subdivided. It is certainly not a basic list of titles which every music library should acquire; but it does provide a list from which the essential materials for a music reference collection can be selected. It can best be described as a bibliography of music bibliographies, its emphasis being on those works which themselves serve as points of departure for further investigations: lists, inventories, alphabetized compilations of facts about music. The one section which falls most conspicuously outside of this pattern of bibliographical emphasis is the section on "Histories and Chronologies." This is the only category in which books are listed for what they contain intrinsically rather than for their function as guides to further information.

In its preliminary forms this book has been put to use in a number of courses in music bibliography throughout the country, and as a result has benefited from the suggestions of several generous-minded critics. I am particularly indebted to Professor Albert T. Luper of the State University of Iowa, and to Professor Otto Albrecht of the University of Pennsylvania for their help in this respect. The form of the annotations owes much to Richard Angell of the Library of Congress, who placed his notes at my disposal. My colleagues in the Music Library of the University of California at Berkeley, Harriet Nicewonger and Minnie Elmer, have made their influence felt on nearly every page in matters that have to do with the selection of titles, the framing of the annotations, and the reading of proof.

One feature which has been introduced for the first time in the current edition is the citation of book reviews. These are offered as practical aids to the evaluation of the items. No effort has been made to achieve complete coverage: reviews are cited only for the more recent items, and are confined largely to those published in the English-language journals.

The entries are numbered throughout this book, and for the most part, each title is entered once. There are some instances of duplicate entries, however, when the content of the item calls for its listing in more than one category. Eitner's *Quellen-Lexikon* is a case in point. This title is entered once as a dictionary of biography, and again as a bibliography of early music.

Abbreviations are used sparingly. What they save in space in a work of this kind is rarely commensurate to the inconvenience caused to the user. They are confind to the standard symbols for the dictionaries and journals most frequently cited in reviews: *Grove* for *Grove's Dictionary of Music and Musicians,* 5th edition; *MGG* for *Die Musik in Geschichte und Gegenwart; Acta M* for *Acta musicologica; JAMS* for *Journal of the American Musicological Society; MQ* for *The Musical Quarterly;* and *Notes* for *Music Library Association Notes,* 2nd series.

A bibliographer's work is never done. Even as this edition goes to press, I am troubled by the submerged voices of would-be entries which may have been overlooked, and entries which may have been misplaced or misrepresented. Other music bibliographers proceed, unconcerned, with their work, the results of which will eventually call for supplements, or even substantial revisions in our present pattern of organization. But if one were too attentive to such considerations a work of this kind would never reach the point of publication. Now that it has made its appearance, I hope that it will attract collaboration, in the form of corrections, additions, or suggestions for improvement, from all who have occasion to use it.

Vincent Duckles
1964

MUSIC
REFERENCE
AND
RESEARCH
MATERIALS

Dictionaries and Encyclopedias

The most comprehensive bibliography of music dictionaries and encyclopedias is James B. Coover's *Music lexicography,* 3rd edition, 1971 (see no. 3047), which offers some 1,800 titles. Other convenient listings appear in the article "Lexika der Musik," by Hans Heinrich Eggebrecht, in *MGG,* vol. 8, and in the "Sachteil" of the Riemann *Musik Lexikon,* 12th edition, 1967. Coover's article in *The New Grove,* "Dictionaries and encyclopedias of music," (see no. 701), includes a selective listing arranged by country or region, a listing by language, and another by subject.

Two works published since the 3rd edition of *Music Reference and Research Materials* are of singular importance. The first is *The New Grove,* edited by Stanley Sadie. (See no. 48) It was wholly based on new research and is the fruit of mainly Anglo-American musical scholarship, though many of the contributors were from other countries. The second is *The New Harvard Dictionary of Music,* edited by Don M. Randel. (See no. 399) Both of these substantial new research tools succeeded in breaking away from the practice of depending heavily upon earlier dictionaries and encyclopedias for their texts.

The present list includes the most important music dictionaries and encyclopedias in current use, in modern languages, cited as far as is possible under their latest editions. It also includes a selection of titles of those early works available in modern reprints or of continuing value for reference purposes.

GENERAL

1. Abert, Hermann J. Illustriertes Musik-Lexikon. Stuttgart: J. Engelhorns Nachf., 1927 542 p.

A popular general dictionary based on *Riemann* (no. 57) and *Das neue Musiklexikon* (no. 109). 503 pictures on 72 plates and numerous short musical examples. Contributing editors: Hermann Abert, Friedrich Blume, Rudolf Gerber, Hans Hoffman, and Theodor Schwartzkopf.

2. Algemene Muziekencyclopedie, onder leiding van A. Corbet en Wouter Paap. J. Robijns: Redactiesecretaris. Antwerpen: Zuid-Nederlandse Uitg., (1957–63). 6 v.

Comprehensive coverage of all aspects of music, including ethno-musicology, popular music, jazz. Brief biographies include performers, musicologists, composers, dancers. Major articles signed by contributors from England, Israel, United States, U.S.S.R., etc. Subject bibliographies and brief lists of works for composers and musicologists. Valuable for its wide biographical range. Illustrated.

3. Allorto, Riccardo and Alberto Ferrari. Dizionario di music. Milano: Casa Editrice Ceschina, 1959. 576 p.
A popular dictionary of terms and biography. Brief biographical entries mentioning representative works of minor composers and giving full tabulations of works of major composers. Well printed and illustrated, 8 plates in color. No bibliographical references.

4. Ammer, Christine. Harper's dictionary of music. N.Y.: Harper & Row, 1972. 414 p.
A dictionary for the general music lover.

5. Arma, Paul and Yvonne Tiénot. Nouveau dictionnaire de musique. Paris: Éditions Ouvrières, 1947. 285 p.
A "pocket" dictionary comprising some 2,000 biographical entries and 6,000 terms. 365 illustrated and short musical examples. Brief articles and summary listings of composers' works. Table of abbreviations.

6. Arnold, Denis. The New Oxford companion to music. Oxford: Oxford University Press, 1983. 2 v.
First published in 1938 and reissued in 10 more editions as the *Oxford companion to music.*
Still intended for the general reader, the *New Oxford Companion* is the work of a team of scholars and writers on music, among them the originator of the *Companion* Percy Scholes, several of whose articles have been incorporated. The *New Companion* is intended to be complete in itself, but bibliographies are appended few articles and *The New Grove* is cited as the source for "more facts." The inclusion of jazz, some popular music, and non-western music signals the broader world-view of the authors and their readers. Nevertheless, the articles on "color and music" by Scholes, any of the geographical articles ("Russia," "Scandinavia") and the articles on several formal terms ("sonata," "symphony") signal somewhat dated styles and intentions.
Review of the 8th ed. by Charles Warren Fox in *Notes,* 8 (1950), p. 177–78; of the 9th ed. by Vincent Duckles in *Notes,* 13 (1955), p. 70–72. For a further evaluation of this work, see the article "Music lexicography" by Vincent Duckles in *College music symposium,* 11 (1971), p. 121 ff.

7. Blom, Eric. Everyman's dictionary of music. 5th edition. Revised by Jack Westrup, John Caldwell, Edward Ollison, and R. T. Beck. London: Dent & New York: St. Martin's Press, 1971. 397 pages.
First pub. in 1946; U.S. ed., 1948, rev. ed., 1965; further rev. ed., 1968.
A popular quick-reference book of terms and biography. Small in size but exceedingly rich in information. Excludes living performers. Summary listings of composers' works.
Review of the 1954 ed. by Vincent Duckles in *Notes,* 13 (1955), p. 70–72.

8. Bonaccorsi, Alfredo. Nuovo dizionario musicale Curci. Milano: Curci, [1954]. 557 p.

Emphasis on terms and forms, but with essential biographies. Brief bibliographies for most articles, including references to modern republications for composers.

Review in *Rassegna musicale,* 24 (1954), p. 389–91.

9. Bonniers Musiklexikon. [Edited by] Folke T. Törnblom. Stockholm: Bonniers Förlag, 1983. 528 p.

First published in 1975 based on entries in the *Bonniers Lexikon* of 1961–64, 446 p.

The end papers carry a chronological chart of music history with parallel columns devoted to art, literature, philosophy and political history.

10. Borba, Tómas and Fernando Lopes Graça. Dicionário de música ilustrado. Lisboa: Edições, 1956. 2 v.

11. Bottenheim, S. A. M. Prisma encyclopedie der muziek. Bewerkt en ingeleid door Wouter Paap. [2. druk.] Utrecht: Het Spectrum, 1957. 2 v.

12. Coeuroy, André. Dicionnaire critique de la musique ancienne et moderne. Paris, Payot: 1956. 413 p.

Primarily biographical, its chief value is in the section "Ecoles modernes" (p. 92–191) which provides chronological lists by country, giving brief stylistic characteristics and one or two works for each composer. Important modern composers are entered in the main alphabet. Appropriate cross references.

Collins Music Encyclopedia. See Westrup, Jack A., and F. L. Harrison. *The new college encyclopedia of music . . . ,* no. 73.

13. Cooper, Martin. The concise encyclopedia of music and musicians. New York: Hawthorne Books, [1958]. 516 p.

English edition: London: Hutchinson, 1958.

It is [the] "average music lover" for whom the present work is designed. The expert and connoisseur are already well catered for with twelve-volume dictionaries and detailed studies of particular musical fields, but my task has been to present in a concise, easily digestible form the history and technical rudiments of an art which plays an increasing part in our life. [*Forward*]

Biographical entries are brief. Longer discussions of major terms and forms. No bibliographies. Well illustrated with 16 color plates and more than 100 in monochrome. 17 contributors in addition to the editor.

14. Della Corte, Andrea and G. M. Gatti. Dizionario di music. 6. ed. Torino: G.B. Paravia, [1959]. 724 p.

First published in 1925.

Includes personal names, subjects, instruments, and cities covering all countries and periods, but with emphasis on Italian names and topics. Brief biographies list major works, with fair coverage of republications of old music, especially for Italian composers.

15. Dahlhaus, Carl and Hans Eggebrecht. Brockhaus Riemann Musiklexikon. Wiesbaden: F.A. Brockhaus and Mainz: Schott, 1978–79. 2 v.

A general music dictionary based on the format laid out in the Musik-Lexikon of Hugo Riemann of 1881.

Rev. by Wolfgang Burde in *Neue Zeitschrift für Musik,* 140 (1979), p. 74–75 and by Hubert Unverricht in *Musik und Bildung,* 11 (1979), p. 127–128.

DBG-Musiklexikon. See Herzfeld, Friedrich. *Ullstein Musiklexikon,* no. 32.

16. Diccionario Enciclopédico de la Música. [Dirección general A. Albert Torrellas]. Barcelona: Central Catalana de Publicaciones, [1947]-52. 4 v.

Supersedes *Diccionario de la musica ilustrado, 1927–29. 2 v.*

Contributors include composers and musicologists from Spain, Portugal, and Latin Americ.

Vol. 1: "Terminología, tecnología, morfología, instrumentos." Technical terms in all languages, including Greek and Oriental (transliterated). No bibliography or documentation.

Vols. 2–3: "Biografís, bibliografía, monografías, historia, argumentos de operas." Biographies of composers, performers, musicologists, with emphasis on Spanish and South American musicians. Lists of works for major composers, classified listing for minor figures. Historical articles under names of countries. Extended articles for Spanish provinces, covering folk music, history, composers, institutions, etc. No bibliographical references.

Vol. 4: "Apéndice, por A. Albert Torrellas. . . ."

17. A Dictionary of modern music and musicians. New York: Da Capo, 1971. 543 p.

Reprint of the edition first published in London and New York in 1924. General editor Arthur Eaglefield Hull.

18. Dizionario enciclopedico universale della musica e dei musicisti: diretto da Alberto Basso. Torino: UTET, 1983– . 4 v. dictionary of terms and v. 1–4 of the biographical parts to date.

Successor to *La Musica* (see no. 44).

Prima parte: *La lessico,* v.1–4 (1983–84).

Seconda parte: *Le biografie,* v. 1– . (1985–86).

The dictionary of terms consists of extensive signed articles with many illustrations, charts, and tables. Cross references.

The biographical section features signed articles on composers, musicians, and other musical figures. Articles on composers have works lists. International in scope. Selective bibliographies.

This is the leading Italian encyclopedia of music.

19. Dizionario Ricordi della Musica e dei Musicisti. [Direttore: Claudio Sartori; redattori: Fausto Broussard, *et al.*]. [Milano]: Ricordi, 1959. 1,155 p.

Wide biographical coverage, including living performers, important composers of light music, musicologists. Concise articles, excellent bibliographies and lists of compositions.

Review by Jack A. Westrup in *Music and letters,* 41 (1960), p. 80–81; by James B. Coover in *Notes,* 17 (1960), p. 564–66.

20. Enciclopēdia da Musica Brasileira erudita, folclōrica, popular. General editor: Marcos Antonio Marcondes. São Paulo: Art Editora, 1977. 2 v.

Includes entries on Brazilian musical persons, terms, genres, and instruments. Extensive lists of works in biographical entries. Many useful appendices: Discography by composer and medium; Chronological list of Brazilian operas; Brazilian music periodicals; Brazilian theatres; first line index of music. General bibliography.

21. Enciclopedia della Musica Ricordi. Direttore: Claudio Sartori; Vice-Direttore: Riccardo Allorto. Milano: Ricordi, 1963–64. 4 v.

22. Enciclopedia Salvat de la Músic. Barcelona; Madrid; Buenos Aires; Mexico; Caracas; Bogotá; Rio de Janeiro: Salvá, 1967. 4 v.

This is a Spanish adaptation of the *Encyclopédie de la musique* published by Fasquelle (see no. 23).

Review by Daniel Devoto in *Revue de musicologie,* 57 (1971), p. 87–88.

23. Encyclopédie de la Musique. [Publié sous la direction de François Michel en collaboration avec François Lesure et Vladimir Fedorov, et un comité de rédaction composé de Nadia Boulanger *et al.*]. Paris: Fasquelle, [1958–61]. 3 v.

Preceding the dictionary proper is a series of essays (vol. 1, p. 1–238) devoted to general information about music in society: festivals, concerts, radio, the music press, education in France, copyright laws, institutions and associations. A "Livre d'Or," p. 35–76, gives portraits and facsimile pages from the manuscripts of leading contemporary composers. Chronological table of music history, p. 203–38.

Much emphasis on ideas and principles rather than on individuals and works. Biographical articles are short. Bibliographical references, many to *MGG*. Lists of works for major composers; fuller treatment of subjects. Many signed articles. Excellent illustrative material, musical and pictorial. Especially valuable for its coverage of modern music.

Review by James B. Coover in *Notes,* 16 (1959), p. 381–83.

24. Encyclopédie de la Musique et dictionnnaire du conservatoire. Fondateur: Albert Lavignac; Directeur: Lionel de La Laurencie. Paris: C. Delagrave, 1913–31. 2 parts in 11 v.

Originally published in fascicles.

Part I: "Histoire de la musique." Part II: "Technique, esthetique, pedagogie."

The work was designed, in the tradition of the French encyclopedists, as a universal repository of musical knowledge. It is international in scope, although most of the contributors are French. Many of the studies are full-scale monographs and still rank among the most important surveys of their fields. History is treated by country. Among the chief contributors are Maurice Emmanuel, Amedee Gastoue, Oscar Chilesotti, Romain Rolland, Henry Expert, and Rafael Mitjana.

Part II deals with music theory, instruction, and aesthetics in all aspects, including acoustics, notation, instrument making, choreography, institutions. Major articles by Charles Koechlin, Paul Rougnon, and Vincent d'Indy. Illustrated; numerous musical examples.

The *Encyclopédie* lacks an index, and for this reason the detailed tables of contents at the end of each part are most useful as a guide to its contents. A partial index, compiled by Robert Bruce and published in *Notes* ser. 1 (May 1936), is not generally available.

25. Encyclopédie methodique, ou par ordre de matières; par une societé de gens de lettres, de savans et d'artistes ... *Musique,* publiee par MM. [Nicholas Etienne] Framery et [Pierre Louis] Ginguene. Paris: Chez Panc-koucke, 1791–1818. 2 v.
   Vol. 1: A-G, 760 pgs. Vol. 2: H-Z, 558 pgs.
   Publisher varies. Tome II, Paris, Chez Mme. veuve Agasse. In this volume the name of Jerome Joseph de Momigny is added to that of the two other compilers. Vol. 1 contains a musical appendix of 74 p.; vol. 2, of 114 p.
   The *Encyclopédie methodique* is a large general reference work of which the two volumes cited are concerned with music. These volumes are of considerable historical importance since they incorporate articles from Rousseau's *Dictionnaire de musique* (no. 401) and from the Diderot —d'Alembert *Encyclopédie* along with more recent commentary. Articles are signed.

26. Encyclopedie van de Muziek. Hoofdredactio: Louis M. G. Arntzenius *et al.* Met bijzondere medwerking van J. Kunst *et al.* Amsterdam: Elsevier, 1956–57. 2 v.
   Vol. 1: A-H. Vol. 2: I-Z.

27. Encyklopedia muzyczna PWM [kolegium red. i komitet red. Zofia Lissa (przewodn.) ... *et al.*]. Krakow: Polskie Wydawn. Muzyczne, 1979–1980. 6 v.
   The modern Polish encyclopedia of music, providing bio-bibliographical information and entries on terms and topics.

28. Entsiklopedicheskii Muzykal'nyi Slovar'. Otvetstvennyi redaktor: G. V. Vsevolodovich sostaviteli B. S. Shteinpress i I. M. Iampol'skii. Moskva: Gos. Nauk. Izd. 'Bol'shaia sovetskaia entsiklopediia', 1959. 326 p.
   A second edition appeared in 1966. 631 pages.
   One of the standard Russian encyclopedias of music.

Everyman's Dictionary of Music. See Blom, Eric, no. 7.

Ewen, David. Popular American composers. ... See no. 249 under 'Jazz, Popular, and Folk Musicians."

29. Gads musikleksikon redigeret af Soren Sorensen, John Christiansen, Finn Slumstrup. Kobenhavn: G.E.C. Gad, 1976. 502 p.
   Based in the *Bonniers musiklexikon* of 1975.

Grove's Dictionary of Music and Musicians See The New Grove Dictionary of Music and Musicians no. 48.

30. Gurvin, Olav and Ø. Anker. Musikkleksikon. Ny revidert utg. Oslo: Dreyer, [1959] 902 cols.
First published in 1949.
Biography, including jazz musicians, performers, and composers. Title entries for dramatic works, familiar art songs, and folk songs. Terms, short articles, partial lists of works, occasional bibliographical references. Popular.

31. Hamburger, Povl. Aschehougs musikleksikon. København: Aschehoug, 1957–58. 2 v.
Supersedes the *Illustreret musikleksikon* (no. 51), edited by Hortense Panum and William Behrend, published in 1940.

32. Herzfeld, Friedrich. Ullstein Musiklexikon. Mit 4500 Stichwörtern, 600 Notenbeispielen, 1000 Abbildungen, und 32 Tafelseiten. Berlin; Frankfurt; Wien: Verlag Ullstein, 1965. 631 p.
Also published under the title *DBG-Musiklexikon* by the Deutsche Buch-Gemeinschaft, Berlin.
A one-volume music dictionary for ready reference. Profusely illustrated with small-scale portraits and musical examples. References to recordings.

33. Honegger, Marc. Dictionnaire de la musique. I: Les hommes et leurs œuvres. II: Science de la musique: techniques, formes, instruments. Paris: Bordas, 1970–76. 4 v.
Part I reprinted in 1974.
The most substantial modern French music encyclopedia. Excellent coverage particuarly of French topics, albeit with brief entries. A handsome, well illustrated work, produced with the collaboration of some 186 authorities; international in scope.

34. Hyojun Ongaku Jiten. [Standard music dictionary. Sansaku Meguro, ed.] Tokyo: 1966.
For a Japanese multivolume encyclopedia of music, see no. 66.

35. Jacobs, Arthur. A new dictionary of music. 2nd edition. Harmondsworth: Penguin, 1967. 425 p.
First published in 1958, followed by a hardcover edition with new introduction and corrections in London and Chicago, 1961.

A pocket dictionary for the inquiring music lover, with brief identifications of people (mostly composers and performers), terms, operatic and other specific titles, and all sorts of musical topics. [*Notes,* 16 (1958), p. 68.]

Review of the 1961 ed. by Harold Samuel in *Notes,* 20 (1963), p. 657–58.

36. Keller, Gerard and Philip Kruseman. Geïllustreerd muzieklexicon, onder redactie van G. Keller en Philip Kruseman, met medewerking van Sam Dresden, Wouter Hutschenruijter, Willem Landre. . . . 's-Gravenhage: J.P. Kruseman, 1932. 966 p.
Supplement of 319 p. published in 1949; then reissued in two volumes (vol. 1, p. 1–664; vol. 2, p. 665–966).
Brief articles, bibliographical references, and lists of major works for

composers. Similar to Abert (no. 1) in form and content, but useful in connection with contemporary Dutch names.

37. Kennedy, Michael. The Oxford dictionary of music. Oxford; New York: Oxford University Press, 1985. 810 p.

An enlargement and revision of the 3rd ed. of the *Concise Oxford dictionary of music* (no 64). Approximately 11,000 entries, of which 4,000 are biographical.

38. Larousse de la musique. [Dictionnaire encyclopédique] en 2 volumes. Publié sous la direction de Norbert Dufourcq, avec la collaboration de Félix Raugel, Armand Machebey. Paris: Larousse, [1957]. 2 v.

Also issued in an Italian edition: *Dizionario musicale Larousse.* A cura di Delfino Nava. Milano: Edizioni Paoline, 1961. 3 v.

A handsome, beautifully illustrated dictionary. Brief but authoritative articles by international contributors. Biographies (composers, performers, musicologists, choreographers); title entries (operas, ballets, manuscripts); subjects (terms, places). Some emphasis on ethnomusicology. Bibliographies given in an appendix to each volume under the same headings as the articles.

Special features: Discography and analysis (vol. 1, 587–626; vol. 2, p. 537–640). Musical examples in analytical section. Two phono-records, "Illustrations sonores," issued with the encyclopedia: (1) Les instruments de musique (with vol. 1) and (2) Principaux termes du langage technique (with vol. 2).

Review by Paul Henry Lang in *MQ,* 45 (1959), p. 120–23; by James B. Coover in *Notes,* 16 (1959), p. 381–83.

39. Malá Encyklopédia Hudby. Spracoval kolektiv autorov. Veduci autorskeho kolektivu Marian Jurik. Vedecký redaktor Dr. Ladislav Mokrý, CSc. Bratislava: Obzor, 1969. 642 p.

A Slovak dictionary of music and bio-bibliography. P. 629–42: bibliography. Illustrated. No bibliographical references with the articles.

40. Mendel, Hermann. Musikalisches Conversations-Lexikon. Eine Encyklopädie der gesammten musikalischen Wissenschaften. Fur Gebildete aller Stände, unter Mitwirkung der Literarischen Commission der Berliner Tonkunstlervereins. ... Berlin: L. Heimann; New York, J. Schuberth, 1870–79. 11 v.

Reprint of the 2nd ed., 12 vols., by Georg Olms, Hildesheim.

2nd ed. with supplementary volume, "Ergänzungsband," Berlin: R. Oppenheim, 1880–83. 3rd ed., "Neue wohlfeile Stereotyp-Ausgabe," Leipzig: List & Francke [1890–91].

Founded by Mendel, continued (vols. 7–11) by August Reissmann. One of the major 19th-century general music encyclopedias. Superseded in most respects, but still useful for obscure names and earlier concepts and criticism. Partial lists of works; few bibliographical references.

41. Meyers Handbuch über die Musik. Herausgegeben und bearbeitet von der Fachredaktion Musik des Bibliographisches Instituts. 2nd ed. Mannheim: Bibliographisches Institut, 1961. 1,062 p.

A miscellaneous assemblage of facts about music, musicians, and musical institutions. Lists of libraries, societies, research institutes, performers, etc. Wide in scope but superficial in coverage. The emphasis is on European musical activities and persons.

P. 493–993: a biographical dictionary of musicians. Combined index of subjects and persons.

42. Moore, John W. Complete encyclopaedia of music, elementary, technical, historical, biographical, vocal and instrumental. Boston: J.P. Jewett, 1854 [copyright notice, 1852]. 1,004 p.

Appendix ... containing events and information occurring since the main work was issued. Boston: Oliver Ditson, 1875, 45 p.

Reprinted by Ditson in 1880.

The first comprehensive American musical dictionary, containing more than 5,000 terms, 4,000 biographical citations, 200 articles, many of which are drawn from Gerber, Choron and Fayolle, Burney, Hawkins, Hogarth, Calcott, Gardiner, Busby, Hamilton, Schilling, and Fetis. Substantial additional material from *Dwight's musical journal* and the *New York Musical Times*. Especially rich in notices of 18th and 19th-century musicians, although somewhat weak in early Americana.

43. Moser, Hans J. Musik Lexikon. Vierte, stark erweiterte Aufl. Hamburg: H. Sikorski, 1955. 2 v.

First published in 1932–35; 2nd ed., 1943; 3rd ed., 1951. Ergänzungsband A-Z. 287 p. (1963).

Brief, authoritative articles, with special emphasis on bibliographies and lists of early music in new editions. Addressed to German readers, but increasingly international in scope with the late editions. The 4th edition, first to appear in two volumes, is extensively revised, with many new articles and bibliographical additions.

44. La Musica, sotto la direzione di Guido M. Gatti, a cura di Alberto Basso. Torino: Unione Tipografico-editrice Torinese, 1966–68. 6 v.

Parte prima: *Enciclopedia storica,* v. 1–4 (1966).

Parte seconda: *Dizionario,* v. 5–6 (1968).

A large-scale, handsomely illustrated reference tool. There are only 196 entries in the *parte prima,* of which 81 are biographies. All of the articles are extended, averaging 16 to 18 pages each. Useful tabulations of composers' works. The contributors are chiefly Italian but include a number of international authorities.

The dictionary, *parte seconda,* serves as an index to the *Enciclopedia* articulating with it and offering brief entries for terms and the biographies of minor musicians.

Review of the *Enciclopedia storica* by Vincent Duckles in *Notes,* 24 (1947), p. 263–64; of the *Dizionario* by Hans Lenneberg in *Notes,* 27 (1970), p. 51–52; and by Georg Karstadt in *Die Musikforschung,* 24 (1971), p. 458–61.

45. Musiikin Tietokirja. Toimituskunta: Tiovo Haapanen *et al.* Helsingissä: Kustannososkeyhtiö Otava, [1948]. 573 p.

Terms, subjects, operas, biographies (including performers, publishers, musicologists, many contemporary composers). Emphasis on Scandinavian musicians. Partial lists of works.

46. Die Musik in Geschichte und Gegenwart. Allgemeine Enzyklopädie der Musik . . . Edited by Friedrich Blume. Kassel u. Basel: Bärenreiter Verlag, 1949–1967. 17 v.

The work continues in two *Ergänzungs Banden,* 19773–79. A *Register Band,* edited by Elisabeth Heckmann and Harald Heckmann was published 1986.

MGG is a comprehensive music reference work of the highest scholarly merit. In German, but international in scope and coverage. Articles contributed by specialists throughout the world. Gives complete listings of composers' works and detailed monographs, and all attempted to embody the latest research. Many illustrations.

The *Ergänzungs Banden* both supplement and correct information in the first 14 volumes. The first supplement volume provides individual entries for composers and musicians who were originally treated in very large family articles. The *Register Band* is an extensive and very valuable index making many otherwise obscured matters accessible.

Reviewed by Willi Apel in *JAMS* 3 (1950), p. 142–45; 5 (1952), p. 56–57, and p. 138–39; by Charles Warren Fox in *Notes,* 7 (1950), p. 466–67, 10 (1953), p. 451–52, 12 (1954), p. 92–93; by Paul Henry Lang in *MQ,* 36 (1950), p. 141–43, 38 (1952), p. 477–79. Reviewed in *Die Musikforschung* by Rudolph Steglich, 6 (1953), p. 260–64; by Hans Ehinger, 8 (1955), p. 92–96; by Kurt von Fischer, 9 (1956), p. 331–36, and 10 (1957), p. 423–28; by Hellmut Federhofer in 12 (1959), p. 338–41.

Publication of the 5th edition of *Grove* in 1954 provided the occasion for some critical comparisons between *Grove* and *MGG.* See Richard S. Hill in *Notes,* 12 (1954), p. 85–92, and A. Hyatt King, "Grove V and MGG" in *The Monthly Musical Record,* 85 (1955), p. 155–19, p. 152–57, and p. 183–85. For a fascinating discussion of the genesis, organization, and production of a great music reference work, see "Die Musik in Geschichte und Gegenwart: a postlude," by Friedrich Blume in *Notes,* 24 (1967), p. 217–44. Blume also wrote a "Preface" to the Supplement to *MGG* published in *Notes,* 26 (1970), p. 5–8. Paul Henry Lang in *"Die Musik in Geschichte und Gegenwart*: Epilogue", in *Notes,* 36 (1979), p. 271–81, presents a panegyric to Blume and others who had worked on *MGG* as well as a comment on the state of musicology.

See also Jack Westrup, "Kritische Anmerkungen zu *Die Musik in Geschichte und Gegenwart,* volumes 9–14," trans. by Ludwig Finscher in *Die Musikforschung,* 22 (1969), p. 217–25.

Two of Blume's major survey articles have been translated by M. D. Herter Norton and published separately by W. W. Norton: 1. *Renaissance and Baroque music, a comprehensive survey* (1967), 180 p. 2. *Classic and romantic music, a comprehensive survey* (1970), 213 p. The former is reviewed by Vernon Gotwals in *Notes,* 24 (1968), p. 488-89.

47. Muzička Enciklopedija. [Glavni redaktor: Josip Andreis]. Zagreb: Izdanje i naklada leksikografskog zavoda, 1958–63. 2 v.

Vol. 1: A-J, 760 pgs. Vol. 2: K-Z, 286 pgs.

Contributors: Yugoslavian musicologists. Major articles signed.

Condensed biographical, extended subject entries. Well-organized bibliographies and lists of works. Living performers excluded. International coverage, with emphasis on Slavic composers. Excellent in content and appearance.

Review by Josef Brozek in *Notes,* 21 (1963–64), p. 128–29.

47.1. Muzykal'naia entsiklopediia. Gl. red. Iurii Vsevolodovich Keldysh. Moscow: Sov. Entsiklopediia—Sov. Kommozitor, 1973–82. 6 v.

The official musical encyclopedia of the U.S.S.R. Extensive, signed articles. Many with bibliographies and works lists. International in scope, but clearly more coverage of figures in socialist countries. Many of the biographical articles cover musical figures cited in no other reference work. Despite the difficulty in reading the Cyrillic characters, the effort is repaid with information and opinion otherwise unavailable.

48. The New Grove Dictionary of Music and Musicians. Edited by Stanley Sadie. London: Macmillan, 1980. 20 v.

First published in 1879–89; 2nd ed., 1904–10, ed. by J. A. Fuller-Maitland; 3rd ed., 1927–28, ed. by H. C. Colles; 4th ed., 1940, ed. by H. C. Colles. A supplementary volume to the 3rd edition appeared in 1940, covering the period from 1928 to 1940, with new information pertaining to earlier entries. An American supplement, edited by W. S. Pratt, containing material on the U.S., Canada, and Spanish America, was published in 1920 and again in 1928. A fifth edition, edited by Eric Blom, was published in 1954 by Macmillan. A supplementary volume to the 5th edition, ed. by Eric Blom; assoc. ed., Denis Stevens, 1961. 493 p.

The set was issued in an unabridged paperback reprint by St. Martin, New York, 1970.

The *New Grove* is the standard comprehensive music encyclopedia in English. It contains entries on music history, theory, and practice, instruments, and terms. The longer biographical entries include lists of works and extensive bibliographies; the shorter ones summarize works lists and bibliographies. Entries are signed. This edition clearly favors the interests of music scholars rather than those of informed amateurs and performers. It succeeds *MGG* as the major reference work supporting and informing musical scholarship. The *New Grove* is marred by the lack of a general index; there is an index to ethnomusicological terms, but a vast body of information is made less accessible by this editorial decision.

The publication of the of the *New Grove* in 1980 brought a flood of commentary, most of it highly favorable. The work was projected on an international scale, with contributions from scholars throughout the world. Stanly Sadie, the general editor, has provided an account of the complexities in such a vast publication in 20 volumes and 20,000 entries in the article "The New Grove" in *Notes,* 32 (1975), p. 259–268. The text of the *New Grove* was set using a computer and parts of it have reappeared, revised, in a series of volumes since 1980.

The editor of the *Musical Quarterly* devoted an entire issue (v. 68, 1982, p. 153–286) to assessments of coverage of certain broad topics in the 6th edition: Bruno Nettl - ethnomusicology; Allen Forte - theory; Robert Cogan - music, science and technology; Lance W. Brunner - Medieval music; Frank Tirro - Renaissance music; Denis Stevens - Baroque music; Bathia Churgin - music of the Classic era; Aubry S. Garlington - Opera; Jon W. Finson - 19th century music; Richard Crawford - music of pre-20th century America; Robert P. Morgan - 20th century music; Billy Taylor - jazz; Paul Wittke - American music theater.

Similar treatment was afforded in *Notes,* 38 (1981) by Susan T. Sommer, William Morris, Virgil Thomson, Michael Tilson Thomas, and the reference staff of the Music Division of the New York Public Library. Joshua Rifkin reviewed the *New Grove* in *JAMS* 35, (Spring, 1982), p.

182–199, as did Desmond Shawe-Tayler in the *New Yorker* (Nov. 23, 1981), p. 218–25. A controversial and perhaps the longest review is that of Charles Rosen in *The New York Review of Books* issue of 28 May 1981; Rosen concentrates mostly upon the treatment of Western art music, focussing principally on biography and theory in *The New Grove.* Donald W. Krummel's review in *Choice* of February 1981, p. 762–66 is well worth reading. There is a review in the *New Statesman* of 27 February 1981 by Andrew Clements. Andrew Jones, Robin Orr, and Michael Greenhalgh reviewed portions of *The New Grove* in the March 1981 issue of the *Musical times* and reviews by Christopher Hogwood and Derrick Puffett appeared in the April 1981 issue.

49. Norlind, Tobias. Almånt musiklexikon. 2 omarbetade uppl. Stockholm: Wahlstrom & Widstrand, 1927–28. 2 v.

First published in parts, 1912–16.

Many biographies, with full lists of compositions, including information om dates and publishers.

50. Nuovo dizionario Ricordi della musica e dei musicisti a cura di Riccardo Allorto; redattori Lily Allorto Bozzano, Franco Armani, Irlando Danieli. Milano: G. Ricordi, 1976. 730 p.

Utilizes parts of the *Dizionario Ricordi* (no. 19 above). The entries are short and the bibliographies brief. Well printed, with handsome color plates; notation practices illustrated.

51. Panum, Hortense and Wiliam Behrend. Illustreret musikleksikon. Nyudgave under redaktion af Povl Hamburger, under medvirken af William Behrend, O. M. Sandvik, Jurgen Balzer. København: Aschehoug, 1940. 735 p.

First issued in parts, 1924–26. Superseded by *Aschehougs musikleksikon,* ed. by Povl Hamburger, 1957.

Designed for popular use. International in coverage, but with emphasis on Scandinavian names and subjects. Based on the first edition of Norlind (no. 49) and the Schytte translation of Riemann.

52. Pena, Joaquín. Diccionario de la música Labor; iniciado por Joaquín Pena, continuado por Higinio Anglés, con la colaboracíon de Miguel Querol y otros distinguidos musicólogos españoles y extranjeros. Barcelona: Labor, 1954. 2 v.

Begun in 1940 as an adaptation of *Riemann,* but developed as a new dictionary of music for Spanish-speaking countries. Contributors are Spanish and Spanish-American. Foreign biographies drawn from *Riemann, Grove, Baker, Schmidl,* etc. Covers bio-bibliography, technique, and history. Designed for professional musicians and for general use.

53. Pratt, Waldo S. The new encyclopedia of music and musicians. New and rev. ed. New York: Macmillan, 1929. 969 p.

First published in 1924.

Originally planned as an abridgement of the second edition of *Grove* but developed as an independent work. Arranged in three main alphabets: terms, biography, institutions and organizations. Appendices for bibliography, musicians before 1700, and operas and oratorios produced since 1900. Covers primarily the 18th and 20th centuries, with emphasis on the living musicians and the American scene. Excellent definitions of musical terms.

54. Randel, Don Michael. Harvard concise dictionary of music. Cambridge, Mass.: Belknap Press, 1978. 577 p.

Published in Mexico by Editorial Diana as *Diccionario Harvard de música, 1984.*

A small, affordable dictionary for student use; entries on terms, compositions, and persons.

55. Reiss, Jósef Wladyslaw. Mala encyklopedia muzyki. [Redaktor naczelny Stefan Sledzinski Wyd. 1] Warszawa: Państwowe Wydawn. Naukowe, 1970. 1,269 p.

First issued in 1924: later editions in 1960 and 1968.

Popular dictionary, international coverage, with definitions of terms, fairly extended articles on topics, brief biographies of composers, performers, critics, etc. Short bibliographies for major subjects. Illustrated. An interesting feature is the biographical index, which assembles all references to individuals.

56. Ricordi Enciclopedia della Music. Direttore: Claudio Sartori. Vice-direttore: Riccardo Allorto. Milano: Ricordi, 1963–64. 4 v.

A major modern Italian encyclopedia of music. Well printed and illustrated, including color plates. Contributions by some 232 international specialists. Long articles signed. Good bibliographical coverage.

57. Riemann, Hugo. Musik-Lexikon. 12. vollig neubearbeitete Auflage in drei Banden. Hrsg. von Willibald Gurlitt. Mainz, B. Schott's Söhne, 1959–1967. 3 v.

Vol. 1: *Personenteil,* A-K, 1959. 986 pgs. Vol 2: *Personenteil,* L-Z, 1961. 976 pgs. Vol. 3: *Sachteil,* 1967. 1,087 pgs. (Vol. 3 ed. by Hans Heinrich Eggebrecht.) Two supplementary volumes, *Ergänzungsbánde* to the *Personenteil* have been published. The first, A-K, appeared in 1972, edited by Carl Dahlhaus. The second, L-Z, appeared in 1975.

The 12th edition is the latest in the series based on Reimann's work, first published in 1882. The present edition is the first in which terms and biography are treated in separate alphabets. Alfred Einstein was editor of the 9th, 10th, and 11th editions and added much to the scope and authority of the work.

Riemann's *Musik-Lexikon* is a universal dictionary of music covering all times and places and incorporating the achievements of German musical scholarship. Superior to *Moser* (no. 43) in typography and organization and to *Baker* (no. 76) in bibliographical coverage. Lists of works are included within the bodies of the articles; modern editions of early works and bibliographical references in separate paragraphs.

The *Ergänzungsbánde* incorporate new information, corrections and additions to the articles and bibliographies in the main volumes. There are new articles as well. The L-Z volume includes a supplementary necrology covering persons in the dictionary who had died up to 1975.

Riemann has been widely translated, and most of the translations have incorporated new materials of national interest. The principal translations are as follows:

Dictionnaire de musique. Traduit d'après la 4me édition par Georges Humbert. Paris: Perrin, 1895–1902. 2me éd., Paris: Perrin, 1913. 3me éd., entièrement refondue et augm. sous la direction de A. Schaeffner, avec la collaboration de M. Pincherle, Y. Rosketh, A. Tessier. Paris: 1931.

Dictionary of music. New edition, with many additions by the author. Trans. by J. S. Shedlock. London: Augener, 1893. Also 1897 as *Encyclopedic dictionary of music. Later editions in 1902 and 1908. Reprint of the 1908 edition by Da Capo Press, 1970.*

Muzykal'nyi slovar'. . . . Moskva: P. Iurgenson, 1901–1904. A Russian translation from the 5th German edition.

Nordisk musik-lexikon, udarbeidet af H. V. Schytte, København: 1888–92, 2 vols. with a *Supplement* (c. 1906).

Reviews of the 12th ed. *Personenteil* by Vincent Duckles in *Notes,* 16 (1959), p. 240–42, and 18 (1961), p. 572–74; by Paul Henry Lang in *MQ,* 45 (1959), p. 563–66; by Hans H. Eggebrecht in *Die Musikforschung,* 12 (1959), p. 221–23; and by Charles van den Borren in *Revue belge de musicologie,* 14 (1960), p. 137–38.

Reviews of the 12th ed. *Sachteil* by Jack Alan Westrup in *Music and letters,* 49 (1968), p. 256–57; by François Lesure in *Revue de musicologie,* 54 (1968), p. 115–16; by Hans Oesch in *Melos (1969),* p. 15; and by Vincent Duckles in *Notes,* 27 (1970), p. 256–58. See also the review-article by Walter Wiora, "Hugo Riemann und der 'neue Riemann'–" in *Die Musikforschung,* 22 (1969), p. 348–55.

The *Ergänzengsbände* were briefly reviewed by Stephen M. Fry in *Notes,* 32 (1976), p. 782.

58. Roche, Jerome and Elizabeth Roche. A dictionary of early music: from the troubadors to Monteverdi. N.Y.: Oxford University Press, 1981. 208 p.

> The aim . . . is to deal . . . with the instruments, musical forms, technical terms, and composers [of the period until the death of Monteverdi]. [*Introduction*]

Some entries include brief bibliographical citations.

59. Rororo Musikhandbuch hrsg. u. bearb. von Heinrich Lindlar in Zusammenarb. mit d. Fachred. Musik d. Bibliograph. Inst. Reinbek bei Hamburg: Rowohlt, 1973. 2 v.

Originally issued as *Meyers Handbuch über die Musik,* 1961.

Contents: Bd. 1. Musiklehre und Musikleben; Bd. 2. Lexikon der Komponisten, Lexikon der Interpreter Gesamtregister.

As is the *Meyers Handbuch,* a miscellaneous array of facts about music and musical life, especially from a European perspective. Lists of libraries, societies, research institutes, performers, etc. Wide scope, shallow coverage.

60. Rubertis, Victor de. Pequeño diccionario musical, tecnologico y biográfico. 6 ed., corregida y aumentada. Buenos Aires: Ricordi Americana, 1962. 349 p.

61. Sandved, Kjell Bloch. Musikkens verden. Musik fra A-Z. Udg. ved Kjell B. Sandved. [Overs. fra norsk] Gennemset og revideret af Vagn Kappel. Redaktionssekrataer: K. Claussen. [Ny udg.] Hovedred.: Sverre Hagerup

Bull. København: Musikkens Verden, 1964. 2,272 columns.

A Danish general dictionary of music.

62. Schilling, Gustav. Encyclopädie der gesammten musikalischen Wissenschaften, oder, Universal-Lexikon der Tonkunst. Stuttgartö F. H. Kohler, 1835–37. 6 v.

Supplement-Band, hrsg. von Gustav Schilling, 1842.

Reprinted by Georg Olms, Hildesheim, including the supplement, in 1974.

One of the leading 19th-century repositories of musical knowledge. A comprehensive work with emphasis on the subject aspects, but including numerous biographies displaced or reduced in later reference works.

63. Schilling, Gustav. Universal-Lexikon der Tonkunst. Neue Hand-Ausgabe in einem Bande. Mit Zugrundlegung des grösseren Werkes neu bearbeitet, ergänzt und theilweise vermehrt von Dr. F.S. Gassner. ... Stuttgart: F. Köhler, 1849. 918 p.

A one-volume condensation of the preceding six-volume work. Remarkably full of information. In many instances the entries are more comprehensive and up to date than in the original printing.

64. Scholes, Percy A. The concise Oxford dictionary of music. 3rd edition by Michael Kennedy, based on the original by Percy Scholes. London & New York: Oxford Univ. Press, 1980. 724 p.

First published in 1952. Second edition published in 1964 and issued as a paperback, 1968.

Primarily a reduction of the *Oxford companion.* Includes "some hundreds of short biographical entries for vocal and instrumental performers and conductors ... and some hundreds of entries concerning individual compositions." About 10,000 entries, 3,500 biographical. The 3rd edition adds many new articles and supplements articles remaining from previous editions.

Review of the 1st ed. of the *Oxford companion* by Charles Warren Fox in *Notes,* 9 (1952), p. 605–06.

65. Seeger, Horst. Musiklexikon in zwei Bänden. Leipzig: Deutscher Verlag fur Musik, 1966. 2 v.

Vol. 1, A-K. Vol. 2, L-Z.

Represents the Marxist (East German) approach to music lexicography. Articles by 44 East European contributors. Summary listings of composers' works; no bibliographies for articles on major topics. Illustrated.

66. Shimonaka, Yasazuro, ed. Ongaku jiten. Tokyo: Heibonsha, 1954–57. 12 v.

The major Japanese encyclopedia of music.

Vol. 12 is an index in Japanese and English.

67. Sohlmans Musiklexikon. Editor-in-chief Hanse Astrand. Stockholm: Sohlmans Förlag 1975–78. 5 v.

A first edition was published 1948–1952.

An extensive dictionary in Swedish providing brief entries on a very wide variety of musical topics, including biographical entries. Pop music, ethnic dance forms, musical technologies and geographical topics are covered. The larger articles are signed and include bibliographies. There are many unusual illustrations, photographs, and charts. Excellent and extensive coverage of the contemporary musical scene. The last volume provides a classified index to topical articles. The major modern Swedish music encyclopedia. Contributions by leading Scandinavian musicologists.

Reviewed by Sven Hansell in *Fontes artis musicae,* 24 (1977), p. 194–96. Briefly reviewed by Stephen M. Fry in *Notes,* 33 (1976), p. 307.

68. Thompson, Oscar, ed. The international cyclopedia of music and musicians. 11th ed. by Bruce Bohle. W: Dodd, Mead, 1985. 2,609 p.

First published in 1939. 8th ed. (1958) edited by Nicolas Slonimsky. 9th ed. (1964) edited by Robert Sabin. 10th edited (1975) edited by Bruce Bohle.

The eleventh edition includes an appendix of additional new articles and new information to articles appearing in the tenth edition; it is, thus, a reprint of the tenth edition with a section of *addenda et corrigenda.*

A good one-volume general dictionary of music in English. Strong list of contributors, with extended signed articles for major persons and subjects. Large numbers of title entries. Particularly valuable for detailed lists, given in tabulated form, of works by major composers. Through the 8th edition the work carried an appendix of opera plots and an extensive bibliography of music literature. The 11th edition includes an appendix of additional new articles and new information to articles appearing in the 10th edition.

Review of the 5th edition by Charles Warren Fox in *Notes,* 7 (1950), p. 291–92; of the 9th edition by Irene Millen in *Notes,* 22 (1965), p. 733–35.

69. Tonkonsten, Internationellt musiklexikon. Stockholm: Nordiska Uppslagsböcker, [1955–57]. 2 v.

Popular, illustrated dictionary giving pronunciations of foreign names, lists of works and bibliographies for major composers, bibliographical references on important topics. Covers popular music. Signed articles by Scandinavian contributors.

70. Tschierpe, Rudolf. Kleines Musiklexikon, mit systematischen Übersichten und zahlreichen Notenbeispielen. [6. ergänzte Auflage.] Hamburg: Hoffman und Campe, 1959. 414 p.

First published in 1946; 2. Aufl., 1948; 3 Aufl., 1949; 4. Aufl., 1951; 5. Aufl., 1955.

Excellent small general dictionary. Brief but inclusive. Representative works listed for major composers. Bibliographical references. Tables illustrating dance forms, theory and history. Appendix lists major writers on music with their fields of specialization; another lists titles of operas, operettas, oratorios, choral and orchestra works.

Ullstein Musiklexikon. See Herzfeld, Friedrich, no. 32.

71. Viotta, Henri Anastase. Lexicon der toonkunst. Met medewerking van de heeren Peter Benoit, Frans Coenen, F. Gernsheim, L. van Gheluwe, F. A. Heinze, Richard Hol, Dan. de Lange, W.F.G. Nicolai, etc. Amsterdam: P. N. van Kampen, 1883–85. 3 v.

First printed in 1881–85.

The standard 19th century Dutch encyclopedia of music. The emphasis is on biography.

72. Walther, Johann G. Musikalisches Lexicon, oder musikalische Bibliothek. Leipzig: Wolffgang Deer, 1732. 659 p., 22 fold. plates.

Facsimile reprint edited by Richard Schaal (1953 and 1986) and published by Barenreiter in the series (*Documenta musicologica*) , Erste Reihe, 3.

Walther's Lexicon established the pattern for modern dictionaries that combine terms and biography, as in Riemann and Moser. It also constitutes a primary source of information about late Baroque musical knowledge and practice.

73. Westrup, Jack A. and Frank L. Harrison. The new college encyclopedia of music. Revised by Conrad Wilson. N.Y.: W. W. Norton, 1976. 608 p.

Published first in England, in 1959, as the *Collins music encyclopedia and then in the U.S. as the New College Encyclopedia of Music* in 1960, 739 p. The present edition was also published in Britain as the *Collins Encyclopedia of Music.* The 1976 American edition was reprinted in 1981.

A dictionary less scholarly than informative. Focus on common practice composers, terms, and titles, but with brief attention to earlier and more modern topics. Most important composers are provided with summaries of works. There are occasional bibliographical references in the articles. Some illustrations with musical quotations. Strong British bias.

Review of the 1960 edition by James B. Coover in *Notes,* 17 (1960), p. 564–66.

74. Willemze, Theo. Spectrum muzieklexicon. Utrecht: Het Spectrum, 1975. 4 v.

Composers, authors and titles of pieces of music, as well as definitions of terms are found in this compendium of very brief entries. Plentiful cross references from the major European languages to Dutch. Extensive coverage of a broad span of Low Countries' musical culture.

75. Zenei Lexikon. [írtak] Bence Szabolcsí [és] Aladár Tóth. Átdolgozott új loadás, förszerkesztö: Dénes Bartha, szerkesztö: Margit Tóth. Budapest: Zenemükiadó Vallalat, 1965. 3 v.

This is a revision and expansion of a work that was first issued in 1930–31.

A general music encyclopedia of high quality. Major articles signed by outstanding musicologists, Hungarian and foreign. Long articles on national music, forms, music for various instruments. Biographical articles discuss major works and list others by category. Short bibliographies.

Revue by J. Gerely in *Revue de musicologie,* 53 (1967), p. 185–87.

BIOGRAPHY, INTERNATIONAL

Listed here are dictionaries and encyclopedias, international in coverage, in which the emphasis is exclusively or mainly on persons engaged in activities related to music: composers, performers, scholars, critics, impresarios, etc. The line that separates biographical dictionaries from volumes of collected biography is a rather arbitrary one. The distinction is essentially between works that contain numerous brief entries, alphabetically arranged, and works that consist of collections of essays on a fairly limited group of musicians. Works in the latter category have been excluded, and for this reason the user should not expect to find entries for such titles as Donald Brook's *Masters of the Keyboard* (London, 1947) or his *Singers of Today* (London, 1949), David Ewen's *Dictators of the Baton* (New York, 1943), or Madeleine Goss's *Modern Music-makers* (New York, 1952).

76. Baker, Theodore. Baker's biographical dictionary of musicians. 7th ed. revised by Nicolas Slonimsky. N.Y.: Schirmer Books, 1984. 2,577 p.

First published in 1900; subsequent editions in 1905, 1919, 1940, 1958 and 1978. The 1958 edition was reprinted in 1965, with a 143-page *Supplement.* There was also a 1971 Supplement of 262 pgs.

Baker's is by far the most authoritative and extensive biographical dictionary in English, a standard work from its beginning. It focuses mainly upon musicians and musical figures in the world of "art music." Through the 3rd edition early figures were treated briefly, with references to Grove and Eitner. For the 4th edition, these biographies were rewritten as independent articles (by Gustave Reese, Gilbert Chase, and Robert Geiger). The 5th edition was greatly enlarged and checked carefully for accuracy. The 6th edition was extensively revised from the 5th ed. and the 7th from the 6th. Lists of works.

Review of 5th edition by Brooks Shepard Jr., in *Notes,* 16 (1959), p. 239–40; by Philip L. Miller in *MQ,* 45 (1959), p. 255–58. Review of the 1971 *Supplement* by Gloria Rose in *Notes,* 29 (1972), p. 253–54.

77. Bertini, Giuseppe. Dizionario storico-critico degli scrittori di musica, e de'piu celebri artisti di tutte le nazioni si' antiche che moderne. Palermo: Dalla Tipografia reale di Guerra, 1814–15. 4 v. in 2.

Tomo primo: Discorso preliminare, p. i-lvi, AA-BU. 167 p.
Tomo secondo: C-KU. 234 p.
Tomo terzo: LA-RU. 245 p.
Tomo quarto: SA-Z. 145 p.

An early Italian dictionary of musical biography. Bertini leans heavily on *Choron and Fayolle* (see no. 81) for his information but adds much new material. His "Discorso preliminare" is a perceptive discussion of the role of bibliography in enhancing musical knowledge.

78. Bingley, William. Musical biography; memoirs of the lives and writings of the most eminent musical composers and writers who have flourished in the different countries of Europe during the last three centuries. London: H. Colburn, 1814. 2 v.

2nd ed., 1834. Reprint of the 2nd ed. by Da Capo Press, New York, 1971.

Brief, anecdotal accounts grouped chronologically and by national schools.

79. Brown, James Duff. Biographical dictionary of musicians, with a bibliography of English writings on music. Paisley and London: A. Gardner, 1886. 637 p.
Reprint by Georg Olms, Hildesheim, 1970.
International in coverage but with pronounced British slant.

80. Carlson, Effie B. A bio-bibliographical dictionary of twelve-tone and serial composers. Metuchen: Scarecrow Press, 1970. 233 p.
Entries for 80 twelve-tone and serial composers, from Gilbert Amy to Bernd Alois Zimmerman.

81. Choron, Alexandre E. and F. J. M. Fayolle. Dictionnaire historique des musiciens, artistes et amateurs, morts ou vivans, qui se sont illustrés en une partie quelconque de la musique et des arts qui y sont relatifs. ... Paris: Valade, 1810–11. 2 v.
Another printing, 1817. Reprint by Olms, Hildesheim, 1970.
The first French biographical dictionary of importance. International in scope. Partial lists of works for major composers. A valuable guide to early 19th-century musical opinion. The dictionary proper (by Fayolle) is preceded by an 81-page 'Sommaire de l'histoire de la musique' by Choron.
Translated and expanded in the English A *dictionary of musicians,* 1824. See no. 84.

82. Cohen, Aaron I. International encyclopedia of women composers. N.Y. & London: R. R. Bowker, 1981. 597 p.
Provides brief biographical coverage with lists of compositions for almost 5,000 women composers. Appendix of composers listed by country and century. Extensive bibliography of works about women composers.

83. A Dictionary of Modern Music and Musicians. Ed. by Arthur Eaglefield-Hull. London: J.M. Dent; New York, E.P. Dutton, 1924. 543 p.
Reprint of the 1924 ed. by Da Capo Press, New York, 1971, and by the Scholarly Press, 1972.
Primarily biographical, although there are entries for terms related to modern music. For the period c. 1880–1920, the best international coverage of any dictionary of its time. Written with the aid of numerous foreign collaborators. Also includes publishers, musicologists, organizations, new instruments, etc. (See also no. 109).

84. A Dictionary of Musicians, from the earliest ages to the present time, comprising the most important biographical contents of the works of Gerber, Choron and Fayolle, Count Orloff, Dr. Burney, Sir John Hawkins, etc. Together with more than 100 original memoirs of the most eminent living musicians and a summary of the history of music. London: Sainsbury, 1824. 2 v.
Reprinted in 1827.
Reprint of the original edition by Da Capo Press, New York, 1966. The

reprint incorporates an essay on the work by H. G. Farmer, originally printed in *Music and Letters,* 12 (1931), p. 384–92.

The Sainsbury *Dictionary* has been shown recently to have been copied and paraphrased from Bingley (see no. 78) and from other contemporaneous English publications. The first major biographical dictionary of musicians in English. Its tone is popular and anecdotal, but the work furnishes an excellent picture of contemporary taste and opinion. The compiler is not identified, but the work has been attributed to its publisher, John Sainsbury.

See the article by Lawrence I. Ritchey "The untimely death of Samuel Wesley; or the perils of plagiarism" in *Music and Letters,* 60 (1984), p. 45–59.

Review of the reprint edition by Vincent H. Duckles in *Notes,* 23 (1967), p. 737–39.

85. Eitner, Robert. Biographisch-bibliographisches Quellen-Lexikon der Musiker und Musikgelehrten der christlichen Zeitrechnung bis zur Mitte des 19. Jahrhunderts. . . . Leipzig: Breitkopf & Hartel, 1898–1904. 10 v.

Eitner's Quellen-Lexikon is mainly a bibliography of primary sources, but it does contain much useful biographical information, often helpful with respect to obscure names. For fuller information on this important reference work, see under Bibliographies of music (no. 1773).

86. The Etude Music Magazine. Portraits of the world's best known musicians, an alphabetical collection of notable musical personalities of the world covering the entire history of music. Compiled and edited by Guy McCoy. Philadelphia: Theodore Presser, [1946]. 251 p.

Portraits and brief identifications of 4,748 composers, performers, and other musicians, largely reprinted from *Etude,* 1932–40. Geographical index of American names.

One of the few dictionaries of its kind. Of limited value, however, since the portraits are reproduced at little more than postage-stamp size.

87. Ewen, David. Composers of yesterday, a biographical and critical guide to the most important composers of the past. New York: H. W. Wilson, 1937. 488 p.

Biographies, lists of works, bibliographies, lists of recordings, and portraits of about 200 composers from Dunstable to the end of the 19th century. Selected on the basis of current acceptance or importance in music history.

88. Ewen, David Composers since 1900: a bibliographical and critical guide. New York: H. W. Wilson, 1969. 639 p.

First supplement. . . . 1981. 328 p.

Supersedes *Composers of today* (1934 and 1936); *American composers of today;* and *European composers today* (1954).

Portraits; listing of major works, and short bibliographies of writings about the composers under consideration.

Reviewed in *The Booklist,* 66 (July 1970), p. 1290–91.

89. Ewen, David. Living musicians. New York: H. W. Wilson, 1940. 390 p. *First supplement.* ... , 1957.

A dictionary of performers, especially American or active in Americ. Portraits. The supplement contains biographies of 147 musicians who have come into prominence since 1940.

90. Ewen, David. Musicians since 1900; performers in concert and opera. N.Y.: H. W. Wilson, 1978. 974 p.

Ewen, David. Popular American composers ... See no. 249 under "Jazz, Popular, and Folk Musicians."

91. Fétis, François J. Biographie universelle des musiciens et bibliographie générale de la musique. 2me éd. Paris: Firmin Didot Freres, 1866–70. 8 v.

First published in 1835–44. *Supplément et complément,* pub. sous la direction de M. Arthur Pougin. Paris, 1878–80. 2 v.

Reprint of the second edition, with the supplements by Arthur Pougin, by Editions Culture et Civilisation, Brussels, (1973) with a critical introduction by L. Weemaels, P. Huyskens, and G. Thines. 10 v.

Fetis's work once set the standard for modern biographical research in music. A significant achievement for its time, it contains biographical and bibliographical information (much of which modern scholarship has shown to be less than accurate), complete lists of works, and—occasionally—annotated lists of books about composers. Although outdated and marred by the author's personal critical bias, it has been a starting point for research.

92. Gerber, Ernst Ludwig. Historisch-biographisches Lexikon der Tonkünstler, welches Nachrichten von dem Leben und Werken musikalischer Schriftsteller, beruhmter Componisten, Sanger, usw. ... enthalt. Leipzig:: J.G.I. Breitkopf, 1790–92. 2 v.

See annotation under no. 93, below.

93. Gerber, Ernst Ludwig. Neues historisch-biographisches Lexikon der Tonkünstler. ... Leipzig: A. Kühnel, 1812–13. 4 v.

The Gerber *lexika* are early biographical dictionaries of great historical importance. The compiler expanded the biographical content of Walther's *Lexikon* (no. 72) and produced the first major self-contained dictionary of musical biography. The four-volume edition of 1812–14 supplements but does not supersede the earlier two-volume edition (no. 92, above). Both compilations must be used for complete coverage.

The two Gerber *lexica* have been reprinted by Akademische Druck- u. Verlagsanstalt, Graz, under the editorship of Othmar Wessely. Wessely has also edited a supplementary volume containing additions and corrections made by Gerber's contemporaries and published in the *Leipzig Allgemeine musikalische Zeitung* and other journals. Also included are the author's manuscript revisions. A full transcription of the title of the reprint edition is given as follows:

Historisch-Biographisches Lexikon der Tonkünstler (1812–14) und Neues historisch-biograpisches Lexikon der Tonkünstler (1812–14). Mit den in den Jahren 1792 bis 1834 veröffentlichten Ergänzungen sowie der

21

Erstvoeröffentlichung handschriftlicher Berichtigungen und Nachträge. Hrsg. von Othmar Wessely. Graz: Akademische Druck- u. Verlagsanstalt, 1966–69. 4 v.

94. Gilder, Eric. The dictionary of composers and their music; a listener's companion. New, revised edition. N.Y.: Holt, Rinehart and Winston, 1986. 592 p.

First published in 1978, 2nd ed. 1985.

Brief biographical entries on 426 composers most likely to be encountered on programs of classical music. Works lists arranged in chronological order for each composer and a survey of compositions listed in chronological order. Time lines for the lives of composers in the book. Includes a time line showing when each cited composer was born and died, and with whom each was contemporaneous.

95. Le Grandi Voci. Dizionario critico-biografico dei cantanti, con discografia operistic. Roma: Istituto per la Collaborazione Culturale, 1964. 1,044 columns.

Published under the direction of Rodolfo Celletti; consultants for the discographies, Raffaele Vegeto and John B. Richards; editor, Luisa Pavolini.

An illustrated dictionary of opera singers, historical and contemporary, with the discographies of the major artists.

96. Greene, David Mason. Greene's Biographical Encyclopedia of composers. Garden City: Doubleday, 1985. 1,348 p.

A popular dictionary limited to composers of art music. Entries arranged chronologically by birth date. Alphabetical list of composers.

97. Griffiths, Paul. The Thames and Hudson encyclopaedia of 20th-century music. New York: Thames and Hudson, 1986. 207 p.

98. Hughes, Rupert. The biographical dictionary of musicians. Originally compiled by Rupert Hughes, completely revised and newly edited by Deems Taylor and Russell Kerr. Over 8,500 entries, together with a pronouncing dictionary of given names and titles and a key to the pronunciation of sixteen languages. New York: Blue Ribbon Books, 1940. 481 p.

Reprinted by Scholarly Press, 1972.

A popular reference work. Brief entries with representative works for composers mentioned. Useful for the abundance of obscure performers entered.

99. International who's who in music and musical gazetteer, a contemporary biographical dictionary and a record of the world's musical activity, edited by Cesar Saerchinger. New York: Current Literature Pub. Co., 1918. 861 p.

The geographical index and directory of schools and organizations are now only of historical interest, but the biographical section is still useful for minor figures of the first two decades of the century. Composers, performers, critics, musicologists, teachers—their education, activity, principal works, addresses.

100. International who's who in music and musicians' directory. 10th ed., 1985. Cambridge, England: International Who's Who in Music of the International Bibliographical Centre; Melrose Press, 1984. 1,178 p.

Began publication in 1935. Title 1962–72, *Who's who in music and musicians' international directory. Resumed under the present title with 7th ed., 1975; 8th ed., 1977; 9th ed., 1980.*

Résumés of almost 8,000 musicians, musicologists, music critics, managers, publishers, librarians, and others in the field. Each entry initially supplied by the subject. Includes addresses of subjects. Emphasis on western European and western hemisphere figures. International lists of organizations with addresses by various categories: orchestras, competitions, libraries, conservatories, etc.

Review of the 1962 ed. by Fred Blum in *Notes,* 19 (1962), p. 442–43.

101. Kurzgefasstes Tonkünstler-lexikon [von] Frank/Altmann; fortegeführt von Burchard Bulling, Florian Noetzel und Helmut Rösner. 15. Aufl. Zweiter Teil: Ergänzungen und Erweiterungen seit 1937. Wilhelmshaven: Heinrichshofen's Verlag, 1974–78. 2 v.

Erste Teil a reprint of Merseburger *Kurzegefasstes Tonkünstler-lexikon,* 14. Aufl. (see no. 104)

This edition corrects and augments the 14th, adding more than 16,000 new entries.

Review by Rudolf Klein in *Össterreichische Musik Zeitschrift,* 30 (1975), p. 422, and by Nyal Williams in *Notes,* 29 (1973), p. 478.

102. Kutsch, K. J. and Leo Riemens. A concise biographical dictionary of singers, from the beginning of recorded sound to the present. Translated from German, expanded and annotated by Harry Earl Jones. Philadelphia: Chilton Book Co., 1969. 487 p.

First printed in German under the title *Unvergängliche Stimmen,* Bern u. München, Francke Verlag, 1962, 1975, 1979, 1982.

Brief biographies of great singers who have flourished since the invention of sound recording. Entries include information on the singers' principal roles, the character of the voice, and the labels under which recordings were made. No detailed discographies.

Review by Philip L. Miller in *Library Journal* (Oct. 15, 1969).

103. Mattheson, Johann. Grundlage einer Ehren-Pforte, woran der tüchtigsten Capellmeister, Componisten, Musikgelehrten, Tonkünstler, etc. erscheinen sollen. Zum fernern Ausbau angegeben von Mattheson, Hamburg, 1740. Vollständiger, originalgetreuer Neudruck mit gelegentlichen bibliographischen Hinweisen und Matthesons Nächtragen, hrsg. von Max Schneider. Berlin: Leo Liepmannssohn, 1910. 428 p. with *Anhang* of 51 p.

Reprints issued in 1969 reprint of the 1910 edition by Bärenreiter, Kassel and by Die Akademische Druck- und Verlagsanthalt, Graz.

Mattheson's work is, strictly speaking, a volume of collected biography rather than a biographical dictionary. But the volume stands first, chronologically, among all self-contained works of musical biography, establishing the precedent for Gerber's *Lexikon* (no. 92 & 93) and subsequent dictionaries of musical biography. Most of the essays were contributed by the subjects themselves.

104. Merseburger, Carl W. Kurzgefasstes Tonkünstler-Lexikon für Musiker und Freunde der Musik. Begründet von Paul Frank [pseud.] Neu bearbeitet und ergänzt von Wilhelm Altmann. 14. stark erweiterte Auflage. Regensburg: G. Bosse, 1936. 730 p.

First published in 1860 as P. Frank's *Kleines Tonkünstler-Lexikon.* Title varies slightly in subsequent editions. Subsequently published as part 1 of the *Frank-Altmann Kurzgefasstes Tonkünstler-Lexikon* in 1974 (see no. 101).

One of the most popular of the pre-war German dictionaries of musical biography. Extremely wide coverage, but with minimum data. Over 18,-000 entries, including composers, librettists, performers, musicologists. Many minor figures. No lists of works or bibliographical references. Useful for quick reference.

Review of the 15th edition by Nyal Williams in *Notes,* 29 (1973), p. 448.

105. Mirkin, Mikhail Iur'evich. Kratkii biograficheskii slovar' zarubezhnykh kompositorov. [Brief biographical dictionary of foreign composers.] Moskva: Sovetskii kompozitor, 1969. 265 p.

A biographical dictionary covering some 2,500 musicians excluding Russian and Soviet composers.

106. Moore, John W. A dictionary of musical information; containing also a vocabulary of musical terms, and a list of modern musical works published in the United States from 1640 to 1875. New York: AMS Press, 1977 211 p.

Reprint of the first edition published by Oliver Ditson, Boston, 1876. Previously reprinted by Benjamin Franklin, 1971.

The "musical information" is chiefly biographical. The "vocabulary of musical terms" is a pronouncing dictionary. The "list of modern musical works" is alphabetical by title.

107. Les Musiciens Célèbres. [Publie sous la direction de Jean Lacroix....]. [Genève]: L. Mazenod, 1946. 385 p.

Also published in German under the title Die berühmten Musiker. Genève, 1946. Reprinted by Magenod, Paris, 1950. 357 p.

An "art" publication, chiefly valuable for its fine full-page portraits of musicians. 66 individual biographies and several group articles, chronologically arranged. P. 293–349: brief identifications of other composers.

108. Musikens Hven-Hvad-Hvor. Politikens Musikleksikon. Udarbejdet af Nelly Backhausen og Axel Kjerulf. København: Politikens Forlag, 1950. 3 v.

Vol 1: "Musikhistorie." Chronology from antiquity to 1900, with composer index. Vols. 2–3: Biographies (composers, performers, musicologists) indicating field of activity and principal works. Vol. 3: p. 141–414. Title list of 15,000 entries, including operas, repertory works, popular and musical comedy songs, folk songs. For each, identification, composer, and date if known.

A new edition of vols. 2–3, the biographies section, appeared in 1961, edited by Ludig Ernst Bramsen Jr.

109. Das Neue Musiklexikon, nach dem *Dictionary of modern music and musicians,* hrsg. von A. Eaglefield-Hull, übersetzt und bearb. von Alfred Einstein. Berlin: M. Hesse, 1926. 729 p.

A German translation of no. 17, with many additions and corrections by Einstein. Most of the information in this revision is incorporated in the 11th edition of the *Riemann Musik-Lexikon.*

110. Parker, John R. A musical biography; with new introd. by Frederick Freedman. Detroit: Information Coordinators, 1975. 250 p.

Reprint of the 1825 ed. published by Stone & Fovell, Boston.

Includes bibliographical references in the introduction.

111. Pedigo, Alan. International encyclopedia of violin-keyboard sonatas and composer biographies. Booneville, Arkansas: Arriaga, 1979. 135 p.

Most useful for the national lists of composers and the brief biographies of composers.

112. Prieberg, Fred K. Lexikon der neuen Musik. Freiburg & Munchen: K. Alber, 1958. 495 p.

Primarily biographical, but with a few articles on aspects of and trends in contemporary music (film music, radio operas, polytonality, 12-tone music, *musique concrete,* etc.) Factual rather than critical, covering education, activities, and principal works of the 20th-century composers.

113. Ricart Matas, José. Diccionario biográfico de la músic. [2nd. ed.] Barcelona: Editorial Iberia, 1966. 1,143 p.

A Spanish dictionary of international musical biography. Brief biographical entries. Lists of works for major composers together with bibliographical references.

114. Rostand, Claude. Dictionnaire de la musique contemporaine. Paris: Larousse, 1970. 256 p.

A pocket dictionary of contemporary music, primarily biographical. Major works are mentioned, but no attempt is made to provide full lists of works.

115. Sakka, Keisei. Meikyoko jiten. [Dictionary of famous music and musicians.] Tokyo: Ongaku no Tomosha, 1969. 702 p.

A general bio-bibliography in Japanese.

116. Schäffer, Boguslaw. Leksykon Kompozytorów XX wieku. Kraków: Polskie Wydawnictwo Muzyczne, 1963–65. 2 v.

Vol. 1: A-L. Vol. 2: M-Z.

A Polish-language dictionary of 20th-century composers. International in coverage but particularly stong in Slavic musicians. Portraits, bibliographies.

117. Schmidl, Carlo. Dizionario universale dei musicisti. Milano: Sonzogno, [1928?-29]. 2 v.

Supplemento, 1938. 806 p.

First pub. 1888–89 in 1 vol.

A major bio-bibliography in Italian and good general biographical source for obscure Italian musicians. Emphasis on native composers, librettists, and performers, with full articles on well-known persons and brief accounts of minor ones. Dates of first productions of dramatic works. Lists of works, including modern republications. Particularly valuable for articles on Italian literary figures and their relation to music. All forenames are Italianized.

118. Schnoor, Hans. Oper, Operette, Konzert. Ein praktisches Nachschlagebuch für Theater- und Konzertbesucher, fur Rundfunkhörer, Fernsehteilnehmer und Schallplattenfreunde. Gütersloh: C. Bertelsmann, 1963. 575 p.

First printed in 1955. Reprinted in 1969 by Rowohlt-Taschbucher-Verlag and in 1970 by Bertelsmann.

Issued also in an edition with additions by Stephan Pflicht entitled *Mosaik-Opernführer, Konzertführer mit Operetten und Musicals.* München: Mosaik-Verlag, 1979, 504 p.

A handbook for the musical amateur and concertgoer. Organized biographically, but with emphasis on the composers' works in the current repertory. Some 347 musical examples and numerous illustrations. With an appended glossary and indexes of persons and subjects.

119. Seeger, Horst. Musiklexikon: Personen A-Z. Leipzig: Deutscher Verlag für Musik, 1981. 860 p.

Very brief biographical sketches followed by categorized lists of major works. International scope, but better coverage for persons from the Eastern Bloc.

120. Simpson, Harold. Singers to remember. Lingfield, England: The Oakwood Press, 1973. 223 p.

I have not attempted an exhaustive survey of these singers' careers or their recordings. Rather it has been my aim to provide data which will encourage searchers in the vocal record field to probe further into the legacy of discs left by the artists mentioned. [Author's *Introduction*]

Biographies of some 100 singers, with selected discographies.

121. Southern, Eileen. Biographical dictionary of Afro-American and African musicians. Westport: Greenwood Press, 1982. 478 p. (Greenwood encyclopedia of Black music)

Biographies include citations of sources. Lists of periods and places of birth, musical occupations. Index.

122. Suppan, Wolfgang. Lexikon des Blasmusikwesens. Im Auftrag des Bundes Deutscher Blasmusikverbände, hrsg. in Zusammenarbeit mit Fritz Thelen und weiteren Fachkollegen. 2., ergänzte und erweiterte Auflage. Freiburg im Breisgau: F. Schulz, 1976. 342 p.

First published in 1973. Also known as *Blasmusikwesen.*

Extensive introductory chapters on history, organizations supporting, arrangements, repertoire, conducting, and bibliography of wind bands. Biographies of composers, conductors and performers, each accompanied by a brief bibliography. Most extensive coverage of German-speaking areas of Europe.

Review by Georg Karstädt in *Die Musikforschung,* 32 (1979), p. 193–94.

Unvergangliche Stimmen. See Kutsch, K. J. (no. 102).

123. Vinton, John. Dictionary of contemporary music. New York: E. P. Dutton; London: Thames and Hudson, 1974. 834 p.

London edition titled *Dictionary of twentieth-century music.*

A dictionary consisting of articles focusing on concert music of the Western tradition. Entries on composers were based on questionnaires completed by the composers. Entries on topics were written by distinguished scholars. "Perhaps a ... way to use this book is to regard it as a slice of history reported in large part by some of its makers." Articles include lists of principal compositions and bibliographies.

Who's Who in Music ... See no. 100 & 126.

124. Willemze, Theo. Componistenlexicon. Utrecht: Spectrum, 1981. 2 v. (785 p.)

A Dutch biographical dictionary with international coverage. Includes bibliographical references.

125. Young, Percy M. Biographical dictionary of composers, with classified list of music for performance and study. New York: Crowell, 1954. 381 p.

Published in England under the title A Critical dictionary of composers and their music. London: Dobson, 1954; British edition reprinted by Hyperion Press of Westport, Connecticut, 1979.

Selective list of 500 composers. Brief critical surveys of each, titles of representative works, and references to further sources of information, usually in English. Intended for the general student rather than the specialist.

BIOGRAPHY, NATIONAL

Any dictionary of musical biography may be expected to be strong in names within its own language group. There are numerous specialized dictionaries of biography devoted specifically to the musicians of particular countries. Only the most important of such dictionaries are listed here, with the emphasis on recent publications. Entries are arranged by country.

126. Who's who in American music: classical. 2nd ed. Edited by Jacques Cattell Press. N.Y.; London: Bowker, 1983. 783 p.

Brief biographical entries comppiled from information provided by the biographees. Entries include resumes of professional careers and mailing addresses. 9, 038 entries in alphabetical order. Geographical and professional classification indexes.

127. Arizaga, Rodolfo. Enciclopedia de la música Argentina. Buenos Aires: Fondo Nacional de las Artes, 1971. 371 p.

Chiefly a biographical dictionary of Argentine musicians but including some terms for dance forms, musical institutions, and the like. Partial lists of composers' works. Chronological tables covering the history of Argentine music from 1901 to 1970.

128. Senillosa, Mabel. Compositores argentinos. 2.ed., a umentada. Buenos Aires: Casa Lottermosser, 1956. 451 p.

First ed. issued as *Homenaje al artista argentino, músicos, 1948.*

Some entries supplied by the composers themselves.

129. MacKenzie, Barbara and Findlay MacKenzie. Singers of Australia from Melba to Sutherland. Melbourne: Lansdowne Press, 1967. 309 p.

Also published in London by Newnes, 1968.

Biographies, with a liberal selection of portraits. Bibliography and index; data on results of vocal competitions in Australia.

130. McCredie, Andrew D. Catalogue of 46 Australian composers and selected works. ... Canberra: Commonwealth Assistance to Australian Composers,1969. 20 p. (Music by Australian Composers, survey no. 1)

131. Knaus, Herwig. Die Musiker im Archivbestand des Kaiserlichen Obersthofmeisteramts (1637–1705). Wien: Hermann Böhlaus Nachf., 1967. 2 v. (Österreichische Akademie der Wissenschaften ... Veröff. der Kommission für Musikforschung, Heft 7 u. 8)

An archive study of early Austrian musicians, made up of transcriptions of documents pertaining to musical activity in Austrian courts, chapels, and municipalities. Each volume has an index of names.

For a similar study based on French archives, see. no. 2302.

132. Suppan, Wolfgang. Steirisches Musiklexikon. Im Auftrage des Steirischen Tonkünstlerbundes unter Benützung der "Sammlung Wamlek" bearb. ... Graz: Akademische Druck- und Verlagsanstalt, 1962–1966. 676 p. 56 plates.

Issued serially between 1962 and 1966.

A biographical dictionary of musicians associated with Graz and other parts of Styria. Comprehensive for pre-1800 names, selective for post 1800. Good bibliographical coverage for composers' works and for writings on the musicians.

Review by Fritz Racek in *Die Musikforschung,* 22 (1969), p. 388–89.

BELGIUM

133. Centre Belge de Documentation Musicale. Music in Belgium: contemporary Belgian composers. Brussels: Published in cooperation with the CeBeDeM, by A. Manteau, 1964. 158 p.

A publication designed to stimulate interest in contemporary Belgian music. Biographical sketches of 48 modern Belgian composers, with lists of their major works. Portraits. Index of names and brief lists of recordings.

134. Hemel, Victor van. Voorname belgische toonkunstenaars uit de 18de, 19de, en 20ste eeuw. Beknopt overzicht van hun leven en œuvre. Derde bijgewerkte druk. Antwerpen: Cupidouitgave, 1958. 84 p.

Brief biographies of 101 Belgian musicians, covering the period from Loeillet to the present.

135. Vannes, René with André Souris. Dictionnaire des musiciens (compositeurs). Bruxelles: Maison Larcier, 1947. 443 p.

Belgian composers from the 15th century to 1830, with comprehensive lists of works, published or in manuscript, and references to other sources of information.

Comments by Richard S. Hill in *Notes,* 6 (1949), p. 607–608.

BULGARIA

136. Entsiklopediia na Bulgarskata Muzikalna Kultura. Ed. by Venelin Krustev. Sofia: Bulgarska Akademiia na Naukite, 1967. 465 p.

A Bulgarian bio-bibliographical dictionary of musicians. Illustrated. Contains much information on Bulgarian instruments and musical institutions.

CANADA

137. Canadian Broadcasting Corporation. Catalogue of Canadian composers. Rev. and enl. ed. Ed. by Helmut Kallman. Ottawa: Canadian Broadcasting Corporation, 1952? 254 p.

Reprint by The Scholarly Press, 1972.

356 brief biographical sketches, giving activities, education, addresses. Listings of works as complete as possible, giving titles, dates of publications, medium, duration, publisher. Unpublished works included. Lists of Canadian publishers and composers' organizations.

138. Encyclopedia of Music in Canada. Edited by Helmut Kallman, Gilles Potvin, and Kenneth Winters. Toronto: University of Toronto Press, 1981. 1,076 p.

French version published in 1982 as *Éncyclopédie de musique au Canada.*

About music in Canada and Canada's musical relations with the rest of the world . . . relates the activities and contributions of Canadian individuals and organizations . . . and discusses general topics in their Canadian aspects. [from the *Introduction*]

Truly encyclopedic in scope. Lengthy articles, many illustrated. Includes tables, lists, and bibliographies. Superb indexes.

CUBA

139. Orovio, Helio. Diccionario de la música cubana; biográfico y técnico. Ciudad de la Habana: Editorial Letras Cubanas, 1981. 442 p.

Primarily a biographical dictionary, but with entries for terms, institutions and organizations, and instruments.

140. Ramírez, Serafín. La Habana artïstica. Apuntes historicos. Habana: Imp. del E. M. de la Capitania general, 1891. 687 p.

Early attempt to record activity in 19th century Cuba, includes notes on 19th century Cuban dances. Includes a 200 p. dictionary of composers and another 100 p. discussing the literature of music.

CZECHOSLOVAKIA

141. Ceskoslovenský Hudebni Slovník, osob a instituci. Praha: Statni hudebni vydavatelstvi, 1963–65. 2 v.

Editors: Gracian Cernusak, Bohumir Stedron, and Zdenko Novacek.

A Czech bio-bibliographical dictionary. Also includes entries under names of places and institutions.

Review by Camillo Schoenbaum in *Die Musikforschung,* 18 (1965), p. 347–49.

142. Dlabač, Jan Bohumir. Allgemeines historisch Künstlerlexikon fur Böhmen und zum Theil auch fur Mähren und Schlesien. Auf Kosten der höchloblichen Herrenstände Böhmens hrsg. Prag: Gedruckt bei G. Hasse, 1815. 3 v.

Reprint by Frits A. M. Knuf, Hilversum, Holland.

An early dictionary of Czech (Bohemian and Moravian) musicians).

143. Gardavsky, Cenek, ed. Contemporary Czechoslovak composers. Prague: *s.n.,* 1965. 562 p.

Biographies and bibliographical information on more than 300 Czech composers. English text. Also published in French.

FRANCE

144. Benoit, Marcelle. Musique de cour, chapelle, chambre, écurie. Recueil de documents 1661–1733. Paris: Éditions A. et J. Picard, 1971. 553 p. (La vie musicale en France sous les rois Bourbons)

A rich documentary study of musicians active in the French court from 1661 to 1733 based on material in the national archives and the Bibliothèque Nationale.

145. Brossard, Yolande de. Musiciens de Paris, 1535–1792; actes d'État civil d'après le Fichier Laborde de la Bibliothèque Nationale. Préf. de Norbert Dufourcq. Paris: A. et J. Picard, 1965. 302 p. (Vie musicale en France sous les rois Bourbons, 11)

A directory of early Parisian musicians based on a card file compiled by Leon de Laborde (d. 1869). Comprises some 6,624 cards listing musicians of all kinds active in Paris during the period covered. Index of musicians arranged chronologically under their specialties.

146. Dictionnaire des musiciens Français. Paris: Seghers, 1961. 379 p.

A pocket, illustrated dictionary of French musicians. Coverage is selective, particularly for contemporary figures. Brief summaries of the major works of composers; no full listings or bibliographical references.

147. Favati, Guido. Le biografie trovadorische, testi provenzali dei secc. XIII e XIV, edizione critica . . . Bologna: Libreria Antiquaria Palmaverdi, 1961. 523 p. (Biblioteca degli studi mediolatine e volgari, 3)

Not a French biographical dictionary in the ordinary sense, but a critical edition of the original 13th and 14th-century biographical descriptions of the troubadour composers.

For specialists in Romance philology and Medieval music; to be used in connection with Gennrich (no. 1783) and Pillet (no. 1812).

Jurgens, Madeleine. Documents du Minutier Central. . . . See 'Catalogs of Music Libraries," no. 2302.

148. Muller, René. Anthologie des compositeurs de musique d'Alsace. Strasbourg: Féderation de sociétés catholiques de chant et de musique d'Alsace, 1970. 190 p.

149. Sevran, Pascal. Le dictionnaire de la chanson française. Paris: M. Lafon, 1986. 379 p.

A biographical dictionary of singers of the French popular song.

150. Tablettes de renommée des musiciens, auteurs, compositeurs, virtuoses, amateurs et ma_itres de musique vocale et instrumentale, les plus connus en chaque genre. Genève: Minkoff Reprints, 1971. 125 p.

Reprint of the edition of Cailleau, Paris, 1785.

A bio-bibliographical work focusing primarily upon musicians of Paris.

GERMANY

151. Fellerer, Karl G., ed. Rheinische Musiker. Köln: Arno Volk-Verlag, 1960–74. (Beitrage zur rheinischen Musikgeschichte, 43, 53, 58, 64, 69, 80, 97)

A series of volumes giving biographical and bibliographical information on musicians of the Rhineland. Issued serially. Each volume is alphabetically complete in itself, but the indexing is cumulative. Numerous contributors. Beginning with Folge 6 (1969), the editor is Dietrich Kamper. The work follows the pattern of Mattheson's *Grundlage einer Ehren-Pforte* (1740) in that many of the biographies of living musicians are self-compiled.

152. Fey, Hermann. Schleswig-Holsteinische Musiker, von den ältesten Zeiten bis zur Gegenwart; ein Heimatbuch. Hamburg: C. Holler, 1922. 126 p.

Dictionary arrangement. Full bibliographies of compositions, with authority references. "Quellennachweis," p. 125–126.

153. Kossmaly, Karl and C. H. Herzel. Schlesisches Tonkünstler-Lexikon, enthaltend die Biographieen aller schlesischen Tonkünstler, Componisten, Cantoren, Organisten, Tongelehrten, Textdicher, Orgelbauer, Instrumentenmacher . . . hrsg. von Kossmaly und Carlo (pseud.). Breslau: E. Trewendt, 1846–47. 332 p.

Reprinted by G. Olms, Hildesheim, 1982.

Issued in four parts, each in a separate alphabet. Long articles giving classified lists of compositions, roles for performers, concert programs.

154. Kürschners Deutscher Musiker-Kalender 1954. Zweite Ausgabe des *Deutschen Musiker-Lexikons. Herausgeber:* Hedwig Mueller von Asow und E. H. Mueller von Asow. Berlin: Walter de Gruyter, 1954. 1,702 columns.

First published in 1929 under the title, *Deutsches Musiker-Lexikon. Ed. by* Erich H. Muller.

Biographies of living German, Austrian, and Swiss musicians in all categories and German-born musicians in foreign countries. Entries give essential biographical information and detailed lists of works. Excessive use of abbreviations. Indexes of names by date of birth (1854–1939) and date of death (1929–1954).

155. Ledebur, Carl F. H. W. P. J., Freiherr von. Tonkünstler-Lexikon Berlins von den ältesten Zeiten bis auf die Gegenwart. Berlin: L. Rauh, 1861. 704 p.

Reprint by Hans Schneider, Tützig, 1965.

An important early dictionary of Berlin musicians. Entries for composers, publishers, performers, amateurs, born or active in Berlin, with detailed bibliographies of compositions.

156. Lipowsky, Felix J. Bairisches Musik-Lexikon. Munchen: Giel, 1811. 338 (438) p.

Reprint of the original edition by G. Olms, Hildesheim, 1982.

An early dictionary of some historical importance. Covers Bavarian composers and performers, listing major compositions. Occasional title-page transcriptions.

157. Musik und Musiker am Mittelrhein: ein biographisches, orts- und landesgeschichtliches Nachschlagewerk in Verbindung mit den Musikwissenschaftlichen Instituten der Universitäten Frankfurt a.M. . . . [et al.] unter Mitarbeit zahlreicher Musik- und Lokalgeschichtsforscher und mit Unterstützung durch Franz Bösken herausgegeben von Hubert Unverricht; Bd. 2 Unter mitwirkung von Kurt Oehl. Mainz: Schott, 1974–1981. 2 v. (Beiträge zur mittelrheinischen Musikgeschichte, 20–21)

A biographical work concentrating upon musical figures from the area around Frankfurt. Bibliographies.

158. Verband Deutscher Komponisten und Musikwissenschaftlicher. Komponisten und Musikwissenschaftlicher der Deutschen Demokratischen Republik. Kurzbiographien und Werkverzeichnisse. Berlin: Verlag Neue Musik, 1959. 199 pgs.

2nd edition expanded, Berlin, 1967. 239 pgs.

Brief biographical sketches of East German composers and musicologists, with listings of their major works. Preceded by a group of essays on musical life and institutions in the Eastern zone. Portraits.

GREAT BRITAIN (INCLUDING IRELAND AND SCOTLAND)

159. Baptie, David. Musical Scotland, past and present. Being a dictionary of Scottish musicians from about 1400 till the present time, to which is added a bibliography of musical publications connected with Scotland from 1611. Paisley: J. and R. Parlane, 1894. 53 p.

Reprint by Georg Olms, Hildesheim, 1972.

160. Brown, James D. and Stephen S. Stratton. British musical biography: a dictionary of musical artists, authors, and composers born in Britain and its colonies. Birmingham: Stratton, 1897. 462 p.

Reprint by Da Capo Press, New York, 1971.

The emphasis is on composers living at the time of publication. Great masters treated briefly to afford room for the obscure. Includes a large number of English names that cannot be found elsewhere, with excellent bibliographies.

161. Highfill, Philip H. A biographical dictionary of actors, actresses, musicians, dancers, managers & other stage personnel in London, 1660–1800. By Philip H. Highfill, Kalman A. Burnim and Edward A. Langhans. Carbondale: Southern Illinois University Press, 1973– . 12 v. to date

When completed this work will comprise perhaps 20 volumes, each containing about 1,000 biographical entries detailing all the facts that exhaustive research has produced about the performers and other theatrical personnel listed.

Humphries, Charles and William C. Smith. *Music publishing in the British Isles* ... See no. 2661.

162. Huntley, John. British film music. Forward by Muir Mathieson. London: Skelton Robinson, 1947. 247 p.

Reprinted by Arno Press, New York, 1972.

P. 189–229: biographical index of British film composers. Lists many names not to be found in other reference sources together with a listing of film scores.

Kidson, Frank. *British music publishers* ... See no. 2667.

163. Palmer, Russell. British music. London: Skelton Robinson, 1948. 283 p.

Biographical index of contemporary British musicians and musical organizations. Portraits.

164. Pulver, Jeffrey. A biographical dictionary of old English music. London: Kegan Paul; New York, Dutton, 1927. 537 p.

Reprints by the Da Capo Press, New York, 1973, with a new introduction by Gilbert Blount, and by Bert Franklin, New York, 1969.

English musicians active from about 1200 to the death of Purcell (1695). Cites manuscript sources, contemporary publications, and occasionally modern editions. Somewhat discursive in style, with lists of works scattered through the bodies of the articles, but useful as a starting point for the study of early English musicians. See also the author's companion volume covering old English musical terms (no. 397).

HOLLAND

See THE NETHERLANDS

HUNGARY

165. Contemporary Hungarian Composers. Responsible editor Gyula Czigány. Fourth, revised and enlarged edition. Budapest: Editío Musica, 1979. 219 p.

First published in 1970.

A bio-bibliographical work including a discography of works by Hungarian composers.

166. Molnár, Imre. A magyar muzsika könyve. Budapest: Merkantil-Nyomda, 1936. 632 p.

Institutions, organizations, and biographical entries for composers, performers, and other musicians.

INDIA

167. Sambamoorthy, P. A dictionary of South Indian music and musicians. Madras: The Indian Music Publishing House, 1952– .

In progress. Vol. 1: A-F. Vol. 2 (1959): G-K. Vol. 3 (1971): L-N.

Portraits of composers and performers.

168. Who's Who of Indian Musicians. New Delhi: Sangeet Natak Akademi, 1984. 160 p.

First published in 1968. 100 p.

Brief biographical data on living Indian musicians, giving date of birth, area of specialization, addresses.

IRELAND

169. Dublin. Music Association of Ireland. A catalogue of contemporary Irish composers. Edgar M. Deale, editor. 2nd ed. Dublin: Music Association of Ireland, 1974. 108 p.

Data on the works of contemporary Irish composers, including brief biographical information, addresses, full descriptions of works: titles, media, timing, instrumentation, availability. List of publishers and list of abbreviations.

ISRAEL (AND JEWISH MUSICIANS IN GENERAL)

170. Gradenwitz, Peter. Music and musicians in Israel: a comprehensive guide to modern Israeli music. 3rd ed. Tel Aviv: Israeli Music Publications, 1978. 227 p.

Originally published in Jerusalem, 1952. Subsequently appeared in Tel Aviv, 1959. 226 p.

Biographies, varying in length, of about 60 composers, grouped by school. Appendix, p. 133–63, contains an alphabetical listing of composers and their works, but without reference to the biography section. Also given is a list of publishers and a group of publishers' catalogs.

171. Saleski, Gdal. Famous musicians of Jewish origin. New York: Bloch, 1949. 716 p.

First published in 1927 under the title, *Famous musicians of a wandering race*. 463 p.

Informal biographies, classified according to type of musical activity: composers, conductors, violinists, etc. About 400 entries. No bibliographies, but major works are mentioned in the articles. Portraits. P. 679–716: Israeli musicians.

172. Shalita, Israel and Hanan Steinitz. Encyclopedia of music. Vol 1: a biographical dictionary of Jewish and world musicians; Vol 2: dictionary of terms, theory, instruments, forms and history of Jewish and world music. Tel Aviv: Joshua Chachik, 1965. 2 v.

In Hebrew with indexes of Hebrew equivalents for English names and terms. International in scope.

173. Stengel, Theophil and Herbert Gerigk. Lexikon der Juden in der Musik, mit einem Titelverzeichnis judischer Werke. Berlin: B. Hahnefeld, 1943. 404 columns. (Veroffentlichungen des Instituts der NSDAP zur Erforschung der Judenfrage . . . , 2)

First published in 1940. 380 p.

Among the more shameful products of German National Socialism were dictionaries of Jewish musicians compiled to further the purposes of anti-Semitism. This one and the Girschner *Repertorium* (see no. 558) are cited as examples of this vicious genre.

174. Who Is Who in ACUM. Authors, composers, and music publishers. Biographical notes and principal works. Compiled and edited by Ravina Ravina and Shlomo Skolsky. Tel Aviv: ACUM Ltd., Société d'auteurs, compositeurs et éditeurs de musique en Israel, 1965. 95 p.

Addenda and corrigenda published 1966, 10 p.

Brief biographies, with lists of works, of authors, composers, and publishers affiliated with ACUM, a performing rights organization in Israel.

ITALY

175. Alcari, C. Parma nella music. Parma: M. Fresching, 1931. 259 p.

A biographical dictionary of musicians born in Parma. Emphasis is placed on 19th-century figures. Extended bibliographies for the most important musicians (e.g.,Verdi, Pizzetti).

176.   Angelis, Alberto de. L'Italia musicale d'oggi. Dizionario dei musicisti: compositori, direttori d'orchestra, concertisti, insegnanti, liutari, cantanti, scrittori musicali, librettisti, editori musicali, ecc. 3rd ed., corredate di una appendice. Roma: Ausonia, 1928. 523, 211 p.
First published in 1918; 2nd edition, 1922.
Living Italian musicians, with comprehensive lists of works.

177.   Berutto, Guglielmo. Il Piemonte e la musica 1800–1984. Torino: Guglielmo Berutto, 1984. 421 p.
A bio-bibliographical dictionary arranged in sections: musicisti, cantanti, editori, impresari, registri, scenografi, danzi-bande musicali, società corali, teatri scomparsi ed esistenti. A final section gives brief historical sketches.

178.   Damerini, Adelmo, and Franco Schlitzer. Musicisti toscani; scritti di G. Barblan *et al.*, settembre 1955. Siena: Ticci, 1955. 81 p.
A publication of the Accademia Musicale Chigiana.
Musicians of Tuscany.

179.   Masutto, Giovanni. I maestri di musica italiani del secolo XIX. Notizie biografiche. . . . Terza edizione, corretta ed aumentata. Venezia: G. Cechini, 1882. 226 p.
First printed in 1880 by Fontana, Venice.

LATIN AMERICA

180.   Mariz, Vasco. Dicionário bio-bibliográfico musical (brasileiro e internacional). Pref. de Renato Almeida. Rio de Janeiro: Livraria Kosmos, 1948. 246 p.
Brief biographies of the best-known figures in music since the Renaissance, including performers. Useful chiefly for Brazilian musicians.

181.   Mayer-Serra, Otto. Música y músicos de Latinoaméric. México, Editorial Atlante, 1947. 2 v.
Primarily biographical, although some terms, dance forms, and instruments are included. Listings of composers' works vary from brief resumes to full tabulations for major composers. Portraits.

182.   Pan American Union. Music Section. Composers of the Americas, biographical data and catalogs of their works. Washington, D.C.: Pan American Union, 1955– . no. 1– .
Each issue contains from 4 to 16 names, alphabetically arranged, with brief biographies in English and Spanish. Portraits. Dates from scores, sometimes autographs. Works are given chronologically within prinicipal media, with dates of composition, timing, publisher, and recordings if any. Lists unpublished works.

THE NETHERLANDS

183. Gregoir, Edouard G. J. Biographie des artistes-musiciens néerlandais des XVIIIe et XIXe siècles, et des artistes étrangers résidant ou ayant résidé en Néerlands à la même époque. Anvers: L. de la Montagne, 1864. 238 p.

Based on an supplementing his *Essai historique sur la musique,* Brussels, 1861.

Brief biographies of Dutch musicians. Careers summarized, major works mentioned for composers, but no full listings.

184. Letzer, J. H. Muzikaal Nederland, 1850–1910. Bio-bibliographisch woordenboek ... 2.uitgaff met aanvulligen en verbeteringen. Utrecht: J.L. Beijers, 1913. 201 p., with 10 p. of additions.

Composers, musicologists, performers, etc., active in The Netherlands 1850–1910. Biographies, lists of works, occasional dates of first performances.

185. Straeten, Edmond S. J. vander. La musique aux pays-bas avant le XIXe siècle. Documents inédits et annotés. Compositeurs, virtuoses, théoriciens, luthiers, opéras, motets, airs nationaux, académies, maitrîses, livres, portraits, etc. Bruxelles: C. Muquardt, 1867–88. 8 v.

Vols. 2–7 published by G. A. Van Trigt; vol. 8 by Schott. Reprint by Dover, New York, 1968, 4 v.

Not strictly a biographical dictionary but an invaluable collection of documents, transcripts of records, biographical and bibliographical notes related to the activities of Flemish musicians (Dutch and Belgian). Vol. 6 is devoted to Flemish musicians in Italy; vols. 7–8, to Flemish musicians in Spain. Rich in information of the greatest interest to students of early European music.

186. Het Toonkunstenaarsboek van Nederland 1956. Edited by Jos. Smits van Waesberghe. Amsterdam: Nederlandse Toonkunstenaarsraad, 1956. 240 p.

A source book of information on Dutch organizations, institutions, and persons connected with music. Members of the Dutch society of composers are listed alphabetically, with addresses and a key to their activities and affiliations. They are also listed by place.

PARAGUAY

187. Boettner, Juan Max. Música y músicos del Paraguay. Asunción: Editorial de Autores Paraguayos Asociados, 1957. 294 p.

Includes biographical dictionary of Paraguayan musicians. Bibliography.

POLAND

188. Chybiński, Adolf. Slownik muzyków dawnej Polski do roku 1800. Krakow: Polskie Wydawnictwo Muzyczne, 1949. 163 p.

Biographical dictionary of musicians (composers and performers) active in Poland in 1800. Brief articles mentioning principal works. List of references for each entry. Preface discusses sources of information such as *Fetis, Eitner,* and many Polish publications and archives.

189. Chybiński, Josef. Slownik muzyków polskich. Ed. Jósef Chominski. Warsaw: Polskie Wydawnictwo Muzyczne, 1962. 2 v.

At head of title: Instytut Sztuki Polskiej Akademii Nauk. Vol. 1: A-L. Vol. 2: M-Z.

190. Sowinski, Wojciech. Les musiciens polonais et slaves, anciens et modernes; dictionnaire biographique ... Précédé d'un un résumé de l'histoire de la musique en Pologne. ... Paris: A. Le Clerc, 1857. 599 p.

Another edition, in Polish, published in 1874. Reprint by the Da Capo Press, New York, 1971.

"Resume de l'histoire de la musique en Pologne," p. 1–44. "Anciens instruments de musique chez les polonais et les slaves," p. 45–58. Long biographical articles, with full bibliographies for major composers.

PORTUGAL

191. Amorim, Eugénio. Dicionário biográfico de musicos do norte de Portugal. Porto: Edições Maranus, 1935. 110 p.

Chiefly 19th century and living musicians. Some extended articles, with compositions listed in the body of the text.

192. Mazza, José. Dicionário biográfico de musicos portugueses, com prefácio e notas do José Augusto Alegria. ... Lisboa: 1945? 103 p.

"Extraido de revista, *Ocidente,* 1944/45."

A dictionary compiled around 1790 and preserved in manuscript in the Biblioteca Publica de Évora. Entries arranged by Christian names; many names of members of religious orders. The dictionary occupies p. 13–40; additional biographical information supplied by the editor from other sources, p. 41–103.

193. Vasconcellos, Joaquim A. da Fonseca E. Os musicos portuguezes. Biographia-bibliographia. Porto: Imprenza Portugueza, 1870. 2 v.

Long biographical articles, lists and discussions of compositions. Useful for early names, library locations of manuscripts, etc. Discussions of operas includes dates and places of first performances.

194. Viera, Ernesto. Diccionario biographico de musicos portuguezes; historia e bibliographia da musica em Portugal. Lisboa: Moreira e Pinheiro, 1900–1904 2 v.

More inclusive than Vasconcellos, above. Comprehensive lists of works for major composers. Vol. 2 includes much supplementary material and a chronological index.

RUMANIA

195. Cosma, Viorel. Muzicieni români. Compozitori si muzicologi. Lexicon. [Rumanian musicians, composers and musicologists; a dictionary.]

Bucuresti: Uniunii Compozitorilor, 1970. 475 p.
Expansion of a work first issued in 1965.
Biographical data and information on the works of the most prominent Rumanian composers and musicologists. Includes musicians of earlier times, but stresses the contemporary scene. Portraits and discographies.

SCANDINAVIA

196. Kappel, Vagn. Contemporary Danish composers against the background of Danish musical life and history. 3rd rev. ed. Copenhagen: Det Danske Selskab, 1967. 88 p.
A public relations document, first issued in 1948 and published in a 2nd ed. in 1950. 116 p.
Biographical sketches of 14 Danish composers. Representative works cited, but no full lists. Discography of Danish music, p. 97–113.

197. Sundelin, Torsten. Norrländskt musikliv. Uppsala: Almqvist u. Wiksell, 1946. 358 p.

SOUTH AFRICA

198. Huskisson, Yvonne. The Bantu composers of southern Afric. s.l.: South African Broadcasting Corporation, 1969. 335 p.
Text in English and Afrikaans.
Portraits of musicians, index of composers, and a study of the traditional instruments of the Bantu.

199. South African music encyclopedia, general editor, Jacques P. Malan. Cape Town : Oxford University Press, 1979–1986. 4 v.
"A publication of the Human Sciences Research Council, Pretoria."
Entries limited to the period 1652–1960. Coverage of the music of European and indigenous South Africans. Biographical entries include comprehensive lists of works. Bibliographies follow many articles.

SPAIN

200. Alcahili y de Mosquera, José Maria Ruiz de Lihori y Pardines, Baron de. La música en Valencia. Diccionario biográfico y crítico . . . Valencia: Domenech, 1903. 445 p.
Biographies of widely varying length, with summary lists of works for major composers. Under "Anonimos," p. 39–170, the compiler introduces long literary digressions concerning liturgical drama, dance, music, military music, etc. with musical examples.

SWITZERLAND

201. Refardt, Edgar. Historisch-biographisches Musikerlexikon der Schweiz. Leipzig/Zürich: Hug u. Co., 1928. 355 p.
Comprehensive biographical coverage for names connected with Swiss music from the Middle Ages to the end of the 16th century. Musicians and instrument makers of the 17th and 18th centuries; composers

only for the 19th and 20th centuries. Lists of works.

202. Schweizer Musiker-Lexikon. Dictionnaire des musiciens suisses.... Im Auftrag des Schweizerischen Tonkunstlervereins bearbeitet von ... Rédigé a la demande de l'Association des Musiciens Suisses par Willi Schuh *et al.* Zürich: Atlantis Verlag, 1964. 421 p.

The expansion of a biographical dictionary of Swiss musicians that appeared originally as vol. 2 of the *Schweizer Musikbuch* (Zürich, 1939). Treats Swiss musicians of all periods as well as foreign musicians resident in Switzerland or associated with the music of that country. Articles in French and German. Excellent bibliographical coverage.

203. Swiss Composers' League. 40 contemporary Swiss composers. Amriswil: Bodensee Verlag, 1956. 222 p.

Brief biographies and critical comment. A few representative works are described and a larger selection listed, with imprints and instrumentation given. Recordings. Portraits.Text in English.

TURKEY

204. Öztuna, T. Yilmaz. Türk musikisi ansiklopedisi. Istanbul: M. E. B. Devlet Kitaplari, 1969–74. 2 v.

Based on his *Türk musikisi lugati.*

Turkish dictionary of terms and biography. Terms are general musical concepts, but the biographies are restricted to Turkish figures. Bibliographical references.

UNITED STATES

205. American Society of Composers, Authors and Publishers. ASCAP Biographical dictionary. Fourth edition. Compiled for the American Society of Composers, Authors and Publishers by Jacques Cattell Press. N.Y.: R. R. Bowker, 1980. 589 p.

1st published 1948. 2nd edition 1952. 3rd edition 1966.

Brief biographies of over 8,000 members of ASCAP, including lyricists and composers of popular and serious music. Major works listed. Separate list of publisher members.

Review by Alan Hoffman in *Notes,* 39 (1982), p. 103–4.

206. Anderson, E. Ruth. Contemporary American Composers: a biographical dictionary. Second edition. Boston: G. K. Hall, 1982. 578 p.

First published in 1976 with 513 p.

Approximately 4,500 composers listed.

Criteria for inclusion: birth date no earlier than 1870; American citizenship or extended residence in the U.S.; at least one original composition published, commercially recorded or performed in an urban area.

Lists representative works; composers' addresses cited.

207. Claghorn, Charles Eugene. Biographical dictionary of American music. West Nyack: Parker Publishing, 1973. 491 p.

5,200 entries covering persons engaged in a wide range of musical styles and genres. Entries also for ensembles listing principal members. Reviewed in ALA *Booklist,* February 1, 1975.

208. Edwards, George Thornton. Music and musicians of Maine. Being a history of progress of music in the territory which has come to be known as the State of Maine, from 1604–1928. N.Y.: AMS Press, 1970.
Reprint of the 1928 edition.
Many illustrations and a biographical dictionary.

209. Ewen, David. American composers, a biographical dictionary. N.Y.: G. P. Putnam's Sons, 1982. 793 p.
Biographical information and stylistic characterizations for 300 American composers from William Billings to the present. Index of titles of music discussed.

Ewen, David. Popular American composers. ... See 249.

210. Granniss, Lewis C. Connecticut composers. New Haven: Connecticut State Federation of Music Clubs, 1935. 125 p.
Brief biographies with lists of major works. Lists early tune book writers. Chronological list of composers.

211. Historical Records Survey. District of Columbia. Bio-bibliographical index of musicians in the United States of America from colonial times ... sponsored by the Board of Commissioners of the District of Columbia. 2nd ed. Washington, D.C.: Music Section, Pan American Union, 1956. 439 p.
First printed in 1941. Unaltered reprint, 1970, by the AMS Press, New York, and the Scholarly Press, St. Clair Shores, Michigan, 1972.
An index to biographical information contained in 66 works (dictionaries, histories, etc.) on American music, with page references to the volumes indexed.

212. Jablonski, Edward. The encyclopedia of American music. N.Y.: Doubleday, 1981. 629 p.
The work is organized in roughly chronological order under the following headings:
1. In the beginning;
2. A time of revolutions;
3. From the second awakening to the second New England School;
4. The Romantics and Classicists;
5. The Twenties;
6. The time of trouble: Depression and war.
Appendix: American music on records.

213. Jacobi, Hugh William. Contemporary American composers based at American colleges and universities. Consultant Margaret DeVoss. Paradise, California: Paradise Arts Publishers, 1975. 240 p.
Biographies interpolating citations of major works. Quotations from composers following each alphabetical section. Supplement, 2. 238–40.
Brief review by Stephen M. Fry in *Notes,* 32 (1975), p. 302.

214. MacCarty, Clifford. Film composers in America: a checklist of their work. Foreward by Lawrence Morton. Glendale: John Valentine, 1953. 193 p.

Reprint by Da Capo Press, New York, 1972.

163 names, with film scores listed by date. Index of film titles; index of orchestrators.

Review by Frederick. W. Sternfeld in *Notes,* 11 (1953), p. 105.

215. Mangler, Joyce Ellen. Rhode Island music and musicians, 1733–1850. Detroit: Information Service, 1965. 90 p. (Detroit studies in music bibliography, 7)

Primarily a directory of early Rhode Island musicians; indexed by profession and by chronology.

Supplement I: organ builders and installations in Rhode Island churches. Supplement II: membership in the Psallonian Society 1816–1832. Bibliography of primary and secondary sources.

Review by Donald W. Krummel in *Notes,* 23 (1966), p. 265.

216. Music and Dance in California and the West. Richard D. Saunders, editor. Hollywood: Bureau of Musical Research, 1948. 311 p.

Earlier editions with slightly varying titles in 1933 and 1940.

This and the following six titles (nos. 217–222) are a series of regional reference works covering different sections of the United States. Long articles on the development of musical and dance activities. Biographical sketches of composers, performers, conductors, educators, etc. Portraits. Pronounced emphasis on the commercial aspects of music.

217. Music and Dance in New York State. Sigmund Spaeth, editor-in-chief. William J. Perlman, director and managing editor. New York: Bureau of Musical Research, 1951. 435 p.

218. Music and Dance in Pensylvania, New Jersey and Delaware. Sigmund Spaeth, editor-in-chief. William J. Perlman, director and managing editor. New York: Bureau of Musical Research, 1954. 339 p.

219. Music and Dance in Texas, Oklahoma and the Southwest. Edited by E.Clyde Whitlock and Richard D. Saunders. Hollywood: Bureau of Musical Research, 1950. 256 p.

220. Music and Dance in the Central States. Richard D. Saunders, editor; William J. Perlman, compiler. Hollywood: Bureau of Musical Research, 1952. 173 p.

221. Music and Dance in the New England States. Sigmund Spaeth, editor-in-chief. William J. Perlman, director and associate editor. New York: Bureau of Musical Research, 1951. 347 p.

222. Music and Dance in the Southeastern States. Sigmund Spaeth, editor-in-chief. William J. Perlman, director and managing editor. New York: Bureau of Musical Research, 1952. 331 p.

223. The New Grove Dictionary of American Music. Edited by H. Wiley Hitchcock and Stanley Sadie. London: Macmillan, 1986. 4 v.

A work consisting of re-worked articles from the *New Grove* and newly commissioned ones "to reflect the essence of American music" (from the Preface). Covers American music and musicians broadly considered, with concise articles summarizing works for lesser known persons, and broad, illustrated pieces with works lists and lengthy bibliographies for well-known persons. Many of the articles bring bits of information together for the first time. Detailed coverage of popular styles and genres, including sketches of important popular groups. Numerous descriptions of uniquely American musical instruments. Historical sketches of musical publishers. Copiously illustrated, provided with an excellent introduction and a list of contributors. Signed articles. The principal reference work on American music, but not without significant flaws and omissions.

An extensive review by Mary Wallace Davidson *et al.* appears in *Notes,* 44 (1988), p. 43–47.

224. North Carolina Federation of Music Clubs. North Carolina musicians, a selective handbook. Chapel Hill: University of North Carolina Library, 1956. 82 p. (Univ. of North Carolina Library Extension pubn., vol. 21, no. 4)

225. Reis, Claire R. Composers in America; biographical sketches of contemporary composers with a record of their works. Rev. and enl. ed. New York: Macmillan, 1947. 399 p.

First published in 1930 under the title *American Composers. . . .*

A survey of music written by American serious composers, 1915 to 1947. Biographies of 332 composers, with a classified listing of their works, manuscripts included (date, publishers, duration). Supplementary list of 424 names without further biographical data.

Review by Lee Fairley in *Notes,* 4 (1947), p. 458–59.

226. Schiavo, Giovanni Ermenegildo. Italian-American history. New York: Arno Press, 1975. 2 v. (The Italian American experience)

Vol. 2 has also a special title: The Italian contribution to the Catholic Church in Americ. Reprint of the ed. published by Vigo Press, New York, 1947–49.

One of a series of volumes devoted to Italian-American cultural relations. The first volume of this set includes a section on Italian music and musicians in America and a *Dictionary of musical biography.*

227. Smith, Julia, ed. Directory of American women composers, with selected music for senior and junior clubs. First edition. Chicago: National Federation of Music Clubs, 1970. 51 p.

> Here is a first *Directory of American Women Composers. . . .* The *Directory* contains the names of over 600 composers who have written, or are now writing music that ranges from very easy to the most difficult and experimental, including electronic music. [Editor's *Foreword*]

No work lists, but type of music composed is indicated for each composer as well as for the publishers who have issued their works. Key to music publishers and distributors (p. 48–51).

228. Thomson, Virgil. American music since 1910. With an introduction by Nicolas Nabokov. New York: Holt, Rinehart and Winston, 1970. 204 p. (Twentieth-century composers, 1)

Primarily a collection of critical essays, but contains a biographical dictionary of 106 American composers, p. 118–185. Brief biographies with stimulating commentary. Principal works cited.

Who's who in American music: Classical See no. 126.

229. Works Projects Administration. Northern California. Celebrities in El Dorado, 1850–1906. Cornel Lengyel, editor. San Francisco: Works Project Administration of California and sponsored by the City and County of San Francisco, 1940. 270 leaves (typescript). (The history of music in San Francisco, 4)

A biographic record of 111 prominent musicians who have visited San Francisco and performed here from the earliest days of the gold rush era to the time of the great fire, with additional lists of visiting celebrities (1909–1940), chamber music ensembles, bands, orchestras, and other music making bodies. [Editor's *Note*]

U.S.S.R.

230. Belza, Igor' Fedorovich. Handbook of Soviet musicians. Edited by Alan Bush. London: Pilot Press, 1944. 101 p.

First printing, 1943. Reprints by the Greenwood Press, Westport, Conn., 1971, and by the Scholarly Press, St. Clair Shores, Michigan, 1972.

40 short biographies. Portraits. Separate bibliographical section giving a list of each composer's works. English titles, dates given when known.

231. Mirkin, Mikhail Iurevich. Kratkii biograficheskii slovar' zarubezhnykh kompozitorov. Moskva: Sov. kompozitor, 1969. 267 p.

A bio-bibliographical dictionary.

232. Sovetskie Kompozitory, kratkii biograficheskii spravochnik. Sostaviteli: G. Bernandt e A. Dolzhanskii. Moskva: Sovetskii Kompozitor, 1957. 695 p.

Biographical sketches of 1,072 composers, with a full listing of their compositions arranged by medium, with dates of first performance for large works. Literary works by the musicians are also listed.

Review by Fred K. Prieberg in *Musical America,* 78 (July 1958), p. 28–29.

233. Vordarsky-Shiraeff, Alexandria. Russian composers and musicians, a biographical dictionary. New York: H.W. Wilson, 1940. 158 p.

Reprint by the Greenwood Press, New York, 1969.

Brief biographies of outstanding figures: composers, performers, teachers, critics. Classified lists of major works, bibliographical references. Cross references to variant spellings of Russian names.

YUGOSLAVIA

234. Kovačević, Krešimir. Hrvatski kompozitori i njihova djela. Zagreb: Naprijed, 1960. 553 p.

Biographies of 50 Croatian composers, for the most part contemporary, with descriptive accounts of their principal works. Summaries in English. Classified index of works analyzed; general index.

235. Savez Kompozitora Jugoslavije. Kompozitori i muzicki pisci Jugoslavije. Clanovi Saveza kompozitora Jugoslavije 1945–1967. Katalog. [Yugoslav composers and music writers. Members of the Union of Yugoslav Composers 1945–1967. Catalogue.] Sastavilia Milena Milosavljevic-Pesic. Beograd: Savez Kompozitora Jugoslaviue, 1968. 663 p.

Contemporary Yugoslav composers and writers on music. Brief biographies; full bibliographies of works. Portraits. Addresses. Preceded by "An introduction to contemporary Yugoslav musical creation," by Krešimir Kovačević, p. 45–75.

DICTIONARIES AND ENCYCLOPEDIAS OF JAZZ, POPULAR, AND FOLK MUSIC

Resources for the reference and research in the areas of jazz, popular, and folk music have increased since the last edition of this work. Numerous dictionaries, encyclopedias, and other, related works are now widely available, though frequently these contain very references to the sources of data for the information provided. The rise of popular music as a commercial enterprise has in turn stimulated an enourmous number of books intended for the uncritical reader; few such works are cited here. Related information will be found in the section, *Jazz* under "Bibliographies of Music Literature," *Jazz* and *Popular Music* under "Bibliographies of Music," and *Collectors' Guide to Jazz Recordings, Collectors' Guide to Popular Recordings,* and *Ethnic and Folk-Music on Records* under "Discographies."

236. Anderson, Robert and Gail North. Gospel music encyclopedia. N.Y.: Sterling, 1979. 320 p.

Illustrated popular biographical work with variable quantities of data presented. Useful lists of winners of awards and broadcast gospel programs.

Discography.

237. Baggelaar, Kristen and Donald Milton. The folk music encyclopedia. London: Omnibus Press, 1977. 419 p.

Also published in the U.S. as *Folk music: more than a song* by Crowell in 1976.

Entries on persons and groups, incorporating biographical, political, social, musical, and discographical information. Does not cite sources. Illustrated.

238. Bane, Michael. Who's who in rock. Researcher, Kenny Kertok. New York: Everest House, 1982. 259 p.

239. Berry, Jr., Lemuel. Biographical dictionary of black musicians and music educators. Volume one. Guthrie: Educational Book Publishers, 1978.
Entries on individuals and ensembles. Many appendices. Indexes to names and specialties.

240. Bogaert, Karel. Blues lexikon. Blues, cajun, boogie woogie, gospel. Antwerp: Standaard, 1972. 480 p.
Biographical information, with discographies for hundreds of blues performers. Bibiography and index. Introduction by John Godrich provides a survey of significant blues literature.

241. Brown, Len and Gary Friedrich. Encyclopedia of rock and roll. N.Y.: Tower Publications, 1970. 217 p.
A bio-bibliographic work.

242. Charters, Samuel B. Jazz: New Orleans. Rev. ed. New York: Oak Publications, 1963. 173 p.
First published in 1958 by Walter C. Allen.
Brief descriptions of musicians and groups, under chronological periods. Appendix of discography; index to names of musicians and bands, to halls, cabarets, and tune titles. Illustrated.

243. Chilton, John. Who's Who of Jazz: Storyville to Swing Street. Philadelphia: Chilton Book Co., 1972. 419 p.
First published in London by The Bloomsbury Book Shop, 1970. 447 p.
Brief biographies of more than 1,000 jazz musicians tracing their affiliations with various groups. Portraits. A partial listing of bandleaders mentioned in the text (p. 416–18).

244. Clifford, Mike. The Harmony illustrated encyclopedia of rock. 5th ed. New York: Harmony Books, 1986. 272 p.
Published in Great Britain as *The illustrated rock handbook. Revised from previous editions of 1981–84. Rev. ed. of The illustrated New musical express encyclopedia of rock, 1978.*

245. Craig, Warren. Sweet and lowdown: America's popular song writers. Metuchen: Scarecrow, 1978. 645 p.
Biographical sketches of Tin Pan Alley figures followed by chronological lists of productions and songs. Claims to rectify factual errors in other works on the same subject. Indexes to song titles and productions.
Review by Julian Hodgson in *Brio,* 16 (1979), p. 23–24. Review by John Shepherd in *Notes,* 36 (1979), p. 372–73.

246. Craig, Warren. The great songwriters of Hollywood. San Diego: A. S. Barnes, 1980. 287 p.
Simultaneously published in London by Tantivy Press.

A biographical work covering composers and librettists. Includes lists of songs and song indices.

247. Davidson, Harry C. Diccionario folclórico de Colombia; musicos, instrumentosy danzas. Bogotá: Banco de la Repúpublica, Departmento de Talleres Gráficos, 1970. 3 v.

248. Dellar, Fred, Roy Thompson, and Douglas B. Green. The illustrated encyclopedia of country music. Foreword by Roy Acuff. New York: Harmony Books, 1977. 256 p.

A publication intended for the enthusiast, but with sufficient information and cross references to be a useful source. Covers personalities, groups, and occasional places. Profusely illustrated. Discographic information provided.

249. Ewen, David. Popular American composers, from revolutionary times to the present. New York: H.W. Wilson, 1962. 217 p.

First Supplement, 1972, 121 pgs.

A bibliographical reference guide to 130 of the most important American composers of popular music, from William Billings to Andre Previn. Portraits. Chronological list of the composers, with an index to some 3,500 songs. The *First supplement* updates the information in 1962 volume and adds 31 new biographies.

250. Feather, Leonard. The encyclopedia of jazz. Completely revised, enlarged and brought up to date. New York: Horizon Press, 1960. 527 p.

First published in 1955. Supplement, 1956. Reprinted by Quartet Books, London & N.Y., 1978 and by Da Capo, N.Y., 1985.

P. 13–90: introductory essays on the history, sociology, and structure of jazz. P. 96–473: biographies of jazz musicians, outlining their careers and summarizing their recording activities. Addresses given.

251. Feather, Leonard. The encyclopedia of jazz in the sixties. Forward by John Lewis. New York: Horizon Press, 1966. 312 p.

Reprinted by Da Capo, N.Y., 1986.

Similar in content and organization to the preceding. Numerous portraits. Biographies stress affiliations with recording companies. Short essays on the state of jazz, the results of jazz polls, etc.

253. Feather, Leonard G. and Ira Gitler. The encyclopedia of jazz in the seventies. Introduction by Quincy Jones. N.Y.: Horizon Press, 1976. 393 p.

Reprinted by Da Capo Press, N.Y. 1987. Also published by Quartet Books, London, 1978.

As in the preceding, a compilation of biographies surrounded with short, topical essays. Covers events from mid-1966 to mid-1976.

"A guide to available jazz films", by Leonard Maltin, p. [382]-386.

Reviews in *Jazz Podium,* 26 (1977), p. 39 and in *Downbeat,* 44 (15 December 1977), p. 52, 60.

254. Gammond, Peter and Peter Clayton. Dictionary of popular music. New York: Philosophical Library, 1961. 274 p.

A dictionary of names, terms, titles of major popular songs. Listing of works and recordings for the principal composers of popular music. Pronounced British slant.

255. Gentry, Linnell. A history and encyclopedia of country, western, and gospel music. 2nd edition, completely revised. Nashville: Claimon Corp., 1969. 598 p.

First published in 1961 by the McQuiddy Press, Nashville.

A major reference work in its field. Part II is an anthology of magazine articles on country, western, and gospel music since 1904. Part III: country musical shows since 1924. Part IV: biographies of country, western, and gospel singers, musicians, and comedians.

256. Gold, Robert S. Jazz talk. Indianapolis: Bobbs-Merrill, 1975. 322 p.

Reprinted by Da Capo, N.Y., 1982.

A dictionary of slang terms providing definitions, sometimes word origins and quotations from the literature.

Brief review by Stephen M. Fry in *Notes,* 32 (1975), p. 302.

257. Harris, Sheldon. Blues who's who: a biographical dictionary of blues singers. New York: Da Capo Press, [1981] c1979. 775 p.

A reprint of the 1979 publication by Arlington House, New Rochelle.

Covering 571 blues singers active from 1900 to 1977. Bibliography of sources. Film, radio, television, theater, song, and names and place indexes. Numerous photographs.

258. Helander, Brock. The rock who's who: a biographical dictionary and critical discography, including rhythm-and-blues, soul, rockabilly, folk, country, easy listening, punk, and new wave. New York: Schirmer Books; London: Collier Macmillan, 1982. 686 p.

Includes articles about non-musical figures. Bibliography and index.

259. Herzhaft, Gérard. Encyclopédie du blues: étude bio-discographique d'une musique populaire négro-americaine. Lyon: Fédèrop, 1979. 346 p.

Entries on individuals, genres, trends, and styles. Occasional discographic citations. General bibliography, but no bibliographies for individuals. Name index.

260. Jasper, Tony and Derek Oliver. The international encyclopedia of hard rock & heavy metal. Revised ed. London: Sidgwick & Jackson, 1986. 388 p.

Previously published in 1983 by Facts on file, N.Y., 400 p.

Entries for almost 1,500 groups and individual musicians. International in scope. Entries include basic biographical facts, some attempts at critical analysis, and a discography.

261. Kienzle, Richard. Great guitarists; the most influential players in jazz, country, blues and rock. New York: Facts on File, c1985. 246 p.

Extensive biographies on about 50 performers in popular genres. Includes discographies and index.

Dictionaries and Encyclopedias / 262

262. Kinkle, Roger D. The complete encyclopedia of popular music and jazz, 1900–1950. New Rochelle: Arlington House, 1974. 4 v.

Contents.: v.1. Music year by year, 1900–1950; v.2. Biographies, A-K; v.3. Biographies, L-Z; v.4. Indexes & appendices.

Covers musicians whose careers began before 1950 and therefore may include works actually written up to the early 1970s. V. 1 contains lists of significant works organized by year of appearance (Broadway musicals, popular songs, movie musicals, representative recordings). Biographies in v. 2 & v. 3 provide works and recordings lists, but no bibliographic citations. V. 4 contains lists of winners of polls and prizes, indexes of names, titles and popular songs. This is an essential reference work for the genre and the period it covers.

263. Lacombe, Alain, and Claude Rode. La musique du film. Paris: Editions Francis Van de Velde, 1979. 516 p.

Preceded by 5 chapters on the nature of film music, there are biographical entries on composers, each with lists of films for which music was provided. Lists of 20th century composers whose music has been adapted to film. Indexes of names and titles.

264. Lawless, Ray McKinley. Folksingers and folksongs in America; a handbook of biography, bibliography, and discography. Illustrated from paintings by Thomas Hart Benton and others and from designs in Steuben glass. New revised edition with special supplement. New York: Duell, Sloan and Pearce, 1965. 750 p.

First published in 1960.

A general book of knowledge for folk song enthusiasts, with information pertaining to singers, song collecting, sources and recordings. The largest part of the work is devoted to biographical information on American folk singers.

Review of the first edition by Rae Korson in *Notes,* 18 (1960), p. 62.

265. Nite, Norm N. Rock on, the illustrated encyclopedia of rock n'roll. New York: T. Y. Crowell, 1974–84. 4 v.

v. 1: *The solid gold years,* 1974. 676 p.

v. 2: *The modern years, 1964-present,* 1978. 590 p.

v. 2, rev.: *The years of change, 1964–1978,* with Ralph M. Newman; published by Harper & Row, N.Y., 1984.

v. 3: *The video revolution, 1978-present,* with Charles Crespo; published by Harper & Row, N.Y., 1985. 444 p.

Brief biographical entries on individuals and groups active in rock and roll and related genres. Includes lists of principal recordings. Indexes of song titles.

266. Panassie, Hughes and Madeleine Gautier. Dictionnaire du jazz. Préface de Louis Armstrong. Nouvelle édition, revue et augmenté. Paris: Albin Michel, 1971. 360 p.

First published by Robert Laffont, Paris, 1954. English translation under the title: *Guide to jazz.* Trans. by Desmond Flower. New York: Houghton Mifflin, 1956.

The *Dictionnaire* is a standard source book on jazz; it is chiefly biographical but with some terms included. Portraits.

267. Paulin, Don. Das Folk-Music-Lexikon. Frankfurt: Fischer-Taschenbuch-Verlag, 1980. 128 p.

A bio-bibliographical work covering individuals and ensembles. Better coverage of European figures. Entries include discographical information. Index and bibliography.

268. Rachlin, Harvey. The encyclopedia of the music business. N.Y.: Harper & Row, 1981. 524 p.

Entries on terms and topics pertinent to the making and marketing of music for commercial reasons. Extensive appendices including winners of some of the more famous awards.

269. Rice, Edward le Roy. Monarchs of minstrelsy, from 'Daddy' Rice to date. New York: Kenny Publishing Co., 1911. 366 p.

Colorful biographical sketches of the leading performers in American minstrel shows of the late 19th century. Illustrated. The information is arranged roughly in chronological order.

270. The Rolling Stone encyclopedia of rock & roll edited by Jon Pareles, consulting editor, and Patricia Romanowski. New York: Rolling Stone Press/Summit Books, 1983. 615 p.

271. Rose, Al and Edmond Souchen. New Orleans jazz family album. Baton Rouge: Louisiana State University Press, 1967. 304 p.

Copiously illustrated with many early photographs. Special sections devoted to the musicians, the ensembles, and the places where they performed.

272. Roxon, Lillian. Rock encyclopedia. Rev. ed. New York: The University Library, Grosset and Dunlap, 1978. 611 p.

First published in 1971, 611 p.

Brief, vividly written biographical sketches of individuals and groups connected with rock. Discographies of albums and of singles.

Review by Gilbert Chase in *Notes,* 28 (1972), p. 196–97.

273. Schmidt-Joos, Siegfried and Barry Graves. Rock-Lexikon; mit Diskographien von Bernie Sigg. Reinbek bei Hamburg: Rowohlt, 1978. 445 p.

Biographical dictionary of rock performers, as individuals and groups. Brief entries with cross references and selected discographies. Appendix of entries on terms and recording companies. Extensive bibliography. Index to names cited in articles.

274. Shaw, Arnold. Dictionary of American pop/rock: rock, pop, rhythm and blues, folk, country, blues, gospel, jazz films, musical theater, recordings and music business. New York: Schirmer Books, 1982. 440 p.

Brief entries on the terminology of the field and on important individuals. Entries on persons discuss style characteristics and contributions. Cross references. Entries on important clubs and locations. Index to names and terms.

275. Shestack, Melvin. The country music encyclopedia. New York: T. Y. Crowell Co., 1974. 410 p.

Contains 200 entries and 250 black-and-white photographs. Describes the institutions and relates the history of country music.

276. Stambler, Irwin. Encyclopedia of pop, rock & soul. New York: St. Martin's Press, 1977. 609 p.

First printed in 1974. Successor to the *Encyclopedia of popular music*, 1965. 359 p.

Preceded by three essays on the genres, the dictionary consists mostly of biographical entries, with a few terms and trends defined or discussed. There are articles on films and musicals included. Lists of winners of various prizes. Bibliography.

277. Stambler, Irwin and Grulun Landon. Encyclopedia of folk, country, and western music. New York: St. Martin's Press, 1969. 396 p.

A source book made up chiefly of biographical entries to performers and groups. Appendices include special articles on "Changing attitudes toward folk music" by Sam Hinton, "The rise and fall of country music" by Bill Anderson, and "Country and pop music: development and relationship" by Ed Kahn. Also, award listings and a selective discography and bibliography.

278. Ténot, Frank. Dictionnaire du jazz. Paris: Larousse, 1967. 256 p. (Les dictionnaires de l'homme du XXe siecle)

One of the Larousse popular, subject-oriented, dictionaries. Good, brief discussions, chiefly biographical but with some jazz terms. Illustrated.

279. Vernillat, France and Jacques Charpentreau. Dictionnaire de la chanson française. Paris: Larousse, 1968. 256 p.

A dictionary of French popular song. Coverage extends from the 13th century to the present day, but with emphasis on singers of the 19th and 20th centuries. The dictionary is preceded by a "petite histoire de la chanson française". Illustrated.

280. York, William. Who's who in rock music. Rev. edition. New York: Scribner, 1982. 413 p.

First published by Atomic in Seattle, 1978. 260 p.

Collates information gleaned from rock album covers and therefore covers "sidemen" broadly, if with dubious authority.

MUSICAL INSTRUMENTS, MAKERS AND PERFORMERS

There is a substantial group of reference books concerned with the construction, performance, and iconography of musical instruments. A great deal of work has been done with respect to the violin, and there is an increasing number of reference tools devoted to keyboard and to wind instruments. For specific descriptions, prices, and illustrations of individual instruments, particularly those of the string family, the student should not neglect the catalogs of various dealers: Hamm, Herrmann, Hill, Lyon & Healy, Wurlitzer, etc. These are not included in our listing. For the iconography of musical instruments, see *Buchner* (no. 293), *Besseler* (no. 601), *Kinsky* (no. 607), and *Komma* (no. 608). See also "Bibliographies of Music Literature" (no. 683 ff.) and "Catalogs of Musical Instrument Collections" (no. 2525 ff.).

281. Ames, David W. and Anthony V. King. Glossary of Hausa music and its social contexts. Evanston: Northwestern University Press, 1971. 184 p. plus 10 p of photographs.

A technical glossary of musical instruments and sound production providing indicators of the socio-cultural context of musical performance of the sub-Saharan Hausa culture. Indexes of Hausa terms and English equivalents.

282. Avgerinos, Gerassimos. Lexikon der Pauke. Frankfurt am M.: Verlag das Musikinstrument, 1964. 105 p. (Das Musikinstrument) , 12

A dictionary of terms, chiefly German, connected with drums and drum playing.

283. Bächi, Julius. Berühmte Cellisten; Porträts der Meistercellisten von Boccherini bis Casals und von Paul Grümmer bis Rostropovitch. 3. Aufl. Zürich : Atlantis, 1981, c1973. 168 p.

284. Bachmann, Alberto A. An encyclopedia of the violin. Translated by Frederick H. Martens, edited by Albert E. Wier. New York: D. Appleton, 1925. 470 p.

Reprinted, with a new preface by Stuart Canin, by Da Capo Press, New York, 1966.

A sourcebook on the violin, its history, construction, literature, and performers. Organized by chapters, many of which contain lexicons and bibliographies: for example, Chap. II, "Violin makers in Europe"; Chap. III, "Violin makers in America"; Chap. XXI, "Glossary of musical terms"; Chap. XXII, "Biographical dictionary of violinists"; Chap. XXIII, "Literature relating to the violin"; Chap. XXV, "A list of music for the violin." Portraits and illustrations.

285. Bachmann, Alberto A. Les grands violinists du passé. . . . Paris: Fischbacher, 1913. 468 p.

Biographies of 40 violinist-composers, varying in length but with lists of works and a number of full or partial thematic catalogs (e.g. Corelli, Kreutzer, Leclair, Rode, Sarasate, Tartini, Viotti, Vivaldi, etc.).

286. Baines, Anthony. European and American musical instruments. London: Batsford, 1966. 824 p.

A "pictorial museum" of musical instruments selected from American and European collections. Instruments are grouped by families: stringed, woodwind, brass, and percussion. Much precise technical information along with historical background. All instruments are identified as to present location.

Review by Albert Protz in *Die Musikforschung,* 21 (1968), p. 388–89.

287. Bechler, Leo and Bernhardt Rahm. Die Oboe und die ihr verwandten Instrumente, nebst biographischen Skizzen der bedeutendsten ihrer Meister. Anhang: Musikliteratur für Oboe und englisch Horn, zusammengelstellt von Dr. Phillip Losch. Leipzig: C. Merseburger, 1914. 98 p., 32 p. (Anhang).

Reprint of the 1914 edition by Sändig, Wiesbaden, 1972 and by Knuf, Buren, 1978.

A history of the oboe and related instruments, with brief biographical sketches of famous players. Supplementary list of works for oboe and English horn, solo and with other instruments.

288. Boalch, Donald H. Makers of the harpsichord and clavichord, 1440 to 1840. Oxford: Clarendon Press, 1974 225 p.

First published by G. Ronald, London, [1956], 169 p.

Lists more than 820 makers of early keyboard instruments and describes over 1,000 of their instruments, giving dates, registers, compasses, histories, and present ownership. Photographs of instruments.

Review by Frank Hubbard in *Notes,* 14 (1957), p. 572–73. Review in the *Times Literary Supplement,* Dec. 21, 1956.

289. Bone, Philip James. The guitar and mandolin: biographies of celebrated players and composers. [2nd ed., enl.]. London & New York: Schott, 1954. 388 p.

First published in 1914. Reprint by Schott, London, 1972.

Performers and composers, including "standard" composers who have written for guitar or mandolin. Major works are mentioned, but there are no complete listings. Portraits.

Review by Richard Capell in *Music and letters,* 35 (1954), p. 254.

290. Bowers, Q. David. Encyclopedia of automatic musical instruments. Cylinder music boxes, disc music boxes, piano players and player pianos, coin-operating pianos, orchestrions, photoplayers, organettes, fairground organs, calliopes, and other self-playing instruments mainly of the 1750–1940 era. Including a dictionary of automatic musical instrument terms. New York: The Vestal Press, 1972. 1,008 p.

Profusely illustrated. Much documentary information. A book for collectors of automatic musical instruments.

291. Bragard, Roger and Ferdinand J. de Hen. Musical instruments in art and history. Preface by G. Thibault. Trans. by Bill Hopkins. New York: Viking Press, (n.d.). 281 p., 119 plates.

Originally published in French. German translation by Dieter Krickeberg, Stuttgart, Belser Verlag, 1968.

An attractive "picture book" of early instruments, with popular commentary.

Review of the German edition by J. H. van der Meer in *Die Musikforschung,* 24 (1971), p. 481–83; of the English edition by Edmund A. Bowles in *Notes,* 25 (1969), p. 735–36, and by Mary Remnant in *Music and Letters,* 50 (1969), p. 301–303.

292. Brinser, Martin. Dictionary of twentieth century Italian violin makers. Irvington, N.J.: American Graphic, 1978. 111 p.

293. Buchner, Alexander. Musical instruments through the ages. Trans. by Iris Urwin. London: Spring Books, [1956]. 37 p., 323 plates.

First published, with the text in Czech, by Artia, Prague. German edition: *Musikinstrumente im Wandel der Zeiten.* Published in a new translation by Borek Vancurel as *Musical instruments, an illustrated history* by Crown Books, New York, 1973, 274 p.

Not a dictionary or encyclopedia, but important as a collection of beautifully reproduced plates, some 323 in number, of musical instruments and representations of musical performance in painting, engraving and sculpture.

294. Buchner, Alexander. Musikinstrumente der Volker. [Ins Deutsche ubers. von O. Guth. Grafische Gestaltung von M. Houska. Notenbeispiele gezeichnet von J. Milota.] [Hanau/Main]: Dausien, [c1968]. 295 p.

Simultaneous publication in Prague, Artia, 1968.

A pictorial work with focus upon European folk music instruments.

295. Carfagna, Carlo and Mario Gangi. Dizionario chitarristico italiano. (Chitarristi, liutisti, tiorbisti, compositori, liutai ed editori.) Ancona: Berben, 1968. 97 p.

In two alphabets, the first devoted to guitarists, lutenists, theorbo players and composers, the second to instrument makers and editors.

296. Clarke, A. Mason. A biographical dictionary of fiddlers, including performers on the violoncello and double bass, past and present, containing sketches of their artistic careers. Together with notes of their compositions. London: W. Reeves, 1895. 390 p.

Reprint of the original edition by Scholarly Press, St. Clair Shores, Michigan, 1972.

Anecdotal accounts.

297. Crane, Frederick. Extant medieval musical instruments: a provisional catalogue by types. Iowa City: University of Iowa Press, 1972. 105 p.

Brief descriptions of the surviving medieval musical instruments in art and archaeological museums throughout the world. The instruments are classified according to the Hornbostel-Sachs system (idiophones, chordophones, and aerophones). 30 of the instruments are illustrated in rather crude pen sketches.

P. 91–105: bibliography.

298. Dictionary of organs and organists. 2nd edition. London: George Mate & Son, 1921. 476 p.

First published in 1912.

A handbook of information concerning the organ. Some of the principal sections are:

Bibliography of the organ;

London organs; provincial organs;

Foreign and colonial organs;

Organists' who's who (p. 297–441).

299. Enciclopedia del rock [di] Massimo Bassoli.... [et al.]. Milano: Teti, 1981. 222 p.
A biographical work covering both individuals and groups. Better coverage of European figures.

300. Enciclopedia rock anni '60 a cura di Riccardo Bertoncelli. Milano: Arcana, 1985. 512 p.
An Italian dictionary on rock music of the 1960s, includes biographical entries with discographic citations. Brief general bibliography.

301. Fairfield, John H. Known violin makers. Coral Gables: Virtuoso Press, 1983. 218 p.
First published by Bradford Press, New York, 1942, 192 p. Reprinted with supplements in 1973 and 1980.
Separate listings of European makers from the 16th century and American makers. For each, a brief biography, description of works, and the current price range of the instruments.

302. Gorgerat, Gerald. Encyclopédie de la musique pour instruments à vent. Lausanne: Éditions Rencontre [1955]. 3 v.
A pretentious work which attempts to cover all information pertaining to the making and performance of wind instruments and much more that has no particular relevance. Useful fingering charts for all winds. Several special lists, as follows:
Vol. 3, p. 243–83: Principal works for wind instruments, solo and ensemble. Vol. 3, p. 285–340: Dictionary of composers cited in the text. Brief identifications; no page references. Vol. 3, p. 341–524: Table of French terms with their equivalents in Italian, German, English, and Spanish.

303. Hamma, Fridolin. German violin makers; a critical dictionary ... translated by Walter Stewart. London: W. Reeves, [1961]. 49 p., 80 plates.
Translated from the 1948 German edition, *Meister deutscher Geigenbaukunst. Stuttgart, 1948.*
Alphabetical listing of 550 names of important German makers, with plates illustrating their work.
Review by Cynthia L. Adams in *Notes,* 19 (1962), p. 261–62.

304. Hamma, Walter. Geigenbauer der deutschen Schule des 17. bis 19. Jahrhunderts. Violin-makers of the German school from the 17th to the 19th century. Luthiers de l'école allemande du 17e au 19e siècle. Tutzing : H. Schneider, 1986. 2 v.
Parallel texts in English, French, and German.

305. Hamma, Walter. Meister italienischer Geigenbaukunst. (Zum 100 jahr. Bestehen der Firma Hamma & Co., Stuttgart, im Jahre 1964. Engl. Übers: Walter J. Stewart. Franz. Übers.: Aristide Wirsta.) München: Schuler, 1976. 727 p.
Revision and expansion of a work first published in 1931. Subsequently published in Stuttgart by Schuler, 1965. 728 p.

Describes more than 300 instruments made by Italian masters. Descriptions arranged alphabetically by makers, with biographical information and photographic plates of details.

306. Handbuch der europäischen Volksmusikinstrumente hrsg. vom Institut für Deutsche Volkskunde Berlin in Zusammenarbeit mit dem Musikhistorischen Museum Stockholm durch Ernst Emsheimer und Erich Stockmann. Leipzig: Deutscher Verlag für Musik, 1967– . 4 v.
Contents: Series I—
Bd. 1. *Die Volksmusikinstrumente Ungarns* von Bálint Sárosi, 1968 (148 p.).
Bd. 2. *Die Volksmusikinstrumente der Tschechoslowakei* von Ludvík Kunz, 1974 (2 v.).
Bd. 4. *Die Volksmusikinstrumente der Schweiz* von Brigitte Bachmann Geiser, 1981 (134 p.).
Bd. 5. *Die Volkmusikinstrumente in Slowenien* von Zmaga Kumer, (Ljubljana: Slovenska akademija znanosti in umetnosti, Znanstvenoraziskovalni center SAZU, Institut za slovensko narodopisje, 1986. 107 p.)
See also Sárosi, Bálint, no. 349.

307. Hartnack, Joachim W. Grosse Geiger unserer Zeit. München: Rütten & Loening, c1967. 335 p.
Includes discography.

308. Haupt, Helga. "Wiener Instrumentenbauer von 1791 bis 1815," in *Studien zur Musikwissenschaft, Beihefte der Denkmaler der Tonkunst in Österreich.* Bd. 24. Graz: Hermann Bohlaus, 1960. p. 120–84.
Alphabetical listing of Viennese instrument makers in all categories. Addresses, dates of activity. A well-documented study.

309. Henley, William. Universal dictionary of violin and bow makers. 2nd ed. [Managing ed., Cyril Woodcock.] Brighton: Amati Pub. Co., 1973 1,268 p.
1st published in 5 v. 1959–60.
Includes a dictionary of contemporary violin and bow makers and a price guide and appendix.
Biographies in the dictionary are of varying length. Long accounts of important figures with descriptions of famous instruments. Maintains a rather subjective and literary tone.
The *Price guide* gives listings for English and for American dealers.

310. Herzog, Hans Kurt. Piano-Nummern deutscher, europäischer und überseeischer Instrument: Klaviere, Flügel, Cembali, Harmonien. Piano serial numbers of German, European and foreign uprights, grands, harpsichords, harpsichords, harmoniums. ... 6., wesentlich erw. und erg. Aufl. Frankfurt/M.: E. Bochinsky, 1984. 100 p. (Schriftenreihe Das Musikinstrument, 2)
First edition published under title *Taschenbuch der Piano-Nummern deutscher, europaischer und uberseeischer Instrumente. Cover title: Europe piano atlas.*
Text in English, French, German, Italian and Swedish.

311. Hirt, Franz Josef. Meisterwerke des Klavierbaus. Stringed keyboard instruments. Geschichte der Saitenklaviers von 1440 bis 1880. Olten: Urs Graf Verlag, 1981. 235 p.

First German edition published in 1955, 521 p. Original German edition translated by M. Boehme-Brown and published as *Stringed keyboard instruments, 1440–1880* in Boston, 1968. 465 p.

Parallel text in English and German.

Beautifully illustrated book with information about the history, design, construction, makers, etc., of keyboard instruments. Full-page photographic plates, useful sections of biography and bibliography.

312. International Council of Museums. Ethnic musical instruments: identification-conservation. . . . Edited by Jean Jenkins. London: H. Evelyn for the International Council of Museums, 1970. 59 p.

Parallel English and French texts.

313. Irwin, Stevens. Dictionary of pipe organ stops. 2nd ed. New York, Schirmer Books, 1983. 422 p.

First edition 1962, 264 p. Revised edition appeared in 1965, 276 p.

Detailed descriptions of more than 600 stops together with definitions of many other terms connected with the organ and an examination of the acoustical properties of many types of pipes and the various divisions of the organ. Illustrated. Includes a short bibliography.

314. Jacquot, Albert. Dictionnaire pratique et raisonne des instruments de musique anciens et modernes. 2nd ed. Paris: Fischbacher, 1886. 280 p.

Many names of Eastern instruments included. Some illustrations. Brief definitions. No bibliography.

315. Jahnel, Franz. Die Gitarre und ihr Bau. 3. Aufl. Technologie von Gitarre, Laute, Mandoline, Sistern, Tanbur und Saite. Frankfurt am Main: Verlag Das Musikinstrument, 1977. 240 p.

English edition *Manual of guitar technology; the history and technology of plucked string instruments,* translated by J. C. Harvey, published by Verlag des Muiskinstrument, 1981, 229 p.

A compendium of information on the construction of the guitar and other fretted instruments. Bibliography, numerous tables and lists, detailed plans and technical data. A handsomely designed and printed volume, invaluable for the musical instrument maker or interested performer.

316. Jalovec, Karel. Enzyklopadie des Geigenbaues. Leiden: E.J. Brill, 1965. 2 v.

Simultaneous publication also by Dausien, Hanau am Main and Artia, Prague.

Vol. 1: 940 p., 51 colored illustrations on 24 plates. Vol. 2: 405 illustrations on 595 plates; 3,000 reproductions of violin makers' labels.

English translation by J. B. Kozak, published by Hamlyn, London, 1968.

317. Jalovec, Karel. German and Austrian violin makers. Translated from the Czech by George Theiner, edited by Patrick Hanks. London: Hamlyn,

1967. 439 p.

318. Jalovec, Karel. Italian violin makers. Rev. edition. London: P. Hamlyn, 1964. 445 p.

First published in Prague, 1952; published in London, 1958, with text in Czech and English.

Accounts of Italian violin makers, with descriptions and dimensions of important instruments. Many illustrations, some in color. Index by place; scale plans, facsimiles of labels.

319. Jalovec, Karel. The violin makers of Bohemia; including craftsmen of Moravia and Slovakia. London: Anglo-Italian Publication, [1959]. 129 p. 392 plates.

Originally published in Czech under the title *Cesti houslari.* Prague, 1959. German ed., 1959.

Covers the work of some 1,200 Czech violin makers. Photographs of instruments, and a section of makers' labels in facsimile.

320. Langwill, Lyndesay Graham. An index of musical wind-instrument makers. 6th ed., rev., enl., and illustrated. Edinburgh, Lyndesay G. Langwill, 1980. 331 p.

First published in 1960; 2nd edition, 1962; 3rd edition, 1972; 4th edition, 1974; 5th edition, 1977.

Alphabetical index of musical wind-instrument makers with accompanying bibliographical references and locations of examples of early instruments in museums and private collections. Bibliography with occasional annotations. List of collections. A short selection of makers' marks. Index of makers by place.

Review of first edition by Josef Marx in *Notes,* 18 (1961), p. 234–36; of the scond edition by Georg Karstadt in *Die Musikforschung,* 18 (1965), p. 90–91; of the third edition by Anthony Baines in *Galpin Society journal,* 25 (July 1975), p. 134–35.

321. Langwill, Lyndesay Graham. Church and chamber barrel-organs: their origin, makers, music and location; a chapter in English church music, by Lyndesay G. Langwill and the late Noel Boston. 2d ed. revised and enlarged. Edinburgh: L. G. Langwill, 1970. 125 p.

First ed. by N. Boston and L. G. Langwill published in 1967. 120 p.

322. Lunelli, Renato. "Dizionario degli organari Veneti o attivi nel Veneto," in *Studi e documenti di storia organaria veneta, p. 145–236.* Firenze: L. S. Olschki, 1973. 279 p. (Studi di musica veneta, 3)

Following the dictionary is a bibliography of sources.

323. Lütgendorff, Willibald Leo. Die Geigen- und Lautenmacher vom Mittelalter bis zur Gegenwart, nach den besten Quellen bearbeitet.... 4. mit der 3. übereinstimmende Aufl. Frankfurt am Main: Frankfurter Verlags-Anstalt, 1922. 2 v.

First published in 1904, in 1 volume. Reprinted by Kraus, Nendeln, 1968 and by H. Schneider, Tützing, 1975.

Vol. 1: History of the making of stringed instruments by country. Index of manufacturers by city, with dates of birth and death. Bibliography, p. 403–20. Many illustrations.

Vol. 2: Biographical dictionary of makers of stringed instruments. P. 583–668: facsimiles of trademarks and labels.

324. Lüttmann, Reinhard. Das Orgelregister und sein instrumentales Vorbild in Frankreich und Spanien vor 1800. Kassel: Bärenreiter, 1979. 365 p. Münster. Universität, Orgelwissenschaftliche Forschungsstelle, Veröoffentlichungen, 10

325. Lyle, Wilson. A dictionary of pianists. New York: Schirmer Books, 1984. 343 p.

Simultaneously published in London by Hale.

International in scope. Covers 4,000 concertizing pianists with brief biographical sketches mentioning instructors and pupils, prizes won, stylistic characteristics. Cites compositions, if any, and lists principal recordings. Performers on historical instruments not covered well. Appendix of winners of international piano competitions and medalists of conservatories and schools. Addresses of competition organizers. No sources cited.

326. Marcuse, Sibyl. Musical instruments; a comprehensive dictionary. Corrected edition N.Y.: Norton, 1975. 608 p.

First published in New York by Doubleday, 1964. 608 p. Reprinted by Country Life, London, 1966.

Intended to serve English readers as Sachs' *Real-Lexikon* (No. 347) does German. World coverage, although the author acknowledges incompleteness with respect to non-European and folk instruments.

P. 603–08: listing of 206 sources of information about instruments.

327. Michel, Norman Elwood. Historical pianos, harpsichords and clavichords. Pico Rivera, Calif., [1963]. 209 p.

Reprinted in 1970. 236 p.

A volume of photographs of pianos. P. 1–46: photos of pianos, birthplaces, family homes, and historical societies related to 35 presidents of the U.S. P. 47–86: pianos and homes of statesmen, actors, etc. P. 87–135: photos from libraries, historical societies, museums, and other institutions. P. 136–209: photos of musical instruments from all over the world. A curious exercise in bibliographical name-dropping.

328. Michel, Norman Elwood. Michel's organ atlas; organs, melodeons, harmoniums, church organs, lap organs, barrel organs. Pico Rivera, Calif.: N.E. Michel [1969] 128 p.

"Book contains 141 photographs, 128 pages, 869 names of organs, etc." Known also as the *Organ atlas.*

329. Michel, Norman Elwood. Michel's piano atlas. Contains names of pianos, dates of manufacture, and serial numbers. Pico Rivera, Calif., [1961]. 272 p.

Subsequently published as Pierce piano atlas, see no. 336.

6,580 names of pianos. For some of these, there is no information other than name; for others, complete lists of serial numbers.

330. Möller, Max. The violin-makers of the low countries (Belgium and Holland). Amsterdam: M. Möller, 1955. 165 p.

A historical survey of violin making in Belgium and Holland.

P. 23–129:photographic plates, chiefly of instruments in detail. P. 131–53: "Alphabetical Register," brief critical comments on the makers and their work. Glossary of terms in English, French, German and Flemish.

331. Morris, W. Meredith. British violin makers, a biographical dictionary of British makers of stringed instruments and bows and a critical description of their work. 2nd ed., revised and enl. London: R. Scott, 1920. 318 p.

First published in 1904.

P. 87–259: alphabetical dictionary of violin and bow makers. Some labels in facsimile. P. 261–94: "A list of present-day makers, and a few old makers recently discovered."

332. The New Grove Dictionary of Musical Instruments. Edited by Stanley Sadie. London: Macmillan, 1984. 3 v.

Articles on western and non-western, historical and modern instruments, their makers and performance practices, many derived, but largely re-written from articles in the *New Grove*. Extensive coverage of folk and ethnic instruments by scholars expert in the regions in which the instruments are located. Extensive cross references linking articles and terms to one another make up for the lack of an index by culture or region. Copiously illustrated. Bibliographies. The dictionary of musical instruments based on modern scholarship and unique in its genre.

333. Niemann, Walter. Klavier-lexikon: Elementarlehre fur Klavierspieler, Anleitung zur Aussprache des italienischen, Tabelle der Abkurzungen in Wort- und Notenschrift, Literaturverzeichnis, ausfuhrliches Fremdworter-, Sach- und Personal-Lexikon. 4. vollig umgearb. und reich verm. Aufl. Leipzig: C. F. Kahnt, 1918. 365 p.

First published in 1912 as *Taschen-Lexikon fur Klavierspieler.*

334. Norlind, Tobias. Systematik der Saiteninstrumente. Stockholm: [Emil Kihlströms Tryckeri], 1936–39. 2 v.

At head of title: Musikhistorisches Museum, Stockholm.

Vol. 1: *Geschichte der Zither* (1936). Vol. 2: *Geschichte des Klaviers* (1939).

Detailed classification and description of stringed instruments based on the archive in the Musikhistorisches Museum in Stockholm, where records of some 40,000 instruments are maintained. Illustrated. Bibliographical references and locations given for specific instruments in European and American collections. The work was projected in four parts, only two of which were completed.

335. Pâris, Alain. Dictionnaire des interprètes et de l'interprètation musicale au XXe siècle. Paris: Robert Laffont, 1982. 875 p.

A collection of essays on the situation and evolution of musical interpretation in the 20th century precedes a biographical section on individual artists and another section covering ensembles. Indexes arranged by performance medium.

336. Pierce piano atlas. 8th ed. Long Beach, Calif.: B. Pierce, 1982. 416 p.
Title varies: 1947–61, *Michel's piano atlas*; also known as *Piano atlas.*
Compiled and published, 1947–61, by Norman Elwood Michel.
Contains "piano names, serial numbers, dates of manufacture."

337. Pincherle, Marc. Les violonistes, compositeurs et virtuoses. Paris: H. Laurens [1922] 126 p.
Not a dictionary, but provides biographical information on a number of violinists and composers for the instrument.

338. Poidras, Henri. Critical and documentary dictionary of violin makers old and modern, translated by Arnold Sewell. . . . Rouen: Imprimerie de la Vicomte, 1928–30. 2 v.
Originally published in French, 1924, with a 2nd edition in 1930. There is also a one-volume English edition, 1928. Reprint edition by Scholarly Press, St. Clair Shores, 1978.
Brief biographical notices with critical comments, arranged alphabetically under national schools: Italian, French, German, etc. Photographic plates of instruments; facsimiles of labels.

339. Powroźniak, Józef. Leksykon gitary. Kraków: Polskie Wydawn. Muzyczne, 1979. 212 p.
Simultaneously published in Berlin by Neue Musik as *Gitarren-Lexikon,* in a translation by Bernd Haag. 165 p.
A dictionary of terms and biography devoted entirely to the guitar and its practitioners.

340. Prat, Domingo. Diccionario biografico, bibliografico, historico, critico de guitarras (instrumentos afines), guittaristas (profesores, compositores, concertistas, lahudistas, amateurs), guitarreros (luthiers), danzas y cantos, terminologia. Buenos Aires: Casa Romero y Fernandez, [1934]. 468 p.
Reprinted as *A biographical, bibliographical, historical, critical dictionary of guitars* (related instruments), guitarists (teachers, composers, performers, lutenists, amateurs), guitar-makers (luthiers), dances and songs, terminology with an introduction by Matanya Ophee by Editions Orphée, Columbus, Ohio, c1986. Known also as the *Dictionary of guitarists.*
The main alphabet contains biographies and lists of compositions. P. 423–52: dance forms. P. 453–64: terminology.

341. Profeta, Rosario. Storia e letteratura degli strumenti musicali. Firenze: Marzocco, 1942. 659 p.
A history of instrumental music, its composers and performers, consisting chiefly of a recital of names of musicians grouped under their instruments and respective national schools. Minimal biographical and bibliographical information given.

342. "Provisional Index of Present-day Makers of Historical Musical Instruments (Non-keyboard)." In the *Galpin Society journal,* 13 (July 1960), p. 70–97.

A useful guide to sources of modern replicas of historical instruments. Makers of historical keyboard instruments are listed in an appendix, p. 86–87.

343. Riley, Maurice W. The history of the viola. [s.l. : s.n.], c1980 (Ann Arbor: Braun-Brumfielüd). 396 p.

"Brief biographies of violists:" p. 312–376. Bibliography: p. 379–384.

344. Roda, Joseph. Bows for musical instruments of the violin family. Chicago: W. Lewis & Son, 1959. 335 p.

Brief history and description of the bow, including statistics as to dimensions and weight.

P. 119–325: biographical list of bow makers, with 47 excellent plates of their work.

345. Roth, Henry. Great violinists in performance; critical evaluations of over 100 twentieth-century virtuosi. Los Angeles: Panjandrum Books, 1986. 266 p.

346. Sachs, Curt. Handbuch der Musikinstrumentenkunde. (Reprografischer Nachdruck der 2. Aufl., Leipzig, 1930.) Hildesheim: Olms; Wiesbaden: Breitkopf u. Hartel, 1967. 419 p. (Kleine Handbucher der Musikgeschichte nach Gattungen, 12)

First published in 1920.

Not precisely a dictionary but a systematic and historical description of musical instruments classified according to their methods of sound production: idiophones, membranophones, chordaphones, aerophones, etc. Much of the same ground is covered in Sachs' *The History of Musical Instruments* (New York, Norton, 1940), in which the approach is chronological and by cultural areas.

347. Sachs, Curt. Real-Lexikon der Musikinstrumente, zugleich ein Polyglossar fur das gesamte Instrumentengebiet. [Rev. and enl. ed.] New York: Dover Publications, 1964. 451 p.

First published in Berlin, 1913; unaltered reprint of the original edition issued by G. Olms, Hildesheim, 1962.

A technical and historical dictionary of instruments of all periods and countries. Names of instruments and parts of instruments in some 120 languages and dialects—European, African, and Asian. Locations of examples in instrument collections. Illustrations; some bibliographies. This is Sachs's great work in this field and one of the best sources of information on instruments.

For a English-language dictionary inspired by the *Real-Lexikon,* see Marcuse's *Musical instruments,* no. 326.

Review by Guy Oldham in *Musical times,* v. 107 (Dec. 1966), p. 1064–65.
Review by J. A. Westrup in *Music and letters,* v. 4:3 (July 1966), p. 277–278.

348. Samoyault-Verlet, Colombe. Les facteurs de clavecins Parisiens, notices biographiques et documents, 1550–1793. Paris: Société Française de

Musicologie, 1966. 191 p. (Publications de la Société Française de Musicologie Ser. 2, ll)
Biographies of some 140 Parisian makers of keyboard instruments, based largely on archival documents.
Review by Maurice A. Byrne in *Galpin Society journal,* 25 (July 1972), p. 136–37.

349. Sárosi, Bálint. Die Volksmusikinstrumente Ungarns. Leipzig: Deutscher Verlag für Musik, 1968. 147 p. (Handbuch der europäischen Volksmusikinstrumente I, 1)
Sárosi's work is the first of a series projected to cover folk instruments in Czechoslovakia, Bulgaria, the Soviet Union, Greece, Portugal, Turkey, and Norway.
The Hungarian folk instruments are grouped according to type, with detailed commentary, illustrations, and transcription of music. Bibliography, and glossary of Hungarian instrument names.
Review by Fritz Bose in *Literature, music, fine arts,* 1 (1968), p. 230–231.

350. Schimmel, Klaus. Piano-Nomenclatur. Ein Bildwörterbuch der Teile von Klavier und Flügel: Dentsch, Englisch, Franz—osisch, Italienisch und Norwegisch. 2. Aufl. (Mitarbeit und Ubersetzungen: Pianofortefabrik Wilhelm Schimmel [u.a.]) Frankfurt a. M.: Verlag Bochinsky/Das Musikinstrument, 1983. 127 p. (Fachbuchreihe Das Musikinstrument, 14)
Terms in German, English, French, Italian, Norwegian, and Spanish.

351. Schwarz, Boris Great masters of the violin; from Corelli and Vivaldi to Stern, Zukerman, and Perlman. New York: Simon and Schuster, c1983. 671 p.
Like Pincherle's *Les violonistes, compositeurs et virtuoses,* not a dictionary, but a valuable source of biographical information about violin virtuosi. Bibliography

352. Shead, Herbert A. The anatomy of the piano. Old Woking: Unwin Brothers Ltd., 1978. 177 p.
An illustrated dictionary of the piano.

353. Stainer, Cecilia. A dictionary of violin makers, compiled from the best authorities. Rev. ed. London: Novello, 1909. 102 p.
First edition 1896, 102 p. Reprinted by Milford House, Boston, 1973 and Longwood Press, Boston, 1977.
A useful biographical dictionary of violin makers with critical evaluations of their work. Still in print. Contains a bibliography of literature on violin making.

354. Stiller, Andrew. Handbook of instrumentation. Illustrations by James Stamos. Berkeley: University of California Press, c1985. 553 p.
A thorough, well illustrated compendium of information about a wide range of instruments. Bibliography.

355. Straeten, Edmund S. J. vander. History of the violoncello, the viol da gamba, their precursors and collateral instruments : with biographies of all the most eminent players of every country. 1st AMS ed. New York: AMS Press, 1976.

Reprint of the 1915 ed. published by W. Reeves, London. Another reprint edition published by W. Reeves, London, 1971, 700 p.

356. Straeten, Edmund S. J. vander. The history of the violin, its ancestors and collateral instruments from the earliest times to the present day; with 48 plates and numerous illustrations in the text. London: Cassell, [1933]. 2 v.

Reprinted by Da Capo, New York, 1968.

Vol. 1, p. 55–416, and the whole of vol. 2 consist primarily of biographies of violinists grouped by period, and under period by country. Biographical index, vol. 2, p. 443–73. Information on many obscure violinist-composers not elsewhere readily accessible, with lists of works by category.

357. Thornsby, Frederick, W. Dictionary of organs and organists. London: G. A. Mate, 1921.476 p.

First published by H. Logan, Bournemouth, 1912(?), 364 p.

Chiefly concerned with 19th-century British organs and organists.

"Brief specifications of the principal organs in the British Isles." "The organist's *Who's who*: Brief biographical notes of the leading British organists." A bibliography on the organ by J. H. Burn.

358. Tintori, Giampiero. Gli strumenti musicali. Ricerca iconografìa di Alberto Basso. Turin: Unione tipografico-editrice torinese, [1971]. 2 v. 138 plates.

The main organization is geographical, with subdivisions covering the various types of instruments. Numerous musical examples, a comprehensive bibliography and glossary; general index.

359. Valdrighi, Luigi Francesco. Nomocheliurgografìa antica e moderna, ossia Elenco di fabbricatori di strumenti armonici con note esplicative e documenti estratti dall'Archivio di Stato in Modena. Bologna: Forni, 1967. 327 p. (Bibliotheca musica Bononiensia, I, 3)

Reprint of the Modena 1884 edition, with supplements originally published 1888–1894.

P. 2–106: an alphabetical listing of 3,516 instrument makers, giving name, nationality, dates of birth and death, name of special instrument, and the school, style, or system. Many of these names are given fuller biographical treatment in the section following, p. 107 to end.

360. Vannes, René. Dictionnaire universel des luthiers. Bruxelles: Les Amis de la Musique, 1979. 2 v. in 1.

Reprint of 2nd edition (1951–59) and 3rd edition (1971–75).

First published in 1932, Paris, Fischbacher, under the title *Essai d'un dictionnaire universel. . . .*

Most comprehensive of all dictionaries of violin makers. Each volume has its own alphabet of biographical entries. Bibliographical references. Both volumes combined give 3,400 facsimiles of makers' labels. Index of makers by place of birth or center of activity.

Review by Doris Commander in *Violins and violinists,* 12 (Nov., 1951), p. 326; review of *Tome second* by Albert van der Linden in *Revue belge de musicologie,* 14 (1960), p. 144, and by William Lichtenwanger in *Notes,* 17 (1960), p. 577.

361. Vercheval, Henri. Dictionnaire du violinist. ... Paris: Fischbacher, 1923. 192 p.

Also published as *Dizionario del violinista.* ... by Casa Musicale Editrice ditta Cesare Sarti, Bologna, 1924. 249 p.

Part I, p. 9–141, includes terms of interest to violinists, history of stringed instruments, etc. Part II, p. 143–92, is a biographical dictionary of violinists, composers, teachers, violin and bow makers, giving dates and nationalities.

362. Winternitz, Emanuel. Musical instruments of the Western world. Photographs by Lilly Stunzi. New York and Toronto: McGraw-Hill Book Co.; London: Thames & Hudson, 1967. 259 p. 60 plates.

This work was published in German under the title, *Die schönsten Musikinstrumente des Abendlandes.*

A magnificent picture book of music.

Review by Howard Mayer Brown in *Notes,* 25 (1968), p. 223–25.

363. Worthmuller, Willi. "Die Nürnberger Trompeten- und Posaunenmacher des 17. und 18. Jahrhunderts." In *Mitteilungen des Vereins für Geschichte der Stadt Nürnberg.* Bd. 46 (1955). p. 372–480.

Also published separately.

A musicological study, the major portion of which is a dictionary of 40 Nuremberg brass instrument makers of the Baroque period with a listing of their surviving instruments. Tracing of monograms and other makers' devices. 5 plates.

364. Wright, Rowland. Dictionnaire des instruments de musique; étude de lexicologie. London: Battley Bros., 1941. 192 p.

An etymological dictionary of names for musical instruments mentioned in French writings from ancient times to the end of the 19th century. Extremely well documented; precise bibliographical references. One of the few dictionaries of terms to employ a thoroughly etymological approach.

365. Zingel, Hans Joachim. Lexicon der Harfe: ein biographisches, bibliographisches, geographisches und historisches Nachschlagewerk von A-Z. Regensburg: Laaber, 1977. 207 p.

An errata slip was issued.

Very brief articles. Fails to cite works for the instrument even when appropriate to do so. Bibliography of sources.

366. Zuth, Josef. Handbuch der Laute und Gitarre. Wien: Verlag der Zeitschrift fur die Gitarre, 1926. 297 p.

Reprinted by Olms, Hildesheim, 1972.

Terms; biographies of performers, instrument makers, and composers giving titles of compositions, publishers, and dates. International coverage for all periods, including many early names. A scholarly work with supported statements and bibiographical references.

TERMS

Dictionaries of terms have a longer history than any other form of music lexicology. Their prototype is Johannes Tinctoris' *Terminorum musicae diffinitorium* (no. 413), a work compiled in the late 15th century. Almost equally significant is Sebastien de Brossard's *Dictionaire de musique,* 1701 (no. 372), one of the first in the long line of "modern" dictionaries of music.

A few specialized dictionaries of terms will be found under other headings in this volume. See no. 313 & 324 (pipe organ stops); no. 364 (names of musical instruments); no. 425 (liturgical music terms).

367. Albina, Diāna. Mūzikas terminu vardnica. Redigejis J. Licitis. Riga: Latvijas valsts izdevnieciba, 1962. 303 p.

A Latvian dictionary of musical terms.

368. Baker, Theodore. Dictionary of musical terms containing upwards of 9,000 English, French, German, Italian, Latin and Greek words and phrases used in the art and science of music ... with a supplement containing an English-Italian vocabulary for composers. New York: G. Schirmer, [1923]. 257 p.

First published in 1895. Reprinted by Saphrograph, N.Y., 1975.

Reprint of the 1923 edition, New York, AMS Press, 1970 & 1975.

Useful small manual, with brief definitions of English and foreign words, especially those used in performance. More extended articles on topics such as pitch, notation, instruments. More than 9,000 terms treated.

369. Balter, G. Fachwörterbuch Musik deutsch-russisch und russisch-deutsch. Moscow; Leipzig: VEB Deutscher Verlag für Musik, 1976. 484 p.

Additional title page in Russian. Basically a bilingual glossary.

370. Bobillier, Marie. Diccionario de la música, historico y técnico. Tradducción de la última edición francesa, revisada y notablemente ampliada con multitud de artículos nuevos ... por Jose B. Humbert, J. Ricart Matas & Aurelio Capmany. Barcelona: Iberia, J. Gil, [1964]. 548 p.

Translation of the 2nd edition of the preceding, revised and with special emphasis on Spanish terms, Latin and South American terminology and folklore. Profusely illustrated.

371. Bobillier, Marie. Dictionnaire pratique et historique de la musique, par Michel Brenet (pseud.). Paris: A. Colin, 1926. 487 p.

2nd edition appeared in 1930.

The standard French dictionary of terms, including terms from Greek and medieval music theory, historical sketches of musical forms. Fairly long articles, excellent small illustrations. No bibliographies.

372. Brossard, Sebastien de. Dictionnaire de musique, contenant une explication des termes grecs, latins, italiens & françois les plus usitez dans la musique. ... Paris: Christophe Ballard, 1703. 112 p.

A preliminary edition appeared in 1701, in octavo format.

The first folio edition (1703 above) has been reprinted in facsimile by Antiqua, Amsterdam, 1964 and translated and edited by Albion Gruber in an edition published by the Institute of Mediaeval Music, Henryville, Pa., c1982. 252 p. (Musical theorists in translation, 12). An octavo edition, Paris 1705, has been reprinted, with an introduction by Harald Heckmann, by Frits A. M. Knuf, Hilversum 1965.

Brossard's Dictionnaire is the prototype for all modern dictionaries of musical terms. It is also a pioneer work in music bibliography, since it contains a listing of more than 900 authors who have written about music from antiquity to Brossard's time.

For an early English music dictionary based on *Brossard,* see *Grassineau* no. 385.

Review of the 1964 (Amsterdam) reprint by Vincent Duckles in *Notes,* 24 (1968), p. 700–701.

373. Carter, Henry H. A dictionary of Middle English musical terms. Bloomington: Indiana Univ. Press, [1961]. 655 p. (Indiana University humanities series, 45)

Reprint by Kraus, New York, 1968.

Terms are not only defined but quoted in their original contexts with citation of their sources. P. 569–604: bibliography of works quoted; p. 605–49: works consulted but not quoted.

Review by Leonard Ellinwood in *Notes,* 19 (1962), p. 262–63.

374. Chetrikov, Svetoslav. Muzikalen terminologischen rechnik. 2. izd. Sofiia, Muzika, 1979. 448 p.

A Bulgarian dictionary of musical terms.

375. Dembski, Stephen. Lexique musical international. International vocabulary of music. Lessico musicale internazionale. Par Stephen Dembski, Gerard Gubisch, Jorge Labrouve, Patrick Marcland. Paris: Editions Transatlantiques, 1979. 151 p.

A polyglot dictionary of terms in English, French, Italian and Spanish. Polyglot dictionaries—Terms

376. Dolzhanskii, Aleksandr Naumovich. Kratkii muzkalnyi slovar. Izd. 4. Leningrad, Muzyka, 1964 517 p.

First published Leningrad, 1952.

377. Eggebrecht, Hans Heinrich. Handwörterbuch der musikalischen Terminologie. Im Auftrag der Kommission fur Musikwissenschaften und der Literatur zu Mainz. ... Wiesbaden: F. Steiner, 1972– .

A work providing the most thorough and scientific treatment of musical terms. An exhaustive historical and etymological analysis of term families, showing their changes in meaning and citing quotations from the literature. The dictionary is compiled in looseleaf format, with dividers and indexes.

By 1986, 13 Auslieferungen in 3 v. including over 100 articles had been issued.

For a preliminary notice and discussion, see *Archiv fur Musikwissenschaft,* 25 (1968), p. 241–77, and 27 (1970), p. 214–22.

378. Eimert, Herbert and Hans Ulrich Humpert. Das Lexikon der electronischen Musik. Regensburg: Gustav Bosse Verlag, 1973. 428 p.

Brief terminological articles citing musical works where appropriate. Bibliography. Index to persons mentioned.

379. Elsevier's Dictionary of Cinema, Sound and Music, in six languages: English/ American, French, Spanish, Italian, Dutch, and German. Compiled and arranged on an English alphabetical base by W. E. Clason. Amsterdam/New York: Elsevier Publishing Co., 1956. 948 p.

One of a series of polyglot technical dictionaries relating to special fields of science and industry. 3,213 terms, with brief definitions and the equivalent phrases in French, Spanish, Italian, Dutch, and German. Indexes in each of the five languages.

380. Fink, Robert and Robert Ricci. The language of twentieth century music: a dictionary of terms. N.Y.: Schirmer Books, 1975. 125 p.

Covering all 20th century music genres and styles. Includes technical terms, instruments, analysis, and performance practice. Appendix of terms aranged topically.

381. Gerigk, Herbert. Fachworterbuch der Musik. Bayreuth: Gondrom, 1983. 213 p.

First published in Münchberg i. Bayern by Hahnefeld in 1954, 206 p.

A small, useful dictionary of German definitions of the most common musical terms in French, Italian, and Latin, with some in English.

Review by Richard Schaal in *Die Musikforschung,* 8 (1955), p. 245.

382. Gold, Robert S. A jazz lexicon. New York: Knopf, 1964. 363 p.

A dictionary of terms from the world of jazz. Both musical and sociological interest. Date of usage is specified where possible. Informative introduction and bibliography.

383. Gold, Robert S. Jazz talk. Indianapolis: Bobbs-Merrill Co., c1975. 322 p.

Reprinted in 1982 by Da Capo.

A dictionary of the colorful language that has emerged from America's own music. [Author's *Preface*]

Extensive bibliography.

384. Grant, Parks. Handbook of music terms. Metuchen: Scarecrow Press, 1967. 476 p.

The availability of several excellent music dictionaries and encyclopedias intended for the scholar, the music professor, and the musicologist points up the need for a book less advanced (though not too brief) intended for persons who make only a modest claim to musical knowledge. [Author's *Preface*]

Review by James W. Pruett in *Notes,* 24 (1968), p. 720–21.

385. Grassineau, James. A musical dictionary; being a collection of terms and characters, as well ancient as modern; including the historical, theoretical, and practical parts of music. . . . London: printed for J. Wilcox, 1740. 347 p.

Reprint by Broude Brothers, New York, 1967 (Monuments of music and music literature in facsimile. Ser. 2, vol. 40).

Grassineau can be described as the first important dictionary of music in English. It is largely an adaptation of Brossard (no. 372), but with some important additions. A later edition, 1769, has an appendix containing additional terms from Rousseau's *Dictionnaire* (no. 401).

386. Grigg, Carolyn Doub. Music translation dictionary. An English, Czech, Danish, Dutch, French, German, Hungarian, Italian, Polish, Portuguese, Russian, Spanish, Swedish vocabulary of musical terms. Westport: Greenwood, 1978. 330 p.

A polyglot glossary of 1,300 musical terms with an index of all terms in one alphabet for words in Roman characters and in another for those in Cyrillic. Bibliography.

387. Hoyle, John. A complete dictionary of music. Ráimpr en facs. de l'éd. de Londres, 1791. Genève: Minkoff Reprint, 1976. 162 p.

First ed. published in 1770 under title: *Dictionarium musica.* Reprint of the 1791 ed. printed for H. D. Symonds, London.

388. Jackson, Barbara Garvey and Joel Berman. The A.S.T.A. dictionary of bowing terms for string instruments. 2nd ed. Urbana, Illinois: American String Teachers Association, 1976. 53 p.

389. Janovka, Tomas Baltazar. Clavis ad thesaurum magnae artis musicae, seu eluciadarium omnium fere rerum & verborum, in musica figurali tam vocali, quam instrumentali obvenietum. Consistens potissimum in definitionibus & divisionibus; quibusdam recentioribus de scala, tono, cantu, & genere musicae &c. sententijs, variisque exqvisitis observationibus . . . alphabetico ordine compositum a Thoma Balthasare Janovka. Vetero-Pragae: in Magno collegio Carolino typis Georgij Labaun, 1701. 324 p.

Reprinted by Frits Knuf, Hilversum, 1973, as vol. 3 of the series *Facsimile reprints of early music dictionaries.*

This volume shares with Brossard (no. 372) the distinction of being one of the first modern dictionaries of musical terms. The two compilers worked simultaneously but independently of each other.

390. Katayen, Leila and Val Telberg. Russian-English dictionary of musical terms. New York: Telberg Book Corp., 1965. 125 leaves (Typescript).

Russian-English equivalents in musical terminology. No definitions, short bibliography.

391. Koch, Heinrich Christoph. Musikalisches Lexikon, welches die theoretische und praktische Tonkunst, encylopädisch bearbeitet, alle alten und neuen Kunstwörter erklärt, und die alten und neuen Instrumente beschrieben, enthält. .... Frankfurt a. M.: A. Hermann dem Jungern, 1802. 2 v.

One of the first of a long line of German dictionaries of terms. Particularly important for definitions and concepts pertaining to late Baroque and classic music and instruments.

A revised edition, by Arrey von Dommer, printed in Heidelberg, 1865, has very little resemblance to the original.

Reprint publication by Georg Olms, Hildesheim, 1964 and 1975.

392. Leuchtmann, Horst. Wörterbuch Musik. Dictionary of terms in music: Englisch-Deutsch/Deutsch-Englisch. 3. [erw.] Aufl. München, etc.: K.G. Saur; Hamden, Conn., Linnet Books, 1981. 560 p.

First published as Langenscheidts Fachwörterbuch, Musik by Langenscheidt, Berlin, 1964, 359 p. 2nd edition published by Verlag Documentation in Munich, 1977, 433 p.

An English-German, German-English dictionary of terms. No definitions, merely verbal equivalents.

393. Levarie, Siegmund and Ernst Levy. Musical morphology: a discourse and a dictionary. Kent, Ohio: Kent State University Press, c1983. 344 p.

An earlier edition of this work [A dictionary of musical morphology] was published by the Institute of Mediaeval Music, Binningen, Switzerland, [and Henryville, Pennsylvania, 1980] despite the objections of the authors, who took the position that it was unauthorized, incorrect, and not truly representative of their work. The present edition is fully authorized. [verso of title page]

A dictionary covering few terms with lengthy entries. Appended illustrations. Index to composers and works cited in the entries.

394. Lichtenthal, Pietro. Dizionario e bibliografia della music. Milano, A. Fontana, 1836. 4 v.

First published in 1826 in 2 v. Reprint of 1836 edition by Forni, Bologna (Biblioteca musica Bononiensis, I, 6), 1970.

The first two volumes of this work are a dictionary of terms, the last two, a bibliography of music literature based on Johann Nikolaus Forkel's *Allgemeine Literatur der Musik* (see no.708). A French edition of the dictionary of terms, "traduit et augmente par Dominique Mondo," appeared in Paris in 1839.

395. Limenta, Fernando. Dizionario lessicografico musicale italiano-tedesco-italiano. Milano: Hoepli, 1940. 391 p.

Designed to provide precise Italian equivalents for German technical terms not adequately treated in most dictionaries.

396. Padelford, Frederick M. Old English musical terms. Bonn, P. Hanstein, 1899. 112 pages. (Bonner Beitrage zur Anglistik, 4)

Reprinted by Milford House, Boston, 1973 and by Longwood Press, Portland, Maine, 1976.

397. Pulver, Jeffrey. A dictionary of old English music and musical instruments. London, Kegan Paul; New York, E.P. Dutton, 1923. 247 p.

Terms used by Tudor and early Stuart musicians. Fairly long articles, with references to early literary and musical sources for the terms. 10 plates of early English instruments.

398. Randel, Don Michael. Harvard concise dictionary of music. Cambridge, Mass.: Belknap Press, 1978. 577 p.

Successor to the *Harvard brief dictionary of music* by Willi Apel and Ralph T. Daniel (Cambridge: Harvard University Press, 1960, 341 p.)

Published in Spanish as *Diccionario Harvard de música* by Editorial Diana, Mexico City, 1984, 559 p.

Intended as a companion for students enrolled in a college-level music appreciation course. Short articles on topics and persons.

399. Randel, Don Michael,, ed. The New Harvard dictionary of music. Cambridge, Mass.: Belknap Press of Harvard University Press, 1986. 942 p.

Completely revised edition of the *Harvard dictionary of music by* Willi Apel, 2nd ed. (Cambridge: Belknap, 1969. 935 p.).

First printed in 1944. The fifth printing, 1947, contains a section of 'addenda and corrigenda to the original entries." The second edition, 1969, was completely reset.

The standard reference work in English for non-biographical information, designed to provide accurate and pertinent information on all musical topics. The emphasis is on the historical approach and on Western art music, but there is coverage of non-Western and popular musics. Good, basic bibliographies; excellent brief historical articles. Signed articles, numerous musical examples and illustrations.

There is a thoughtful article on the place of music lexicography in musicology by Don Randel entitled "Defining music" in*Notes,* 43 (1987), p. 751–66.

Review of the second edition by Charles Rosen in *The New York Review of Books,* 14 (Feb. 1970), p. 11–15; in *The Booklist,* 66 (May, 1970), p. 1055-1061); by Vincent Duckles in *Notes,* 27 (1970), p. 256–58.

400. Reid, Cornelius L. A dictionary of vocal terminology: an analysis. New York: Joseph Patelson Music House, 1983. 457 p.

Definition of principal terms "in common use by the vocal profession from the early 17th century to the present . . ." Includes scientific terms and cross references. Bibliography.

401. Rousseau, Jean J. Dictionnaire de musique. Paris: Duchesne, 1768. 548 [i.e., 556] p., 13 folded plates.

Reprint by G. Olms, Hildesheim, and by Johnson Reprint Corp., New York, 1969.

Several editions published in Paris and Amsterdam during the 18th century. An English edition, translated by William Waring, published under the title *A complete dictionary of music,* 2nd edition, London, 1779. Reprint of the 1779 Waring edition by AMS Press, New York, 1975, 470 p. Reprint of the Aubree edition of Paris, 1832 by Art & Culture, Paris, 1977, 2 v.

Based on articles written by Rousseau for the Diderot and d'Alembert *Encyclopedie* but not included in that work. Reflects the stimulating and highly personal views of an 18th-century man of letters. Wide influence and considerable historical importance.

402. Sacher, Jack, ed. Music A to Z. Based on the work of Rudolf Stephan. [Translators: Miecslaw Kolinski and others.] New York: Grosset & Dunlap, 1963. 432 p.

A translation, with additions and corrections, of Rudolf Stephan's music dictionary in the Fischer Lexikon series, see no. 410.

Review by Theodore Karp in *JAMS,* 17 (1964), p. 394–395; by Harold Samuel in *Notes,* 20 (1963), p. 658–59.

403. Schaal, Richard. Abkurzungen in der Musik-Terminologie. Eine Ubersicht. Wilhelmshaven: Heinrichshofen's Verlag, 1969. 165 p. (Taschenbucher zur Musikwissenschaft, 1)

A dictionary of the abbreviations most frequently used to refer to musical practice, bibliography, insitutions. Intended primarily for German music students, but of general utility.

404. Schaal, Richard. Fremdwörterlexikon Musik. Englisch-Franzosisch-Italienisch. Wilhelmshaven: Heinrichshofen's Verlag, 1970. 2 v. (Taschenbucher zur Musikwissenschaft, 2, 3)

Vol. 1: A-Ist. Vol. 2: Jac-Zur.

A polyglot dictionary of English, French, and Italian terms with their German equivalents. Contains more than 15,000 foreign terms.

405. Seagrave, Barbara G. and Joel Berman. The A.S.T.A. dictionary of bowing terms for string instruments. 2nd ed. Urbana: American String Teachers Association, 1976. 53 p.

First published in 1968.

406. Siliakus, H. J. 500 German musical terms and their English translations together with 500 useful phrases. Adelaide: University of Adelaide, 1968. 113 p.

This booklet is not a dictionary, but a special word list for musicologists who need a reading knowledge of German. It will only be useful for those who have mastered the elements of the German language, since we assume a knowledge of basic grammar and familiarity with about 1,000 basic words. [Author's *Preface*]

407. Sinzig, Pedro. Dicionärio musical. Rio de Janeiro: Kosmos, 1947. 613 p.

A Portuguese-language dictionary of terms. Based largely on Apel and Riemann. Bibliographical references.

408. Smith, W. J. A dictionary of musical terms in four languages. London: Hutchinson, [1961]. 195 p.

English terms with equivalents in French, Italian, and German. Pronunciations given in phonetic symbols. No definitions.

409. Stainer, Sir John and W. A. Barrett. Dictionary of musical terms. Hildesheim: Olms, 1970. 456 p.

Reprint of the 2nd ed., Novello, 1898. Reprint of 1889 ed. by Scholarly Press, St. Clair Shores, 1974.

Terms in Italian, French, Latin, German, Hebrew, Greek, Russian, Spanish, and Arabic, with brief English definitions.

410. Stephan, Rudolf. Musik. [Frankfurt am Main]: Fischer Verlag, [1957]. 382 p.

This work has been translated and expanded in Sacher's *Music A to Z;* see no. 402.

General articles cover major topics, with more detailed information approached through an index. Topical bibliographies, p. 355–64. 10 plates. A scholarly summation of musical knowledge for the general reader.

411. Terminorum musicae index septem linguis redactus; Polyglottes Wörterbuch der musikalischen Terminologie; Polyglot dictionary of musical terms . . . [Prepared by a joint committee of the International Musicological Society and the International Association of Music Libraries; Editor: Horst Leuchtmann] Budapest, Akademiai Kiado; Kassel, Bärenreiter, 1978. 798 p.

A polyglot dictionary of musical terms in English, German, French, Italian, Spanish, Russian, and Hungarian. Also know as the *Terminorum Musicae Index.* German is the basic language, but all terms in all seven languages are indexed. Introductory material in each of the 7 languages. Cyrillic index. Diagrams.

Review by Dale Higbee in *American recorder,* 19 (1979), p. 173.

412. Thiel, Eberhard. Sachwörterbuch der Musik. 4. verb. Aufl. Stuttgart: Alfred Kroner Verlag, 1984. 739 p.

1st ed. 1962; 2nd ed. 1973; 3rd ed. 1977.

Review by Harold Samuel in *Notes,* 20 (1963), p. 658.

413. Tinctoris, Johannes (Jean). Dictionary of musical terms. An English translation of Terminorum musicae diffinitorium together with the Latin text. Translated and annotated by Carl Parrish [with a bibliographical essay by James B. Coover]. New York: Free Press, [1963]. 108 p.

A 15th-century dictionary of musical terms, and one of the first books on music to be printed. 291 terms defined. Important for an understanding of Renaissance music theory and practice. The Latin text was reprinted in Coussemaker's *Scriptorum* (1867), in Forkel's *Allgemeine Literatur der Musik* (1792), and with a German translation in Chrysander's *Jahrbuch der Musikwissenschaft,* I (1863).

It appeared in a French translation with introduction and commentary by Armand Machabey (Paris, 1951), and in an Italian translation by Lionello Cammarota (Rome, 1965). The Free Press edition of 1963 was reprinted in 1978 with an introduction by James W. McKinnon. A facsimile edition was published in 1983 by Bärenreiter, Kassel with an introduction by Heinrich Bellermann and and afterword by Peter Gülke (Documenta musicologica, I, 37).

414. Tovey, Donald F. Musical articles from the *Encyclopaedia Britannica.* London, New York: Oxford Univ. Press, 1944. 256 p.

Paperback edition: New York, Meridian Books, 1956, as *The forms of music.* Reprint of *The Forms ...* by Oxford University Press, London, 1967. Reprint of the *Musical articles ...* by Scholarly Press, St. Clair Shores, 1977.

28 articles on the larger aspects of music. Shorter ones (madrigal, sonata, etc.) are briefly historical; others (harmony, sonata forms, etc.) are comprehensive and analytical. Reprinted from Tovey's contributions to the 11th edition of the *Britannica. Encyclopedia Britannica* (11th ed.)— Music articles

415. Vannes, René. ... Essai de terminologie musicale. Dictionnaire universel comprenant plus de 15,000 termes de musique en italien-espagnol-portugais-francais -anglais-allemand-latin et grec. ... Thann: "Alsatia," c. 1925. 230 p.

Reprint by Da Capo Press, New York, 1970.

Most extensive manual of its kind, containing 15,000 entries in eight languages. Includes forms, terms, instruments in current use. Brief definitions given under the original or characteristic language, with equivalents in other languages. No explanatory or historical material.

416. Wörterbuch Musik: englisch-deutsch, deutsch-englisch. Dictionary of terms in music: English-German, German-English. Herausgegeben von Horst Leuchtmann. 3., erw. Aufl. München; New York; London; Paris: Saur; Hamden, Conn.: Linnet Books, 1981. 560 p.

Brief definitions, chiefly verbal equivalents. Some unusual features: a list of 950 popular titles of musical works and a section devoted to the vocabulary of change ringing.

417. Wotton, Tom S. A dictionary of foreign musical terms and handbook of orchestral instruments. Leipzig: Breitkopf & Hartel, 1907. 226 p.

Reprint by Scholarly Press, 1972.

Less comprehensive than Vannes (no. 312). Designed as an aid to score reading, including orchestral terms, instruments, tempo indications, etc. Primarily in French, German, and Italian.

CHURCH MUSIC

This section begins with a list of several general dictionaries relating to church music. This is followed by a list of handbooks on the hymnology of various Protestant groups, with citations under the denominations represented. Such handbooks are essentially bibliographies of sacred music, but most of them contain enough biographical and factual information to justify listing them among the encyclopedias and dictionaries of church music.

418. Carroll, J. Robert. Compendium of liturgical music terms. Toledo: Gregorian Institute of America, 1964. 86 p.

An attempt to provide a single source for information most frequently requested by students and working church musicians. [*Preface*]

419. Davidson, James Robert. A dictionary of Protestant church music. Metuchen: Scarecrow Press, 1975. 349 p.

Brief entries on terms and subjects, most with bibliographies.

Brief review by Stephen M. Fry in *Notes,* 32 (1975), p. 301.

420. Encyclopédie des Musiques Sacrées. Publiée sous la direction de Jacques Porte. Paris: Éditions Lagergerie, 1968–1970. 4 v. [vol. 4 consists of sixteen 7-in. phonodiscs.]

Vol. I: "L'expression du sacré en Orient, Afrique, Amérique du Sud."

Vol. II: "Traditions chrétiennes—des premiers siècles aux cultes révolutionnaires."

Vol. III: "Traditions chrétiennes (suite et fin)—essence, nature et moyens de la musique chrétienne."

A handsomely designed publication. Numerous full-page color plates. The editor is assisted by a large group of authorities, chiefly French. The contributions are all extended articles; no definitions of terms.

421. Fischer, Albert. F. W. Kirchenlieder-Lexikon; hymnologisch-literarische Nachweisungen über c. 4500 der wichtigsten und verbreititsten Kirchenlieder aller Zeiten in alphabetischer Folge nebst einer Übersicht der Liederdichter. Hildesheim: Georg Olms, 1967. 2 v. in 1 ; 25 cm.

Originally published in Gotha, 1878–1879.

Contents: I. A-J—II. K-Z ; Alphabetisches Verzeichnis der Dichter.

422. Foote, Henry W. Three centuries of American hymnody. [Hamden, Conn.]: Shoe String Press, 1961 [c1940]. 418, [23] p.

Not a dictionary, but a history which can serve as a kind of handbook.

423. Hatfield, Edwin Francis. The poets of the church; a series of biographical sketches of hymn writers with notes on their hymns. Detroit: Gale Research, 1978. 719 p.

A reprint of the 1884 edition.

424. Hayden, Andrew J. and Robert F. Newton. British hymn writers and composers; a check-list giving their dates & places of birth & death. Croydon: Hymn Society of Great Britain and Ireland, 1977. [94] p.

425. Hughes, Anselm. Liturgical terms for music students; a dictionary. Boston: McLaughlin & Reilly, [1940]. 40 p.

Reprint (1972) by the Scholarly Press, St. Clair Shores, Michigan.

Concise definitions of terms likely to occur in the literature of ancient ecclesiastical music of the West. Tables give structure of mass and office. Includes terms from the church calendar, terms referring to notation, texts with explanations of their places in the liturgy.

426. Julian, John. A dictionary of hymnology, setting forth the origin and history of Christian hymns of all ages and nations. Rev. ed. with new suppl. London: J. Murray, 1907. 1,768 p.

Unaltered reprint in two volumes, New York, Dover, 1957 and by Kregel Publications, Grand Rapids, Michigan in 1985.

First published in 1892.

Entries under authors, titles, and subjects of hymn texts. Brief but adequate biographical notices. Long articles on American, English, Latin, etc. hymnody. For individual hymns gives original publication and location in other hymnals. Contains a vast amount of information on musical and literary aspects of Christian hymnody.

427. Key words in church music ; definition essays on concepts, practices, and movements of thought in church music. Edited by Carl Schalk. St. Louis: Concordia Pub. House, c1978. 365 p.

Focusing principally on Lutheran practices, but of general relevance. Includes bibliographical references.

428. Kornmüller, P. Utto. Lexikon der kirchlichen Tonkunst. . . . 2. verb. und verm. Aufl. Regensburg: A. Coppenrath, 1891–95. 2 v. in 1.

First published in 1870. Reprint by Olms, Hildesheim, 1975.

Vol. 1: Dictionary of subjects, terms, and instruments connected with Catholic church music, with a subject index of topics discussed in extended articles.

Vol. 2: Biogrpahical dictionary of church musicians. Published works cited for early names, categories of compositions for recent ones.

429. Kümmerle, Salomon. Encyclopädie de evanglischen Kirchenmusik. Gütersloh: E. Bertelsmann, 1888–95. 4 v.

Originally published in Lieferungen, 1883–95.

Reprinted by Olms, Hildesheim, 1974.

Terms and biographies related to Protestant church music. Entries for chorale titles, with full musical quotations of the melodies. The author was responsible for basic research on the melodies of the Lutheran chorale.

Review by Friedrich Spitta in *Vierteljahrschrift fur Musikwissenschaft,* 1 (1885), p. 235–38.

430. McCutchan, Robert G. Hymn tune names, their sources and significance. Nashville: Abingdon Press, [1957]. 206 p.

Reprinted by Scholarly Press, St. Clair Shores, 1976.

Alphabetical listing of tunes, giving their metrical structures and thematic incipits in letter notation. Commentary related to authors, composers, and sources. Numerous cross references. Melodic index. First line index of texts, with author, translator, and tune name.

431. Miller, Josiah. Singers and songs of the church; being biographical sketches of the hymn-writers in all the principal collections, with notes on their psalms and hymns. 2nd ed. Louisville: Lost Cause Press, 1981. 617 p.

A microfiche edition of the original published in London by Longmans, Green in 1869.

432. Mizgalski, Gerard. Podreczna encyklopedia muzyki kościelnej. Poznan; Warszawa; Lublin: Ksiegarnia Sw. Wojciecha, 1959. 566 p.

A Polish dictionary of sacred music. Biographical articles all stress contributions to church music. Illustrated.

433. Nulman, Macy. Concise encyclopedia of Jewish music. New York: McGraw-Hill Book Co., 1975. 276 p.

A highly selective work including both terms and biography. Information is presented in chronological order, with emphasis on current practices. Includes a four page "Highlights in the history of Jewish music." Brief review by Stephen M. Fry in *Notes,* 32 (1976), p. 556.

434. Ortigue, Joseph Louis d'. Dictionnaire liturgique, historique et théorique de plain-chant et de musique d'église, au moyen âge et dans les temps modernes. Paris: J. P. Migne, 1853. 1,563 p.

Reprinted by Da Capo, New York, 1971.

A pioneer reference work on liturgical music, of considerable historical importance. Documented with frequent references to the works of the leading 18th- and 19th-century specialists in church music.

435. Perry, David W. Hymns and tunes indexed by first lines, tune names, and metres compiled from current English hymnbooks. Croydon, England : Hymn Society of Great Britain & Ireland: Royal School of Church Music, 1980. 310 p.

436. Richter, Gottfried Lebrecht. Allgemeines biographisches Lexikon alter und neuer geistlicher Liederdichter. Leipzig: Zentralantiquariat de Deutschen Demokratischen Republik, 1970. 487 p.

A reprint of the Leipzig, 1804 edition.

437. Stubbins, George W. A dictionary of church music. London: Epworth Press, [1949]. 128 p.

A practical reference book for the use of church organists and choir directors. Short explanations of technical terms and concise information on topics related to church music.

438. Thomson, Ronald W. Who's who of hymn writers. London: Epworth Press, 1967. 104 p.

Brief biographies of the principal Protestant hymn text writers with a representative selection of their hymns.

439. Weissenbäck, Andreas. Sacra musica; Lexikon der katholischen Kirchenmusik. Klosterneuburg: Augustinus Druckerei, [1937]. 419 p.

Biography, terms, and subjects in one alphabet. Articles on religious organizations and music publishing houses. More comprehensive in coverage than Kornmüller (no. 428), but the articles are briefer.

Congregational

440. Companion to Congregational Praise. Edited by Kenneth L. Parry, with notes on the music by Erik Routley. London: Independent Press, [1953]. 580 p.

P. 1–336: *Notes* on the words and music for 884 hymns and chants. P. 337–550: biographical notes on hymn writers and composers. Chronological listing of 396 musical sources. Index of tune names and first-line index of hymns.

Episcopal

441. Church of England. Historical companion to Hymns ancient and modern. Edited by Maurice Frost. London: Printed for the Proprietors by William Clowes & Sons, [1962]. 716 p.

The latest revision of a work compiled in 1909 by W. H. Frere under the title *Historical edition of Hymns ancient and modern;* revised in 1950.

P.1–124: Introduction, with contributions by Egon Wellesz, Ruth Massenger, C. E. Pocknee, and Lowther Clarke covering the history of hymnody and of the Anglican hymnal. P. 125–478: Texts and commentary for 636 hymns, including the language of the original if translated. Index of first lines, brief biographies of hymn writers, chronological list of authors and translators, alphabetical index of tunes, index of plainsong, Notes on the composers, with chronology, list of publications and tunes, metrical index.

442. Moorsom, Robert Maude, ed. A historical companion to Hymns ancient and modern: containing the Greek and Latin; the German, Italian, French, Danish and Welsh hymns; the first lines of the English hymns; the names of all authors and translators; notes and dates. 2nd ed. London: C. J. Clay, 1903. 380 p.

Includes bibliographic references.

443. Protestant Episcopal Church in the U.S.A. The Hymnal 1940 companion. [3rd ed. rev.] New York: Church Pension Fund, 1956. 741 p.

First published in 1949.

Contains historical essays on texts and tunes; biographies of authors, composers, translators, and arrangers. List of organ works based on hymn tunes, with publishers. Index of scriptural texts; general index; melodic index; index of tunes; first-line index.

444. Yeats-Edwards, Paul. English church music; a bibliography. London: White Lion, 1975. 217 p.

A selective bibliography, the "object of which is to indicate, under subject headings what books, pamphlets and tracts have been published in England on English church music." There is a general index to the 1.220 entries.

Evangelical and Reformed

445. Haeussler, Armin. The story of our hymns: the handbook to the hymnal of the Evangelical and Reformed Church. St. Louis: Eden Publishing House, 1952. 1,088 p.

Commentary on 561 hymns and other liturgical pieces. Biographies of hymn writers and notes on sources. Bibliography. Index of scriptural texts, topical index, metrical index, indexes of tune names, composers, arrangers, and sources. First-line index.

446. Handbuch zum evangelischen Kirchengesangbuch. Hrsg. von Christhard Mahrenholz und Oskar Sühngen, unter Mitarbeit von Otto Schliske. Gottingen: Vanderhoeck & Ruprecht, 1956–1970. Band I-III (5 v.).

Supplementary volume: *Die Lieder unserer Kirche,* by Johannes Kulp. Gottingen, 1958.

A compendium of information related to the German Lutheran hymnal, in five volumes.

Summary of contents: Bd. 1. 1.T. *Wort- und Sachkonkordanz* (Word and subject concordance) 2. durchgesehene Aufl. (1956) Bd. 1. 2.T. *Die biblischen Quellen der Lieder* (The biblical sources of the songs) von Rudolf Köhler (1957). Bd.2. 1.T. *Lebensbilder der Liederdichter und Melodisten* (Biographical sketches of the poets and the composers). Bd.2. 2. T. *Geschichte des Kirchenliedes* (History of the songs). Bd.3. 1.T. *Liederkunde, Lied 1 bis 175* (Studies of the individual songs and their melodies) (1975).

447. Hustad, Don. Dictionary-handbook to Hymns for the living church, with The history of Hope Publishing Company.... by George H. Shorney Jr. Carol Stream, Il.: Hope Pub. Co., c1978. 364 p.

Lutheran

448. Key words in church music; definition essays on concepts, practices, and movements of thought in church music; edited by Carl Schalk. St. Louis: Concordia Pub. House, 1978. 365 p.

A dictionary of ideas that relate to the history and use of music in the Christian church. Includes bibliographical references.

449. Polack, William G. The handbook of the Lutheran hymnal. 3rd and rev. ed. St. Louis: Concordia, [1958]. 681 p.

Texts of and commentary on 660 Lutheran hymns. Biographical and historical *Notes* on the authors and composers. Index of biblical references, table of hymns for feasts and festivals, first-line index, including stanzas of hymns; index of tunes, metrical index, topical index, index of authors and translators.

Mennonite

450. Hostetler, Lester. Handbook to the Mennonite hymnary. Newton, Kansas: General Conference of the Mennonite Church of North America, Board of Publications, 1949. 425 p.

Commentary on 623 Mennonite hymns and other liturgical pieces. Bibliography. Indexes.

Methodist

451. Gealy, Fred Daniel. Companion to the hymnal; a handbook to the 1964 Methodist hymnal. Nashville: Abingdon Press, [1970]. 766 p.

452. McCutchan, Robert G. Our hymnody, a manual of the Methodist hymnal. 2nd ed. New York: Abingdon Press, [1942]. 619 p.
First published in 1937.
Commentary on 664 hymns and other liturgical pieces. Hymn calendar, bibliography, and nine special indexes.

453. Rogal, Samuel J. Guide to the hymns and tunes of American Methodism. Westport: Greenwood Press, c1986. 318 p. (Music reference collection, 7)

Mormon

454. Cornwall, J. Spencer. Stories of our Mormon Hymns. 4th enlarged printing. Salt Lake City, Deseret Book Co., 1975. 304 p.
A popular companion to the Mormon hymnal, giving information on composers and writers of texts for approximately 311 hymns used in the Mormon church.

Presbyterian

455. Covert, William Chalmers. Handbook to the Hymnal. Calvin Weiss Laufer, associate editor. Philadelphia: Presbyterian Board of Christian Education, 1935. 566 p.

Unitarian

456. Foote, Henry W. American Unitarian hymn writers and hymns. Compiled for the Hymn society of America for publication in the Society's proposed Dictionary of American Hymnology. Cambridge, Mass. [Author], 1959. 270 leaves (typescript).
Contains an historical sketch of American Unitarian hymnody, a catalog of American Unitarian hymn books, alphabetical list of hymn writers, biographical sketches, and first-line index of published hymns.

United Church of Christ

457. Ronander, Albert C. and Ethel K. Porter. Guide to the Pilgrim hymnal. Philadelphia: United Church Press [1966]. 456 p.

OPERA AND THEATER MUSIC

Dictionaries of opera and theater music are of two principal kinds: (1) compilations of facts related to the history or of the production of musical dramatic works, in which case they can be cited as dictionaries or handbooks of opera, or (2) listings of operatic works, often in chronological order, associated with a particular place: city, country, or opera house. Works of the latter kind can properly be described as "Bibliographies of Music," and will be found cited under that heading in the subdivision "Local Opera Repertoires."

Listeners' guides to opera and collections of opera plots have been excluded.

One encyclopedia of theater arts demands mention at this point, although its coverage extends far beyond the realm of music. This is the *Enciclopedia dello spettacolo,* Roma, Casa Editrice le Maschere, 1954–62. 9 vols. This great illustrated reference work was published under the auspices of the Cini Foundation and covers all aspects of the theater, with contributions by outstanding authorities in the field.

Other reference works related to opera will be found cited under the entries Kutsch (no. 102), Le Grandi Voci (no. 95), and Highfill (no. 161).

458. Altmann, Wilhelm. Katalog der seit 1861 in den Händel gekommenen theatralischen Musik (Opern, Operetten, Possen, Musik zu Schauspielen, usw.) Ein musikbibliographischer Versuch ... Wolfenbüttel: Verlag fur musikalische Kultur and Wissenschaft, 1935. 384 p. (incomplete)

This work was published in *Lieferungen,* of which four appeared carrying the entries through 'Siegmund, Josef."

Operas, ballets, and incidental music since 1861, arranged under composer with references from librettist, etc. Gives brief titles of works, type, librettist, date of first performance if known, type of score, language of text, and publisher. There is no key to the abbreviations of publishers' names, but most of these can be readily identified.

459. Bernandt, Grigorii B. Slovar' oper. Vpervye postavlennykh ili izdannykh v dorevoliutsionnoi rossii i v SSSR, 1736–1959. Moskva: Sovetskii Kompozitor, 1962. 554 p.

A dictionary of operas first performed or first published in Russia during the period 1736–1959. Entries are alphabetical by title. Information includes genre of the work, composer, first performance, librettist, literary source, and many details that relate to production. Indexed by composer, librettist, and author of the original literary source.

460. Bloom, Ken. American song: the complete musical theater companion. New York: Facts on File, 1985. 2 v.

Provides information on over 5,000 productions, on- and off-Broadway. Indexes individual songs in each production.

461. Bordman, Gerald. American musical theatre: a chronicle. Expanded edition. New York: Oxford University Press, 1986. 782 p.

First published in 1978. 749 p.

Includes a chronologically ordered discussion of all sorts of musical theatre presented in America from 1735 to 1986. Information about each production includes opening date and theatre, plot synopsis, characters and names of performers, and critical comments based on contemporaneous reviews. Title index. Index to sources upon which shows were based. Index to songs mentioned in the book, but not to all songs in each show. Index to persons.

462. Brockpähler, Renate. Handbuch zur Geschichte der Barockoper in Deutschland. Emsdetten: Verlag Lechte, 1964. 394 p.
A handbook of historical information related to German Baroque opera. Organized by place (47 municipalities), each entry includes a bibliography of relevant literature, sections devoted to the history of music or opera in particular in the place, and a listing of the works performed. Indexed by place, musicians, poets, and dancing masters.

463. Burton, Jack. The blue book of Broadway musicals; with additions by Larry Freeman. Watkins Glen: Century House, [1975?] c1969. 335 p.
Lists title, date, composer, author, principals, and musical numbers for more than 1,500 operettas, musical comedies, and revues from the 1890s to 1951. Arranged by decades, with a general introduction to each period.
The second book in a trilogy on popular music, the first of which was *The blue book of Tin Pan Alley (see no.1545) and the third* The blue book of Hollywood musicals (see no. 464).

464. Burton, Jack. The blue book of Hollywood musicals; songs from the sound tracks and the stars who sang them since the birth of the talkies a quarter-century ago. Watkins Glen: Century House, [1953]. 296 p.

Complementing *The blue book of Tin Pan Alley* (1951) and *The blue book of Broadway musicals* (1952), this present anthology completes a trilogy on popular music. [*Introduction*]

See also *The blue book of Tin Pan Alley* (1962), entered under "Bibliographies of Music: Popular" (see no. 1545) and *The Index of American popular music* (see no. 1546).

465. Busby, Roy. British music hall; an illustrated who's who from 1850 to the present day. London/Salem, New Hampshire: Paul Elek, 1976. 191 p.
A biographical dictionary of British popular entertainers.

466. Caselli, Aldo. Catalogo delle opere liriche pubblicate in Italia. Firenze: Leo S. Olschki, 1969. 891 p. (Historiae musicae cultores, Biblioteca, 27)
An ambitious attempt to cover all operas produced in Italy from 1600 to the present. Organized to permit approaches through the composer, city and theatre, title, librettist. The effort to achieve comprehensiveness leads to some sacrifice in accuracy.
Review by Thomas Walker in *Notes,* 26(1970), p. 758–59.

467. Clément, Félix and Pierre Larousse. Dictionnaire des opéras (Dictionnaire lyrique) contenant l'analyse et la nomenclature de tous les opéras, opéras-comiques, opérettes et drames lyriques représentes en France et è l'étranger depuis l'origine de ces genres d'ouvrages jusqu'è nos jours. ... Rev. et mis è jour par Arthur Pougin. Paris: Librairie Larousse, [1905]. 1,203 p.

First published in 1869 under the title *Dictionnaire lyrique*. Reprint of the 1905 ed. by Da Capo Press, New York, 1969. 2 v.

Title entries (frequently under the French form, with references to other forms) for operas and comic operas presented in France and elsewhere from the beginnings to the date of publication. For each entry: language of text, number of acts, authors of words and music, place and date of first performance, brief sketch of plot, occasional criticism. Index of composers. A comprehensive work.

468. Dassori, Carlo. Opere e operisti (dizionario lirico 1541–1902). Elenco nominativo universale dei maestri compositori di opere teatrali, col prospetto cronologico dei loro principali lavori e catalogo alfabetico generale delle opere serie, semiserie, buffe, comiche e simili rappresentate ... dall'origine dell'opera in musica fino ai d'i nostri, coll'indicazione di data e di luogo della prima rappresentazione, avuto speciale riguardo al repertorio italiano. Bologna: A. Forni [1979] 977 p. (Bibliotheca musica Bononiensis; III, 64)

Reprint of the orignal edition of Tipografia editrice R. Istituto Sordomuti, Genova, 1903.

Includes 15,406 operas by 3,628 composers. Author and title lists only, no descriptive and critical matter.

Part I: Alphabetical list of composers, with dates of birth and death, chronological list under composer of operas, with dates and places of first performances.

Part II: Title list of all operas that have been performed in Italy.

469. Directory of American and foreign contemporary operas and American opera premieres, 1967–1975. New York: Central Opera Service, Metropolitan Opera, 1975. 66 p. (Central Opera Service bulletin, vol. 17, no. 2 (Winter, 1975)))

A listing of operas by American composers premiered and operas by foreign contemporary composers presented in the period 1967–1975.

470. Directory of American Contemporary Operas. N.Y.: Central Opera Service, 1967. 79 p.

A listing of operas by American composers premiered since 1930; arranged alphabetically by composer with information as to place of first performance, librettist, cast and number of acts, availability (from composer, publisher, etc).

A special issue of the Central Opera Service Bulletin, v. 10, no. 2, (Dec. 1967); editor, Mrs. Maria F. Rich.

471. Drone, Jeanette Marie. Index to opera, operetta, and musical comedy synopses in collections and periodicals. Metuchen: Scarecrow Press, 1978. 171 p.

" ... An index to 74 collections and four periodical titles ... including 1,605 titles by 627 composers." [from the *Preface*]

Includes a bibliography of additional sources of synopses not indexed. Review by Frits Noske in *Fontes Artis Musicae,* 26 (1979), p.92–3.

472. Eaton, Quaintance. Opera, a pictorial guide. New York: Abaris Books, 1980. 528 p.

473. Eaton, Quaintance. Opera production: a handbook. Minneapolis: University of Minnesota Press, [1961–74] 2 v.

Reprint of v. 1 by Da Capo, New York, 1974 with title *Opera production I: a handbook,* 266 p ...

V. 1 contains useful information on 224 "long" and 148 "short" operas, including timings, difficulty of leading roles, instumentation, source and cost of scores and parts, photographs of productions, lists of performing groups.

V. 2 treats more than 350 lesser known operas and includes *Production problems of Handel's operas,* by Randolph Mickelson.

474. The Encyclopedia of opera edited by Leslie Orrey; advisory editor, Gilbert Chase. London: Pitman; N.Y.: Charles Scibner's Sons, 1976. 376 p.

Signed articles of very short duration on people, characters, titles, terms, places, and subjects. Brief summary plots and descriptions of characters. Preceded by a short history of the bibliography of opera.

Review by Irwin Kraus in *Notes,* 34 (1977), p. 340–2. Review by Egon Voss in *Neue Zeitschrift für Musik,* 40 (1979), p. 421–22.

476. Ewen, David. New complete book of the American musical theatre. New York: Holt, Rinehart, and Winston, 1970. 800 p.

A sourcebook of information about American musical comedies and revues.

477. Ewen, David. The new encyclopedia of opera. New York: Hill and Wang, 1971. 759 p.

First published in 1955; reissued with a supplement in 1963.

Composers, text incipits, terms, plots, singers, librettists, theatres, all in one alphabet.

Review by Piero Weiss in *Notes,* 28 (1972), p. 697–80.

478. Forbes, Elizabeth. Opera from A to Z. London: Kaye & Ward; South Brunswick, N.J.: A.S. Barnes, 1977. 153 p.

A dictionary of opera including bibliographical references.

479. Gänzl, Kurt. The British musical theatre: volume 1 1865–1914 and volume 2 1915–1984. London: Macmillan Press Music Division; N.Y.: Oxford University Press, 1986. 2 v.

A survey of British light musical theatre, confining itself to works with texts and scores written particularly for the shows in question, excluding opera. Organized chronologically, each year's entries are preceded by a brief essay on the character of the times. Entries provide performance information and history, including references to TV/video productions. Characters and players are cited. Appendices listing printed and recorded works. Index of names, titles, theatres, and titles of journals or newspapers cited. A substantial guide to this genre.

480. Green, Stanley. Broadway musicals, show by show. Milwaukee: Hal Leonard Books, 1985. 316 p.

Organized chronologically, 300 entries provide brief histories, information on each production, and photographs. Indexes to titles, composers, lyricists, librettists, directors, choreographers, principal members of casts, and theaters.

481. Green, Stanley. Encyclopaedia of the musical film. New York: Oxford University Press, 1981. 344 p.

Bibliography and discography: p. 335–344.

482. Green, Stanley. Encyclopedia of the musical theatre: an updated reference guide to over 2,000 performers, writers, directors, productions, and songs of the musical stage, both in New York and London. New York: Da Capo Press, 1984. 492 p.

Reprint of the ed. published by Dodd, Mead, New York, supplemented with photographs and addenda, 1976.

Bibliography and discography, p. 472–488. Supplementary listing of awards and prizes and long runs.

483. Green, Stanley. Rodgers and Hammerstein fact book: a record of their works together and with other collaborators. New York: Lynn Farnol Group, 1980. 762 p.

Bibliography: pp. 709–720. Discography: p. 721–734. Categorical listing of songs.

484. Green, Stanley. The world of musical comedy; the story of the American musical stage as told through the careers of its foremost composers and lyricists. Foreword by Deems Taylor. New York: Grosset & Dunlap, 1962. 397 p.

First published in 1960.

Not properly a dictionary, this work nonetheless contains valuable information about the creators of this American genre. Musical productions & discography: p. 318–382.

485. Gruber, Clemens M. Opern-Uraufführungen: ein internationales Verzeichnis von der Renaissance bis zur Gegenwart; hrsg. von der Gesellschaft für Musiktheater. [Wien: Österreichische Verlagsanstalt, c1978-] 3 v. to date.

Projected in 15 to 18 volumes. Will contain information on about 40,000 operatic world premieres.

V. 3. Komponisten aus Deutschland (der Bundesrepublik Deutschland, der Deutschen Demokratischen Republik) 1900–1907, 319 p.

Entries by composer giving dates and places of world premieres for each title. Title and location indexes. *Anhang* and supplement.

Review by Gustav Pichler in the *Österreichisches Musikzeitschrift,* v. 34 (1979), p. 388.

486. Herders Musiklexikon; Oper Operette Musical. 4. Aufl. Freiburg; Basel; Wien: Herder, 1976. 370 p.

Three sections with a brief history of each genre, followed by descriptions of the works including plot summaries, arranged by composer. Heavily weighted to German language productions. There is a brief bio-bibliographical dictionary and a dictionary of terms. Indexes to arias, and to names and titles.

487. Johnson, H. Earle. Operas on American subjects. New York: Coleman-Ross Co., 1964. 125 p.

An alphabetical listing, by composer, of operas from the 17th century to the present based on American subject matter or involving American characters. The entries supply much interesting information related to plot, performance, and estimates by contemporary critics. Topical, title, and general indexes.

Also see Julius Mattfeld's *A handbook of American operatic premieres*, no. 3141.

488. Kürschners Biographisches Theater-Handbuch. Schauspiel, Oper, Film, Rundunk: Deutschland, Österreich, Schweiz. Hrsg. von Herbert A. Frenzel and Hans Joachim Moser. Berlin: W. de Gruyter, 1956. 840 p.

Names, addresses, activities of singers, music directors, actors, critics, dancers, choreographers, composers, librarians of theater collections, etc. Entries are for persons living as of 1956.

Also know as *Biographisches Theater-Handbuch.*

489. Lessing, Gotthold. E. Handbuch des Opern-Repertoires. [Neubearbeitung.] London; New York: Boosey & Hawkes, 1952. 393 p.

An organized compilation of facts related to the performance of 392 operas in the current repertoire, including casts of characters, locales of action, instrumentation, duration of acts, dates of first performance, and publishers of music.

A work reference intended for the use of theatrical managers, conductors, dramatists and in libraries. [Author's *Preface*]

490. Lewine, Richard, and Alfred Simon. Encyclopedia of theater music: a comprehensive listing of more than 4,000 songs from Broadway and Hollywood, 1900–60. New York: Random House, [1961]. 248 p.

A guide to the song repertory of the American musical theater.

Part I: Theater songs, 1900–24. Part II: Theater songs, 1925–60. Part III: Motion picture songs. Part IV: Show chronology, 1925–60.

Songs are listed alphabetically by title, with composer, lyricist, show, and year given. List of published vocal scores and index of shows.

491. Loewenberg, Alfred. Annals of opera, 1597–1940, compiled from the original sources; with an introduction by Edward J. Dent. 3rd ed., rev. and corrected. Totowa: Rowman and Littlefield; London: J. Calder, 1978. 1756 columns.

First published in 1943 by W. Heffer, Cambridge, 879 p. and subsequently published in a 2nd revised and corrected edition by Societas Bibliographica, Geneva, 1955 in 2 v. The 1955 edition was reprinted by Rowman and Littlefield, New York, 1970 and by Scholarly Press, St. Clair Shores, 1972.

Part 1: chronological listing of operas by dates of first performance, including (with a few exceptions) only works known to have been produced. The list is limited to older operas that are extant and modern ones that have created interest outside their countries of origin. Each entry includes composer's name, original title of the work, English translation for all languages except German, French, and Italian. Librettist identified; place and date of first performance given.

Part 2: indexes by title, composer, librettist, and a general index for other names, places, and subjects.

A work of distinguished scholarship; essential for the historical study of opera.

Review of 2nd ed. by Edward N. Waters, in *Notes,* 13 (1956), p. 285–86.

492. Manferrari, Umberto. Dizionario universale delle opere melodramatiche. Firenze: Sansoni, 1954–55. 3 v. (Contributi alla biblioteca bibliografica italica, 4, 8, 10)

One of the most comprehensive of all listings of opera before the work of Franz Steiger (see no. 510). Entries under composer, giving title, librettist, place and date of first performances in other opera houses.

There is a typescript index of librettists cited in entries for operas composed before 1801 which was prepared in Venice in 1966.

493. Martin, George W. The companion to twentieth century opera. New York: Dodd, Mead & Co., 1984. 653 p.

Previously published as *The opera companion to twentieth-century opera, 1979.*

Synopses of 78 opera plots, with statistics on repertoires of 23 major opera houses around the world.

494. Moore, Frank L. Crowell's handbook of world opera. New York: Thomas Y. Crowell, 1961. 683 p.

Reprinted by Greenwood, Westport, 1974.

Pub. in England under title: *The handbook of world opera,* London, Arthur Baker, [1962], with introduction by Darius Milhaud.

Rich accumulation of facts under headings such as the operas, the people in opera, the characters in opera, first lines and titles of famous musical numbers, chronology of opera, glossary, themes of most famous musical numbers, recordings of complete operas. Numerous special indexes.

495. Northouse, Cameron. Twentieth century opera in England and the United States. Boston: G. K. Hall, 1976. 400 p.

A chronological list of first performances, 1900–74 with another list organized by composer of operas lacking information to include them in the chronological list. Appendices: a list of operas based on literary works and published operas. Index to composers, librettists, opera titles, literary titles, and literary authors.

496. L'Opera : repertorio della lirica dal 1597. Capo redattore Riccardo Mezzanotte]. Milano: A. Mondadori, 1977. 512 p.

Issued in an English version as *The Simon and Schuster book of the opera; a complete reference guide—1597 to the present* by Simon and Schuster, New York, 1978, 512 p. Issued in a German version as *Oper; eine illustrierte Darstellung der Oper von 1597 bis zur Gegenwart* (Übersetzung aus dem Italienischen von Brigitte de Grandis Grossmann und Sigrid Oswald) by Laaber-Verlag, Laaber, and by Drei Lilien Verlag., Wiesbaden, both c1981 and both 508 p. Issued in a Spanish version as *La Ópera; enciclopedia del arte lírico* [traducción del texto original en italiano por Juan Novella Domingo] by Aguilar, Madrid, 1981, 514 p.

497. Opera Manual: a handbook of practical operatic information. Edited by Mrs. Charles A. Matz and Marguerite Wickersham. New York: Central Opera Service, 1956. 36 p.

Contains lists of operas in modern translation; chamber operas, citing voices and instruments needed, sets, duration, source of music. Information on costume and scenery rentals. Bibliography of stagecraft materials; lists of awards for singers; opera activity in the U.S., 1955–56; addresses of publishers, opera groups; unpublished translations, sources of chamber operas, etc.

498. Osborne, Charles. The dictionary of opera. New York: Simon & Schuster, 1983. 382 p.

499. Phaidon book of the opera, a survey of 780 operas from 1597. Oxford: Phaidon, 1979. 511 p.

Published originally as *L'Opera: repertorio della lirica dal 1597* by Mondadori in Milano, 1977.

Chronologically ordered descriptions and synopses, including first cast if known. Copiously illustrated. Indexes of titles and composers, librettists and sources.

500. Pipers Enzyklopädie des Musiktheaters: Oper, Operette, Musical, Ballet herausgegeben von Carl Dahlhaus und dem Forschungsinstitut für Musiktheater der Universität Bayreuth unter Leitung von Sieghart Döhring. München; Zürich: Piper, 1986– . 8 v. intended, 1 v. issued to date.

V. 1–5 will contain lengthy articles on composers and their works. Each entry provides information on individual works: authors of texts. First performances, characters, performing forces, performance characteristics. The origins of the story are described and discussed. A plot outline, commentary on the work, and a performance history are provided. There is bibliographical information on sources and editions as well as the literature about each work. Illustrated. An index and supplement volume is planned as are two volumes defining terms and discussing concepts. V. 1 treats composers through Donizetti in 726 p. There is an index to titles in v. 1 and the articles are signed.

501. Regler-Bellinger, Brigitte, Wolfgang Schenck and Hans Winking. Knaurs grosser Opernführer. Redaktion, Brigitte Mudrak-Trost. München: Droemer Knaur, c1983. 672 p.

Earlier edition *Knaurs Opernführer* by Gerhart von Westermann and Karl Schumann and published by Dromer/Knaur, Munchen & Zurich, 1969, 511 p. *Opera guide* edited, with an introd., by Harold D. Rosenthal and translated by Anne Ross was adapted from the 1969 *Knaurs Opernführer* and published by E. P. Dutton, N.Y., 1965, 584 p.

Known as *Opernführer.*

Includes bibliographical references, discography (p. 633–650) and indexes.

502. Rich, Maria F. Who's who is opera: an international biographical directory of singers, conductors, directors, designers, and administrators, also including profiles of 101 opera companies. New York: New York Times Co., 1976. 684 p.

Provides information on 2,300 artists in 144 opera companies. Profiles of opera companies include recent repertories and budgets. There is a also a directory of international agents.

503. Rieck, Waldemar. Opera plots, an index to the stories of operas, operettas, etc., from the sixteenth to the twentieth century. New York: The New York Public Library, 1927. 102 p.

Reprinted March 1927 from the *Bulletin of the New York Public Library* of January, February, March, April 1926.

Over 200 books and editions published in English, French, German, and Danish during the past 80 years have been indexed; 998 composers are represented by more than 2,775 works in operatic form. [*Introduction*]

504. Riemann, Hugo. Opern-Handbuch. Repertorium der dramatisch-musikalischen Litteratur (Opern, Operetten, Ballette, Melodramen, Pantomimen, Oratorien, dramatische Kantaten, usw.). Leipzig: H. Seemann Nachfolger, [n.d.]. 862 p.

Reprint of the reissue of the 1887 edition with the addition of the second supplement of 1893 by Olms, Hildesheim, 1979, 862 p.

Originally published by C. A. Koch, Leipzig, 1887. Intended as an opera supplement to Riemann's *Lexikon*.

Title articles give genre, number of acts, composer, librettist, first performance. Composer articles give dates, chronological list of operas. Librettist entries give dates and chief activity.

505. Rosenthal, Harold D. and John Warrack. Concise Oxford dictionary of opera. 2d ed., Reprinted with corrections. Oxford; New York: Oxford University Press, 1986. 561 p.

First published in 1964, subsequently issued in a corrected 1st ed. in 1972. 2nd ed. issued in 1971.

A richly informative pocket dictionary of opera. Special emphasis laid on the growth of opera in Eastern Europe, on literary backgrounds and relationships, and on singers.

Enlarged version of the earlier edition, considerably enhanced by a corss-referencing system, by more coverage of the development of opera in all countries, and by better coverage of localities. Singers are especially well-represented. Includes a brief bibliography for further study.

Review by David Z. Kushner in *Notes,* 22 (1965–66), p. 906. Review by Clifford Bartlett in *Brio,* 16 (1979), p. 18.

506. Ross, Anne. The opera directory. London: John Calder; New York: Sterling Pub. Co., [1961]. 566 p.

A source book of current opera facts and figures. Introductions and headings in six languages (English, French, German, Italian, Spanish, Russian). Material organized under 13 headings, the most important of which are opera singers, conductors, producers and designers, technical staff, theaters and producing organizations, festivals, living composers, works by living composers, librettist, colleges and schools of music, casting index, glossary.

The identical volume is issued with various foreign title pages under the imprints of publishers in Paris, Geneva, Berlin, London, New York, etc.

507. Schumann, Otto. Opernführer: von Monteverdi bis Penderecki Unter Mitarbeit von Viktor Kreiner. Reinbeck bei Hamburg: Rowohlt, 1982, c1978. 963 p.

Originally published in 1935 under the title *Meyers Opernbuch.*

508. Seeger, Horst. Opern Lexikon. Mitarbeit für die Gebiete Opernfiguren und -zitate, Eberhard Schmidt. 3., erw. Aufl. Wilhelmshaven: F. Noetzel Verlag "Heinrichshofen Bücher," 1978. 702 p.

"Lizenzausgabe für die Bundesrepublik Deutschland, Berlin (West), Österreich und die Schweiz."

Review by Egon Voss in *Neue Zeitschrift für Musik,* 40 (1979). p. 422.

509. Smith, William C. The Italian opera and contemporary ballet in London, 1789–1820; a record of performances and players with reports from the journals of the time. London: The Society for Theatre Research, 1955. 191 p. (Society for Theatre Research. Annual publication, 1953–54)

Cites 618 works produced in the London theaters during the period under consideration, with commentary by the author and quotations from contemporary sources. Indexes of operas, burlettas, cantatas; of ballets and divertissements; of singers, ballet personnel, composers, and instrumentalists.

510. Steiger, Franz. Opernlexikon. Opera catalogue. Lexique des opéras. Dizionario operistico. Mit e. Einf. von Franz Grasberger. Tutzing: Schneider, 1975–1983. 4 pts. in 11 v.

Contents: Titelkatalog, 3 v.; Komponisten, 3 v.; Librettisten, 3 v.; Nachträge, 2 v.

Each of the main volumes presents permutations of the same information: opera title, composer, librettist(s), premiere date & place, genre or opus number. All information is taken from the sources.

The *Nachträge* provide various chronolgical lists: opera composed before 1700; composers who were also librettists; an index to composers with additional full entries included; German opera and singspiele, by period; Italian opera in Italy and elsewhere, by period; etc.

511. Suskin, Steven. Show tunes, 1905–1985: the songs, shows, and careers of Broadway's major composers. New York: Dodd, Mead, 1986. 728 p.

A study of 30 composers with a section on notable Broadway scores by other composers, a chronological list of productions, a collaborator reference listing, and a bibliography. Indexes to song titles, show titles and persons.

512. Towers, John. Dictionary-catalogue of operas and operettas which have been performed on the public stage. Morgantown: Acme Pub. Co., [1910]. 1,045 p.

Reprint by Da Capo Press, New York, 1967. 2 v.

Title lists of 28,015 operas, giving for each composer his nationality and birth and death dates. Alternative or translated titles included. Composer index. No information on librettists, no historical or descriptive material.

Review by Donald Krummel in *Notes,* 24 (1968), p. 502–3.

513. La Vallière, Louis César de La Baume Le Blanc, duc de. Ballets, opera, et autres ouvrages lyriques, par ordre chronologique depuis leur origine; avec une table alphabetique des ouvrages et des auteurs. Paris: Cl. J. Baptiste Bauche, 1760. 300p.

Reprint ed. London, H. Baron, 1967.

514. Várnai, Péter. Operalexikon. Budapest: Zenemúkiadó, 1975. 533 p.

A Hungarian dictionary of opera, especially strong on Eastern European opera.

515. Wallace, Mary Elaine and Robert Wallace. Opera scenes for class and stage. Carbondale, Illinois: Southern Illinois University Press, 1979. 260 p.

Ready reference to over 700 excerpts from 100 operas by voice categories. A guide to opera ensembles for opera workshop use. Information includes identification of excerpts, duration, summary of the dramatic situation. Bibliography, index of operas, index of composers, index of arias and ensembles, index to editions of piano-vocal scores.

516. White, Eric Walter. A register of first performances of English operas and semi-operas: from the 16th century to 1980. London: The Society for Theatre Research, 1983. 130 p.

517. Who's who in opera; an international biographical directory of singers, conductors, directors, designers, and administrators, also including profiles of 101 opera companies. Maria F. Rich, editor. New York: Arno Press, 1976. 684 p.

Provides information on 2,300 artists in 144 opera companies. Profiles of opera companies include recent repertories and budgets. There is a also a directory of international agents.

MISCELLANEOUS

518. Barlow, Harold and Sam Morgenstern. A dictionary of musical themes. Rev. ed. New York: Crown, 1975. 642 p.

First published in 1948. Reissued in 1957 and 1966. This edition also published by E. Benn, London.

Contains 10,000 themes from instrumental works, arranged alphabetically by composer. Indexed by scale degrees in letter notation with all themes transposed to C major or minor. Title index.

519. Barlow, Harold and Sam Morgenstern. A dictionary of opera and song themes: including cantatas, oratorios, lieder, and art songs. Originally published as A dictionary of vocal themes. Rev. ed. New York: Crown Publishers, 1976. 547 p.

First published in 1950 and reissued in 1960. This edition also published by E. Benn, London.

Contains themes from operas, cantatas, oratorios, art songs, and miscellaneous vocal works, arranged alphabetically by composer. Indexed by scale degrees as in the preceding work. Title and first-line index.

Review by Harold Spivacke in *Notes,* 8 (1951), p. 334–5.

520. Berger, Kenneth W. Band encyclopedia. Evansville: Distributed by Band Associates, 1960. 604 p.

A compendium of information useful to band directors. Includes revisions of the author's earlier publications: *Band bibliography; Band discography;* and *Bandmen,* a biographical dictionary of band musicians.

Review by Keith Polk in *Notes,* 18 (1961), p. 424–26; by J. M. Lundahl in *Journal of research in music education,* 10 (1962), p. 81–82.

521. Burrows, Raymond M. and Bessie C. Redmond. Concerto themes. New York: Simon and Schuster, 1951. 296 p.

More inclusive than Barlow and Morgenstern (no. 518) for concertos. Alphabetical arrangement by composer. Indexed by concerto titles, keys, and solo instruments.

522. Burrows, Raymond M. and Bessie C. Redmond. Symphony themes. New York: Simon and Schuster, 1942. 295 p.

523. Cobbett, Walter W. Cyclopedic survey of chamber music. 2nd ed. London: Oxford Univ. Press, 1963. 3 v.

First published in 2 volumes, 1929–1930.

Cobbet's Cyclopedia is a biographical and subject dictionary of chamber music, giving full lists of works in this category under composer. Solo works and piano compositions excluded. The main emphasis is critical and analytical. Excellent critical and bibliographical material, with signed articles by outstanding authorities.

The second edition is a reissue of the original two volumes with minor corrections, plus a third volume which brings the information up to date.

Volume 3 of the 1963 edition is made up of extended articles surveying chamber music since 1929 in Europe, Great Britain, Russia, and Americ. Editor and principal contributor is Colin Mason. The chapter on *"Chamber music in America"* is by Nicolas Slonimsky; on *"Soviet chamber music"* by I. I. Martinov. Classified bibliography on chamber music; index of composers.

Review of the second edition by Homer Ulrich in *Notes,* 21 (1963–64), p. 124–26.

524. Comuzio, Ermanno. Film music lexicon. Pavia: Amministrazione Provinciale di Pavia, 1980. 304 p.

International in scope, providing biographical information on 580 musicians, listing the motion pictures for which they composed. "Filmografia" with entries from 1906–1980 on films with original music judged of particular value, films of a musical character (with subjects on symphonies, operas, ballets, or biographies of great musicians), musicals, and films featuring jazz, pop, and rock music. Index of names. Bibliography.

525. **Heinzel, Erwin.** Lexikon der Kulturgeschichte in Literatur, Bildender Kunst und Musik. Wien: Verlag Bruder Hollinek, 1962. 493 p.

A supplement to the succeeding work.

526. **Heinzel, Erwin.** Lexikon historischer Ereignisse und Personen in Kunst, Literatur und Musik. Wien: Verlag Bruder Hollinek, 1956. 782 p.

A dictionary treating the artistic, literary, and musical works based on the lives of historical persons or events. Entries arranged alphabetically with persons and events interfiled. The information includes a summary of the historical details followed by a classified listing of the art works in which the person or event is represented.

527. **Hodgson, Julian.** Music titles in translation; a checklist of musical compositions. London: CLive Bingley; Hamden: Linnet Books, 1976. 370 p.

A list of titles in one alphabetical sequence giving "the original or English language translation followed by the translation or original" of titles of musical compositions. The last name of the composer is included for each title. Excerpts are denoted by connection to the larger work.

528. **Leipoldt, Friedrich.** Lexikon der musischen Künste: Begriffe, Namen, Themen aus Musik, Malerei und Dichtung. Unter Mitarbeit von Clemens M. Gruber. Herrsching: M. Pawlak, [1986?] 382 p.

A fascinating attempt to provide access to musical works by theme or reference to extra-musical ideas. See also the work of E. Heinzel (no. 525 and 526).

529. **Parsons, Denys.** The directory of tunes and musical themes. Introd. by Bernard Levin. Cambridge, Eng.: S. Brown, 1975. 288 p.

Identifies about 15,000 vocal and instrumental themes by representing the pitch direction of the first sixteen notes in each theme. Includes a directory of popular tunes and a section on national anthems in musical notation coded to demonstrate the identification scheme.

Brief review by Stephen M. Fry in *Notes,* 32 (1976), p. 556–57.

530. **Rachlin, Harvey.** Encyclopedia of the music business. N.Y.: Harper & Row, 1981. 524 p.

400 articles on the "business of selling music." Cross referenced, but no index. Appendix of winners of certain awards. Focus on the American scene.

531. **Read, Gardner.** Thesaurus of orchestral devices. New York: Pitman, 1953. 631 p.

Reprint by the Greenwood Press, New York, 1969.

Intended to be a lexicon of instrumentation which will serve the student and/or professional orchestrator in the same manner and to the same degree that Bartlett's *Familiar quotations* or Roget's *Thesaurus* aid both the student of literature and the established writer. [*Preface*]

Nomenclature in English, Italian, French, and German, with ranges of instruments, lists of devices, with reference to the page and measure number of the score. List of music publishers and their U.S. agents. Index of nomenclature and terminology. Also known familiarly as *Orchestral devices*.

532. Reallexikon der Akustik herausgegeben von Michael M. Rieländer. Frankfurt am Main: Bochinsky, 1982. 461 p.
A technical dictionary with numerous diagrams and photographs. Bibliographic citations drawn almost entirely from German language sources. There is a list of principal sources.

533. Risatti, Howard A. New music vocabulary. A guide to notational signs for contemporary music. Urbana, etc.: University of Illinois Press, 1975. 219 p.

This book has been organized into six chapters: Chapter I surveys general material pertinent to many instruments; succeeding chapters deal with one of the instrumental groups, and the sixth and final chapter deals with the voice. [*Author's Introduction*]

All the signs are graphically displayed, with explanation as to their meanings. There is a list of composers cited, a bibliography, and a general index.

534. Schillinger, Joseph. Encyclopedia of rhythms: instrumental forms of harmony; a massive collection of rhythm patterns (evolved according to the Schillinger theory of interferences arrayed in instrumental form). N.Y.: Da Capo, 1976. 250 p.
Reprint of edition of C. Colin, N.Y., 1966.

This is a practical handbook of rhythm patterns ... it presents ... the entire range of rhythm resources, making accessible to all who are interested in music the most normal, the most complex, and the most simple rhythm forms.

Arranged in 2 sections: rhythmic resultants; analyzing rhythmic resultants with fractioning.

535. Slonimsky, Nicolas. Thesaurus of scales and melodic patterns. New York: Coleman-Ross, 1947. 243 p.
Reprinted by Duckworth, London, 1975.
Described by the author as "a reference book for composers in search of new materials." Contains nearly 1,000 scales, both traditional and contrived.

536. Vernillat, France and Jacques Charpentreau. Dictionnaire de la chanson francaise. Paris: Librairie Larousse, 1968. 256 p.
A dictionary of French popular song. Full historical coverage, but with

emphasis on the early 19th and 20th centuries. Includes both terms and biography. Illustrated. No bibliographical references.

Also entered as no. 279.

Histories and Chronologies

We have been particularly selective in this area. The titles include only the standard general histories of music in the major European languages together with some of the more recent outline histories. Excluded are all histories devoted to the music of a particular national group and most early histories (pre-1850) unless—as in the case of Burney, Hawkins, Forkel, or Martini—they are of extraordinary interest and are currently available. Also excluded are histories of special periods and forms except as they occur as part of a comprehensive series. Music histories come and go, and few of those designed for the general reader, or for the music student, may be expected to outlive their time. This will account for the fact that some of the familiar occupants of library shelves, such as Dommer, Naumann, Rowbotham, and Rockstro, are missing from this list.

It is true of the early histories as it was of the early dictionaries that a number of titles have been restored to availability through modern reprint publication. We have indicated in the annotations which histories are available in reprint editions.

Those who want a chronological listing of histories will find one in the appendix to Warren Allen's *Philosophies of music history* (no. 3015), under the title "Bibliography of literature concerning the general history of music in chronological order." See also the article "Histories" by S. T. Worsthorne in *Grove's* 5th edition, vol 4, p. 296–306, for both a chronological and a systematic listing.

HISTORIES

537. Abbiati, Franco. Storia della music. 2nd ed. Milano: Garzanti, 1944–54. 5 v.

A general history of music for Italian readers. Numerous pictorial and musical illustrations. Each major section is followed by an anthology of excerpts from the writings of modern authorities on the period under consideration. There is a bibliography at the end of each volume.

Contents: Vol. I: Roma, Medio Evo, Rinascimento. Vol. II: Seicento. Vol. III: Settecento. Vol. IV: Ottocento. Vol. V: Novecento.

A revision was published in 1967–69 with a somewhat different organization of the material, compacting the Seicento and Settecento volumes into one.

538. Abraham, Gerald. The concise Oxford history of music. London; N.Y.; Melbourne: Oxford University Press, 1979. 968 p.

A work that extends far beyond a condensation of *The new Oxford history of music* (see no. 579). It is one of the most informative of all one-volume histories, with extensive bibliographical references and an index.

Rev. by Paul Henry Lang in *Notes,* 37 (1980), p. 42–43, and by Kurt von Fischer in *Music and Letters,* 62, (1981), p. 68–70.

539. Adler, Guido. Handbuch der Musikgeschichte. . . . 2, vollständig durchgesehene und stark ergänzte Aufl. Berlin-Wilmersdorf: H. Keller, 1930. 2 v.

Unaltered reprint of the 2nd ed., Schneider, Tutzing, 1962 and Deutscher Taschenbuch-Verlag, München, 1975.

First printed in 1924 in one volume. Adler's *Handbuch* is the standard compendium of music history representing the fruits of German scholarship in its an early period of expansion and influence. Major articles contributed by such authorities as Alfred Einstein, Wilhelm Fischer, Robert Haas, Friedrich Ludwig, Curt Sachs, Arnold Schering, Peter Wagner, and Egon Wellesz.

Contents: Bd. 1. Die Musik der Natur- und orientalischen Kulturvölker. Antike. Erste Stilperiode. Zweite Stilperiode.—Bd. 2–3. Dritte Stilperiode.

540. Ambros, August Wilhelm. Geschichte der Musik. . . . 3. gänzlich umbearb. Aufl. Leipzig: Leuckart, 1887–1911. 5 v.

Republication by Olms, Hildesheim, 1968.

One of the last major one-man histories of music. The author did not live to carry the fourth volume past the beginning of the 17th century. Based on original research, the work is particularly important for its coverage of the sources of Medieval and Renaissance music.

Bd. I: Ancient music. 1862. 2nd ed., 1880. 3rd ed., 1887 (B. v. Sokolowsky, ed.).

Bd. II: Music of the Middle Ages. 1864. 2nd ed., 1880 (Otto Kade). 3rd ed., 1891 (Heinrich Riemann).

Bd III: The Renaissance to Palestrina. 1868. 2nd ed., 1893 (Otto Kade).

Bd. IV: (not completed by Ambros) Italian music, 1550–1650. 1878 (Gustav Nottebohm and Carl F. Becker). 2nd ed., 1881. 3rd ed., 1909 (Hugo Leichtentritt).

Bd. V: Musical examples for Bd. III, 1882 (Otto Kade). 2nd ed., 1887. 3rd ed. 1911.

The work by Wilhelm Langhans (see no. 572) was intended to complete the Ambros history from the 17th through the 19th century.

541. Bernard, Robert. Histoire de la musique. [Paris]: Fernand Nathan, 1969–71. 5 v.

First published 1961–63, 3 v.

A history of music distinguished for its fine printing and rich illustrative material, including numerous plates in full color. The work lacks a bibliography or other documentation. Vol. 1 treats the history of European music to the end of the 18th century; vols. 2 and 3 are concerned with the 19th- and 20th-century developments in Europe and the Americas, with brief discussions of Oriental music.

A *Complément à l'histoire de la musique,* containing indexes and glossary, appeared in 1971.

542. Bourdelot, Pierre and Pierre Bonnet. Histoire de la musique et des ses effets. Paris: J. Cochart, 1715. 487 p.

Editions were also printed in Amsterdam, 1725, and The Hague, 1743. The Paris edition (1715) has been reprinted by Slatkine, Genève, 1969; the Amsterdam edition (1725) has been reprinted by the Akademische Druck- und Verlagsanstalt, Graz, 1966.

This is one of the first general histories of music. It was begun by Pierre Bourdelot, continued by his nephew, Pierre Bonne, and finally completed and published by the brother of the latter, Jacques Bonnet.

543. Bücken, Ernst, ed. Handbuch der Musikwissenschaft. Wildpark-Potsdam: Akademische Verlagsgesellschaft Athenaion [1927–31]. 13 v. in 10.

First issued serially in parts.

A series of monographs on various periods and aspects of music history by the leading German musicologists of the period. Well printed and profusely illustrated, including plates in color.

Reprinted by Musurgia, New York, 1949. 13 v. in 9.

[Vol. I] Heinrich Besseler. *Die Musik des Mittelalters und der Renaissance* [1931], 337 p.

[Vol. 2] Friedrich Blume. *Die evangelische Kirchenmusik* [1931], 171 p. Re-edited under the title *Geschichte der Evangelischen Kirchenmusik.* ... herausgegeben unter Mitarbeit von Ludwig Finscher, Georg Feder, Adam Adrio und Walter Blankenburg. Kassel: Bärenreiter, 1965.

Also published in an English translation as *Protestant church music: a history* with a foreword by Paul Henry Lang. (London: Victor Gollancz Ltd., 1975. 831 p.)

Review article by Werner Braun in *Die Musikforschung,* 21 (1968), p. 50–57.

Review of Blume's *Geschichte der evangelischen Kirchenmusik* by U. S. Leupold in *Notes,* 23 (1966), p. 45–46.

[Vol. 3] Ernst Bücken. *Geist und Form im musikalischen Kunstwerk* [1929], 195 p.

[Vol. 4] Ernst Bücken. *Die Musik des 19. Jahrhunderts bis zur Moderne* [1929], 319 p. Reprinted by Laaber Verlag, Laaber, 1979.

[Vol. 5] Ernst Bücken. *Die Musik des Rokokos und der Klassik* [1927], 247 p.

[Vol. 6] Robert Haas. *Aufführungspraxis der Musik* [1931], 298 p.

[Vol. 7] Robert Haas. *Die Musik des Barocks* [1929], 290 p.

[Vol. 8, Pt. 1] Wilhelm Heinitz. *Instrumentenkunde* [1929], 159 p.

[Vol. 8, Pt. 2] Robert Lachmann. *Die Musik der aussereuropäischen Natur- und Kulturvölker* [1929, 33 p.

[Vol. 8, Pt. 3] Curt Sachs. *Die Musik der Antike* [1928], 32 p.

[Vol. 8, Pt. 4] Peter Panóff. *Die Altslavische Volks- und Kirchenmusik* [1930], 31 p.

[Vol. 9] Hans Mersmann. *Die moderne Musik seit der Romantik* [1928], 225 p.

[Vol. 10] Otto Ursprung. *Die katholische Kirchenmusik* [1931], 312 p.

544. Burney, Charles. A general history of music, from the earliest times to the present period. London: printed for the author, 1776–1789. 4 v.

Reprinted with critical and historical notes by Frank Mercer. London: Foulis; New York: Harcourt, 1935. 4 v. in 2. Reprint of the Mercer edition by Dover, New York, 1965. Reprinted by the Folio Society, London, 1969 and Eulenberg, London, 1974.

Burney shares with Sir John Hawkins (see no. 564) credit for the emergence of music historiography in the latter part of the 18th century. In addition to its merits as a source of musical informmion, Burney's work is marked by high literary quality. It set a precedent for generations of music historians to follow.

545. Cannon, Beekman C., Alvin H. Johnson, and William G. Waite. The art of music, a short history of musical styles and ideas. New York: Crowell, [1960]. 484 p.

Reprinted by Crowell in 1966.

Designed as an introduction to the history of music, presupposing little background. The "basic principles of music" are covered in an appendix. No bibliography. Brief musical examples in the text.

Review by Warner Imig in *Jounral of research in music education* 9 (1961), p. 172.

546. Chailley, Jacques. 40,000 years of music. Translated from the French by Rollo Myers, with a preface by Virgil Thomson. London: Macdonald; N.Y.: Farrar, Strauss & Giroux, 1964. 229 p.

Reprinted by Da Capo, N.Y., 1975.

Originally published by Libraries Plaon, Paris, under the title *40,000 ans de musique* (1961).

A provocative if somewhat disorganized approach to music history; treats the subject within the framework of sociology and the history of ideas.

547. Chi, Lien-k'ang. Ch'un ch'iu chan kuo yin yüeh shih liao. Hong Kong (?): s.n., 1980 or 1981. 104 p.

This is a selection of source readings from various Chinese classics of the Spring and Autumn period (722—481 B.C.) and the Warring States period (403–221 B.C.) concerning music. There is a bibliography of sources.

548. Combarieu, Jules. Histoire de la musique des origines au début du XXe siècle. Paris: A. Colin, 1946–60. 5 v.

Reprinted by Minkoff, Geneva, 1972

Vols. 1–3 originally published 1913–19.

I: Des origines à la fin du XVIe siècle. II: Du XVIIE siècle à la mort de Beethoven. III: De la mort de Beethoven au bébut du XXe siècle. IV: L'aube du XXe siècle (by René Dumesnil, 1958). V: La première motié du XXe siècle (by René Dumesnil, 1960).

549. Confalonieri, Giulio. Storia della musica. Nuova edizione riveduta e aggiornata a cura di Alfredo Mandelli. Firenze: Sansoni; Milano: Accademia, 1968. 872 p.

First issued in 1958 by Nuova accademia editrice, Milano. 2 v. A popular general history, lavishly printed on glossy paper, with 34 plates in full color and hundreds of black-and-white illustrations. No musical examples. Essential bibliography listed by chapter at the end of the second volume, where there is also a general index and an index of illustrations.

550.   Contemplating music; source readings in the aesthetics of music selected and edited by Carl Dahlhaus and Ruth Katz. New York: Pendragon Press, 1986– . 4 v. (projected) (Aesthetics in music, no. 5–)

Projected in 4 v.

Contents: v. 1. Substance (1986); v. 2. Import; v. 3. Essence; v. 4. Community of discourse. Will include indexes.

551.   Crocker, Richard L. A history of musical style. New York: McGraw-Hill, 1966. 573 p.

Reprinted by Dover, N.Y., 1986.

One of the few histories of music to focus attention consistently on musical style.

Crocker's book is discussed critically by Leo Treitler in "The present as history,"an article in *Perspectives of new music* (Spring-Summer, 1969), p. 1–58.

Review by Martin Chusid in *Notes,* 23 (1967), p. 732–33; by Gwynn McPeek in *Journal of research in music education,* 15 (1967), p.333–36. Review by Henry Leland Clarke in *JAMS,* 21 (1968), p. 103–5.

552.   Della Corte, Andrea. Antologia della storia della musica, dalla Grecia antica all'ottocento. 4. ed., rinnovata in uno volume. Torino, G. B. Paravia [1945]. 491p.

First published in 1926 in 2 volumes.

An anthology of writings on music history, chiefly by modern European scholars, but with a few early documents (excerpts from Zarlino, Galilei, Caccini, Peri, etc.).

553.   Della Corte, Andrea and Guido Pannain. Storia della music. 4. riv. ed ampliata ed. Torino: Unione Tipografico-Editrice Torinese, 1964. 3 v.

First published in 1935; 2nd ed., 1942; reprinted, 1944.

The standard general history of music for Italian readers.

I: Dal medioevo al seicento. II: Il settecento. III: L'ottocento e il novecento.

554.   Einstein, Alfred. A short history of music. 3rd American edition. New York: Knopf, 1947. 438 p.

Also issued as a paperback. Originally published in German, 1934.

One of the most perceptive and authoritative concise histories of music. Published in numerous editions and translations. Most editions incorporate a useful anthology of 39 musical examples, orignally issued in 1917 as "Beisielsammlung zur älteren Musikgeschichte." A handsome illustrated edition (London: Cassell, 1953) edited by A. Hyatt King unfortunately does not contain the musical supplement.

555.   Ferguson, Donald N. A history of musical thought. 3rd ed. New York: Appleton-Century-Crofts [1959] 675 p.

Reprinted by Greenwood, Westport, 1975. First published in 1935; 2nd ed., 1948.

An influential one volume work designed for music history courses at college level. One of the first to propagate the results of German scholarship in Americ.

556. Finney, Theodore M. A history of music. Rev. ed. New York: Harcourt, 1947. 720 p.

Reprinted by Greenwood, Westport, 1976.

First published in 1935. A well organized student's history.

557. Forkel, Johann Nikolaus. Allgemeine Geschichte der Musik. Leipzig: im Schwikertschen Verlag, 1788–1801. 2 v.

Reprint by Olms, Hildescheim, 1962 and by the Akademische Druck-und Verlagsanstalt, Graz, 1967. Ed. by Othmar Wessely in the series *Die grossen Darstellungen der Musikgeschichte* . . .

The first full-scale history of music in German, by the scholar who has been called "the father of modern musicology." The work is incomplete, covering only as far as the early 16th century.

558. Girschner, Otto. Repetitorium der Musikgeschichte. Elfte Auflage. Koln, P.J. Tonger, 1941. 438 p.

A question-answer survey of music history produced during the Nazi era in Germany. Contains numerous anti-semitic elements including on p. 350–411 "Juden in der Musik," a biographical supplement first introduced in the 9th edition, 1936. See also the Stengel *Lexikon* (no. 173) as another example of a shameful practice.

559. Gleason, Harold. Music literature outlines. 2nd ed. Series 1–5. Bloomington: Frangipani Press, 1981. 5 v.

First published in Rochester by Levis Music Stores, 1949–55.

Ser. 1: Music in the Middle Ages and Renaissance. 2nd ed., 1951.
Ser. 2: Music in the Baroque.
Ser. 3: Early American music from 1620–1920.
Ser. 4: Contemporary American music.
Ser. 5: Chamber music from Haydn to Bartok.

Historical outlines, or syllabi, with copious bibliographical references including discography. The organization of Seris 1 and 2 follows closely that of the corresponding works by Reese and Bukofzer in the *Norton history of music series* (see no. 581).

560. Grout, Donald Jay and Claude V. Palisca. A history of Western music. 3rd ed. New York: Norton, 1980.

First published in 1960, revised edition published in 1973.

All editions were also published in shortened form for use as a text, 1964, 1973, 1981. A fourth edition by Claude Palisca is underway.

Intended for undergraduate college music students or for the general reader. "An elementary knowledge of musical terms and of harmony . . . has been assumed." Based on a stylistic approach. Contains numerous musical and pictorial illustrations. Annotated bibliography for further reading, a chronology of musical and historical events, and a glossary of terms.

Review of the 1960 edition by Albert T. Luper in *Notes,* 18 (1960), by Warren Allen in *Journal of research in music education,* 8 (1960), p. 124–26; by Alec Harman in *Musical times* (Dec. 1962), p. 845–47.

561. Gruber, Roman Il'ich. Istoriia muzykal'noi kyl'tury. Moskva: Gosudarstvennoe muzykal'noi izdatel stvo, 1941–1959. 2 v.

A translation into Rumanian by Tatiana Nichitin was issued in Bucarest, 1963– .

A general history of music from antiquity to the beginning of the 17th century, for Russian readers. Vol. 1, pt. 1 deals with Egypt, Mesopotamia, India China, etc. as well as Greece and Rome. The final chapter of vol. 2 is concerned with the musical culture of the Western Slavs to the 17th century.

562. Handschin Jacques. Musikgeschichte in Überblick. 2. ergänzte Auflage. Hrsg. von Franz Brenn. Luzern: Räber: 1964. 442 p.

First published in 1948. Reprint edition by Heinrichshofen, Wilhelmshaven, 1981, 450 p.

A stimulating short history weighted in the direction of Medieval and Renaissance music. Chronological tables and a classified bibliography.

Review of the 2nd ed. by Joseph Müller-Blattau, in *Die Musikforschung,* 18 (1965), p. 441.

563. Harman, Alec and Wilfrid Mellers. Man and his music, the story of musical experiences in the West. New York & Oxford: Oxford University Press, 1962. 1,172 p.

First published in 1957–59 in four volumes covering Medieval music through 20th century music. Reprinted in London by Barrie & Rockcliffe, 1969, and by Barrie and Jenkins, 1977 and 1980.

A history designed for the intelligent layman, stressing the social and cultural backgrounds. Comparative choronology and a list of recommended books and music.

Review of vol. 2 by J. Merrill Knapp in *Notes,* 17 (1960), p. 569–70; of vols. 3 and 4 by William S. Newman in *Notes,* 15 (1957), p. 99–101; of the composite volume by Jack A. Westrup in *Music and letters,* 43 (1962), p. 265–66.

564. Hawkins, Sir John. A general history of the science and practice of music. London: Payne and Son, 1776. 5 v.

New edition "with the author's posthumous notes," published by Novello, London, 1853, 3 v. (vol. 3 is an atlas of portraits); reprinted by Novello in 1875. Unabridged republication of the 1853 edition, with a new introduction by Charles Cudworth, N.Y.: Dover, 1963. 2v. Reprint by the Akademische Druck- und Verlagsanstalt, Graz, 1969, 2 v.

Hawkin's history appeared in the same year that the first volume of Charles Burney's history (no. 544) was published. The two works inevitably invite comparison, largely to Hawkin's disadvantage. His history, however, has much to recommend it. It contains extensive translations of excerpts from early theory works and includes many examples of early music.

Review of the Dover reprint by Bernard E. Wilson in *Notes,* 22 (1966), p. 1026–27.

565. Honolka, Kurt, ed. Knaurs Weltgeschichte der Musik. München/Zürich: Th. Knaur Nachf., 1968. 640 p.

Reprinted by the Rheingauer Verlagsgesellschaft, Wiesbaden, 1976 and by Doremer-Knaur, München and Zürich, 1979.

A general history with 500 illustrations and musical examples. 30 color plates.

Contributors: Hans Engel, Paul Nettl, Kurt Reinhard, Lukas Richter, and Bruno Stäblein.

566. Keisewetter, Raphael Georg. Geschichte der europäisch-abendländischen oder unserer heutigen Musik. Darstellung ihres Wachsthumes und ihrer stufenweisen Entwicklung von dem ersten Jahrhundert des Christenthums bis auf unsere Zeit. Leipzig: Breitkopf und Härtel, 1834. 116 p.

A second, enlarged edition appeared in 1846; this has been reprinted by Sändig, Wiesbaden, 1972. The work appeared in an English translation by Robert Müller, London: Newby, 1848. This, in turn, has been reprinted by Da Capo, New York, 1973, with a new introduction by Frank Harrison.

Kiesewetter's work is the first popular outline history of music in the modern sense. The author organizes his information in 17 different epochs, each characterized by the activity of one or more dominant musical individuals.

567. Knepler, Georg. Geschichte als Weg zum Musikverständnis: zur Theorie, Methode und Geschichte der Musikgeschichtsschreibung. 2., überarbeitete Aufl. Leipzig: Reclam, 1982. 664 p.

First published in 1977.

Knepler's *Geschichte presents a thoroughly Marxist view of musical scholarship. Extensive bibliography.*

568. Kretzchmar, Hermann. Kleine Handbücher der Musikgeschichte nach Gattungen. Leipzig: Breitkopf und Härtel, 1905–1922. 14 v. in 15.

All the volumes in this set have been reprinted by Olms, Hildesheim, 1967–72.

The Kretzschmar *Handbücher* are a series of historical monographs dealing with the development of specific musical forms or disciplines. Although superseded in many respects, these volumes remain basic studies in the areas with which they are concerned.

[Vol. 1] Arnold Schering. *Geschichte des Instrumentalkonzerts.* ... 1905. 226 p. 2nd Aufl., 1927. Reprinted by Olms, Hildesheim, 1965 and 1972.

[Vol. 2] Hugo Leichtentritt. *Geschichte der Motette.* 1908. 453 p. Reprinted by Olms, Hildesheim, 1967 and Breitkopf und Härtel, Wiesbaden, 1967.

[Vol. 3] Arnold Schering. *Geschichte de Oratoriums.* 1911. 647 p. *Notenanhang,* 39 p. Reprinted by Olms, Hildesheim, 1966.

[Vol. 4.] Hermann Kretzschmar. *Geschichte des neuen deutschen Liedes.* Teil 1. Von Albert biz Zelter (all published). 1911. 354 p. Reprinted by Olms, Hildesheim and Breitkopf und Härtel, Wiesbaden, 1977.

[Vol. 5] Eugen Schmitz. *Geschichte der Kantate und des geistlichen Konzerts.* Teil 1. Geschichte der weltlichen solokantate (all published). 1914. 327 p. 2nd. Aufl., 1955. Reprinted by Olms, Hildesheim, 1966.

[Vol. 6] Hermann Kretzschmar. *Geschichte der Oper.* 1919. 286 p. Reprinted by Sändig, Wiesbaden, 1970.

[Vol. 7] Hermann Kretzschmar. *Einführung in die Musikgeschichte.* 1920. 82 p.

[Vol. 8] Johannes Wolf. *Handbuch der Notationskunde.* Teil 1. Tonschriften des Altertums und des Mittelalters. ... Teil 2. Tonschriften des Neuzeit, Tabulaturen, Partitur, Generalbass und Reformversuche. 1913–1919. 2 v. Reprinted by Olms, Hildesheim, 1963.

[Vol. 9] Hugo Botstiber. *Geschichte der Ouvertüre und der freien Orchesterformen.* 1913. 274 p. Reprinted by Sändig, Wiesbaden, 1969.

[Vol. 10] Georg Schünemann. *Geschichte des Dirigierens.* 1913. 359 p. Reprinted by Olms, Hildesheim, 1965.

[Vol. 11] Peter Wagner. *Geschichte der Messe.* Teil 1. Bis 1600 (all published). 1913. 548 p. Reprinted by Olms, Hildesheim, 1963.

[Vol. 12] Curt Sachs. *Handbuch der Musikinstrumentenkunde.* 1920. 412 p. Reprinted by Olms, Hildesheim, 1967.

[Vol. 13] Adolf Aber. *Handbuch der Musikliteratur.* ... 1922. 696 cols. Reprinted by Olms, Hildesheim, and Breitkopf und Härtel, 1967.

[Vol. 14] Karl Nef. *Geschichte der Sinfonie und Suite.* 1921. 344 p. Reprinted by Sändig, Wiesbaden, 1970 & 1981.

569. De La Fage, J. Adrien. Histoire générale de la musique et de la danse. Tome premier. Paris: Antiquité Comptoir des Imprimeurs, 1844. 614 p.

30 p. of musical examples published separately with 28 plates of illustrations.

Noteworthy for its wide range of interest in music of other cultures, a forerunner of ethnomusicology.

570. Laborde, Jean Benjamin de. Essai sur la musique ancienne et moderne. Paris: Impr. de P. D. Pierres, et se vend chez E. Onfroy, 1780. 4 v.

Reprint by the Akademische Druck- und Verlagsanstalt, Graz, and by the AMS Press, N.Y., 1978.

Laborde's work is the major French contribution to music historiography of the 18th century, but it suffers by comparison to Burney and Hawkins because it is not a chronoogical history. The *Essai* is a vast assemblage of information on musical ethnology, iconography, organology, history, biography, and other humanistic concerns. Much attention is directed toward French lyric poetry and the chanson.

571. Lang, Paul Henry. Music in Western civilization. N.Y.: Norton, 1941. 1,107 p.

This work has been widely translated (into German, Spanish, Portuguese, Czech and Japanese, etc.).

Music in the context of the social, political and cultural currents of Western civilization. One of the most influential of all music histories produced in America, it coincided with, and contributed to, the general acceptance of music history in American higher education. Bibliography of literature in all languages in one alphabet, p. 1045–65.

572. Langhans, Wilhelm. Die Geschichte der Musik des 17. 18. und 19. Jahrdunderts in chronologischen Anschlusse an die Musikgeschichte von A. W. Ambros. Leipzig: F. E.C. Leuckart, 1884. 2 v.

Written as a continuation of Ambros' unfinished history, no. 540.

Manuel, Roland. See Roland-Manuel, no. 590.

573. Martini, Giovanni Battista. Storia della music. Bologna: Lelio dalla Volpe, 1757–81. 3 v.

Reprint by the Akademische Druck- und Verlagsanstalt, Graz, 1967. Edited and supplied with an index by Othmar Wessely.

In spite of its archaic methodology, and the fact that Martini did not live to carry his history beyond the music of the ancients, it was an influential work and a source book for later historians.

Review of the reprint edition by Jack A. Westrup in *Music and letters,* 49 (1968), p. 55–57; and by Werner Kümmel in *Die Musikforschung,* 22 (1969), p. 238–39.

574. Music in early Christian literature. Edited by James McKinnon. Cambridge, [England]; New York: Cambridge University Press, 1987. 180 p. (Cambridge readings in the literature of music)

Translations of writings from the Patristic period about music. This work is a Strunk *Source Readings* for the early Medieval period. Bibliography. Index.

575. Music in the Western World, a history in documents; selected and annotated by Piero Weiss and Richard Taruskin. New York: Schirmer Books; London: Collier Macmillan, 1984. 556 p.

A collection of source readings.

576. Muzykal'nia zhizn' Moskvy v pervye gody posle Oktiabria. Oktiabr 1917–1920. Khronika. Dokumenty. Materialy. Musical life of Moscow in the first years after October. [Compiled by] Svetlana Romanova Stepanova. Moskva: Sov. Kompozitor, 1972. 336 p.

A collection of source materials. Includes bibliographical references.

577. Muzykalnaia éstetika Rossii odinadtsatogo-vosemnadtsatogo vekov. [Dokumenty i materialy]. Sost. tekstov, perevody i obshchaia vstupit. stat'ia. [Compiled by] Aleksandr Ivanovich Rogova. Moskva: Muzyka, 1973. 245 p. (Pamiatniki muzykalno-esteticheskoi mysli)

A collection of source documents on Russian musical aesthetics in the 11th-18th centuries. Includes bibliographical references.

578. Nef, Karl. An outline of the history of music. Trans. by Carl Pfatteicher. N.Y.: Columbia Univ. Press, 1935. 400 p.

Originally published as *Einführung in die Musikgeschichte* in 1920. Many reprintings. An augmented French edition by Yvonne Rokseth appeared in 1931.

An excellent outline history for use in college or university courses. Brief yet comprehensive, readable yet scholarly. Rich in bibliographical information and musical examples in the text.

579. The New Oxford History of Music. London & New York: Oxford Univ. Press, 1954– . 10 v. to date.

Each volume is a composite work made up of contributions by scholars of international repute and edited by a specialist in the period. The set is planned in 10 volumes plus a volume of chronological tables and a general index.

There is an accompanying set of recordings issued uunder the title *The history of music in sound* with illustrated booklets designed for teaching purposes. All recordings and pamphlets have appeared.

Vol. 1: *Ancient and oriental music,* ed. by Egon Wellesz, 1957. 530 p.

Review by Curt Sachs in *Notes,* 16 (1957), p. 97–99; by Roy Jesson in *MQ,* 44 (1958), p. 245–53; by Charles Seeger in *Ethnomusicology,* 3 (1959), p. 96–97.

Vol. 2: *Early medieval music up to 1300,* ed. by Anselm Hughes, 1951. 434 p.

Review by Charles Warren Fox in *MQ,* 41 (1955), p. 534–47; by Jeremy Noble in *Music and letters,* 36 (1955), p. 65–70.

Vol. 3: *Ars Nova and the Renaissance (1300–1540),* ed. by Anselm Hughes and Gerald Abraham, 1960. 565 p.

Review by Richard H. Hoppin in *MQ,* 47 (1961), p. 116–25; by Thurston Dart in *Music and letters,* 42 (1961, p. 57–60.

Vol. 4: *The age of humanism, 1540–1630,* ed. by Gerald Abraham, 1968. 978 p.

Review byHoward M. Brown in *Notes,* 26 (1969), p. 133–36; by Paul Doe in *Music and letters,* 51 (1970), p. 66–69; by Claude V. Palisca in *JAMS,* 23 (1970), p. 133–36.

Vol. 5: *Opera and church music (1630–1750),* ed. by Anthony Lewis and Nigel Fortune, 1975, 869 p.

Vol 6: *Concert music (1630–1750),* ed. by Gerald Abraham, 1986. 786 p.

Vol 7.: *The age of enlightenment (1745–1790),* ed. by Egon Wellesz and Frederick Sternfeld, 1973. 724 p.

Review by Daniel Heartz in *The Musical times,* (April, 1974), p. 295–301.

Vol. 8: *The age of Beethoven (1790–1830),* ed. by Gerald Abraham, 1982. 747 p.

Vol. 10: *The modern age (1890–1960),* ed. by Martin Cooper, 1974. 764 p.

Vol. 9: Romanticism (1830–1890) and Vol. 10: Chronological tables and general index not yet published.

580. Nijenhuis, Emmie te. Musicological literature. Wiesbaden: Harrassowitz, 1977. 51 p. (A History of Indian literature, 6: Scientific and technical literature, Fasc. 1)

An essay on musicological works in India with a bibliography.

581. The Norton History of Music Series. N.Y.: Norton, 1940– .

A publisher's series consisting of independent works on different periods in the history of music. The volumes by Reese, Austin, and Bukofzer are particularly rich in bibliographical content.

Curt Sachs: *The rise of music in the ancient world, East and West,* 1943. 324 p.

Gustave Reese: *Music in the Middle Ages,* 1940. 502 p.

Also published in an Italian edition under the title *La musica nel medioevo* (Florence: Sansoni, 1964. 642 p.). Much new illustrative material has been added to this edition.

Gustave Reese: *Music in the Renaissance,* 1954. 1,022 p. Revised edition, 1959.

Review by Denis Stevens in *Music and letters,* 36 (1955), p. 70–73; by Edgar H. Sparks in *Notes,* 17 (1960), p. 569.

Manfred Bukofzer: *Music in the Baroque era, from Monteverdi to Bach,* 1947. 489 p.

William W. Austin: *Music in the 20th century from Debussy through Stravinsky,* 1966. 708 p.

Also printed by Dent, London, 1967.

Review by Peter Evans in *Music and letters,* 49 (1968), p. 43–47; by Henry Leland Clarke in *Journal of research in music education,* 15 (1967), p. 174–76.

582. The Oxford History of Music. 2nd ed. London: Oxford University Press, 1929–38. 7 v. (plus an introductory volume).

First printed in 1901–1905 in six volumes. Volumes 4–6 of the 2nd edition are reprints of the original volumes.

Introductory volume, edited by Percy C. Buck, 1929. 239 p.

A symposium by nine scholars covering Greek and Hebrew music, notation, musical instruments, theory to 1400, plainsong, folk song, social aspects of music in the Middle Ages. Chapter bibliographies, p. 233–39.

Vols. 1–2: H. E. Wooldridge. *The polyphonic period.* 2nd rev. ed by Percy C. Buck, 1928–32.

Vol. 3: C. Hubert Parry. *The music of the 17th century,* 1938. 486 p.

Vol. 4: A. J. Fuller-Maitland. *The age of Bach and Handel.* 2nd ed., 1931. 362 p.

Vol 5: W. H. Hadow. *The Viennese period,* 1931. 350 p.

Vol 6: Edward Dannreuther. *The romantic period,* 1931. 374 p.

Vol. 7: H. C. Colles. *Symphony and drama, 1850–1900,* 1934. 504 p.

583. The Pelican History of Music. Edited by Alec Robertson and Denis Stevens. Harmondsworth, Middlesex: Penguin Books, 1960–69. 3 v.

Reissued by Barnes and Noble, N.Y. under the title *A history of music.*

Vol. 1: Ancient forms to polyphony. Vol 2: Renaissance and Baroque. Vol. 3: Classical and romantic.

A popular history of music with contributions from leading authorities, including the editors: Alec Robertson, "Plainchant"; Denis Stevens, "Ars antiqua"; Gilbert Reaney, "Ars nova"; Peter Crossley-Holland, "Non-Western music"; Hugh Ottaway, "The 19th century"; etc.

Review of vol. 3 by William S. Newman in *Notes,* 26 (1970), p. 504–06.

584. The Prentice-Hall History of Music Series. Englewood Cliffs: Prentice-Hall, 1965– .

A publisher's series for which H. Wiley Hitchcock serves as general editor. Short, one-volume surveys by leading American scholars covering the major historical periods as well as folk and non-Western music. The numbering of the volumes below is arbitrary.

[Vol. 1] Bruno Nettl: *Folk and traditional music of the Western continents* with chapters on Latin America by Gárhard Báhague, 2nd ed. 1973. 258 p.

Review by Alfred W. Humphreys in *Journal of research in music education,* 13 (1965), p. 259–60; by Fritz Bose in *Die Musikforschung,* 21 (1968), p. 107–08; by Wolfgang Suppan in *Jahrbuch für Volksliedforschung,* 12 (1967), p. 217–18.

[Vol. 2] William P. Malm: *Music cultures of the Pacific, the Near East, and Asia,* 2nd ed. 1977. 236 p.

[Vol. 3] Albert Seay: *Music in the medieval world,* 2nd ed. 1975. 182 p.

Review by Leo Treitler in *Journal of research in music education,* 14 (1966), p. 235–36; by Peter Gülke in *Die Musikforschung,* 21 (1968), p.

108–09.

[Vol. 4] Claude V. Palisca: *Baroque music,* 2nd ed. 1981. 300 p.
Review by David Burrows in *Notes,* 25 (1969), p. 717–18.
[Vol. 5] Reinhard G. Pauly: *Music in the classic period,* 2nd ed. 1973. 206 p.
Review by Eugene Helm in *Notes,* 25 (1968), p. 40–41.
[Vol. 6] Rey M. Longyear: *Nineteenth-century romanticism in music,* 2nd ed., 1973. 289 p.
[Vol. 7] Eric Salzman: *Twentieth-century music: an introduction,* 2nd ed., 1974. 242 p.
[Vol. 8] Wiley H. Hitchcock: *Music in the United States: a historical introduction,* 2nd ed., 1974. 286 p.
Review by Ross Lee Finney in *Notes,* 26 (1969), p. 271–72.
[Vol. 9] Howard M. Brown *Music in the Renaissance,* 1976. 384 p.
[Vol. 10] Bonnie C. Wade *Music in India : the classical traditions,* 1978. 252 p.
[Vol. 11] Gérard Béhague. *Music in Latin America, an introduction,* 1979. 369 p.

585. Printz, Wolfgang Caspar. Historische Beschreibung der edelen Sing- und Kling-kunst. . . . Dresden: J. C. Mieth, 1690. 240 p.
Reprint by the Akademische Druck- und Verlagsanstalt, Graz, 1964. Edited and indexed by Othmar Wessely.
This work has been described as the first history of music. Printz's observations are based largely on Biblical authority and legend, but his work exercised considerable influence on 18th century lexicographers and historians.

586. Prunières, Henry. A new history of music; the Middle Ages to Mozart. Trans. and ed. byEdward Lockspeiser. N.Y.: Macmillan, 1943. 413 p.
Originally published as *Nouvelle histoire de la musique. Patis, 1934–36. 2 v. Reprint by Vienna House, N.Y., 1972.*
Valuable for its emphasis on the earlier periods.

587. Readings in the history of music in performance. Selected, translated and edited by Carol MacClintock. Bloomington: Indiana University Press, 1979. 432 p.
Selected sources on the history of performance practice. Lacks index.
Review by James Pruett in *Notes,* 36 (1980), p. 892–893.

588. Renner, Hans. Geschichte der Musik. Stuttgart: Deutsche Verlags-Anstalt, 1965. 704 p.
Also published as *Musikgeschichte der Büchergilde.*
A well-illustrated student's history. Traditional chronological arrangement with useful appendices devoted to notation, voice ranges, the composition of orchestras, musical instruments, and glossary. Index of names and subjects.

589. Riemann, Hugo. Handbuch der Musikgeschichte. 2nd ed. [Edited by Alfred Einstein.] Leipzig: Breitkopf und Härtel, 1920–23. 2 v. in 4.
First published in 1904–1913. Reprint by Johnson Reprint Corporation, N.Y., 1972.

A product of one of the most vigorous and stimulating minds in German musicology, always provocative, frequently misleading. Extensive chapter bibliographies and sections devoted to brief biographies of musicians; the emphasis, however, is on musical styles and forms. Numerous transcriptions of early music, all of which must be viewed in the light of Riemann's unorthodox editorial methods.

590. Roland-Manuel, ed. Histoire de la musique. Nouv. ed. Paris: Gallimard, 1981. 2 v. (Encyclopédie de la Pléiade, 9 and 16)

First published 1960–63 and reprinted in 1977.

Vol 1: "Des origines à Jean-Sebastian Bach." 2,238 p. Vol. 2: "Du XVIIIe siècle à nos jours." 1,878 p.

An important work. The language is French but the approach is international, consisting of contributions by specialists from many different countries. Vol. 1 begins with a chapter on "Elements et genres," followed by surveys of the music of non-Western cultures, of ancient and oriental music, and of the music of the Moslem world. Thereafter the organization is chronological within individual countries. At the end of col. 2 there are chapters devoted to contemporary music and to the history of musicology and of criticism. Each volume has a chronological table and index, plus an analytical table of contents.

591. Rowen, Ruth Halle. Music through sources and documents. Englewood Cliffs: Prentice-Hall, 1979. 386 p.

Following in the tradition of Strunk's *Source readings,* chronologically ordered translations of excerpts of 103 source documents, each provided with historical and bibliographical background. Index of names and subjects.

Review by James W. Pruett in *Notes,* 36 (1980), p. 892–93.

592. Sachs, Curt. Our musical heritage, a short history of music. 2nd ed. Englewood Cliffs: Prentice-Hall, 1955. 351 p.

First published in 1948. Reprinted by Greenwood, Westport, 1978.

Designed as a textbook for introductory courses in music history. References to essential bibliography.

593. Salazar, Adolfo. La mùsica en la sociedad europea. [México]: El Colegio di México, 1942–46. 9 parts in 4 v.

Reprinted by Alianza, Madrid, 1982.

A general history for Spanish readers, from antiquity to the end of the 19th century.

594. Smijers, Albert, ed. Algemeene muziekgeschiedenis; geïlustreerd overzicht der Europeesche muziek van de oudheid tot heden. 4. bijgewerkte druk. Utrecht: W. de Haan, 1947. 518 p.

1st edition, 1938; 2nd edition, 1940.

A composite history in eight books, each written by a different Dutch or Flemish scholar. Short bibliographies after each book. Plates and numerous musical illustrations.

595. Strunk, W. Oliver. Source readings in music history from classical antiquity through the romantic era. N.Y.: Norton, 1950. 919 p.

Reissued in a paperback edition, 1965. 5 v.

87 items extracted from the writings of theorists, composers, teachers, critics, and practical musicians, arranged chronologically under topics. Each item is introduced with a few concise and illuminating comments by the editor. The translations are excellent, the editorial work exemplary. An indispensable volume in any library of music history.

Review by Manfred Bukofzer in *Notes,* 8 (1951), p. 517–18; by Erich Hertzmann in *MQ,* 37 (1951), p. 430–32; by Leo Schrade in *JAMS,* 4 (1951), p. 249–51.

596. Subirá, José. Historia de la músic. 3. ed. reformada, amplicada, y puesta al dia. Barcelona: Editorial Salvat, 1958. 4 v.

First published in 1947; 2nd edition, 1951.

Handsomely printed and illustrated, musically and pictorially. Some emphasis on ethnomusicology. The approach is generally chronological, but with chapters on the development of notation, 17th century theory, and performance practice.

597. Time, place and music. An anthology of ethnomusicological observation c.1550 to c.1800, by Frank L. Harrison. Amsterdam: Frits Knuf, 1973. 221 p. (Source materials and studies in ethnomusicology, 1)

A compendium of written observations by travelers on non-Western musical cultures.

598. Ulrich, Homer and Paul Pisk. A history of music and musical style. N.Y.: Harcourt, 1963. 696 p.

The authors' purpose in writing this history of music has been to offer a clear, straightforward presentation of historical developments in musical style. [*Preface*]

Review by Susan Thiemann in *Notes,* 20 (1963), p. 638–42.

599. Wiora, Walter. The four ages of music. Translated by M.D. Herter Norton. N.Y.: Norton, 1965. 233 p.

Originally issued by W. Kohlhammer Verlag, Stuttgart, 1961, under the title *Die vier Weltalter der Musik* (Urban-Bücher, 56). Also published in France as *Les quatres ages dela musique, de la préhistoire à l'éra de la technique.*

An original approach to music history and its periodization, treating the subject in the context of universal history and anthropology.

Review by Johannes Riedel in *Journal of research in music education,* 13 (1965), p. 260–61; by Rose Brandel in *Notes,* 24 (1968), p. 695–97.

600. Wörner Karl H. Geschichte der Musik. Ein Studien- und Nachschlagebuch. 7. durchgesehene und erg. von Ekkehard Kreft. Göttingen: Vandenhoeck u. Ruprecht, 1980. 692 p.

First published in 1954; 2nd ed., 1956; 3rd ed., 1961; 4th ed., 1965; 5th ed., 1972; 6th ed. 1975.

A well-organized outline history of music with excellent bibliographical information. Utilizes a variety of aproaches: stylistic, national, biographical. Paragraphs are numbered for easy reference.

A 5th edition, in English translation, has been issued by the Free Press, N.Y., 1973.

MUSICAL ICONOGRAPHY

The change in the title of this section is meant to convey the change in emphasis in historical musicology. Increasingly musical iconography has become a branch of scholarship with its own principles, methodologies, and literature. At the same time, writers of histories of music have become more conscious of the value of including numerous well-chosen images in their texts. The tradition, begun in 1929 by George Kinsky in his *Geschichte der Musik in Bildern* (see no. 607), is very much alive and flourishing. Meanwhile other scholars and publishers have compiled anthologies of images incorporating some reference to music as important adjuncts to the study of music by period, place, and genre; the extensive series *Musikgeschichte in Bildern* is an example of this activity.

There is an international body devoted to all aspects of musical iconography, the Répertoire Internationale d'Iconographie Musicale, with headquarters at the Graduate Center of the City University of New York. RIdIM produces a *Newsletter* which publishes important articles on the subject, relates the activities of the organization, and reports on scholarship in musical iconography underway or published elsewhere.

BAND IV: NEUZEIT

601. Besseler, Heinrich and Max Schneider, ed. Musikgeschichte in Bildern. Leipzig: Deutscher Verlag für Musik, 1961– . v. 1– .

A multivolume work projected to cover all periods in the history of music as well as some of the systematic branches. Publication of the volumes and their respective subsections (Lieferungen) has not necessarily followed in chronological order. Each issue contains numerous plates, with commentary, a bibliography, chronological tables, and indexes. The following issues have been released to date:

Lief. 1: Paul Collaer. *Ozeanien,* 1965. 234 p.

Review by Dieter Christensen in *Die Musikforschung,* (1967), p. 339–41; by Bruno Nettl in *Notes,* 23 (1966), p. 276; by Wolfgang Suppan in *Jahrbuch für Volksliedforschung,* 16 (1971), p. 262–64.

Lief. 2: Paul Collaer. *Amerika: Eskimo und indianische Bevolkerung,* 1967. 211 p.

Review by Fritz Bose in *Die Musikforschung,* 22 (1969), p. 522–23; by Bruno Nettl in *Notes,* 24 (1968), p. 717–18.

Lief. 3: Paul Collaer, unter Mitarbeit von Emmy Bernatzik ... [*et al.*] *Südostasien,* 1979. 181 p.

Lief. 4: Alain Daniélou, trans. by Fritz Bosel. *Südasien: die indische Musik und ihre Traditionen,* 1978. 146 p.

Lief. 8: Paul Collaer [und] Jürgen Elsner; unter der Mitarbeit von Brahim Bahloul, [*et al.*] ... *Nordafrika,* 1983. 205 p.

Lief. 10: Gerhard Kubik unter Mitarbeit von Jim de Vere Allen ... [*et al.*]. *Ostafrika,* 1982. [252] p.

Lief. 1: Hans Hickmann. *Ägypten,* 1961. 187 p.
Review by Caldwell Titcomb in *JAMS,* 17 (1964), p. 386–91; by Fritz Bose in *Die Musikforschung,* 17 (1964), p. 184–85.

Lief. 2: Subhi Anwar Rashid. *Mesopotamien,* 1984. 182 p.

Lief. 4: Max Wegner. *Griechenland,* 1964. 143 p.
Review by Emanuel Winternitz in *JAMS,* 19 (1966), p. 412–15.

Lief. 5 Gunter Fleischhauer. *Eturien und Rom,* 1965. 195 p.

Lief. 7: Samuel Marti. *Alt-Amerika; Musik der Indianer in präkolumbischer Zeit,* 1970. 195 p.
Review by Wolfgang Suppan in *Jahrbuch fur Volkliedforschung,* 16 (1971), p. 262–64.

Lief. 8: Walter Kaufmann unter Mitarb. von Joep Bor, Wim van der Meer, und Emmie te Nijenhuis. *Altindien,* 1981. 208 p.

Lief. 2: Henry George Farmer. *Islam,* 1966. 206 p.
Review by Emmy Wellesz in *Music and letters,* 49 (1968), p. 73–74; by Essa Zonis in *JAMS,* 22 (1969), p. 293–96.

Lief. 3: Joseph Smits van Waesberghe. *Musikerziehung, 1969. 214 p.*
Review by Hans Oesch in *Literature, music, fine arts,* 5 (1972), p. 232–33.

Lief. 4: Bruno Stäblein. *Schriftbild der einstimmigen Musik,* 1975. 257 p.

Lief. 5: Heinrich Besseler und Peter Gülke. *Schriftbild der mehrstimmigen Musik,* 1973. 183 p.

Lief. 8: Edmund A. Bowles. *Musikleben im 15. Jahrhundert,* 1977. 189 p.

Lief. 9: Walter Salmen. *Musikleben im 16. Jahrhundert,* 1976. 205 p.

Lief. 1: Hellmuth Christian Wolff. *Oper, Szene und Darstellung von 1600 bis 1900,* 1968. 214 p.
Review by Karl Michael Komma in *Literature, music, fine arts,* 1 (1968), p. 220–22; by Christoph-Hellmut Mahling in *Die Musikforschung,* 23 (1970), p. 97–99.

Lief. 2: Heinrich W. Schwab *Konzert: Offentliche Musikdarbietung vom 17. bis 19. Jahrhundert,* 1971. 230 p.

Lief. 3: Walter Salmen. *Haus- und Kammermusik zwischen 1600 und 1900,* 1969. 203 p.

602. Cohen, H. Robert. Les gravures musicales dans *l'Illustration.* 1843–1899. Avec la collaboration de Sylvia L'Ecuyer Lacroix et Jacques Léveillé. Québec: Presses de l'Université Laval, 1983. 3 v.

Reproductions of 3,360 engravings from the important 19th century French periodical *l'Illustration* with a thesaurus of images to direct the reader to appropriate images. A treasure of 19th century French musical life. *L'Illustration*—Engravings

603. Collaer, Paul and Albert Van der Linden. Historical atlas of music: a comprehensive study of the world's music, past and present ... with the collaboration of F. van den Bremt. Pref. by Charles van den Borren. Trans. by Allan Miller. Cleveland: World Pub. Co., 1968. 175 p.

Also published by Harrap, London and Toronto, 1968. Originally published as*Atlas historique de la musique by Elsevier, Paris, 1960.*

An illustrated survey of music history, with 15 full-page maps and more than 700 illustrations.

Review by Robert E. Wolf in *MQ,* 47 (1961), p. 413–16.

604. Crane, Frederick. A bibliography of the iconography of music. Iowa City: University of Iowa, 1971. 41 p.

Typescript bibliography of secondary sources.

605. Dufourcq, Norbert, ed. La musique des origines à nos jours. Préface de Claude Delvincourt. Nouv. ed., rev., augm. Paris: Larousse, 1954. 591 p.

The reprinting of a work first published in 1946 and carried through seven editions.

Richly illustrated compendium of music history and related fields, the work of 44 scholars, chiefly French. Organized in 5 books, of which the third (p. 83–431) deals with the history of Western music. Other books treat of the voice and instruments, ancient and Near Eastern music, non-European music, and musical aesthetics. A series of 17 appendices covers special topics such as notation, theory, criticism, libraries and other institutions. 6 colored plates and numerous black-and-white illustrations.

606. Dufourcq, Norbert. La musique, les hommes, les instruments, les œuvres. Paris: Larousse, 1965. 2 v.

Tome 1: "La musique, des origines à la mort de Rameau." Tome 2: "La musique, de l'aube du classicisme à la periode contemporaine."

This work is an expansion of the preceding. The articles are contributed by leading authorities, chiefly French. A fine, visually oriented history of music. It also serves as the basis for another Larousse publication: *Larousse encyclopedia of music,* ed. by Jeoffrey Hindley (New York: World Publishing Co., 1971).

607. Kinsky, Georg. A history of music in pictures. New York: Dutton, 1937. 363 p.

Originally published in German in 1929; first English edition, 1930. Reprint, New York, Dover, 1951. There is also a French edition.

Pictures include musicians' portraits, music in painting, drawing and sculpture; facsimile pages of early musical and theoretical works. Pictures of early instruments. Arranged chronologically from antiquity to the early 20th century. Index to instruments, place names, and personal names.

608.   Komma, Karl Michael. Musikgeschichte in Bildern. Stuttgart: Alfred Kroner, 1961. 332 p.

743 well-reproduced illustrations covering the history of music from ancient times to the present; detailed commentary on each illustration. Review by Hans Engel in *Die Musikforschung,* 18 (1965), p. 440–41.

609.   Lang, Paul Henry and Otto Bettmann. A pictorial history of music. New York: Norton, 1960. 242 p.

The text is based on Lang's *Music in Western civilization,* no. 571, with selected illustrations. Inferior reproduction technique.

610.   Leppert, Richard D. The theme of music in Flemish painting of the seventeenth century. München; Salzburg: E. Katzbichler, 1977. 2 v.

A catalog of 770 paintings with indexes to instruments and themes as well as a plethora of ancillary data. Review by François Lesure in *Fontes artis musicae,* 25 (1978), p. 197.

611.   Lesure, François. Musik und Gesellschaft im Bild. Zeugnisse der Malerei aus sechs Jahrhunderten.... Aus dem Französischen von Anna Martina Gottschick. Kassel: Barenreiter, 1966. 245 p. 105 plates, 24 in color.

Skillful use of pictorial materials to illuminate the musical-social structure of European culture from the 14th through the 19th centuries. Review by Steven J. Ledbetter in *Notes,* 24 (1968), p. 702–4.

612.   Michels, Ulrich. DTV-Atlas zur Musik: Taf. u. Texte. München: Deutscher Taschenbuch-Verlag; Kassel: Bärenreiter, 1980–1985. 2 v.

Published also by Alianza, Madrid (1982–), as *Atlas de música.*

Includes music. Includes bibliographies and indexes. Also known as *Atlas zur Musik.*

Contents: Bd. 1. Systematischer Teil. Historischer Teil: von den Anfängen bis zur Renaissance. 5. Aufl.—Bd. 2. Historischer Teil: vom Barock bis zur Gegenwart.

613.   Pincherle, Marc. An illustrated history of music. Ed. by Georges Bernier and Rosamond Bernier. Trans. by Rollo Myers. Rev. ed. New York: Reynal; London: Macmillan, 1962. 230 p.

Published in France under the title *Histoire illustreé de la musique* (Paris: Gallimard, 1959).

A beautifully designed volume, with 200 illustrations in black and white, 40 in full color. The text is planned as an introduction to music history but maintains a high standard of accuracy and critical comment. The work lacks a bibliography or any other documentation apart from the illustrations.

Review by Denis Stevens in *The Musical times,* 101 (Aug. 1960), p. 493; by Emanuel Winternitz in *Notes,* 18 (1960), p. 48–50; by Jack A. Westrup in *Music and letters,* 41 (1960), p. 388.

CHRONOLOGIES

615. Burbank, Richard. Twentieth century music. Introduction by Nicolas Slonimsky. N.Y.: Facts on file, 1984. 485 p.

"The books reports and describes musical events . . . between January 1900 and December 1979. It includes events in opera, dance, instrumental and vocal music, births, deaths, debuts and related events, thoughts, ideas, declarations and statements on music . . ."(from the author's preface). Bibliography. Index to names and titles.

616. Chailley, Jacques. Chronologie musicale en tableaux synoptiques. Paris: Centre de Documentation Universitaire et S.E.D.E.S. réunis, 1955 – . 140 p.

Part I: 310 to 1600.

A workbook of musical chronology, with parallel tables of political, literary, and artistic events. Most detailed for the period prior to the 15th century.

617. Cullen, Marion Elizabeth. Memorable days in music. Metuchen: Scarecrow, 1970. 233 p.

A chronology of musical events by day of year with popular quotations regarding music inserted for each day. Lists importants persons' birth and death days, premieres, and other significant days.

618. Detheridge, Joseph. Chronology of music composers. Birmingham: J. Detheridge, 1936–1937. 2 v.

Reprint, 1972, by Scholarly Press, St. Clair Shores, Michigan.

Vol. I: 820–1810. Vol. 2: 1810–1913.

More than 2,500 names of composers arranged chronologically by date of birth. Brief comments on their activity, fields of composition, nationality. Numerous inaccuracies and misleading statements, but valuable for its comprehensive coverage. Alphabetical list of names.

619. Dufourcq, Norbert, Marcelle Benoit, and Bernard Gagnepain. Les grandes dates de l'histoire de la musique. 2e. éd. Paris: Presses Universitaires de France, 1976. 127 p.

Dates of events, with historical commentary, from the first century A.D. to 1960. Organized according to periods: Middle Ages, Renaissance, 17th, 18th, 19th and 20th centuries.

620. Eisler, Paul E. World chronology of music history. Dobbs Ferry, N.Y.: Oceana Publication, 1972– . Vol. 1– .

An ambitious multivolume survey of the chronology of music, projected in eight to ten volumes. According to the publisher it will contain, when completed, over 100,000 entries covering all significant dates in music history: composers, compositions, performers, premieres, and other pertinent dates.

Contents: v. 1. 30,000 B.C.-1594 A.D.; v. 2. 1594–1684.; v. 3. 1685–1735.; v. 4. Name index (v.I-III); v.5 1736–1786.; v. 6. 1771–1796.

621. Gangwere, Blanche. Music history from the late Roman through the Gothic periods, 313–1425: a documented chronology. Westport: Greenwood Press, 1986. 247 p. (Music reference collection, 6)

A synopsis of important topics arranged chronologically and in outline form. References from each topic are provided to sources and secondary works cited in the principal bibliography. Maps and "supplemental sources" are provided for each period. The outline for the Romanesque period, for instance, covers background, philosophy, the birth of polyphony, St. Martial period, and terms. There are appended: a general bibliography; a discography; an author-composer index; and a subject index, the last not providing any cross-references for common names of manuscripts. The bibliographies, general and supplemental, consist primarily of English-language sources.

This is an interesting, if somewhat simplistic, concept and potentially quite useful in providing an overview to non-specialists or as a foil to specialists. The author intends to produce similar works on other periods. The text is occasionally difficult to read because of the quality of reproduction.

622. Hall, Charles J. Hall's musical years; the twentieth century 1900–1979. A comprehensive, year-by-year survey of the fine arts. Northbrook, Illinois: Opus, 1980. 1 v. unnumbered p.

In outline form, lists historical events, debuts, prizes, works of art, books on music and other subjects, births and deaths of musicians and others, and musical compositions for each year. A useful concatenation of facts, musical and otherwise. Derived from the author's years of compiling program notes for WAUS, Michigan's fine arts radio station.

623. Hendler, Herb. Year by year in the Rock Era: events and conditions shaping the rock generations that reshaped Americ. Westport: Greenwood Press, 1983. 350 p.

Essentially a chronicle of political, social, and popular musical events. Bibliography: p. 339–350.

624. Lahee, Henry Charles. Annals of music in America; a chronological record of significant musical events from 1640 to the present day, with comments on the various periods into which the work is divided. Freeport, N.Y.: Books for Libraries Press, 1970. 298 p.

Reprint of a work first published in 1922. Also reprinted by AMS Press, N.Y., 1969.

625. Manson, Adele P. Calendar of music and musicians. Metuchen: Scarecrow Press, 1981. 462 p.

A day-by-day list of important musical events. Indexes to personal and corporate names and to titles.

626. Mattfeld, Julius. Variety music cavalcade, 1620–1961; a chronology of vocal and instrumental music popular in the United State. With an introduction by Abel Green. 3rd edition. Englewood Cliffs: Prentice-Hall, 1971. 766 p.

Originally appeared in a modified form as *Variety radio directory 1938–39,* supplemented in weekly issues of the periodical *Variety.* First issued as *Variety music cavalcade 1620–1950* in 1952. A revised edition appeared in 1962.

A chronological bibliography of American popular music, with parallel social and historical events listed for each year. Index of musical works by title, with dates of first publication.

Review by Irving Lowens in *Notes,* 20 (1963), p. 233–34.

627. Mies, Paul and Norbert Schneider. Musik im Umkreis der Kulturgeschichte. Ein Tabellenwerk aus der Geschichte der Musik, Literatur, bildenden Kunste, Philosophie und Politik Europas. Koln: P. J. Tonger, 1953. 2 v.

Vol. 1: chronological tables of musical periods and events. Vol. 2.: parallel tables of history, philosophy, literature, art, and architecture.

628. La Revue Musicale. La musique 1900–1950. Documents du demi-siècle; tableau chronologique des principales œuvres musicales de 1900 à 1950, étable par genre at par année. Paris: 1952. 1 v. (various pagings)

629. Saathen, Friedrich. Musik im Spiegel der Zeit: synchronoptische Taf. zur Musikgeschichte Europas mit einem lexikalischen Personen- u. Sachverzeichnis. Wien: Universal Edition, 1975. 47 p. & 3 tables

Tables showing European musical events in chronological order. A brief dictionary of persons and topics is included.

630. Schäffer, Boguslaw. Maly informator muzyki XX wieku. Wyd. 3 nowe. Krakow: Polskie Wydaw. Muzyczne, 1975. 384 p.

A chronology of musical events of the 20th century.

631. Schering, Arnold. Tabellen zur Musikgeschichte, ein Hilfsbuch beim Studium der Musikgeschichte. Fünfte Auflage bis zur Gegenwart ergänzt von Hans Joachim Moser. Wiesbaden: Breitkopf & Härtel, 1962. 175 p.

First published in 1914; 3rd edition, 1921; 4th edition, 1934.

Chronological tables outlining the important events in music history from antiquity to 1962, including birth and death dates of musicians, the principal events of their lives, significant publications and performances, dates marking the activity of important music centers, and stylistic developments. Parallel historical and cultural events given. The 4th edition contained a 30-page supplement giving the contents of the major *Denkmaler* and *Gesamtausgaben* published by Breitkopf & Härtel. The 5th edition deletes this but offers an index of names and subjects.

632. Slonimsky, Nicolas. Music since 1900. 4th edition. New York: Charles Scribner's Sons, 1971. 1,595 p.

Supplement to Music since 1900, 1986. 390 p. Includes additions, amplifications, and corrections. Appendix of formerly secret U.S. Army

633 / **Histories and Chronologies**

documents and documents from the Cultural Revolution of the Peoples Republic of China. Index.

First published by Norton, New York, 1937; 2nd edition, 1938; 3rd edition, 1949.

Contains a "Tabular view of stylistic trends in music, 1900–1969." "Descriptive chronology: 1900–1969." Letters and documents. There is an index to the descriptive chronology. The first two editions contained a "Concise biographical dictionary of 20th-century musicians," omitted in later editions.

The chronology records significant events in the development of contemporary music: dates of composition and first performance, the founding of institutions and societies, births and death of contemporary musicians. International in scope, but with increased emphasis on American music for the past two decades. An appendix quotes many of the major documents in the history of contemporary music.

The 4th edition includes a dictionary of terms (p. 1421–1502).

Review by Jack A. Westrup in *Music and letters,* 53 (1972), p. 447–48.

633. Thompson, Oscar. Tabulated biographical history of music. New York: Harcourt, Brace, 1936.

13 folding charts tracing the major events in the careers of more than 100 musicians from Guido d'Arezzo (c. 995) through 1936.

Guides to Systematic and
Historical Musicology

This chapter cites works intended to introduce the student to the methods, materials, and philosophy of musical research, as well as some current issues in some of the sub-disciplines. These works vary widely in pattern and approach, some concerned with the content, others with the method of the discipline. Some emphasize the historical aspects of research, others the systematic. A few anthologies addressing "state of the art" are included. Especially in this chapter is the compilation *not* intended to be exhaustive. The reader will find useful bibliographies of writings on musicology in the article "Musicology" by Vincent H. Duckles *et al.* in *The New Grove,* in Lincoln Spiess's *Historical musicology, Appendix I,* by Ernst C. Krohn (see no. 674), and in *Perspectives in musicology,* compiled by Barry S. Brook (see no. 639). A useful assemblage of articles is *Musicology in the 1980s: Methods, Goals, Opportunities* (see no. 668). Perhaps the most important and stimulating book to appear recently on the subject is Joseph Kerman's *Contemplating Music: Challenges to Musicology* (see no. 660).

The general discussion of musical scholarship "Musikwissenschaft" by Walter Wiora and Hans Albrecht in *MGG* with its excellent, but now dated bibliography can no longer be regarded as the single best statement of the goals, aspirations, structure, and philosophy of musical scholarship. More than ever diversity is the rule, and no single work can be said to encompass the myriad of possibilities inherent in musical scholarship. Psychohistory, semiotics, information theory, computer science and linguistics have joined other non-musical disciplines with influence upon the musical subjects we take up and the ways we approach and report them. A comprehensive definition of the field may not be possible and perhaps is not even desirable.

634. Adler, Guido. Methode der Musikgeschichte. Leipzig: Breitkopf & Hartel, 1919. 222 p.

Reprint by Gregg International, 1971.

This, along with the author's *Der Stil in der Musik* (1929), is a basic study of the content and method of historical musicology. Contains a bibliographical supplement, "Verzeichnis von bibliographischen Hilfswerken fur musikhistorischen Arbeiten," zusammengestellt von Wilhelm Fischer, now outdated but of interest as a listing of music references prior to World War I.

635. Barbag, Seweryn. Systematyka muzykologji. Lwow: "Lwowskie Wiadomości Muzyczne i Literackie," 1928. 111 p.

A Polish manual of musicological method, with bibliographical supplements: p. 56–91, general works of musicological interest; p. 91–98, Polish works of musicological interest.

636. Benestad, Finn. Musikk og tanke: Hovedretininger i musikkestetikkens historie fra antikken til vår egen tid. Oslo: H. Aschehoug, 1976. 468 p.

Sub-title is "Main currents in the history of music aesthetics from ancient times to our own."

A survey of the aesthetics of music.

Review by Sven Hansell in *Notes,* 34 (1977), p. 81–84.

637. Bengtsson, Ingmar. Musikvetenskap, en översikt. Stockholm: Kungl. Boktrycheriet P.A. Norstedt u. Söner, 1973. 448 p.

An outstanding Swedish survey of the content and methods of musicology. Bibliography.

638. Broeckx, Jan L. Methode van de muziekgeschiedenis, met een inleiding door Prof. Dr. F. Van der Mueren. Antwerpen: Metropolis, 1959. 368 p.

A comprehensive survey of the methods and content of historical musicology. The three major divisions of the work treat (1) basic concepts, (2) working procedures, and (3) terminology. Numerous bibliographical references in the text and in a bibliographical appendix, p. 329–339.

639. Brook, Barry S., Edward O. D. Downes, and Sherman Van Solkema. Perspectives in musicology. The inaugural lectures of the Ph.D. program in music at the City University of New York. New York: W. W. Norton, 1972. 363 p.

Reprinted by Pendragon, N.Y., 1985.

15 scholars, American and European, assess the position of their discipline and project its future.

P. 335–46: "Musicology as a discipline: a selected bibliography."

640. Chailley, Jacques. Precis de musicologie. Nouvelle éd. Paris: Presses Universitaires de France, 1984. 490 p.

First published in 1958. 431 p.

A syllabus published under the auspices of the Institute of Musicology of the University of Paris. Contributions by 25 French musicologists covering varied aspects of musical research. The emphasis is historical. Main approach is chronological, but there are chapters devoted to music bibliography, ethnomusicology, instruments, dance, philosophy, and aesthetics. Bibliography is stressed throughout. Indexed.

641. Crawford, Richard. American studies and American musicology: a point of view and a case in point. Brooklyn: Institute for Studies in American Music, Brooklyn College of the City University of New York, 1975. 33 p. (Institute for Studies in American Music, I. S. A. M. monographs, 4)

Includes a second essay A hardening of the categories: Vernacular, cultivated, and reactionary in American psalmody.

642. Current thought in musicology edited by John W. Grubbs, with the assistance of Rebecca A. Baltzer, Gilbert L. Blount, and Leeman Perkins. Austin: University of Texas Press, 1976. 313 p.
Contents:
Charles Seeger: "Tractatus esthetico-semioticus; model of the systems of human communication".
Charles Hamm: "The ecstatic and the didactic; a pattern in American music".
Elliot Carter: "Music and the time screen".
Howard M. Brown: "Instruments and voices in the fifteenth-century chanson".
Lewis Lockwood: "Nottebohm revisited".
Daniel Heartz. "The chanson in the humanist era".
Gilbert Chase: "Musicology, history, and anthropology; current thoughts".
Gilbert Reaney: "The prospects for research in Medieval music in the 1970s".
Vincent H. Duckles: "The library of the mind; observations on the relationship between musical scholarship and bibliography".

643. Dahlhaus, Carl. Einführung in die systematische Musikwissenschaft. Unter Mitarbeit von Tibor Kneif, Helga de la Motte-Haber und Hans-Peter Reinecke. Köln: Musikverlag Hans Gerig, 1971. 202 p.
Chapters on "Naturwissenschaftlicher Grundlagen der Musik;" "Musikpsychologie;" "Musiktheorie;" "Musikästhetik;" "Musiksoziologie." These essays introduce the sub-disciplines, present some of the current thinking, problems and situations, and conclude with bibliographies.

644. Dahlhaus, Carl. Foundations of music history. Translated by J. A. Robinson. Cambridge: Cambridge University Press, 1983. 177 p.
Translation of *Grundlagen der Musikgeschichte,* first published by Musikverlag Hans Gerigk, Cologne, 1967 and subsequently by Laaber-Verlag, Laaber, 1982. Published in an Italian translation by Discanto Edizioni in Forence as *Fondamenti di storiografia musicale* in 1980 (212 p.).

> The following . . . historiographic reflections, which were occasioned, or rather provoked, by the obvious and disproportionate lack of theory in my own discipline as compared to the veritable welter of theoretical writings in general history, sociology and epistomologically oriented philosophy, are not meant to be an introduction to the basic facts of music history. Nor are they intended as a textbooks of historical method . . .

645. Druesedow, John E. Library research guide to music; illustrated search strategy and sources. Ann Arbor: Pierian Press, 1982. 86 p.
An introductory guide for undergraduate students which includes a list of basic reference sources for courses in music.
Ann P. Basart describes this work as "the first book on library research strategy and sources specifically designed for music undergraduates," in *Cum notis variorum,* 63 (June, 1982), p. 13.

Review by Ann P. Basart in *Notes,* 39 (1982), p. 153.

646. Duckles, Vincent H. "Musicology," in *The New Grove Dictionary of Music and Musicians,* edited by Stanley Sadie, v. 12, p. 836–863 by Vincent H. Duckles with Howard Meyer Brown, George S. Buelow, Marc Lindley, Lewis Lockwood, Miloš Velimirovic and Ian D. Bent. London: Macmillan, 1980.
An essay on the nature, disciplines and national traditions of musicology, approached historically and systematically. Discusses the various specialties within the discipline and notes stellar achievements. Bibliography arrayed in chronological order.

647. Eggebrecht, Hans Heinrich. Reflexionen über Musikwissenschaft Heute, ein Symposium. Kassel: Bärenreiter, 1972. 80 p.
First printed in the proceedings of the international congress of the Gesellschaft für Musikforschung, Bonn, 1970.
Statements by 11 musicologists on their views of the state of the discipline, with discussion from the floor.

648. Erdely, Stephen. Methods and principles of Hungarian ethnomusicology. Bloomington: Indiana University; The Hague: Mouton and Co., 1965. 150 p. (Indiana University Publications, Uralic and Altaic Series, 52)
Review by Benjamin Rajaczky in *Jahrbuch fur Volkliedforschung,* 12 (1967), p. 233–34 and by John S. Weissmann in *Ethnomusicology,* 11 (1967), p. 129–31.

649. Fellerer, Karl G. Einführung in die Musikwissenschaft. 2. neubearb. und erweiterte Aufl. Münchberg: B. Hahnefeld, 1953. 190 p.
First published in 1942.
Historical musicology plays a comparatively minor role in this survey of the content of musical knowledge. Emphasis is on the systematic areas: acoustics, aesthetics, psychology, sociology, and pedagogy. Extensive bibliographies for each chapter.
Review by Glen Haydon in *Notes,* 11 (1953), p. 111–12; anon. in *Die Musikforschung,* 8 (1955), p. 96–97.

650. The Garland library of the history of western music. General editor: Ellen Rosand. New York; London, Garland Publishing, 1985. 14 v.
Reprint of articles originally published between 1940–1982.
This anthology of modern musicological writings is neither history nor handbook or guide to the practice of musicology. It may serve as a convenient anthology for the practicing scholar and as a repertory of exemplars for the student of musicology.
Text chiefly in English including articles in French, German and Italian. Includes bibliographical references.
Contents: v.1. Medieval music I: monophony; v.2. Medieval music II: polyphony.; v.3. Renaissance music, part I.; v.4. Renaissance music, part II.; v.5. Baroque music I: seventeenth century.; v.6. Baroque music II: eighteenth century.; v.7. Classic music.; v.8. Eighteenth and nineteenth-century source studies.; v.9. Nineteenth-century music.; v.10. Twentieth-century music.; v.11. Opera I: up to Mozart.; v.12. Opera II: Mozart and

after.; v.13. Criticism and analysis; v.14. Approaches to tonal analysis.

651. Garrett, Allen M. An introduction to research in music. Washington: Catholic University of America Press, 1958. 169 p.

A rather superficial attempt to survey the content and methods of musicology in a course intended for first-year graduate students in music.

Review by Donald J. Grout in *Notes,* 16 (1959), p. 247–49.

652. Harrison, Frank Ll. ,   Mantle Hood, and Claude V. Palisca. Musicology. Englewood Cliffs, N.J., Prentice-Hall. 1963. 337 p. (The Princeton studies: humanistic scholarship in America.)

Reprinted by Greenwood, Westport, 1974.

Harrison writes on "American musicology and the European tradition," Palisca on "American scholarship in Western music," and Hood on "Music, the unknown." Stimulating, thoughtful statements on the place of musicology in the world of learning. The work has already exercised a wide influence on discussions of the nature and purposes of musical scholarship in Americ. See Joseph Kerman's paper on "A profile for American musicology," in *JAMS,* 18 (1965), p. 61–69, and the reply by Edward Lowinsky, "Character and purposes of American musicology," in the same journal, p. 222–34.

Review by Jan La Rue in *JAMS,* 17 (1964), p. 209–14; by Vincent Duckles in *Notes,* 21 (1964), p. 368–69; by Paul Henry Lang in a review editorial in *MQ,* 50 (1964), p. 215–26. Joint review by Charles Seeger, Lincoln B. Spiess, and David McAllester in *Anuario, inter-American institute for musical research,* 1 (1965), p. 112–18.

653. Haydon, Glen. Introduction to musicology: a survey of the fields, systematic and historical, of musical knowledge and research. New York: Prentice-Hall, 1941. 329 p.

Unaltered reprint by the Univ. of North Carolina Press, Chapel Hill, 1969, and by Greenwood Press, Westport, 1978.

Systematic musicology (acoustics, psychology, aesthetics, theory and pedagogy) occupies the major emphasis of this work. Historical musicology is treated only in the last 54 pages. Chapter bibliographies, with a general bibliography at the end, p. 301–13.

654. Helm, Eugene and Albert T. Luper. Words and music: form and procedure in theses, dissertations, research papers, book reports, programs, and theses in composition. Rev. ed ... Totowa, N.J.: European-American Music Corporation, 1982. 91 p.

First published in Hackensack, N.J., by Joseph Boonin, 1971, 78 p. and then in an edition with new copyright information in 1978 by the European-American Music Corporation, Clifton, N.J., 79 p.

A manual emphasizing the technical and mechanical aspects of academic literature.

655. Herndon, Marcia and Norma McLeod. Field manual for ethnomusicology. Norwodd: Norwood Editions, 1983. 137 p.

A handbook of suggestions ofr "minimizing the subjectivity of synchronic field investigations" and conducting ethnomusicological field work. Brief bibliography.

656. Hood, Mantle. The ethnomusicologist. New ed. Kent: Kent State University Press, 1982. 400 p.
First published by McGraw-Hill, N.Y., 1971. 386 p.
A stimulating and practical exposition of what ethnomusicologists are and do. Illustrated.
Review by Willard Rhodes in *MQ*, 58 (1972), p. 136–41.

657. Husmann, Heinrich. Einfuhrung in die Musikwissenschaft. 3e. Aufl. Wilhelmshaven: Heinrichshofens Verlag, 1980. 291 p.
First published in Heidelberg by Quelle und Meyer, 1958. 268 p. Subsequently published in 2nd ed. by Heinrichshofen, 1975.
An introduction to systematic musicology. Much attention is given to the acoustical and psychological aspects of the subject. The approach embraces all musical phenomena in all cultures. Extensive bibliography organized by chapter headings, p. 235–55.
Review of the first edition by Werner Korte in *Die Musikforschung* 13 (1960), p. 340–42.

658. Irvine, Demar B. Writing about music, a style book for reports and theses. Second edition, revised and enlarged. Seattle and London: Univ. of Washington Press, 1968. 211 p.
A much enlarged edition of a work first published in 1956.
A guide to the preparation of the research report in music, with detailed instructions regarding the preparation of the manuscript, documentation, use of illustrations, abbreviations, and the improvement of literary style.

659. Karbusicky, Vladimir. Systematische Musikwissenschaft: eine Einführung in Grundbegriffe, Methoden und Arbeitstechniken. München: W. Fink, 1979. 250 p.
An introduction to the fundamentals, methods and working practices of musicological studies. This book is used as a text in the musicology program of the University of Hamburg.

660. Kerman, Joseph. Contemplating music; challenges to musicology. Cambridge, MA: Harvard University Press, 1985. 255 p.
Simultaneously published by Fontana, London, as Musicology.

This book is, ultimately, one musician's analysis of modern ideas and ideologies of music. It deals with musicology and other fields of music study mainly as he has apprehended them in the United States and Britain in the years since the Second World War." [from the author's *Acknowedgments*]

One of the most important books about the discipline of musicology and the relationships of that discipline to other musical disciplines and to related non-musical disciplines. It serves as a personal survey of the most important recent developments in Anglo-American musical scholarship and as a polemical commentary on the practice of musicology. Bibliography of main works cited.
Reviews by Erich Leinsdorf in *The New York Times Book Review* (26 May 1985), p. 19; Robert Winter in the *New York Review of Books* (18 July

1985), p. 23; by Christopher Wintle in the *Times Literary Supplement* (10 May 1985), p. 525; and by Julie E. Cumming in *Cum notis variorum,* no. 88 (December 1984), p. 7–11.

661. Kretzschmar, Hermann. Einführung in die Musikgeschichte. Leipzig: Breitkopf & Hartel, 1920. 82 p. (Kleine Handbucher der Musikgeschichte, 7)

Reprinted by Sändig, Wiesbaden, 1970.

A brief, narrative account of the content of and sources for the historical study of music. Relevant literature is mentioned in context. Chapter I traces the development of music historiography through the 19th century.

662. Kunst, Jaap. Ethnomusicology; a study of its nature, its problems, methods and representative personalities to which is added a bibliography. 3d much enl. ed. of *Musicologica.* The Hague: M. Nijhoff, photomechanical reprint, 1969. 303 p.

Reprint of the 1959 edition. Supplement to the third edition of *Ethnomusicology,* 2nd ed. published 1969, 46 p.

A fundamental work with an extensive bibliography (p. 79–215) based on Kunst's own collection of materials.

663. Lehrbuch der Musikwissenschaft herausgegeben von Ekkehard Kreft; Redaktion, Erhard Johannes Bücker. Düsseldorf: Schwann, 1985. 699 p.

664. Lissa, Zofia. Wstep do muzykologii. Wyd. 1. Warszawa: Panstwowe Wyda Wnictwo Naukowe, 1974. 277 p.

Appeared first in 1970. 228 p.

A Polish guide to musicological method by one of the leading musicologists of that nation. Covers both the historical and the systematic aspects of the discipline. Extensive chapter bibliographies.

665. Machabey, Armand. La musicologie. 2. éd. Paris: Presses Universitaires de France, 1969. 128 p. (Que sais-je?, 978)

Brief, popular survey of the scope, content, and methods of musicology treated under five headings: "Sources," "Les elements," "Les formes," "Les instruments," "Diffusion." Highly selective bibliography.

666. Madsen, Clifford K.and Charles H. Madsen Jr. Experimental research in music. Englewood Cliffs, N.J.: Prentice-Hall, 1970. 116 p.

Reprinted by Contemporary Publishing Co., Raleigh, 1978.

A research manual emphasizing the quantitative and descriptive aspects of musical scholarship.

667. Mixter, Keith E. General bibliography for music research. 2d ed. Detroit: Information Coordinators, 1975. 135 p. (Detroit studies in music bibliography, 33)

The purpose of this study is to present in an organized manner references to general bibliographical tools that may be of aid to those engaged in research in music. ... The emphasis ... is on titles from North America and Europe.

Coverage includes books, but is not extended to articles. [from the *Introduction*]

This is an excellent introduction to non-musical reference works, albeit somewhat dated. Organized in chapters according to reference genres, there are indexes to names and to titles.

Brief review by Stephen M. Fry in *Notes,* 32 (1976), p. 781–82.

668. Musicology in the 1980s; methods, goals, opportunities. Edited by D. Kern Holoman and Claude V. Palisc. New York: Da Capo Press, 1982. 160 p.

Proceedings of 2 panel discussions held at the fall 1981 meeting of the American Musicological Society in Boston.

Contents: *Musicology I—Current methodology, opportunities and limitations*

"Editor's introduction"—Claude V. Palisc.

"Reflections on musical scholarship in the 1960s"—Claude V. Palisc.

"Archival research"—Jeremy Noble.

"Applications of the history of ideas"—Maria Rika Maniates.

"Sketch studies"—Joseph Kerman.

"Structural and critical analysis"—Leo Treitler.

"Iconography"—James McKinnon.

Musicology II : The musicologist today and in the future

"Editor's introduction"—D. Kern Holoman

"The musicologist and the performer"—Richard Taruskin.

"Publishing and/or perishing"—D. Kern Holoman.

"Teaching music history in different environments"—Anne V. Hallmark.

"Musicology and criticism"— Rose Rosengard Subotnik.

Includes bibliographical references.

669. Neues Handbuch der Musikwissenschaft; hrsg. von Carl Dahlhaus. Wiesbaden: Akademische Verlagsgesellschaft Athenaion; Laaber, Laaber-Verlag Müller-Buscher, 1980– . 10 v.

Contents:

v.4: *Die Musik des 17. Jahrhunderts* hrsg. von Werner Braun.

v.5: *Die Musik des 18. Jahrhunderts* [hrsg. von] Carl Dahlhaus, unter Mitarbeit von Ludwig Finscher, et al.

v.6: *Die Musik des 19. Jahrhunderts* [hrsg. von] Carl Dahlhaus.

v.7: *Die Musik des 20. Jahrhunderts* [hrsg. von] Hermann Danuser.

v.8–9: *Aussereuropäische Musik* (Teil 1–2) [hrsg. von] Hans Oesch, unter Mitarbeit von Peter Ackermann [und] Max Haas, et al.

v.10: *Systematische Musikwissenschaft* [hrsg. von] Carl Dahlhaus [und] Helga de la Motte-Haber.

Each volume serves as a kind of Baedeker to the study of the period or realm of musicology which is the topic of the volume, with each chapter prepared by an expert or team of experts in the specialty. In addition to discussions of methodology, problems, and directions, there are bibliographies, maps, discographies, tables of pertinent information, and indexes.

670. Pruett, James W. and Thomas P. Slavens. Research guide to musicology. Chicago: American Library Association, 1985. 175 p. (Sources of information in the humanities, 4)

James Pruett's guide to musicology is a traditional, conservative even, exposition of the development of the discipline. Thomas Slavens' bibliography of the research literature is limited almost entirely to English-language publications and seems not to have been coordinated with the essay.

Reviews by Lenore Coral in *Notes,* 43 (1986), p. 42–22 and by James Scholter in *Music educators journal,* 72 (February, 1986), p. 69–71.

671. Riemann, Hugo. Grundriss der Musikwissenschaft. 4. Aufl. durchgesehen von Johannes Wolf. Leipzig: Quelle und Meyer, 1928. 160 p. (Wissenschaft und Bildung, 34)

672. Samuel, Harold. "Musicology and the music library" in Trends in the scholarly use of library resources [ed. by] Donald W. Krummel *et al.*: *Library trends,* 25/4 (1977).

An exposition on the expansion of the horizons of musicology and related disciplines with a concomitant widening of the scope of collection building and services in music libraries.

673. Schiedermair, Ludwig. Einführung in das Studium der Musikgeschichte: Leitsätze, Quellen, Übersichten und Ratschläge. 4. umbearb. und erweiterte Aufl. Bonn: F. Drummlers Verlag, 1947. 167 p.

First published in 1918.

Brief surveys, with bibliographies, of the major historical periods. Concluding chapters deal with methodology, institutions, advice to students, etc. A useful appendix lists major *Gesamtausgaben* and the contents of publishers' series devoted to early music.

674. Spiess, Lincoln B. Historical musicology, a reference manual for research in music ... with articles by Ernst C. Krohn, Lloyd Hibberd, Luther A. Dittmer, Tsang-Houei Shu, Tatsuo Minagawa, and Zdenek Novacek. Brooklyn: Institute of Medieval Music, 1963. 294 p.

Reprinted by Greenwood, Westport, 1980.

A text and reference book of musical research, includes lists of suggested topics for class and seminar reports, term papers, and dissertations; with a copious bibliography, index of publishers, etc. [*Publishers' preface*]

The bibliography consists of 1,980 numbered items, in all categories, distributed throughout the text. Ernst C. Krohn's essay, "The development of modern musicology", p. 153–172, provides a useful bibliography of the history of the discipline.

Review by Vincent Duckles in *Notes,* 20 (1963), p. 469–71.

675. Stevens, Denis. Musicology: a practical guide. London: Macdonald Futura, 1980. 224 p. (Yehudi Menuhin Music Guides)

"This book is not for musicologists; they already know it all" (from the author's introductory remarks).

Reviews by Clifford Bartlett in *Brio,* 17 (1980), and by David Fallows in *Early music,* 9 (1981), p. 243–44

676. Suppan, Wolfgang. Musica humana: die anthropologische und kulturethologische Dimension der Musikwissenschaft. Wien: H. Böhlau, 1986. 121 p. (Forschen, Lehren, Verantworten, 8)

Bibliography: p. 94–115.

677. Systematische Musikwissenschaft [hrsg. von] Carl Dahlhaus, Helga de la Motte-Haber. Wiesbaden: Akademische Verlagsgesellschaft Athenaion; Laaber: Laaber-Verlag Müller-Buscher, 1982. 367 p. (Neues Handbuch der Musikwissenschaft, 10)
Contents:
"Umfang, Methode und Ziel der Systematischen Musikwissenschaft" von Helga de la Motte-Haber.
"Musikwissenschaft und Systematische Musikwissenschaft" von Carl Dahlhaus.
"Begründungen Musiktheoretischer Systeme" von Helga de la Motte-Haber und Peter Nitsche.
"Ästhetik und Musikästhetik" von Carl Dahlhaus.
"Musiksoziologische Reflexionen" von Carl Dahlhaus und Günter Mayer.
"Musikalische Hermeneutik und empirische Forschung" von Helga de la Motte-Haber.
"Sozialpsychologische Dimensionen des musikalischen Geschmacks" von Ekkehard Jost.
"Begabung, Lernen, Entwicklung" von Klaus-Ernst Behne, Eberhard Kötter und Roland Meissner.
"Wissenschaft und Praxis" von Günter Kleinen und Helga de la Motte-Haber.

678. Wallon, Simone. La documentation musicologique. Paris: Beauchesne, 1984. 142 p. (Guides musicologiques, 3)
A brief handbook to the practice of musicology

679. Watanabe, Ruth T. Introduction to music research. Englewood Cliffs, N.J., Prentice-Hall, 1967. 237 p.
A discussion of the procedures, resources, and techniques preliminary to research activity in music. The main subdivisions are as follows: Part I, library orientation. Part II, the research paper. Part III, survey of research materials.
Review by Donald W. Krummel in *Notes,* 24 (1968), p. 481–82.

680. Weber, Édith. La recherche musicologique: objet, méthodologie, normes de présentation. Paris: Beauchesne, 1980. 171 p. (Guides musicologiques. 1)
An introduction to the field, to the variety of methods used in pursuing musicological research, and to report writing in musicology.

681. Westrup, Jack A. An introduction to musical history. 2nd ed. London: Hutchinson University Library, 1973. 176 p.
First published in London, 1955, as a volume in the Hutchinson Unversity Library. Subsequently in New York by Harper and Row, 1964. 174 p.

This is not a history of music. It is simply an attempt to outline some of the problems which historians and students have to face, and to give some idea of the conditions in which music has come into existence. [Author's *Preface]*

Although intended as a layman's guide to music history, this little book is one of the few clear treatments of the problems of music historiography in English.

Review by Allen P. Britton in *Journal of research in music education,* 3 (1955), p. 154.

682. Wiora, Walter. Historische und systematische Musikwissenschaft; ausgewählte Aufsätze von Walter Wiora. Hrsg. von Hellmut Kühn und Christoph-Hellmut Mahling. Tutzing: H. Schneider, 1972. 480 p.

Prof. Wiora was the leading exponent of the systematic approach to musical scholarship. This volume contains his writings on musicology and a bibliography of his later writings.

Bibliographies of Music Literature

The term "music literature" as applied here refers to writings on music as opposed to musical scores. Such writings may appear as periodical articles or monographs; they may be cited in complete, self-contained bibliographical works or in serial publications; and they can be organized in terms of a variety of subject field. Nearly every dissertation or research study will have its appended bibliography of relevant literature, and most of the authoritative dictionaries or encyclopedias have subject bibliographies connected with their articles. It would be impossible to cite all of these resources, but the titles selected are numerous and various enough to form a substantial sample of the available titles. Following is an outline of the subdivisions employed.

Bibliographies of Music Literature
   General
   Current or Annual
   Indexes to Periodical Literature
   Lists of Periodicals

   Special and Subject Bibliographies
   Contemporary Music
   Dissertations
   Ethnomusicology
   Musical Instruments
   Jazz
   Popular Music
   Medieval and Renaissance Music
   Baroque and Classical Music
   Music Education
   National Music
   Opera and Theater Music
   Primary Sources: Early Music Literature
   Sacred Music
   Writing on Individual Composers

See also "Catalogs of Music Libraries and Collections." Many of the published catalogs of major libraries contain separate volumes or sections devoted to holdings in books on music.

GENERAL

683. Aber, Adolf. Handbuch der Musikliteratur in systematisch-chronologischer Anordnung. Leipzig: Breitkopf & Härtel, 1922. 696 p. (Klein Handbücher der Musikgeschichte nach Gattungen, 13)

Reprints by Olms, Hildesheim, and Breitkopf & Härtel, Wiesbaden, 1967.

A classified bibliography for students of music history. International coverage, although strongest in German materials. Entries from at least 13 important musicological journals are included. Subject and author indexes.

Also listed as part of the *Kretzschmar* series of music history, no. 568.

684. Adams, John L. Musicians' autobiographies; an annotated bibliography of writings available in English, 1800 to 1980. Jefferson, North Carolina: McFarland, 1982. 126 p.

Arranged by author. Excludes letters, oral histories, diaries, and articles in reference works. Chronological, title and subject indexes.

685. Adlung, Jacob. Anleitung zu der musikalischen Gelartheit, 1758. Faksimile-Nachdruck hrsg. von. H. J. Moser. Kassel: Bärenreiter, 1953. 814 p. (Documenta Musicological, Erste Reihe, 4)

2nd ed., revised by J. A. Hiller, 1783.

Chronologically one of the first important critical bibliographies of music literature. The author proposed to list all works on musical subjects necessary to "educated music lovers, and particularly to lovers of keyboard music," as well as builders of organs and other instruments.

See the description of this work in Gustav Reese's *Fourscore classics of music literature* (no. 1158). N.Y.: Liberal Arts Press, 1957. p. 74–75.

686. Azhderian, Helen Wentworth. Reference works in music and music literature in five libraries of Los Angeles County. Los Angeles: Published for the Southern California Chapter of the Music Library Association by the University of Southern California, 1953. 313 pp.

A partial supplement of holdings in the USC Library, January 1952-June 1962. Prepared by Joan M. Meggett. 1962. 13 p.

A bibliography of musicological literature, approx. 4,500 entries. International coverage. Full bibliographical citations. Classified listing with author index. The libraries represented are The Henry E. Huntington Library, The William Andrews Clark Memorial Library, The Los Angeles Public Library, and the libraries of the University of Southern California and the University of California at Los Angeles.

Review by Otto Albrecht, in *Notes*, 11 (1954), p. 468–69; by Vincent Duckles in *JAMS*, 7 (1954), p. 242–43.

687. Baily, Dee. A checklist of music bibliographies and indexes in progress and unpublished. 4th ed. Philadelphia: Music Library Association, 1982. 104 p. (MLA index & bibliography series, 3)

Rev. ed. of *A checklist of music bibliographies and indexes, in progress and unpublished.* 3rd ed. compiled by Linda Solow. 1974.

The results of a survey.

688. Battier, Marc and Jacques Arveiller. Documents musique et information matique: une bibliographie indexée. Réedition augmentée. Paris: Editeur Elmeratte, 1978. 178 p.
First published in 1976.
A bibliography of computer applications to music research and practice. 1,485 numbered items, including many periodical articles. Among the tables at the end of the column are a list of sigla, a list of programs an systems, a list of computer languages, and a list of subjects.

689. Becker, Carl F. Systematisch-chronologisch Darstellung der musikalischen Literatur von der frühesten bis auf die neueste Zeit. . . . Leipzig: R. Friese, 1836. 571 cols. and 34 p.
Nachtrag Chroalsammlungen aus dem 16. 17. und 18. Jahrhundert, 1839.
Reprint by Frits A. M. Knuf, Hilversum, 1964.
Becker presents a classified bibliography of many now obscure works. His work fills the gap, chronologically, between *Lichtenthal,* (no. 725) and Eitner's *Bücherverzeichnis,* 1885, (no. 705). Includes news paper and periodical articles. Gives place of publication, date, pagination, with brief annotations; 33 page index by subject, author, etc.

690. Beiträge zur Musikwissenschaft. Sonderreihe: Bibliographien, musikwissenschaftliche Literatur sozialistischer Länder. Berlin: Verlag neue Musik, 1973– .
Band III *Deutsche Demokratische Republik 1945–1970.* 334 p. A classified bibliography of 3,495 published writings on musicology by German and foreign authors. Not indexed.
Band IV *Sowjetunion 1945–70,* 1976. 312 p. A classified bibliography, transliterated from Russian. 4,007 entries.
Band IV Anhang *Verzeichnis der Autoren und der publiziarten Titel in russischer Spracher,* 1976. 166 p. An index of authors with titles in Cyrillic characters to Band IV.
Chief editor: Georg Knepler.
See also no. 693.

691. Besterman, Theodore. Music and drama: a bibliography of bibliographies. Totowa: Rowman and Littlefield, 1971. 365 p.
A listing extracted by the publisher from the 4th edition of the author's *World bibliography of bibliographies* (1965).

692. Bibliography of discographies. New York: R. R. Bowker, 1977–1983. 3 v.
Contents:
v. 1. *Classical music, 1925–1975 [by]* Michael H. Gray and Gerald D. Gibson, 1977.
v. 2. *Jazz [by]* Daniel Allen, 1981.
v. 3. *Popular music [by] Michael H. Gray, 1983.*
These three volumes are the most complete bibliographies of discographies to date. Gray and Gibson were responsible for the annual cumulation of citations of discographies in the *Association for Recorded Sound Collections Journal.*
Also entered as no. 2768.

693. Blechschmidt, Renate. "Bibliographie der Schriften über Musik aus der Deutschen Demokratischen Republik, 1945–59." In *Beiträge zur Musikwissenschaft,* Jahrg. 1 (1959), Heft 3, p. 51–75; Jahrg. 2 (1960), Heft 1, p. 50–68; Heft 2, p. 64–78.

Classified list covering the writings on music produced in East Germany for the 15-year period. Complemented by no. 690.

694. Block, Adrienne Fried and Carol Neuls-Bates. Women in American music; a bibliography of music and literature. Westport: Greenwood, 1979. 302 p.

A classified bibliography of 5,024 entries organized as in the RILM model with abstracts. Author-subject index to the literature. Composer-author index to music. Index to recordings. Very thorough indexing and annotating.

695. Blom, Eric. A general index to modern musical literature in the English language, including periodicals for the years 1915–1926. London; Philadelphia: Curwen, [1927]. 159 p.

Reprint by Da Capo, N.Y., 1970.

Entries for books by author and for parts of books by catchword subject in one alphabet.

696. Blum, Fred. Music monographs in series: a bibliography of numbered monograph series in the field of music current since 1945. N.Y.: Scarecrow, 1964. 197 p.

Gives contents of more than 259 monographic series originating from some 30 countries.

> Over one-third of them may best be described as broadly musicological in content, many issued under the auspices of universities or scholarly societies; others, ranging in tone from the academic to the popular, cover the gamut of musical subject matter . . . [*Preface*]

Review by Thomas Watkins in *Current Musicology* (Fall, 1965), p. 227–29; by Richard Schaal in *Die Musikforschung,* 22 (1969), p. 521.

697. Briquet, Marie. La musique dans les congrès internationaux (1835–1939). Paris: Heugel, 1961. 124 p. (Publications de la Société Française de Musicologie, 2ème sér. Tome X)

A bibliographical survey of the contributions on music made at international congresses from 1835 to 1939. Classified listing of 164 congress reports with papers on music itemized. Indexed by place of meeting, by chronology, by author, and by subject.

Review by Richard Schaal in *Die Musikforschung,* 17 (1964), p. 183.

698. Büchting, Adolf. Bibliotheca musica. Verzeichnis aller Bezug auf die Musik . . . 1847–66, im deutschen Buchhandel erschienenen Bücher und Zeitschriften. Nebst Fortsetzung 1: die Jahre 1867–71 umfassend. Nordhausen: A. Büchting, 1867–72. 2 v.

A bibliography of music literature covering German publications from 1847 to 1871. The work takes its place chronologically after that of Becker (no. 689) in this history of music bibliography. The gap of eight years in coverage between *Becker* and *Büchting* has been filled by Robert Eitner.

See no. 705.

699. Carl Gregor, Duke of Mecklenburg. Bibliographie einiger Grenzgebiete der Musikwissenschaft. Baden-Baden: Librarie Heitz, 1962. 197 p. (Bibliotheca bibliographica Aureliana, 6)

A bibliography devoted to areas peripheral to the traditional emphasis on historical musicology. Includes books and periodical articles on aesthetics; psychology; sociology of music; relations between music and the other arts; musical interests of poets, writers, philosophers, etc. 3,519 entries, alphbetically by author, with indexes of subjects and of persons as subjects.

Review by Wolfgang Schmieder in *Die Musikforschung,* 20 (1967), p. 461–62.

700. Chicorel, Marietta. Chicorel bibliography of books on music and musicians. N.Y.: Chicorel, 1974. 500 p.

A mechanically compiled list of currently available books.

701. Coover, James B. "Dictionaries and encyclopedias of music," in *The New Grove Dictionary of Music and Musicians,* edited by Stanley Sadie, v. 5, p. 430–59. London: Macmillan, 1980.

An extensive essay on the early history of dictionaries broken into several chronological spans, each with a bibliography of the dictionaries published in the time under examination. There is a separate section on encyclopedias, with a bibliography organized by country followed by a section on terminological dictionaries. International biographical and then national or regional biographical dictionaries are listed and discussed. Dictionaries devoted to specific topics are listed. There is a chronology "Landmarks in musical lexicography," and a bibliography. This article is the distillate of a lifetime of bibliographic work on the genre by the author.

Beginning with no. 115 (September 1987), *Cum notis variorum* has published James B. Coover's "Lacunae in music dictionaries and encyclopedias," a two-part essay and beginning with no. 117 (November 1987) in *CNV* Coover's "A non-evaluative checklist of music dictionaries and encyclopedias," a five-part classified bibliography has appeared. Together these complement the article and bibliography in *The New Grove.*

702. Coover, James B. Provisional checklist of priced antiquarians' catalogs containing musical materials. Buffalo: Music Library, State University of New York, 1981. 150 p. (typescript)

Organized by name of firm, then chronologically, with title or brief summary, number of lots to be sold or pages in the catalog, and location.

703. Crane, Frederick. A bibliography of the iconography of music. Iowa City: University of Iowa, School of Music, 1971. 40 *l.*

Distributed at the IAML meeting of 1971. Cites articles, catalogs, illustrated histories and other studies.

704. Diamond, Harold J. Music criticism: an annotated guide to the literature. Metuchen: Scarecrow Press, 1979. 316 p.

A bibliography of critical writings on music in English. A new edition is projected.

705. Eitner, Robert. Bücherverzeichnis der Musikliteratur aus den Jahren 1839 bis 1846 im Anschlussan Becker und Büchting . . . Leipzig: Breitkopf & Härtel, 1885. 89 p. (Monatshefte für Musikgeschichte. Beilage. 17. Jahrgang)

Intended to bridge the gap between Becker's bibliography, no. 689, and Büchting's, no. 698.

706. Elste, Martin. Verzeichnis deutschsprachigen Musiksoziologie 1848–1973. Hamburg: Verlag der Musikalienhandlung Karl Dieter Wagner, 1975. 201 p.

Part one is a classified bibliography with indexes to names and periodicals. Part two is a keyword in context index (KWIC) to titles.

707. Floyd, Samuel A. and Marsha J. Reisser. Black music in the United States: an annotated bibliography of selected reference and research materials. Millwood, N.Y.: Kraus International Publications, 1983. 234 p.

Cites bibliographies and indexes, catalogs, discographies, biographical dictionaries, and anthologies. Includes a directory of archives holding materials relevant to the subject. Indexes to names, titles, and subjects.

708. Forkel, Johann N. Allgemeine Litteratur der Musik, oder Anleitung zur Kenntniss musikalischer Bücher, welche von den ältesten bis auf die neusten Zeiten bey den Griechen, Römern und den meisten neuern europäischen Nationen sind geschrieben worden. Leipzig: Schwickert, 1792. 540 p.

Reprint by Olms, Hildesheim, 1962.

The first comprehensive bibliography of music literature and still a work of great utility. Classified listing of some 3,000 works on all aspects of musical knowledge, with brief biographical notices on all of the authors and descriptive annotations. Complete tables of contents are given for most important books.

Forkel's classification system has served as a model for many subsequent bibliographies. See Scott Goldthwaite, "Classification problems, bibliographies of literature about music," in *Library quarterly* (October 1948), p. 255 ff.

Forkel's work was expanded and translated into Italian by Pietro Lichenthal in 1826. See no. 725.

709. Gardeton, César. Bibliographie musicale de la France et de l'étranger, ou Répertoire général systématique de tous les traités et œuvres de musique vocale et instrumentale, imprimés ou gravés en Europe jusqu'à ce jour avec l'indication de lieux de l'impression, des marchands et des prix . . . Paris: Noigret, 1822. 608 p.

Reprinted by Minkoff, Genève, 1978 as part of the series (Archives de l'édition musicale française, 6.)

An early 19th century bibliography of music and music literature, chiefly French although titles from other European countries are listed. There is a section devoted to reviews, biographies, analysis and musical news, and a directory of musicians of all kinds active in Paris.

710. Gerboth, Walter. An index to musical Festschriften and similar publications. N.Y.: W. W. Norton, 1969. 188 p.

Expanded version of a bibliographical work first appearing in *Aspects of Medieval and Renaissance music, a birthday offering to Gustave Reese* (N.Y.: W. W. Norton, 1966), p. 183–307.

The most comprehensive treatment of music *Feschriften* available. In three parts: A. List of *Festschriften* under the name of the individual or institution honored; B. Subject listing of more than 2,700 articles; C. Author and secondary-subject index. *RILM* provides coverage of articles in musical *Festschriften* published after 1967.

Review by Donald Seibert in *Notes,* 26 (1970), p. 760–61. *Festschriften* —Indexes

711. Heaton, Wallace and Charles W. Hargens. An interdisciplinary index of studies in physics, medicine, and music related to the human voice. Bryn Mawr: T.Presser, 1968. 61 p.

A bibliography of articles.

712. Heussner, Horst. Collectio musica: Musikbibliographie in Deutschland bis 1625 [von] Horst Heussner [und] Ingo Schultz. Kassel: Internationale Vereinigung der Musikbibliotheken / Internationale Gesellschaft für Musikwissenschaft, 1973. 254 p. (Catalogus musicus, 6)

A classified bibliography of music and music literature published in Germany before 1625. Arranged in two langauge groups, Latin and German. Indexes to: names composers, authors of texts, editors and collectors; printers, publishers and dealers; names of presses; titles appearing twice. Corrigenda and addenda. Provided with a bibliography of contemporaneous bibliographies amd a bibliography of modern secondary literature.

713. Honigsheim, Paul. Music and society; the later writings of Paul Honigsheim. Edited, with additional material and bibliographies, by K. Peter Etzkorn. Foreword by J. Allan Beegle. New York: J. Wiley, 1973. 327 p.

Reprinted 1979. First published as *Sociology of music: titles selected and annotated by Paul Honigsheim* by the University of Missouri, St. Louis, 1970. 196 l.

Sociology and music: additional and recent bibliographic entires, p. 299–320.

714. Index of Music Theory in the United States, 1955–1970. Richmond Browne, supervising editor. v. 3, nos. 7–11 of *In theory only;* journal of the Michigan Music Theory Society. Ann Arbor: Michigan Music Theory Society, 1978. 170 p.

An index of articles, books, dissertations, reviews, etc. published 1955–70 on music theory: terms and concepts, analyses, and "technical music theory" (e.g. orchestration, notation). Includes some works on ethnomusicology, musicology, aesthetics, philosophy, and theory pedagogy. Author and subject indexes. Index of musical compositions pieces analyzed. Index of historical theorists whose work is treated as a subject.

715. Kahl, Willi, und Wilhelm-Martin Luther. Repertorium der Musikwissenschaft. Musikschrifttem, Denkmäler und Gesamtausgaben in Auswahl

(1800–1950) mit Besitzvermerken deutscher Bibliotheken und musikwissenshaftlicher Institute. Kassel: Bärenreiter, 1951. 271 p.

A comprehensive bibliography of music literature, broadly classified, including useful lists of *Festschriften*, conference reports, and critical editions. International in scope. Prepared as a union list of musicological holdings in postwar German libraries. 2,795 items. Indexed persons, subjects, and geographical locations.

Review by Otto Albrecht in *Notes*, 11 (1954), p. 468–69; by Vincent Duckles in *JAMS*, 7 (1954), p. 242–45.

716. Kananov, Pavel Khristoforovich and Ida Pinkhasovna Vulykh. Zarubezhnaia literatura o muzyke: referativnyi ukazatel za 1959–1966. [Foreign literature about music: annotated bibliography 1959–66] Moskva: Sovetskii Kompozitor, 1972. 604 p.

A bibliography of general literature on the methodology and history of musical knowledge, covering theoretical and historical disciplines. Titles given in Russian and in the original language.

717. Kananov, Pavel Khristoforovich and Ida Pinkhasovna Vulykh. Zarubezhnaia literatura o muzyke: referativnyi ukazatel za 1954–1958. [Foreign literature about music: annotated bibliography from 1954–1958]. Moskva: Sovetskii Kompozitor, 1962.

A bibliography of general literature on the methodology and history of musical knowledge, covering both theoretical and historical disciplines. Titles are given in Russian and in the original foreign language.

718. Keller, Michael A. "Music and dance" in The Reader's Adviser. New York; London: R. R. Bowker, 1986. p. 484–525.

A briefly annotated list of currently available, English language books intended to introduce the non-specialist to topics in music and dance.

719. Kostka, Stefan M. A bibliography of computer applications in music. Hackensack: J. Boonin, 1974. 58 p. (Music indexes and bibliographies, 7)

720. Krohn, Ernst C.. The history of music: an index to the literature available in a selected group of musicological publications. St. Louis: Washington University, 1952. 463 p. (Washington University Library Studies, 3)

Reissued by Baton Music, Co., St. Louis, 1958.

Classified index of articles on music history in 39 leading musicological publications, chiefly German and English. Chronological arrangement, with subdivisions by subject. Includes book reviews.

Review by Richard Appel in *Notes*, 10 (1952), p. 105–06; by Scott Goldthwaite in *JAMS*, 6 (1953), p. 250–51; by Wolfgang Schmieder in *Die Musikforschung*, 6 (1953), p. 278–80.

721. Krohn, Ernst C.. "Musical Festschriften and related publications." In *Notes*, 21 (1964), p. 94–108.

A useful listing of *Festschriften*, cited chronologically under four headings: A. works of major musicological interest; B. works compiled in homage to individual musicians, living or in the past; C. commemorative volumes consisting of original music; and D. those celebrating a particular institution, school, society, or performing group.

For a more complete bibliography of *Festschriften,* see no. 710, above.

Festschriften—Bibliography

722. Laskowski, Larry. Heinrich Schenker: an annotated index to his analyses of musical works. New York: Pendragon Press, 1978. 157 p.

723. De Lerma, Dominique-René. "Black music: a bibliographic essay" in *Music and fine arts in the general library,* edited by Guy A. Marco and Wolfgang M. Freitag, vol. 23, no. 3 of *Library trands* (January, 1975), p. 517–32.

A bibliography citing bibliographies of Black music and literature about Black music and musicians, as well as discographies of Black music. Organized by genre and subject.

724. De Lerma, Dominique-René. Bibliography of Black music. Foreword by Jessie Carney Smith. Westport: Greenwood Press, 1981–84. 4 v. (The Greenwood encyclopedia of Black music)

Contents: v.1. Reference materials; v.2. Afro-American idioms; v.3. Geographical studies; v.4. Theory, education, and related studies.

Annotated bibliography, international in scope and including articles, books, graduate student papers, and journals, on many areas of Black musical life. Arrangement and citations based on the *RILM* model. Indexes in v. 3 and 4 only.

725. Lichtenthal, Pietro. Dizionario e bibliografia della musica. Milano: A. Fontana, 1826. 4 v.

Reprinted by Forni, Bologna, 1970.

Vols. 3 and 4 are a translation of Forkel's *Allgemeine Litteratur der Music* (no. 708) with additions to 1826. Vols. 1 and 2 are the dictionary as cited as no. 394.

726. Marco, Guy A. Information on music: a handbook of reference sources in European languages; with the assistance of Sharon Paugh Ferris; foreword by James Coover. Littleton, Colo.: Libraries Unlimited, 1975–1984. 3 v. (to date)

A six volume work is projected:

v.1. *Basic and universal sources,* 1975. 164 p.

v.2 *The Americas,* with Ann M. Garfield and Sharon Paugh Ferris, 1977. 296 p.

v.3. *Europe* with Sharon Paugh Ferris, and Ann G. Olszewski, 1984. 519 p.

An annotated guide to music reference works with the intention of providing comprehensive access to information about music. Each entry provides complete bibliographic information, an LC cassification, references to other guides to music reference and research materials, and an introduction. There are indexes to names and titles, and to subjects.

727. Marks, Martin. "Film music: the material, literature, and present state of research" in *Notes,* 36 (1980),p.282–325.

A survey of the source material and research on it including numerous citations for secondary works and criticism. Includes "a selective bibliography of film music publications."

728. Materialy do Bibliografii Muzyki Polskiej. (Series editor: Tadeusz Strumillo). Kraków: Polskie Wydawnictwo Muzyczne, 1954–78. 5 v.

A series of bibliographies related to Polish music and music literature.

Vol. 1 by Kornel Michalowski: *Opery polskie,* 1954. 227 p. (Polish operas and foreign operas with Polish settings or subjects, listed by title, giving composer, librettist, date and place of first performance.)

Vol. 2 by Erwin Nowaczyk: *Piésni solowe S. Moniuszki, katalog tematyczny,* 1954. 332 p. (Thematic catalog of 304 songs by Moniuszki, giving authors of text, lists of editions.)

Vol. 3 by Kornel Michalowski: *Bibliografia polskiego piśmiennictwa muzycznego,* 1955. 280 p. (Classified bibliography of books on music in Polish. Lists of theses and dissertations, 1917–1954.)

A supplement to vol. 3, published in 1964 as vol. 4, contains classified listings of new Polish books on music published between 1955 and 1963, with some addenda from earlier years. A second supplement to vol. 3, published as vol. 5, was issued in 1978 and covers the period 1964 to 1974.

729. Mathiesen, Thomas J. A bibliography of sources for the study of ancient Greek music. Hackensack: J. Boonin, 1974. 59 p. (Music indexes and bibliographies, 10)

730. Matthew, James E. The literature of music. London: E. Stock, 1896. 281 p.

Reprint by Da Capo, N.Y., 1969.

Essays on the literature of music in historical sequence to the 18th century, thereafter by topics: histories, biographies, dictionaries, sacred music, opera, instruments, music as a science, biibliography. Narrative style. Matthew, although out of date, presents a useful survey of the earlier literature of music.

731. Mrygon, Adam and Eva Myrgon. Bibliografia polskiego piśmiennictwa muzykologicznego (1945–1970). [Wyd. 1.] Warszawa: Państwowe Wydawn. Naukowe, 1972. 208 p.

Authors known also as Adam Mrygoniowie and Ewa Mrygoniowie.

A classified bibliography of 3,398 items, covering all aspects of musicology practiced in Poland.

732. Ogawa, Takashi, ed. Honpo yogaku kankei tosho mokuroku. A list of books about foreign music in the Japanese language. 3d ed. Tokyo: Ongaku no Tomo Sha, 1965. 267 p.

733. Paxinos, S. "Select bibliography of harmony and counterpoint," in *Ars nova, magazine of the Department of Musicology, University of South Africa,* 6, 2 (August 1974), p. 3–31.

361 item bibliography arranged alphabetically in two sections: books and articles. Full bibliographical entries, but no annotations.

734. Performing arts 1876–1981 books, including an international index of current serial publications. N.Y.: R. R. Bowker, 1981. 1,656 p.
A retrospective bibliography of Library of Congress cataloged entries of works published or distributed inthe U.S . . . Derived from the *American book publishing record.* About one-third of the work is devoted to works about music. Indexes to subjects, authors, and titles for books and serials.

735. Petermann, Kurt. Tanzbibliographie. Verzeichnis der in deutscher Sprache veröffentlichten Schriften und Aufsätze zum Bühnen-, Gesellschaft-, Kinder-, Volks-, und Turniertanz sowie zur Tanswissenschaft, Tanzmusik und zum Jazz. Hrsg. vom Institut für Volkskunstforschung beim Zentralhaus für Kulturarbeit. Leipzig: VEB Bibliographisches Institut, 1966–81. 7 v.
A supplement of 2 v. was published in 1981. A second edition encompassing, unchanged, all entries to 1981, was published in 2 v. by K. G. Saur, Munich, in 1981, edited by the Akademie der Künste Tanzarchive der DDR, Leipzig.
This is a classified bibliography of writings on the dance.

736. Refardt, Edgar. Verzeichnis der Aufsätze zur Musik in den nicht-musikalischen Zeitschriften der Universitätsbibliothek Basel. Leipzig: Breitkopf & Härtel, 1925. 105 p.
A classified list of writings on music in over 500 non-musical newspapers and periodicals, arranged alphabetically by author. One of the few efforts to compile a bibliography of musical literature in journals outside of the field.

737. Sakkyokuka zenshu, gakufu sosho shozai mokuroku Union check list of collected editions, historical sets, and monuments of music in Japanese music libraries. Sakkyokuka Zenshu Gakufu Sosho Shozai Mokuroku Henshu Iinkai hen. Zoho kaiteiban. Tokyo: Ongaku Toshokan Kyogikai & Sohatsubaimoto Akademia Myujikku, 1983. 2 v.
Compiled by the Working Group of Union Checklist in Music Library Association of Japan.
First published in 1975, indexes holdings of 25 music libraries in Japan.

738. Tripp, Wendell. "Folk song and dance" in The Reader's Adviser. New York; London: R. R. Bowker, 1986. p. 593–594.
A briefly annotated list of currently available, English language books intended to introduce the non-specialist to topics within the discipline.

739. Tyrrell, John, Rosemary Wise. A guide to international congress reports in musicology, 1900–1975. New York: Garland Pub., 1979. 353 p.
A bibliographical guide to locating and identifying congress reports and an index to papers published in those reports. Covers congress published reports, so some reports for congresses held in the period 1970–75 but not yet published at the time of compilation are not included. Organized chronologically. Indexed by place, by titles, series and sponsors, by authors and editors, and by subject.
Review by Walter Gerboth in *Notes,* 36 (1980), p. 902–03.

740. Vinquist, Mary and Neal Zaslaw. Performance practice: a bibliography. N. Y.: W. W. Norton, 1971. 114 p.

First appeared as issue 8 (1969) of *Current Musicology; this issue was supplemented in issue 10 (1970).*

The books is supplemented in *Current Musicology,* 12 (1971), p. 129–49, under the title "Performance practices bibliography", but this is labeled "Second supplement" and was edited by Thomas W. Baker and Robert Kline. A third supplement was published in *Current Musicology,* 15 (1973), p. 126–33, edited by Richard Koprowski and JAmes Hines.

Not including the supplements, this is a bibliography of about 1,200 entries; includes both primary sources and secondary sources. International in scope. The index brings out writings on major sub-topics. Includes, on p. 6, a bibliography of performance practice bibliographies (chiefly unpublished dissertations).

741. Vorreiter, Leopold. "Musikikonographie des Altertums im Schrifttum 1850,1949 und 1950–1974", in *ActaM,* 46 (1974), p. 1–42.

A narrative bibliography of 532 titles devoted to writings providing information on the iconography of ancient music. Part 2 treats writings related to the inconography of ethnic musics in general.

742. Wenk, Arthur B. Analyses of nineteenth-century music: 1940–1980. 2nd ed. Boston: Music Library Association, 1984. 83 p. (MLA index and bibliography series, 15)

First published in 1976/

A bibliography of works analyzing nineteenth century music and appearing in books, periodicals, or anthologies.

743. Wescott, Steven D. A comprehensive bibliography of music for film and television. Detroit: Information Coordinators, 1985. 432 p. (Detroit studies in music bibliography, 54)

An extensive bibliography (6,340 entries) of articles and a wide variety of other sources on the subject. Filmography: pp. 375–377. Discography: pp. 377–379. Index to names and subjects.

Additions to Steven D. Westcott: A comprehensive bibliography of music for film and television by Gillian B. Anderson published 1986, Library of Congress, Washington. c. 68 p. Anderson has used Wescott's headings, numbering, and format, added substantially to Wescott's index, and provided an index to film titles.

744. Wettstein, Hermann. Bibliographie musikalischer thematischer Werkverzeichnisse. Laaber: Laaber-Verlag, 1978. 408 p.

A bibliography of thematic catalogs, alphabetical by composer. Content and organization of each catalog are described.

745. Winick, Steven. Rhythm: an annotated bibliography. Metuchen: Scarecrow Press, 1974. 157 p.

Lists about 500 English-language sources written in 1900–72. Three categories: general background; psychology of rhythm; pedagogy of rhythm. Index of authors, editors and reviewers. Focus seems to be on music education.

CURRENT OR ANNUAL, INCLUDING PERIODICALS LISTING MUSIC LITERATURE

746. Sovetskaia Literatura o Muzyke] 1918–1947; bibliograficheskii ukazatel knig.: Ivan I. Startsev; redaktor S. D. Uspenskaia. Moskva: Sovetskii kompozitor, 1963. 293 p.

A classified list of books and periodical articles in Russian.

747. [Sovetskaia Literatura o Muzyke] 1948–53. Compilers S. L. Uspenkaia and B. Yagolim. Moskva: Sovetskii kompozitor, 1955. 343 p.

A classified list of books and periodical articles in Russian. A bibliographical series, issued irregularly; further volumes have appeared as follows:

1958, covering the years 1954–56
1959, covering the year 1957
1963, covering 1958–59
1967, covering 1960–62
1971, covering 1963–65
1974, covering 1966–67
1979–84, covering 1968–70

Title and imprint varies. Name index; list of periodicals.

748. Acta Musicologica. V. 1–24. Internationale Gesellschaft für Musikwissenschaft, 1928–52.

"Index novorum librarum," a department appearing in most issues of this journal, is one of the best sources of bibliographical information for the period between 1930 and 1950. It gives a classified listing of books on music in all languages. The department was discontinued after 1952.

See *An index to Acta Musicologica, Fall 1928-Spring 1967, by* Cecil Adkins and Alis Dickinson. Basel, Bärenreiter. Author and subject index.

749. African Music. Journal of the African music society. V. 1– . Roodepoort, Transvaal, Union of South Africa: 1954– .

Each annual issue has a section of "books and pamphlets received" as well as reviews of current publications in ethnomusicology.

750. American Bibliographic Service. Quarterly checklist of musicology. An international index of current books, monographs, brochures, and separates. Darien, Connecticut: American Bibliographic Service, 1959–77. V. 1–19.

V. 1–10 reprinted by Johnson Reprint Corporation, 1977.

An unclassified numbered listing of current writings on music. The selection is broad and rather uncritical. Full bibliographical information, including prices. Indexed by authors, editors, and translators in the last issue of each volume.

751. Bibliographia Musicologica, a bibliography of musical literature. Utrecht: Joachimsthal, 1970–77. 7 v.

An international bibliography of books about music, listed alphabetically by author, with a subject index. V. 1 is devoted to literature published in 1968, 2,170 items. V. 2, covering literature for 1969, runs to 2,057 items. V. 7 covers about 2,000 titles. The listings give publisher, pagination, and price and include current reprints, facsimile editions, and revised editions.

752. Bibliographic guide to music. Boston: G.K. Hall, 1975– .
An annual listing publications cataloged each year by the Research Libraries of the New York Public Library and the Library of Congress. Also serves as an annual supplement to the *Dictionary catalog of the music collection of the Research Libraries of the New York Public Library* (see no. 2276). Music and works about music in all languages and all forms are included. Entries provided under personal and corporate names, titles, and subjects.
Brief review by Stephen M. Fry in *Notes,* 33 (1976), p. 305.

753. Bibliographie des Musikschrifttums. Jahrgang 1936– . (Herausgegeben im Auftrage des Instituts für Musikforschung Preussischer Kulturbesitz, Berlin.) Leipzig; Frankfurt a.M.: F. Hofmeister, 1936– .
Editors: 1936–37, Kurt Taut; 1938–39, Georg Karstädt; (1940–49, suspended publication); 1950–59, Wolfgang Schmieder; 1960 Werner Bollet, Dieter J. Frecot, Bärbel Schleyer; 1961–64 Dieter J. Frecot, Bärbel Schleyer; 1965 Dieter J. Frecot, Heinz-Lothar Fichter. 1966–68 Dieter J. Frecot; 1969–75 Elisabeth Wilker; 1976 Claudia Wegner; 1977–78 Norbert Bökerheil Claudia Wegner.
A bibliography of books and an index to periodical literature in all European languages. A large number of nonmusical journals included. Classified by broad subjects with an index of names (author and subject) and places. The emphasis is on "serious" music.
This bibliography follows in a direct line of descent from the listings in the Peters *Jahrbuch,* no. 764.
Review of *Jahrgang 1950–51* by Richard Schaal in *Die Musikforschung,* 8 (1955), p. 371–72; by Richard S. Hill in *Notes,* 11 (1954), p. 555–57; by Scott Goldthwaite in *JAMS,* 8 (1955), p. 55–57. Review of *Jahrgang* 1952–53 by Richard Schaal in *Die Musikforschung,* 10 (1957), p. 440.

754. Bollettino Bibliografico Musicale. Milan. V. 1:1 (Sept. 1926)-v. 8:4/5 (April/May 1933). N.S. v. 1:1 (Jan./Feb. 1952)- v. 1:7/8 (Aug./Sept. 1952).
A journal devoted to matters of bibliographical interest in music; each issue customarily contains a bibliography of the works of one composer, early or contemporary, chiefly Italian. Regular departments give listings of current music publications, the contents of music journals, music and book reviews.

755. Brass Quarterly. Milford, N.H.: The Cabinet Press, 1967– . V. 1– .
Edited by Mary Rasmussen.
Contains in each issue review of recordings and scores of brass music as well as a section of "Current publications" classified by instrument or ensemble.

756. Bulgarski Muzikalen Knigopis: trimesechen bibliografskibiuletin za novoizliazla literatura po muzika i noti. Soffia: Bulgarski Bibliografski Institut "Elin Pelin," 1958– .
Quarterly, classified list of books and periodical articles on music and publications in musical notation issued in Bulgaria. Cumulative index,

the October-December issue containing index for the entire year.

757. Cum Notis Variorum. Edited by Ann P. Basart. Berkeley: University of California, Music Library, 1976– . no. 1– .
One of the most distinguished of music library newsletters issued. This journal lists recent acquisitions and provides brief reviews of new reference works. There are regular features on music in the Bay Area, on conferences, on music libraries and music collections in northern California, and on news culled from journals on librarianship. By 1981, each issue contains at least one substantial article, frequently upon a subject in the sphere of music bibliography. *Cum Notis Variorum* is issued 10 times each year, but lately the acquisitions lists have appeared as supplements less frequently.

758. Deutsche Musikbibliographie. Leipzig: F. Hofmeister, 1829– . Jahrgang 1– .
Title varies: 1829–1942, *Hofmeisters musikalisch-literarischer Monatsbericht.*
Lists German, Swiss, and Austrian publications of music and music literature. Alphabetical by author, giving date and place of publication, pagination, and price. A monthly publication useful chiefly for its listings of music. Indexed by publisher. Entries are cumulated in Hofmeister's *Jahresverzeichnis . . .* (no. 767)

759. Deutsche Staatsbibliothek (Berlin). Neuerwerbungen ausländischer Musikliteratur. Berlin: Deutsche Staatsbibliothek, 1956– . v. 1– (Bibliographische Mitteilungen, Nr. 12, 1954–55; Nr. 16, 1956–57; Nr. 19, 1958–60)
Classified lists of books on music and foreign publications acquired by the Deutsche Staatsbibliothek (East Berlin). Issued at irregular intervals as part of the library's series of *Bibliographische Mitteilungen.* The three volumes appeared in 1956, 1958, and 1962 respectively.

760. Ethnomusicology. Journal of the Society for ethnomusicology. Middletown, Ct.: Wesleyan Univ. Press, 1953– . Vol. 1– .
Title varies: 1953–57, *Ethno-Musicology Newsletter.*
Imprint varies: after Jan. 1972, "Published by the Society for Ethnomusicology, Inc."
Each issue contains a section of "current bibliography," listing books, dissertations, films, exchange publications, and and periodical articles related to the field. After January, 1967 the lists include "discography," and were compiled by Joseph C. Hickerson *et al..* Organized by geographical areas and occasional topics, e.g., "dance." The journal also publishes from time to time special bibliographies devoted to the work of leading ethnomusicologists.

761. Fontes Artis Musicae. Review of the International Association of Music Libraries. Paris: International Association of Music Libraries, 1954 – . V. 1– .
Until 1976, each issue contained a "Liste internationale selective" of music publications classified by country; music literature appears under the sub-heading "Ouvrages sur la musique et ouvrages didactiques."

Thereafter several times each year a bibliography titled "Publications à caractère bibliographique" appears; this is a classified list.

762. Hofmeisters Handbuch der Musikliteratur. Leipzig: F. Hofmeister, 1844 – . Bd. 1– .

Cumulation of the *Jahresverzeichnis der deutschen Musikalien und Musikschriften (no. 767)*.

Preceded by a similar work compiled by C. F. Whistling and published by Anton Meysel, Leipzig, 1817, listing music and music literature through 1815, with 10 supplements (1 published by Meysel, 2–8 by Hofmeister, 9–10 by Whistling) to 1827. This initial volume, with its 10 supplements, has been reprinted by Garland in 1975 with an excellent introduction by Neil Ratliff explicating the history and relationships of these important bibliographies. There was an earlier 2 v. reprint by Vienna House, New York, 1972, under the title *Handbuch der musikalischen Litteratur*.

Title varies: Vols. 1–3 (to 1844), C. F. Whistling's *Handbuch der musikalischen Literatur*. Vols. 4–6 (1844–67), *Handbuch der musikalischen Literatur*. Vols. 4–18 (1844–1933), also called *Ergänzungsband 1–15*.

There is also an Olms reprint (1975, 1,298 p.) of the first three *Ergänzungsbanden* (originally published 1828–39) of the Whistling *Handbuch* up to 1838.

Publication interrupted in Vol. 19 (1943) covering the years 1934–40, through the letter "L" in the alphabet.

The Handbuch is of greatest importance for its music (score) listings, but each volume contains an *Anhang* devoted to books and writings on music. The long life of the series, plus the leading position occupied by German music publishing houses during the period covered, make it one of the major reference tools.

For a detailed description of the organization of this complex trade bibliography, see "*A survey of the music catalogues of Whistling and Hofmeister,*" by Rudolf Elvers and Cecil Hopkinson, in *Fontes artis musicae*, 19 (1972), p. 1–7.

The entry is also cited under "Bibliographies of music", by virtue of its music listings.

Review of the Ratliffe edition of the Whistling *Handbuch* by François Lesure in *Fontes artis musicae, 24 (1977), p. 102.*

763. Imago Musicae; International yearbook of musical iconography. Official organ of the International repertory of musical iconography. Edited by Tillman Seebass, assisted by Tilden Russell. Basel, etc. :Bärenreiter; Durham, North Carolina: Duke University Press, 1985– . v. I– .

Includes articles on specific artistic works and collections of works, on cultural life, especially as concerned with music and the visual arts, catalogs and inventories of collections (real and synthetic), of art works which incorporate musical images; and a bibliography of writings on musical iconography. "Bibliografia" in v. I covers 1975–81; in v. 2 covers 1981–83.

764. Jahrbuch der Musikbibliothek Peters. Leipzig: C. F. Peters, 1895–1941. V. 1–47.

Most issues contain a section entitled "Verzeichnis der in allen Kulturländern erschienenen Bücher und Schriften über Musik," edited at various times by Rudolf Schwartz, Emil Vogel, Eugen Schmitz, and Kurt Taut. Does not include periodical literature. This section, expanded to include periodical articles, has been continued as the *Bibliographie des Musikschrifttums,* published separately (no. 753)

765. Jahrbuch für Liturgik und Hymnologie. Kassel: Johannes Stauda-Verlag, 1955– . Bd. 1– .

Each volume contains an extensive "Literaturbericht," classified, frequently annotated, and covering all aspects of liturgics and hymnology.

766. Jahrbuch fur Volksliedforschung. Im Auftrag des Deutschen Volksliedarchivs. Berlin & Leipzig: Walter De Gruyter, 1928– . Erster Jahrgang- .

Editors vary. The yearbook ceased publication between 1951 and 1964.

From 1965 to date it has carried an extensive section devoted to reviews ("Besprechungen") covering the important literature in the field of folk song research.

767. Jahresverzeichnis der Deutschen Musikalien und Musikschriften. Leipzig, F. Hofmeister, 1852– . Jahrgang 1– .

An annual listing which cumulates the material in the *Deutsche Musikbibliographie* (no. 758) and is, in turn, cumulated in *Hofmeisters Handbuch der Musikliteratur* (no. 762).

Title varies: Vols. 1–77 (1852–1928), *Verzeichnis der im Jahre ... erschienen Musikalien.* Vols. 78–91 (1929–42), *Hofmeisters Jahresverzeichnis.*

768. Journal of Music Theory. New Haven: Yale School of Music, 1957– . V. 1– .

Each issue contains a "Bibliography of current periodical literature" covering articles related to music theory.

769. Journal of the International Folk Music Council. Published with the assistance of the International Music Council under the auspices of UNESCO, 1949–68 . V. 1–19.

Superseded by the council's *Yearbook,* 1969– . Urbana, Univ. of Illinois Press.

Each volume of this yearly publication contains a section 'Publications received," which gives a brief, authoritative survey of a wide range of publications in the field, including periodicals, recordings, and important articles.

770. Literature, Music, Fine Arts: a review of German-language reseach contributions on literature, music, and fine arts. With bibliographies. Tubingen, 1968– . Vol. 1– . (German studies, Section 3)

Appears twice a year. A journal devoted to reviews and listings of cultural studies in the German language. All titles and reviews are given in English. The music section provides a useful tool for acquisition purposes.

Some 15 to 20 titles are selected for review, followed by a listing of 75 to 100 other new titles. Information includes prices.

771. Music Article Guide. A comprehensive quarterly reference guide to significant signed feature articles in American music periodicals. Philadelphia: Music Article Guide, 1966– . V. 1– .

Until 1972 published a separate *Annotated guide to periodical literature on church music.*

Indexes (as of 1970) about 150 music periodicals, including many of local or highly specialized interest. Entries are grouped by subject and numbered consecutively within each issue. Indexed by title and author. Brief annotations. Nearly every issue until 1970 contains a "Dictionary of American music periodicals" listing the journals by title with their addresses.

The *Guide* changed in format after the first volume, from a small loose-leafed volume to full-page typescript.

Published quarterly in 10 categories, one of which is "Musicology."

Review by Bennet Ludden in *Notes,* 24 (1967), p. 719–20, and anon. in *ALA Booklist,* 65 (1969), p. 1,239–41.

772. The Music Index; the key to current music periodical literature. Detroit: Information Service, Inc., Jan. 1949– . V. 1, no. 1– .

Issued monthly with annual cumulations. Beginning with 1979, the annual cumulations are doubled up so that 1979–80 (vol 31–32) appears together in a larger format. The most recent monthly issue is for April of 1987 as this entry is written (vol. 33, no. 4).

The founding editor was Florence Kretschmar. Currently the editors are Esther Dombrow, Elain Gorzelski, Sonja Hempseed, and Nadia A. Stratelak.

Currently indexes more than 500 periodicals by subject and author. Published in 12 monthly numbers, with an annual cumulation. Reviews are indexed under "Book reviews."

Review of 1954 annual cumulation by Richard Appel in *Notes,* 14 (1957), p. 364–65; of the 1955 and 1956 cumulations by James B. Coover in *Notes,* 16 (1958), p. 45–46. Review by Richard Schaal in *Die Musikforschung,* 10 (1957), p. 442–43 and anon. in *ALA Booklist,* 65 (1969), p. 123–24.

773. Music Library Association Notes, a magazine devoted to music and its literature. The Music Library Association, 1948– . (2nd ser.) 1– .

Subsequently *Notes*; the quarterly journal of the Music Library Association.

Notes "Book reviews," a department compiled and edited by a variety of editors and supplemented by a list of current publications on music, is the most comprehensive listing of current music literature available. Since December 1950, the list has been international in scope; classified by language. "Music received" edited by Ruth Watanabe is one of the most extensive and most current lists of currently available scores.

774. Music Teachers National Association. Committee on Literature about Music. "Report." In its Proceedings (annual), 1906– . 1906– .

Classified lists of books on music in English, giving author, title, publisher, pagination, and price. Includes some translations, new editions, and reprints. Excellent listings of material in English; carefully selected, some annotations. Listed by authors and subjects.

775. Musica Disciplina. A yearbook of the history of music. American Institute of Musicology, 1946– . V. 1– .
Title varies: Vol. 1, *Journal of Renaissance and Baroque music.*
Most of the volumes contain a bibliography of books, periodical articles, and editions related to early music, doctoral dissertations included; compiled since 1958 by Wolfgang Schmieder.

776. Musica/Realtà. Rivista quadrimestale. Milano: Edizioni Unicopli, 1979– . V. 1.
There is an annual "Supplemento libri: Libri d'interesse musicale stampati in Italia . . ." with brief reviews arrayed in categories ("Analisi musicale," "Cataloghi," "Musica antica," "Musica del '900," etc). Reviews are prepared by musicologists associated with the *Dipartimento di Musica e Spettacolo dell'Università di Bologna,* principal among them Professor Maria Baroni and Laura Callegari. A list of books issued but not reviewed is appended to each category.

777. "Musical Literature." In *The British catalogue of music. London: Council of the British National Bibliography, 1957– .*
An annual listing, broadly classified, of all books about music published in Great Britain. "Musical literature" appears first in the classified section. Scores, however, occupy the greater part of the volumes. Indexed by author and title.

778. The Musical Quarterly. New York: G. Schirmer, 1915– . V. 1– .
The "Quarterly Book-List" in each issue is a selection of books of musicological interest in all languages. Less comprehensive than the current listings in *Notes* (no. 773, above). Edited successively by Carroll C. Wade, Fred Blum, Frank Trafficante, Jon Newsom, Carolyn Bryant.

779. Musik-Information; bibliographische Titelübersicht. Jahrg. 1– , 1971– . Berlin: Leitstelle für Information und Dokumentation "Musik" an der Deutschen Hochschule Für Musik "Hanns Eisler".
An introductory number called Jahrg. O, Heft A, was issued in 1970.
A monthly publication covering "important international titles in the sphere of musicology in books and journals." Subject and author indexes.

780. Periodica musica. Vol. 1, no. 1 (spring 1983)- Vancouver, B.C.: Centre international de recherche sur la presse musicale; Department of Music of the University of British Columbia, 1983– .
An annual Newsletter of the Répertoire international de la presse musicale du XIXe siècle, of the Centres internationaux de recherche sur la presse musicale. Covers research and publications relating to the music periodical publications of the 19th century.
The Répertoire international de la presse musicale du XIXe siècle with headquarters in Vancouver, Canada and Parma, Italy has as its goal the provision of access to the enormous periodical literature about music published in the 19th century.

781. Svensk Tidskrift för Musikforskning. Stockholm, 1919– . V. 1– .
Since 1927 the *Tidskrift* has maintained an annual listing of "Svensk

musikhistorisk bibliografi," compiled since 1946 by Åke Davidsson. Broadly classified. Indexes Swedish periodicals.

INDEXES OF MUSIC PERIODICALS AND TO PERIODICAL LITERATURE ABOUT MUSIC

782. Aarhus. Denmark. Statsbiblioteket. Indeks til danske periodiske musik-publicationer 1795–1841: kumulevet og annoteret indeks til *Apollo, Norden Apollo, Nye Apollo, Odeon, Musikalsk Theatre Journal* og *Vaudeville Journal.* . . . by Joergen Poul Erichsen. Aarhus: Statsbiblioteketforlaget, 1975. 113 p.
Bibliography p. 129–132.

783. Anderson, Gillian B. "Unpublished periodical indexes at the Library of Congress and elsewhere in the United States of America" in *Fontes artis musicae,* 31 (1984), p. 54–60.
Covering the card indexes at the Library of Congress, the W.P.A. index now at Northwestern University, and the Boston Public Library. Lists periodicals and periods of publication indexed. Cites indexes at Washington University in St. Lousi, Howard University in Washington, D.C., and at the Sibley Music Library in Rochester, N.Y.

784. Anderson, Gillian B. Music in New York during the American Revolution: An inventory of musical references in Rivington's New York gazette. With the editorial assistance of Neil Ratliff. Boston: Music Library Association, 1987. 135 p. (MLA index and bibliography series, 24)

785. "Articles Concerning Music in Non-musical Journals 1949–64." In *Current Musicology* (Spring, 1965), p. 121–27; (Fall, 1965), p. 221–26.
The first installment stresses articles on historical subjects; the second articles under various systematic headings: acoustics, philosophy and aesthetics, music in literature, psychology, sociology, etc.

786. Artículos sobre música en revistas espaünolas de humanidades recopilados por Flora Arroyo . . . [et al.] ; editor-coordinador, Jacinto Torres. Madrid: Instituto de Bibliografía Musical, 1982– . v. 1– .
A bibliography of articles about music appearing in major intellectual Spanish journals published from the end of the 19th century to 1980. Includes indexes.

787. Arts & Humanities Citation Index. Philadelphia: Institute for Scientific Information, 1976– .
Issued three times each a year, the third being an annual cumulation. Issued in 3 parts: pt. 1, Citation index; pt. 2, Source index/Corporate index; pt. 3, Permuterm index. Includes supplement with title: "Guide & journal lists."
The "Source Index" lists by author articles published during the period of coverage; thge "Citation Index" lists by authoir, composer or artist works referred to in the source articles (whether in footnotes, end notes, or in the body of the article); the 'Permuterm Index" arranges meaning-

ful words in the titles of the source articles to allow access by pairing of such words. There is also a 'Corporate Index" listing source article authors by institution of affiliation.

About 60 music periodicals are regularly indexed, but numerous essays in conference reports and other anthologies are indexed as well.

This complex bibliographic tool provides a kind of access new to musical studies and is available as an on-line file through the Institute for Scientific Information in Philadelphia.

Review and explanation by Michael A. Keller and Carol A. Lawrence in *Notes,* 36 (1980), p. 575–600.

788. Basart, Ann Phillips. Perspectives of new music, an index, 1962–1982. With a foreword by Benjamin Boretz. Berkeley: Fallen Leaf Press, c1984. 127 p. Fallen Leaf reference books in music *Perspectives of new music* —Indexes

789. Belknap, Sara Y. The guide to the performing arts, 1957–68. New York: Scarecrow Press, 1960–72. V. 1–11.

Annual periodical index to the performing arts. Began as a supplement to the compiler's *Guide to the musical arts.* Contains a "general" section and a "television arts" section. References to performing groups and performers as well as general subject headings.

790. "Bibliographie der Aufsätze zur Musik in aussermusikalischen Italienischen Zeitschriften." In *Analecta Musicologica,* Veröffentlichungen der Musikabteilung des Deutschen Historischen Instituts in Rom. Bd. I (1963), p. 90–112. Bd. II (1965), p. 144–228.

A bibliography of writings on music in Italian non-musical journals. Part 1 by Paul Kast. Part 2 by Ernst-Ludwig Berz. The two installments are organized somewhat differently and indexed independently. The first contains 237 entries, the second, 1,074.

791. A Bibliography of Periodical Literature in Musicology. . . . Washington, D.C.: American Council of Learned Societies, 1940–43. Nos. 1–2 (1938–39, 1939–40).

Indexes approximately 240 periodicals, all European languages, musical and nonmusical, from Oct. 1938 through Sept. 1940. Signed abstracts or annotations for most of the articles. Vol. 1 contains a list of graduate theses accepted in American colleges, universities, and conservatories, Oct. 1, 1939-Sept. 1, 1939.

Vol. 1 compiled by D. H. Dougherty. Vol. 2, added compilers: Leonard Ellinwood and Richard S. Hill.

792. Brio. Journal of the United Kingdom Branch of IAML.

"Index of articles published in selected musical periodicals," compiled by Christel Wallbaum. In *Brio,* 1964–72.

A biannual subject index to articles in some 23 English-language music periodicals. The listings cover the periods January to June and July to December for each year.

793. Deutscher Büchereiverband. Arbeitsstelle fur das Buchereiwesen. Zeits-chriftendienst Musik. (ZD Musik). Berlin: Deutscher Buchereiverband, 1966– . 1. Jahrgang– .

From 1977, a bimonthly and until that year, a monthly periodical index of articles from about 50 music periodicals, cheifly German. Approximately 3,000 articles are indexed per year. The editors are Burchard Bulling and Sibylle Schneider. Monthly number 12 is a cumulative volume for the year. Titles are arranged in alphabetical order under subject headings. The listings can also be purchased in card-size format for filing.

794. Fellinger, Imogen. Periodica musicalia (1789–1830); im Auftrag des Staatlichen Instituts für Musikforschung PreuBischer Kulturbesitz. Regensburg: G. Bosse, 1986. 1,259 p. (Studien zur Musikgeschichte des 19. Jahrhunderts, 55)

Index to compositions appearing in periodicals from 1789–1830.

795. "Index to music obituaries in *Notes*.

Formerly titled *"Index to music necrology"*.

An index to deaths of musicians which began with coverage of 1965 in 1966 in *Notes*. From 1965 through 1979, the column indexes a standard list of 16 to 18 journals. Beginning with 1980, the current editor, Kären Nagy, indexes as many sources as possible, becoming somewhat more selective in the inclusion of names. Currently over 65 periodicals and newspapers are scanned for death notices of musicians. In addition, references to music dictionaries and encyclopedias where biographical entries may be found are included.

Previous editors have been Sivart Poladian, Dale L. Hudson, Patricia Mtusky, Janet Rhoads Pinkowitz, Dale L. Good, Barbara Henry, and Patsy Felch Monokoski.

International Inventory of Musical Literature. See Répertoire International de Littérature Musicale no. 808.

796. Jazz Index. Bibliographie unselbständiger Jazzliteratur. Bibliography of jazz literature in periodicals and collections. Compiled by Norbert Ruecker and C. Reggentin-Scheidt. v.1, n.1– May, 1977– . Frankfurt: N. Ruecker, 1977– .

First volume quarterly, subsequently semi-annually.

Indexes about 50 jazz periodicals and anthologies of essays by author and subject. Beginning in 1978 began a blues section. There is an especially useful "list of unconventional literature" at the end of each issue.

Review by Roger Cottrell in *Jazz forum*, 12 (1978), p. 52; by Carl Gregor Herzog zu Mecklenburg in *Jazz podium* 27 (1978), p. 44; and by Harold Rauter in *Jazzforschung*, 9 (1977), p. 183.

797. Journal of Aesthetics and Art Criticism, 1941–1964 ... an index by Peter L. Ciurczak, of articles and book reviews pertaining to music. Emporia: Kansas State Teachers Coll., 1965. *Journal of Aesthetics and Art Criticism*—Indexes

798. Meggett, Joan M. Music periodical literature: an annotated bibliography of indexes and bibliographies. Metuchen: Scarecrow Press, 1978. 116 p.

Covers more than 250 indexes to music periodicals in general works and works devoted to the subject of music. Provides a bibliography of lists of periodicals and a guide to the literature of the history of music periodicals. Index to authors, compilers and editors. Indexes of subjects and titles.

Review by Patricia Felch in *Notes,* 35 (1979), p. 637–38 and by Rita Benton in *Fontes artis musicae,* 25 (1978), p. 417–18.

799. Music and Letters. Index to volumes 1–40, 1920–59. London: Oxford University Press, [1962]. 140 p.

An index compiled largely by Eric Blom before his death in 1959 and completed by Jack A. Westrup. Two major sections. 1: articles (filed by author and subject in one alphabet). 2: reviews (similarly treated). Reviews of music are not indexed. *Music and Letters*—Indexes

800. Music psychology index. V. 2– . (*sic*) Denton, Texas: Institute for Therapeutics Research, 1978– .

Edited by Charles T. Eagle. Successor to *Music therapy index.*

The "international, interdisciplinary index of the influence of music on behavior: references to the literature from the natural and behavioral sciences and the fine and therapeutic arts for the years 1976– ." Like the *Music therapy index,* an author and keyword index to articles from 10 primary source journals and 24 secondary source journals, and 14 secondary source indexes.

Review by Michael A. Keller and Carol A. Lawrence *"Music literature indexes in review: RILM abstracts (on-line) and the Arts and Humanities Citation, Music Therapy, Music Psychology, and Recording Industry Indexes"* in *Notes,* 36 (1980), p. 575–600.

801. Music therapy index. V. 1. Lawrence, Kansas: National Association for Music Therapy, 1976.

Edited by Charles T. Eagle. Succeeded by *Music psychology index.*

"An international, interdisciplinary index to the literature of the psychology, psychopsychology, psychophysics and sociology of music, contains titles of pertinent articles published ... between 1960 and 1975 inclusively." This is an author and keyword index to about 2,100 articles in six periodicals of primary importance and other articles selected from a variety of sources of secondary importance.

Review by Michael A. Keller and Carol A. Lawrence *"Music literature indexes in review: RILM abstracts (on-line) and the Arts and Humanities Citation, Music Therapy, Music Psychology, and Recording Industry Indexes"* in *Notes,* 36 (1980), p. 575–600.

802. The Musical Quarterly. Cumulative Index. 1915 thru 1959 [v. 1–45]. Compiled by Herbert K. Goodkind. New York, Goodkind Indexes, [1960]. 204 p.

Cumulative index supplement, 1960 thru 1962. New York, 1963.

The main volume indexes by author and subject in separate alphabets, the *Supplement* in one alphabet. Indexes book reviews and "Current chronicle" as well as articles. *Musical Quarterly—Indexes*

803. Muzykalnaia bibliografiia russkoi periodicheskoi pechati xix veka. [Bibliography of Russian music periodicals printed in the 19th century]. Sostavila Tamara Livanova [of the] Akademiia nauk SSSR Institut istorii iskusstv. Moskva: Gos. muzykalnoe izdvo, 1960– .

V. 4– published by Sovetskii kompozitor, Moskva.
V 1: 1801–1825.
V.2: 1826–1840.
V.3: 1841–1850.
V.4: 1851–1860, 2 pts.
V.5: 1861–1870, with O. A. Vinogadov.
V.6: 1871–1880.

804. The Organ. Index to The Organ. A complete index to all the articles in *The Organ, 1921–1970, from the first issue to date.* Compiled by Betty Matthews. Bournemouth, K. Mummery, 1970. *The Organ*—Indexes

805. Popular music periodicals index, 1973–1976 by Dean Tudor and others. Metuchen: Scarecrow Press, 1974–77. 4 v.

V. 1 with Nancy Tudor, v. 2 & 3 with Andrew D. Armitage; v. 4 with Linda Biesenthal.

A complement to the author's *Annual index to popular music record reviews.* Provides coverage of about 55 journals (fully indexed) and another 12 journals (partially indexed), primarily published in the U.S., Canada, and Great Britain. Subject and author sections each provide full bibliographic information for citations. Cross references.

806. La Rassegna Musicale. Indice generale delle annate 1928–52 [v. 1–22]. Torino, Roggero & Tortia, [1953]. 174 p.

An index, compiled by Riccardo Allorto, of articles, musical performances reviewed, book reviews, record reviews, and musical subjects. *La Rassegna Musicale*—Indexes

807. Recording industry index. v.1–3. Cherry Hill, N.J.: National Association of Recording Manufacturers, 1977–79.

"A cumulative subject index of trade and consumer publications of interest, published in the United States. The main body consists of a subject index arranged alphabetically."

The 20 sources indexed complement the indexing in the *Music Index, RILM, Music Article Guide, ZD Musik,* and *Popular Music Periodical Index.*

808. Répertoire International de Littérature Musicale International Inventory of Music Literature. RILM abstracts of music literature. New York: International RILM Center, 1967– . v. 1– .

The most recent volume out is v. 16 (1982), part 3; there is no part 4 (the index) yet. There is also no cumulation for v. 11–15 yet.

An international quarterly journal devoted to abstracts of current literature on music. Published under the aegis of the International Musicological Society and the International Association of Music Libraries.

Contents are in a clear, classified arrangement. Abstracts are all given in English. Foreign titles are translated, including those in the Cyrillic alphabet. Each issue contains an author index, and every fourth issue includes a name, title and subject index to the entries for the year.

RILM is available for on-line searching for the years 1971– to the present, about 56,000 abstracts, on the Dialong Information Retrieval Service. For a review of *RILM on-line see* Michael A. Keller and Carol A. Lawrence *"Music literature indexes in review: RILM abstracts (on-line) and the Arts and Humanities Citation Index, Music Therapy, Music Psychology, and Recording Industry Indexes"* in *Notes,* 36 (1980), p. 575–600. See also Naomi Steinberger in "Selected problems in searching the *RILM* database" in *Proceedings of the National Online Meeting, 1981,* p. 455–60.

For a full discussion of the RILM project and its implications, see Barry S. Brook, *"Music literature and modern communication; revolutionary potential of the ACLS/CUNY/RILM project,"* in *College Music Symposium,* 9 (1969), p. 48–59.

Review in the *ALA Booklist,* 65 (1969), p. 1,239–41.

RILM Abstracts of Music Literature. See Répertoire International de Littérature Musicale no. 808.

809. Rivista Musicale Italiana. Indici dei volumi I a XX (1894–1913). Compiled by Luigi Parigi. Torino: Fratelli Bocca, 1917. 256 p.

Indici dei volumi XXI a XXXV (1914–1928). Compiled by A. Salvatori and G. Concina. Torino, 1931. 195 p.

Indici dei volumi XXXVI a LVII (1929–1955). Compiled by Francesco Degrada. Firenze: Leo S. Olschki, 1966. 144 p. (Quaderni della Rivista Italiana di Musicologia a cura della Societa Italiana di Musicologia, 1)

Review of the Degrada index by Ludwig Finscher in *Die Musikforschung,* 21 (1968), p. 365–66. *Rivista Musicale Italiana*—Indexes

810. Royal Musical Association. Index to papers read before the members ... 1874–1944. Leeds, Printed by Whitehead & Miller for the Royal Association, 1948. 56 p.

A subject and an author index to the first 70 volumes of the *Proceedings of the Association.* Compiled by Alfred Lowenberg and Rupert Erlebach.

811. Shirley, Wayne D. *Modern Music* published by the League of Composers, 1924–1945; an analytic index. Edited by William Lichtenwanger and Carolyn Lichtenwanger. N.Y.: AMS Press, 1976. 246 p.

Brief review by Stephen M. Fry in *Notes,* 33 (1976), p. 306–07. *Modern Music*—Index

812. Tilmouth, Michael. "A calendar of references to music in newspapers published in London and the provinces (1660–1719)" in *R.M.A. Research Chronicle,* 1, p. 1–107.

Index published in *R.M.A. Research Chronicle,* 2, p. 1–15.

Crucial introduction, list of titles examined. Organized chronologically. Cites advertisements, lists, notices, availability of music, concerts.

813. Vierteljahrschrift für Musikwissenschaft. Ed. by Friedrich Chrysander & Philipp Spitta. Leipzig, 1885–94. V. 1–10.

Each volume contains a section, "Musikalische Bibliographie," compiled by F. Ascherson, which usually includes a listing of scholarly music books, critical editions, and the contents of current scholarly periodicals in all European languages.

814. Williams, Michael D. *Source: music of the avant garde*; annotated list of contents and cumulative indices. Ann Arbor: Music Library Association, 1978. 52 p. (MLA index and bibliography series, 19) *Source; music of the avant garde*—Indexes

815. Wolff, Arthur S. Speculum: an index of musically related articles and book reviews. 2nd ed. Philadelphia: Music Library Association, 1981. 64 p. (MLA index and bibliography series, 9)

First edition published 1970, 31 p. Originally published as *Speculum: a journal of mediaeval studies, 1926–1962 . . . a checklist of articles and book reviews pertaining to music* in Denton, Texas by North Texas State University in 1965. *Speculum*—Indexes

816. Zeitschrift der Internationalen Musikgesellschaft. Leipzig, 1899/1900–13/14. V. 1–15.

Most issues contain departments under the headings, "Kritische Bücherschau" and "Zeitschriftenschau." The latter indexes approximately 84 periodicals, chiefly musical, in many languages. Vols. 1–11 by author only. Vols. 12–15 by subject with "see' references from the author.

817. Zeitschrift für Müsikwissenschaft. Leipzig, 1918–35. V. 1–17.

Indexes once a year the periodical literature on music in some 200 journals, in many languages. 1914–18 covered retrospectively in the 1918 index, thus articulating with no. 816 above.

LISTS OF MUSIC PERIODICALS

One of the most comprehensive lists of music periodicals is to be found in the article "Zeitschriften" compiled by Imogen Fellinger for *MGG* (see no. 818). Dr. Fellinger's bibliography of 19th-century music periodicals (no. 836) gives virtually complete coverage for the century under her consideration. Even more up to date and valuable is the article "Periodicals," in *The New Grove* (no. 835). The best chronological survey of the early music periodicals is offered by Wilhelm Freystätter (no. 838) but this has been supplemented and expanded in certain respects by the historical study by Eckart Rohlfs (no.851).

Musicians should also be aware of the resources of a number of general reference works devoted to periodicals, such as Ulrich's *International periodicals directory and the Union List of serials.*

818. **"Zeitschriften."** Imogen Fellinger, comp. In *Die Musik in Geschichte und Gegenwart,* Band 14 (1968), col. 1041–1188.

One of the most comprehensive listings of music periodicals available. Organized by country. Extensive bibliographies of literature on music periodicals.

819. **"Europäische Musikzeitschriften 1945–48."** In *Jahrbuch der Musikwelt.* Bayreuth: J. Steeger, 1949–50. p. 111–23.

A listing useful chiefly as an indication of the periodicals current during the period after World War II. Organized by country. Information brief and inconsistent, with German periodicals given most complete coverage; Russian, Czech, and others very incomplete.

820. **"Periodicals Indexed."** In *The music index annual cumulation.* Detroit: Information Service, 1949– .

Regularly indexes about 500 current periodicals. Addresses and subscription prices given. In its first year (1949) the *Index* treated only 81 titles. Since that time there has been a constant increase in the number of periodicals covered to c. 500.

821. **"Zeitschriften."** In *Riemann Musiklexikon.* 12th ed. Band 3: *Sachteil,* p. 1073–78.

Historical introduction followed by a selective list, organized by country.

822. **Basart, Ann P.** "Editorial practice and publishing opportunities in serious English-language music journals; a survey" in *Cum notis variorum,* no. 79 (January-February 1984), p. 9–51.

An extensive survey with charts and tables. Annotated bibliography of 81 serials participating in the survey.

823. **Basart, Ann P.** "Serials devoted to individual composers and musicians: a checklist" in *Cum notis variorum,* no. 83 (June 1984), p. 14–22.

824. **Bibliografia muzyczna polskich czasopism niemuzycznych** pod redakcjá Kornela Michalowskiego. Krakow: Polskie Wydawn. Muzyczne, 1962–1979. v. 1–5.

Contents: t. 1. *Muzyka w polskich czasopismach niemuzycznych w latach 1800–1830* opracowal Stanislaw Papierz; t. 2. *Muzyka w polskich czasopismach literackich i spolecznych, 1831–1863* opracowal Sylwester Dziki; t. 3. *Muzyka w polskich czasopismach literackich i spolecznych, 1864–1900* opracowala Elzbieta Szczawinska; t. 4. *Muzyka w polskich czasopismach literackich i artystycznych, 1901–1918* opracowala Elzbieta Szczawinska; t. 5. *Muzyka w czasopismach polskich, 1919–1939* opracowal Kornel Michalowski.

825. **Blum, Fred.** "East German music journals: a checklist." In *Notes,* 19 (1962), p. 399–410.

100 periodicals listed in alphabetical order (including secondary titles, former titles, and subsequent titles). Gives a critical description of a variety of East German music serials.

826. The British Union Catalogue of music periodicals; compiled by Anthony Hodges and edited by Raymond McGill. London: Library Association Publishing, 1985. 145 p.

"The Library Association in association with The International Association of Music Libraries, Archives and Documentation Centres: United Kingdom."

827. Campbell, Frank C. A critical annotated bibliography of periodicals. New York, American Choral Foundation, 1962. 14 p. (American choral foundation, Memo 33)

Evaluates 44 periodicals that treat choral music and materials, giving pertinent details (addresses, price, emphasis, etc.)

828. Canadian Library Association. Union list of music periodicals in Canadian libraries. Compiled by a committee of the Canadian Library Association. Ottawa, 1964. 32 p.

Committee chairman: Jean Lavander.

Gives data on holdings in music periodicals of 66 Canadian libraries. Brief annotations on the nature and content of each periodical listed.

829. Clough, F. F. and G. J. Cuming. "Phonographic periodicals, a survey of some issued outside the United States." In *Notes,* 15 (1958), p. 537–58.

A critical description of some 30 foreign periodicals devoted to recordings, with comments on record coverage in general periodicals.

830. Coover, James B. "A bibliography of East European music periodicals." In *Fontes artis musicae* (1956) p. 219–26; (1957) p. 97–102; (1958) p. 44–45, 93–99; (1959) p. 27–28; (1960) p. 16–21, 69–70; (1961) p. 75–90; (1962) p. 78–80.

"This bibliography is an attempt at a comprehensive and authoritative listing of all music periodicals which have been and which are being published in the countries of Bulgaria, Czechoslovakia, Estonia, Finland, Hungary, Latvia, Lithuania, Poland, Rumania, the U.S.S.R., and Yugoslavia." [Compiler's introduction]

831. "Directory of American Music Periodicals," in *Music article guide,* vol. 1 – . Philadelphia: Music Article Guide, 1966– .

Nearly every issue of the *Guide* carries a list of periodicals, indexed, with the addresses of editors or publishers given. A useful guide to current American music periodicals.

832. Douglas, John R. "Publications devoted to individual musicians; a checklist," in *Bulletin of bibliography and magazine notes,* 33 (1976), p. 135–39.

List of periodicals published by 52 societies, each devoted to a single musician.

833. Fairley, Lee. "A check-list of recent Latin American music periodicals." In *Notes,* 2 (1945), p. 120–23.

Treats 23 periodicals from the collections of the Library of Congress and the Pan American Union, with brief comments on each. Covers publications between 1940 and 1947.

834. Fellinger, Imogen. "List of union catalogues of (music) periodicals" in *Fontes artis musicae,* 28 (1981), p. 323–27.

A bibliography of 54 lists from 30 countries, arranged by country, of union lists of serials, most of them general with a music section or music entries scattered. Full bibliographic information provided.

835. Fellinger, Imogen. "Periodicals," in *The New Grove Dictionary of Music and Musicians,* edited by Stanley Sadie, v. 14, p. 407–535. London: Macmillan, 1980.

> The present article provides a general account of music periodicals and their history; it is supplemented by a comprehensive list of musical periodicals (not periodic editions of music), arranged by continent and country, with an alphabetical index.

The "general account" is followed by an excellent bibliography which includes brief but essential annotations. Included in the bibliography are citations for indexes to periodicals.

836. Fellinger, Imogen. Verzeichnis der Musikzeitschriften des 19. Jahrhunderts. Regensburg: Gustav Bosse, 1969. 557 p. (Studien zur Musikgeschichte des 19. Jahrhunderts, 10)

Locates and lists chronologically more than 2,300 music periodicals, with a rich supply of bibliographical information. Actual coverage extends through journals established as late as 1918.

P. 10–28: historical survey of 19th-century music periodicals. P. 33–37: a bibliography of literature on periodicals. Five indexes: titles, editors, places of publication, printers and publishers, subjects.

Since the initial publication, a series of supplements have appeared in *Fontes artis musicae*: Nachträge, Folge 1, in vol. 17 (1970), p. 2–8; Nachträge, Folge 2, in vol. 18 (1971), p. 59–62; Nachträge, Folge 3, in vol. 19 (1972), p. 41–44; Nachträge Folge 4, in vol. 20 (1973), p. 108–111; Nachträge Folge 5, vol. 21 (1974), p. 36–38; Nachträge Folge 6, vol. 23 (1976), p. 62–66.

Review by J. A. Westrup in *Music and letters,* 50 (1969), p. 400–03; by Philip Gossett in *Notes,* 26 (1970), p. 740–41; by Willi Reich in *Literature, music, fine arts,* 2 (1969), p. 200.

837. Fredricks, Jessica M. "Music magazines of Britain and the U.S." In *Notes,* 6 (1949), p. 239–63, 457–59; 7 (1950), p. 372–76.

Lists 200 music periodicals arranged alphabetically by title, with a subject and type index. Brief descriptions of character and contents.

838. Freystätter, Wilhelm. Die musikalischen Zeitschriften seit ihrer Entstehung bis zur Gegenwart. Chronologisches Verzeichnis der periodischen Schriften über Musik. Munchen: T. Riedel, 1884. 139 p.

Unaltered reprint of the original edition by Frits A. M. Knuf, Hilversum, 1963.

Based on E. Gregoir's *Recherches historiques concernant les journaux de musique,* Antwerp, 1872.

A chronological listing, from 1722 to 1844, with extensive annotations as to content, editors, contributors, etc. Still valuable as a convenient source of information on early music periodicals.

839. Kallman, Helmut. "A century of musical periodicals in Canada." In *The Canadian music Journal,* 1:1 (1956), p. 37–43, 1:2 (1957) p. 25–35.

The last installment contains a section entitled: *"A checklist of Canadian periodicals in the field of music,"* p. 30–36.

840. Malm, William P. "A bibliography of Japanese magazines and music." In *Ethnomusicology,* 3 (1959), p. 76–80.

Annotated bibliography of 25 Japanese periodicals related to music and the dance. Place, publisher, date of first issue, and price given.

841. Mekkawi, Carol Lawrence. "Music periodicals: popular and classical record reviews and indexes" in *Notes,* 34 (1978), p. 92–107.

Brief reviews of about 40 reviewing and indexing periodicals concerned with recorded music. Especially valuable for the coverage of titles devoted to popular music.

842. Michalowski, Kornel. Bibliografia polskich czasopism muzycznych. Kraków, Polskie Wydawnictwo Muzyczne, 1955– .

A bibliography of Polish music periodicals; classified listings of their contents from 1820 to 1939. 10 vols. to 1964.

843. "Music Periodicals, United States." In *The Music Industry Guide, formerly the Musican's Guide* 7th edition, 1983 , p. 321–350. Chicago: Marquis Professional Publications, 1983.

U.S., Canadian, and international periodicals are listed alphabetically within each country. Phone number, editor's name, frequency of publication, description of coverage/audience, and subscription rate are given for most publications . . .

844. Ongaku kankei chikuji kankobutsu shozai mokuroku. Union list of periodicals in music [henshu Ongaku Toshokan Kyogikai, 1979 -nenban Henshu Iinkai]. 1979-nenban. Tokyo: Do Kyogikai, 1980. 129 p.

This edition supplements the third ed. of 1969. Lists 970 periodicals in 25 Japanese music libraries in 2 sections, one for Japanese language titles and another for Western titles. Japanese and Russian titles are romanized. Conventional entry includes location of libraries and extent of holdings.

845. Ongaku kankei ehikuji kankōbutsu sōgō mokuroku. Union lists of periodicals in music. 3rd ed. Tokyo: Music Library Association of Japan, 1979.

846. Ongaku Toshokan Kyogikai. Ongaku kankei chikuji kankobutsu sogo mokuroku Union list of periodicals in music. 1974-ban. Tokyo: Ongaku Toshokan Kyogikai, Showa 49, 1974. 40 p.

Published in 1972 under title: *Chikuji kankobutsu sogo mokuroku.*

Contents: Wabunhen.—Obunhen. Covers music periodical holdings in 7 Japanese music libraries. 624 titles in 2 sections, one for Japanese titles and another for Western titles.

847. Ongaku Toshokan Kyogikai. Ongaku kankei chikuji kankobutsu sogo mokuroku. Union list of periodicals in music. 1976-ban. Tokyo: Ongaku Toshokan Kyogikai, 1976. 60 p.

Published in 1972 under title: Chikuji kankobutsu sogo mokuroku.

Contents: Wabunhen.—Obunhen. A numbered list of 793 titles in 13 Japanese music libraries. Divided into Japanese and Western language sections.

848. "Periodische Schriften." In *Jahrbuch der Musikbibliothek Peters.* Leipzig: C.F. Peters, 1894–1941. V. 1–47.

A regular section of the annual "Verzeichnis . . . Bücher und Schriften über Musik," listing new periodicals and other serial publications that have been issued during the year. Compiled by a variety of editors.

849. "Revistas Musicales." In *Diccionario de la musica Labor.* Barcelona: Labor, 1954. V. 2, p. 1863–70.

An extensive listing of music periodicals, classified by country, with a short bibliography on musical journalism. *Journalism—Bibliography*

850. Riedel, A. Répertoire des periodiques musicaux belges. Bruxelles: Commission belge de bibliographie, 1954. 48 p. (Bibliographia belgica)

330 items, of which the first 130 are music serials, the remainder are periodicals in the usual sense.

851. Rohlfs, Eckart. Die deutschsprachigen Musikperiodica, 1945–57. Regensberg: G. Bosse, 1961. 108 p. (Forschungsbeiträge zur Musikwissenschraft, 11)

A source book of information about music periodicals, their history, coverage, distribution, and subject emphasis. Not confined to German journals as the title might suggest. The systematic bibliographic *Anhang,* p. 5–64, lists 589 periodicals in 12 categories. Indexed by chronology, place, title.

Review by Fred Blum in *Notes,* 19 (1961), P. 77–78. By Wolfgang Schmieder in *Die Musikforschung,* 21 (1968), p. 105–107.

852. Savig, Norman. A check-list of music serials in 18 libraries of the Rocky Mountain region. Greely, Colorado: Kastle Kiosk, 1970. 45 p. (typescript)

"This list includes music serials in the general sense of the word: periodicals, newspapers, annuals, proceedings, transactions of societies and some monograph series and publishers' series." [Compiler's introduction]

This work supersedes a *Check-list of music serials in nine libraries of the Rocky Mountain region,* compiled by William M. McClellan in 1963.

The present work lists over 800 title entries and 250 cross references.

853. Solow, Linda I. "Index to 'music periodicals' reviewed in *Notes* (1976–1982)" in *Notes,* 39 (1983), p. 585–90.

A title index to music periodicals reviewed in a regular column in

Notes, principally by Charles Lindahl.

854. Svobodová, Marie. "Music journals in Bohemia and Moravia 1796–1970." In *Fontes artis musicae,* 19 (1972), p. 22–41.

259 journals listed alphabetically by title, with a chronological index. Most of the Czech titles are translated into English, or some indication is given of their content. Items are identified by their number in Fellinger's *Verzeichnis* (no. 836) where applicable.

855. Svobodová. Marie and Juraj Potúček. "Music journals in Slovakia, 1871–1970," in *Fontes artis musicae, 21 (1974), p. 32–36.*

A list of 27 titles, with a chronological index. Titles are translated into English and there is a brief description of contents.

856. Thoumin, Jean-Adrien. Bibliographie rétrospective des périodiques français de littérature musicale 1870–1954. Preface de Madame Elizabeth Lebeau. Paris: Éditions documentaires industrielles et techniques, 1957. 179 p.

Alphabetical listing of 594 French music periodicals. Chronological index; indices of persons and places of publications.

857. A union list of music periodicals in the libraries of Northern California, edited by Ann Basart, Garrett Bowles, Richard Colvig, and Harriet Nicewonger for the Northern California Chapter of the Music Library Association, 6th edition, 1979.

Covers periodicals held by 17 libraries.

858. Union List of Periodicals in Music in the libraries of the University of London and some other London libraries. M. A. Baird., comp. London, 1969. 56 p.

Based on the periodical holdings of 23 London libraries, excluding the British Museum.

859. "Verzeichnis der Zeitschriften und Jahrbucher." In *Hofmeisters Jahresverzeichnis,* v. 100. Leipzig: F. Hofmeister, 1953. p. 334–39.

Lists more than 100 German and Austrian periodicals and yearbooks available in 1951. Since 1953, periodicals are listed in a subsection of the "Anhang: Musikschriften."

See also earlier issues of the *Jahresverzeichnis.*

860. Weichlein, William J. A check-list of American music periodicals, 1850–1900. Detroit: Information Coordinators, 1970. 103 p. (Detroit studies in music bibliography, 16)

Review by Dena J. Epstein in *Notes,* 27 (1971), p. 489.

861. Zecca-Laterza, Agostina. Catalogo dei periodici musicali delle biblioteche lombarde. Milano: Biblioteca del Conservatorio Giuseppe Verdi, 1979. 50 p.

A union list of music periodicals held in libraries in Lombardy. Arranged alphabetically by title, including in each entry a list of libraries where copies are held. Periodicals published in Lombardy in a chronological index arranged in alphabetical order by city.

Review by Gisella de Caro in *Associazione italian bibliotechne bolletino,* 19 (1979), p. 234.

862. "Zeitschriften." In Mendel's *Musikalisches Conversations-Lexikon,* v. 11. Berlin: Heimann, 1879. p. 443–462.

An early listing, but still useful for its detailed descriptions of 18th- and 19th-century journals.

SPECIAL AND SUBJECT BIBLIOGRAPHIES

Contemporary Music

863. Basart, Ann Phillips. Serial music, a classified bibliography of writings on twelve-tone and electronic music. Berkeley and Los Angeles: Univ. of California Press, 1961. 151 p. (University of California Bibliographic Guides)

A classified bibliography of 823 items treating the literature of 12-tone music, electronic music, the Viennese school (Schonberg, Berg, and Webern) and 20 other contemporary composers using serial techniques. Author and subject indices.

Review by Dika Newlin in *Notes,* 19 (1961), p. 256–257; by James B. Coover in *Journal of music theory,* 6 (1962), p. 316–317; by Donald Mitchell in *Tempo,* 63 (Winter 1962–63), p. 46–48; and by Josef Rufer in *Die Musikforschung,* 17 (1964), p. 315–16.

864. Betz, Annaliese. Auftragskompositionen im Rundfunk 1946–1975. Frankfurt am Main: Deutsches Rundfunk Archiv, 1977. 210 p.

List of works commissioned, taped, and broadcast by German radio stations. Information provided on performers, dates, and durations.

865. The Boston composers project, a bibliography of contemporary music, [compiled by the] Boston Area Music Libraries; editor: Linda I. Solow, associate editors: Mary Wallace Davidson, Brenda Chasen Goldman, Geraldine E. Ostrove. Cambridge, Mass.: MIT Press, 1983. 775 p.

Lists compositions by art music and jazz composers in the Boston area during the latter half of the 1970s. Arranged by composer. Index to names and titles.

866. Bull, Storm. Index to biographies of contemporary composers. New York: Scarecrow Press, 1964–74. 2 v.

V. 1 indexes 69 sources of biographical information for 5,800 composers (dictionaries, who's whos, publishers' lists, etc.) indicating whether the composer under consideration is mentioned. No page references given. V. 2 indexes 108 reference works for 8,000 composers, one-half of which appeared in v. 1.

867. Cross, Lowell M. A bibliography of electronic music. Toronto: University of Toronto Press, 1967. 126 p.

A bibliography of writings on electronic music. Some 1,562 articles entered.
Review by Otto Luening in *Notes,* 25 (1969), p. 502–503.

868. Deliège, Celestin. "Bibliographie" (of serial and experimental music) in *Revue belge de musicologie,* 13 (1959), p. 132–48.
Broadly classified bibliography of contemporary music with an introduction surveying the literature of the field.

869. Edmunds, John and Gordon Boelzner. Some twentieth-century American composers, a selective bibliography . . . With an introductory essay by Peter Yates. New York: The New York Public Library, 1959–60. 2 v.

This bibliography has been made with the purpose of bringing together in a single body separately published writings by and about a representative group of 20th-century American composers . . . conservative, moderate, dodecaphonic, and experimental. [*Preface*]

Vol. 1 includes bibliographies for 15 composers, vol. 2 for 17 (with an introductory essay by Nicolas Slonimsky). There are two appendices, one a listing of composers cited in at least one of 21 standard reference works and the other for composers not cited but who are under 35 and merit some attention.
Both volumes are reprinted with additions from *The bulletin of the New York Public Library.*

870. Tjepkema, Sandra L. A bibliography of computer music: a reference for composers. Iowa City: University of Iowa Press, 1981. 276 p.
"Intended to be a comprehensive listing of books, article, dissertations and papers relating to the use of computers by composers." There are indexes to subjects, to names not appearing in the alphabetical array of authors' names, and to studios or centers of activity.

871. Warfield, Gerald. Writings on contemporary music notation: an annotated bibliography. Ann Arbor: Music Library Association, 1976. 93 p.
A comprehensive bibliography of books and articles on new music published between 1950 and 1975. Selectively includes works published earlier in the century and works referring to new notation, but not entirely devoted to the subject. Brief annotations and complete bibliographic information are included. Arrayed alphabetically by author with a brief subject index.

872. Wenk, Arthur B. Analyses of twentieth-century music, 1940–1970. Ann Arbor: Music Library Association, 1975. 94 p. (MLA index and bibliography series, 13, 14)
Supplement published 1984. 132 p.
"The checklist covers some hundred fifty composers represented in thirty-nine periodicals . . . in addition an attempt has been made to gleen as many analyses as possible from biographies, book-length surveys, doctoral dissertations, and Festschriften."

Dissertations

Doctoral dissertations, along with articles in scholarly periodicals, represent the growing edge of research activity in any field. We are currently well-supplied with bibliographies of doctoral studies in music for the United States (see no.875), for Germany (no.s 873, 874, 896 & 897), for France (see no. 882) and for Great Britain (see no. 895), but studies produced in other countries are less easy to locate. Included here are only those reference tools concerned exclusively with studies in music. There are a number of comprehensive national bibliographies of dissertations from which music titles can be extracted. For these, the user should consult Sheehy's *Guide to reference books,* 10th edition (see no. 3203) and Keith Mixter's *General bibliography for music research* (see no. 667).

873. "Im Jahre ... angenommene musikwissenschaftliche Dissertationen." In *Die Musikforschung,* v. 1– . 1948– .
A listing, annual or at more frequent intervals, of doctoral dissertations completed in German, Austrian, and Swiss institutions during the current year. Beginning with vol. 18 (1965), a special section is devoted to reviews of selected dissertations.

874. "Verzeichnis der im Berichtsjahr ... bei der Deutschen Bucherei zu Leipzig registrierten musikwissenschaftlichen Dissertationen und Habilitationsschriften." (Compiled by Ortrun Landmann) In *Deutsches Jahrbuch der Musikwissenschaft.* Leipzig: Peters, 1957– .
Continues a bibliography of dissertations originally published in the *Peters Jahrbuch.* Primarily those completed in East German institutions.

875. Adkins, Cecil and Alis Dickinson. Doctoral dissertations in musicology. 7th North American edition / 2nd International edition. The second combined publication of the American-Canadian *Doctoral dissertations in musicology* (7th cumulative edition) and the *International Doctoral Dissertations in Musicology (2nd cumulative edition).* Philadelphia: American Musicological Society; [Basel]: International Musicological Society, 1984. 545 p.
First published in 1951 in photo-offset from typed copy, issued jointly by a Committee of the Music Teachers' National Association and the American Musicological Society.
2nd edition, 1958; 3rd edition, 1961; 4th edition, 1965, all compiled by Helen Hewitt, who also edited supplements that appeared in *JAMS* and in the *American Music Teacher.* 5th edition, 1971 compiled by Cecil Adkins. 6th edition issued as *International index of dissertations and works in progress* compiled by Adkins and Alis Dickinson in 1977.
This edition supplemented by pamphlets covering January 1983 - April 1984 (1984), May 1984 - November 1985 (1986), and December 1985 - November 1986 (1987).
Throughout the first four editions, entries are grouped by historical periods under the institutions where the degree was completed. The 5th and following editions abandon listings under institutions. Organized as the previous editions into broad historical periods and then classified by topic. Covers dissertations until December 1982. Entries provide University Microfilm numbers, *Dissertation Abstracts* reference numbers, and

RILM references.

This edition covers only dissertations, completed and in progress. *Musicological works in progress* included in the 6th edition appears annually in *Acta Musicologica.*

This list is international, covering dissertations from 30 different countries, but only those begun or completed since 1972. Earlier, non-American, dissertations are covered by Schall's *Verzeichnis musikwissenschaftlicher Dissertationen* (see no. 896 & 897) and annual lists in *Die Musikforschung* for German language dissertations. For earlier British dissertations, see the lists in the Royal Musical Association's *Research Chronicle* beginning with no. 3 (1963) *et passim* (see no. 895). French dissertations are covered by Gribenski's *Thèses de doctorat ...* (see no. 882).

876. Approved doctoral dissertations in progress in music education (as of January 1, 1977), compiled by the Council of Research in Music Education, School of Music, University of Illinois. Urbana: Council for Research in Music Education, 1977. 43 p.

877. Bradley, Ian L. A selected bibliography of musical Canadiana. Revised edition. Victoria: University of Victoria, 1978. 177 p.

First published in 1974.

Classified contents: bibliographies, theses, biographies, compositions, education, ethnomusicology, histories, miscellaneous. The listing of theses written at Canadian academic institutions is of particular interest.

878. Comprehensive dissertation index, 1861–1972. Vol. 31 : Communications and the arts. Ann Arbor: Xerox University Microfilms, 1973. 961 p.

Includes a section covering dissertations on music. Dissertations cited in this list, with some few exceptions, can be obtained on microfilm from Xerox University Microfilms on microfilm or on paper. Includes a computer-generated index based on keywords from dissertation titles. Author index.

879. "Dissertations." In *Current musicology,* no. 1– . New York: the Music Department, Columbia University, 1965–

An occasional feature printed in the journal. Offers critical reviews of selected doctoral studies and listings of current dissertations, European as well as American.

880. Dundes, Alan. Folklore theses and dissertations in the United States. Austin: Published for the American Folklore Society by the University of Texas Press, 1976. 610 p.

Cited even though the bulk of the dissertations listed fall outside the discipline of music, because access to some of these titles is difficult.

Chronological list of theses and dissertations, indexes of subjects, authors, and institutions.

881. Gillis, Frank and Alan P. Merriam. Ethnomusicology and folk music: an international bibliography of dissertations and theses. Middletown, Connecticut: Wesleyan University Press, 1966. 148 p.

Cites 873 entries for graduate theses in the field of ethnomusicology, including both master's and doctor's degrees. This bibliography developed from an earlier listing in the journal *Ethnomusicology,* 4 (1960), p. 21–35, with a supplement in the same journal, 6 (1962), p. 191–214.

Review by William Malm in *Notes,* 24 (1968), p. 499–500.

882. Gribenski, Jean. Thèses de doctorat en langue française relatifs à la musique: bibliographie commentée. French language dissertations in music: an annotated bibliography. New York: Pendragon Press, 1979. 270 p. (RILM Retrospectives, 2)

Doctoral dissertations written in French between 1883 and 1976 on music and defended in Belgian, Canadian, French and Swiss universities are included. Arrayed on a variant of the *RILM* classification system. Each entry is extensively annotated in French. Indexes to authors, subject, dates and universities. Addenda.

Reviewed by Geraldine Ostrove in *Notes,* 36, (1979), p. 377–78.

883. Hartley, Kenneth R. Bibliography of theses and dissertations in sacred music. Detroit: Information Coordinators, Inc., 1967. 127 p. (Detroit studies in music bibliography, 9)

884. International Center of Musicological Works in Progress. "Musicological works in progress." Edited by Cecil Adkins. In *Acta Musicologia,* 44 (1972), p. 146–69.

A listing of active research projects, including not only dissertations but post-doctoral studies as well. The entries are classified within major chronological divisions. In many cases the scholar's address is given to encourage communication. Subject index.

For a description of the scope of this project and the techniques employed, see Cecil Adkins's report in *Acta Musicologica,* 43 (1971), p. 103–106.

885. International directory of aproved music education dissertations in progress. Richard J. Colwell, editor, and John Chenault, assistant. Urbana: Council for Research in Music Education, 1986.

Previously published in 1984 & 1985. Successor to *Approved doctoral dissertations in progress in music education.*

A classified directory with entries which give name and address of candidates, institution at which enrolled and title of dissertation. Indexes to names and to institutions.

886. De Lerma, Dominique-René. A selective list of masters' theses in musicology. Compiled for the American Musicological Society. Bloomington, Indiana: Denia Press, 1970. 42 p.

Entries for 257 titles submitted by 36 institutions. Indexes of names, topics and participating institutions. Entries give information as to availability by photoreproduction or interlibrary loan.

887. Meadows, Eddie S. Theses and dissertations on Black American music. Beverly Hills: Theodore Front Musical Literature, 1980. 19 p.

A classified and briefly annotated bibliography of 119 doctoral, 120 master's and a few other dissertations. Lacks references to *Dissertations abstracts.* No author or subject indexes.

888. Melange of dissertations in music. Ann Arbor: University Microfilms International, 1977? 22 p.

A listing of doctoral dissertations, written in 1974, 1975, 1976 and some from 1977. Includes a title collection of master's theses abstracted in the quarterly publication "Master's abstracts" volumes I-XIV, 1962–1976. A list of American doctoral dissertations written 1974–77.

889. Music, a catalog of selected doctoral dissertation research. Ann Arbor: University Microfilms International, 1984. 38 p.

Contains citations to 1,335 doctoral dissertations and 233 master's theses completed between 1978 and 1983.

890. Music Educators' National Conference. Bibliography of research studies in music education, 1932–48. Compiled by William S. Larson. Chicago: Music Educators National Conference, 1949. 119 p.

An earlier edition, compiled by Arnold M. Small, appeared in 1944, State Univ. of Iowa Press.

This, and the following five entries, provide continuing documentation for research in music education from 1932 to 1971. From 1957 on the bibliographies have appeared in issues of the *Journal of research in music education.*

891. Music Educators' National Conference. Bibliography of research studies in music education, 1949–1956. Compiled by William S. Larson. In *Journal of research in music education,* 5:2 (1957). 225 p.

892. Music Educators' National Conference. Doctoral dissertations in music and music education, 1963–1967. Compiled by Roderick D. Gordon. In *Journal of research in music education,* 16 (Summer 1968), p. 87–218.

893. Music Educators' National Conference. Doctoral dissertations in music and music education, 1968–1971. Compiled by Roderick D. Gordon. In *Journal of research in music education,* 20 (1972), p. 2–185.

In the above MENC bibliographies, coverage includes dissertations submitted for the degree Doctor of Philosophy, Doctor of Education, Doctor of Musical Arts, Doctor of Music Education, and Doctor of Music. No clear distinction is made between research studies in education and those engaging other research areas.

894. Music Educators' National Conference. Doctoral dissertations in music education, 1957–1963. Compiled by Roderick D. Gordon. In *Journal of research in music education,* 12 (Spring 1964). 112 p.

895. "Register of theses on music in Britain and Ireland" by Nick Sandon in *R.M.A. Research Chronicle,* 15 (1979), p. 38–116.

"Supplements" in v. 16 (p. 110–34), v. 17 (p.117–33), v. 18 edited by Ian Bartlett (p. 85–118), v. 19 including an index (p.59–90). Previous versions

had appeared under the editorship of Paul Doe and Michael Downey.
2,155 Entries arranged by period, then author.

896. Schaal, Richard. Verzeichnis deutschsprachiger musikwissenschaftlicher Dissertationen, 1861–1960. Kassel: Bärenreiter, 1963. 167 p.
(Musikwissenschaftliche Arbeiten, hrsg. von der Gesellschaft für Musikforschung, 19)
An alphabetical listing, by author, of 2,819 music dissertations in the
German language. Publications data given for works in print. Subject
index.
Review by Erich Schenk in *Die Musikforschung*, 17 (1964), p. 421–23,
supplying numerous additional entries.

897. Schaal, Richard. Verzeichnis deutschsprachiger musikwissenschaftlicher Dissertationen, 1961–1970, mit Ergänzungen zum Verzeichnis
1861–1960. Kassel: Bärenreiter, 1974. 91 p.
A supplement of 1,271 dissertations, most written between 1961 and
1970, listed alphabetically by author. Publication dates indicated for
works subsequently published. Subject index.

898. Texas Music Educators Association. A bibliography of master's theses
and doctoral dissertations in music completed at Texas colleges and
universities, 1919–1972. Rev. ed. Houston: Texas Music Educators Association, 1974. 152 p.
First ed. published in 1964 covered only until 1962.
Listings chronological by institution. Research studies in music education completed in 14 Texas colleges or universities. Subject and author
indexes.

899. University Microfilms International. Music: a dissertation bibliography
[edited by Kay Long]. Ann Arbor: University Microfilms, 1979. 36 p.
A list of master's theses and doctoral dissertations written between
1974 and 1978.

Ethnomusicology

Vigorous growth in the field of ethnomusicology in recent years has
prompted numerous bibliographical studies. No attempt has been made
to list the many useful bibliographies appended to monographs, dissertations, and periodical articles in this field. Attention has been called to the
listings of current literature and recordings in *Ethnomusicology, journal
of the Society for Ethnomusicology* (see no. 759). One of the most comprehensive bibliographies in this area is found in Jaap Kunst's *Ethnomusicology, a study of its nature, its problems ...* (no. 918).
Additional references will be found under "Bibliographies of Music:
Folk song and ballad," and under "Discographies: Ethnic and folk music."

**900. Aning, B. A. An annotated bibliography of music and dance in English-
speaking Afric.** Legon: Institute of African Studies, University of Ghana,

1967. 47 p.
A bibliography of 132 items, including both books and periodical articles. Index of authors. Organized regionally.
Review by Alan P. Merriam in *Ethnomusicology,* 16 (1972), p. 544–545.

Annual Bibliography of European Ethnomusicology See Musikethnologische Jahresbibliographie Europas. (no. 931).

901.   Baumann, Max Peter. Bibliographie zur ethnomusikologischen Literatur der Schweiz: mit einem Beitrag zu Geschichte, Gegenstand und Problemen der Volksliedforschung. Winterthur: Amadeus, 1981. 312 p.
Includes bibliographical references and indexes.

902.   Bose, Fritz. Musikalische Völkerkunde. Freiburg: Atlantis-Verlag, 1953. 197 p. (Atlantis-Musikbücherei)
"Bibliographie," p. 144–63. 393 items.

903.   Cavanagh, Beverly. "Annotated bibliography : Eskimo music," in *Ethnomusicology,* 16 (1972), p. 479–87.
Cites works on Eskimos in Alaska, Greenland, and the Canadian Arctic.

904.   Christensen, Nerthus. Hornbostel opera omnia Bibliographies Hornbostel opera omnia herausgegeben von Klaus P. Wachsmann, Dieter Christensen, Hans-Peter Reinecke. The Hague: Nijhoff, 1976. 114 p.
An unnumbered volume in the *Hornbostel Opera Omnia.*
Part I: Chronological bibliography of Erich Moritz von Hornbostel's published writings, p. 3–20.
Part II: Comprehensive bibliography of references, p. 23–114.
This work is included as the bibliography of references provides access to many titles encountered in the ethnomusicological guides commonly used in the U.S. This volume thus forms a bibliography of ethnomusicological writings to about 1935. In English and German.

905.   Colvig, Richard. "Black music." In *Choice,* a publication of the Association of College and Research Libraries, 6 (Nov. 1969), p. 1169–79.
"A representative selection of English language monographs dealing with the contribution made to music by members of the Negro race on both sides of the Atlantic." 71 items, classified and mostly annotated.
Also published separately by the Oakland Public Library, 1969, 18 p.

906.   "Current Bibliography and Discography." In *Ethnomusicology,* Journal of the Society for Ethnomusicology. Edited by Joseph C. Hickerson, Neil V. Rosenberg, and Frank Gillis.
Editors vary, but the above three names have been active since May 1970.
The best current listing of literature and phonorecords in the field of ethnomusicology. This excellent current listing has never been cumulated, classified and indexed.

907. Densmore, Frances. "The study of Indian music in the nineteenth century." In *American Anthropologist,* 29 (1927), p. 77–86.
A survey of early studies in the field of American Indian music; generally valuable, although it contains some errors.

908. Emsheimer, Ernst. "Musikethnographische Bibliographie der nicht-slavischen Völker in Russland." In *Acta M,* 15 (1943), p. 34–63.
A bibliography of 433 items concerned with the music of the non-Slavic peoples of Russia. Classified according to ethnic groups. German translations for Slavic titles. Some editions of folk music cited, but chiefly concerned with periodical literature and monographs. Full bibiographical information.

909. Gaskin, Lionel. A select bibliography of music in Africa; compiled at the International African Institute by L. J. P. Gaskin under the direction of Prof. K. P. Wachsmann. London: International African Institute, 1965. 83 pgs.
Review by Leonard Vohs in *Die Musikforschung,* 22 (1969), p. 390–391. Review by Douglas Varley and Alan Taylor, in *Ethnomusicology,* 11 (1967), p. 125–28.

910. Gillis, Frank and Alan P. Merriam. Ethnomusicology and folk music: an international bibliography of dissertations and theses. Middletown, CT: Published for the Society for Ethnomusicology by the Wesleyan University Press,1966. 148 p.

911. Guèdon, Marie-Francoise. "Canadian Indian ethnomusicology: selected bibliography and discography." In *Ethnomusicology,* 16 (1972), p. 465–78.
Subdivided by five cultural areas: (1) Eastern woodlands-Great Lakes, (2) Plains, (3) Yukon-Mackenzie basins, (4) Plateau, (5) Northwest coast.

912. Haywood, Charles. A bibliography of North American folklore and folksong. Second rev. ed. New York: Dover Publications [1961]. 2 v.
First published in one volume by Greenberg, New York, 1951.
Vol. 1, p. 1–748: concerned with the non-Indian Americans north of Mexico. Vol. 2, p. 749–1,159: with the American Indians north of Mexico. Subdivisions in Vol. 1 include general bibliography. Vol. 2 is subdivided by cultural areas. Entries for folklore and for folk music are separated under each heading; recordings included. General index. Endpapers are maps of regional and cultural areas.
Review of first edition by Duncan Emrich in *Notes,* 8 (1951), p. 700–701.

913. Henry,Mellinger Edward. A bibliography for the study of American folk songs, with many titles of folk songs (and titles that have to do with folk songs) from other lands. London: Mitre Press [1937]. 142 p.
Studies and collections of music interfiled in one alphabet. The emphasis is on the English-Scottish ballad and its derivatives.

914. Herzog, George. Research in primitive and folk music in the U.S., a survey. Washington, D.C.: American Council of Learned Societies, 1936.

97 p.

Surveys U.S. resources for the study of primitive and folk music as of 1936. Record archives are described and their holdings tabulated; collections of primitive musical instuments listed. Bibliographies given for each of the main sections.

915. Huerta, Jorge A., ed. A bibliography of Chicano and Mexican dance, drama, and music. Oxnard, California: Colegio Quetzalcoatl, 1972. 59 p.

P. 36–59: Music Pre-Columbia, Mexican, Aztlan. Includes references to books, journals, and photograph records (for Mexico only).

916. Kendadamath, G. C. Indian music and dance: a select bibliography. Varanasi: Indian Bibliographic Centre, 1986. 261 p.

917. Krader, Barbara. "Ethnomusicology," in *The New Grove Dictionary of Music and Musicians,* edited by Stanley Sadie, v. 6, p. 275–82. London: Macmillan, 1980.

After a brief historical overview, this article poses the chief problems of the field and addresses some of the approaches taken in addressing them. Classified bibliography of works on the discipline.

918. Kunst, Jaap. Ethnomusicology, a study of its nature, its problems, methods and representative personalities, to which is added a bibliography. 3rd ed. enl. The Hague: Nijhoff, 1959. 303 p.

First published in 1950 under the title *Musicologica.* . . . The 2nd edition, 1955, contains a selective bibliography. 2nd ed. reprinted in 1977 by Scholarly Press. Reprint of the 3rd ed. and its *Supplement* in 1969.

Bibliography of the 3rd edition, p. 79–215, lists 4,552 items, most of them with location symbols referring to libraries in Western Europe. Entries which contain extensive bibliographies within themselves are marked with an asterisk. Portraits of ethnomusicologists.

Supplement to the 3rd edition, 1960, 45 p., adds some 500 items to the bibliography; new record listings through 1958, more portraits.

Review of the 3rd ed. by Bruno Nettl in *Notes,* 16 (1959), p. 560–61; of the *Supplement* by William Lichtenwanger in *Notes,* 19 (1961), p. 79.

919. Kuppuswamy, Gowri and Muthuswamy Hariharan. Indian dance and music literature. New Delhi: Biblia Impex Private Ltd., 1981. 156 p.

920. Laade, Wolfgang. Gegenwartsfragen der Musik in Afrika und Asien. Eine grundlegende Bibliographie. Baden-Baden: V. Koerner, 1970. 120 p. (Sammlung musikwissenschaftlicher Abhandlungen, 51.)

A regionally organized bibliography of 874 items taken chiefly from current periodical literature. this work also serves a a useful directory of institutions, societies, broadcasting stations involved in the study of Asian-African music.

Lawless, Ray McKinley. Folksingers and folksongs in America . . . See no. 264.

921. Laws, George M. Native American balladry; a descriptive study and a bibliographical syllabus. Philadelphia: American Folklore Society, 1950. 276 p. (Publications of the American Folklore Society. Bibliographical Series, 1)

922. League of Nations. International Institute of Intellectual Cooperation. Folklore musical; répertoire international des collections et centres de documentation avec notices sur l'état actuel des recherches dans les différents pays et références bibliographiques. Paris: Département d'Art, d'Archéologie et d'Ethnologie, Institut International de Coopération Intellectuelle, [1939]. 332 p.

Organization similar to the following item. Special section devoted to the international phonorecord archive in Berlin, Paris, and Vienna. P. 307–22: supplement of additions and corrections to the 1934 volume, below.

923. League of Nations. International Institute of Intellectual Cooperation. Musique et chanson populaires. Paris: Institut International de Coopération Intellectuelle, 1934. 257 p.

A reference book intended to establish an international listing of museums, archives, libraries, and other institutions, public and private, concerned with research or collection in the field of popular music, with descriptions of their facilities. Contributions by leading specialists arranged alphabetically by country. Most of the essays contain bibliographies of studies and editions and a list of names and addresses of specialists.

924. De Lerma, Dominique-Réne and Michael Phillips. "Entries of ethnomusicology interest in *MGG*: a preliminary listing." In *Ethnomusicology,* 13 (1969), p. 129–38.

Attention is directed to eight areas in the German reference work that contain articles of interest to ethnomusicologists: The Americas (7 entries), Africa (13), Asia and Oceania (23), Europe (33), Dance (35), Instruments (47), Miscellaneous (24), and biographies and index of contributors (134). *Die Musik in Geschichte und Gegenwart*—Ethnomusicology- -Indexes

925. Liebermann, Fredric. Chinese music, an annotated bibliography. 2nd ed., revised and enlarged. New York: Garland, 1979. 257 p.

First edition published by the Society for Asian Music, 1970. 157 p.

"This bibliography attempts exhaustive coverage of publications in Western languages as well as critical annotation." [Author's *Preface*]

A bibliography of 1,483 items arranged alphabetically by author. Index of periodicals, of names, and of topics for selected readings. Includes discographies.

926. Lomax, Alan and Sidney R. Cowell. American folksong and folklore, a regional bibliography. New York: Progressive Education Association, 1942. 59 p.

927. Marks, Paul F. Bibliography of literature concerning Yemenite-Jewish Music. Detroit: Information Coordinators, 1973. 50 p. (Detroit Studies in Music Bibliography, 27)

928. Mattfeld, Julius. The folk music of the Western hemisphere; a list of references in the New York Public Library. New York: New York Public Library, 1925. 74 p.

Reprinted with additions from the Bulletin of the New York Public Library, November and December 1924.

929. McLean, Mervyn. An annotated bibliography of Oceanic music and dance. Wellington, N.Z.: Polynesian Society, 1977. 252 p. (Memoir of the Polynesian Society, 41)

A 74 p. supplement by the same author was issued in 1981.

In a single alphabet, with an index to areas covered by each cited work. There are area codes based on Murdoch's *Outline of world cultures.* No subject or title index. References to books, articles, reviews, record album notes, manuscripts and theses in commonly read western European languages are included. Trivial items, collections of songs with piano accompaniment, publications of or about "acculturated music" omitted.

Supplement adds 500 entries to the earlier 2,200 and brings coverage up to 1980.

930. Merriam, Alan P. "An annotated bibliography of African and African-derived music since 1936." In *Africa,* 21 (1951), p. 319–30.

931. Musikethnologische Jahresbibliographie Europas. Annual bibliography of European ethnomusicology. Hrsg. von Slowakischen Nationalmuseum in Verbindung mit dem Institut für Musikwissenschaft der Slowakischen Akademie der Wissenschaften und dem Institut für deutsche Volkskunde der Deutschen Akademie der Wissenschaften Berlin unter Mitwirkung des International Folk Music Council durch Oskár Elschek, Erich Stockmann und Ivan Macák. Bratislava: Slovenské národné múzeum, 1967–76. 10 v.

Introduction in Czech and English. An annual bibliography of periodical articles, books and other materials on ethnic music in Europe. Bibliographical entries are printed in the original language only.

Review of v. 1 by Rolf W. Brednich in *Jahrbuch für Volksliedforschung,* 15 (1970), p. 182–83, and by Frank J. Gillis in *Ethnomusicology,* 16 (1972), p. 138–39.

932. Nettl, Bruno. Reference materials in ethnomusicology. Second edition, revised, 1967. Detroit: Information Coordinators, 1967. 40 p. (Detroit studies in music bibliography, 1)

First published in 1961.

A narrative and critical discussion of the leading reference works in the field, organized in terms of the structure of the discipline. On p. 37–46 a list of publications is cited, with full bibliographical information.

Review by William Lichtenwanger in *Notes,* 19 (1962), p. 428–30; by Marius Schneider in *Die Musikforschung,* 19 (1964), p. 88–89.

933. Nettl, Bruno. The study of ethnomusicology; 29 issues and concepts. Urbana: University of Illinois Press, 1983. 410 p.

A discussion of issues central to the field of ethnomusicology. Each essay "deals with a concept or an aspect of theory or procedure affecting the field of ethnomusicology as a whole, and not specific to any one world area or culture." Extensive bibliography p. 363–96.

934. Nettl, Bruno. Theory and method in ethnomusicology. New York, The Free Press, 1964. 306 p.

Chapter 2 is a history of the field, focusing on bibliography. Each chapter is followed by a list of publications cited.

Review by David P. McAllester in *MQ,* 51 (1965), p. 425–28.

935. Sandberg, Larry and Dick Weissman. The folk music source book. New York: Knopf, 1976. 260, p.

This book treats North American folk music in both the popular sense and the ethnic sense. There is information on blues as well as on North American indian musics. Styles and genres are discussed, each with a discography. There are biographical entries, an annotated list of song books, and a list of reference works. There is a list of periodicals and a directory of organizations, centers, archives, and festivals.

936. Smith, Donna Ridley. Non-Western music: a selected bibliography of materials in the California State University, Sacramento Library. 3rd ed. Sacramento: Library, California State University, 1982. 45 p.

Second ed. by Sheila J. Johnson, 1973. 40 p.

A bibliography of works about African, Asian and Oceanic musics held in the California State University, Sacramento Library.

937. Song, Bang-Song. An annotated bibliography of Korean music. Providence, R.I.: Brown University, 1971. 250 p. (Asian music publications, ser. A, no. 2.)

A bibliography of 1,319 items. Part I cites writings on Korean music in the Korean language; Part II, writings in foreign languages. Indexes of bibliographical sources and of names and subjects. The annotations are brief but informative.

938. Stein, Evan. The use of computers in folklore and folk music: a preliminary bibliography. Washington, D. C.: Library of Congress, Archive of Folk Song, 1979. 12 p.

939. Thieme, Darius L. African music, a briefly annotated bibliography. Washington, D.C.: Library of Congress, Reference Department, Music Division, 1964. 55 p. (typescript)

"The present work lists sources discussing the music of sub-Saharan Afric. The work is divided into two main sections, the first listing periodicals and serial articles, the second listing books." [*Preface*]

A bibliography of 597 items, with an author and linguistic area index.

940. Tsuge, Genichi. Japanese music: an annotated bibliography. New York: Garland Pub., 1986. 161 p. (Garland bibliographies on ethnomusicology, 2)

This bibliography includes publications on Japanese music in Western languages which appeared through 1983. Although its scope is limited primarily to publications dealing with traditional Japanese music, some writings concerning dance, drama, and/or perofrming arts of ritualistic nature are inevitably included, as certain aspects of Japanese music are indeed inseparable from such areas. [*Introduction*]

881 annotated entries in a single alphabet. Subject index in three sections: fields of study; genres of traditinal Japanese music; Japan and the West. Name, and format indexes. Indexing does not reveal the presence of reference works, especially bibliographies.

941. Varley, Douglas H. African native music: an annotated bibliography. 1st ed. reprinted; with additional note. Folkestone: Dawsons, 1970. 116 p.
  Reprint of 1st ed. by the Royal Empire Society, London, 1936.
  "Confined to the Negro and Bantu cultures, roughly south of the Sahara."
  Two sections of general bibliography followed by local bibliographies relating to 30 African countries. Special sections on "African survivals in the New World" and the drum language. List of museums containing collections of African instruments. Author index. Brief but informative annotations.

942. Vetterl, Karel. A select bibliography of European folk music. Published in cooperation with the International Folk Music Council by the Institute for Ethnography and Folklore of the Czechoslovak Academy of Sciences. Prague, 1966. 144 p.
  "The bibliography attempts to list the most useful publications, both books and articles, and especially those of a scholarly nature, that bear on the folk music of particular European countries." [*Introduction*]
  Organized alphabetically by country. Strong on East European entries, particularly Russian.
  Brief review by Rolf Wilh. Brednich in *Jahrbuch für Volksliedforschung,* 14 (1969), p. 175.
  Review by Ann Briegleb in *Ethnomusicology,* 12 (1968), p. 161–62.

943. Waterman, Richard. [*et al.*] "Bibliography of Asiatic musics." In *Notes,* 5:1–8:2 (Dec. 1947-March 1951). 181 p. in all.
  A classified bibliography, published serially, of 3,488 books, monographs, articles, sections of larger works, texts, transcriptions and recordings, arranged geographically and ethnologically. All European languages, including Russian and Romanized Turkish.

Musical Instruments

The literature on musical instruments is to be found in a variety of reference books. The reader in search of further information should look under the following additional headings: "Dictionaries of Musical Instrument Makers and Performers" (no. 281 ff.) and "Catalogs of Musical Instrument Collections" (no. 2525 ff.). Many of the reference tools contain appended bibliographies on the subject.

944. Bakus, Gerald J. The Spanish guitar: a comprehensive reference to the classical and flamenco guitar. Los Angeles: Gothic Press, 1977. 204 p.
Includes bibliography and index.

945. Blades, James. Percussion instruments and their history. New and revised edition. London: Faber, 1975. 509 p.
Bibliographies and indexes.

946. Blades, James and Jeremy Montagu. Early percussion instruments: from the Middle Ages to the Baroque. London: Oxford University Press, 1976. 77 p.
Bibliography.

947. Blaetschacher, Richard. Die Lauten- und Geigenmachwerk des Füssener Landes. Hofheim am Taunus: Friedrich Hofmesiter, 1978. 239 p.
Beautiful plates of instruments, chiefly viols and violins. Bibliography.

948. Boalch, Donald H. Makers of the harpsichord and clavichord, 1440 to 1840. 2nd edition. Oxford: Clarendon Press of Oxford University Press, 1974. 225 p. with 12 p. of plates.
First published in 1956 (169 p.).
Lists over 1,000 makers of early keyboard instruments and describes many of their instruments in tabular form, giving dates, register, composers, histories, and present ownership. Geographical and chronological conspectus of makers. Bibliography. Glossary. Addenda.

949. Chou, Ch'ing-yün. Ch'in shih pu. [History of the Ch'in, Supplement]. [China]: Meng-p'o shih ts'ang pan, cchi wei, [1919]. 5 v.
On double leaves, Oriental style, in case. In Chinese.
collection of quotations from various Chinese texts in which people connected with the ch'in as musicians, ch'in makers, etc. are mentioned. Arranged chronologically by the person's name, beginning with legendary times and continuing into the 10th century, totaling over 100 names. Each person is identified briefly, the quotation is cited, and the source named.
Another two titles are included in this publication. The first is *Ch'in shih hsü [Continuation of the History of the Ch'in]*, a 3 volume work containing the names of anther 400 people associated with the ch'in who lived from the Sung dynasty (beginning in 960 A.D.) to the 19th century. There are appendices devoted to Buddhists and women. The second is *Ch'in shu pieh lu [Bibliography of works on the Ch'in*, a one volume annotated list of 200 books and manuscripts on the ch'in from the Chou (1122 B.C.) to the Ch'ing (1644–1911) dynasties.

950. Coover, James B. Musical instrument collections; catalogues and cognate literature. Detroit: Information Coordinators, 1981. 464 p. (Detroit Studies in Music Bibliography, 47)
An annotated bibliography citing locations of the works cited. Part one concerns musical instrument collections owned by institutions or gathered to an exposition, in order by place. Part 2 concerns collections owned by individuals, in order by name.

Chronological indexes to early inventories and expositions and exhibitions. General index and index to auctioneers, antiquarians and firms. Review by Paula Morgan in *Notes,* 39 (1982), p. 198. Review by Jeremy Montagu in *Eraly music,* 11 (1983), p. 100–02.

951. Crane, Frederick. Extant medieval musical instruments: a provisional catalogue by types. Iowa City: University of Iowa Press, 1972. 105 p.
Bibliography p. 91–105.

952. Evans, Tom and Mary Anne Evans. Guitars: music, history, construction, and players from the Renaissance to rock. New York: Facts On File, [1982?] 479 p.
Previously published by Padington Press, 1977. Published in a French edition by A. Michel, Paris, 1979 as *Le grand livre de la guitare, de la Renaissance au rock. 354 p.*
A source book including biographical information.

953. Fallou, Robert and Norbert Dufourcq. Essai d'une bibliographie de l'histoire de l'orgue en France. Paris: Fischbacher, 1929. 74 p.

954. Graaf, G. A. C. de. Literatuur over het orgel. Literature on the organ, principally in Dutch libraries. Amsterdam: G. A. C. de Graaf; Uitgeverij, F. Knuf, 1957. 71 p. (Bibliotheca organologica, 51)
Lists over 1,250 titles of books, brochures, and reprints concerning the use, the history, and the construction ot organs. Does not include books on organ playing.
Introduction and title page in Dutch, English, German, French, Spanish, and Italian.

955. Handbuch der europäischen Volksmusikinstrumente. Hrsg. von Ernst Emsheimer und Erich Stockmann. Leipzig: Deutscher Verlag für Musik, 1967– .
A series of volumes devoted to the folk instruments of Europe. The work is projected in five series of five or six volumes each. The following volumes have appeared, all in the first series:
Bd. 1: Bálint Sárosi. Die Volksmusikinstrumente Ungarns (1968) 148 p.
Bd. 2, T. 1: Ludvík Kunz. Die Volksmusikinstrumente der Tschechoslowakie. (1974)
Bd. 2, T. 2: Oskar Elschek. Die slowakischen Volksmusikinstrumente. (1983)
v. 4: Brigitte Bachman Geiser. Die Volksmusikinstrumente der Schweiz. (1981) 134 p.
Bd. 5: Zmaga Kumer. Die Volksmusikinstrumente in Slowenien. Lubljana: Slovenska akademija znanosti in umetnosti, Znanstvenoraziskovalni center SAZU, Institut za slovensko narodopisje, 1986. 107 p.

956. Hermann, Judy. "Violin makers: a selective bibliography" in *Cum notis variorum,* no. 96 (October 1985), p. 5–9.
Published in a abbreviated version in *Metrodata, the newsletter of the Los Angeles Metropolitan Cooperative Library System,* November-December, 1984.

An annotated bibliography.

957. Heron-Allen, Edward. De fidiculis bibliographia: being an attempt towards a bibliography of the violin. . . . London: Griffith Farran and C., 1890–94. 2 v.

Reprint by Holland Press, 1961.

Classified bibliography of literature on the violin in all its aspects. Full bibliographical data with copious annotations. The work was issued in parts, printed on the recto only, and concludes with four supplements.

958. Hinson, Maurice. The piano teacher's source book: an annotated bibliography of books related to the piano and piano music. 2d ed. Melville, N.Y.: Belwin Mills Pub. Corp., 1980. 187 p.

First published in 1974 and supplemented in 1976.

A categorized bibliography of English-language books. Indexes to authors and composers.

959. Hutschenruyter, Willem. Bijdrage tot de bibliographie der muziekliteratuur. Een zooveel mogelijk aangevulde samenvatting der boek- en tijdschrift-overzichten, die sedert 1885 zijn opgenomen in het *Vierteljahrschrift für Musikwissenschaft,* het *Zeitschrift der Internationalen Musikgesellschaft,* en het *Jahrbuch der Musikbibliothek Peters.* Vol. 1: Instrumenmtale muziek, mechanische muziek, electrische muziek, klokken. Zeist, 1941. 513 p. (typescript)

An incomplete project, intended to be a comprehensive bibliography of music literature, but progressed only so far as to cover writings on instrumental music, electrical music, and bells.

960. Liebenow, Walther M. Rank on rank; a bibliography of the history and construction of organs. Minneapolis: Martin Press, 1973. 171 p.

Brief entries organized geographically with separate sections on history and construction. Indexed.

961. Lyons, David B. Lute, vihuela, guitar to 1800; a bibliography. Detroit: Information Coordinators, 1978. 214 p. (Detroit Studies in Music Bibliography, 40)

A bibliography of music for and articles and books on the instruments listed in the title and theorbo, orpharion, bandora, and mandolin, including a list of editions featuring tablature. Organized in 28 chapters. Cross referenced and author index. Addenda of 231 more sources, separately indexed.

Review by Thomas F. Heck in *Notes* 36 (1979), p. 107–08, and by François Lesure in *Fontes artis musicae,* 26 (1979), p. 297.

962. Meer, John Henry van der. "Ältere und neuere Literatur zur Musikinstrumentenkunde," in *ActaM,* 51 (1979), p. 1–50.

An extensive discussion of the literature of musical instruments, citing 415 titles and ranging from important catalogs of exhibitions to monographs on the development of individual instruments. A *tour de force.*

963. Miller, Dayton C. Catalogue of books and literary material relating to the flute and other musical instruments, with annotations. Cleveland, privately printed, 1935. 120 p.

Catalog of the literary portion of one of the largest collections ever assembled on the flute and related instruments. Now in the Music Division of the Library of Congress (see no. 2600).

Includes material on all wind instruments, in the form of books, pamphlets, periodical articles, newspaper clippings, concert programs, makers' catalogs and price lists, etc. Brief annotations.

964. Oberkogler, Friedrich. Vom Wesen und Werden der Musikinstrumente. 2. Aufl. Schaffhausen: Novalis Verlag, 1985. 175 p.

First published in 1976.

Narrative bibliography on the nature and development of musical instruments; a well made book.

965. Overton, Friend Robert. Der Zink: Geschichte, Bauweise und Spieltechnik eines historischen Musikinstrumentes. Mainz; New York: Schott, 1981. 260 p.

In addition to the historical study there is a valuable bibliography and list of compositions for the Zink.

966. Pohlmann, Ernst von. Laute, Theorbe, Chitarrone. Die Lauten-Instrumente, ihre Musik und Literatur von 1500 bis zur Gegenwart. Zweite Auflage. Bremen: Edition Eres, 1972. 416 p.

First printed in 1968. The 2nd edition is much enlarged.

A source book of information about instruments of the lute family, including sources, composers, literature, descriptions of tablatures, locations of existing instruments, makers.

Review by Stanley Buetens in *Journal of the lute society of America,* 5 (1972), p. 114–16.

967. Reuter, Rudolf. Bibliographie der Orgel; Literatur zur Geschichte der Orgel bis 1968. Kassel:Bärenreiter, 1973. 256 p. (Münster. Universität. Orgelwissenschaftliche Forschungsstelle. Veröffentlichungen, 3)

A bibliography of 8,574 books and articles, not including works about organists or reviews of performances. Arranged alphabetically by authors, but provided with indexes by location, names of persons, and subjects. List of periodicals devoted to literature on the organ.

968. Schlesinger, Kathleen. A bibliography of musical instruments and archaeology. . . . London: W. Reeves, 1912. 100 p.

Only the first 20 plates are devoted to works on musical instruments and the orchestra. Short sections on catalogs of instrument collections and general works on music. The greater part of the volume is concerned with classical and medieval antiquities.

969. Schulz, Ferdinand F. Pianographie: Klavierbibliographie der lieferbaren Bücher und Periodica sowie der Dissertationen in deutscher, englischer, französischer und italienischer Sprache. 2., verb. und erheblich erw. Aufl. Recklinghausen: Piano-Verlag, 1982. 458 p.

First published in 1978.

A classified bibliography of about 2,000 works about pianos, music for pianos, and composers of piano music. There is a short *Nachtrag*, extensive lists of addresses of publishers, libraries, piano competitions, and music societies. No title or subject index.

970. Schwarz, Werner. Guitar bibliography: an international listing of theoretical literature on classical guitar from the beginning to the present ... München: K. G. Saur, 1984. 257 p.

A classified bibliography of 4,705 entries.

971. Skei, Allen Bennet. Woodwind, brass, and percussion instruments of the orchestra, a bibliographic guide. New York: Garland, 1985. 271 p.

Selected titles on instruments annotated. Intended as a guide to research for a professional audience. A classified list of 1,195 items. Index of names and subjects.

972. Torri, Luigi. La costruzione ed i costruttori degli istrumenti ad arco. Bibliografia liutistica storico-tecnic. 2a edizione. ... Padova: G. Zanibon, 1920. 43 p.

Brief critical and descriptive annotations. Alphabetically arranged, with a subject index.

973. Warman, John Watson. The organ: writings and other utterances on its structure, history, procural, capabilities, etc.: with criticisms, and depositories preceded by an analytical consideration of general bibliographical and catalogual construction. Thornton Heath, Surrey: J.W. Warman, 1898–1904. 4 pts. (287 p.)

At head of title: *The organ: a comprehensive treatise on its structure.*

974. Warner, Thomas E. An annotated bibliography of woodwind instruction books, 1600–1830. Detroit: Information Coordinators, 1967. 138 p. (Detroit studies in music bibliography, 11.)

Jazz

The literature of jazz continues to proliferate rapidly. Readers will find relevant information in several different sections of this book, under "Bibliographies of Music: Jazz and Popular Music," and, above all, under "Discographies: Collectors's Guides to Popular Recordings." The *Jazz Index* provides good coverage of the current literature of jazz (see no. 796).

975. Carl Gregor, Duke of Mecklenburg. International bibliography of jazz books. Volume I: 1921–1949. Compiled with the assistance of Norbert Rucker. Baden-Baden: Valentin Koerner, 1983. 108 p. (Collections D'Etudes Musicologiques, 67)(Sammlung musikwissenschaftlivher Abhandlungen, 67)

The first of a projected four volumes intended to revise and expand the author's earlier bibliography and its two supplements (see no. 976).

Arranged alphabetically including brief transcriptions of tables of contents. List of phantom titles. Index of collaborators. Index of keywords and persons named in titles. Index of subjects. Index of collections and series. Index of countries of publication. Chronological survey of years of publications.

976. Carl Gregor, Duke of Mecklenburg. International jazz bibliography: jazz books from 1919 to 1968. Strasbourg: Heitz, 1969. 198 p. (Sammlung musikwissenschaftlicher Abhandlungen, 49.)

1970 Supplement. . . . Graz: Universal Edition, 1971. 109 p. (Beiträge zur Jazzforschung, 3.) *1971/72/73 Supplement.* . . . Graz: Universal Edition, 1975. 246 p. (Beiträge zur Jazzforschung, 6.)

Review of the 1969 edition by Ekkehard Jost in *Die Musikforschung,* 24 (1971), p. 330–31; by Alan P. Merriam in *Ethnomusicology,* 14 (1970), p. 177. Review of the *1970 Supplement* by James Patrick in *Notes,* 29 (1972), p. 236–39. Review of the *1971/72/73 Supplement* in *Jazz* odium, 24 (1975), no. 3, p. 34.

977. Chilton, John. Who's who of jazz: Storyville to Swing Street. Philadelphia: Chilton, 1972. 419 p.

A bio-bibliographical dictionary.

978. Haselgrove, J. R. and D. Kennington. Readers' guide to books on jazz. 2d ed. London: Library Association, 1965. 16 p.

A popular, but informed bibliography. Still valuable.

979. Hefele, Bernhard. Jazz-bibliography. Jazz-bibliographie. International literature on jazz, blues, spirituals, gospel and ragtime music with a selected list of works on the social and cultural background from the beginning to the present. München; New York: K. G. Saur, 1981. 368 p.

A superb bibliography including 6,600 entries arranged by topic, some citing reviews. Name index.

Review by Nina Davis-Millis in *Notes,* 39 (1981), p. 102–03.

980. Kennington, Donald and Danny Read. The literature of jazz, a critical guide. 2nd edition, revised. Chicago: American Library Association, 1980.

Nine short chapters discussing various aspects of jazz documentation, each follwed by an annotated bibliography. Title index and name index.

A work first published in England, 1970, by The Library Association.

Review, unfavorable, of the first American edition by Eileen Southern in *Notes,* 29 (1972), p. 35–36.

981. Meadows, Eddie S. Jazz reference and research materials: a bibliography. New York: Garland Publishing, 1981. 300 p. (Critical studies on Black life and culture, 22)

Arranged in 2 sections: "Jazz and its genres;" and "Reference materials," the latter organized by reference or research genre (e.g. bibliography, histories, discographies, etc.). Each section is separately indexed by name and subject.

982.   Meeker, David. Jazz in the movies. New, enlarged edition. N.Y.: Da
Capo, 1981. unnumbered pages.
   Original edition published by the British Film Institute, London, 1972.
Subsequent edition co-published by Talisman Books, London, and Ar-
lington House, New Rochelle, 1977.
   Cites and describes 3,724 films, including television films, mentioning
jazz musicians responsible for the musical elements of the sound track.
Index to names.

983.   Merriam, Alan P. A bibliography of jazz. With the assistance of Robert
J. Benford. Philadelphia: American Folklore Society, 1954. 145 p. (Publications of the American Folklore Society, Bibliographical series, 4.)
   Reprint by Da Capo Press, New York, 1970.
   3,324 numbered entries, arranged alphabetically by author, with subject emphasis indicated by a code system. Lists 113 jazz periodicals. Subject index.
   Review by Marshall W. Stearns in *Notes,* 12 (1955), p. 436–37; of the
reprint edition by Eileen Southern in *Notes,* 29 (1972), p. 34–35.

984.   Reisner, Robert G. The literature of jazz; a selective bibliography.
With an introduction by Marshall W. Stearns. New York: The New York
Public Library, 1959. 63 p.
   A preliminary edition appeared in the *Bulletin of the New York Public
Library,* March-May, 1954.
   Cites some 500 books on jazz, 850 periodical articles, and 125 jazz maga-
zines.
   Review by William Lichtenwanger in *Notes,* 16 (1959), p. 398.

Popular Music

984.1.   Dimmick, Mary L. The Rolling Stones: an annotated bibliography.
Pittsburgh: University of Pittsburgh, Graduate School of Library and
Information Sciences, 1972. 73 p. (Pittsburgh studies in library and infor-
mation sciences.)
   Liberal annotations, some critical, some descriptive. As a collection of
documents and commentary, this is a model of its kind.

985.   Hoffmann, Frank W. The literature of rock, 1954–1978. Metuchen:
Scarecrow Press, 1981. 337 p.
   Supplement issued: *The literature of rock, II, 1979–1983,* with additional material for the period 1954–1978; by Frank Hoffmann and B. Lee
Cooper, with the assistance of Lee Ann Hoffmann. 1986. 2 v.
   A classified and annotated bibliography with a brief historical survey
of the literature. Annotated list of popular music periodicals. Basic stock
list of rock recordings. Bibliography and index to persons and groups.
   The supplement is a selective bibliography arranged according to an
historical outline of the genre. There are additioinal categories for
materials not fitting into the historical framework. Includes a list of
books cited in the bibliography, a basic stock list of rock recordings
ordered according to the historical outline, list of periodicals covering
the genre, and index of artists, groups, genres, concepts and trends.

986. Kuhnke, Klaus, Manfred Miller, and Peter Schulze. Schriften zur populären Musik: eine Auswahl-Bibliographie. Bremen: Archiv für Populäre Musik, 1975–77. 2 v. (Archiv für Populäre Musik. Schriften, 1–2)
Classified list of titles about a broad range of popular musics. Indexes by author and translator, subject and period.

987. Lowe, Leslie. Directory of popular music, 1900–1965. Droitwich: Peterson Publishing Co. Ltd, 1975. 1,034 p.
" . . . intended to be a standard work of reference for popular music in Great Britain." Chronological section recording information about popular songs, including citation of recordings. Following sections treat stage shows, films, music publishers, award-winning songs, and theme songs. Index to song titles.

988. Shapiro, Nat and Bruce Pollock. Popular music, 1920–1979: a revised cumulation. Detroit: Gale Research Co., 1985. 3 v.
Supplements the nine-volume 1st edition, overlapping in some respects.

An annotated index of over 18,000 American popular songs, cumulating and updating eight volumes of *Popular music* and including introductory essays, lyricists and composers index, important performances index, award index, and list of publishers. [Author's *Preface*]

989. Stanley, Lana. Folk rock: a bibliography on music of the 'sixties. San Jose, Calif.: San Jose State College Library, 1970. 80 p. (typescript) (San Jose State College Library, Bibliography series, 3.)
Classified under topical headings and writings on particular groups or individual artists.

990. Stevenson, Gordon. "The wayward scholar: resources and research in popular culture" in Trends in the scholarly use of library resources [ed. by] Donald W. Krummel *et al.*: *Library trends,* 25/4 (1977).
A discussion of the directions of and support for research in popular culture as an academic discipline.

991. Tamm, Eric. "Materials of rock music research" in *Cum notis variorum,* no. 90–94.
A thoughtful annotated bibliography arranged in classified order. Introductory comments to each section of the classified arrangement describe some of the issues and quandries in which scholars of rock find themselves.

992. Taylor, Paul. Popular music since 1955; a critical guide to the literature. London; N.Y.: Mansell, 1985. 533 p.
Intends "to provide a critical, bibliographical guide to the literature of popular music published in English since 1955." (*Preface*)
An annotated, categorized bibliography: generalia; social aspects; artistic aspects; business; genres; lives and works; fiction; periodicals.

993. Terry, Carol D. Here, there & everywhere: the first international Beatles bibliography, 1962–1982. Ann Arbor: Pierian Press, 1985. 282 p. (Rock and Roll reference series, 11)

Medieval and Renaissance Music

994. Gallo, F. Alberto. "Philological works on musical treatises of the Middle Ages: a bibliographical report." In *Acta Musicologica,* 44 (1972), p. 78–101.

A narrative bibliography treating the work recently accomplished in the editing and description of medieval treatises. The material is discussed chronologically and by country, with copious notes.

995. Gleason, Harold. Music in the Middle Ages and Renaissance. 2nd ed. Rochester, N.Y.: Levis Music Stores, 1951. 158 p. (Music literature outlines, ser. 1.)

The outline follows the organization in Reese's *Music in the Middle Ages,* but each section is accompanied by numerous bibliographical references to books, periodical articles, scores, and recordings.

996. Hughes, Andrew. Medieval music: the sixth liberal art. Rev. ed. Toronto; Buffalo: University of Toronto Press, 1980, c1974. 360 p. (Toronto medieval bibliographies, 4)

First published in 1974, 326 p. Also published in London by E. Benn.

A classified, annotated bibliography of the literature on medieval music. Index of authors and editors, and a general index. Author's preface is a guide to the bibliographical conventions adopted, and a "Key to the bibliography" provides a useful guide to the subject matter. A new classic.

997. Lütolf, Max. Analecta hymnica medii aevi ... Register. .... Zusammenarbeit mit D. Baumann, E. Meier, M. Römer, und A. Wernli. Bern und München: Francke Verlag, 1978. 2 v. (Musikwissenschaftliches Seminar der universität Zürich, 1)

An index to the massive *Analecta hymnica medii aevi* by G. M. Dreves, Cl. Blume, and H. M. Bannister. In four sections: an index to the incipits, A-Z; and three indexes—to literary genres, to liturgical feasts, and to authors (presumed or attributed).

Review by Marie-Noëlle Colette in *Fontes artis musicae,* 26 (1979), p. 246–47. *Analecta hymnica medii aevi*—Index

998. Reese, Gustave. "Bibliography." In his *Music in the Middle Ages.* New York: Norton, 1940. p. 425–63.

Lists books, periodical articles, facsimiles, and editions. Difficult to use because the material is grouped by chapter headings. One of the most influential bibliographies available to students of early music.

999. Reese, Gustave. "Bibliography." In his *Music in the Renaissance.* Rev. ed. New York: Norton, 1959. p. 884–946.

An important bibliography of monographs, editions, and periodical literature related to Renaissance music. Unclassified, alphabetical arrangement.

1000.　Smith, Carleton Sprague and William Dinneen. "Recent work on music in the Renaissance." In *Modern philology,* 42:1 (Aug. 1944), p. 41–58.

A bibliographical article in narrative style citing and evluating research and editorial activity in Renaissance music from about 1900 to date of publication.

1001.　Smits van Waesberghe, Joseph. "Die gegenwärtige Geschichtsbild der mittelalterlichen Musik." In *Kirchenmusikalisches Jahrbuch,* 46–49, 1962–65.

A narrative survey and discussion, under major topics, of the contributions on medieval music in 19 current musicological and historical journals.

For 1957–60, in Jahrgang 46 (1962), p. 61–82.
For 1960–62, in Jahrgang 47 (1963), p. 11–38.
For 1963, in Jahrgang 48 (1964), p. 1–26.
For 1964, in Jahrgang 49 (1965), p. 9–33.

1002.　Suñol, Grégorio María. "Bibliographie generale." In his *Introduction à la paléographie musicale grégorienne.* Paris: Desclee, 1935.p. 511–65.

This bibliography first appeared in 1925 in the original edition of the author's work on Gregorian paleography. Entries are broadly classified and listed in order of publication.

1003.　Velimirovic, Milos. "Present status of research in Byzantine music." In *Acta musicologica,* 43 (1971), p. 1–20.

A narrative bibliography citing the important work accomplished in this area since 1950.

Baroque and Classical Music

1004.　Gleason, Harold. Music in the Baroque. Rochester, N.Y.: Levis Music Stores, 1950. (Music literature outlines, ser. 2)

The outline is based on Bukofzer's *Music in the Baroque era* (1947), with much additional documentation.

1005.　Hill, George R. A preliminary checklist of research on the classic symphony and concerto to the time of Beethoven (excluding Haydn and Mozart). Hackensack, N.J.: Joseph Boonin, 1970. 58 p. (Music indexes and bibliographies, 2.)

1006.　Surian, Elvidio. A checklist of writing on 18th-century French and Italian opera (excluding Mozart). Hackensack, N.J.: Joseph Boonin, 1970. 121 p. (Music indexes and bibliographies, 3.)

1007.　Weaver, Robert L. and Norma W. Weaver. A chronology of music in the Florentine theater, 1590–1750; operas, prologues, finales, intermezzos, and plays with incidental music. Detroit: Information Coordinators, 1978. 421 p. (Detroit Studies in Music Bibliography, 38)

Numerous bibliographic references.
Review by Thomas Walker in *Notes,* 36 (1979), p. 90–2.

Music Education

1008. Harris, Ernest E. Music education : a guide to information sources. Detroit: Gale Research Co., 1978. 566 p.

An exemplary work, one of the best of its kind. The author extends his range to include many entries not found in ordinary bibliographies. Arranged in 74 sections, titles are divided into 5 categories: generalia, music in education, subject matter areas, uses of music, and multimedia and equipment. There are appendices listing library holdings and music periodicals.

1009. International Society for Music Education. International listing of teaching aids in music education. Edited by Egon Kraus. Cologne: International Society for Music Education (distributing agent: Moseler Verlag, Wolfenbuttel), 1959. 52 p.

A classified bibliography of materials, since 1945, concerned with music instruction.

Review by Theodore Normann in *Journal of research in music education,* 8 (1960), p. 55–56.

1010. Modisett, Katherine C. "Bibliography of sources, 1930–1952, relating to the teaching of choral music in secondary schools." In *Journal of research in music education,* 3 (1955), p. 51–60.

A classified bibliography of 236 items, with a brief introductory survey of the field and its problems.

1011. Music Educators' National Conference. Selected bibliography, music education materials. (Prepared for the U.S. Department of State by a special committee of the M.E.N.C.) Chicago: M.E.N.C., 1952. 64 p.

Contains five bibliographies, classified, partially annotated: music education materials for elementary schools, collections for junior high, collections for senior high, instrumental music materials, textbooks on music education. The emphasis is on school music performance materials.

1012. Music Educators' National Conference. Committee on Bibliography. "Music education materials, a selected bibliography." Published as volume 7, no. 1 of the *Journal of research in music education,* 1959. 146 p.

A classified listing of materials. Major groupings are elementary music education, junior high school, choral materials, instructional materials for instrumental music, music appreciation guides and reference materials, music theory texts and workbooks, audio-visual aids, teacher training.

1013. Music Educators' National Conference. Curriculum Committee. Music education source book (no. 1). Edited by Hazel N.Morgan. Chicago: M.E.N.C., 1951. 268 p.

First printed in 1947.

Various sections contain brief bibliographies; the 1951 printing has an appendix of revisions and additions. Much of the bibliographical information in the first four printings is now out of date.

1014. Music Educators' National Conference. Music in American Education Committee. Music in American Education. Music education source book (no. 2). Edited by Hazel N.Morgan. Chicago: M.E.N.C., 1955. 365 p.
Brief bibliographies to various chapters and subchapters concerned with aspects of American public school music.

1015. Phelps, Roger P. A guide to research in music education. 3rd ed. Metuchen: Scarecrow Press, 1986. 368 p.
First published in 1969 by W. C. Brown, Dubuque, Iowa. 2nd ed. published by Scarecrow, 1980. 385 p.
Aimed at the graduate student in music education. Covers bibliography and research procedures.

1016. Smits van Waesberghe, Joseph. "Chronologische Übersicht der Musiktraktate, und Literaturverzeichnis." In *Musikerziehung: Lehre und Theorie der Musik im Mittelalter.* Leipzig: 1969. p. 195–202. (Musikgeschichte in Bildern, III, 3)
Provides a bibliographical key to the historical study of music education. The "Chronologische Übersicht" cites the most important treatises devoted to music theory and instruction from the 5th to the 15th century. The "Verzeichnis" is an extensive bibliography of books and articles on medieval music instruction.

1017. Sollinger, Charles. String class publications in the United States, 1851–1951. Detroit: Information Coordinators, 1974. 71 p. (Detroit Studies in Music Bibliography, 30)

National Music

The first 47 entries in this section call attention to a series of articles that have appeared in *Acta musicologica,* the journal of the International Musicological Society, since 1957. These articles survey the bibliographical and research activities in music in various countries since the end of World War II. Most of them cite major scholarly publications, dissertations, and important music reference works.

National Musicological Trends

AUSTRALIA

1018. Kartomi, Margaret. "Musicological research in Australia, 1979–1984" in *ActaM,* 51 (1984), p. 109–45.

AUSTRIA

1019. Flotzinger, Rudolf. "20 Jahre Musikforschung in Österreich," in *ActaM,* 51 (1979), p. 268–78.

1020. Wessely, Othmar. "Die österreichische Musikforschung nach dem zweiten Weltkrieg." In *Acta M,* 29 (1957), p. 111–19.

BELGIUM

1021. Clercx-Lejeune, Suzanne. "La musicologie en Belgique depuis 1945." In *Acta M,* 30 (1958), p. 199–214.

CANADA

1022. Maniates, Maria Rika. "Musicology in Canada 1963–1979," in *ActaM,* 53 (1981), p. 1–14.

CZECHOSLOVAKIA

1023. Strakova, Theodora. "Die tschechische Musikwissenschaft in den Jahren 1945–1975" in *ActaM,* 49 (1977), p. 103–20.

DENMARK

1024. Schousboe, Torben. "Dänische musikwissenschaftliche Publikationen seit 1958." In *Acta M,* 44 (1972), p. 1–11.

FINLAND

1025. Ringbom, Nils-Eric. "Die Musikforschung in Finnland seit 1940." In *Acta M,* 31 (1959), p. 17–24.

FRANCE

1026. Lesure, François. "La musicologie française depuis 1945." In *Acta M,* 30 (1958), p. 3–17.

GERMANY

1027. Heckmann, Harald. "Musikwissenschaftliche Unternehmungen in Deutschland seit 1945." In *Acta M,* 29 (1957), p. 75–94.

GREAT BRITAIN

1028. Cooper, Barry. "Musicology in Great Britain (1982–1985)" in *ActaM,* 58 (1986), p. 1–8.

1029. Fallows, David. "Musicology in Great Britain, 1979–1982," In *Acta M,* 55 (1983), p. 244–53.

1030. Fallows, David, Nigel Fortune, Arnold Whittal, and John Blacking. "Musicology in Great Britain since 1945" in *ActaM,* 52 (1980), p. 38–68.
In 4 parts: Introduction (Fortune); Historical musicology (Fallows); Analysis (Whittal); Ethnomusicology (Blacking).

IRAN

1031. Massoudieh, Mohammad Tagli. "Die Musikforschung in Iran" in *ActaM,* 52 (1980), p. 79–83.

IRAQ

1032. Qassim Hassan, Scheherazade. "Die Entwicklung und der gegenwörtige Stand der Musikforschung im Irak" in *ActaM,* 52 (1980), p. 148–61.

ISRAEL

1033. Gerson-Kiwi, Edith. "Musicology in Israel." In *Acta M,* 30 (1958), p. 17–26.

1034. Gerson-Kiwi, Edith and Amnon Shiloah. "Musicology in Israel, 1960–1980" in *ActaM,* 53 (1981), p, 200–216.

ITALY

1035. Allorto, Riccardo e Claudio Sartori. "La musicologia italiana dal 1945 a oggi." In *Acta M,* 31 (1959), p. 9–17.

1036. Gallo, F. Alberto, Agostino Ziino, Giulio Cattin, Lorenzo Bianconi, Elvidio Surian, Antonio Serravezza, e Tullia Magrini. "Vent'anni di musicologia in Italia" in *ActaM,* 54 (1982), p. 7–83.
An extensive review includes numerous bibliographical footnotes.

JAPAN

1037. Nomura, Francesco Yosio. "Musicology in Japan since 1945." In *Acta M,* 35 (1963), p. 45–53.

1038. Suppan, Wolfgang and Hachirō Sakarishi. "Musikforschung in und für Japan" in *ActaM,* 54 (1982), p. 84–123.
Includes numerous bibliographical references.

KOREA

1039. Song, Bang-Song. "Musikwissenschaft in Korea seit 1950" in *ActaM,* 57 (1985), p. 141–50.

LATIN AMERICA

1040. Devoto, Daniel. "Panorama de la musicología Latinoamericana." In *Acta M,* 31 (1959), p. 91–109.

THE NETHERLANDS

1041. Dunning, Albert. "Musikwissenschaft in Holland seit 1960" in *ActaM,* 55 (1983), p. 58–69.

1043. Reeser, Eduard. "Musikwissenschaft in Holland." In *Acta M,* 32 (1960), p. 160–74.

NORWAY

1043. Schjelderup-Ebbe, Dag. "Neuere norwegische musikwissenschaftliche Arbeiten." In *Acta M,* 44 (1972), p. 25–31.

1044. Schjelderup-Ebbe, Dag. "Norwegische musikwissenschaftliche Arbeiten" in *ActaM,* 52 (1980), p. 68–73.

PHILIPPINES

1045. Dioquino, Corazon C. "Musicology in the Philippines" in *ActaM,* 54 (1982), p. 124–47.
Includes an extensive bibliography of writings on music in the Philippines.

PORTUGAL

1046. De Brito, Manuel Carlos. "Musicology in Portugal since 1960" in *ActaM,* 51 (1984), p. 29–47.

1047. Kastner, Macario Santiago. "Veinte años de musicologia en Portugal (1940–60)." In *Acta M,* 32 (1960), p. 1–11.

SCANDINAVIA

1048. Rosenberg, Herbert. "Musikwissenschaftliche Bestrebungen in Dänemark, Norwegen, und Schweden in den letzten c. 15 Jahren." In *Acta M,* 30 (1958), p. 118–37.

SOUTH AFRICA

1049. Paxinos, Socrates. "Musicology in South Africa" in *ActaM,* 58 (1986), p. 9–23.
Includes a list of dissertations in order by author.

SOUTH AMERICA

1050. Bose, Fritz. "Südamerikanische Musikforschung" In *Acta M* 29 (1957), p. 43–45.

SPAIN

1051. Querol, Manuel. "Die Musikwissenschaft in Spanien (1964–1979)" in *ActaM,* 52 (1980), p. 75–78.

SWEDEN

1052. Lönn, Anders. "Trends and tendencies in recent Swedish musicology." In *Acta M,* 44 (1972), p. 11–25.

SWITZERLAND

1053. Schanzlin, Hans Peter. "Musikwissenschaft in der Schweiz (1938–58)." In *Acta M,* 30 (1958), p. 214–24.

UNITED STATES

1054. Buelow, George. S. "Musicology in the United States in 1981–1982" in *ActaM,* 55 (1983), p. 253–266.

1055. Goldthwaite, Scott. "The growth and influence of musicology in the United States." In *Acta M,* 33 (1961), p. 72–79.
With a "Codetta: some details of musicology in the United States," by Jan LaRue, p. 79–83.

1056. Haar, James. "Musicology in the United States in 1979" in *ActaM,* 52 (1980), p. 84–87.

1057. Haar, James. "Musicology in the United States in 1978 " in *ActaM,* 51 (1979), p. 279–82.

1058. Palisca, Claude. "Report on the musicological year 1974 in the United States," in *ActaM,* 47 (1975), p. 283–89.

1059. Steiner, Ruth. "Musicology in the United States in 1980" in *ActaM,* 53 (1981), p. 216–23.

U.S.S.R.

1060. Jarustovsky, Boris. "Soviet musicology," in *ActaM,* 46 (1974), p. 50–57.

VIETNAM

1061. Tran Van Khe. "Situation de la musique en République Socialiste du Viêt-Nam," in *ActaM,* 49 (1977), p. 121–30.

YUGOSLAVIA

1062. Cvetko, Dragotin. "Der gegenwärtige Stand der jugoslawischen Musikwissenschaft" in *ActaM,* 51 (1979), p. 151–60.

1063. Cvetko, Dragotin. "Les formes et les résultats des efforts musicologiques yugoslaves." In *Acta M,* 31 (1958), p. 50–62.

National music

1064. American music before 1865 in print and on records: a biblio-discography. Preface by H. Wiley Hitchcock. Brooklyn: Institute for Studies in American Music, Dept. of Music, School of Performing Arts, Brooklyn College of the City University of New York, 1976. 113 p. (I.S.A.M. monographs, no. 6)

Supplemented by *"American music before 1865 in print and on records: a biblio-discography:* supplement to music on records" by James R. Heintze in *Notes,* 34 (1978), p. 571–80 and by the same author *"American music before 1865 in print and on records: a biblio-discography:* second supplement to music on records" in *Notes,* 37 (1981), p. 31–36.

Review by James R. Heintze in *Notes,* 33 (1977), p. 842–43.

1065. American Music Recordings, a discography of 20th-century U.S. composers. A project of the Institute for Studies in American Music for the Koussevitsky Music Foundation, Inc. Carol J. Oja, editor. Brooklyn: Institute for Studies in American Music, 1982. 368 p.

Lists over 13,000 disc recordings of 8,000 works by almost 1,300 American composers. No jazz, folk, or popular musics are included. Bibliography. Indexes to performing groups, ensembles, vocalists and narrators, and instrumentalists.

1066. Behague, Gerard. Music in Latin America: an introduction. Englewood Cliffs: Prentice-Hall, 1979. 369 p.

Translated by Miguel Castillo Didier and published in Spanish in 1983 (502 p.).

"The most comprehensive and reliable general history of Latin American music written to date." [Malena Kuss]

1067. Beiträge zur Musikwissenschaft. Sonderreihe: Bibliographien. I. SR Rumanien (1945–1965). II. VR Polen (1945–1965). 1966. I, 66 p. II, 192 p.

Rumania and Poland are the first two countries covered in this series of bibliographies devoted to musicological literature in the East

European countries. Printed in a subseries of the leading musicological journal of the German Democratic Republic.

Subsequent volumes cited at no. 690.

1068. Bericht über die musikwissenschaftlichen Arbeiten in der Deutschen Demokratischen Republik 1968. Herausgegeben vom Zentralinstitut für Musikforschung beim Verband Deutscher Komponisten und Musikwissenschaftler. Berlin, Verlag Neue Musik, 1969. 150 p.

Abstracts of scholarly papers and dissertations by East German musicologists.

1069. Bradley, Ian L. A selected bibliography of musical Canadiana. Revised edition. Victoria: University of Victoria, 1978. 177 p.

First published in 1974.

Classified contents: bibliographies, theses, biographies, compositions, education, ethnomusicology, histories, miscellaneous. The listing of theses written at Canadian academic institutions is of particular interest.

1070. Burt, Amanda. Iceland's twentieth-century composers and a listing of their works. Annandale, Va.: Charles Baptie Studios, 1977. 71 p.

1071. Chung-kuo ku-tai yin-yüeh shu-mu. Compiled by the Institute of Chinese music at the Central Conservatory of Music, Pei-ching. Pei-ching: Yin yüeh ch'u pan she, 1962. 142 p.

A bibliography of works about ancient Chinese music divided into three parts: books on music commonly available; books known to be in existence but not seen by the author; known lost works. Works on histories and theory, vocal music, dance music, music to accompany storytelling, theatrical music, instruments, religious and ceremonial music, ch'in and music technique are covered. Each entry provides titles, author or editor imprint information, and call numbers in the Library of Musical Research in the Central Music Conservatory in Pei-ching.

1072. Chung-kuo yin yüeh shu p'u chih. Pei-ching: Peoples Music Press, 1984. 200 p.

This is a union catalog of holdings of Chinese music titles in 37 Chinese libraries covering the period from 722 B.C. to 1949. It is a classified catalog in two parts, one for the period from 722 B.C. to 1911 and another for 1912–1949. There is an index to all titles.

1073. Compositeurs Canadiens Contemporains. Éditions françis dirigée par Louise Laplante. Traduction de Véronique Robert. Montréal: Les Presses de l'Université du Québec, 1977. 382 p.

English edition published in 1975 by Oxford University Press as *Contemporary Canadian Composers,* 248 p. by Keith MacMillan and John Beckwith.

A biographical work including bibliographical references and index. Analyses of most important works provided for major composers.

Lists of Canadian musical organizations of all sorts.

Review by Kathleen Toomey in *Notes,* 35 (1978), p. 86.

1074. Correia de Azevedo, Luis H. Bibliografia musical brasileira (1820–1950). Rio de Janeiro, 1952. 252 p. (Ministerio da Educacao e Saude. Instituto Nacional do Livro, Col. Bl. Bibliografia 9)
1,639 titles under 13 subject sections. Includes writings by Brazilian authors on non-Brazilian music. Publications containing music only are omitted.
Review by A. Hyatt King in *Music and letters,* 35 (1954), p. 67–68; by Charles Seeger in *Notes,* 11 (1954), p. 551–52.

1075. Davidsson, Åke. Bibliografi över Svensk musiklitteratur, 1800–1945. Bibliography of Swedish music literature, 1800–1945. 2. suppl. utökad med ett suppl. Uppsala, Almqvist & Wiksell1980. 267 p.
First published in 1948, 215 p.
A classified bibliography of general works, general music histories, histories of music in Sweden, works on musicians of all nationalities, and theoretical works. Restricted to writings by Swedish authors except for subjects connected with Swedish music. 5,432 items in all. Index.

1076. Davis, Martha Ellen. Music and dance in Latin American urban contexts: a selective bibliography. Brockport, N.Y., 1973. 20 p. (Urban anthropology bibliographies, 1)

1077. De Lerma, Dominique-René. Bibliography of black music. Westport: Greenwood Press, 1981– . (The Greenwood Encyclopedia of Black Music.)
Vol. 1: Reference materials
Vol. 2: Afro-American idioms
Vol. 3: Geographical studies
Vol. 4: Theory, education, and related studies
Bibliographies of books and articles, international in scope. Arranged after the RLIM classification, with coverage particularly intense up to 1975. Vol. 3 includes an extensive bibliography on acculturation and an index to authors amd editors in that volume. Volume 4 has a similar index.

1078. Delli, Bertrun. Music, [Section R] in volume 3 of *Arts in America, a bibliography*, edited by Bernard Karpel. Washington, D.C.: Smithsonian Institution, 1979. 4 v.
A 655 item classified bibliography of American musical literature. Other entries on music scattered throughout. General index in volume 4.

1079. Dordevič, Valdimir R. Ogled srpske muzicke bibliografije do 1914 godine. (An essay on the Serbian musical bibliography until 1914.) Beograd: Nolit, 1969. 281 p.
P. 57–280: a bibliography of 2,350 items, with separate sections for printed music, music literature, and manuscripts. Indexes of authors and titles.

1080. Ford, Wyn K. Music in England before 1800: a select bibliography. London, The Library Association, 1967. 128 p.
Classified bibliography in two major divisions: Part I, music and its

environment; Part II, persons. Confined to literature published in the 20th century in English, French, and German. The major critical editions of composers' works are cited in Part II.

1081. Fukuda, Naomi, ed. Bibliography of reference works for Japanese studies. Ann Arbor: Center for Japanese Studies, University of Michigan, 1979. 210 p.
Includes on p. 48–50 annotated entries on Japanese music. Reference works, dictionaries, handbooks, directories, chronologies, annuals, and books on instruments and folk music are covered.

1082. Giovine, Alfredo. Bibliografia ed emerografia; a cura di Felice Giovine e Nicola Roncone. Bari: Edizioni F.lli Laterza, 1980. 32 p. (Biblioteca dell'archivio delle tradizioni popolari baresi. Civiltà musicale pugliese)
A bibliography, including periodical and newspaper articles, on music in the province of Bari.

1083. Heard, Priscilla S. American music, 1698–1800: an annotated bibliography. Waco: Baylor University Press, Markham Press Fund, 1975. 246 p.
"Includes all entries pertaining to music from the *American bibliography* by Evans and Shipton, and the supplement by the American Antiquarian Society which covers the addenda of Bristol." *American bibliography*—Excerpts.

1084. Heintze, James R. American music studies; a classified bibliography of master's theses. Detroit: Information Coordinators, 1984. 312 p. (Bibliographies in American Music, 8)
With indexes to authors, places and subjects.

1085. Heskes, Irene. The resource book of Jewish music, a bibliographical and topical guide to the book and journal literature and program materials. Westport: Greenwood Press, 1985. 302 p. (Music reference collection 3)
An annotated bibliography of published English language sources on Jewish music. Classified by type of publication, but with a topical index. Author index. Glossary of Judaic.

1086. Horn, David. The literature of American music in books and folk music collections: a fully annotated bibliography. Metuchen: Scarecrow Press, 1977. 556 p.
First published in 1972 as a catalog of holdings in the Exeter University Library.
A classified work organized on historical and cultural bases. Almost 2,000 entries. Index to names and titles. Appendix of works discovered while the book was in preparation.
Reviews by Dan Morgenstern in *Journal of jazz studies,* 5 (1979), p.93–95, by Eileen Southern in *Black perspectives in music* 6 (1978), p. 94–96, and by Stephen M. Fry in *Notes,* 34 (1977), p. 89–90.

1087. Johnson, H. Earle. First performances in America to 1900. Detroit: Information Coordinators, 1979. 470 p. (Bibliographies in American Music, 4)

A source book for statistics on first performances of orchestral music. Entries in alphabetical order by composer give title and date of first performance in major cities. Choral performances with orchestra as well as some chamber music performances are included. Annotations frequently derive from contemporary reviews.

Review by Mary Jane Corry in *Notes,* 36 (1980), p. 653–54.

1088. Kassler, Jamie Croy. The science of music in Britain, 1714–1830: a catalogue of writings, lectures, and inventions. New York: Garland Pub., 1979. 2 v. (1,339 p.)

An extensively annotated bibliography arranged by author of English language writings on four areas of musical knowledge: technical, mathematical, critical, and physical. Works on sacred and theatrical music, singing, and playing are omitted. Location of sources and supporting bibliography are provided for each source. Three appendices cover genres of publication issued in Britain 1714–1830, encyclopedias and dictionaries, and musical periodicals. Indices of names, tradesmen, places, and genres and subjects.

1089. Kinscella, Hazel G. "Americana index to *The Musical Quarterly,* 1915–57." Published as vol. 6:2 (1958), of *The journal of research in music education.* 144 p.

Indexes all articles related to American music and musical events.

1090. Kjellberg, Erik. "Svenska Sanfundet för Musikforskning." [Swedish Society for Musicology] in *ActaM,* 47 (1975), p. 290–92.

1091. Kokusai Bunka Shinkokai. K. B. S. bibliography of standard reference books for Japanese studies descriptive notes. Vol. II (B): Theatre, dance and music. Tokyo: 1960. 182 p.

Kokusai Bunka Shinkokai is the "Society for International Cultural Relations."

Part of a multi-national "annotated bibliography of standard reference works in Japanese for the use of foreign students of Japanese culture who want to get access to original sources." The music titles were selected and annotated by Kishibe Shigo. There is an appendix: "selected bibliography of works in Western languages on Japanese drama, music and dance." There are extensive annotations with titles in *kanji,* romanized and translated.

1092. Koltypina, Galina B. and N. G. Pavlova. Sovetskaia literatura o muzyke: bibliograficheskii ukazatel knig, zhurnalnykh statei i retsenzii za 1968–1970 gg. Moskva: Sovetskii kompozitor, 1979–84. 2 v.

A bibliography of Russian music literature including periodical articles.

1093. Krautwurst, Franz. Das Schrifttum zur Musikgeschichte der Stadt Nürnberg. Hrsg. im Auftrag der Stadt Nürnberg Schul- Kulturreferat von der Stadtbibliothek. Nürnberg: Stadtbibliothek Nürnberg, 1964. 68 p. (Veröffentlichungen der Stadtbibliothek Nürnberg, 7)

A bibliography of writings about music in the city of Nürnberg.

1094. Kuss, Malena. "Current state of bibliographic research in Latin American music" in *Fontes artis musicae,* 31 (1984), p. 206–28.

An extensive prose bibliography with bibliographical supplements. Invaluable for the information conveyed, but merely a precursor to her book-length bibliography which will be forthcoming.

1095. Leguy, Jean. Catalogue bibliographique des livres de langue française sur la musique. Avant-propos de Norbert Dufourcq. Avec un supplément 1954–1959. Paris: E. Ploix, 1959. 59, 43 p.

Organized as the *Répertoire bibliographique,* below.

1096. Leguy, Jean. Répertoire bibliographique des ouvrages en français sur la musique. Chambray-lès-Tours: Musica reservata, 1975. 175 p.

Supplément 1975–1978 au Répertoire bibliographique des ouvrages en français sur la musique (1975) published in Tours by Ars Musicae in 1978. 63 p.

A classified list of works about music, most of them published in France in the mid-20th century up to 1975. Arranged by author in each section. Intended as a sales catalog, but with practical bibliographic application.

1097. Lieberman, Fredric. Chinese music, an annotated bibliography. 2nd edition. New York: Garland Pub., 1979. 257 p. (Asian music publications. Series A: Bibliographies and research aids, 1)

First edition published 1970 and supplemented 1973.

Annotated bibliography providing "exhaustive coverage of publications in Western languages." 2,441 entries covering all aspects of Chinese music, including the topic of music of emmigrant Chinese. Principal sources are Chinese journals. Index to sources and to names.

Review by Judith J. Johnson in *Notes,* 36 (1979), p. 370–71.

1098. Lissa, Zofia. "Die Musikwissenschaft in Volkspolen (1945–56)." In *Die Musikforschung,* 10 (1957), p. 531–47.

Translated from the Polish by Werner Kaupert.

In narrative style with many titles quoted. Discusses the state and organization of Polish musicology since World War II.

Materialy do Bibliografii Muzyki Polskiej. See no. 728.

1099. Maultsby, Portia K. "Selective bibliography: U.S. Black music" in *Ethnomusicology,* 19 (1975), p. 421–449.

Organized by genres and styles. Within each broad divison are citations of general works, works on composers, and works on performers.

1100. Mead, Rita H. Doctoral dissertations in American music: a classified bibliography. Brooklyn: Institute for Studies in American Music, Brooklyn College of the City University of New York, 1974. 155 p. (I.S.A.M. monographs, 3)

A classified bibliography of 1,226 entries covering dissertations on American music, but in many cases written within disciplines other than music (e.g. sociology, theater, anthropology, history, American studies, theology, literature, and education). Includes University Microfilm and Library of Congress microfilm numbers and references to *Dissertation Abstracts.* Author and subject indexes.
Review by Geoffrey C. Weston in *Notes,* 32 (1976), p.548.

1101. Michaelides, Solon. The music of ancient Greece: an encyclopaedia. London: Faber & Faber, 1978. 365,
Published in Greek as *Enkyklopaideia tés archaias Hellénikés mousikés* in Athens by Morphótiko Hidryma Ethnikés Trapezés, 1982. 364 p.

1102. Moldon, David. A bibliography of Russian composers. London: White Lion Publishers, 1976. 364 p.
Covers English language books and articles on Russian music (entries 1–368 in chronological order) and Russian composers (entries on generalia and works, each in chronological order). Indexes of authors, editors, and compilers, of translators and illustrators, and subjects. A poorly designed book.

1103. Murdoch, James. Australia's contemporary composers. Melbourne: Sun Books, 1975. 223 p.
Extended essays with discographies. Includes bibliography and index.

1104. "Music Section," in *Handbook of Latin American studies.* Cambridge, Mass.: Harvard Univ. Press, 1936–50; Gainesville: University of Florida Press, 1951–78; Austin: University of Texas Press, 1979– . v. 1 – .
Volumes for 1936–50 reprinted by the University of Florida Press.
The first issue to include anything about music was that for 1937, in which Irma Goebel Labastille published "The music of Mexico and Central America."
In 1939, William Berrien prepared the bibliography. In 1940–42, Gilbert Chase was responsible. From 1943 to 1953, Charles Seeger prepared the section. Richard A. Waterman compiled the bibliography from 1954–59. In 1959–63, Bruno Nettl was editor. Gilbert Chase returned to active duty from 1964–68. Gerhard Béhague took over from 1970–74 and Robert Stevenson has been responsible from 1976 until the current issue (1984).
From 1939, there has been a brief introductory essay and a classified bibliography of practically anything having to do with Latin American music. There is a section for generalia and then entries arranged by country or region. Anthologies are analyzed and periodical articles cited. Each volume indexes titles, subjects, and authors; title lists of journals indexed are supplied. Since 1965, the *Handbook* has been divided, social sciences being treated in odd-numbered years and humanities in even-numbered years.

1105. La Música de México Julio Estrada, editor. Guía bibliográfica [por] Sylvana Young Osorio. México: Instituto de Investigaciones Estéticas, Universidad Nacional AutÓnoma de México, 1984– .
Part 2 of a a history of music in Mexico.

1106. Muzíková, Ruzena. Selective bibliography of literature on Czech and Slovak music. Prague: Czechoslovak Music Information Centre, 1969. 124 p.

A useful bibliography of Czechoslovakian music literature for English readers. Czech titles are given in English translation, with brief descriptions of content and bibliographical features. Classified in nine major sections: bibliography, catalogs, dictionaries, periodical publications, history of Czech and Slovak music, monographs, anthologies, instruments, and notation.

1107. Napier, Ronald. A guide to Canada's composers, new, enl. and rev. ed. Ontario: Avondale Press, 1976. 56 p.

Includes a list of Canadian music publishers.

1108. Nef, Karl. Schriften über Musik und Volksgesang. Bern: K. J. Wyss, 1908. 151 p. (Bibliographie der schweizerischen Landeskunde, Faszikel V.)

Classified bibliography of literature on Swiss music, its history and practice. Index of names.

1109. Nihon no Saukō Tosho Henshū Inkai. [Guide to Japanese reference works]. Chicago: American Library Association, 1966. 303 p.

Includes on p. 49–52 29 annotated entries on Japanese music. Titles are provided in kanji, romanized and translated. Annotations are in English. Covers bibliography, dictionaries, biographies, chronology, yearbooks, illustrations, recorded music, and folk music.

1110. Orlov, Georgii P. Muzykalnaia literatura; bibliograficheskii ukazatel knizhnoi i zhurnalnoi literatury o muzyke na russkom iazyke. Leningrad: Leningradskaia filarmoniia, 1935. 222 p. (Knigi o simfonicheskoi muzyke)

A bibliography of music literature in Russian.

1111. Pavlova, N. G. Ukazatelw bibliograficeskix posobii po muzyke: annotirovannyi perecenw ukazatelei literatury, izdannyx na russkom iazyke. Moskva: Gos. biblioteka SSSR im. V.I. Lenina, Otdelnotnyx izdanii i zvukozapisei, 1978. 109 p.

This work supplements the earlier published *Bibliografii muzykalnoi bibliografii* compiled by G.B. Koltypinoi in 1963 and also a work of the same title compiled by N.G. Pavlova and published in 1970.

1112. Potúček, Juraj. Súpis slovenských hudobnín a literatúry o hudobníkoch. (Catalog of Slovak printed music and books on musicians.) Bratislava: Slovenská akademie vĕd a unmĕní, 1952. 435 p.

Lists musicians active in Slovakia to 1949 or mentioned in Slovak periodical literature. Bibliographies of works with Slovak texts, 1881 to 1949. Chronological index, classified index, name index.

1113. Potúček, Juraj. Súpis slovenskych hudobno-teoretických prác. (Catalog of Slovak musico-theoretical works.) Bratislava: Slovenská akademie vĕd, 1955. 467 p.

Classified bibliography of literary and theoretical works on Czech music, including periodical articles (p. 15–216). List of theoretical works in chronological order, 1519–1853 (p. 219–25). Biographical section, including, under composers' names, both publications of music and critical articles (p. 223–380). Classified list of music published 1950–52 (p. 383–403).

1114. Potuček, Juraj. Výberofá bibliografia zo slovenskej hudobnovednej literatúry 1862–1962. (Selective bibliography of Slovak musicological literature from 1862–1962.) Cyclostyled: Bratislava, Slovenská akademie věd, 1963. 116 p.

1115. Pruett, Lillian. "Music research in Yugoslavia" in *Notes,* 36 (1980), p. 23–49.

1116. Průvodce po pramench k dějinám hudby. Fondy a sbírky uložené v Čechách. [Guide to the sources of the history of music] Zpracovali: Jaroslav Bužga, Jan Kouba, Eva Mikanová a Tomislav Volek. Praha: Academia Nakladateleství Československé adademie ved, 1969. 323 p.
An annotated bibliography of music history for Bohemia.

1117. Rajeczky, B. "Musikforschung in Ungarn 1936–1960. (Bibliographischer Bericht.)" In *Studia musicologica,* 1 (1961), p. 225–49.
A brief survey of recent Hungarian musical scholarship, with a classified bibliography of music literature. Hungarian titles given with German translations. Sections on folk music, Hungarian music history, general music history, collective works.

1118. Ratliff, Neil. "Resources for music research in Greece—an overview" in *Notes,* 36 (1980), p. 50–64.

1119. Resources of American music history: a directory of source materials from colonial times to World War II [by] D. W. Krummel, Jean Geil, Doris J. Dyen [and] Deane L. Root. Urbana: University of Illinois Press, 1981. 463 p.
Geographically organized listing of source materials, including printed and mansucript music, programs and catalogs, institutional and personal papers, pictures and sound recordings. This was an American Bicentennial project with hundreds of local correspondents. There is a bibliography of reference works and an index to names, titles and subjects.
See D. W. Krummel's "Little RAMH, who made thee?," in *Notes,* 37 (1980), p. 227–38 for an exegesis on its genesis.

1120. Rocha da Silva Guimarãaes, Bertino D. Primeiro esboco duma bibliografia musical portuguesa, con uma breve notícia histórica de música no nosso país. Porto, 1947. 174 p.
The bibliographical section includes works on music by Portuguese authors, works on music in Portugal by native or foreign authors, old Portuguese pedagogical works, special bibliographies, and music periodicals.

1121. Schaal, Richard. Das Schrifttum zur musikalischen Lokalges-chichtsforschung. Kassel: Bärenreiter, 1947. 62 p.

A bibliography of studies of music in various European cities and provinces, arranged alphabetically by place. Includes articles from a few leading periodicals. Very brief citations. Much of this information is complemented by the bibliographies in articles on cities in *MGG* and *The New Grove*.

1122. Sendrey, Alfred. Bibliography of Jewish music. New York: Columbia University Press, 1951. 404 p.

Reprint by Kraus Reprint Co. in 1969.

A classified bibliography of 5,854 items; writings on Jewish music and musicians. Includes periodical articles.

Part II of this work is a bibliography of music, entered as no. 1291.

Review by Milton Feist in *MQ*, 37 (1951), p. 432–35; by Ernst C. Krohn in *JAMS*, 7 (Summer 1954), p. 150–52.

1123. Skowronski, JoAnn. Black music in America: a bibliography. Metuchen: Scarecrow, 1981. 723 p.

A list of books and articles about black music and musicians in the U.S. from colonial times through 1979. Entries are listed chronologically in each section and under each musician's name. Sections are: selected musicians and singers; general references; reference works. Author index.

1124. Stevenson, Robert Murrell. "The Americas in European music encyclopedias; part I: England, France, Portugal" in *Inter-American music review*, 3 (1981), p. 159–207.

A review of lexicographical coverage of Latin Americ. Extensive discussion of coverage in *The New Grove*.

1125. Stoneburner, B. C. Hawaiian music: an annotated bibliography. Westport: Greenwood, 1986. 100 p. (Music Reference Collection, 10)

The present work, which lists and annotates writing on Hawaiian music, musicians, and music life, covers the years 1831 through 1980. It is limited to sources in English, German, French, Spanish . . .

Arranged by author, 564 historical and critical works are cited. Appendices: glossary of Hawaiian terms, location of periodicals cited. Subject index.

Review in *The Sonneck Society Bulletin for American Music*, 3 (1987), p. 75–76.

1126. Thompson, Annie Figueroa. An annotated bibliography of writings about music in Puerto Rico. Ann Arbor: Music Library Association, 1974. 34 p. (MLA index and bibliography series, 12)

1127. Thompson, Leila Fern. Selected references in English on Latin American music, a reading list. Washington, D. C.: Music Division, Pan American Union, 1944. 20 p. (Pan American Union. Music Division. Music series, 13)

1128. Toomey, Kathleen M. and Stephen C. Willis. Musicians in Canada, a bio-bibliographical finding list. Musiciens au Canada, index bio-bibliographique. Ottawa: Canadian Association of Music Libraries, 1981. 185 p. (Canadian Association of Music Libraries, Publications, 1)(Association Canadienne des bibliothèques musicales, Publications, 1)

Previous edition published as *Bio-bibliographical finding list of Canadian musicians,* 1962.

An index to biographical and/or bibliographical information on over 1,700 Canadian musicians in 218 sources. Lists of musicians by specialty.

1129. Urturbey, Pola Suárez. La música en revistas argentinas. Buenos Aires: Fondo Nacional de las Artes, 1969. 70 p.

A bibliography of 652 entries for articles on music in four Argentine periodicals: *La Gaceta musical* (1874–87), *La Moda* (1837–38), *Revista de estudios musicales* (1949–54), and *La Revista de musica* (1927–30). Index of names. *La Gaceta musical*—Index *La Moda*—Index *Revista de estudios musicales*—Index *La Revista de musica*—Index

1130. Van der Merwe, F. Z. Suid-Afrikaanse musiekbibliografie: 1787–1952. En 1953–1972 bygewerk vir die Raad vir Geesteswetenskaplike Navorsing deur Jan van de Graaf. Kaapstad: Tafelberg-uitgewers vir die Instituut vir Taal, Lettere en Kuns, Raad vir Geesteswetenskaplike Navorsing, 1974. 297 p.

A bibliography concerning music in South Africa covering the period 1787–1952, with a supplement bringing the coverage of bibliography up to 1972.

1131. Vyborny, Zdenek. "Czech music literature since World War II." In *Notes,* 16 (1959), p. 539–46.

Translated from the German by William Lichtenwanger.

A classified bibliography, each section preceded by a brief descriptive statement. Titles given in Czech and English.

1132. Weisser, Albert. Bibliography of publications and other resources on Jewish music. New York: National Jewish Music Council, 1969. 117 p.

"Revised and enlarged edition based in part upon *"The bibliography of books and articles on Jewish music"* prepared by Joseph Yasser and published in 1955."

1133. Woodfill, Walter L. "Bibliography." In his *Musicians in English society.* Princeton: Princeton Univ. Press, 1953. p. 315–61.

Unabridged reprint by Da Capo Press, New York, 1959.

A substantial listing of the primary and secondary sources for the study of English music of the late 16th- and early 17th-centuries. Separated as to works before and after 1700.

The Woodfill bibliography is a fine example of the kind of information to be found in histories of national music or monographs related to the music of a local school or development.

Opera and Theater Music

1134. Abert, Anna Amalie. "Die Barockoper. Ein Bericht über die Forschung seit 1945," In *Acta M*, 41 (1969), p. 121–164.

A narrative account of recent research on Baroque opera in its major national schools, with extensive bibliographies for each section.

1135. Abert, Anna Amalie. "Die Opera zwischen Barock und Romantik: Ein Bericht über die Forschung seit dem Zweiten Weltkrieg." In *Acta M*, 49 (1977), p. 137–193.

A study of research since 1945 on classic period opera, constructed in a similar fashion to her work *Die Barockoper*.

1136. Bustico, Guido. Bibliografia della storia e cronistorie dei teatri italiani. Milano: Bollettino bibliografici musicale, 1929. 82 p.

Subtitle: "Il teatro musicale italiano."

Part I (p. 19–27): a general bibliography of the Italian musical theater. Part II (p. 31–83): a bibliography of the musical theater in specific Italian cities, arranged alphabetically by place. Includes periodical articles. Some brief descriptive annotations.

1137. Cohen, H. Robert and Marie-Odile Gigon. Cent ans de mise en scène lyrique en France (env. 1830–1930). One hundred years of operatic staging in France. Catalogue descriptif des livrets de mise en scène, des libretti annotés et des partitions annotées dans la Bibliothèque dl l'Association de la régie théâtrale (Paris). Préface de Philip Gossett. N.Y.: Pendragon Press, 1986. 334 p. (LA vie musicale en France au XIXe siècle)

"This catalogue limits itself to documents present in the central depository for Parisian staging manuals, the Bibliothèque de l'Association ... [and] it provides an indispensable base upon which later investigations of other collections can build."

Arranged by the title of staged work, supplies name of composers and librettists, and dates of premieres, and describes the *libret de mise en scène*. Indexes to composers, librettists, other names, and to theatres by country and city.

1138. Cowden, Robert H. Concert and opera singers; a bibliography of biographical materials. Westport: Greenwood, 1985. 278 p. (Music Reference Collection, 5)

An annotated bibliography treating collective works and separate monographs. Includes an index to singers in *The New Grove Dictionary of Music and Musicians*. Index of authors. Bibliography. *The New Grove* —Singers—Index

1139. Farkas, Andrew. Opera and concert singers: an annotated international bibliography of books and pamphlets. With a foreword by Richard Bonynge. New York: Garland Pub., 1985. 363 p. (Garland reference library of the humanities, 466)

1140. Fuld, James J. The book of world-famous libretti: the musical theater from 1598 to today. New York: Pendragon Press, 1984.

Extensive descriptions of libretti for 168 operas designated by Fuld as operas of first importance in the current world repertory or for their historical significance.

Review by Marita P. McClymonds in *Fontes artis musicae,* 32 (1985), p. 140–41.

1141. Giovine, Alfredo. Bibliografia di teatri musicali italiani (storia e cronologie) di Alfredo Giovine. Bari: Edizioni Fratelli Laterza, 1982. 67 p. (Biblioteca dell'Archivio delle tradizioni popolari baresi)

A bibliography of histories and chronologies of Italian theaters used for staged musical events, including opera.

1142. Grout, Donald J. "Bibliographies, lexicons, guides, histories, and other works dealing with opera. . . ." In his *A short history of opera. 2nd ed.* New York: Columbia Univ. Press, 1965. p. 585–768.

A 3rd edition appeared in 1987 with Hermine Williams as co-author.

One of the most comprehensive bibliographies of literature on the opera of its time. Includes both books and articles in leading European and American periodicals. Arranged alphabetically by author.

1143. Marco, Guy A. Opera: a research and information guide. New York: Garland Pub., 1984. 373 p.

A classified, annotated bibliography of 704 core titles on opera. Works about operetta and singspiele are included selectively; works on the American musical theater are omitted. All items included are in western European languages. This guide is especially good to studies of individual operas and opera in specific countries and regions. Excludes bibliographies of individuals. Includes as an appendix a checklist of opera composers and their major works. Author-title index and subject index.

1144. "Opern-Uraufführungen in den USA und Kanada seit 1945," in *Musik-bühne,* (1975) p. 189–[242].

A list of American and Canadian opera premieres.

1145. Quellentexte zur Konzeption der europäischen Oper im 17. Jahrhundert. Kassel, etc.: Bärenreiter, 1981. 200 p. (Musikwissenschaftliche Arbeiten, no. 27)

Recent historians have directed their attention to source documents on which our knowledge of music is based. In this case the subject is 17th-century opera. Responsibility for its coverage is shared among Wolfgang Osthoff, Herbert Schneider, and Hellmuth Christian Wolff. Includes bibliographical references and indexes.

1146. Sartori, Claudio. Primo tentativo di catalogo unico dei libretti italiani a stampa fino all'anno 1800. [Milano: Biblioteca nazionale braidense & Ufficio Ricerca Fondi Musicali, 1973–1981]. unnumbered leaves, bound variously by subscribers.

Photocopies of cards gathered by the compiler as a union catalog of printed Italian libretti. Originally intended as a RISM project. The most extensive union catalog of Italian opera.

1147. Senelick, Laurence, David F. Cheshire, and Ulrich Schneider. British music-hall, 1840–1923: a bibliography and guide to sources, with a supplement on European music-hall. Hamden, Conn.: Archon Books, 1981. 361 p.
A bibliography of 3,863 items.

1148. Surian, Elvidio. A checklist of writings on 18th-century French and Italian opera (excluding Mozart). Hackensack: Joseph Boonin, 1970. 121 p. (Music indexes and bibliographies, 3)

1149. Wildbibler, Hubert and Sonja Völklein. The musical; an international annotated bibliography; eine internationale annotierte Bibliographie. München: K. G. Saur, 1986. 320 p.
"An overview . . . of the entire theoretical literature on the stage and film musical from its beginnings to 1986," consisting of 3,629 entries arranged in a classified order. Includes sections on general references, predecessors, history and development, production, "musicals and the public," musicals outside of North America, the film musical, and people associated with musicals. Excludes citations for libretti, scores and reviews of performances. Only citations for the most important works are annotated. Lists of sources and periodicals consulted. Author and subject index.

Primary Sources: Early Music Literature

The entries in this section are concerned with writings on music that appeared before 1800. For further listings of early music literature, one should consult the general bibliographies compiled before 1840, such as Becker (no. 689), Forkel (no. 708), and Lichtenthal (no. 725). See also the narrative bibliography by James E. Matthew (no. 730) and the catalogs of libraries with noteworthy holdings in early music theory, such as the U.S. Library of Congress (no. 2472), the library of Alfred Cortot (no. 2503), and the Paul Hirsch Library in the British Museum (no. 2178). The *RISM* volume, *Écrits imprimés concernant la musique,* is the international union catalog covering separate publications on music (no. 1159).

1150. Bircher, Martin. "Von Boethius bis Hindemith. Eine Züricher Samm-lung von Erstausgaben zur Geschichte der Musiktheorie," in *Librarium,* 13 (1970), p. 134–161.
A description of the Erwin Jacobi collection of first editions of works on music theory.

1151. Bukofzer, Manfred F. "Check-list of Baroque books on music." In his *Music in the Baroque era.* New York: Norton, 1947. p. 417–31.
Theory treatises, instruction books, and histories written between c. 1590 and 1770. Modern facsimiles and reprints indicated. Arranged al-phabetically by author.

1152. Cohen, Albert and Leta E. Miller. Music in the Paris Academy of Sciences, 1666–1793; a source archive in photocopy at Stanford Universi-ty. Detroit: Information Coordinators, 1979. 69 p. (Detroit Studies in Mu-

sic Bibliography, 43)
An index of proceedings of the *Academie Royale des Sciences.*
A study based on these documents has been published under the title
*Music in the French Royal Academy of Sciences: a study in the evolution
of musical thought.* (Princeton, 1981)

1153. Coover, James B. "Music theory in translation; a bibliography." In
Journal of music theory, 3 (1959), p. 70–96; and 13 (1969), p. 230–49.
Cites only English translations of early theory works. Alphabetical
listing, by author, of works from antiquity to the present day.

1154. Davidsson, Åke. Bibliographie der musiktheoretischen Drucke des
16. Jahrhunderts. Baden-Baden: Heitz, 1962. 99 p. (Bibliotheca bibliographica aureliana, 9)
A bibliography of 16th-century theory works; more than 600 titles, arranged alphabetically by author, with bibliographical reference to literature on the sources. Index of persons, including printers, editors, etc.
Bibliography, p. 85–88. 25 facsimile plates.
Review by Fred Blum in *Notes,* 20 (1963), p. 234.

1155. Davidsson, Åke. Catalogue critique et descriptif des ouvrages théoriques sur la musique imprimés au XVIe et XVIIe siècles et conservés
dans les bibliothèques suédoises. Upsala: Almquist & Wiksells, 1953. 83
p. (Studia musicologica upsaliensia, 2)
A union catalog of early works on music theory in Swedish libraries.
108 items, fully described, with locations and references to relevant literature. P. 77–83: bibliography of works cited.

1156. Farmer, Henry G. The sources of Arabian music: an annotated bibli-
ography of Arabic manuscripts which deal with the theory, practice, and
history of Arabian music from the eighth to the seventeenth century.
Leiden: E. J. Brill, 1965. 71 p.
First issued privately by the author in 1940.
Entries arranged chronologically by century, preceded by a brief gen-
eral discussion of Arabian music and its sources.
Review by Jorg Martin in *Die Musikforschung,* 25 (1972), p. 372–73.

1157. Mandyczewski, Eusebius. "Bucher und Schriften uber Musik. Druckwerke und Handschriften aus der Zeit bis zum Jahre 1800." In *Geschichte
der K.K. Gesellschaft der Musikfreunde in Wien. . . .* Wien, 1912. p. 55–84.
An extremely useful listing of the pre-1800 writings on music in the
library of the Gesellschaft der Musikfreunde in Vienna.

1158. Reese, Gustave. Fourscore classics of music literature; a guide to
selected original sources on theory and other writings on music not available in English, with descriptive sketches and bibliographical references. New York: The Liberal Arts Press, 1957. 91 p.
Reprinted by the Da Capo Press, New York, 1970.
80 works presented in chronological order, with illuminating commentary. This bibliography, sponsored by the American Council of Learned
Societies, was intended to stimulate new English editions and transla-

tions of important early theory works. Index of titles.

1159. Répertoire International des Sources Musicales. Ecrits imprimes concernant la musique. Ouvrage publié sous la direction de François Lesure. Munchen: G. Henle, 1971. 2 v. (RISM ser. B VI, 1/2.)

Vol. 1: A-L. Vol. 2: M-Z.

A comprehensive bibliography of writings on music printed before 1800, comprising all theoretical, historical, aesthetic, or technical literature. Location symbols identify copies held in European and American libraries. Brief introduction; listing of the institutions that have contributed information on their holdings.

Anonymous works are listed by title in a separate section and there is an addendum. Index of printers and publishers and a chronological index.

For supplementary information see François Lesure "Ecrits inprimés sur la musique; addenda et corrigenda," in *Fontes artis musicae, 26 (1979), p. 1–4.*

1160. Répertoire International des Sources Musicales. Hebrew writings concerning music in manuscripts and printed books from Geonic times up to 1800 by Israel Adler. München: G. Henle, 1975. 389 p. (RISM, ser. B, pt IX, 2)

"This volume presents a corpus of Hebrew writings concerning music, and not only a catalogue of these sources." The entries for the 276 manuscripts and 384 books are arranged alphabetically by author. Bibliography. Indexes of quotations and references, Hebrew and Arabic titles. There is a general name, title, and subject index.

1161. Répertoire International des Sources Musicales. The theory of music from the Carolingian era up to 1400; descriptive catalogue of manuscripts. Edited by Joseph Smits van Waesberghe, with the collaboration of Peter Fischer and Christian Maas. V. 1– . Munchen: G. Henle, 1961 – . (RISM, ser. B, v. 3:1.)

Offers a description of all manuscripts in which are preserved Latin treatises, however small, dealing with the theory of music which was in use from the Carolingian era to 1400. [*Preface*]

V. 1: Austria, Belgium, Switzerland, Denmark, Fance, Luxembourg, and The Netherlands. (1961) 155 p.

V. 2: Italy. Edited by Peter Fischer. (1968) 148 p. Includes some manuscripts dating from the 15th and even the 16th century when these are sole surviving sources of the earlier tradition.

V. 3: *Manuscripts from the Carolingian era up to c. 1500 in the Federal Republic of Germany, edited by* Michel Huglo and Christian Meyer. (1986)

Each volume includes an index of libraries and an index of authors and of incipits of anonymous treatises.

Review by James B. Coover in *Journal of music theory,* 6 (1962), p. 314–15.

1162. Répertoire International des Sources Musicales. The theory of music in Arabic writings (c. 900–1900): descriptive catalogue of manuscripts in libraries of Europe and the U. S.A. by Amnon Shiloah. München: G.

Henle Verlag, 1979. 512 p. RISM, ser. B, 10

Preceded by an historical introduction and classification of the sources, 341 sources are arrayed by author, analyzed and described. Each entry includes an incipit, an explicit, and bibliographical references. there is a bibliography of library catalogs, a general bibliography, and an Arabic bibliography. There is a general index to names, titles, terms, and subjects.

English or Arabic; pref. in English, French, and German.

1163. Riley, Maurice W. "A tentative bibliography of early wind instrument tutors." In *Journal of research in music education*, 6 (1958), p. 3–24.

The listing is chronological under the various instruments: flute, oboe, clarinet, bassoon, horn, trumpet, trombone, tuba, and related instruments. Annotated.

1164. Vivell, Cölestin. Initia tractatuum musices ex codicibus editorum; collegit et ordine alphbetico disposuit. Genève: Minkoff Reprints, 1979. 352 p.

Reprint of the edition of J. Meyerhoff, Graz, 1912.

Indexes the first lines of each chapter in each treatise in Martin Gerbert's *Scriptores ecclesiastici de musica sacra* and in Edmund de Coussemaker's *Scriptorum de musica medii aevi* and to musical treatises in eleven other 19th-century collections. Includes analytical indexes to sources indexed, an index to authors of treatises (and to titles of anonymous treatises), and a chronological index to treatises. *Scriptores ecclesiastici de musica sacra*—Index *Scriptorum de musica medii aevi*—Index

1165. Warner, Thomas E. An annotated bibliography of woodwind instruction books, 1600–1830. Detroit: Information Coordinators, Inc., 1967. 138 p. (Detroit studies in music bibliography, 11)

A bibliography of 450 items arranged chronologically; includes a number of 'unlocated' titles. Contains a list of modern works cited; indexed by author and anonymous titles and by type of instrument.

1166. Williams, David Russell. A bibliography of the history of music theory. 2nd ed. Fairport, N.Y.: Rochester Music Publishers, 1971. 58 p.

First printed in 1970.

A bibliography of selected theory works and writings devoted to them. Organized chronologically in study units, as in a syllabus. Indexes of treatises and names.

Sacred Music

Bibliographies of writings on sacred music are surprisingly few. Additional references will be found in the various handbooks to hymnology (nos. 418 ff.). See also current listings in the *Jahrbuch fur Liturgik und Hymnologie* (no. 765) and Gregorio Suñol's bibliography of works related to Gregorian chant (no. 1002). Kenneth Hartley's *Bibliography of theses and dissertations in sacred music* (no. 1169) provides information on academic works, each with extensive bibliographies.

1167. Buszin, Walter [*et al.*]. A bibliography on music and the church. Prepared for the Commission on Music, Department of Worship and the Arts, National Council of Churches of Christ in the U.S.A. New York: National Council of Churches, 1958. 16 p.

1168. Daniel, Ralph T. and Peter Le Huray. The sources of English church music 1549–1660. London: Published for the British Academy by Stainer and Bell, 1972. 2 v. (Early English Church Music; supplementary volume 1)

> This is the first attempt to compile a complete inventory of sacred music in English covering the period from the early years of the Reformation to the mid-17th century. [*Preface*]

Part I is a listing of the sources, printed or in manuscript, thematic catalog of all anonymous works, and a first-line index of anthems.

Part II lists services and anthems arranged in alphabetical order by composer with data as to sources and locations.

1169. Hartley, Kenneth R. Bibliography of theses and dissertations in sacred music. Detroit: Information Coordinators, Inc., 1967. (Detroit studies in music bibliography, 9.) 127 p.

1170. Jackson, Irene V. Afro-American religious music: a bibliography and catalogue of gospel music. Westport: Greenwood Press, 1979. 210 p.

The bibliography covers "music of the established Black churches or denominations in the United States and the Caribbean as well as Afro-American cults in the Caribbean and South Americ." Religious music indigenous to west Africa is covered as well. Indexed by subject.

the catalog is arranged by composer and covers music by Afro-Americans written 1938–65 and is based on the collections and catalogs of the Library of Congress.

Review in *Journal of Negro history,* 65 (1980), p. 89–90.

1171. Powell, Martha C. A selected bibliography of church music and music reference materials compiled and annotated by Martha C. Powell; assisted by Deborah C. Loftis. Louisville: Southern Baptist Theological Seminary, 1977. 95 p.

Supplement (10 p.) bound at end.

Oriented to American Protestant denominations.

1172. Szövérfly, Joseph. A guide to Byzantine hymnography: a classified bibliography of texts and studies. Brookline, Massachusetts: Classical Folia Editions; Leyden: E. J. Brill, 1978. 2 v.

An analytical guide to over 6,000 entries and 2,000 separate titles. This is a classified work with titles cited in Roman and non-Roman characters. A third volume completing the bibliography and including indices is anticipated.

1173. Von Ende, Richard C. Church music: an international bibliography. Metuchen: Scarecrow Press, 1980. 453 p.

A classified list of 5,445 works focused almost entirely on works about Christian church music, international in scope. Some anthologies of music are cited. There is an index to authors, editors and compilers.

Individual Composers

In this section are a few representative examples of bibliograpies devoted to writings about specific composers. These are to be distinguished from bibliographies made up of entries for the composer's own works, which will be found in "Bibliographies of Music" under the heading "Music of Individual Composers" (see no. 1595 ff.).

1174. Adams, John L. Musicians' autobiographies; an annotated bibliography of writings available in English 1800 to 1980. Jefferson, N.C.: McFarland, 1982 126 p.

Arranged by author, excluding letters, histories, diaries, and articles in reference works. There are chronological, title, and subject indexes.

1175. Green, Richard D. Index to composer bibliographies. Detroit: Information Coordinators, 1985. 86 p. (Detroit Studies in Music Bibliography, 53)

Deals solely with bibliographies of secondary literature.

BEETHOVEN, LUDWIG VAN

1176. Gyimes, Ferenc and Veronika Vavrineca, ed. Ludwig van Beethoven; a magyar konyvtarakban es gyujtemenyekben. Bibliografia I-III. Budapest: Allami Gorkij Konyvtar, 1970–1972. 3 v.

A union catalog of Beethoven documentation in Hungarian libraries.

V. 1: a bibliography of literature on Beethoven.

V. 2: a discography of 738 items, with index of performing artists and organizations.

V. 3: a bibliography of Beethoven compositions, 1,378 items, with indexes of titles, editors, and publishers.

1177. MacArdle, Donald W. Beethoven abstracts. Detroit: Information Coordinators, 1973. 446 p.

Abstracts of articles about Beethoven from the 18th century through 1964 in four sections: primary periodicals, secondary periodicals, newspapers, catalogs.

BRUCKNER, ANTON

1178. Grasberger, Renate. Bruckner-Bibliographie (bis 1974). Graz: Akademische Druck- u. Verlagsanstalt, 1985. 296 p. (Anton Bruckner Dokumente und Studien, 4)

BUXTEHUDE, DIETRICH

1179. Wettstein, Hermann. Dietrich Buxtehude (1637–1707): eine Bibliographie mit einem Anhang über Nicolaus Bruhns. Freiburg i. Br.: Universtätsbibliothek, 1979. 98 p. (Schriften der Universitätsbibliothek Freiburg i. Br., 2)

Two bibliographies: one about Dietrich Buxtehude and another about

Nicolaus Bruhns.

CHOPIN, FREDERIC

1180. Michalowski, Kornel. Bibliografia chopinowska. Chopin bibliography 1849–1969. Krakow: Polske Wydawnictwo muzyczne, 1970. 268 p.
A well-organized bibliography of literature about Chopin, covering documentary evidence, life, works, interpretation, studies of Chopin's reception, and bibliographical publications.
3,970 items. Text in Polish and English. Indexes of subjects, Chopin's works, and authors.

COPLAND, AARON

1181. Skowronski, JoAnn. Aaron Copland: a bio-bibliography. Westport: Greenwood Press, 1985. 273 p. (Bio-bibliographies in music, 2)
Includes a discography.

COWELL, HENRY

1182. Manion, Martha L. Writings about Henry Cowell: an annotated bibliography. Brooklyn: Institute for Studies in American Music, Conservatory of Music, Brooklyn College of the City University of New York, 1982. 368 p. (I.S.A.M. monographs, 16)

DEBUSSY, CLAUDE

1183. Abravanel, Claude. Claude Debussy; a bibliography. Detroit: Information Coordinators, 1974. 214 p. (Detroit Studies in Music Bibliography, 29)
A broad survey of the literature about Debussy.

HANDEL, GEORGE FREDERIC

1184. Sasse, Konrad. Händel Bibliographie. Zusammengestellt von Konrad Sasse unter Verwendung des im Handel-Jahrbuch 1933 von Kurt Taut veroffentlichten Verzeichnisses des Schrifttums über Georg Friedrich Handel. Abgeschlossen im Jahre 1961. Leipzig: Deutsche Verlag fur Musik, 1963. 352 p.
The expansion of a bibliography compiled by Kurt Taut for the 1933 Handel-Jahrbuch, with a supplement by Sasse published in the 1955 Jahrbuch. A highly organized work citing literature on every aspect of the composer's life and work. Author index.
Review by Willi Reich in *Literature, music, fine arts,* 1 (1968), p. 87–89.

HAYDN, JOSEPH.

1185. Lowens, Irving with Otto E. Albrecht. Haydn in Americ. Detroit: Information Coordinators, 1979. 144 p. (Bibliographies in American Music, 5)
Documents performances and publications in America of Haydn's works. Includes Albrecht's *Haydn autographs in the United States.*

JOSQUIN DES PRES

1186. Charles, Sydney Robinson. Josquin des Prez; a guide to research. N.Y.: Garland, 1983. 235p. (Garland Composer Resource Manuals, 2)(Garland Reference Library of the Humanities, 330)

This work summarizes the contemporaneous documents presenting facts of Josquin's life with references to the literature discussing each document. It provides a categorical list of works about Josquin's music with a list of compositions showing sources, bibliography, recordings, and modern editions of each work. There is a list of sources with modern editions and literature about each cited. Discography with title index. Bibliography of works cited. Index to names of persons, places, and titles. This work serves as an introduction to research on Josquin.

LISZT, FRANZ

1187. Suttoni, Charles . "Franz Liszt's published correspondence: an annotated bibliography" in *Fontes artis musicae,* 26 (1979), p. 191–234.

A good example of the kind of focused bibliographic research that is much needed on the letters of many important composers. Indexes of correspondents and to authors and editors.

MAHLER, GUSTAV

1188. Vondenhoff, Brun and Eleonore Vondenhoff. Gustav Mahler Dokumentation, Sammlung Eleonore Vondenhoff: Materialien zu seinem Leben und Werk. Tutzing: Schneider, 1978. 676 p. (Institut für Österreichische Musikdokumentation, 4)

A 4 p "Ergänzung des Nachtrags" was issued and has been inserted in many copies.

Catalog of the Vondenhoff collection held by the Musiksammlung of the Nationalbibliothek in Vienna.

MENDELSSOHN-BARTHOLDY, FELIX

1189. Bodleian Library. Catalogue of the Mendelssohn papers in the Bodleian Library, Oxford. [By Margaret Crum] Tutzing: Hans Schneider, 1980 – . 2 v. (Musikbibliographische Arbeiten, 7)

Contents: v. 1. Correspondence of Felix Mendelssohn Bartholdy and others; v.2. Music and papers.

MOZART, WOLFGANG AMADEUS

1190. Angermüller, Rudolph and Otto Schneider. Mozart-Bibliographie (bis 1970). *Mozart-Jahrbuch* 1975. Kassel: Bärenreiter, 1976. 362 p. (Mozart-Jahrbuch 1975 des Zentralinstitutes für Mozartforschung der Internationalen Stiftung Mozarteum Salzburg.)

Supplemented by *Mozart-Bibliographie 1976–1980 mit Nachträgen zur Mozart-Bibliographie bis 1975,* by the same authors, published by Bärenreiter, 1982. 175 p.

Over 6,600 entries arranged by author, but indexed by work, persons, places, and subjects. Coverage best for German language works, adequate for works in French and Italian, but clearly less than satisfactory for works in English. The supplement adds over 2,300 entries to the bibliography.

Reviews by A. Hyatt King in *Fontes artis musicae,* 24 (1977), p. 101–02 and in *Fontes artis musicae,* 30 (1983), p. 170. Review by William P. Robinson in *Notes,* 34 (1977), p. 67–70.

PLEYEL, IGNACE

1191. Benton, Rita. Ignace Pleyel: a thematic catalogue of his compositions. N.Y.: Pendragon Press, 1977. 482.

Review by Floyd K. Grave in *JAMS,* 33 (1980), p. 204–10. Review by Lenore Coral in *Notes* 35 (1978), p. 75–76.

RACHMANINOFF, SERGEI

1192. Palmieri, Robert. Sergei Vasilevich Rachmaninoff: a guide to research. N.Y.: Garland, 1984. 335 p. (Garland composer resource manuals, no. 3)

Extensive bibliography, discography, list of compositions, and repertoire list. Indexed.

REGER, MAX

1193. Rösner, Helmut. Max-Reger-Bibliographie. Das internationale Schrifttum über Max Reger 1893–1966. Bonn; Hannover; Munchen: Dummler, 1968. 138 p. (Veroffentlichungen des Max-Reger-Institutes, 5.)

RODGERS, RICHARD

1194. Richard Rodgers Fact Book. New York: Lynn Farnol Group, Inc., 1965. 582 p.

A compendium of facts related to the career of Richard Rodgers. Largest section devoted to his stage, film, and television scores; works entered chronologically from 1920 to 1965, with production information, story, cast, musical numbers, and excerpts from contemporary reviews. General bibliography and discography; indexes of musical compositions and productions.

SCHOENBERG, ARNOLD

1195. Kimmey, John A. The Arnold Schoenberg-Hans Nachod Collection. Detroit: Information Coordinators, 1979. 119 p. (Detroit Studies in Music Bibliography, 41)

Annotated catalog of the collection of correspondence, proof sheets and holographs in the Music Library of North Texas State University, Denton, Texas.

1196. Satoh, Tetsuo. A bibliographic catalog with discography and a comprehensive bibliography of Arnold Schoenberg. Tokyo: Kunitachi Music College Library, 1979. 156 p.

Accompanied by an English guide to the work. 8 p.
In Japanese and English. 2,116 entries in the bibliography of writings about Schoenberg. indexes to titles of compositions, opus numbers, subjects, places, and names. List of periodicals from which articles were drawn.

SCHUMANN, ROBERT

1197. Munte, Frank. Verzeichnis des deutschsprachigen Schrifttums uber Robert Schumann 1956–1970. Hamburg: Wagner, 1972. 151 p.p (Schriftenreihe zur Musik, 1)
Anhang: "Schrifttums über Clara Schumann."

SCHÜTZ, HEINRICH

1198. Skei, Allen B. Heinrich Schütz, a guide to research. New York: Garland, 1981. 186 p. (Garland composer resource manuals, 1)

SIBELIUS, JEAN

1199. Blum, Fred. Jean Sibelius, an international bibliography on the occasion of the centennial celebrations, 1965. Detroit: Information Coordinators, 1965. 114 p. (Detroit studies in music bibliography, 8)
P. 1–11: books and dissertations devoted to Sibelius; p. 13–45: books partially devoted to Sibelius; p. 47–71: music journals; p. 73–94: nonmusic journals. Index of names.
Review by Gerhard Hahne in *Die Musikforschung,* 22 (1969), p. 100; by Ruth Watanabe in *Notes,* 23 (1966), p. 279.

STRAUSS, RICHARD

1200. Ortner, Oswald and Franz Grasberger. Richard-Strauss-Bibliographie. Teil 1: 1882–1944. Wien: Georg Prachner; Kommission bei Verlag Brüer Hollinek, 1964–73. 2 v. (Museion, Veröffentlichungen der Österreichischen Nationalbibliothek, neue Folge, dritte Reihe, 2)
V. 1: 1882–1944; v. 2: 1944–1964.
V. 2 complied by Günther Brosche.
A bibliography organized in terms of various aspects of Strauss's career. The largest section is devoted to writings related to individual works, operas, etc.

WAGNER, RICHARD

1201. Internationale Wagner-Bibliographie 1945–1955. International Wagner bibliography 1945–1955. Bibliographie internationale de la littérature sur Wagner 1945–1955. Hrsg. von Herbert Barth. Bayreuth: Edition Musica, 1956. 56 p.
Second printing issued 1974.
Contains selective listings of German, English, and French writings on Wagner. The appendix offers an international Wagner discography, statistics of performances by major opera companies, and a survey of impor-

tant Wagner collections.

1202. Internationale Wagner-Bibliographie 1956–1960. International Wagner bibliography 1956–1960. Bibliographie internationale de la littérature sur Wagner 1956–1960. Hrsg. von Herbert Barth. Bayreuth: Edition Musica, 1961. 142 p.

This volume follows the same pattern of organization as the preceding but also includes a tabulation of the casts of all the Bayreuth Festivals from 1876 to 1960.

1203. Internationale Wagner-Bibliographie 1961–1966. International Wagner Bibliography 1961–1966. Bibliographie internationale de la littérature sur Wagner 1961–1966 (und Wieland-Wagner-Bibliographie). Bayreuth: Edition Musica, 1968. 99 p.

Includes a bibliography on Wieland Wagner.

1204. Internationale Wagner-Bibliographie 1967–1978. International Wagner bibliography 1967–1978. Bibliographie internationale de la littérature sur Wagner 1967–1978. Hrsg. von Herbert Barth. Bayreuth: Mühl'scher Universitätsverlag W. Fehr, 1979. 175 p.

1205. Kastner, Emerich. Wagner-Catalog. Chronologisches Verzeichniss der von und über Richard Wagner erschienenen Schriften, Musikwerke, etc., etc., nebst biographischen Notizen. Offenbach z.M.: Andre, 1878. 140 p.

Reprint, 1966, by Frits A. M. Knuf, Hilversum.

Chronological listing of Wagner's works and the literature about them from 1813 to 1877.

1206. Oesterlein, Nikolaus. Katalog einer Richard Wagner-Bibliothek; nach den vorliegenden Originalien systematisch-chronologisch geordnetes und mit Citaten und Anmerkungen versehenes authentisches Nachschlagebuch durch die gesammte Wagner-Literatur. Leipzig: Breitkopf & Hartel, 1882–1895. 4 v.

Vols. 1 and 2 of this work consist of a bibliography of late 19th-century writings on Wagner. The remaining volumes consist of a catalog of the holdings of the Richard Wagner-Museum in Eisenach. (See also item no. 1232.)

Bibliographies of Music

In this category are listed bibliographies of *musical scores* as distinct from *writings about music.* This section lends itself to fewer subdivisions than the preceding assemblage of "Bibliographies of Music Literature," the major approaches being that of the performer in search of music appropriate to his particular instrument or ensemble, on the one hand, and that of the student of early music on the other.

Not included here, except for a token listing of some recent titles, are the numerous listings of the works of individual composers. One of the best apporaches to information of this kind is through the biographical dictionaries such as *Baker's* (no. 76) and *Riemann* (no. 57), or such comprehensive encyclopedias as *MGG* (no. 46) and *The New Grove* (no. 48). For thematic catalogs, a useful guide is found in Barry Brook's *Thematic catalogues in music; an annotated bibliography* (no. 3035).

Two significant on-line catalogs with extensive, but not yet exhaustive, coverage of printed music are OCLC (no. 1223) and RLIN (no. 1226). These bibliographic giants are usually not available to the scholar directly, but must be interrogated through intermediaries, knowledgeable music librarians and bibliographers.

This section excludes the catalogs of individual music publishing firms except where their coverage extends beyond the output of a single business house, as in the case of Hofmeister (no. 1217.1) or Pazdirek (no. 1227). Bibliographies of the work of early music publishers are found in the section "Histories and Bibliographies of Music Printing and Publishing."

GENERAL

1207. Aronowsky, Salomon. Performing times of orchestral works. Foreword by Percival R. Kirby. London: E. Benn, 1959. 802 p.

Covers both standard and minor composers of all countries and periods, with some emphasis on British names. Arrangements listed under both composer and arranger. Operas, orchestral versions of single songs, and opera excerpts appear frequently. No precise indication of edition or publisher, but lists of publishers and publishers' organizations are given. The work is a more lavish and expensive publication than seems warranted by its contents.

Review by Howard Mitchell in *Notes,* 17 (1960), p. 237–39.

1208. Berkowitz, Freda P. Popular titles and subtitles of musical compositions. 2nd ed. Metuchen: Scarecrow Press, Inc., 1975. 209 p.

Alphabetical listing of 740 works by title, with brief accounts of the origins of their popular titles. Bibliography. Composer index.

Review by Stephen M. Fry in *Notes,* 32 (1976), p. 554.

1209. Board of Music Trade of the United States of America. Complete catalog of sheet music and musical works. New York: Board of Music Trade, 1970. 575 p.

Reprinted by Da Capo, N.Y., 1973.

Classified catalog of music and books about music published by members of the Board of Music Trade and in print at the time of publication. Scanty bibliographic information provided and not indexed. Excludes numerous publishers not members of the Board.

Review by Don Hixon in *American reference books annual* (1975), no. 1,121.

1210. Bonner Katalog: Verzeichnis reversgebundener musikalischer Aufführungsmateriale. Bearbeitet und herausgegeben vom Deutschen Musikarchiv der Deutschen Bibliothek in Verbindung mit dem Deutschen Musikverleger-Verband e.V.—2., neubearbeitete Aufl. München; New York: K.G. Saur, 1982. 530 p.

A catalog of performance materials available through German music dealers. See no. 1279 for a full description.

1211. Boustead, Alan. Music to Shakespeare, a practical catalogue of current incidental music, song settings and other related music.... London:, printed by Novello and Co., sole distributor. Oxford Univ. Press, 1964. 40 p.

Shakespearean works entered alphabetically, with music given under three headings: (1) incidental music, (2) songs, (3)other music. Minimal bibliographical information. Indexes of song titles and of composers. No key to publishers.

For other listings of Shakespeare music, see no. 1213, below.

1212. British Broadcasting Corporation. Central Music Library. [Catalogues] London: BBC, 1965–67. 9 v.

[1] *Chamber music catalogue:* chamber music, violin and keyboard, 'cello and keyboard, various (1965). 1 v., various pagings.

[2] *Piano and organ catalogue* (1965). 2 v., various pagings.

[3] *Song catalogue* (1966). 4 v. Vols. 1–2, composers; vols. 3–4, titles.

[4] *Choral and opera catalogue* (1967). 2 v. Vol. 1, composers; vol. 2, titles.

[5] *Orchestral catalogue* (1982) 4 v. Edited by Sheila Compton.

These volumes record the holdings of one of the world's great radio libraries and are known as the *BBC catalogs.* Each volume is devoted to a special category of materials. Entries include composer's full name, dates if known, title of the work, score or parts, duration, publisher. A bibliography of relevant reference works and a listing of the principal music publishers are given in each volume. The chief value of this set lies in the information it offers as a reference tool. The BBC Music Library is not a lending library.

Published under the supervision of John H. Davies, former BBC Music Librarian; with an introduction by William Glock.

Review of vol. 1 (Chamber music catalogue) by Donald W. Krummel in *Notes,* 23 (1966), p. 46–48.

1213. Catalogue of Musical Works Based on the Plays and Poetry of Shakespeare. In *Shakespeare in Music. Compiled by* Winton Dean, Dorothy Moore, and Phyllis Hartnoll. London: Macmillan, 1964. p. 243–321.

Works listed under the titles of the plays, in three categories: opera, incidental music, song settings. Check-list of composers. The bibliography of operatic settings, by Winton Dean, is also published in *Shakespeare survey,* no. 18 (1965), p. 75–93.

1214. Coover, James B. "Composite music manuscripts in facsimile" in *Notes,* 38 (1981), p. 275–95.

A guide to manuscript sources accessible in printed books. The manuscripts are listed alphabetically by location. Index to personal names, to items represented in RISM, an to those in series.

1215. Cudworth, Charles. "Thematic index of English eighteenth-century overtures and symphonies", in the Appendix to *Proceedings of the Royal Musical Association,* 78 (1953), 9 p.

Appendix to his paper *"The English symphonists of the eighteenth century".*

1216. Cudworth, Charles. "Ye olde spuriosity shoppe, or, Put it in the Anhang." In *Notes,* 12 (1954–55), p. 25–40, 533–53.

A lively discussion of the problems of plagiarism, hoaxes, misattribution, and the use of pseudonyms in the field of music. The article contains three useful supplements: (1) spuriosities proper, listed under their supposed composers; (2) nicknames and falsely titled compositions; (3) pseudonyms, altered forms of names, and nicknames.

For a work covering similar material, see nos. 2389.

1217. Documents du Demi-Siècle. Tableau chronologique des principales œuvres musicales de 1900 a 1950 etabli par genre et par annee. Numero special. *La revue musicale,* no. 216 (1952), 146 p.

A listing, year by year, of the important musical works of the first half of the 20th century, together with miscellaneous information relating to music for each year. Catalogs of six publishers, with significant work issued by them between 1900 and 1950: Heugel, Costallat, Amphion, Ricordi, Choudens, Ouvrieres. Minimal bibliographical information.

1217.1. Hofmeister, Friedrich. Verzeichnis der in Deutschland seit 1868 erschienenen Werke russischer Komponisten. Leipzig: Druck der Buchdruckerei Frankenstein, 1949. 253 p.

Alphabetical listing of composers, with their works in order of opus number. Detailed bibliographical information including price but lacking date of publication.

1218. McCarty, Clifford. Film composers in America: a check-list of their work. Foreword by Lawrence Morton. Glendale, Calif.: John Valentine, [1953]. 193 p.

Reprint by Da Capo Press, New York, 1972.

163 names, with film scores listed by date. Index of film titles; index of orchestrators.

Review by Frederick W. Sternfeld in *Notes,* 11 (1953), p. 105.

1219. Meggett, Joan M. Keyboard music by women composers: a catalog and bibliography; foreword by Nancy Fierro. Westport: Greenwood Press, 1981. 210 p.

A catalog of the work of 290 coposers including brief biographies and lists of sources. Discography. Extensive, annotated bibliography of sources referring to more than one woman composer.

1220. Mies, Paul. Volkstumliche Namen musikalischer Werke. Bonn: Musikhandel-Verlags, [1960]. 32 p.

Nicknames and popular titles for musical compositions listed under composers, with an alphabetical index of titles. Similar compilations are cited as nos. 1208, 1216.

1221. Music Educators' National Conference. Selective Music Lists. Reston, Virginia: Music Educators National Conference.

From time to time, the MENC has issued lists of compositions especially suited to meet the needs of school musical ensembles. Some of these lists cover sufficiently unusual repertories to warrent inclusion here.

Vocal solos, vocal ensembles. Compiled cooperatively with the American Choral Directors Association and the Society for the Preservation and Encouragement of Barber Shop Quartet Singing in America, 1974. 86 p.

Music for children's choirs. Compiled under the direction of the Boy and Children's Choirs Standing Committee of the American Choral Directors Association, 1977. 44 p.

1222. Music in print Series. Philadelphia: Musicdata, 1974– . 6 volumes and annual supplements (1979–).

v.1: Choral music in print Sacred choral music. 1st ed, 1974. 2nd ed. Sacred choral music in print by Gary S. Eslinger and F. Mark Daugherty, 1985. 2 v.

v. 2: Choral music in print Secular choral music. 1974.

Supplement v.: Choral music in print: 1976 supplement.

Supplement v.: Sacred choral music in print: 1981 supplement, by Nancy K. Nardone.

Supplement v.: Secular choral music in print: 1982 supplement.

v. 3: Organ music in print, ed. by Thomas R. Nardone.1st ed., 1975. 2nd ed. by Walter A. Frankel, 1984.

v. 4: Classical vocal music in print. 1976.

Supplement v.: Classical vocal music in print: 1985 supplement, ed. by Gary R. Eslinger.

v. 5: Orchestral music in print, ed. by Margaret K. Farish. 1979.

Supplement v.: Orchestral music in print: 1983 supplement.

Supplement v.: Educational section of orchestral music in print. 1978.

v. 6: String music in print, ed. by Margaret K. Farish. 2nd ed., 1980.
Supplement v.: String music in print: 1984 supplement.

Using the information supplied by cooperating publishers, the series lists
specific editions which are available from a publisher ... in appropriate
categories. ... The *Music-in-print series* is kept up to date by means of the
... *Annual supplements.* Each year's *Supplement* contains a separate section
updating each volume already published in the series. The updates are
cumulative ..." [from the *Introduction*]

Within categories, entries are arranged by composer, then title. Instrumentation, duration, publisher, and availability of parts are indicated. Many collections are analyzed. Cross references are provided. Each
volume contains a directory of publishers. Volumes devoted to a single
category include a composer-title index.

1223. OCLC. 1971– .
The first of on-line bibliographic utilities in the United States, OCLC
presently connects about 3,000 libraries, some from Europe and the rest
American, to a computer and bibliographic data base of immense size
near Columbus, Ohio. Among the important music libraries which have
contributed to the OCLC data base are those at the University of Illinois
at Champaign/Urbana, Indiana University, the Eastman School of Music, the University of Texas, the University of California at Los Angeles,
Oberlin College Conservatory, University of Wisconsin at Madison, The
Newberry Library the University of California at San Diego, North Texas
State University, Florida State University, Ohio State University, New
England Conservatory of Music, Westminster Choir College, and the University of Maryland.

Although cataloging on OCLC began in 1971, numerous retrospective
conversion projects have proceeded and the data base is extraordinarily
rich in music imprints of all periods. Current cataloging from the Library of Congress is loaded into the data base continuously. There are
presently over 17,300,000 works represented by bibliographic records in
the data base.

In the OCLC data base, a bibliographic record is stored only once and
sigla indicating which libraries hold the item in question are added.
Catalog records for scores, sound recordings, books, microforms, video
disks and tapes, and other library materials are included in the data base.
There are over 490,000 bibliographic records for sound recordings and
over 357,000 for scores.

Access to bibliographic records in the OCLC data base is accomplished
through the use of "search keys," truncated versions of author or composer name and/or initial title words. Lately through a special service, one
may use subject headings as access terms for the last several years'
entries to the data base. Soon access by subjects will be possible for the
entire data base.

The fundamental basis for the OCLC data base was the creation of
catalog cards for traditional North American card catalogs in libraries.
For this reason, scholars generally have not been encouraged to use the
data base directly for their own purposes; reference librarians usually
have had to act as intermediaries between the researcher and the data
base. A number of articles on the OCLC data base have been written,
principal among them being "Music in the OCLC online union catalog:
a review" by Richard P. Smiraglia and Ralph R. Papakhian. Music
catalogers, reference librarians, and others who use the OCLC services

have formed a "users group" and have published the *Music OCLC Users Group Newsletter.*

The extensive data base and telecommunications network among libraries has made interlibrary loan more efficient and effective for libraries connected to the OCLC computers, both in the United States and in Europe. Last year over 3 million requests were handled to the great benefit of, among others, musical scholars.

1224. Olmsted, Elizabeth H. Music Library Association catalog of cards for printed music, 1953–1972; a supplement to the Library of Congress catalogs. Totowa, N. J.: Rowman and Littlefield, 1974. 2 v.

Entries for printed music reported to the *National Union Catalog* for the period 1956–72. Complements cataloging in the Library of Congress catalogs treating music (see nos. 1252, 1253). Photocopies of cards supplied with attendent reproduction difficulties. Name of library holding each title not included.

1225. Reddick, William. The standard musical repertoire, with accurate timings. Garden City, N.Y.: Doubleday & Co., 1947. 192 p.

Reprint by the Greenwood Press, New York, 1969.

A classified list of overtures, orchestral works, works for piano and for violin, songs, and choral compositions, with timings to the nearest five seconds. Designed primarily for program directors of radio stations.

1226. Research Libraries Information Network (RLIN).

RLIN is the on-line bibliographic service of the Research Libraries Group, a partnership of about 40 American libraries, many of them the largest in the country. Among the important music libraries contributing to RLIN are those at the New York Public Library, Yale University, the University of California at Berkeley, Stanford University, Cornell University, Princeton University, University of Michigan, the University of Pennsylvania, Peabody Conservatory, Dartmouth College, State University of New York at Buffalo, and lately Harvard University and the Eastman School of Music. Current cataloging from the Library of Congress is loaded into the data base continuously. Numerous retrospective conversion projects have been carried out and the data base is quite rich in music imprints of all periods.

In the RLIN data base, each library's catalog records are stored uniquely, but clustered in most of the files around a single version of the record. The data base is segmented by form, so there are separate files for scores, sound recordings, serials, books and so forth. There is no way of knowing how many of the 26,681,000 catalog records in the books file are related to books about music, but there are about 210,000 bibliographic records for sound recordings and 436,500 bibliographic records for scores. RLIN ennumerates every repetition of a bibliographic record, so the number of unique bibliographic records is considerably smaller than the figures above suggest.

Access to the data base is possible through personal and corporate names, title phrases, words in titles, and/or subject phrases. Names, words, and phrases may be truncated. Indexes may be combined using the Boolean operators and, or, & and not. Once a search on any of these indexes has been accomplished, it may be further modified by date or range of dates of imprint, by publisher, by language, by place of publication, by publisher, by words in subject phrases, and by the holdings of a specific library.

The RLIN data base is driven not only by the desire to share cataloging information among the partner libraries and the other libraries the network serves, but also by the programs of the various standing and special committees of the Research Libraries Group, of which the Music Program Committee is one. Among the many services offered by RLIN, like OCLC interlibrary loan is a particularly effective service to users of the network.

1227. Universal-Handbuch der Musikliteratur aller Zeiten und Volker. Als Nachschlagewerk und Studienquelle der Welt-Musikliteratur. Wien: Pazdirek & Co., [1904–10?] 14 v.

Reprint 34 v. in 12 by Knuf, Hilversum, [1966?]

Known as *Pazdirek,* the nearest thing to a comprehensive listing of 'music in print' ever published. Primarily useful for 19th-century material in establishing the existence of and dates of editions. Arrangement under composer by opus number, if known; otherwise by title.

1228. Wettstein, Hermann. Thematische Sammelverzeichnisse der Musik: ein bibliographischer Führer durch Musikbibliotheken und -archive. Laaber: Laaber-Verlag, 1982. 268 p.

A unique bibliography focused on collections found in some of the major music libraries and archives. The choice of collections is highly selective and the compiler may mean collections down to a single volume with multiple contents. 4 p. name and place index is appended.

1229. Yogaku sakuin: sakkyokusha to gendai to yakudai o hikidasu tame no. Music index: for reference to original composers, foreign titles and Japanese titles, compiled by Takashi Ogawa. Tokyo: The Min-On Music Library, 1975. 769 p.

Text in English and Japanese characters.

P. 1–294, entries by composer, alphabeticaly arranged. P. 297–503, entries by titles in Western languages.

. 507–765, entries by title in Japanese.

CURRENT

The current music bibliographies listed below restrict their entries to music only. For a full coverage, one should be acquainted with the various national bibliographies in which music appears in company with listings from other fields. An excellent introduction to the use of these major bibliographical tools is an article by Donald W. Krummel and James B. Coover, "Current national bibliographies, their music coverage," in *Notes,* 17 (1960), p. 375–88.

See also the current listings and reviews in such periodicals as *Notes, Fontes artis musicae, Acta Musicologica,* the *Music review* and the *Musical times.*

1230. Le Bibliograph Musical. Paraissant tous les deux mois avec le concours d'une Reunion d'artistes et d'erudits. Premiere Annee (1872)—Cinquieme Annee (1876), Numero 1-29. Paris: 1872-76. Continuous pagination, 499 p.

Reprint of the complete set by Schnase, 1968.

A bibliographical journal issued bimonthly by a group of scholars, librarians, and musicians (the number varies). Contains short articles of bibliographical interest, reports of auction sales, reviews, descriptions of music institutions, etc. The most frequent contributor is Arthur Pougin.

1231. Bibliographia Hungarica 1945–1960. Catalogus systematicus notarum musicarum in Hungaria editarum. Edidit Bibliotheca Nationalis Hungariae a Francisco Szechenyi fundata. Budapest: Országos Széchényi Konyvtár, 1969. 361 p.

A classified listing of all Hungarian music publications between 1945 and 1960. Indexed by composers and by first line of texts. P. 353–61: a schematic outline of the classification system. A publication of the National Szechenyi Library; the principal editors are Ivan Pethes, Veronika Vavrineca, and Jeno Vecsey.

1232. Bibliographie Musicale Francaise, publiée par la Chambre Syndicale des Éditeurs de Musique. Annee 1–26, Numero 1–192. Paris: La Chambre Syndicale des Editeurs de Musique, 1875–1920. 47 v. in 23.

Reprint of the original edition by Annemarie Schnase, Scarsdale, N.Y., 1968.

A monthly trade list of music issued by the major French publishers over a period of 45 years. The lists are classified by performing media. Some of the publishers represented are: Colombier, Choudens, Lemoine, Brandus, Durand, Gauthier, Grus, Heugel, Le Bailly, Leduc, and E. Mathieu.

1233. The British Catalogue of Music. London: The Council of the British National Bibliography, 1957– . 1– .

Published quarterly; the last issue of each year is a cumulated annual volume. Organized in two parts: a classified and an alphabetical section. There is also a section devoted to musical literature. Lists of music publishers with their British agents specified.

The classification scheme used in this catalog has been published separately; see no. 3034.

1234. Brünn. Universita. Knihovna. Prírustky hudebnin v ceskoslovenských knihovnäch. Spracoval Zdeněk Zouhar. Praha: Statni Pedagogicke Nakladatelstvi, 1953– .

Joint accession list of 10 principal music libraries in Czechoslovakia, listing 2,000–3,000 items per year. Classified by medium, without index.

1235. Central Opera Service Bulletin. Directory of operas and publishers, in two parts. New York : Central Opera Service, 1976. 2 v. in 1. (118 p.)

Issued as Volume 18, numbers 2 & 3 of the Central Opera Service Bulletin.

A bibliography of opera scores currently available.

1236. Composium Directory of New Music. V. 1– . Los Angeles, Crystal Record Company, 1971– .

Composium, a quarterly index of contemporary compositions, is a list of recent works by living composers, and includes both published and currently unpublished compositions. The *Directory of new music,* published annually, includes all the works that have been listed in the Quarterly during the preceding year. These are indexed here by instrumentation as well as by composer. Also included are brief biographical sketches of each of the composers listed. [From the *Preface* by Peter Christ, Editor, *Composium,* President, Crystal Record Co.]

Title and frequency vary: *Annual index of contemporary compositions, editor* Carol Cunning (1979).

1237. Deutsche Musikbibliographie. Jahrgang 1– . Leipzig, F. Hofmeister, 1829– .
see no. 758 for full annotation.

1238. Deutscher Büchereiverband. Arbeitsstelle für das Büchereiwesen. Musikbibliographischer Dienst (MD). 1.-13. Jahrgang. Berlin, Deutscher Buchereiverband, 1970–82.
A periodical publication that was issued six times yearly, the sixth issue being a cumulation listing all of the current publications of serious music. International in scope, but German in practice since information was reported by 12 German public libraries. The editors were Burchard Bulling and Helmut Fosner. Entries printed in catalog card format on one side of the page so that they could be cut and filed in a card tray. The publication was also available in loose sheets for this purpose.

1239. Fontes Artis Musicae. Review of the International Association of Music Libraries. 1954– .
Until 1976 each issue contains a "Liste internationale selective" largely devoted to listings of current music publications by country, compiled by a series of national editors. Thereafter there is an occasional shorter, annotated list entitled "Publications à caractère bibliographique."
This entry is also found under "Bibliographies of Music Literature: Current or Annual," no. 761.

1240. Hofmeisters Handbuch der Musikliteratur. Bd. 1– . Leipzig: F. Hofmeister, 1844– .
see no. 762 for full annotation.

1241. Jahresverzeichnis der Deutschen Musikalien und Musikschriften. Jahrgang 1– . Leipzig: F. Hofmeister, 1852– .
see no. 767 for full annotation.

1242. Letopis' Muzykal'noi Literatury; organ gosudarstzennoi bibliografii SSSR. Izdtsia s 1931 goda; vykhodit 4 raza v god. Moskva: Izdatel'stvo vsesoiuznoi knizhnoi palaty, 1931– .
Quarterly. Organization and content vary slightly. In 1960 a classified list of publications in musical notation. Includes literary works with musical supplements or extensive musical illustrations, and music is-

sued in periodicals. Index by composer for each issue, and separate lists of books, magazines, newspapers containing music. Annual index of vocal works by title and first line, and by language of text. Entries give full bibliographical information, including complete contents, price, size of edition.

1243. National Union Catalog: Music and phonorecords. 1953–57—1968–72. A cumulative list of works represented by Library of Congress printed cards. Ann Arbor: J. W. Edwards, 1958–73. 11 v. (The Library of Congress catalogs)

The quinquennial cumulation of Library of Congress catalog: *Music and phonorecords.* Continued by: National union catalog: *Music, books on music and sound recordings.*

Originally issued semi-annually with annual cumulations, contains entries for scores, recordings (musical and otherwise), libretti, and books about music and musicians.

1244. National Union Catalog. Music, books on music, and sound recordings. Washington: Library of Congress, 1973– . (Library of Congress catalogs)

Semi-annual, with annual (the 2nd issue of each year) and quinquennial cumulations (published by Rowman and Littlefield, Totowa, N.J., 8 v. covering 1973–77 and 7 v. covering 1978–80).

Continues the Library of Congress catalog *Music and phonorecords.*

Contains bibliographic records created by the Library of Congress and by participating libraries whose collection efforts are sufficiently broad and their cataloging standards sufficiently worthy.

1245. The New Music repertoire directory. N.Y.: American Music Center and Chamber Music America, 1981– . 2 v.

Second volume edited by Margaret Jory.

A list of "interesting or successful" new music solicted from a number of ensembles and composers' organizations. Each entry supplies title, instrumentation, source of score and performance materials, and the name of the ensemble recommending it. Arranged by composer with lists of participating ensembles and "resource oraganizations."

1246. U.S. Copyright Office. Catalog of copyright entries. Music. Washington, D.C.: Governnment Printing Office, 1947–77. Third series, v. 1–31, 1947–77.

In the series from 1906 to 1946 a music catalog was published separately. In 1946 it was subdivided into separate sections: published music, unpublished music, and renewal registrations, with main entries by composer and a classified index. This arrangement was maintained until vol. 11 of the third series (1958), when the listings were grouped under "current registrations" and "renewal registrations," with the main entry under title and a name index for composers.

Cites all music deposited for copyright in the U.S. whether published in the U.S. or elsewhere. Arranged by title with index to names of composers, authors, editors, compilers, arrangers and so forth. The *Catalog of copyright entries* is the most comprehensive catalog of music of its time.

In 1978, the *Catalog of copyright entries* went into a fourth series, issued only in microfiche. Music entries are included in two sections: part 3, Performing arts, issued quarterly, for scores; and part 7, Sound recordings, issued semi-annually. Each part is provided with an index of names cited in it. Citations include basic bibliographic information.

1247. U.S. Copyright Office. Catalog of copyright entries . . . pt. 3: Musical compositions. Washington, D.C.: Government Printing Office, 1906–46. n.s. v. 1–41.

From 1891 to 1906, the quarterly copyright index was issued by the Treasury Department and musical compositions were included as part of the general series. From 1906 to 1945, music (published or not) was entered by title in each monthly issue, followed by renewals, with an annual index. In 1946 this arrangement was succeeded by a division into: unpublished music; published music; renewals; title index to the first two sections.

This section of the *Catalog of copyright entries,* including some entries covering registrations beginning in 1891, was issued in 65 reels of microfilm by the Library of Congress Photoduplication Service in 1980. Reels 1–13 consist of copy of every index, weekly, quarterly, and annual covering years 1898–1946 to facilitate copyright searches. Actual entries for 1891–1946 begin with reel 14.

This is a reproduction of the *Catalog of copyright entries, pt. 3: musical compositions.*

1248. U.S. Copyright Office. Catalog of copyright entries . . . 4th series, part 3: Performing arts. Washington, D.C.: Government Printing Office, 1978 – .

This new series began with the implementation of the Copyright Act of 1976. Musical works (published and otherwise) are entered by title and there is an index of authors, claimants, and other names associated with each work. Entries for sound recordings appear in part 7. This is a microfiche catalog.

1249. U.S. Library of Congress. Library of Congress catalog, Music and phonorecords, a cumulative list of works represented by Library of Congress printed cards. Washington, D.C., The Library of Congress, 1954–72. A semi-annual publication.

Current music accessions, printed or sound recordings, of the Library of Congress and of libraries participating in its cooperative cataloging program. Includes purchased current or retrospective materials and a selection of recent copyright deposits. Entries are reproduced from the library's printed cards. Name and subject index. Semi-annual, with annual cumulation.

NATIONAL MUSIC

In this section are to be found bibliographies of music (scores) concerned with the music of particular nations. Many of these bibliographies originate in various national music centers that exist for the purpose of promoting the works of native composers. For a survey of such organizations, their history, services, publications, see "Directory of national music centers," (no. 2972).

Several of the works cited in the section "Bibliographies of music literature: National Music" also include listings of composers' works.

AUSTRALIA

1250. Australasian Performing Rights Association. Catalogue of major musical compositions by Australian and New Zealand composers. Sydney: 1967? 53 p.

Supplementary catalogue of New Zealand composers. 9 p.

BELGIUM

1251. Auda, Antoine. La musique et les musiciens de l'ancien pays de Liége. Essai bio-bibliographique sur la musique liégeoise depuis ses origines jusqu' à la fin de la principauté (1800). Bruxelles: Librairie Saint-Georges [etc.], 1930. 291 p.

A study of composers active in Liège until about 1800. Works and publications are cited.

1252. Centre Belge de Documentation Musicale. Catalogus van werken van Belgische componisten. Bruxelles: Centre Belge de Documentation Musicale, 1953–57.

An irregularly published series of catalogs averaging 20 pages each, devoted to contemporary Belgian composers and their works. Some in French, others in Flemish.

CANADA

1253. Canadian Music Centre. Catalogue of Canadian choral music available for perusal from the library of the Canadian Music Centre. [3rd ed.] Toronto:, Canadian Music Centre, 1978.

First issued in 1966, with an *Addendum* bringing the coverage up to 1970.

Classified listing with colored paper identifying sections devoted to mixed voices, female voices, and male voices. Composer listing and list of publishers.

Other Canadian Music Centre publications:

Canadian music for orchestra. (1976)
  Canadian chamber music. (1971, supplement 1976)
  Canadian keyboard music. (1976)
  Canadian vocal music. 3rd ed. (1976)
  List of Canadian operas. . . . (1978)
  List of Canadian music for guitar. (1980)

1254. Contemporary Canadian composers edited by Keith MacMillan and John Beckwith. Toronto; New York: Oxford University Press, 1975. 248 p.

A bio-bibliographical work concerning composers productive since 1920. Entries reviewed by subjects.

1255. Jarman, Lynn. Canadian music: a selected check-list 1950–73. La musique canadienne: une liste sélective 1950–73. A selective listing of Canadian music from *Fontis artis musicae*, 1954–73 based on the catalogued entries of *Canadiana* from 1950. Foreword by Helmut Kallmann. Toronto; Buffalo: University of Toronto Press, 1976. 170 p.

A Canadian Association of Music Llibraries bibliographical project cumulating entries for Canadian music in *Fontes artis musicae* in a classified arrangement. Index to composers and authors.

CHINA

1256. Chung-kuo ku-tai yin-yüeh shu-mu. Compiled by the Institute of Chinese music at the Central Conservatory of Music, Pei-ching. Pei-ching: Yin yüeh ch'u pàn she, 1962. 142 p.

A bibliography of works about ancient Chinese music divided into three parts: books on music commonly available; books known to be in existence but not seen by the author; known lost works. Works on histories and theory, vocal music, dance music, music to accompany storytelling, theatrical music, instruments, religious and ceremonial music, ch'in and music technique are covered. Each entry provides titles, author or editor imprint information, and call numbers in the Library of Musical Research in the Central Music Conservatory in Pei-ching.

1257. Chung-kuo yin yüeh shu p'u chih. Pei-ching: Peoples Music Press, 1984. 200 p.

This is a union catalog of holdings of Chinese music titles in 37 Chinese libraries covering the period from 722 B.C. to 1949. It is a classified catalog in two parts, one for the period from 722 B.C. to 1911 and another for 1912–1949. There is an index to all titles.

1258. Yüan, T'ung-li. Chung-kuo yin yüeh shu p'u mu lu. [Bibliography on Chinese music]. T'ai-pei: Chung hua kuo yüeh hui, [1956]. 24, 49, 4 p.

In Chinese and English.

DENMARK

1259. Dansk Komponistforening. Danske komponister af i dag; ben vaerkfortegnelse. Danish composers of today; a catalogue of works. Dänische Komponisten von Heute; ein Werkverzeichnis. København: Dansk Komponistforening, 1980– . 2 v. (loose leaf)

Works, including information on publisher and performing forces necessary, cited in chronological order. Includes separate list of members of the Danske Komponistforening with addresses and telephone numbers; separate listing for music publishers. No biographies.

The catalogue will be constantly updated with new works, and new composers. Revised and additional pages will be sent automatically to those who possess a copy of the catalogue. [*Forward*]

1260. Dansk Musikfortegnelse 1931–1979. Compiled by the Music Department of the Danish Royal Library and edited by Susanne Sugar. Copenhagen: Ballerup, the Danish Library Bureau, 1980– .

The Danish national bibliography of music. Appears originally as monthly listings, and then is published separately as an annual cumulation. Five-year cumulations will be provided with both alphabetical and classified entries.

Coverage is not only for music published in Denmark, but also music by Danish composers or edited by Danes published anywhere, music with a Danish text in Danish or in translation, and music based on Danish themes or the works of Danish authors.

1261. Samfundet Til Udgivelse af Dansk Musik 1871–1971. The Society for Publishing Danish Music. Catalogue. København: Dan Fog Musikforlag, 1972. 115 p.

A similar listing was published in 1956 by Knud Larsen Musikforlag, with a *Supplement* in 1968.

The catalog is preceded by a history of the society. Contents: *An outline of Danish music history;* the composers; catalogue of publications; chronological list of publications; cystematical list of publications; Samfundet's LP-Records.

P. 20–38: brief biographies of the composers; p. 39–85: the catalog, arranged alphabetically by composer. Chronological and systematic lists of publications; recordings issued by the society, a general index, and a 1972 price list.

FINLAND

1262. Säveltäjain Tekijänoikeustoimisto Teosto. Catalogue of Finnish orchestral and vocal compositions. Helsinki:, Teosto (Composers' copyright bureau), 1961. 88 p.

Lists works by 57 Finnish composers giving titles, instrumentation, timings, publishers. Brief biographical sketches. English translations of Finnish titles.

1263. Suomalaista musiikkia. Suomalaista musiikkia: suomalainen orkesterimusiikki, orkesterisaestyksellinen vokaalimusiikki, oopperamusiikki, balettimusiikki. Finnish music: Finnish orchestral works, vocal works with orchestra, operas, ballets. Helsinki: Luovan Saveltaiteen Edistamissaatio, 1973. 282 p.

A bibliography of works by Finnish composers in English and Finnish.

FRANCE

1264. Boll, André. Répertoire analytique de la musique française des origines à nos jours. Paris: Horizons de France, 1948. 299 p.

Not as comprehensive as the title suggests. Part I: a list of composers of the French school, with dates, arranged alphabetically within historical periods. Part II: classified list of published French secular music, alphabetical by composer, followed by a similar listing of sacred music. Publishers given; indexed by works and by composers.

1265. Pierreuse, Bernard. Catalogue général de l'édition musicale en France: livres, méthodes et partitions de musique sérieuse en vente. General catalog of music publishing in France: books, methods, and scores of serious music on sale. Paris: Editions Jobert; Distribution, Editions musicales transatlantiques, 1984. 476 p.

A classified listing of available works arranged by composer or author in each section. Title, version, publisher and occasionally date of composition are indicated. There is an index to composers. Coverage to 1982. For the choral and band sections, only classical works are listed.

GERMANY (DEUTSCHE DEMOKRATISCHE REPUBLIK)

1266. Bibliographie der deutschen Arbeiterliedblätter 1844–1945: Akademie der Künste der Deutschen Demokratischen Republik. Sektion Musik. Abteilung Arbeiterliedarchiv. Bearb. von e. Kollektiv d. Arbeiterliedarchivs; unter Leitung von Inge Lammel. 1. Aufl. Leipzig: Deutscher Verlag für Musik, 1975. 320 p.

A bibliography, including indexes to collections, of songs of working persons in Germany, 1844–1945.

GERMANY (BUNDESREPUBLIK DEUTSCHLAND)

1267. Dupont, Wilhelm. Werkausgaben Nürnberger Komponisten in Vergangenheit und Gegenwart. Nürnberg: Selbstverlag der Stadtbibliothek, 1971. 378 p. (Beiträge zur Geschichte und Kultur der Stadt Nürnberg, 18)

A list of editions of music by composers from Nürnberg.

1268. Deutscher Musikverleger-Verband. Bonner Katalog. Verzeichnis reversgebundenem Aufführungsmateriale. 2., neubearbeitete Auflage. Bearbeitet und herausgegeben vom Deutschen Musikarchiv der Deutschen Bibliothek in Verbindung mit dem Deutschen Musikverleger-Verband e.V. München; N.Y.; London; Paris: K. G. Saur, 1982. 530 p.

First published in 1959.

Not a catalog of German music, strictly speaking, but a listing by composer of musical works marketed in Germany and protected by international copyright under the Bern Convention. Copyright editions of works by early composers included. Types of works indicated by symbols; duration and publishers given. Excellent source of information on published contemporary music. Entries under authors of text, editors, arrangers and translators.

GERMANY (DEUTSCHE DEMOKRATISCHE REPUBLIK)

1269. Simbriger, Heinrich. Werkkatatlog zeitgenössischer Komponisten aus den deutschen Ostgebieten. Esslingen-Necker: Kunstlergilde, 1955. 203 p. *Erganzungsband,* 1961. 151 p.

A classified bibliography of works by East German composers. Entries give title of work, instrumentation, publisher if any, and timing. A preliminary section is devoted to biographical sketches of the composers.

1270. Was Wir Singen. Katalog des in der Deutschen Demokratischen Republik erschienenen weltlichen Lied- und Chormaterials. Band I: 1945–58 Auswahl. Herausgegeben vom Zentralhaus fur Volkskunst. Leipzig: Friedrich Hofmeister, 1959. 255 p.

Title listing of 6,582 entries, supplemented by lists of collections and of cantatas and oratorios. Indexed by subtitles or working titles, by voice combination and by affective theme, and by national character. Further indexes by writer of text and composer.

GREAT BRITAIN

1271. British Music Catalogue 1945–1981. Volume I:Works for piano [by] Paul Griffiths. London: Warwick Arts Trust, 1983. 39 p.
The first volume is a classified catalog restricted to British published music and music by British composers some of whose works are published, including educational music.

1272. The Composers' Guild of Great Britain. British orchestral music. Vol. I of the catalogue of works by members of The Composers' Guild of Great Britain. London: Composers' Guild, 1958. 55 p.
Part 1: works for full, small, or chamber orchestra.
Part 2: works for string orchestra.
The listings give composer, title of work, orchestration, publisher or agent, and availability of the material.

1273. The Composers' Guild of Great Britain. British orchestral music. Vol. II. By living British composers. London: British Information Centre, 1970. 82 p.
A sequel to the preceding catalog. Adds a listing of works for brass or military bands.

1274. The Composers' Guild of Great Britain. Chamber music by living British composers. London: British Music Information Centre, 1969. 42 p.
Alphabetical listing of composers and their works for three or more instruments. Information tabulated includes instrumentation, duration, publisher or agent, and availability of the material. Unpublished works also included.

1275. The Composers' Guild of Great Britain. Instrumental solos and duos by living British composers. London: British Music Information Centre, 1972. 96 p.
Sections for solos, duos with and without keyboard, and miscellaneous solos and duos. Follows the model of the Guild's other catalogs.

1276. The Composers' Guild of Great Britain. Keyboard solos and duos by living British composers. London: British Music Information Centre, 1974. 63 p.
Two sections, one for keyboard solos for piano, organ and other keyboards and another for duets (one piano, two pianos, other).

1277. Hopkinson, Cecil and Cecil B. Oldman. Thomson's collections of national song: with special reference to the contributions of Haydn and Beethoven. [Edinburgh : printed by R. & R. Clark, 1940] 64 p. (Edinburgh bibliographical society; Transactions, 2:1)

Contents: Haydn thematic catalogue: p. 25–47; Beethoven thematic catalogue: p. 48–64.

1278. The Music Trader's Guide to Works by Twentieth-Century British Composers, together with the names of their publishers; comprising instrumental works, songs, textbooks and manuals up to and including June, 1955. Compiled by L. D. Cibbin. London: Boosey and Hawkes, 1956. 132 p.

Brief entries for works by 76 composers; a listing alphabetical by title under the composers' names. Supplementary listing for "other British composers and their principal publishers."

1279. Swanekamp, Joan. English ayres: a selectively annotated bibliography and discography. Westport: Greenwood Press, 1984. 141 p.

HUNGARY

1280. Bibliographia Hungarica 1945–1960. Catalogus systematicus notarum musicarum in Hungaria editarum . . . edit. Bibliotheca Nationalis Hungariae. Budapest: 1969. 360 p.
see no. 1231.

1281. Dedinsky, Izabella K. Zenemüvek, 1936–40. Budapest: Kiadja az országos széchényi könyvtár, 1944. 286 p.

Classified bibliography of music published in Hungary, 1936–1940. Includes both popular and serious music.

1282. Kroo, Gyorgy. "New Hungarian music," in *Notes,* 39 (1982), p. 43–71.

Some 100 works are described in detail, together with a discussion of the place of Hungarian music in the Western tradition.

1283. Magyar nemzeti bibliográia: Zenemüvek bibliográfiája. 8. évf., 3.- füzet; szept. 30, 1977– Budapest: Országos Széchényi Könyvtár.

The current Hungarian national bibliography on music, supplement to *Magyar nemzeti bibliográfia: Könyvek bibliográfiája.* Quarterly.
Continues *Magyar zenemüvek bibliográfiája.*

1284. Magyar zenemüvek bibliográfiája. 1.-8. évf., 2. füzet; júl. 15, 1970-jún. 30, 1977. Budapest: Országos Széchényi Könyvtár. 8 v.

A quarterly supplement on music to *Magyar nemzeti bibliográfia; Bibliográfia Hungarica, the Hungarian national bibliography. Continued by Magyar nemzeti bibliográfia. Zenemüvek bibliográfiája* (see no. 1283, preceding).

INDIA

1285. Kaufmann, Walter. The ragas of South India: a catalogue of scalar material. Bloomington: Indiana University Press, 1976. 723 p.

Simultaneously published in Calcutta by Oxford and IBH Publishing Co.

This is both an historical work and a thematic catalog to South Indian ragas.

1286. Kuppuswamy, Gowri and Muthuswamy Hariharan. Index of songs in south Indian music. Delhi: B.R. Pub. Corp.; New Delhi: Distributed by D.K. Publishers' Distributors, 1981. 970 p.

The general index gives, with regard to each published song, the beginning, raga, tala, language, composer and details of availability. There are separate indices for raga, tala, language and composer.

1287. Subba Rao, B. Bharatiya sangeet: raga nidhi; Encylopedia of Indian ragas, a comparative study of Hindustani & Karnatak ragas. With a foreward by M. Bhawanishankar Niyogi. Poona:, V. Patwardhan, Chairman, Vishnu Digambar Smarak Samiti, 1956–66. 4 v.

V. 2–4 have title: *Raganidhi and imprint Madras: Music Academy.*

ISRAEL

1288. Goldberg, Ira S. Bibliography of instrumental music of Jewish interest. Part 2: Ensemble and solo. Compiled by Ira s. Goldberg. Rev. and enl. ed. New York: National Jewish Music Council, 1970. 181 p.

1289. National Jewish Welfare Board. Bibliography Committee. Bibliography of Jewish instrumental music. New York: National Jewish Music Council, 1948. 16 p.

Addenda, 1950. 7 leaves.

A selective list of the "best and most interesting works that are easily available . . . either in published form or through rental." Classified according to various combinations of instruments. Publishers indicated.

1290. National Jewish Welfare Board. Bibliography Committee. Bibliography of Jewish vocal music. New York: National Jewish Music Council, c. 1948. 36 p.

Addenda, 1950. 15 leaves.

A selective list of available Jewish vocal music "in good taste, and suited for programming." Classified by genre. Language or languages of text; publishers indicated.

1291. Sendrey, Alfred. Bibliography of Jewish music. New York: Columbia Univ. Press, 1951. 404 p.

Part I of this work is concerned with writings on Jewish music. Part II, p. 209–339, is a classified list of about 4,000 pieces of Jewish music, alphabetical by composer within classifications, giving scoring, author, and language of text. Publisher and date indicated for published works; some manuscripts also listed.

JAPAN

1292. Kokusai Bunka Shinkokai. K. B. S. bibliography of standard reference books for Japanese studies descriptive notes. Vol. II (B): Theatre, dance and music. Tokyo: 1960. 182 p.

Kokusai Bunka Shinkokai is the "Society for International Cultural Relations."

Part of a multi-national "annotated bibliography of standard reference works in Japanese for the use of foreign students of Japanese culture who want to get access to original sources." The music titles were selected and annotated by Kishibe Shigo. There is an appendix: "selected bibliography of works in Western languages on Japanese drama, music and dance." There are extensive annotations with titles in *kanji,* romanized and translated.

LATIN AMERICA

1293. Bibliografía de música latino americana: integrada con fichas del catálogo formado por la Biblioteca Nacional 'José Martí', la Biblioteca Central 'Rubén Martínez Villena' de la Universidad de la Habana y la Biblioteca 'José Antonio Echeverría' de la Casa de las Américas. La Habana, Cuba: Casa de las Américas, 1972. 37 leaves

A union catalog of music from three major libraries in Cuba.

1294. Chase, Gilbert. A guide to the music of Latin America. A joint publication of the Pan American Union and the Library of Congress. 2nd ed., rev. and enl. Washington: Pan American Union, 1962. 411 p.

First published in 1945 under the title *Guide to Latin American music.* Reprint by AMS Press, New York, 1962 and 1972.

A general bibliography of Latin American music, followed by listings related to individual composers. Index of authors, names, and subjects.

1295. Indiana University. School of music. Latin-American Music Center. Music from Latin America available at Indiana University: scores, tapes, and records. Edited by Juan A. Orrego-Salas. Bloomington: Latin American Musica Center, School of Music, Indiana University, 1971. 412 p.

A catalog of one of the most important repositories of Latin American scores and recordings in the United States. Includes a listing of materials available at the Indiana University Archives of Traditional Music.

1296. Kuss, Malena. Latin American music in contemporary reference sources: a study session. Paramount, Calif.: Academy Print. and Pub. Co., c1976. 19 p.

Report of a study session of the National meeting of the American Musicological Society in Washington, D.C., 1974. Bibliography: p. 10–19.

Review by Robert Stevenson in the "Music Section" of the *Handbook for Latin American Studies,* v. 40 (1978), p. 537.

1297. List of Latin American music: vocal, piano, instrumental, orchestral and band, which can be purchased in the United States. 2nd ed., rev. and enl. Washington, D.C.: Pan American Union, 1983. 60 leaves

Typescript.

1298. Lotis, Howard. Latin American music materials available at the University of Pittsburgh and at Carnegie Library of Pittsburgh. Pittsburgh: Center for Latin American Studies, University of Pittsburgh, 1981.

145 p.

1299. Pan American Union, Music Section. Latin American orchestral music
available in the United States. Washington: Pan American Union, 1956.
79 p.

Suspersedes a shorter list issued in 1955.

Part I: classified list of Latin American music available through publishing houses and other agencies. Part II: Latin American music in the
Edwin A. Fleisher Collection in the Free Library of Philadelphia.

1300. Thompson, Leila Fern. Partial list of Latin American music obtaina-
ble in the U.S., and Supplement. 3rd ed., revised and enlarged. Washington: Pan American Union, 1948. 56 leaves.

Supplement, 17 leaves.

The first and second editions were prepared by Gilbert Chase, 1941 and
1942.

Concerned with concert music to the exclusion of popular and folk
music. Classified by genre and country. Scoring, language of text, and
publisher indicated. Indexed by country and by composer.

MEXICO

1301. Huerta, Jorge A. A bibliography of Chicano and Mexican dance,
drama and music. Oxnard, Calif.: Colegio Quetzalcoatl, 1972. 59 p.

The three major subdivisions of the bibliography cover dance, drama,
and music subdivided to Pre-Columbian, Mexican, and Aztlan sections.

NORWAY

1302. Society of Norwegian Composers. Contemporary Norwegian orchestral and chamber music. s.l.: Johan Grundt Tanam Forlag, 1970. 385 p.

Lists, with portraits, timings of the works, instrumentation.

PAPUA NEW GUINEA

1303. Gourlay, Kenneth A. A bibliography of traditional music in Papua
New Guinea. Port Moresby: Institute of Papua New Guinea Studies, 1980.
176 p.

Covers Papua New Guinea, Torres Strait islands, parts of Java, and the
Solomon Islands. Comprehensive index.

POLAND

1302. Hordynski, Wladyslaw. Katalog polskich druków muzycznych 1800–
1863. Catalogue des imprimés musicaux polonais de 1800–1863. Krakow:
Polskie Wydawnictwo Muzyczne, 1968. 1 v.

Contents: 1. Biblioteka Uniwersytecka w Poznaniu i Biblioteka Kór-
nicka Polskiej Akademii Nauk.

A catalog of Polish printed musical works for the period 1800–36.

PORTUGAL

1305. Catálogo geral da música portuguesa, repertório contemporâneo. Lisboa: Direcüçao-General do Património Cultural, A Secretaria, 1978– . 1 v. (loose-leaf)

Biographical sketches of contemporary Portuguese composers in English, French, and Portuguese. Also includes lists of works, bibliographies and discographies of each composer.

SCOTLAND

1306. Scottish Music Archive. Catalogue of printed and manuscript music, May 1970. Glasgow: Scottish Music Archive. 74 p.

Supplement issued 1972.

A classified list of music by contemporary Scottish composers giving instrumentation, duration, publisher, and availability of the material. The archive is centered at the University of Glasgow, but its policies are dictated by a committee made up of a number of Scottish musical institutions.

SPAIN

1307. Libros de músic. 2. ed. Madrid: Instituto Nacional del Libro Español, Ministerio de Cultura, 1982. 327 p.

The Spanish national bibliography of music and music literature.

A classified bibliography of books in Spanish. Includes sections on pedagogy, folklore, and popular music, as well as scholarly topics. Indexes to names, subjects, and institutions.

SWEDEN

1308. Föreningen Sveska Tonsättäre. Nyare svenska orkesterverk samt instrumental- och vokalverk med orkester. Katalog of Swedish orchestral works (20th century) including instrumental soli and vocal works with orchestra. Stockholm: Society of Swedish Composers, 1956. 109 p.

Supplement, 1959. 15 p.

Earlier lists were issued in 1937 and 1944 under a slightly varied title.

Classified listings of works under composers' names. Information includes publisher, instrumentation, timings.

1309. Nordiska Musikforlaget. Swedish orchestral works. Annotated catalogue. Commentary by Edvin Kallstenius. Stockholm: Nordiska Musikforlaget, 1948. 85 p.

This catalogue is intended to guide conductors, members of programme committees and other music lovers who wish to learn something about Swedish composition. [*Foreword*]

Selected works by 25 Swedish composers. Portraits and brief biographical sketches.

SWITZERLAND

1310. Archives Musicales Suisses. (Schweizerisches Musikarchiv). Liste des œuvres. Werkverzeichnis. Zurich: Archives musicales suisses, 1968– . Vol. 1– .

A series of pamphlets reproduced from typescript, each devoted to the work of a contemporary Swiss composer. Information includes instrumentation, timings, and availability of the works whether printed or in manuscript. Following is a list of publictions through August 1971:

Adolf Brunner (1961)
Rudolf Moser (1962)
Carlo Hennerling (1963)
Will Eisenmann (1966)
Richard Flury (1966)
Georges Haenni (1966)
Henri Gagnebin (1966)
Peter Mieg (1966)
Max Kuhn (1966)
Walter Lang (1966)
Wladimir Vogel (1966)
Walther Geiser (1967)
René Matthes (1967)
Jean Daetwyler (1968)
Paul Müller-Zürich (1968)
Fernande Peyrot (1968)
Edward Staempfli (1968)
Frank Martin (1969)
Jean Binet (1970)
Luc Balmer (1970)
Richard Sturzenegger (1970)
Hans Haug (1970)

Robert Oboussier (1970)
Aloys Fornerod (1970)
Raffaele d'Alessandro (1970)
Robert Blum (1970)
Roger Vuataz (1970)
Bernard Reichel (1971)
Othmar Schoeck (1971)
Hans Vogt (1972)
Czeslaw Marek (1972)
Othmar Schoeck (1972)
Hugo Pfister (1973)
Julien-François Zbinden (1974)
Arthur Honegger (1975)
André-François Marescotti (1979)
Rudolf Kelterborn (1980)
Klaus Huber (1980)
Robert Suter (1980)
Haller, Hermann (1981)
Frank Martin (1981)
Hans Ulrich Lehmann (1981)
Albert Moeschinger (1982)
Jacques Wildberger (1982)

Albert Jenny (1985)

UNITED STATES

1311. American Society of Composers, Authors and Publishers. ASCAP index of performed compositions. N.Y.: American Society of Composers, Authors and Publishers, 1978. 1,423 p.

Supplement issued in 1981. First appeared in 1942 as the *ASCAP Index* for use of radio braodcasting stations. Subsequently published in 1952, 1954, and 1963 under the present title.

An unedited alphabetical listing of compositions in the ASCAP repertory which have appeared in the Society's survey of radio, television and wired music performances, including easy listening, soul, country, religious, children's, gospel, rock, pop, film, folk, educational, classical, jazz, and musical theatre genres. Alphabetical listing by title citing composer and publisher.

See the *ASCAP Symphonic Catalog* (1977) for more complete coverage of the ASCAP classical repertory (see no. 1312).

1312. American Society of Composers, Authors and Publishers. ASCAP Symphonic catalog. 1977. 3rd edition. N.Y.: R. R. Bowker, 1977. 511 p.

Previous editions in 1959 and 1966.

Alphabetical listing, by composers and arrangers, of symphonic literature controlled by ASCAP. Entries give instrumentation, duration, publisher. List of publishers' addresses.

1313. **Broadcast Music Inc.** Symphonic catalogue. Rev. ed. New York: Broadcast Music Inc., 1971. 375 p.

First appeared 1963. *Supplement* to the rev. ed., 1978. 138 p.

An alphabetical listing, by composer, of symphonic works the performing rights of which are controlled by Broadcast Music Inc. Entries give instrumentation, duration, and publishers of the works.

1314. **De Lerma, Dominque-René.** Black concert and recital music, a provisional repertoire list. Bloomington: Afro-American Opportunities Association, 1975. 40 p.

Brief review by Stephen M. Fry in *Notes,* 32 (1975) p. 301–2.

1315. **Eagon, Angelo** Catalog of Published Concert Music by American Composers. Second edition. Metuchen: Scarecrow Press, 1969. 348 p.

Supplement to the second edition, 1971 (150 p.). *Second supplement* issued 1974 (148 p.).

This work first appeared as a publication of the U.S. Office of Information (1964), with a *Supplement* in 1965. The Scarecrow Press publication is an unacknowledged descendant.

Classified bibliography, including vocal and instrumental music; much relevant information as to performing groups required, instrumentation, publisher, etc.

1316. **Freedom's voice in poetry and song** compiled and edited by Gillian B. Anderson. Wilmington: Scholarly Resources Inc., 1977. 888 p.

Contents:

Pt. 1. An inventory of political and patriotic lyrics in colonial American newspapers, 1773–1783.

Pt. 2. Song book.

Includes bibliographical references and indexes.

1317. **Hixon, Donald L.** Music in early America: a bibliography of music in Evans. Metuchen: The Scarecrow Press, Inc., 1970. 607 p.

"An index to the music published in 17th and 18th-century America as represented by Charles Evans' *American Bibliography and the Readex Corporation's microprint edition of Early American Imprints, 1639–1800.*" The major part of the work is devoted to entries for the music under composer, editor, or compiler. There is also a valuable section of biographical sketches, followed by indexes of names, titles and Evans' serial numbers. *American Bibliography*—Indexes *Early American Imprints, 1639–1800*—Indexes

1318. **Jackson, Richard.** United States music; sources of bibliography and collective biography. 2nd printing. Brooklyn: Institute for Studies in American Music, Dept. of Music, Brooklyn College of the City University of New York, 1976. 80 p. (I.S.A.M. monographs, 1)

First printing 1973.

A generic bibliography (reference works, historical studies, regional studies) with a topical section. Each entry is extensively annotated. Name index.

1319. Jackson, Richard. U.S. Bicentennial music. Brooklyn: Institute for Studies in American Music, Dept. of Music, School of Performing Arts, Brooklyn College of the University of New York, 1977. 20 p. (I.S.A.M. special publications, 1)
470 entries for music composed or reprinted for the American Bicentennial.

1320. Lawrence, Vera Brodsky. Music for patriots, politicians, and presidents: harmonies and discords of the first hundred years. New York: Macmillan, 1975. 480 p.
A well organized source book for information related to early American music. Numerous facsimiles of title pages and excerpts from texts. Includes bibliographical references and index.

1321. Phemister, William. American piano concertos; a bibliography. Detroit: Published for the College Music Society by Information Coordinators, 1985. 323 p. (Bibliographies in American Music, no. 9)

1322. Rabson, Carolyn and Kate Van Winkle Keller. The national tune index; 18th century secular music (and user's guide). N.Y.: University Music Editions, 1980. 80 microfiche (and 96 p.)

> ... An extensive listing of representative sources of [American] secular music, consisting of cross-referenced indexes of source contents, sorted by text, and my music incipits represented in scale degrees, stressed notes, and interval sequences.

Source indexes by genre. The user's guide includes a short title index, a bibliography of sources, and an index to the various elements of the bibliography of sources.

1323. Tischler, Alice. Fifteen black American composers; a bibliography of their works. Detroit: Information Coordinators, 1981. 328 p. (Detroit Studies in Music Bibliography, 45)
A biographical sketch, classified works lists, and indexes for each of the composers.

YUGOSLAVIA

1324. Dordevič, Vladimir R. Ogled srpske muzicke bibliografije do 1914. godine: [za shtampu priredila Ksenija B. Lazic]. [Essay on Serbian musical bibliography until 1914]. Beograd: Nolit, 1969. 281 p.
An annotated bibliography with 2,350 entries in Serbo-Croatian. Summary in English and French.

1325. Kompozitori i Muzicki Pisci Jugoslavije. (Yugoslav composers and music writers. Members of the Union of Yugoslav Composers, 1945–1967.) Catalogue. Edited by Milena Milosavljević-Pesić. Beograd: SAKOJ, 1968. 663 p.
An introduction to contemporary Yugoslav musical creation by Kresimir Kovacevic.
Portraits, brief biographical accounts and lists of works. Text in Serbo-Croatian and English.

MUSIC FOR INSTRUCTION AND PERFORMANCE

The reference tools listed here are designed for the musician who has a specific objective in view; namely, the selection of material for performance purposes, whether for solo or ensemble use. The need for such tools, incorporating the latest publications, is a perpetual one that has given rise to a generous number of resources. Titles are organized by instrument, although, of course, there are bibliographies principally focused on violin music including viola music, for instance. The entries are arranged in a classified order.

1326. Brüchle, Bernhard. Musik-Bibliographien für alle Instrumente. Music bibliographies for all instruments. [English translation by Colleen Gruban.] München: Bernhard Brüchle Edition, 1976. 96 p.

In German and English. Cites some 297 bibliographies of music for instruments, solo and chamber ensembles. List of music publishers, followed by a list of special journals and societies devoted to instruments. Lists of bibliographic tools and music information centers. Index of instruments covered.

Review by Stephen M. Fry in *Notes*, 34 (1977), p. 87.

Bagpipes

1327. Bagpipe Music Index. Current alphabetical tune listing. Glen Ridge, N.J.: Bagpipe Music Index, 1966. [unpaged]

Reproduced from typescript. Contains 2,430 listings from 35 tune books. Tunes identified by title, location in tune book, tune type, meter and number of parts.

1328. Cannon, Roderick D. A bibliography of bagpipe music. Edinburgh: John Donald, 1980. 295 p.

Treats the literature of the bagpipe in its various local styles. Four sections devoted to different pipe practices: Union pipes, Northumbrian bagpipes, Scots highland pipes, Irish warpipes and Brien Born pipes. 126 titles described. Prose bibliographies of the literature on bagpipes. Contents of anthologies not analyzed.

Review by Amy Aaron in *Notes,* 37 (1980), p. 60–61.

Chamber Ensemble

1329. Altmann, Wilhelm. Kammermusik-Katalog; ein Verzeichnis von seit 1841 veröffentlichten Kammermusikwerken. 6., bis August 1944 ergänzte Auflage. Leipzig: F. Hofmeister, 1945. 400 p.

Reprinted by Hofmeister, Hofheim am Taunus, 1967.

Succeeded by Richter's *Kammermusik-Katalog.* ... See no. 1341.

Chamber music published since 1841, separate works or works in collections. Classified by medium, with composer indexes. International coverage.

Bote & Bock
Verlagsarchiv
Berlin

avierquartettspieler ... mit 237
g für musikalische Kultur und

ndbuch.
quartets, arranged chronologi-
man works curtailed in an effort
scriptive and critical commen-

Klavierquintettspieler ... mit 343
ür musikalische Kultur und Wis-

andbuch.
on piano quintets.

ir Klaviertriospieler; Wegweiser
nd Violoncell. Mit fast 400 Noten-
nusikalischer Kultur und Wissen-

s on piano trios.

r Streichquartettspieler. ... Berlin:
bucher, 86, 87, 92, 94.)
Verlag, Wilhelmshaven, (1972–74)
sband von 1935 bis zur Gegenwart.
tring trios, quintets, sextets, octets,
strings and winds. Vol. 5 brings all
printing.

A companion to quartet literature giving brief descriptions and analyses of works in the standard repertory as well as lesser known works. Arrangement within each category is chronological.

1334. Aulich, Bruno. Alte Musik für Liebhaber. 3. verbesserte Auflage. München: Artemis Verlag, 1981. 320 p. plus 17 plates.
Previously published as *Alte Musik für Hausmusikanten, 1968.*
An extensive introduction to the performance factors and genres of early instrumental music. Bio-bibliographical section listing modern editions of music originally intended or arranged to become chamber music. Index to terms and to names.

1335. Australia Music Centre. Catalogue of instrumental and chamber music. Sydney: Australia Music Centre, 1976. 142 p. (Catalogues of Australian compositions, 2)
Includes Australian music for solo instruments and chamber ensembles.

1336. Feinland, Alexander. The combination violin and violoncello without accompaniment. [Paramaribo, Surinam: Printed by J. H. Oliviera, 1944.] 121 p.
Classified catalog, including manuscripts, of music from the Baroque to the present. Original publisher or location given. Biographical sket-

ches of the composers represented.

1337.   Forsyth, Ella Marie. Building a chamber music collection: a descriptive guide to published scores. Metuchen: Scarecrow Press, 1979. 191 p.
Descriptions of formal and stylistic traits of basic chamber music repertory. Bibliography and indexes.

1338.   Lemacher, Heinrich. Handbuch der Hausmusik. Graz: A. Pustet, 1948. 454 p.
The second part of the volume, p. 219 to end, lists works for solo instruments and various chamber ensembles. Many lesser known works included. Arranged alphabetically by composer within various categories. Publisher and brief description of works given. Bibliography, p. 435–39. Index.

Chamber music

1339.   Raaben, Lev Nikolaevich. Sovetskaia kamerno-instrumental'naia. Leningrad: Muzyka, 1963. 339 p.
History of Soviet chamber music with bibliographical footnotes.

1340.   Raoul, Oscar Lotti. Violin and violoncello in duo without accompaniment. . . . based on the work of Alex Feinland. Detroit: Information Coordinators, 1972. 122 p. (Detroit Studies in Music Bibliography, 25.)
A substantially enlarged work based on Feinland's 1947 publication. (see no.1336)

1341.   Richter, Johannes F. Kammermusik-Katalog. Verzeichnis der von 1944 bis 1958 veröffentlichten Werke für Kammermusik und für Klavier vier- und sechshandig sowie für zwei und mehr Klaviere. Leipzig: F. Hofmeister, 1960. 318 p.
Successor to Wilhelm Altmann's work of the same title (no. 1329). Covers chamber music from 1945 through 1958. A classified bibliography, including chamber works with voice, piano four-hands, etc. Alphabetical index of composers and titles of collections. List of publishers.

Harpsichord

1342.   Alker, Hugo. Literatur für alte Tasteninstrumente; versuch einer Bibliographie für die Praxis. 2te verm. und verg. Aufl. Wien: Wissenschaftliches Antiquariat H. Geyer, 1967. 79 p. (Wiener Abhandlungen zur Musikwissenschaft und Instrumentenkunde, 2)
First published in 1962.
The main division is between music for harpsichord and music for organ (without pedals). Brief entries, with publishers and editors given. Collections are entered by title and filed in the same alphabet with composers. The emphasis is on music currently available in practical editions.

1343. Bedford, Frances, and Robert Conant. Twentieth-century harpsichord music: a classified bibliography. Hackensack: Joseph Boonin, 1974. 95 p. (Music Indexes and Bibliographies)

Entries classified by ensembles: harpsichord and one stringed instrument, harpsichord and one other keyboard instrument, etc. Composer and title indexes. List of publishers.

1344. Arneson, Arne J. and Stacie Williams. The Harpsichord book: being a plaine and simple index to printed collections of musick by diffrent masters for the harpsichord, spinnet, clavichord, and virginall. Madison: Index House, 1986. 119 p.

An index to multiple composer anthologies of compositions that include early music (to 1800) for a harpsichord or its kindred instruments, excluding works for organ or pianoforte. Bibliography of anthologies. Composer title and editor indexes.

Orchestra

1345. Altmann, Wilhelm. Orchester-Literatur-Katalog; Verzeichnis von seit 1850 erschienenen Orchester-Werken.... Leipzig: F. E. C. Leuckart, 1926 –36. 2 v.

Reprinted by M. Sändig, Walluf bei Wiesbaden, 1972.

Orchestral music published since 1850, listing scores, miniature scores, parts, and arrangements. Vol. 2 gives, in addition, instrumentation and timing and contains a composer index to both volumes. Thematic quotations given for works whose serial numbers are often confused, e.g. Haydn's symphonies, Handel's concertos, etc.

1346. Basart, Ann P. "Finding orchestral music" in *Cum notis variorum,* 59 (January/February, 1982), p. 14–24.

An annotated, indexed check-list of bibliographies of orchestral music for performance. Includes a section on finding orchestral program notes.

1347. Beck, Georges H. Compositeurs contemporains: œuvres d'orchestre. Paris: Heugel & Cie, [1960]. 35 p.

A descriptive listing of recent orchestral works by 27 composers, chiefly French. Brief biographies of the composers. Entries give instrumentation, timings. Scores and performance materials available on rental from Heugel.

1348. Breitkopf & Härtel. Catalogo delle sinfonie, partite, overture, soli, trii, quattri e concerti per il violino, flauto traverso, cembalo ed altri stromenti, che si trovano in manuscritto nella officina musica di Giovanni Gottlob Breitkopf in Lipsia. Leipzig: 1762–65. 6 parts.

Supplemento I-XVI (1766–87).

Reprint by Dover Publications, New York, with an introduction by Barry S. Brook (1966).

An 18th-century thematic catalog of great importance. Chiefly instrumental music, but some vocal, from the archives of Breitkopf & Härtel. Useful in tracing or identifying works of the period.

1349. Buschkotter, Wilhelm. Handbuch der internationalen Konzert-literatur. Berlin: Walter de Gruyter & Co., 1961. 374 p.

Compiled as a successor to Theodor Müller-Reuter's. *Lexikon der deutschen Konzertliteratur* (no.1356). Works listed chronologically under composer. Information includes performance time, instrumentation, date of composition, performance, publisher.

Review by Richard Schaal in *Die Musikforschung,* 17 (1961), p. 84–85.

1350. Daniels, David. Orchestral music; a handbook. 2nd edition. Metuchen: Scarecrow Press, 1982. 413 p.

"The purpose of this work is to gather together in one volume the diverse information about orchestral works needed to plan programs and organize rehearsals: instrumentation, duration, and source of performance materials." [Editor's *Foreword*]

Entries arranged by composer. Particularly useful is the listing of works by performing forces, the list of orchestral works by duration, and the list of composers by nationality or ethnic group.

1351. Eagon, Angelo. Catalog of published concert music by American composers. Second edition. Metuchen: Scarecrow Press, 1969. 348 p.

This work was issued originally in 1964 as a publication of the Music Branch of the U.S. Information Agency. 175 p.

Supplement issued 1971 (150 p.). *Second Supplement* issued 1974 (148 p.).

Works are entered alphabetically by composer under a classified arrangement: vocal solo, instrumental solo, instrumental ensembles, concert jazz, percussion, orchestra, etc. There is a key to publishers and an author index. Information includes duration of orchestral works, author of text for vocal compositions. A useful, well-organized publication.

Review by Karl Kroeger, of the 1964 edition, in *Notes,* 22 (1966), p. 1032–33; by Richard Hunter, of the 1969 edition, in *Notes,* 26 (1970), p. 759–60,

1352. The Edwin A. Fleisher collection of orchestral music in the Free Library of Philadelphia; a cumulative catalog, 1929–1977. The Fleisher collection in the Free Library of Philadelphia. Boston: G. K. Hall, 1979. 956 p.

First published in 1933–45 in 2 v., with a *Supplementary list, 1945–1955* published in 1956. Revised edition published 1965.

Catalog of a loan collection of over 4,000 pieces of orchestral music, much of the material unpublished. Classified; information includes composers' dates, title of each work in the original language with English translation, publisher, instrumentation, timing, date of composition, and information about the first performance. Occasional thematic incipits included. Indexed by performing forces needed.

Review by Joseph M. Boonin in *Notes,* 36 (1979), p. 92–93.

1353. Emery, Frederic B. The violin concerto through a period of nearly 300 years, covering about 3,300 concertos with brief biographies of 1,000 composers. Chicago: The Violin Literature Publishing Co., 1928. 615 p., with index p. i-xl.

Brief discussions of concerto composers grouped chronologically and by nationality. A mass of somewhat indiscriminate fact and information.

Illustrated with portraits of musicians.

1354. International Music Council. Répertoires internationaux de musique contemporaine à l'usage des amateurs et des jeunes. I. Musique symphonique de 1880 à 1954. Frankfurt, New York: C. F. Peters, 1957– . (v. 1, 63 p.)

A catalog of recently composed symphonic works suitable for young people's and amateur orchestras. Material listed alphabetically by country; publisher, date, and instrumentation given. Indexes of composers, types of ensemble. List of publishers.

1355. Laughlin, James E. The Alexander Broude comprehensive guide to orchestral literature: a catalogue. New York: A. Broude, 1975. 116 p.

A handy catalog of available orchestral music.

1356. Müller-Reuter, Theodor. Lexikon der deutschen Konzertliteratur; ein Ratgeber für Dirigenten, Konzertveranstalter, Musikschriftsteller und Musikfreunde. Leipzig: G. F. Kahnt nachf., 1909. V. 1, 626 p.

Nachtrag zu Band I. Leipzig, Kahnt, 1921. 238 p. Reprinted by Da Capo, New York, 1972.

The standard guide to orchestral and chamber music by the major composers of the romantic period, with detailed information as to date of composition, first performance, duration, instrumentation, relation to the composer's other works. Band I covers the following composers: Schubert, Mendelssohn, Schumann, Berlioz, Liszt, Raff, Wagner, Draseke, Reinecke, Bruch, Gernsheim, and Richard Strauss. The *Nachtrag* is devoted to Beethoven, Brahms, and Haydn (symphonies only).

Buschkotter's *Handbuch* ... (no. 1349) is intended to supplement Müller-Reuter and bring it up to date.

1357. Orchestra Music Guide. ... Evanston, Illinois: Instrumentalist Co., n.d. 98 p.

Lists over 5,000 titles including full and string orchestra music, also vocal and instrumental solos, ensembles with orchestral accompaniment.

1358. Saltonstall, Cecilia Drinker and Henry Saltonstall. A new catalog of music for small orchestra. Clifton, N.J.: European American Music Corp., 1978. 323 p. (Music indexes and bibliographies, 14)

Supersedes the *Catalog of music fo small orchestra,* Washington, D.C., 1947.

Not indexed! 6,380 compositions listed, indicating performing forces needed and duration. List of publishers.

Review by James N. Berdahl in *Notes,* 36 (1979), p. 374–75.

1359. Sartorius, Richard H. Bibliography of concertos for organ and orchestra. Evanston, Illinois:, Instrumentalist Co., [1961]. 68 p.

Includes primary sources as well as modern publications. Extensive annotations, biographical and descriptive of the music. Locatins of original materials given. The list includes much material not exclusively for organ, i.e. concertos for 'harpsichord or organ."

1360. Stein, Franz A. Verzeichnis der Orchestermusik von 1700 bis zur Gegenwart. Bern und München: Francke Verlag, [1963]. 126 p.

A pocket guide to orchestral literature. Selective list of composers and their principal orchestral works. Entries give title, instrumentation, date of composition, movements if a composite work. No publishers given.

1361. Svensk musik för orkester (hyresmaterial) 1985. Swedish music for orchestra (hire material) 1985. Stockholm: STIMS informationscentral för svensk musik, 1985. 150 p.

A catalog produced by the Swedish music information service covering orchestral scores and parts for hire of music written by Swedes.

1362. Tuthill, Burnet C. "The concertos for clarinet." In *Journal of research in music education,* 10 (1962), p. 47–58.

Brief introduction to the history of the clarinet concerto and its literature, followed by annotated listing of such concertos from the 18th century to the present.

This list has been supplemented by Robert A. Titus in an article in the *Journal of research in music education,* 13 (1965), p. 169–76.

1363. Australia Music Centre. Catalogue of orchestral music. Sydney: Australia Music Centre, 1976. 109 p.

Listing the orchestral works of Australian composers.

Organ

1364. Alker, Hugo. Literatur für alte Tasteninstrumente; versuch einer Bibliographie für die Praxis. 2te verm. und verg. Aufl. Wien: Wissenschaftliches Antiquariat H. Geyer, 1967. 79 p. (Wiener Abhandlungen zur Musikwissenschaft und Instrumentenkunde, 2)

First published in 1962.

The main division is between music for harpsichord and music for organ (without pedals). Brief entries, with publishers and editors given. Collections are entered by title and filed in the same alphabet with composers. The emphasis is on music currently available in practical editions.

1365. Arnold, Corliss Richard. Organ literature: a comprehensive survey. 2nd ed. Metuchen: Scarecrow Press, 1984. 2 v.

First published in 1973 with 656 p.

Part I: Historical survey with accompanying bibliographies.

Part II: Biographical catalog, providing basic information about composers and their published works.

Bibliography.

1366. Edson, Jean Slater. Organ preludes, an index to compositions on hymn tunes, chorales, plainsong melodies, Gregorian tunes and carols. Metuchen: Scarecrow Press, 1970. 2 v.

Supplement, including corrections and additions to the first volumes, published in 1974. 315 p.

Vol. I: composer index, with settings listed alphabetically under composer's name. Publishers are identified.

Vol. II: index of tune names, identified by thematic incipits. Each tune name is followed by a list of the composers who have set it.

1367. Kratzenstein, Marilou. Survey of organ literature and editions. Ames: Iowa State University Press, 1980. 246 p.

A survey of organ music arranged by country with essays on the development of the instrument, major composers, and schools for each country. Each essay precedes a bibliography of editions arranged by composer or, in the case of anthologies, by title. Originally a series of articles in *The Diapason.*

1368. Lohmann, Heinz. Handbuch der Orgelliteratur. Wiesbaden: Breitkopf & Härtel, 1975. 206 p.

A work in three parts: an index to settings of chorale melodies, both German and others, arranged alphabeticaly by the "name" of the chorale; an index of editions of works for organ; and a series of indexes to chorale tunes, melody names, and first lines. International in scope, but focused on the German Protestant tradition.

1369. Lukas, Viktor. Orgelmusikführer. Stuttgart: Philipp Reclam Jun., [1963]. 271 p.

A listener's guide to concert organ literature, quite selective and confined to European repertory. Brief biographies of the composers; numerous thematic quotations. Contains a section on the organ with other instruments, a glossary of organ terms, and a description of the mechanics of the instrument. Index of composers and works.

1370. Münger, Fritz. Choralbearbeitungen für Orgel. Verzeichnis zu den Choralen des Deutschen Evangelischen Kirchengesangbuches und des Gesangbuches der evang.-reform. Kirchen der deutschsprachigen Schweiz. Kassel: Bärenreiter, [1952]. 148 p.

Alphabetical listing by chorale text incipit, locating each in the German or Swiss chorale books and indicating the organ settings available in some 56 collections of chorale preludes.

1371. Opp, Walter. Verzeichnis der Orgelvorspiele zum Evangelischen Kirchengesangbuch. Berlin: Verlag Merseburger, 1974. 1 v. (loose-leaf)

An index to organ preludes by the melodies in the order of appearance in the *Evangelischen Kirchengesangbuch,* giving composers and titles of the preludes based on the chorale tunes. Bibliograpy of publications containing the various settings of the chorale melodies.

1372. Stellhorn, Martin H. Index to hymn preludes ... and other organ compositions, based on hymns, chorales, and carols. A listing of 2,200 selections of various publishers according to key, difficulty, and length. St. Louis: Concordia Publishing House, [1948]. 151 p.

1373. Weigl, Bruno. Handbuch der orgelliteratur. Vollständige Umarbeitung des Führers durch die Orgelliteratur, herausgegeben von [Theophil] Kothe-Forchhammer, neubearbeitet von Otto Burkert. Leipzig: F. E.

C. Leuckart, 1931. 318 p.

Classifed listing of compositions for organ solo or organ with orchestra, instruments, or voices. Original works and transcriptions listed separately. International coverage.

Piano

1374. Altmann, Wilhelm. Verzeichnis von Werken für Klavier vier- und sechshändig, sowie für zwei und mehr Klaviere. Leipzig: F. Hofmeister, 1943. 133 p.

Classified catalog of works for piano, 4 and 6 hands, and for 2 and more pianos with and without other instruments. Original works and arrangements included. Alphabetical by composer within classification. Index.

1375. Australia Music Centre. Catalogue of keyboard music. Sydney: Australia Music Centre, 1976. 90 p.

Includes Australian music for organ, harpsichord, and piano.

1376. Basart, Ann P. "Guides to piano music: a check-list" in *Cum notis variorum,* 53 (June, 1981), p. 13–21.

An annotated, indexed check-list to bibliographies providing information about piano music.

1377. Butler, Stanley. Guide to the best in contemporary piano music; an annotated list of graded solo piano music published since 1950. Metuchen: Scarecrow, 1973. 2 v.

Valuable less for the qualitative judgments than for the bibliographic citations.

1378. Chang, Frederic Ming and Albert Faurot. Team piano repertoire; a manual of music for multiple players at one or more pianos. Metuchen: Scarecrow, 1976. 184 p.

A classified, annotated list of music with cryptic bibliographical information. Lists arrangements and transcriptions as well as some recordings.

Review by Stephen M. Fry in *Notes,* 34 (1977), p. 87.

1379. Fuszek, Rita M. Piano music in collections; an index. Detroit: Information Coordinators, 1981. 895 p.

Covering 496 collections in two sections: an index to the collections by composer and a list of the contents of the collections. Title index, lists of editors, catalogs, and editions of composers' works.

1380. Gillespie, John and Anna Gillespie. A bibliography of nineteenth-century American piano music with location sources and composer biography index. Westport: Greenwood, 1984. 358 p. (Music Reference Collection, 2)

A selective, classified bibliography including some music from the late 18th century and extending into the first part of the 20th century. Occasional comments on the music.

1381. Gratia, E. L. Répertoire pratique du pianiste. . . . Préface de I. Philipp. Paris: Delagrave, 1931. 117 p.

A list of 2,500 piano pieces by 271 composers arranged alphabetically by composer, with categories of varying degree of difficulty. Four-hand pieces, p. 112–17.

1382. Hinson, Maurice. Guide to the pianist's repertoire. 2nd, rev. and enl. ed. Bloomington: Indiana University Press, c1986. 856 p.

First published in 1973 and supplemented in 1979.

Lists the piano compositions of individual composers, providing brief information on publisher and ocasional critical remarks. There is a classified list of major anthologies, with an annotated bibliography, and an index to editors, arrangers, and transcribers. Attempts to address three questions: "What is there?" "What is it like?" and "Where can I get it?"

There are occasional citations of literature *about* the music cited.

Indexes: composers by national designations, Black composers, women composers, compositions for tape and piano, compositions for prepared piano, titles in anthologies and collections.

1383. Hinson, Maurice. Music for more than one piano: an annotated guide. Bloomington: Indiana University Press, c1983. 218 p.

Includes works originally written for piano and other forces if arranged by the composer. Includes transcriptions of important composers. Critical comments and publisher information provided. Indexes of special ensembles.

1384. Hinson, Maurice. Music for piano and orchestra: an annotated guide. Bloomington: Indiana University Press, 1981. 327 p.

Provides cryptic bibliographical information as well as more extensive analytical comments on the works cited. Includes not only the standard repertoire, but also numerous contemporary works. Lists many of the cadenzas written for the Beethoven and Mozart concertos. Secondary references occasionally cited. Indexes by performing forces.

1385. Hinson, Maurice. The piano in chamber ensemble: an annotated guide. Bloomington: Indiana University Press, 1978. 570 p.

A classified bibliography covering music from c. 1700 to the present, with considerable attention to contemporary music. There is a brief, annotated bibliography of suggested readings on the subject and an index of composers.

Reviews by Bennett Ludden in *Notes,* 35 (1979), p. 891–92, and by Peter Ward Jones in *Music and letters,* 60 (1979), p. 335.

1386. Kennard, Daphne. "Music for one-handed pianists" in *Fontes artis musicae,* 30 (1983), p. 117–31.

Revision of a list published first in *Brio,* 13, 2 (1976), p.39–42.

A comprehensive list of music for one-handed pianists. Short lists of duets for one and two pianos, references to anthologies, an article, and a thesis.

1387. McGraw, Cameron. Piano duet repertoire: music originally written for one piano, four hands. Bloomington: Indiana University Press, 1981. 334 p.

Arrangements or adaptations from other media are excluded except in rare cases where the composers themselves have made the transcriptions or where such adaptations have long been considered part of the standard four hand repertoire." [from the *General explanation*]

Indexes of music publishers and library locations.

1388. Moldenhauer, Hans. Duo-pianism; a dissertation. [Chicago: Chicago Musical College Press, 1951.] 400 p.

Contains a list of original two-piano music arranged alphabetically by composer. Publishers indicated. The main part of the dissertation concerns itself with practical rather than historical aspects of the subject. Also contains a list of recorded two-piano music.

1389. Parent, Charlotte F. H. Répertoire encyclopédique du pianiste; analyse raisonnée d'œuvres choisies pour le piano, du XVIe siècle au XXe siècle, avec renseignements pratiques de degré de difficulte, nombre de pages, éditeur et prix. . . . Paris: Hachette et Cie., (1900–1907). 2 v.

1390. Phemister, William. American piano concertos; a bibliography. Detroit: Information Coordinators, 1986. (Bibliographies in American Music, 9)

A source book of information about over 1,100 concertos composed in the United States.

1391. Rezits, Joseph. The pianist's resource guide, 1978–79: piano music in print and literature on the pianistic art [by] Joseph Rezits and Gerald Deatsman. Parke Ridge, Illinois: Pallma Music Co./Neil A. Kjos, 1978. 1,491 p.

First published in 1974.

Composed of three major sections: a classified and computer-generated list of music for piano with a title index; a classified list of books on the subject of pianos with an author index; a piano reader's guide consisting of reviews of 118 books and a topical index to books listed in section 2. Publisher information is provided.

1392. Rowley, Alec. Four hands—one piano. A list of works for duet players. London/New York: Oxford Univ. Press, 1940. 38 p.

Classified list, with composer index, of original works for the medium, 1750 to date. Alphabetical arrangement within each class (the classics, the French school, etc.). Entries give composer's name and dates, title— usually in the original language, opus number, publisher.

1393. Ruthardt, Adolf. Wegweiser durch die Klavier-Literatur. 10. Aufl. Leipzig; Zürich: Hug & Co., 1925. 398 p.

First published in 1888.

Selective list of keyboard music including works for four or more hands from the Renaissance to the early 20th century. Classified according to genre and degree of difficulty. Brief descriptions of lesser-known works. Bibliography of writings on keyboard music, p. 359–76. Index.

1394. Teichmuller, Robert and Kurt Herrmann. Internationale moderne Klaviermusik, ein Wegweiser und Berater. Leipzig und Zürich: Hug & Co., 1927. 300 p.
Supplement, 1934.
Critical and selective bibliography of piano music from about 1890 to date of publication, arranged alphabetically by composer, with an index by country. Gives date of composition, opus number, title, publisher, price, grade, and critical comment.

1395. Wolters, Klaus. Handbuch der Klavierliteratur: Klaviermusik zu zwei Händen. 2., rev. und erw. Aufl. Zürich: Atlantis-Verlag, 1977. 660 p.
First published in 1967.
Intended as a guide and aid to piano teachers, this work is an extensive bibliography of editions interspersed with commentaries on the editions themselves, and upon the composers and compositions. Arrangements for piano are included, especially from earlier periods. The section on contemporary music treats, among other genres and styles, jazz, modern dance, avant-garde music, and various national musics. Index to names only.

Choral Music

1396. Burnsworth, Charles C. Choral music for women's voices: an annotated bibliography of recommended works. Metuchen: Scarecrow Press, 1968. 180 p.
Detailed critical and descriptive annotations given for some 135 choral works for women's voices and a like number of arrangements. Indexed by title, number of voice parts, grade of difficulty, extended compositions, and collections. The work is overloaded with apparatus and verbosity which serve to diminish its value.

1397. Challier, Ernst. Ernst Challiers grosser Chor-Katalog, mit Nachträgen I bis III. Ein alphabetisch geordnetes Verzeichnis sämtlicher Gemischter Chöre mit und ohne Begleitung. Wiesbaden: M. Sändig, 1979. 482 p.
Reprint of the 1903 edition and its 1905–1913 supplements.

1398. Challier, Ernst. Ernst Challiers grosser Männergesang-Katalog. Ein alphabetisch geordnetes Verzeichnis sämtlicher Männer-Chore mit und ohne Begleitung. Wiesbaden: M. Sändig, 1979.
Reprint of the 19002 edition and its 6 supplements through 1912.
Cites over 10,000 compositions, arranged by title.

1399. DeVenney, David P. Nineteenth-century American choral music: an annotated guide. Berkeley: Fallen Leaf Press, c1986. 182 p. (Fallen Leaf reference books in music)
Extensive bibliography: p. 97–116.

1400. Edwards, J. Michel. Literature for voices in combination with electronic and tape music: an annotated bibliography. Ann Arbor: Music Library Association, 1977. 194 p. (MLA index and bibliography series, 17)

1401. Knapp, J. Merrill. Selected list of music for men's voices. Princeton: Princeton University Press, 1952. 165 p.

Original works and arrangements, published and unpublished. Alphabetical by composer within main classification scheme. Each entry gives birth and death dates of composer, scoring, language, publisher, and editor. Index of composers.

Review by Archibald Davison in *Notes,* 10 (1952), p. 104–5.

1402. Locke, Arthur W. and Charles K. Fassett. Selected list of choruses for women's voices. 3rd ed., revised and enlarged. Northampton, Mass.: Smith College, 1964. 253 p.

First published in 1927; 2nd edition, 1946, edited by A. W. Locke.

Principal section is an alphabetical catalog by composers, with titles of choruses, voice combination, publishers, or source in a collection. Foreign titles usually translated. Collections listed separately and their contents given. Indexes include a chronological list of composers, compositions by categories, authros and sources of texts, first lines and titles.

Review by Karl Kroeger in *Notes,* 23 (1966), p. 63–64.

1403. May, James D. Avant-garde choral music: an annotated selected bibliography. Metuchen: Scarecrow Press, 1977. 258 p.

Treats music readily available in the U.S. Extensive information on musical characteristics. Indices classified by performing forces. Composer index. Bibliography.

1404. Roberts, Kenneth C. A check-list of 20th-century choral music for male voices. Detroit: Information Coordinators, 1970. 32 p. (Detroit studies in music bibliography, 17)

1405. Schünemann, Georg. Führer durch di deutsche Chorliteratur. Wolfenbuttel: Verlag für musikalische Kultur und Wissenschaft, 1935–36. 2 v.

Vol. 1: Männerchor. Vol. 2: Gemischter Chor.

Classified according to type of composition. Entries give composer, title, publisher, grade of difficulty, number of parts, duration. Indexed by first line of text, title, composer and arranger, author of text. Includes both secular and sacred works.

1406. Temperley, Nicholas and Charles G. Manns. Fuguing Tunes in the eighteenth century. Detroit: Information Coordinators, 1983. 504 p. (Detroit Studies in Music Bibliography, 49)

Analytical census of fuguing tunes with indexes to texts, tune names, persons.

1407. Tortolano, William. Original music for men's voices: a selected bibliography. 2d ed. Metuchen: Scarecrow Press, 1981. 201 p.

First published in 1973.

Arrayed by composer, provides information on performing forces and duration. Section on music found in collections. There are 6 essays on the subject. Indexes of authors and sources of text, and of first lines and titles.

1408. Vagner, Robert. "A selective list of choral and vocal music with wind and percussion accompaniments," in *Journal of research in music education,* 14 (1966), p. 276–88.

"Selections are included for mixed chorus and instrumental ensemble, mixed voices and obbligato instrument, treble or male voices with obbligato instrument, men's chorus with ensemble, women's chorus with ensemble, solo voices with ensemble, solo voice with keyboard and a variety of solo instruments." A list of solo cantatas and arias by Teleman and J. S. Bach is added. Publishers' names and sometimes editors' are provided.

1409. Valentin, Erich. Handbuch der Chormusik. Hrsg. im Auftrag der Arbeitsgemeinschaft deutscher Chorvebände. Regensburg: G. Bosse, [1953–58]. 2 v.

These volumes serve as general source books of information useful to choral directors. Special sections include a discography of choral music, listings of the contents of *Denkmäler,* writings on choral conducting. Major sections devoted to classified bibliographies of choral music, with full performance details. Each volume has a composer index.

1410. White, Evelyn Davidson. Choral music by Afro-American composers; a selected, annotated bibliography. Metuchen: Scarecrow, 1981. 167 p.

Arranged by composer, entries cite title, copyright date, voicing, range, degree of difficulty, performing forces, publisher, and publisher's catalog number. Index to titles. There is a section of analyzed citations from collections of spirituals. Biographical sketches of composers. Appendices: selected source readings and selected discography.

1411. Australia Music Centre. Vocal and choral music. Sydney: Australia Music Centre, 1976. 264 p. (Catalogues of Australian compositions, 4)

Listing of music for solo voices, vocal ensembles, and choruses by Australian composers.

Vocal Music (Solo and Chamber)

1412. Basart, Ann P. "Finding vocal music" in *Cum notis variorum,* 55 (September, 1981), p. 5–15 and 56 (October, 1981), p. 14–22)

An annotated, indexed check-list to bibliographies providing information on vocal music and choral for performance.

1413. Berry, Corre. Vocal chamber duets; an annotated bibliogrphy. *s.l.:* National Association of Teachers of Singing, 1981. 71 p.

With indexes to voice combinations, poets, and titles and first lines.

1414. Brunnings, Florence E. Folk song index; a comprehensive guide to the Florence E. Brunnings Collection. N.Y.: Garland Publishing, 1981. 357 p.

A title index to the 49,399 songs in the printed and recorded anthologies of folk songs in the Brunnings Collection with references from first lines to titles. There is a list of the 1,305 anthologies indexed.

1415. Carmen, Judith E., William K. Gaeddert, and Rita M. Resch. Art-song in the United States, 1801–1976; an annotated bibliography. With a special section Art-song in the United States, 1759–1810 by Gordon Myers. National Association of Teachers of Singing, 1976. 308 p.

A *First Supplement* was published in 1978 (46 p.).

A practical tool for teachers of singing. Limited to music for a single solo voice with English text commercially available at the time of compilation. Extensive information on each publication provided. Arranged by composer. Index to broad subjects and poets. Indexes to composer and titles.

1416. Challier, Ernst. Ernst Challiers grosser Duetten-Katalog. Ein alphabetisch geordnetes Verzeichnis sämtlicher zweistimmiger Lieder mit Begleitung. Nendeln: Kraus-Thompson, 1979. 182 p.

Reprint of the the 1898 publication.

1417. Challier, Ernst. Ernst Challiers grosser Lieder-Katalog. Ein alphbetisch geordnetes Verzeichnis sämtlicher Einstimmiger Lieder mit Begleitung des Pianoforte. Nendeln: Kraus-Thompson, 1979. 2,415 p.

A reprint of the 1885 publication and its 15 *Nachträge*.

1418. De Charms, Desiree and Paul Breed. Songs in collections, an index. Detroit: Information Service, Inc., 1966. 588 p.

Indexes 411 collections of solo songs published between 1940 and 1957. Entries for more than 9,400 songs. Composed songs entered under composer, with anonymous and folk songs entered alphabetically by title under nationality. Separate sections for carols and for sea chanties. Complete title and first line index.

This work articulates with the Sears *Song Index,* no. 1439.

Review by Donald Ivey in *Journal of research in music education,* 15 (1967), p. 169–70; by Imogen Fellinger in *Die Musikforschung,* 23 (1970), p. 96–97; by Ellen Kenny in *Notes,* 23 (1966), p. 269–70.

1419. Coffin, Berton. Singer's repertoire. 2nd ed. New York: Scarecrow Press, 1960. 4 v.

First published in one volume, 1956.

Classified catalog of solo songs, each volume devoted to a particular voice range; information on subject, accompaniment, publisher.

Review by Arnold Caswell in *Journal of research in music education,* 9 (1961), p. 76.

1420. Coffin, Berton and Werner Singer. Program notes for the singer's repertoire. Metuchen: Scarecrow Press, 1962. 230 p.

1421. Cushing, Helen G. Children's song index, an index to more than 22,000 songs in 189 collections comprising 222 volumes. New York: H. W. Wilson, 1936. 798 p.

A dictionary catalog of children's song literature. Main entry is by song title, with subordinate entries under composer, author of the words, and subject. References from first line to title. Foreign titles given in the original language. There is a preliminary "catalog of collections indexed," and a "directory of publishers" at the end of the volume.

1422. Day, Cyrus L. and E. B. Murrie. English song-books, 1651–1702; a bibliography with a first-line index of songs. London: Bibliographical Society, 1940 [for 1937]. 439 p.

Lists and describes the contents of 252 secular song books published in England and Scotland. Arrangement is chronological, nonextant works included. First-line index of 4,150 songs by about 250 composers. Also indexed by composer, author of text, performer, tunes and airs, sources, titles of collections, printers, publishers, and booksellers. A model of descriptive bibliography, particularly valuable for its coverage of the publishing activity of John and Henry Playford and their contemporaries.

1423. Dunlap, Kay, and Barbara Winchester. Vocal chamber music; a performer's guide. N.Y.: Garland, 1985. 140 p.

Cites music written from 1650 to 1980 for at least one voice and one instrument other than guitar and up to twelve solo voices and twelve solo instruments. Index by performing forces.

1424. Edwards, J. Michel. Literature for voices in combination with electronic and tape music: an annotated bibliography. Ann Arbor: Music Library Association, 1977. 194 p. (MLA Index and Bibliography Series, 7)

An historical listing to 1975 and a finding aid, with extensive information about each composition. There are appendices covering publishers, music information centers, foreign and hard-to-find record labels, studios, & bibliography. There is also an index to the entries by medium.

Review by Peter Ward Jones in *Music and letters,* 60 (1979), p. 229.

1425. Espina, Noni. Repertoire for the solo voice; a fully annotated guide to works for the solo voice published in modern editions and covering material from the 13th century to the present. With a forward by Berton Coffin. Metuchen: Scarecrow Press, 1977. 2 v. (1,290 p.)

Arranged in sections: art songs by nationality of composer; excerpts from operas; florid display songs; traditional songs. Entries provide information on source of text, degree of difficulty, accompaniment, publisher, and references to collections. Remarks are made on the general style and the musical and vocal requirements of each song. Indexes to sources of texts (poets and literary titles) and composers.

Review by Stephen M. Fry in *Notes,* 34 (1978), p. 620.

1426. Espina, Noni. Vocal solos for Christian Churches; a descriptive reference of solo music for the church year including a bibliographical supplement of choral works. 3rd ed. Metuchen: Scarecrow Press, 1984. 241 p.

First published in 1965 and again in 1974 under the title *Vocal solos for Protestant services.*

Indexes to "occasions," voices, titles and composers.

1427.   Geenhill, James, William A. Harrison and Frederick J. Furnivall. A list of all the songs and passages in Shakespeare which have been set to music. The words in old spelling, from the quartos and first folios, edited by F. J. Furnival and W. G. Stone. Folcroft, Pennsylvania: Folcroft Library editions, 1974. 112 p.
Reprint of the 1884 edition published for the New Shakespeare Society by N. Trübner in London.

1428.   Gooch, Bryan N. S. and David S. Thatcher. Musical settings of British Romantic literature; a catalogue. Editorial assistant, Odean Long. New York: Garland Pub., 1982. 2 v. (1,768 p.)
Lists published and unpublished compositions setting British Romantic texts by authors born after 1750 who lived to 1800 or later. Organized by author and literary title with information on composers and settings following. Bibliographical information on poetry and settings provided. Index of authors, first lines and titles, and composers.

1429.   Gooch, Bryan N. S. and David S. Thatcher. Musical settings of Early and mid-Victorian literature; a catalogue. Editorial assistant, Odean Long. New York: Garland Pub., 1979. 946 p.
Considers published and unpublished settings of prominent British authors born after 1800 and who lived to 1850 or later, excluding writers asssociated with the Romantic movements. Information on performing forces and publication details for both the poetry and the musical settings is provided. Listed by author, indexed by composer, title and first line.

1430.   Gooch, Bryan N. S. and David S. Thatcher. Musical settings of late Victorian and modern British literature: a catalogue. Editorial assistant, Odean Long. New York: Garland Pub., 1976. 1,112p.
Review by Stephen M. Fry in *Notes,* 34 (1977), p. 8–89.

1431.   Havlice, Patricia Pate. Popular song index. Metuchen: Scarecrow Press, 1978. 933p.
First supplement indexing collections appearing in 1970–75 published 1978, 386 p. Second supplement indexing collections appearing in 1974–1981 published 1984.
Indexes to folk songs, pop tunes, spirituals, children's songs, sea chanteys, and blues in several hundred song anthologies published since 1940. Bibliography of sources. Indexes of titles, first lines, first linbes of choruses, and composers and lyricists.
Brief review by Stephen M. Fry in *Notes,* 32 (1976), p. 781. Review of the first supplement by Patricia Felch in *Notes,* 35 (1979), p. 637–38.

1432.   Hovland, Michael A. Musical settings of American poetry: a bibliography. Westport: Greenwood Press, 1986. 531 p. (Music reference collection, 8)
Lists 5,800 musical settings of 99 American authors by 2,100 composers, providing bibliographical information as well as brief remarks on performing forces. Recordings are occasionally cited. Extensive list of works cited. Arranged by author with indexes to composers and to titles of literary works.

1433. Kagen, Sergius. Music for the voice, a descriptive list of concert and teaching material. Revised edition. Bloomington: Indiana University Press, 1968. 780 p.

First published in 1949 by Rinehart, New York, as no. 3 in the "Field of music" series.

Songs are listed alphabetically by composer and nationality within four large categories: (1) songs and airs before the 19th century; (2) songs of the 19th and 20th centuries; (3) folk songs; (4)operatic excerpts. Each section has its own bibliography, and there are numerous biographical sketches of song writers. Data include title, compass, tessitura, type, with descriptive remarks.

1434. Kuppuswamy, Gowri and Muthuswamy Hariharan. index of songs in South Indian music. Delhi: B. R. Publishing; New Delhi: D. K. Publisher, 1981. 970 p.

The general index gives, with regard to each published song, the beginning, raga, tala, language, composer and details of availability. There are separate indices for raga, tala, language and composer.

Cites sources of songs.

1435. Lax, Roger and Frederic Smith. The great song thesaurus. N.Y.: Oxford University Press, 1984. 665 p.

The intent was to select, from all divisions of song literature, the 10,000 best-known popular and/or significant songs in English-speaking countries and to cross index the pertinent data.

One section organized chronologically beginning with 1226. Second section devoted to listing award winning songs by year beginning with 1932. Third section lists "trademark" songs, theme and signature songs. Fourth section lists songs based on pre-existent musical sources. Fifth section provides complete title listing citing composers, dates and sources (if from a show). Sixth section lists British titles. Indexes to composers' and lyricists' names and to sources (including film, radio and television shows). Thesaurus of song titles by subject, keyword, and category.

1436. Leigh, Robert. Index to song books, a title index to over 11,000 copies of almost 6,800 songs in 111 song books published between 1933 and 1962. Stockton, Calif.: Robert Leigh, 1964. 273 p.

Reprint published by Da Capo Press, New York, 1972.

Intended to supplement the Sears *Song Index,* no. 1439.

1437. Citation omitted.

1438. Lust, Patricia D. American vocal chamber music, 1945–1980: an annotated bibliography. Foreword by Phyllis Bryn-Julson. Westport: Greenwood Press, 1985. 273 p. (Music reference collection, 4)

Annotations consist of descriptions of unusual features of the music, including non-traditional notation. Appendices classify the works by performing forces. Index to titles and to names of persons and ensembles.

1439. Sears, Minnie E. Song index: an index to more than 12,000 songs in 177 song collections. ... New York: H. W. Wilson, 1926. 650 p.

Supplement: an index to more than 7,000 songs in 104 collections. ... 1934. 366 p. Reprint by the Shoe String Press.

Contains titles, first lines, authors' names, and composers' names in one alphabet. Each song is cited under title, with added entry under composer and author, and cross references for first line and variant or translated titles. Classified and alphabetical listings of the song collections indexed.

The work of Sears has been continued in *Songs in collections* by De Charms and Breed (1966). see no. 1418.

1440. Stewart-Green, Miriam. Women composers: a check-list of works for the solo voice. Boston: G. K. Hall, 1980. 296 p.

In the general section, lists 3,746 women composers who have composed "classical" music. Cites song titles and publishers or locations when known. Separate lists for: operas, cantatas, oratorios, masses, cycles and collections, works for voice with instruments, dramatic scenes. Bibliography and index of names.

1441. Swan, Alfred J. The music director's guide to musical literature (for voices and instruments). New York: Prentice-Hall, 1941. 164 p.

P. 117–64: A selected list of works from the early Middle Ages through the 20th century. Arranged chronologically, with subdivisions by genre and country. Occasional annotations. The earlier part of the book contains brief comments on the composers represented in the bibliography.

1442. University of Tennessee, Knoxville. Song Index. Compiled by Pauline S. Bayne and Patricia Barkalow. Knoxville: University of Tennessee Library, 1981. 30 microfiche and accompanying booklet.

An index to songs in 554 anthologies with indexes to song titles, composers, genres, langauge of texts, authors, geographic or ethnic sources, and performance forces.

String Ensemble

1443. Altmann, Wilhelm. Kleiner Führer durch die Streichquartette für Haus und Schule. ... Berlin/Halensee: Deutscher Musikliteratur-Verlag, [1950]. 166 p.

An abridgement of the author's *Handbuch für Streichquartettspieler* (no. 1333) concentrating on the classical literature for the ensemble, curtailing all post-Brahms works.

1444. Farish, Margaret K. String music in print. N.Y.: R. R. Bowker, 1965. 420 p.

Supplement to string music in print published by Bowker, 1968 (204 p.).

The work was first published in a "preliminary" edition in 1963. The work is

... a guide to published music for the violin, viola, violoncello and double-bass. It contains information on solo music, accompanied and unaccompanied; chamber music, including combinations of stringed instruments with wind instruments, keyboard instruments, harp, guitar, percussion and voice; methods and studies. [Author's *Preface*]

Arrangement is alphabetical by composer within each category; composer's dates given. Brief titles, with instrumentation. Publishers indicated by symbols, with a comprehensive list of publishers, p. 411–20.

Succeeded by *String music in print* 2nd ed. published by in the *Music in print* series, see no. 1221.

Review of the preliminary edition by Joal H. Berman in *Notes,* 20 (1963), p. 229; of the 1965 edition by Katherine Holum in *Journal of research in music education,* 13 (1965), p. 190–91; of the *Supplement* by Dena J. Epstein in *Notes,* 25 (1969), p. 746.

1445. Grünberg, Max. Fuhrer durch die Literatur der Streichinstrumente ... Kritisches, progressiv geordnetes Repertorium von instruktiven Solo- und Ensemble-Werken. ... Leipzig: Breitkopf & Hartel, 1913. 218 p. (Handbucher der Musiklehre ... hrsg. von) X. Scharwenka, 10

Reprinted by Martin Sandig, Niederwalluf bei Wiesbaden, 1971.

A listing of music for violin, viola, cello, and ensemble from the Baroque through the 19th-century classified according to genre and degree of difficulty. Publishers and prices indicated. Bibliography, p. 207–9. Index.

Violin

1446. Basart, Ann P. "Finding string music" in *Cum notis variorum,* 57 (November, 1981), p. 6–16.

An annotated, indexed check-list of bibliographies of string music for performance.

1447. Baudet-Maget, A. Guide du violoniste; œuvres choisies pour violon, ainsi que pour alto et musique de chambre, classées d'apres leur degré de difficulté. Lausanne, Paris, [etc.]: Foetisch Freres, [n.d.] 295 p.

Selective list of violin, viola, and string ensemble music from mid-17th century to the present. Classified according to genre and degree of difficulty.

1448. Farish, Margaret K. String music in print. 2nd ed. N.Y.: R. R. Bowker, 1973. 464 p.

First published in 1965. A *Supplement* was published in 1968. The work appeared originally in a preliminary edition in 1963.

This is a guide to music for violin, viola, violoncello, double bass, and viols. Arranged broadly by performing forces with cryptic bibliographical information. Composer index and list of publishers.

See the successor volume in the *Music-in-print* series (no. 1222).

Review of the preliminary edition by Joal H. Berman in *Notes,* 20 (1963), p. 229; of the 1965 edition by Katherine Holumin *Journal of research in music education,* 13 (1965), p. 190–91; of the *Supplement* by Dena J. Epstein in *Notes,* 25 (1969), p. 746.

1449. Iotti, Oscar Raoul. Violin and violoncello in duo without accompaniment based on the work by Alexander Feinland. Detroit: Information Coordinators, 1972. 73 p. (Detroit studies in music bibliography, 25)

A bibliography based on Feinland's *The combination violin and violoncello without accompaniment.*

1450. Letz, Hans. Music for violin and viola. New York: Rinehart, [1948]. 107 p. (The field of music, 2)

Selective, graded list of music for unaccompanied violin, or violin and piano (p. 1–94); followed by a similar list of music for the viola (p. 96–107).

1451. Toskey, Burnett R. Concertos for violin and viola, a comprehensive encyclopedia. Seattle: B. R. Toskey, 1983. 992 p.

"... a listing of more than 8,400 concertos for a solo violin or viola ..." In addition to information on the composer and the music, a descriptive review is provided for most works. Numerous indexes and a bibliography.

1452. Tottmann, Albert. Führer durch die Violin-Literatur. ... 4. wesentlich vervollständigte, bis auf die Gegenwart seit 1901 forgeführte und neu bearbeitete Auflage von Wilhelm Altmann. Leipzig: J. Schuberth, 1935. 472 p.

Title varies: first published as *Führer durch den Violin-Unterricht, 1873; 2nd ed., 1886; 3rd ed., 1902.*

Classified bibliography including etudes, solo or accompanied violin works, duos, trios, quartets, etc., for violins. Gives full bibliographical information and brief critical comments. Supplements Altmann's *Kammermusik-Katalog* (no. 1329) for solo works.

Viola

1453. Altmann, Wilhelm and W. Borissowsky. Literaturverzeichnis für Bratsche und Viola d'amore. Wolfenbuttel: Verlag für musikalische Kultur und Wissenschaft, 1937. 148 p.

Classified catalog, including solo works, duos, and other combinations in which the viola has the leading role. Lists some works in manuscript and all known editions of published works, with dates. Includes transcriptions as well as original works.

1454. Drüner, Ulrich. "Das Viola-Konzert vor 1840" in *Fontes artis musicae,* 28 (1981), p. 153–76.

A bibliography documenting the development of the viola concerto in its first stage. Works of 141 composers are listed, and locations of the sources given.

1455. Ewald, Konrad. Musik für Bratsche, Führer durch die heute Zugangliche Literatur für Viola. Liestal, Switzerland: author, 1975. 153 p.

Arranged by composer in three broad chronological sections. Each chronological division is divided into a section in which the music is discussed and another in which it is just listed. Includes publication information. Classified index to performing forces and an index to composers.

1456. Williams, Michael D. Music for viola. Detroit: Information Coordinators, 1979. 362 p. (Detroit Studies in Music Bibliography, 42)

A classified bibliography attempting to be comprehensive. Provides complete bibliographic information for each work cited.

1457. Zeyringer, Franz. Literatur für Viola: Verzeichnis der Werke für Viola-Solo, Duos mit Viola, Trios mit Viola, Viola-Solo mit Begleitung, Blockflöte mit Viola, Gesang mit Viola und der Schul- und Studienwerke für Viola. Literature for viola: catalogue of works for viola solo, duos with viola, trios with viola, solo viola with accompaniment, recorder with viola, voice with viola, and methods, etudes and exercises for viola. Neue, erw. Ausg. Hartberg, Austria: J. Schönwetter Jun., 1985. 446 p.

First published in 1963 (151 p.) with a supplement in 1965 (82 p.). 2nd edition published in 1976 (418 p.).

Indexes of publishers and composers.

Violoncello

1458. Kenneson, Claude. Bibliography of cello ensemble music. Detroit: Information Coordinators, 1974. 59 p. (Detroit Studies in Music Bibliography, 31)

Cites works for 'cello music for two 'celli to orchestra works, including works with piano. Classified.

1459. Nogué, Edouard. La littérature du violoncelle . . . Preface de M. Paul Bazelaire. . . . Paris: Delagrave, 1925. 151 p.

Lists nearly 2,000 works for violoncello, solo or with other instruments. Classified and graded, with short descriptions of most of the works. Publishers indicated.

1460. Weigl, Bruno. Handbuch der Violoncell-Literatur; systematisch geordnetes Verzeichnis der solo- und instruktiven Werke. . . . 3. Auflage. Wien: Universal-Edition, 1929. 357 p.

Classified listing of compositions of cello and orchestra, cello and piano, cello solo, or accompanied by other instruments. Comparable in arrangement and content to his *Handbuch der Orgelliteratur* (see no. 1372).

Double Bass

1461. Grodner, Murray. Comprehensive catalogue of available literature for the double bass. 3rd ed. Bloomington: Lemur Musical Research, 1974. 169 p.

First published in 1958. 2nd edition, 1964, 84 p.

Lists works in print, 1974. Solos and ensembles for from 2 to 14 instruments, using string bass. Each entry gives composer, title, instrumentation, grade of difficulty, publisher, price, with occasional annotations as to availability. A short bibliography of works about the bass and bass playing. Index of names.

Review of the first edition by Darius Thieme in *Notes,* 16 (1969), p. 258.

1462. Planyavsky, Alfred. Geschichte des Kontrabasses. 2., wesentlich erw. Aufl. unter der Mitarbeit von Herbert Seifert. Tutzing: Hans Schneider, 1984. 917 p.

First printed in 1970, 537 p.

Primarily a historical study of the string bass from the 16th century to the present—its construction, technique, and repertoire.

P. 433–506: classified catalog of string bass music, treating the instrument as solo and in a variety of ensembles. The work also contains a bibliography of relevant literature, a discography of string bass music, and an index of names and subjects.

Viols

1463. Dodd, Gordon. Thematic index of music for viols. *s.l.*: The Viola da Gamba Society of Great Britain, 1980–82. 2 v.

Third installment issued in 1984.

The intent of the index is to provide thematic incipits and locations in manuscript sources of music for viols by British composers or found mainly in British sources. Each installment includes a list of entries, a bibliography, and, for each composer, a brief essay on style. There are frequent remarks on the sources.

See the brief article by Gordon Dodd on the genesis of the *Index* in *Fontes artis musicae,* 25 (1978), p. 239–42.

1464. De Smet, Robin. Published music for the viola da gamba and other viols. Detroit: Information Coordinators, 1971. 105 p. (Detroit studies in music bibliography, 18)

Wind Ensemble and Band

1464.1. American Music Center. Library. Music for orchestra, band and large ensemble. New York: American Music Center, 1982. 196 p. (Catalog of the American Music Center Library, 3)

A catalog of the holdings of large instrumental ensemble by American composers in the American equivalent of a national music information center.

1465. Australia Music Centre. Military and brass band music [in the] Australia Music Centre. Sydney: Australia Music Centre, 1977. 28 p. Catalogues of Australian compositions, 6

A catalog of the holdings of the Australia Music Centre in this genre.

1466. Band music guide: alphabetical listing of titles and composers of all band music. 8th ed. Evanston: Instrumentalist Co., 1982. 408 p.

The 7th edition appeared in 1978. 367 p.

An attempt at a comprehensive listing intended to aid school band directors in the United States in program preparation.

1467. Gillespie, James E. The reed trio: an annotated bibliography of original published works. Detroit: Information Coordinators, 1971. 84 p. (Detroit studies in music bibliography, 20)

1468. Heller, George N. Ensemble music for wind and percussion instruments: a catalog. Washington, D.C.: Music Educators' National Conference, 1970. 142 p.

1469. Helm, Sanford Marion. Catalog of chamber music for wind instruments. Revised reprint. New York: Da Capo Press, 1969. 85 p.
First printed in 1952 at Ann Arbor, Michigan.
Chamber music for from 3 to 12 instruments employing at least one wind instrument. classified according to the size of the ensemble and instrumentation. Gives publisher, date, American agent for currently available editions. Composer index.

1470. Hošek, Miroslav. Das Bläserquintett. The woodwind quintet; [Englisch von Colleen Gruban]. Grünwald: B. Brüchle, 1979. 234 p.
Bibliography of woodwind quintets by categories. Essays on origin, acoustics and performance practice. Bibliography. Lists of personnel in professional woodwind quintets.

1471. Peters, Harry B. The literature of the woodwind quintet. Metuchen: Scarecrow Press, 1971. 174 p.
A basic listing of woodwind quintet music, followed by a section devoted to the quintet with one, two, three, four, or five additional performers.

1472. Selective music list for band. 1986 revision. Nashville: National Band Association, 1986. 71 p.
A bibliography of band music.

1473. Suppan, Armin. Repertorium der Märsche für Blasorchester. Tutzing: H. Schneider, 1982. 346 p, (Alta musica, 6)
An alphabetical listing by composer giving titles and publishers of marches. Index to titles. A second volume is projected.

1474. Voxman, Himie and Lyle Merriman. Woodwind ensemble music guide. Evanston, Illinois: Instrumentalist Co., 1984. 280 p.
Classified lists with brief title and publisher codes.

1475. Wallace, David and Eugene Corporon. Wind ensemble/band repertoire. Greeley: University of Northern Colorado School of Music, 1984. c. 248 p. (not continuously paged)
A broadly classified list citing composer, title, instrumentation, and, by reference, publisher. Includes work for voice and wind ensemble/band. There is a list of composers and their addresses, but no index.

1476. Whitwell, David. Band music of the French revolution. Tutzing: Schneider, 1979. 212 p. (Alta musica, 5)

A history with an extensive bibliography and a thematic catalog.

1477. Whitwell, David. The history and literature of the wind band and wind ensemble. Northridge, Calif.: Winds, 1982–84. 9 v.

Contents:

v. 1. *The wind band and wind ensemble before 1500.*

v. 2. *The Renaissance wind band and wind ensemble.*

v. 3. *The Baroque wind band and wind ensemble.*

v. 4. *The wind band and wind ensemble of the Classic Period, 1750–1800.*

v. 5. *The nineteenth century wind band and wind ensemble in western Europe*

v. 6. *A catalog of multi-part instrumental music for wind instruments or for undesignated instrumentation before 1600.*

v. 7. *A catalog of Baroque multi-part instrumental music for wind instruments or for undesignated instrumentation.*

v. 8. *Wind band and wind ensemble literature of the classic period.*

v. 9. *Wind band and wind ensemble literature of the nineteenth century.*

A monumental history and bibliography.

1478. Ziegenrücker, Wieland. Literaturberater Blasmusik: e. Wegweiser bei d. Repertoire- u. Programmgestaltung auf d. Grundlage d. Notenausg. d. Musikverlage d. DDR. Leipzig: Zentralhaus für Kulturarbeit der DDR, 1975. 74 p.

A guide to the repertory and bibliography of music for bands and wind ensembles available in the Deutsches Demokratisches Republik.

Flute

1480. Bowers, Jane. "A catalogue of French works for the transverse flute, 1692–1761," in *Recherches sur la musique francaise classique," XVIII (1978), p. 89–125.* Paris: Editions A. et J. Picard, 1978.

1481. Girard, Adrien. Histoire et richesse de la flûte. Paris: Libraire Grund, 1953. 143 p.

A handsome, illustrated volume printed in an edition of 1,500 copies. Chapter IV, "Les flûtistes," lists the principal performers from the 15th to the 20th centuries, with brief comments on each. Chapter V, "Littérature," is a chronological listing of the important composers of flute music with their works, from Louis Couperin to the present, followed by an alphabetical listing, by composer, of works for solo flute accompanied by keyboard, harp, or orchestra. Manuscript works included.

1482. Kongelige Bibliothek. Catalogue of Giedde's music collection in the Royal Library of Copenhagen. Compiled by Inge Bittmann. Copenhagen: Edition Egtved, 1976. 198 p.

A catalog of "a fairly comprehensive collection, mostly of flute music from the second half of the 18th century." [from the Preface]

Arranged alphabetically by composer with thematic incipits. There is a classified list of titles, a list of publishers, and a bibliography.

1483. Pellerite, James J. A handbook of literature for the flute (a list of graded method materials, solos, and ensemble music for the flute). Bloomington: Zalo Publications, 1978. 408 p.

First published in 1963, 96 p.

This listing of flute literature is specifically designed to familiarize the music teachers, music educators, and students of the flute with a portion of available materials presently appearing in publishers' catalogs. [*Foreword* to the 1963 edition]

Graded and annotated.

1484. Pierreuse, Bernard. Flûte litterature; catalogue général des œuvres éditées et inédités par formations instrumentales. General catalog of published and unpublished works by instrumental category. Paris: Éditions Musicales Transatlantiques, 1982. 670 p.

An international catalog with a composer index, a list of publishers, and a list of major libraries.

1485. Vester, Frans. Flute music of the 18th century, an annotated bibliography. Monteux: Musica Rara, 1985. 573 p.

Entries include information on location of works, when known. As with the *Flute repertoire catalog* (1976), there are indexes to the composer listing arranged by performing forces. This work omits music including voice, studies, methods and instruction books, literature about the flute, and a list of publishers.

1486. Vester, Frans. Flute repertoire catalogue. 10,000 titles. London: Musica Rara, 1967. 383 p.

Lists music for flute alphabetically under composer, with indexes directing the user to music for flute in combinatin with other instruments and with orchestra and voice. There is a short bibliography of literature on the flute and a listing of publishers of flute music.

1487. Wilkins, Wayne. The index of flute music including the index of Baroque trio sonatas. Magnolia, Arkansas: Music Register, 1974. 131 p.

Supplements issued in 1975 (25 p.) and 1978 (14 p).

Classified lists of works citing composer and publisher.

Oboe

1488. Gifford, Virginia Snodgrass. Music for oboe, oboe d'amore, and English horn; a bibliography of materials in the Library of Congress. Westport: Greenwood, 1983. 431 p. (Music Reference Collection, 1)

A bibliography of cataloged and uncataloged holdings at the Library of Congress. Essentially a locating device for L.C. holdings in specified classes. Includes a detailed table of contents, an index of publishers, an index of instruments, and an index of composers.

1489. Haynes, Bruce. Music for oboe, 1650–1800: a bibliography. Berkeley: Fallen Leaf Press, 1985. 394 p. (Fallen Leaf reference books in music, 4.)

"This book is a complete revision of Music for oboe to 1800 (interim edition, June 1982) published privately by the author" in The Hague, 1980, 65 p.

Covers over 9,400 pieces for oboe, oboe d'amore, and F-oboe in printed and manuscript editions. Also lists chamber music up to 8 parts, concertos with up to 3 solo parts, vocal music with obbligato oboe parts, and oboe method books containing music. Cites lost works.

Arranged by composer, each entry includes title, key, opus and/or thematic index information, instrumentation, imprint, location of source, modern edition, and occasionally notes.

1490. Hošek, Miroslav. Katalog der Oboenliteratur tschechischer und slowakischer Autoren. Herausgegeben vom Tschechoslowakischen Musikinformationszentrum. Praha: 1969. 89 p.

Alphabetical listing by composer of chamber works for oboe and as many as 13 other instruments. Concertos and other orchestral works featuring the oboe are also included. Indexes of libraries, publishers, and instrumental combinations.

1491. Hošek, Miroslav. Oboen-Bibliographie. 2. Aufl. bearb. von Rudolf H. Führer. Wilhelmshaven: Heinrichshofen, 1984. 403 p.

Essentially a reprint of the edition of 1975.

A bibliography of modern, published oboe music, international in scope. Includes a separate bibliography of oboe methods. Arranged alphabetically by composer, with an index by instrumentation, a list of publishers, and a short bibliography of works about the oboe.

1492. Wilkins, Wayne. The index of oboe music including the index of Baroque trio sonatas. Magnolia, Arkansas: Music Register, 1976. 96, 11 p.

Supplement issued in 1977 and 1978.

Classified lists of works for solo oboe and oboe in ensemble citing composer and publisher.

1493. Bigotti, Giovanni. Storia dell'oboe e sua letteratura. Padova: G. Zanibon, 1974. 77 p.

Historical survey of the instrument in its varied forms. Brief entries, alphabetical by composer, classified by instrumentation.

Clarinet

1494. Brixel, Eugen. Klarinetten-Bibliographie. 2. Aufl. Wilhelmshaven: Heinrichshofens Verlag, 1978. 493 p.

A classified listing, international in scope, citing composer, title and publisher of music for solo clarinet and as a member of an ensemble. There is a short bibliography of literature about the clarinet and an index to composers listed.

1495. Gee, Harry. Clarinet solos de concours, 1897–1980: an annotated bibliography. Bloomington: Indiana University Press, 1981. 118 p.

A bibliography of clarinet music approved by the Paris Conservatoire.

1496. Gillespie, James E. Jr. Solos for unaccompanied clarinet; an annotated bibliography of published works. Detroit: Information Coordinators, 1973. 79 p. (Detroit Studies in Music Bibliography, 28)

The annotations feature composers' comments on performance and include biographical information.

1497. Kroll, Oskar. The clarinet. Revised, and with a repertory by Diethard Riehm. Translated by Hilda Morris. New York: Taplinger Pub. Co., 1968. 183 p.

Translation of *Die Klarinette; ihre Geschichte, ihre Literatur, ihre grossen Meister.*

Bibliography: p. 133–35. "Repertory of the clarinet": p. 136–75.

1498. Opperman, Kalmen. Repertory of the clarinet. New York:, Ricordi, [1960]. 140 p.

Classified index of music for the clarinet, including methods, etudes, and music for the instrument as solo and in combination with other instruments. List of publishers given, and a short bibliography of books on the clarinet.

Review by Roger P. Phelps in *Notes,* 18 (1960), p. 63–64.

1499. Tuthill, Burnet C. "The sonatas for clarinet and piano." In *Journal of research in music education,* 14 (1966), p. 197–212.

An annotated listing of sonatas from the 18th century to the present. A few transcriptions and works in manuscript are included.

Bassoon

1500. Langwill, Lyndesay Graham. The bassoon and the contrabassoon. London: E. Benn; New York, W.W. Norton [1965]. 269 p.

A history of the development of the bassoon and countrabassoon with a list of solo music for each and a discography. Numerous bibliographical footnotes.

1501. Risdon, Howard. Musical literature for the bassoon; a compilation of music for the bassoon as an instrument in ensemble. Seattle: Berdon, [1963]. 24 p.

1502. Wilkins, Wayne. The index of bassoon music including the index of Baroque trio sonatas. Magnolia, Arkansas: Music Register, 1976. 76, 11 p.

Supplements published in 1976–77 and 1978.

Classified lists of works citing composer and publisher.

Horn

1503. Brüchle, Bernhard. Horn Bibliographie. Wilhelmshaven: Heinrichshofen, 1970–83. 3 v.

First volume published with a 14-page supplement of plates.

Entries classified according to ensembles; horn solo, horn and keyboard, various duo combinations, trios, quartets, etc. The work contains a bibliograhy of literature on the instrument, list of publishers, and index of names.

1504. Gregory, Robin. The horn, a comprehensive guide to the modern instrument and its music. New York: Praeger, 1969. 410 p.

First printed in 1961 in London.

P. 181–393: Appendix C. A list of music for the horn. A classified list of music for horn solo or in combination with various ensembles, instrumental or vocal. Entries give composer, title, ensemble, and publisher.

Recorder

1505. Alker, Hugo. Blökflöten-Bibliographie. Neuausgabe. Wilhelmshaven: Heinrichshofen's Verlag, 1984. 2 v.

1st edition published 1960 with a supplement appearing in 1961. 2nd edition appeared in 1966 and was supplemented in 1969.

Band I: Systematischer Teil

Band II: Alphbetischer Teil

Band I includes a classified listing by composer and title with imprint of music for recorder. There is a section devoted to articles about performance practice and other works relating to the recorder.

Band II contains an alphabetical index to composers in volume I and a list of publishers' names and addresses.

1506. McCowan, Richard A. Italian Baroque solo sonatas for the recorder and the flute. Detroit: Information Coordinators, 1978. 70 p. (Detroit Studies in Music Bibliography, 37)

In two sections, the first listing and describing 18th century manuscripts and editions and the second containing modern editions.

1507. Winterfeld, Linde H. von and Harald Kunz. Handbuch der Blockflöten-Literatur. Berlin/Wiesbaden: Bote & Bock, 1959. 139 p.

Listings of music for recorder, solo, ensemble, and in combination with other instruments. Publisher and price given. Composer and title index, and a short list of books on the recorder.

Saxophone

1508. Londeix, Jean-Marie. 125 ans de musique pour saxophone. Répertoire général des œuvres et des ouvrages d'enseignement pour le saxophone. 125 years of music for the saxophone. General repertory of pieces and educational literature for the saxophone. Paris: Alphonse Leduc, 1971. 398 p.

A general listing of works involving saxophone by composer, followed by indexes under individual instruments (soprano, alto, tenor, baritone) and by ensembles. Composers are identified, and rather full biographical information, with critical quotations, is given for major composers. Supplementary lists of addresses for composers and publishers of saxophone music.

1509. Wilkins, Wayne. The index of saxophone music. Magnolia, Arkansas: Music Register, 1979. 59 p.

Classified lists of works for saxophone and for saxophone in ensembles citing composer and publisher.

Brass Instruments (Solo and Chamber)

1510. Bell, William J. amd R. Winston Morris. Encyclopedia of literature for the tuba. New York: C. Colin, 1967. 161 p.

A bibliography of tuba music and music for the tuba.

1511. Carnovale, Robert. Twentieth-century music for trumpet and orchestra; an annotated bibliography. Nashville: Brass Press, 1975. 55 p. (Brass Research Series, 3)

A guide to 179 works with imprint information, duration, range and reviews cited.

Briefly reviewed by Stephen M. Fry in *Notes,* 32 (1976), p. 780.

1512. Decker, Richard G. A bibliography of music for three heterogeneous brass instruments alone and in chamber ensembles. Oneonta: Swift-Dorr Publications, 1976. 82 p.

1513. Devol, John Brass music for the church; a bibliography of music appropriate for church use. New York: H.Branch, 1974. 102 p.

Lists "a total of 1,309 works, including brass parts for one trumpet up to a twenty-piece brass choir."

1514. Everett, Thomas G. Annotated guide to bass trombone literature. 3rd ed., revised and enlarged. Nashville: Brass Press, 1985. 94 p. (Brass Research Series, 6)

1st published in 1973 and again in 1978.

726 entries of published and manuscript music. Bibliography, list of recordings, index to composers.

Review by Peter B. Brown in *Notes,* 36 (1979), p. 103–04.

1515. Morris, R. Winston. Tuba music guide. Evanston: The Instrumentalist Co., 1973. 60 p.

A classified and annotated bibliography of solo and chamber music for the tuba.

1516. Anderson, Paul G. Brass ensemble music guide. Evanston: Instrumentalist Co., 1978. 259 p.

Classified lists with brief titles and publisher codes.

Composer index.

1517. Anderson, Paul G. and Larry Bruce Campbell. Brass music guide: solo and study guide material in print. 1985 edition. Northfield, Ill.: Instrumentalist Co., 1984. 294 p.

First published as *Brass solo and study material music guide, 1976.*

Classified lists with brief titles and publisher codes. Composer index.

269

1518. Arling, Harry J. Trombone chamber music; an annotated bibliography. Second edition (revised and enlarged). Nashville: Brass Press, 1983. 43 p.

First published in 1978.

The majority of works cited in this guide were composed in the twentieth century. Most of the works cited involve trombone as the only brass instrument.

Reviewed by Peter B. Brown in *Notes,* 36 (1979), p. 103–04.

Electronic and Computer Music

1519. Australia Music Centre. Electronic music. Sydney: Australia Music Centre, 1977. 65 p. (Catalogues of Australian compositions, 7)

Catalog of Australian electronic music.

1520. Davies, Hugh. Répertoire international des musiques electroacoustiques. International electronic music catalog. A cooperative publication of le Groupe de recherches musicales de l'O.R.T.F., Paris, and the Independent Electronic Music Center, New York. Cambridge, Mass.: distributed by M.I.T. Press, 1968. 330 p. (Electronic music review, nos. 2/3, April/July 1967.)

Text in French and English.

The aim of this new catalog is to document all the electronic music ever composed in the almost 20 years since composers first began to work in this media.

Main alphabet is by country, subdivided by city and state (if in U.S.A.). Gives data on composers, titles of work, functions, dates of composition, duration, and number of tape tracks involved.

Some 5,000 compositions listed. Appendixes include a discography, a directory of permanent studies, and an index of composers.

Review by Jon Appleton *Notes,* 25 (1968), p. 34–35.

1521. Melby, Carol, comp. Computer music compositions of the United States, 1976. Prepared for the first International Conference on Computer Music, October 28–31, 1976, Massachusetts Institute of Technology. 2d ed. Urbana: *s.n.,* 1976. 28 p.

First ed. prepared for the Music Computation Conference II, held at the University of Illinois at Urbana-Champaign, November 7–9, 1975. 42 p.

1522. Storey, Cheryl Ewing. A bibliography of computer music. Denton, Texas: North Texas State University Music Library, 1981. 41 p.

'Compiled for the North Texas State University Music Library and the International Computer Music conference held at NTSU November 5–8, 1981." Includes a discography.

Wind Instruments (Chamber)

1523. Basart, Ann P. "Bibliographies of wind music: a check-list" in *Cum notis variorum,* 37 (November, 1979), p. 10–13 and 39 (February, 1980), p.9–13.

An annotated check-list to bibliographies providing information on music for wind instruments.

1524. Chapman, James, Sheldon Fine, and Mary Rasmussen. "Music for wind instruments in historical editions, collected works, and numbered series: a bibliography" in *Brass and Woodwind Quarterly,* 1 (1968), p. 115–149, and 2 (1969), p. 17–58.

Part I: Music, without voices, for specified instrumentations with basso continuo;

Part II: Music with voices, for specified instrumentation;

Part III: Music without voices, for unspecified instrumentation;

Part IV: Music with voices, for unspecified instrumentation.

1525. Houser, Roy. Catalogue of chamber music for woodwind instruments. 2nd ed. Bloomington: Indiana University, 1960. 158 leaves (typescript)

Reprinted by Da Capo, 1973.

Supplement: *Woodwind ensembles bibliography.*

Material for from 3 to 10 instruments, classified according to ensemble. P. 147–48: a list of woodwind music found in the Moravian archives at Winston-Salem, North Carolina, and at Bethlehem, Pennsylvania. P. 152–55: Selected publications from the catalog of the Donemus Foundation, Amsterdam.

1526. National Association of Schools of Music. Solo literature for the wind instruments. The Bulletin of the National Association of Schools of Music, no. 31. January, 1951. 32 p.

Lists of solos, including concertos, for flute, oboe, clarinet, bassoon, French horn, cornet and trumpet, trombone. Graded as to difficulty; brief critical or descriptive annotations. Publishers indicated.

1527. Rasmussen, Mary. A teacher's guide to the literature of brass instruments. Durham, N.H.: Brass Quarterly, 1964. 84 p.

General discussion of music available for brass ensembles and solos, followed by extensive listings giving publisher, price, instrumentation, and grade level of the works cited.

1528. Rasmussen, Mary and Donald Mattran. A teacher's guide to the literature of woodwind instruments. Durham, N.H.: Brass and Woodwind Quarterly, 1966. 226 p.

Bibliographies of woodwind music for solos or ensembles.

1529. Voxman, Himie and Lyle Merriman. Woodwind music guide, solo and study material in print. 1984 ed. Evanston, Illinois: Instrumentalist Co., 1984. 499 p. (Music guide series, 3)

Updated edition of *Woodwind solo and study material music guide, 1975.*

Classified list with brief titles and publisher codes.

Percussion

1530. Combs, F. Michael. Solo and ensemble literature for percussion. Knoxville: Percussive Arts Society, 1978. 93 *l.*
Originally published in 1967, reissued in enlarged form in 1972, and supplemented in 1976.
A classified list of music for various percussion instruments. Includes information on publishers and sources.

Lute, Vihuella, Guitar and Other Plectoral

1531. Gilmore, George and Mark Pereira. Guitar music index: a cross-indexed and graded listing of music in print for classical guitar and lute. Honolulu: Galliard Press, 1976. 108 p.

1532. International Music Service. A catalog of music for the harp ... New York: International Music Service, 1981. 1 v. (unpaged loose-leaf)
A distributor's catalog.

1533. Moser, Wolf. Gitarre Musik; ein internationaler Katalog. Hamburg: Joachim Trekel-Der Volksmusikverlag, 1974–77. 2 v.
A classified list by performing forces, with separate sectors for etudes, collections, books about the guitar, and Flamenco guitar music. There is a composer index. V. 2 supplements v. 1.

1534. Ragossnig, Konrad. Handbuch der Gitarre und Laute. Mainz: Schott, 1978. 256 p.
A brief and superficial bibliography appended to a work intended to inform students of the instruments. Valuable comments upon editions of music.
Review by Thomas F. Heck in *Notes,* 36 (1979), p. 107–08.

1535. Rensch, Roslyn. The harp; its history, technique and repertoire. New York: Praeger Publishers, 1969. 246 p.
An historical monograph with discographies and bibliographies.

1536. Rezits, Joseph. The guitarist's resource guide: guitar music in print and books on the art of guitar. San Diego: Pallma Music Co./Distributed by N. A. Kjos Music Co., 1983. 574 p.
Includes sections on lute, mandolin, and vihuela music. Each section has a composer and title index. The guitar section is further sub-divided by performing forces.

1537. Rudén, Jan Olof. Music in tablature: a thematic index with source descriptions of music in tablature notation in Sweden. Stockholm: Svenskt musikhistoriskt arkiv, 1981. 257 p. (Musik i Sverige, 5)(Music in Sweden, 5)
One of the first national catalogs of music in tablature. Includes bibliographical references and index.

1538. Zingel, Hans Joachim. Harfenmusik; Verzeichnis der gedruckten und zur Zeit greifbaren Literatur für Pedalharfe. Harp music. Musique de la harpe. Harp muziek. Musica per arpa. Hofheim am Taunus: F. Hofmeister 1965. 35 p.

1539. Zingel, Hans Joachim. Harfenmusik im 19. Jahrhundert: Versuch einer historischen Darstellung. Wilhelmshaven: Heinrichshofen, 1976. 95 p. (Veröffentlichungen zur Musikforschung, 2)

An historical monograph with bibliographical references.

JAZZ

Jazz has become a fully accepted scholarly specialty and bibliographical resources have expanded concomitantly. Some of the principal items in this area are listed below. Others will be found in the section on "Dictionaries and Encyclopedias," e.g., Leonard Feather's *The encyclopedia of jazz* (nos. 250–253). Others are cited under "Collectors' guides to jazz recordings" (nos. 2832 ff.).

1540. Australia Music Centre. Jazz. Sydney: Australia Music Centre, 1978. 280 p. (Catalogues of Australian compositions, 8)

Catalog of Australian jazz compositions.

1541. Lewine, Richard and Alfred Simon. Songs of the theater. New York: H. W. Wilson Co., 1984. 897 p.

Succeeds the authors' *Songs of the American theater,* 1973. 820 p.

An alphabetical list of songs from American musical theater from 1891 to 1983, each entry giving composer, lyricist, and title of the show from which the song originated. List of shows listing all songs with references to sources and adaptations. Index of composers, lyricists, and authors.

1542. Panassie, Hughes, and Madeleine Gautier. Dictionnaire du jazz. Préface de Louis Armstrong. Nouvelle édition, revue et augmenté. Paris: Albin Michel, 1980. 378 p.

First edition published in 1954. Revised and enlarged in 1971. This edition is a reprint of the 1971 edition with a supplement of 9 pages of new entries and a postface. There is a 1956 English translation reprinted in 1973 by Greenwood Press.

1543. Voigt, John. Jazz music in print and jazz books in print. 3rd ed. Boston: Hornpipe Music Pub. Co., 1982. 195 p.

Revised edition of *Jazz music in print,* 2nd ed., 1978. First edition in 1975.

Organized by individual artist. Contents of anthologies provided. Publisher and catalog distribution numbers cited. List of publishers.

Reviews of 2nd ed. by Lewis Porter in *Black perspective in music,* 7 (1979), p. 121–23; Dan Morgenstern in *Journal of jazz studies,* 5 (1979), p. 97–98.

POPULAR MUSIC

The study of popular music and popular culture is beginning to permeate academic curricula. There is an international scholarly society devoted to it, the International Association for the Study of Popular Music, and that society produces a journal, *Popular Music Perspectives.* Still, popular music reference works by and large continue to be the product of the work of dedicated amateurs. Roger Kinkle's *Complete encyclopedia of popular music and jazz* (no. 262) and the *Encyclopedia of musical theater* (no. 482) by Stanley Green are good examples what is being produced. In the 20th century, popular music has come to mean "mass-disseminated music" and is really distinct from "folk music" and other "music of the people."

1544. Brooks, Elston. I've heard those songs before; the weekly top ten tunes for the past 50 years. N.Y.: Morrow Quill, 1981. 444 p.

Titles of the most played popular songs on American radio in chronological order with an index to titles cited.

1545. Burton, Jack. The blue book of Tin Pan Alley, a human interest encyclopedia of American popular music. Expanded new edition Vol. 1: 1776–1860–1910; Vol 2. 1910–1960, with a *1950–1965 supplement* by Larry Freeman. Watkins Glen, N.Y.: Century House, 1962–65. 2 v.

First published in 1951.

The approach is chronological, with detailed listings of songs by the principal popular composers. Covers jazz and its musicians as well as popular music.

1546. Burton, Jack. The index of American popular music; thousands of titles cross-referenced to our basic anthologies of popular songs. Watkins Glen, N.Y.: Century House, 1957. 1 v.

Contents: 1. *Blue book of Tin Pan Alley.* 2. *Blue book of Broadway musicals.* 3. *Blue book of Hollywood musicals.* 4. *The melodies linger on.*

1547. Chipman, John H. Index to top-hit tunes (1900–1950) . . . with a foreword by Arthur Fiedler. Boston: Bruce Humphries, [1962]. 249 p.

An alphabetical index, by title, of the most popular American songs of the first half of the 20th century. Gives key, composer and author, publisher and original publication date, source in film or musical comedy. Chronological index, short bibliography.

1548. 80 years of American song hits 1892–1972; a comprehensive yearly reference book listing America's major hit songs and their writers. s.l.: Chappel, 1973. 106 p.

1549. Ewen, David. American popular songs: from the Revolutionary War to the present. New York: Random House, 1966. 507 p.

Provides information on more than 3,600 songs popular in America from 1775 to 1966. Cites composer, lyricist, place, medium, and date, including the performer who made the song popular.

Review by Ruth Hilton in *Notes,* 24 (1968), p. 501.

1550. Folio-Dex II: choral, orchestral, band. Loomis, c.: Folio-Dex Co., 1980
– . v. (loose-leaf)
"Index of all types of music (popular, classical, sacred, etc.) . . . listing
. . . those songs that are published for choral, band and orchestra music."
Updated by revised and new loose-leaf pages.

1551. Fuld, James J. American popular music (reference book) 1875–1950.
Philadelphia: Musical Americana, 1955. 94 p.
Supplement. . . . 1956. 9 p.
A bibliography of some 250 selected American popular songs. Detailed
information as to first printing, copyright date, description of cover. 20
plates of song covers. An interesting attempt to approach American
popular song with the methods of descriptive bibliography.

1552. Fuld, James J. The book of world-famous music; classical, popular
and folk. 3rd ed., rev. and enlarged. N.Y.: Dover, 1985. 714 p.
First published in 1966; 2nd edition published in 1971.
Considerable new information has been incorporated to this new edition of a work which traces the lineage, in printing or manuscript, of the
most familiar ("world-famous") compositions of the Western world. A
thematic index with detailed commentary on sources, composers, history. An admirable exercise in bibliography.
Not all of the author's revisions could be incorporated in the main body
of the text, so there is a supplement suction beginning on p. 669 keyed by
symbols to the main text. Index to names and titles.
Review of the 1966 edition by Ruth Hilton in *Notes,* 23 (1966), p. 56–57.
Review of the 1971 edition by Nyal Williams in *Notes,* 29 (1973), p. 448–49.

1553. Gargan, William and Sue Sharma. Find that tune; an index to rock,
folk-rock, disco and soul in collections. N.Y.: Neal-Shumann, 1984. 303 p.
An index to over 4,000 songs in 203 published collections of rock, folk-
rock, soul and disco music from 1950–81. List of collections indexed. Title
index including information on composer and lyricist, performers, publisher and copyright date. Index to first lines. Index to composers and
lyricists. Index to performers.

1554. Havlice, Patricia Pate. Popular song index. Metuchen: Scarecrow
Press, 1978. 933p.
First supplement indexing collections appearing in 1970–75 published
1978, 386 p. Second supplement indexing collections appearing in 1974–
1981 published 1984.
Indexes to folk songs, pop tunes, spirituals, children's songs, sea chanties, and blues in several hundred song anthologies published since 1940.
Bibliography of sources. Indexes of titles, first lines, first lines of choruses, and composers and lyricists.
Brief review by Stephen M. Fry in *Notes,* 32 (1976), p. 781. Review of
the first supplement by Patricia Felch in *Notes,* 35 (1979), p. 637–38.

1555. Iwaschkin, Roman. Popular music, a reference guide. New York: Garland Pub., 1986. 658 p. (Music research and information guides, 4)

Classified and annotated bibliography of 5,276 works covering the broadest range of popular music styles and genres. Includes a bibliography of bibliographies. Lists periodicals about popular music. Index of names, groups, and some titles.

1556. Lax, Roger and Frederic Smith. The great song thesaurus. N.Y.: Oxford University Press, 1984. 665 p.

> The intent was to select, from all divisions of song literature, the 10,000 best-known popular and/or significant songs in English-speaking countries and to cross index the pertinent data.

One section organized chronologically beginning with 1226. Second section devoted to listing award winning songs by year beginning with 1932. Third section lists "trademark" songs, theme and signature songs. Fourth section lists songs based on pre-existant musical sources. Fifth section provides complete title listing citing ocmposers, dates and sources (if from a show). Sixth section lists British titles. Indexes to composers' and lyricists' names and to sources (including film, radio and television shows). Thesaurus of song titles by subject, keyword, and category.

1557. Lewine, Richard and Alfred Simon. Songs of the theater. N.Y.: H. W. Wilson, 1984. 897 p.

A title listing of songs from virtually all the shows appearing on- and off-Broadway from 1891 to 1983. Each entry includes names of composer(s) and lyricist(s), name and dates of the show. Indexes to names, titles of shows, and film and television productions. Chronological list of shows.

This work based on and largely superseding the author's *Encyclopedia of theater music* (1961) and *Songs of the American theater* (1973).

1558. Limbacher, James L. Film music: from violins to video. Metuchen: Scarecrow Press, 1974. 835 p.

Part one is an anthology of essays on the subject, with a bibliography. Part two is divided into four sections: film titles and dates; films and their composers; composers and their films; discography of recorded movie music. Name and title index to part one.

1559. Limbacher, James L. Keeping score, film music 1972–1979. Metuchen: Scarecrow Press, 1981. 510 p.

Continues *Film music: from violins to video,* superseding individual entries with corrected information. This is a book of lists: winners of Academy Awards for best original film scores, 1935–1979; a necrology of film music composers; a bibliography of recent books on the subject of film music; film music titles and dates; films and their composers/adaptors; composers and their films; and recorded musical scores.

1560. Lynch, Richard Chigley. Musicals! a directory of musical properties available for production. Chicago: American Library Association, 1984. 197 p.

Lists 400 titles and supplies vital information: title, date of original production, author, composer, lyricist, plot, cast requirements, licensing agent, recordings available.

1561. Mattfeld, Julius. Variety music cavalcade, 1620–1961; a chronology of vocal and instrumental music popular in the United States. With an introduction by Abel Green. 3rd ed. Englewood Cliffs, N.J.: Prentice-Hall, 1971. 766 p.

First issued in 1952 as *Variety music cavalcade, 1620–1950*. Originally appeared in a modified form as *Variety radio directory 1938–39, supplemented in weekly issues of the periodical Variety*. A revised edition appeared in 1962.

A chronological bibliography of American popular music, with parallel social and historical events listed for each year. Index of musical works by title, with dates of first publication.

Review by Irving Lowens in *Notes,* 20 (1963), p. 233–34.

1562. Naha, Ed. Lillian Roxon's rock encyclopedia, revised edition. N.Y.: Grosset & Dunlap, 1978. 565 p.

An updated version of Lillian Roxon's *Rock Encyclopedia (q.v.)* covering the growth of the industry and the eclectic branching of the genre. Lists of albums and single titles. Index.

1563. Ragtime, its history, composers, and music; edited by John Edward Hasse. New York: Schirmer Books, 1985. 400 p.

Brief history of the genre. Biographical essays on principal figures (e.g. Scott Joplin, James Scott). Essay on use of ragtime elements in other genres. check-list of compositions; bibliography; list of ragtime music folios and method books; discography; list of ragtime compositions by women.

1564. Rapee, Erno. Encyclopedia of music for pictures. New York: Arno Press, 1970. 510 p. (The literature of cinema)

Reprint of the 1925 edition.

An anthology of music.

1565. Rapee, Erno. Motion picture moods for pianists and organists. New York: Arno Press, 1970. 678 p.

Reprint of the 1925 edition.

This and the preceding volume are reference works that were designed to assist musicians of the 1920s and early 1930s to select the appropriate musical themes, or moods, to accompany motion pictures.

1566. Shapiro, Nat. Popular music: an annotated index of American popular songs. New York: Adrian Press, 1964–84. 9 v.

Vol. 1: 1950–59. Vol. 2: 1940–49. Vol. 3: 1960–64. Vol. 4: 1930–39. Vol. 5: 1920–29. Vol 6: 1965–69. Vol. 7: 1970–74. Vol. 8: 1975–79. Vol. 9: 1980–84.

A series which aims "to set down in permanent and practical form a selective annotated list of the significant popular songs of the 20th century." (author's preface)

Songs are listed alphabetically by title under each year of the decade.

Each volume has its own index of titles and list of publishers.
Review by Ruth Hilton in *Notes,* 25 (1968), p. 247–48, and 27 (1970), p. 60–61.

1567. Stecheson, Anthony and Anne Stecheson. The Stecheson classified song directory. Hollywood: Music Industry Press, 1961. 503 p.
Supplement issued 1978, 69 p.
About 100,000 songs popular in the U.S. are arranged under 400 topics or catchwords. Composers, titles, publishers, and sometimes dates are cited. There is no title index.

1568. Swanekamp, Joan. Diamonds & rust: a bibliography and discography on Joan Baez. Ann Arbor: Pierian Press, 1980. 75 p.

1569. Woll, Allen L. Songs from Hollywood musical comedies, 1927 to the present: a dictionary. New York,:Garland Pub., 1976. 251 p.
Contents: The songs; The films; A chronology of the Hollywood Musical; Composers and lyricists.
Covers American musicals and foreign films of musicals which had appeared on Broadway. There is an alphabetical list of song titles with references to the films for which they were written. Only musicals produced after 1950 with soundtrack recordings are included. Chronological list of shows. Index of composers and lyricists. In no one entry in this work does all information about a film appear.

REGIONAL AND LOCAL OPERA REPERTOIRES

A useful type of reference work is that which traces the chronology of opera as it has been performed in a particular region, place or theater: New York, Milan, Rome, Paris, Bologna, etc. Many of the leading opera companies of the world have been provided with such chronicles, which often include valuable data about first productions, the original cast of singers and dancers, information about the frequency of performance, etc.
These works are, strictly speaking, bibliographies of music, and they can be distinguished from other reference tools devoted to the musical theater; namely, dictionaries of opera and theater music and bibliographies of music literature devoted to the same subject.

1570. Allacci, Leone. Drammaturgia di Lione Allacci, accresciuta e continuata fino all'anno MDCCLV. Venezia: Presso G. Pasquali, 1755. 1,016 columns.
First edition, Rome, 1666. Revised and continued by Giovanni Cendoni, Apostolo Zeno, and others. Reprint of the 1755 edition by Bottega d'Erasmo, Torino, 1966.
A listing, alphabetical by title, of dramatic works produced in the Italian theater from the late 15th century to 1755. Not restricted to music but includes many operas and oratorios. See introduction to the facsimile reprint by Francesco Bernardelli.

1571. Bauer, Anton. Opern und Operetten in Wien; Verzeichnis ihrer Er-
staufführungen in der Zeit von 1629 bis zur Gegenwart. Graz-Köln: Hermann Böhlaus Nachf., 1955. 156 p. (Wiener musikwissenschaftliche
Beiträge, 2)

4,856 stage works, listed by title, with indexes by composer, author, and
chronology.

1572. Bignami, Luigi. Cronologia di tutti gli spettacoli rappresentati al
Teatro Comunale di Bologna della sua apertura 14 maggio 1763 a tutto
l'autunno 1881. Bologna: Mattiuzzi, 1882. 248 p.

The entries consist of transcriptions of theater bills for the period
under consideration. All types of dramatic works are included, but by far
the largest part of the repertory is opera. Numerous indexes of performers, composers, authors, and other categories of theater personnel.

1573. Bolongaro-Crevenna, Hubertus. L'Arpa festante; die Münchner Oper
1651–1825, von den Anfängen bis zum *Freyschützen*. München: Callwey,
1963. 272 p.

A cultural history of the Munich opera from its beginnings to 1825. P.
209–272: a chronological listing of the repertory, with factual information drawn from the Munich theater archives.

1574. Brenner, Clarence D. A bibliographical list of plays in the French
language 1700–1789 with a new foreword and an index by Michael A.
Keller and Neal Zaslaw. N.Y.: AMS Press, 1979. 229 p.; index 43 unnumbered pages.

Reprint of the first edition published by the University of California,
Berkeley in 1947.

Brenner construed play to mean all stage works, including operas,
ballets, and divertissements as well as *opéras-comique*. He provided in
the *List* of 1947 all the information on his sources' title pages, libretti in
Parisian libraries, archives and published collections. The names of
composers responsible for the continuous and incidental music mentioned on the title pages were thus provided in the original publication,
but not indexed. This reprint edition indexes composers' names.

The entries preceded with asterisks in the *List* are those for which
Brenner could not verify attributions conclusively.

1575. Burcher, Suellen. Australia Music Centre. Dramatic music. Sydney: Australia Music Centre, 1977. 212 p. (Catalogues of Australian compositions,
5)

Listing Australian operas and other staged dramatic music.

1576. Falk, Marguerite. Les parodies du nouveau Theatre Italien (1731);
répertoire systématique des timbres. Bilthovenö A.B.Creyghton, 1974?
213 p.

An index to vocal music in the 25 vaudevilles in the source volumes
and a concordance to nine other 18th century collections. Arranged by
first line of text with an alphabetical representation of the melody, followed by a thematic index to the music arranged as in Barlow and Mor-
ganstern. Appendices of extracts of the "Parodies" showing the
placement of the airs and of the musical incipits in order of appearance.

1577. Filippis, Felice de and R. Arnese. Cronache del Teatro di S. Carlo (1737–1960). Napoli Edizioni Politica Popolare, 1961. 466 p.

P. 25–112: chronological listing, by year, of first performances of operas given at the San Carlo Opera in Naples from 1737 to 1960.

P. 113–304: a biographical dictionary of opera composers, with lists of their major works.

Indexes of librettists and singers; a summary of the seasons in which each work was performed. 76 full-page illustrations.

1578. Florimo, Francesco. La scuola musicale di Napoli e i suoi conservatorii, con uno sguardo sulla storia della musica in Italia. Bologna: Forni editore, 1969. 4 v. (Bibliotheca musica Bononiensis, III, 9)

Reprint of the edition of Stabilimento Tipografico di Vinc. Moreno, Naples, 1881–83. First appeared in 1869–71 in 2 v. as *Cenno storico sulla scuola musicale di napoli.*

Contents: v. I. Come venne la musica in Italia; v. II-III. Cenno storico sulla scuola musicale di Napoli e suoi conservatorii, con le biografie dei maestri useiti dai medesimi; v. IV. *Elenco di tutte le opere in musica rappresentate nei teatri di Napoli.*

In v. 4, information is organized under the name of the individual theater, citing title of opera, poet, composer, performers, and general observations.

1579. Fog, Dan. The Royal Danish Ballet, 1760–1958, and August Bournonville. A chronological catalogue of the ballets and ballet-divertissements performed at the Royal Theatres of Copenhagen, and a catalogue of August Bournonville's works. Copenhagen: Dan Fog, 1961. 79 p.

Lists 516 ballet works performed by the Royal Danish Ballet, citing the choreographer, composer, and publisher of the music if available. Index of titles and of persons. Facsimile plates of music title pages.

1580. Gatti, Carlo. Il teatro alla Scala, nella storia e nell'arte (1778–1963). Milano: Ricordi, 1964. 2 v.

A handsome set, the second volume of which contains the chronicles of La Scala—complete inventories of the opera, ballet, and concert performances from 1778 to the present, with an analytical index. The chronologies were compiled by Giampiero Tintori.

1581. Groppo, Antonio. "Catalogo di tutti i drammi per musica recitati ne' Teatri di Venezia dall'anno 1637, in cui ebbere principio le pubbliche rappresentazioni de' medesimi fin all'anno presente 1745." In *Bollettino bibliografico musicale,* Nuova serie. Milano, 1952.

Published serially in four installments.

Lists 811 operas performed in Venice between 1637 and 1745, in chronological order, with title, librettist, composer, theater, and date of performance. Index of titles.

1582. Lajarte, Théodore de. Bibliothèque musicale du Theâtre de l'Opéra. Paris: Libr. des Bibliophiles, 1878. 2 v.

Reprint by Olms, Hildesheim, 1969.

Descriptive list of 594 stage works arranged in order of first production at the Paris Opera, 1671–1876. Classified by period. Each period concludes with a biographical section listing composers and librettists alphabetically. Composer and title index to works in the repertoire.

1583. Mooser, Robert-Aloys. Opéras, intermezzos, ballets, cantates, oratorios joués en Russie durant le XVIIIe siècle. ... Essai d'un rèpertoire alphabètique et chronologique. 3e édition revue et complétée. Bâle: Bärenreiter, 1964. 177 p.
First published in 1945; 2nd edition, 1955.
Gives librettist, translators of work, date and place of first performance, language of performance, date of publication of the libretto, etc. Sources of information are well documented. Indexes.
Review of the 2nd ed. by Anna A. Abert in *Die Musikforschung,* 9 (1956), p. 106.

1584. Radiciotti, Giuseppe. "Teatro e musica in Roma nel secondo quarto del secolo XIX (1825–50)." In *Storia dell'arte musicale e drammatic. Sezione 4.* Roma: Tip. della R. Academia dei Lincei, 1906. P. 157–318.
Parte seconda: A chronicle of the musical-dramatic productions given in the three major theaters in Rome during the early 19th century: Teatro Valle, Teatro Argentina, and Teatro Apollo.

1585. Salvioli, Giovanni. I teatri musicali di Venezia nel secolo XVII (1637–1700). Memorie storiche e bibliografiche di Livio Niso Galvani [pseud. for Giovanni Salvioli]. Milano: Ricordi, 1878. 193 p.
Reprint by A. Forni, Bologna, 1984 in the series (Biblioteca musica bononiensis, III, 32.)
Operas performed in Venice during the 17th century, listed chronologically under 16 different theaters or opera houses. Entries listed by title, with composer, librettist, publication data of libretti, dedicatee, and much useful information. Indexes of names, titles, librettists, and composers.

1586. Salvioli, Giovanni and Carlo Salvioli. Bibliografia universale del teatro drammatico italiano con particolare riguardo alla storia della musica italiana ... Volume primo. Venezia, C. Ferrari, 1903. 932 col.
Issued in parts, 1894–1903. Only v. 1 was published.
"Contenente i titoli e l'analisi di tutte le produzioni drammatiche pubblicate per la stampa in lingua italiana e nei vari dialetti in Italia ed all'estero dalle origini del teatro italiano e del dramma musicale sino ai nostri giorni, con note illustrative, indici copiosi, appendici e supplementi periodici per mantenere quest' opera nello stato di attualità."
Contents: v. 1. A-C. Aggiunte e rettifiche.

1587. Seltsam, William H. Metropolitan Opera annals. New York: H. W. Wilson Co., 1947. 751 p.
Chronological listing of Metropolitan Opera performances, with casts, from the initial season (1883–84) through 1946–47. Coverage for each season includes roster, excerpts from press reviews of noteworthy performances. Indexed by artist, opera.
Supplements issued annually in the final issue of each volume of the periodical *Opera news. First supplement, 1957,* cumulates information for 1945–57. *Second supplement: 1957–1966—a chronicle of artists and*

performers. Foreword by Francis Robinson. New York, H. W. Wilson, 1968. 126 p.

1588. Strohm, Reinhard. Die italienische Oper im 18. Jahrhundert. Wilhelmshaven: Heinrichshofen, 1979. 398 p. (Taschenbücher zur Musikwissenschaft, 25)

Like the following study, this one includes a very useful index and bibliography.

1589. Strohm, Reinhard. Italienische Opernarien des frühen Settecento (1720–1730). Köln: Volk, 1976. 2 v. (Analecta musicologica, 16)

Attached to this study of the Italian opera aria is an index to the genre for the period. V. 1. Studien; v. 2. Notenbeispiele und Verzeichnisse.

1590. Trezzini, Lamberto. Due secoli di vita musicale. Storia del Teatro Comunale di Bologna. Bologna: Edizioni ALFA, 1966. 2 v.

Vol. 1 contains a series of essays on the history of various aspects of musical life in Bologna, chiefly related to the theater.

Vol. 2 consists of a *Repertorio critico degli spettacoli e delle esecuzioni musicali dal 1763 al 1966,* by Sergio Paganelli. This is a chronological listing of opera, oratorio, and symphony productions, giving the names of members of the casts, soloists, and conductors represented.

1591. La Vallière, Louis César de la Baume Le Blanc, duc de. Ballets, opera, et autres ouvrages lyriques, par ordre chronologique depuis leur origine; avec une table alphabetique des ouvrages et des auteurs. Paris: Cl. J. Baptiste Bauche, 1760.

Unaltered reprint by H. Baron, 1967.

The chronological list is preceded by catalogs of poets and composers.

1592. Wiel, Taddeo. I teatri musicali veneziani del settecento. Catalogo delle opere in musica rappresentate nel secolo XVIII in Venezia (1701–1800). Venezia: Fratelli Visentini, 1897. 600 p.

Reprinted by A. Forni, Bologna, 1978 as part of (Biblioteca musica bononiensis, III, 51. New edition with an introduction and updated bibliography by) Reinhard Strohm published by Peters, Leipzig, 1979. 635 p.

Chronological listing of operas performed in Venice during the 18th century. 1,274 items. Entries give librettist, composer, place of performance, cast if known, ballet if included. Indexes of titles, librettists, composers, singers, dancers, etc. Introductory essay of 80 pages on the Venetian musical theater.

1593. Wolff, Stéphane. L'Opéra au Palais Garnier, 1875–1962: les œuvres, les interprètes. Paris: "L'Entr'acte", [1963]. 565 p.

A book of facts related to the Paris opera and its productions from 1875 to the present.

I, p. 23–378: productions listed in several alphabets according to type ("œuvres lyriques et oratories, œuvres choregraphiques, œuvres dramtiques," etc.). II, p. 379–552: persons affiliated with the opera (singers, conductors, dancers, composers, administrative personnel).

1594. Wolff, Stéphane. Un demi-siècle d'opéra comique (1900–50): les œuvres, les interprètes. Paris: Éditions André Bonne, 1953. 339 p.

I. p. 15–231: the works arranged alphabetically by title, with much detailed information as to cast, production, etc. II. p. 233–339: the interpreters and their roles, a series of biographical sections treating the singers, dancers, conductors and other personnel involved in *opéra-comique* productions. *Opéra-comique—20th century—Bibliography*

MUSIC OF INDIVIDUAL COMPOSERS

A large number of bibliographical tools have been created to serve as guides to the music of individual composers; work lists and thematic catalogs exist in abundance. To cite them all would extend the present work beyond reasonable limits. For an exhaustive listing of thematic catalogs the reader can be referred to Barry Brook's compilation (see no. 3035). Important nonthematic inventories are to be found in the major encyclopedias, such as The *New Grove, MGG,* and *La Musica.* Often important information about catalogs of music of individual composers can be found in the bibliographies of literature *about* individual composers (see the entries 1174–1206).

The entries in the following section have been selected as representative of recent compilations of composers' work lists.

1595. Composers' collected editions from Europe. 4th rev. ed. 1987. Wiesbaden: Otto Harrassowitz, 1987. 179 p. plus 11 p.

A dealer's catalog of composers' complete works, ranging from Albinoni to Zajc valuable for its completeness of coverage and currency.

ABEL, KARL FRIEDRICH

1596. Knape, Walter. Bibliographisch-thematisches Verzeichnis der Kompositionen von Karl Friedrich Abel (1723–1787). Cuxhaven: W. Knape, (1972?) 299 p.

ARNE, THOMAS AUGUSTINE

1597. Parkinson, John A. An index to the vocal works of Thomas Augustine Arne and Michael Arne. Detroit: Information Coordinators, 1972. 82 p. (Detroit studies in music bibliography, 21)

BACH, JOHANN SEBASTIAN

1598. Whaples, Miriam K. Bach aria index. Ann Arbor: Music Library Association, 1971. (MLA index series, 11)

The main index classifies the arias by performing forces. Works are identified by text incipit, location in the Bach *Thematisch-systematisches Verzeichnis,* and in the principal editions. Alphabetical index of first lines and of instruments.

BANCHIERI, ADRIANO

1599. Mischiati, Oscar. "Adriano Banchieri (1568–1634): Profilo biografico e bibliografia delle opere." In *Annuario* (1965–1970) Conservatorio di Musica "G. B. Martini," Bologna. Bologna, 1971. p. 39–201.

Also printed as separate by Casa Editrice Patron, Bologna, 1971.

A model bibliographical study of one of the most versatile composers and theorists of the Bolognese school of the early 17th century. Preliminary biographical essay followed by a systematic bibliography of Banchieri's sacred music, instrumental music, secular music, music theory, and literary writings. Copies of the works are located in major European libraries and the Library of Congress. Facsimile plates.

BARBER, SAMUEL

1600. Hennessee, Don A. Samuel Barber, a bio-bibliography. Westport: Greenwood Press, 1985. 404 p. (Bio-bibliographies in music, 3)

BEETHOVEN, LUDWIG VAN

1601. Dorfmüller, Kurt. Beiträge zur Beethoven Bibliographie. Studien und Materialen zum Werkverzeichnis von Kinsky-Halm. München: G. Henle Verlag, 1978. 452 p.

An indispensable adjunct to the Kinsky-Halm *Verzeichnis,* bringing entries on each Opus and WoO number up to date.

1602. Hess, Willy. Verzeichnis der nicht in der Gesamtausgabe veröffentlichten Werke Ludwig van Beethovens. Wiesbaden: Breitkopf & Hartel, 1957. 116 p.

Cites 335 works not included in the complete edition, plus 66 doubtful works.

BERLIOZ, HECTOR

1603. Bibliography Committee, New York Chapter, MLA. An alphabetical index to Hector Berlioz: *Werke.* Ann Arbor: Music Library Association, 1963. (MLA Index series, 2)

1604. Hopkinson, Cecil. A bibliography of the musical and literary works of Hector Berlioz, 1803–1869: with histories of the French music publishers concerned. 2nd ed. edited by Richard MacNutt; with a new foreword by Alec Hyatt King. Tunbridge Wells: R. MacNutt, 1980. 230 p.

First published in Edinburgh by the Edinburgh Bibliographical Society, 1951. 205 p. The 2nd ed. incorporates the author's corrections and additions.

One of the finest bibliographical studies on any composer.

BILLINGS, WILLIAM

1605. Nathan, Hans. William Billings; data and documents. Detroit: Information Coordinators, 1976. 69 p. (Bibliographies in American Music, 2)

A bio-bibliographical study covering Billings' life, musical and literary works.

BLOCH, ERNEST

1606. Ernest Bloch: creative spirit. A program source book prepared by Suzanne Bloch, in collaboration with Irene Heskes. N.Y.: Jewish Music Council of the National Jewish Welfare Board, 1976. 146 p.

A source book of information related to Ernest Bloch and his music. Contains a brief biography, reviews and descriptions of his works, a discography, and a bibliography.

BOCCHERINI, LUIGI

1607. Gérard, Yves. Thematic, bibliographical, and critical catalogue of the works of Luigi Boccherini. Trans. by Andreas Mayor. London: Oxford Univ. Press, 1969. 716 p.

Review by Ellen Amsterdam in *JAMS*, 24 (1971), p. 131–33.

BRAHMS, JOHANNES

1608. Bozarth, George S. "The first generation of Brahms manuscript collections" in *Notes*, 40 (1984), p. 239–62.

A bibliographical study intended to "reassemble ... sources (at least in catalogue format and on microfilm), to establish the 'source situations' of individual compositions, and to ascertain the value of the various manuscripts in source-critical studies ... The Appendix to this article details the contents of these large collections, as well as many of the smaller private holdings."

1609. Dedel, Peter. Johannes Brahms: a guide to his autographs in facsimile. Ann Arbor: Music Library Association, 1978. 86 p. (MLA index and bibliography series 18)

Review by Otto E. Albrecht in *Notes*, 35 (1979), p. 892.

1610. Deutsch, Otto Erich. "The first editions of Brahms," in *The Music Review*, 1 (1940), p. 123–43; 255–278.

1611. Hofmann, Kurt. Die Erstdrucke der Werke von Johannes Brahms: Bibliographie mit Wiedergabe von 209 Titelblättern. Tutzing: Schneider, 1975. 414 p. Musikbibliographische Arbeiten, 2

BRITTEN, BENJAMIN

1612. Benjamin Britten: a complete catalogue of his published works. London: Boosey & Hawkes, ltd., 1973. 52 p.

A "Supplement to a Complete catalogue of his published works, 1978," 2 l. was issued.

The catalog produced by his major publisher. Indexed

BRUCKNER, ANTON

1613. Grasberger, Renate. Werkverzeichnis Anton Bruckner. Tutzing: Schneider, 1977. 309 p. (Institut für Österreichische Musikdokumentation. Publikation, 7)
Review by Robert Winter in *Notes,* 35 (1979), p. 640–41.

BUXTEHUDE, DIETRICH

1614. Karstädt, Georg. Thematisch-Systematisches Verzeichnis der musikalien Werke von Dietrich Buxtehude: Buxtehude-Werke-Verzeichnis (BuxWV). Wiesbaden: Breitkopf & Härtel, 1974.
Review by Kerala J. Snyder in *Fontes artis musicae,* 23 (1976), p. 148–49.

CARISSIMI, GIACOMO

1615. Buff, Iva M. A thematic catalog of the sacred works of Giacomo Carissimi. Clifton, N.J.: European American Music Corp., 1979. 159 p. (Music indexes and bibliographies, 15)

1616. Sartori, Claudio. Giacomo Carissimi, catalogo delle opere attribuite. Milano: Finarte, 1975. 143 p.
Review by Iva M. Buff in *Notes,* 33 (1977), p. 584–86.

CEBALLOS, RODRIGO DE

1617. Snow, Robert J. The extant music of Rodrigo de Ceballos and its sources. Detroit: Information Coordinators, 1980. 155 p. (Detroit Studies in Music Bibliography, 44.)

CHOPIN, FRÉDERIC

1618. Kobylańsk, Krystyna. Fréderic Chopin. Thematisch-bibliographisches Werkverzeichnis. Munich: G. Henle Verlag, 1979. 362 p.
Published previously in Polish as Rękopisy utworów Chopina; Katalog. [Manuscripts of Chopin's works; Catalogue] by Polskie Wydawnictwo Muzyczne, Cracovia, 1977. 2 v.
Reviewed by Jean-Jacques Eigeldinger in *Fontes artis musicae,* 29 (1982), p. 142–45; this review includes a bibliographic addendum to the Chopin thematic catalog. Another review by Eigeldinger in *Fontes artis musicae,* 26 (1979), p. 142–44.
Review by Jeffrey Kallberg in *JAMS,* 34 (1981), p. 357–65.

CLARKE, JEREMIAH

1619. Taylor, Thomas. Thematic catalog of the works of Jeremiah Clarke. Detroit: Information Coordinators, 1977. 134 p. (Detroit Studies in Music Bibliography, 35)

CLEMENTI, MUZIO

1620. Tyson, Alan. Thematic catalogue of the works of Muzio Clementi. Tutzing: Hans Schneider, 1967. 136 p.
Review by Donald W. Krummel in *Notes,* 25 (1969), p. 725–26.

COPLAND, AARON

1621. Skowronski, JoAnn. Aaron Copland: a bio-bibliography. Westport: Greenwood Press, 1985. 273 p. (Bio-bibliographies in music, 2)

D'ORDOÑEZ, CARLO

1622. Brown, A. Peter. Carlo d'Ordoñez, 1734–1786; a thematic catalog. Detroit: Information Coordinators, 1978. 234 p. (Detroit Studies in Music Bibliography, 39)
Includes watermark and copyists indexes.

DEBUSSY, CLAUDE

1623. Lesure, François. Catalogue de l'œuvre de Claude Debussy. Genève: Minkoff, 1977. 167 p. (Centre de documentation Claude Debussy. Publications, 3)
The first scientific bibliography of the works of Claude Debussy.
Review by James R. Briscoe in *Notes,* 34 (1978), p. 862–65.

DELIUS, FREDERICK

1624. Lowe, Rachel. A descriptive catalogue with checklists of the letters and related documents in the Delius collection of the Grainger Museum, University of Melbourne, Australia. London: Delius Trust, 1981. 233 p.

1625. Lowe, Rachel. Frederick Delius, 1862–1934: a reprint of the catalogue of the music archive of the Delius Trust, 1974, with minor corrections. London: Delius Trust & Boosey & Hawkes Music Publishers [distributors], 1986. 183 p.
First published in 1974.
"List of printed music held by the Delius Trust as part of the original accession:" p. 177–179.

DMITRI SHOSTAKOVICH

1626. MacDonald, Malcolm. Dmitri Shostakovich; a complete catalogue, revised edition. London: Boosey & Hawkes, 1985. 56 p.
Contains a chronological listing of works, with a classified index and alphabetical index.

EISLER, HANNS

1627. Notowicz, Nathan and Jürgen Elsner. Hanns Eisler Quellennachweise. Hrsg. im Auftrag des Hanns-Eisler Archives bei der Deutschen Akademie der Künste zu Berlin. Leipzig: Deutscher Verlag für Musik, 1966. 174 p.

A bibliographical source book of the work of Hanns Eisler (1898–1962) based on the holdings of an archive in East Berlin. Coverage includes a listing of his compositions, an annotated bibliography of his literary work, and a discography of his music.

FARWELL, ARTHUR

1628. A Guide to the music of Arthur Farwell and to the microfilm collection of his work. Prepared by his children; Brice Farwell, editor. Limited ed. Briarcliff Manor, N.Y.: Issued by B. Farwell for the estate of Arthur Farwell, 1972. 138 p.

First issued 1971, 130 p.

Bibliography: pp. 108–111. Music supplement.

FIELD, JOHN

1629. Hopkinson, Cecil. A bibliographical thematic catalogue of the works of John Field, 1782–1837. London: 1961. 175 p.

FOOTE, ARTHUR

1630. Cipolla, Wilma Reid. A catalog of the works of Arthur Foote, 1853–1937. Detroit: Published for the College Music Society by Information Coordinators, 1980. 193 p. (Bibliographies in American Music, no. 6)

FRANZ, ROBERT

1631. Boonin, Joseph M. An index to the solo songs of Robert Franz. Hackensack: Joseph Boonin, Inc., 1970. 19 p. (Music indexes and bibliographies, 4)

A listing of Franz's songs by opus numbers; a brief survey of their publishing history, including the various collections issued in the late 19th century; title and first-line index and a listing of the poets set by the composer.

GASSMANN, FLORIAN LEOPOLD

1632. Hill, George R. A thematic catalog of the instrumental music of Florian Leopold Gassmann. Hackensack: J. Boonin, 1976. 171 p. (Music indexes and bibliographies, 12)

Review by Malcolm S. Cole in *Notes,* 34 (1977), p.596–97.

GERSCHWIN, GEORGE

1633. George Gerschwin; a selective bibliography and discography. Detroit: Information Coordinators, 1974. 118 p. (Bibliographies in American Music, 1)

Includes a chronology. The discography covers concert and operatic works, song collections and musicals.

GLUCK, GHRISTOPH WILLIBALD

1634. Hopkinson, Cecil. A bibliography of the printed works of C. W. von Gluck, 1714–1787. 2nd, rev. and augm. ed. New York, Broude Bros., 1967. 96 p.

First published in 1959. 79 p.

GOTTSCHALK, LOUIS MOREAU

1635. Doyle, John G. Louis Moreau Gottschalk 1829–1869. Detroit: Information Coordinators, 1983. 396 p. (Bibliographies in American Music, 7)

Lists works by Gottschalk. Extensive bibliography of literature about the composer.

1636. Offergeld, Robert. The centennial catalogue of the published and unpublished compositions of Louis Moreau Gottschalk. Prepared for *Stereo Review*. New York: Ziff-Davis Pub. Co., 1970. 34 p.

The introduction discusses Gottschalk's output and the state of research based on the source materials. This is followed by an annotated listing of 298 compositions. The annotations are entertaining and informative; a model of bibliographical technique.

GRIFFES, CHARLES T.

1637. Anderson, Donna K. Charles T. Griffes; an annotated bibliography-discography. Detroit: Information Coordinators, 1977. 255 p. (Bibliographies in American Music, 3)

Includes chronologies of Griffes' life and works.

HANDEL, GEORGE FREDERIC

1638. Bell, A. Craig. Handel: a chronological thematic catalogue. Greenock: The Grain-Aig Press, 1972. 452 p.

First published as *Chronological catalogue of Handel's work* in 1969. 68 p.

Contains some 3,000 thematic incipits. Appendices list spurious and doubtful works, unpublished and lost works, and works with opus numbers. Indexed by librettists, instrumental and vocal titles, instrumental interludes. Classified index and first-line index.

1639. Händel-Handbuch in 4 Bd., gleichzeitig Suppl. zu Hallische Händel-Ausgabe (Kritische Gesamtausgabe). Hrsg. vom Kuratorium d. Georg-Friedrich-Händel-Stiftung von Walter Eisen u. Margret Eisen. Kassel, etc.: Bärenreiter, 1978–86

4 v.
Contents:
Bd. 1. Siegfried Flesch. *Lebens- und Schaffensdaten.* Bernd Baselt. *Thematisch-systematisches Verzeichnis, Bühnenwerke.*
Bd. 2. Bernd Baselt. *Thematisch-systematisches Verzeichnis, oratorische Werke, vokale Kammermusik, Kirchenmusik.*
Bd. 3. Bernd Baselt. *Thematisch-systematisches Verzeichnis, Instrumentalmusik, Pasticci und Fragmente*
Bd. 4. Otto Erich Deutsch. *Dokumente zu Leben und Schaffen.*
Review by Hugh Cobbe in *Notes,* 36 (1980), p.883–84.

1640. Kinnear, Betty and Robert Illing. An illustrated catalogue of the early editions of Handel in Australia. Adelaide: The Authors, 1976, 255 p.
A first supplement was issued in 1986, 33 p.

1641. Smith, William Charles. Handel: a descriptive catalogue of the early editions. 2nd ed. with suppl. Oxford: B. Blackwell, 1970. 378 p.
First published in 1960 by Cassell, London.
The *Supplement,* p. 331–340, serves to bring the 1960 work up to date.

HARTMANN, KARL AMADEUS

1642. McCredie, Andrew D. Karl Amadeus Hartmann, thematic catalogue of his works. Wilhelmshaven; New York: Edition Heinrichshofen; New York, N.Y.: C.F. Peters, 1982. 227 p. (Catalogues of musical sources; 18)(Quellenkataloge zur Musikgeschichte, 18)

HASSE, JOHANN ADOLF

1643. Hansell, Sven Hostrup. Works for solo voice of Johann Adolf Hasse (1699–1783). Detroit: Information Coordinators, 1968. 110 p. (Detroit studies in music bibliography, 12)
Review by Robert L. Marshall in *Die Musikforschung,* 24 (1971), p. 463–64; by Owen Jander in *Notes,* 25(1969), p. 722–23.

HAYDN, JOSEPH

1644. Bryant, Stephen C. and Gary W. Chapman. Melodic index to Haydn's instrumental music: a thematic locator for Anthony van Hoboken's Thematisch-bibliographisches Werkverzeichnis, volumes I and III. New York: Pendragon Press, 1982. 100 p. (Thematic catalogues, 8) *Joseph Haydn, Thematisch-bibliographisches Werkverzeichnis,* Bd. 1 & 3—Indexes *Joseph Haydn, Thematisch-bibliographisches Werkverzeichnis,* Bd. 1 & 3—Indexes

1645. Haydn, Joseph. Thematisches Verzeichnis sämtlichen Kompositionen ... zusammengestellt von Aloys Fuchs 1839. Facsimile-Ausgabe. Hrsg. von Richard Schaal. Wilhelmshaven: Heinrichshofen's Verlag, 1968. 204 p. (Quellen-Kataloge zur Musikgeschichte, 2)
Thematic catalog of Haydn's works compiled by the Viennese collector Aloys Fuchs in 1839. Reproduced in facsimile.

Review by H. C. Robbins Landon in *Haydn yearbook,* 6 (1969), p. 217–18.

1646. Hoboken, Anthony van. Joseph Haydn; thematisch-bibliographisches Werkverzeichnis. Mainz: B. Schott's Söhne, 1957–78. 3 v.
The standard thematic catalog to the works of Joseph Haydn.
Beilage zu Band I, Beilage zu Band I und II.
Contents: Bd. 1. Instrumentalwerke. Bd. 2. Vokalwerke. Bd. 3. Register; Addenda und Corrigenda.
Review of Bd. 3. by George R. Hill in *Notes,* 36 (1979), 102–03.

1647. Holm, Anna-Lena, comp. Index of titles and text incipits to Anthony Van Hoboken *Joseph Haydn, Thematisch-bibliographisches Werkverzeichnis, [Bd.] 2, Vokalwerke (Mainz 1971).* Stockholm: Swedish Music History Archive, 1978. 53 leaves. *Joseph Haydn, Thematisch-bibliographisches Werkverzeichnis,* Bd. 2—Indexes

HENZE, HANS WERNER

1648. Hans Werner Henze: list of works. Mainz; New York: Schott, 1983. 64 p.
Bibliographical sketch of Henze by Gerhard R. Koch.

1649. Der Komponist Hans Werner Henze: ein Buch der Alten Oper Frankfurt, Frankfurt Feste '86, herausgegeben von Dieter Rexroth. Mainz; New York: Schott, 1986. 382 p.
"Hans Werner Henze Werkverzeichnis," p. [341]-382.
This work includes material by Henze and bibliographical references.

HEWITT, JOHN HILL

1650. Hoogerwerf, Frank W. John Hill Hewitt: sources and bibliography. Atlanta: Emory General Libraries, 1981. 42 p.
A 19th century composer of songs and ballads. Active in all aspects of the popular theater. This work is a guide to a special collection in the Emory Univerity Woodruff Library.

HOLST, GUSTAV

1651. Holst, Imogen. A thematic catalogue of Gustav Holst's music. London: Faber Music Ltd. in association with G. and I. Holst Ltd., 1974. 285 p.

IVES, CHARLES

1652. De Lerma, Dominique-Rene. Charles Edward Ives, 1874–1954: a bibliography of his music. Kent: Kent State University Press, 1970. 212 p.
Works listed alphabetically by title, with indexes of publishers, medium, chronology, arrangers, poets and librettists, phonorecords, and performers.

JIRAK, KAREL BOLESLAV

1653. Tischler, Alice. Karel Boleslav Jirak; a catalog of his works. Detroit: Information Coordinators, 1975. 85 p. (Detroit Studies in Music Bibliography, 32)

Brief review by Stephen M. Fry in *Notes,* 36 (1975), p. 303.

KUHLAU, FRIEDRICH

1654. Fog, Dan. Kompositionen von Friedrich Kuhlau. Thematisch- Bibliographischer Katalog. Copenhagen: Dan Fog Musikforlag, 1977. 203 p.

233 numbered items. Index of titles and text incipits. Index to persons cited.

Review by June C. Ottenberg in *Notes,* 35 (1978), p. 85–86.

LISZT, FRANZ

1655. Eckhardt, Mária P. Franz Liszt's music manuscripts in the national Széchényi Library, Budapest. [Translated by Erzsébet Mészáros; translation revised by Rena Mueller]. Budapest: Akadémiai Kiadó; Stuyvesant, N.Y.: Pendragon Press, 1986. 252 p. (Studies in Central and Eastern European music, 2)

LOCKE, MATTHEW

1656. Harding, Rosamund. A thematic catalogue of the works of Matthew Locke; with a calendar of the main events of his life. Oxford: R. E. M. Harding; distributed by Blackwell, 1971. 177 p.

Review by Jack A. Westrup in Music and Letters, 53 (1972), p. 442–44; an anonymous review in *Times Literary Supplement,* no. 3,658 (April 1972), p. 387; by Michael Tilmouth in *The Musical Times,* 113 (1972), p. 561–62; by Gloria Rose in *Notes,* 29 (1973), p. 457.

LULLY, JEAN-BAPTISTE

1657. Schneider, Herbert. Chronologisch-thematisches Verzeichnis sämtlicher Werke von Jean-Baptiste Lully (LWV). Tutzing: Schneider, 1981. 570 p. (Mainzer Studien zur Musikwissenschaft, 14)

Covers printed and manuscript sources. False attributions and lost copies are identified. Musical incipits are provided in treble and bass parts. A splendid thematic catalog.

MARCELLO, BENEDETTO

1658. Fruchtman, Caroline S. Checklist of vocal chamber works by Benedetto Marcello. Detroit: Information Coordinators, 1967. 37 p. (Detroit studies in music bibliography, 10)

Review by Owen Jander in *Notes,* 24 (1968), p. 491–92.

MIGOT, GEORGES

1659. Honegger, Marc. Catalogue des ouvres musicales de Georges Migot. Strasbourg: Amis de l'ouvre et de la pensée de Georges Migot, Institut de musicologie, 1977. 126 p.

MONTEVERDI, CLAUDIO

1660. Bibliography Committee, New York Chapter, MLA. An alphabetical index to Claudio Monteverdi: Tutte le opere. Ann Arbor: Music Library Association, 1963. (MLA Index series, 1)

MOSCHELES, IGNAZ

1661. Kistner, Friedrich, firm, Leipzig. Thematisches Verzeichniss im Druck erschienener Compositionen von Ignaz Moscheles. London: H. Baron, 1966. 66 p.

MOZART, WOLFGANG AMADEUS

1662. Haberkamp, Gertraut. Die Erstdrucke der Werke von Wolfgang Amadeus Mozart, Bibliographie. Tutzing: H. Schneider, 1986. 2 v. (Musikbibliographische Arbeiten, 10/11)
v.1. Textband, v.2. Bildband.

1663. Hill, George R. and Murray Gould, *et al..* A thematic locator for Mozart's works as listed in Kochel's *Chronologisch-thematisches Verzeichnis*, 6th edition. Hackensack: Joseph Boonin, 1970. 76 p. (Music indexes and bibliographies, 1)

The thematic locator contained in this volume presents the incipits of Mozart's musical works systematically, enabling the user to determine quickly the Kochel number and movement of any piece by Mozart. [*Preface*]

In two sections, one arranging the themes by interval size, the other arranging them by pitch name.

1664. Schlager, Karl-Heinz. Wolfgang Amadeus Mozart, Verzeichnis von Erst- und Frühdrucken bis etwa 1800. Kassel: Bärenreiter, 1978. 2 v. (RISM, ser. A, pt. I, supplement)

"Sonderdruck aus Répertoire International des Sources Musicales A/I, Einzeldruck vor 1800. Redaktion Karlheinz Schlager. Bd. 6: Montalbano-Pleyel." The second volume includes the directory of sigla of libraries contributing to the catalog.

MUSGRAVE, THEA

1665. Hixon, Donald L. Thea Musgrave, a bio-bibliography. Westport: Greenwood Press, 1984. 187 p. (Bio-bibliographies in music, 1)

First number of a series, each devoted to a single composer. There is a lengthy biographical section followed by a critical bibliography of the composer's works and a discography.

NICHELMANN, CHRISTOPH

1666. Lee, Douglas A. The works of Christoph Nichelmann: a thematic index. Detroit: Information Coordinators, 1971. 100 p. (Detroit studies in music bibliography, 19)

PALESTRINA, GIOVANNI PIERLUIGI DA

1667. Hall, Alison. Palestrina: an index to the Casimiri, Kalmus, and Haberl editions. Philadelphia: Music Library Association, 1980. 82 p. (MLA index and bibliography series, 22)

PALLAVICINO, BENEDETTO

1668. Flanders, Peter. A thematic index to the works of Benedetto Pallavicino. Hackensack: J. Boonin, 1974. 85 p. (Music indexes and bibliographies, 11)

PERGOLESI, GIOVANNI BATTISTA

1669. Paymer, Marvin E. Giovanni Battista Pergolesi, 1710–1736; a thematic catalogue of the opera omnia with an appendix listing omitted compositions. N.Y.: Pendragon Press, 1977. 99 p. (Thematic catalogues, 1)

PEZEL, JOHANN

1670. Weinandt, Elwyn. Johann Pezel (1639–1694): a thematic catalogue of his instrumental works. New York: Pendragon Press, 1983. 102 p. (Thematic catalogue series, 9)

PLEYEL, IGNACE

1671. Benton, Rita. Ignace Pleyel: a thematic catalogue of his compositions. New York: Pendragon Press, 1977. 482 p. (Thematic catalogues, 2)
Exhaustive coverage of the voluminous works of a popular composer of the late 18th and early 19th centuries.

PUCCINI, GIACOMO

1672. Hopkinson, Cecil. A bibliography of the works of Giacomo Puccini, 1858–1924. New York, Broude Bros., 1968. 77 p.
A close bibliographical study.

REGER, MAX

1673. Rösner, Helmut. Max-Reger-Bibliographie. Das internationale Schrifttum über Max Reger 1893–1966. Bonn: Ferd. Dummlers Verlag, 1968. 138 p.
Review by Gerd Sievers in *Die Musikforschung*, 24 (1971), p. 93–95.

REGNART, JACOB

1674. Pass, Walter. Thematischer Katalog samtlicher Werke Jacob Regnarts [c. 1540–1599]. Wien; Köln;, Graz: Bohlau in Komm., 1969. 244 p. (Tabulae musicae Austriacae, 5)
Review by John Graziano in *Notes,* 27 (1971), p. 493–94; by Wilhelm Schepping in *Jahrbuch für Volksliedforschung,* 16 (1971), p. 186; by Jurgen Kindermann in *Die Musikforschung,* 25 (1972), p. 371–72.

ROSETTI, ANTON

1675. Kaul, Oskar. Thematisches Verzeichnis der Instrumentalwerke von Anton Rosetti. Wiesbaden: Breitkopf & Hartel, (1968). 27 p.

ROSSI, SALAMONI

1676. Newman, Joel and Fritz Rikko. A thematic index to the works of Salamon Rossi. Hackensack: J. Boonin, 1972. 143 p. (Music indexes and bibliographies, 6)

SAMMARTINI, GIOVANNI BATTISTA

1677. Jenkins, Newell and Bathia Churgin. Thematic catalogue of the works of Giovanni Battista Sammartini: orchestral and vocal music. Cambridge, Mass.: Published for the American Musicological Society by Harvard University Press, 1976. 315 p.
Review by Eugene K. Wolf in *Notes,* 34 (1978), p.850–52, and by Howard Brofsky in *JAMS,* 32 (1978), p.365–67.

SCHUBERT, FRANZ

1678. Deutsch, Otto Erich. Die Originalausgaben von Schuberts Goethe-Liedern; Ein musikbibliographischer Versuch. Wien: Antiquariat V. A. Heck, 1926. 23 p.
A pamphlet distributed to the participants in the Jubelfeier der Nationalbibliothek (25. bis 29. Mai 1926).
Precise bibliographical descriptions of 26 Goethe settings by Franz Schubert.

1679. Deutsch, Otto Erich. Franz Schubert: Thematisches Verzeichnis seiner Werke in chronologischer Folge. Neuasgabe in deutscher Sprache bearbeitet und herausgegeben von der Editionleitung der Neuen Schubert-Ausgabe und Werner Aderhold. Kassel: Bärenreiter, 1978. 712 p. (Neue Schubert Ausgabe, Serie VIII, Bd. 4.)
Review by L. Michael Griffel in *Notes,* 36 (1979), p. 83–86.

1680. Hilmar, Ernst. Verzeichnis der Schubert-Handschriften in der Musiksammlung der Wiener Stadt-und Landesbibliothek. Kassel: Bärenreiter, 1978. 144 p. (Catalogus musicus, 8)
Review by Michael Griffel in *Notes,* 36 (1979),p. 83–86.

SCHUMANN, ROBERT

1681. Hofmann, Kurt. Die Erstdrucke der Werke von Robert Schumann: Bibliographie mit Wiedergabe von 234 Titelblättern. Tutzing: H. Schneider, 1979. 464 p. (Musikbibliographische Arbeiten, 6)

1682. Ochs, Michael. Schumann index, part 1: an alphabetical index to Robert Schumann: *Werke*. Ann Arbor: Music Library Association, 1967. (MLA Index series, 6)

1683. Weichlein, William. Schumann index, part 2: an alphabetical index to the solo songs of Robert Schumann. Ann Arbor: Music Library Association, 1967. (Music index series, 7)

SCHÜTZ, HEINRICH

1684. Miller, D. Douglas and Anne L. Highsmith. Heinrich Schütz: a bibliography of the collected works and performing editions. N.Y.: Greenwood, 1986. 278 p. (Music Reference Collection, 9)
This is an annotated guide to the very complex bibliography of modern editions of the works of Schütz. Source and title indexes. Index to performing forces.

STRADELLA, ALESSANDRO

1685. Jander, Owen H. A catalogue of the manuscripts of compositions by Alessandro Stradella found in European and American libraries. Wellesley, Mass.: Wellesley College, 1962. 72 leaves (typescript).
First issued in 1960.
A classified catalog of Stradella's works with locations of the manuscript sources. The principal divisions are instrumental music, vocal music with sacred texts, vocal music with secular texts.

STRAUSS, RICHARD

1686. Mueller von Asow, Erich Hermann. Richard Strauss; thematisches Verzeichnis. Wien, L. Doblinger, 1955–74. 3 v. (1,688 p.)
V. 3: "Nach dem Tode des Verfassers vollendet und hrsg. von Alfons Ott und Franz Trenner.
Contents: Bd. 1. Opus 1–59; Bd. 2. Opus 60–86; Bd. 3. Werke ohne Opuszahlen.

1687. Trenner, Franz. Richard Strauss: Werkverzeichnis. Wien: Doblinger, 1985. 153 p.
This is a shortened works list based upon the Mueller von Asow thematic catalog (see no. 1686, above).

STRAVINSKY, IGOR

1688. DeLerma, Dominque—René and Thomas J. Ahrens. Igor Fedorovitch Stravinsky, 1882–1971; a practical guide to publications of his music.

Kent: Kent State University Press, 1974. 158 p.

1689. Shepard, John. "The Stravinsky *Nachlass*: a provisional checklist of music manuscripts" in *Notes,* 40 (1984), p. 719–50.
An inventory including extensive descriptions of "223 music manuscript items for 98 works by Stravinsky" including arrangements and copies of the works of other composers.

1690. White, Eric Walter. Stravinsky, the composer and his works. London: Faber and Faber, 1966. 608 p.

SULLIVAN, ARTHUR

1691. Poladian, Sirvart. Sir Arthur Sullivan: an index to the texts of his vocal works. Detroit: Information Coordinators, 1961. 91 p. (Detroit studies in music bibliography, 2)
A comprehensive index of first lines, titles, and refrains to the composer's vocal works, sacred and secular.
Review by William Lichtenwanger in *Notes,* 19 (1962), p. 428–30.

1692. Presenting in word and song, score and deed, the life and work of Sir Arthur Sullivan. Composer for Victorian England from *Onward, Christian soldiers* to Gilbert and Sullivan opera. Compiled by Reginald Allen in collaboration with Gale R. d'Luhy. New York: The Pierpont Morgan Library, 1975. 215 p.
Catalog of an exhibition of some of the extensive Gilbert and Sullivan collection at the Pierpont Morgan Library.

TELEMANN, GEORG PHILIPP

1693. Menke, Werner. Thematisches Verzeichnis der Vokalwerke von Georg Philipp Telemann. Frankfurt am Main: V. Klostermann, 1982–83. 2 v.
Contents: Bd. 1. *Cantaten zum gottesdienstlichen Gebrauch—Thematisches Werkverzeichnis.*

THOMSON, VIRGIL

1694. Meckna, Michael. Virgil Thomson, a bio-bibliography. New York: Greenwood Press, 1986. 203 p. (Bio-bibliographies in music, 4)

VERDI, GIUSEPPE

1695. Chusid, Martin. A catalog of Verdi's operas. Hackensack: Joseph Boonin, 1973. 125 p. (Music indexes and bibliographies, 5)

1696. Hopkinson, Cecil. A bibliography of the works of Giuseppe Verdi, 1813–1901. New York: Broude Bros., 1973–78. 1 v.
Contents: v. 1. Vocal and instrumental works; v. 2. Operatic works.
Review of v. 2 by James J. Fuld in *Notes,* 35 (1979), p. 626.

VICTORIA, TOMAS LUIS DE

1697. Bibliography Committee, New York Chapter, MLA. An alphabetical index to Tomas Luis de Victoria: Opera omnia. Ann Arbor: Music Library Association, 1966. (MLA Index series, 5)

VIVALDI, ANTONIO

1698. Coral, Lenore. A concordance of the thematic indexes to the instrumental works of Antonio Vivaldi. Ann Arbor: Music Library Association, 1965. (MLA Index series)
2nd edition, Ann Arbor, 1972.

1699. Fanna, Antonio. Opere strumentali di Antonio Vivaldi (1678–1741); catalogo numerico-tematico. Secondo la catalogazione Fanna. 2a edizione riveduta e ampliata. Milano: Ricordi, 1986. 185p.
Introductory material in Italian and English.

1700. Martin, Arlan Stone. Vivaldi violin concertos; a handbook. Metuchen: Scarecrow Press, 1972. 278 p.
A thematic catalog of the Vivaldi concertos with indexes coordinating various numbering systems: Fanna, Ricordi, Pincherle, Rinaldi. Appendix E. lists recorded versions of the works.

1701. Ohmura, Noriko. A reference concordance table of Vivaldi's instrumental works. Tokyo: Academia Music, 1972. 267 p.
Review by Seymour Kesten in *JAMS,* 28 (1975), p. 153–6.

1702. Ryom, Peter. Verzeichnis der Werke Antonio Vivaldis (RV) Kleine Ausg., 2., verb. und erw. Aufl. Leipzig: Deutscher Verlag für Musik, 1977. 226 p.
First printed in 1974.
Erratum slip inserted. "Chronologische Übersicht der Vivaldi-Werkverzeichnisse" p. [213]-217.

WAGENSEIL, GEORG

1703. Scholz-Michelitsch, Helga. Das Orchester- und Kammermusikwerk von Georg Christoph Wagenseil. Thematischer Katalog. Wien: Hermann Bohlaus Nachf., 1972. 228 p.
The incipits reflect all parts and movements in the works. Sources are located in libraries throughout the world. Bibliographical references.

WAGNER, RICHARD

1704. Hopkinson, Cecil. Tannhäuser. An examination of 36 ed. Tutzing: H. Schneider, 1973. 48 p. (Musikbibliographische Arbeiten, 1)

1705. Klein, Horst F. G. Erst- und Frühdrucke der Textbücher von Richard Wagner: Bibliographie. Tutzing: Schneider, 1979. 63 p. (Musikbibliographische Arbeiten, 4)

1706. Klein, Horst F. G. Erstdrucke der musikalischen Werke von Richard Wagner: Bibliographie. Tutzing: H. Schneider, 1983. 236 p. (Musikbibliographische Arbeiten, 5)

WEBERN, ANTON VON

1707. Roman, Zoltan. Anton Webern; an annotated bibliography. Detroit: Information Coordinators, 1983. 219 p. (Detroit Studies in Music Bibliography, 48)

Covers over 100 journals in numerous languages.

EARLY MUSIC IN MODERN EDITIONS (INCLUDING COLLECTIONS AND MONUMENTS)

The purpose of the bibliographies listed in this category is to direct the user to new editions of old music—one of the most pressing needs of the performer, the teacher, and the music historian. Some of the items listed below are focused on the contents of the major critical editions (*Denkmaler, Gesamtausgaben*); others emphasize the more practical, performing editions of early music. In either case, listings of this kind are soon out of date. To keep abreast of new publications in this area, one should consult the music review sections of a variety of current periodicals: *Notes, Music and Letters, Die Musikforschung,* and *JAMS,* as well as such regular listings as may be found in *Fontes artis musicae.* See also the entries in this volume under "Guides to Systematic and Historical Musicology." Many of the works listed there have bibliographical supplements which cite and evaluate historical editions and monuments.

By far the most useful guide to the contents of the historical sets and critical editions is Heyer, no. 1722 below.

1708. Basso, Alberto. "Repertorio generale dei 'monumenta musicae,' delle antologie, raccolte e pubblicazioni di musica antica sino a tutto il 1970." In *Rivista italiana di musicologia,* 6 (1972), p.3–135.

Introduction treats the history of the publication of monumental sets, providing inventories of the contents of 33 sets of anthologies published before 1850. There follows a description with a listing of contents of 61 international sets, then national sets grouped alphabetically by country. The last section is devoted to minor collections or single-volume anthologies, also organized by country.

1709. Bennwitz, Hanspeter, ed. Musikalisches Erbe und Gegenwart: Musiker-Gesamtausgaben in der Bundes Republik Deutschland. Im Auftrag der Stiftung Volkswagenwerk herausgegeben von Hanspeter Bennwitz, Georg Feder, Ludwig Finscher, und Wolfgang Rehm. Kassel: Bärenreiter, 1975. 147 p.

A survey of eleven complete editions in progress in West Germany. Contents of each set are given along with sample pages illustrating the editorial process.

1710. Bukofzer, Manfred. "A check-list of instrumental ensemble music before Haydn." In *Music Teachers' National Association Proceedings,* 1946. P. 470–79.

Includes only practical editions available through American publishers at the time of compilation.

1711. Bukofzer, Manfred. "List of editions [of Baroque music]." In his *Music in the Baroque era.* New York: Norton, 1947. P. 461–69.

A selective list organized under 4 main headings: (1) general anthologies; (2) historical collections; (3) smaller collections and performing editions; and (4) complete or collected editions of individual composers. Minimum bibliographical information.

1712. Chapman, James, Sheldon Fine, and MAry Rasmussen. "Music for wind instruments in historical editions, collected works and numbered series: a bibliography." In *Brass Quarterly,* v. 1, nos. 3 & 4 (Spring-Winter, 1968), p. 115–49.

Part I: Music, without voices, for specified instrumentation, and for unspecified instrumentation with basso continuo, in historical editions and numbered series.

Indexes 42 historical editions and series.

Classified by instruments, ensembles, and forms.

1713. Charles, Sydney Robinson. "Editions, historical," in *The New Grove Dictionary of Music and Musicians,* edited by Stanley Sadie, v. 5, p. 848–69. Julie Woodward assisted with the bibliography. London: Macmillan, 1980.

Extensive bibliographies of single composer complete editions, other collected editions, editions of theoretical works, anthologies (extended, small vocal, small instrumental, small general) and a short bibliography on the subject.

1714. Charles, Sydney Robinson. A handbook of music and music literature in sets and series. New York: Free Press, 1972. 497 p.

Useful guide to the contents of critical editions, both collective and devoted to the works of individual composers. Two further sections treat (1) monographs and facsimile series and (2)music periodicals and yearbooks.

1715. Coover, James B. "Composite music manuscripts in facsimile" in *Notes,* 38 (1981), p. 275–95.

A guide to manuscript sources accessible in printed books. The manuscripts are listed alphabetically by location. Index to personal names, to items represented in RISM, an to those in series.

1716. Coover, James B. Gesamtausgaben: a checklist. n.p., Distant Press, 1970. 27 leaves.

A practical listing, alphabetical by composer, of 376 *Gesamtausgaben.* The list was designed to help with acquisitions in a college or university music library. Includes all works "for which completeness was the professed goal, disregarding failure to accomplish it."

1717. "Denkmaler und Gesamtausgaben." In *Repertorium der Musikwissenschaft.* . . . bearb. von Willi Kahl und Wilhelm-Martin Luther. Kassel & Basel: Bärenreiter, 1953. P. 232–43.

140 entries for major historical sets. Full bibliographical information, but no listing of contents.

1718. "Editions et Reeditions de Musique Ancienne (avant 1800)." In *Fontes artis musicae,* no. 1–22. Paris: Assoc. Internationale des Bibliotheques Musicales, 1954–75.

One of the few listings of new editions of early music. International coverage. Full bibliographical information, including price.

1719. "Editions, Historical." In *Reference works in music and music literature in five libraries of Los Angeles County.* Edited by Helen W. Azhderian. Los Angeles: Univ. of Southern California, 1953. P. 116–37.

360 editions listed, both critical and practical. No detailed content analysis, but good coverage of the important sets.

1720. Eitner, Robert. Verzeichnis neuer Ausgaben alter Musikwerke aus der frühesten Zeit bis zum Jahre 1800. Berlin: Trautwein, 1871. 208 p. (Monatshefte für Musikgeschichte. Beilage. 1871)

Nachträge, published in *Monatshefte,* 9 (1877); "Register zu den Nachtragen" as its *Beilage, 1877;* and 10 (1878).

Still useful as a guide to the contents of early historical collections, including music in histories. *Abtheilung I:* annotated list of collections and literary works containing music; *Abtheilung II:* index of composers and their works, with separate listings of anonymous works and of German secular song through the 16th century.

1721. Hall, Alison. E.H. Fellowes, an index to the *English Madrigalists* and the *English School of Lutenist Song Writers.* Boston: Music Library Association, 1984. 100 p. (MLA index and bibliography series, 23)

An analytic index to the *English Madrigalists* and the *English School of Lutenist Song Writers. English Madrigalists*—Indexes *English School of Lutenist Song Writers*—Indexes

1722. Heyer, Anna Harriet. Historical sets, collected editions, and monuments of music; a guide to their contents. 3rd ed. Chicago: American Library Association, 1980. 2 v.

First published in 1957. 2nd edition published in 1969, 563 p.

An indispensible guide to editorial work in the field of early music. Approximately 1,300 entries in this edition. Detailed listings of the contents of sets, including important publisher's series (e.g. Bärenreiter's *Hortus musicus,* Nagel's *Musik-Archiv,* Kistner und Siegel's *Organum,* etc.). Numerous cross references. Comprehensive index of composers, editors, titles.

A team of scholar-bibliographers under the direction of George Hill are preparing a continuation of this work using computers; distribution of this new work is expected to take place in one of the newer electronic forms, perhaps CD-ROM, in the foreseeable future.

Review of the first edition by Irene Millen in *Notes,* 15 (1958), p. 390–91; by Harriet Nicewonger in *The Library Journal* (Sept. 1958), p. 2,380. Of the second edition by Lenore Coral in *JAMS,* 24 (1971), p. 308–9; by Richard H. Hunter in *Notes,* 26 (1969), p. 275–77.

1723. Hilton, Ruth B. An index to early music in selected anthologies. Clifton: European American Music Corporation, 1978. 127 p. (Music indexes and bibliographies, 13)

Review by Susan T. Sommer in *Notes,* 35 (1979), p.641–42.

1724. Hirsch, Paul and Kathi Meyer. "Sammelwerke und Gesamtausgaben." In their *Katalog der Musikbibliothek Paul Hirsch, Bd. IV.* Cambridge: Cambridge Univ. Press, 1947. P. 331–409.

Lists 90 complete editions and collections, with a detailed survey of their contents.

1725. "Novae Editiones Musicae Classicae." In *ActaM,* v. 3– . Leipzig & Copenhagen: Internationale Gesellschaft für Musikwissenschaft, Jan. 1931–52.

Regular listing of the new editions of early music arranged alphabetically by composer, giving title, scoring, editor, place, publisher, date, and price. Discontinued after 1952.

1726. Ochs, Michael. An index to Das Chorwerk, volumes, 1–110. Ann Arbor: Music Library Association, 1970. 38 p. (MLA Index series, 10)

Composer index and title index. Information includes volume, page, type of composition and vocal ensemble. *Das Chorwerk—*Index

1727. Petrov, Stoian V. and Khristo Kodov. Starobulgarski muzikalni pametnitsi. [Old Bulgarian musical documents] Sofia: Nauka i izkustvo, 1973. 360 p.

Facsimiles of most of the musical notation preserved in Bulgarian manuscripts.

Review by Miloš Velimirovic in *Notes,* 32 (1976), p. 531–33.

1728. Samuel, Harold E. "Editions, historical." In the *New Harvard dictionary of music,* edited by Don M. Randel. Cambridge, Mass.: Harvard Univ. Press, 1986. P. 264–76.

Lists 427 important serial publications of early music, from plainsong through the 18th century. Organized in three check-lists: Collected works, *Denkmäler,* Series of performing editions.

1729. Schering, Arnold. "Übersicht über die musikgeschichtlichen Sammelwerke und kritische Gesamtausgaben der Werke der grossen Meister der Musik aus dem Verlage von Breitkopf & Härtel." In his *Tabellen zur Musikgeschichte.* Leipzig, Breitkopf & Hartel, 1934. *Anhang,* 30 p.

A useful breakdown of the contents of the critical editions published by Breitkopf & Härtel. This supplement is omitted from the 1962 edition of the *Tabellen. Breitkopf & Härtel* editions—Index

1730. Schiedermair, Ludwig. "Gesamtausgaben und Publikationsreihen in Übersichten." In his *Einfuhrung in das Studium der Musikgeschichte.* Bonn: F. Bummlers Verlag, 1947. *Anhang,* p. 104–61.

Surveys the contents of the major sets and publishers' series.

1731. Schmeider, Wolfgang. "Gesamtausgaben.". In *MGG,* v. 4, col. 1850–76.

A valuable discussion of the historical development of critical editions of the work of individual composers followed by entries for 84 such editions, with detailed listings of contents.

1732. Schmieder, Wolfgang. "Denkmaler der Tonkunst". In *MGG,* v. 3, col. 164–92.

Lists 213 major editions, practical and scholarly, with contents given in considerable detail. Classified as to national or international coverage.

1733. The Symphony, 1720–1840: a comprehensive collection of full scores in sixty volumes: reference volume, contents of the set and collected thematic indexes. Preface by Barry S. Brook. New York: Garland Publishing, 1986. 627 p.   •

A thematic catalog of the 549 works of 244 composers in the collection, *The Symphony, 1720–1840,* including 13 thematic indexes not included in the individual volumes when originally published. Includes thousands of incipits with copious information on each symphony and its sources. Organized by composer, but not indexed. Bibliography of catalog references. *Symphony, 1720–1840*—Indexes

1734. Verzeichnis der Neudrucke alter Musik. Herausgegeben im Auftrage des Staatlichen Instituts für deutsche Musikforschung von Walter Lott. Leipzig, F. Hofmeister, 1937–43. 7 v.

An annual bibliography of new editions of music composed before 1800, covering the years of publication 1936–42. Includes separate works and contents of collections. German publications emphasized. Works listed by composer; medium and title index.

PRIMARY SOURCES OF EARLY MUSIC: MANUSCRIPTS AND PRINTED BOOKS

This section will direct users to bibliographies of original source materials, chiefly those prior to 1800. The list is highly selective. Nearly every dissertation or research study devoted to early music contains its bibliography of primary sources. Some of these bibliographies are of great value, but any attempt to cite them all would extend far beyond the scope of the present work. The user should be reminded that the major reference works such as *The New Grove, MGG* or Riemann's *Lexicon* contain abundant listings of primary sources. See, for example, the *MGG* articles under "Ars antiqua," "Ars nova," or "Chanson" and the "Sources" article in *The New Grove.* Since the third edition of the present work was published, several important volumes in the *Repertoire International des Sources Musicales (International Inventory of Musical Sources)* have made their appearance (see nos. 1159–1162, 1817–1826, 1876, 1889).

It should be obvious that one of the most direct approaches to primary sources will be found in the section entitled "Catalogs of Music Libraries and Collections." Another useful approach, although not employed here apart from one or two exceptions, is through the catalogs of antiquarian music and book dealers such as H Baron, Richard MacNutt, J. & J. Lubrano, etc.

See also the section "Histories and Bibliographies of Music Printing and Publishing" for bibliographies of the output of some of the major music publishing houses from the 16th through the 18th centuries.

1735. Abravanel, Claude. "A checklist of music manuscripts in facsimile edition" in *Notes,* 34 (1978), p. 557–70.

A selected bibliography of facsimiles of entire works.

Substantially supplemented by James B. Coover in "Music manuscripts in facsimile edition: supplement" in *Notes,* 37 (1981), p. 533–56. Coover's bibliography includes a helpful section on facsimiles appearing in series included in the bibliography.

See also no. 1901 for a bibliography of composite music manuscripts in facsimile.

1736. Anderson, Gordon A. "Notre Dame and related conductus: a catalogue raisonne." In *Miscellanea musicologic. Adelaide studies in musicology,* 6 (1972), p. 153–229; 7 (1975), p. 1–81.

A "work in progress" designed to give systematic coverage to all pieces which may be designated conductus and which issue from c. 1170 to the close of the 13th century." Sources are identified and bibliographical references cited.

1737. Becker, Carl Ferdinand. Die Tonwerke des XVI. und XVII. Jahrhunderts, oder systematisch-chronologische Zusammenstellung der in diesen zwei Jahrhunderten gedruckten Musikalien. Zweite Ausgabe. Leipzig: E. Fleischer, 1855.

First published in 1847. Reprint of the second edition by Olms, Hildesheim, 1969.

An early classified bibliography of musical source materials, chronologically arranged under categories, with an index of composers and a general index to the whole. Attempts to list all musical compositions published in the 16th and 17th centuries to which actual or approximate dates could be assigned. An abridgement of Rimbault's *Bibliotheca madrigaliana* (no. 1829) is included as a supplement.

1738. Besseler, Heinrich. "Studien zur Musik des Mittelalters: 1. Neue Quellen des 14. und beginnenden 15. Jahrhunderts. 2. Die Motette von Franko von Köln bis Philipp von Vitry." In *Archiv für Musikwissenschaft,* 7 (1925), p. 167–252, and 9 (1927), p. 137–258.

Two articles that are basic source studies for the music of the late medieval period, containing numerous inventories and descriptions of ars nova manuscripts. They supplement the work of Friedrich Ludwig covering the ars antiqua sources (see no. 1800).

1739. Bibliotheca Musico-Liturgica. A descriptive handlist of the musical and Latin-Liturgical mss. of the Middle Ages preserved in the libraries of Great Britain and Ireland. Drawn up by W. H. Frere . . . and printed for the members of The Plainsong and Mediaeval Music Society. . . . London: Quaritch, 1901–1932. 2 v.

A union list of manuscript sources of early music in Great Britain. Vol. 1 (nos. 1–545): manuscripts at Lambeth and Oxford. Vol. 2 (nos. 546–1,031): manuscripts in cathedral chapter libraries and at Manchester, Dublin, Cambridge, etc. Full descriptions of the manuscripts; 17 plates. Indexes of service books, places, persons, and of Oxford Bodleian and Cambridge University Library manuscripts.

1740. Boetticher, Wolfgang. Handschriftlich überlieferte Lauten- und Gitarrentabulaturen des 15. bis 18. Jahrhunderts.

Dinko Fabris provides a supplement of 18 previously unknown lute tablatures from 11 Italian cities in *"Prime aggiunte Italiane al volume RISM B/VII" in Fontes artis musicae,* 29 (1982),p. 103–21.

1741. Bohn, Emil. "Bibliothek des gedruckten mehrstimmigen weltlichen deutschen Liedes vom Anfange des 16. Jahrhunderts bis c. 1640." In the author's *Fünfzig historische Concerte in Breslau, 1881–1892.* Breslau: Hainauer, 1893. p. 77–188.

A bibliography of German printed secular polyphonic song. The collections are listed chronologically to 1625; the volumes containing works by individual composers are listed alphabetically. Detailed bibliographical information, but contents not given. A useful guide to the printed sources of early German song.

1742. Bolle, W. Die gedruckten englischen Liederbucher in der Zeit Shakespeares. Mit Abdruck aller Texte aus den bisher noch nicht neugedruckten Liederbuchern und den zeitgenossischen deutschen Übertragungen. Berlin: 1903.

Reprint by Johnson Reprint Co., 1969.

1743. Boorman, Stanley. "Sources, MS," in *The New Grove Dictionary of Music and Musicians,* edited by Stanley Sadie, v. 17, p.590–702 by Stanley Boorman, John A. Emerson, David Fallows, David Hiley, Ernest H. Sanders, Ursula Günther, Gilbert Reaney, Kurt von Fischer, Charles Hamm, Jarry Call, and Herbert Kellman. London: Macmillan, 1980.

After an introduction to the nature, function, preparation, history and study of musical manuscripts, there follows eight extensive bibliographies of manuscript sources of western music: *Western plainchant; Secular monody; Organum and discant; Early motet; English polyphony 1270–1400; French polyphony 1300–1400; Italian polyphony c1325-c1430; and Renaissance polyphony.*

Each section presents and describes manuscripts, citing modern editions and secondary literature for each source. The introductory sections is followed by a brief bibliography.

1744. Borren, Charles van den. "Inventaire des manuscrits de musique polyphonique qui se trouvent en Belgique." In *ActaM,* 5 (1933), p. 66–71, 120–27, 177–83; 6 (1934), p. 23–29, 65–73, 116–21.

An inventory of the manuscript sources of early polyphony in Belgian libraries. Detailed descriptions, with listing of contents, of manuscripts in the libraries in Brussels, Ghent, Liege, Louvain, Malines, and Tournai.

1745. Bowers, Jane. "A catalogue of French works for the transverse flute, 1692–1761," in *Recherches sur la musique francaise classique," XVIII (1978), p. 89–125.* Paris: Editions A. et J. Picard, 1978.

1746. The Breitkopf Thematic Catalogue. The six parts and sixteen supplements, 1762–1787. Edited and with an introduction and indexes by Barry S. Brook. New York: Dover, 1966. 888 p.

Facsimile reproduction of the major 18th-century thematic catalog, giving almost 15,000 musical incipits and 1,300 first lines of texts representing over 1,000 composers. Preceded by an informative essay and an outline of the contents. Index of first lines of texts and a general index of names and topics.

Review by Bernard E. Wilson in *JAMS,* 21 (1968), p. 400–404; by Donald W. Krummel in *Notes,* 24 (1968), p. 697–700; by H. C. Robbins Landon in the *Haydn yearbook,* 6 (1969), p. 218.

1747. Breslauer, Martin (Firm, Booksellers, Berlin). Das deutsche Lied, geistlich und weltlich bis zum 18. Jahrhundert. Berlin: M. Breslauer, 1908. 304 p. (Documente frühen deutschen Lebens, Reihe 1)

Reprint by Olms, Hildesheim, 1966.

An important music dealer's catalogue listing 556 items in the field of early German song. Full bibliographical entries with descriptive annotations. Numerous facsimiles of title pages. Prices given. Index of first lines of song texts, melodies, persons.

1748. Bridgman, Nanie. "Musique profane italienne des 16e et 17e siècles dans les bibliothèques françaises." In *Fontes arties musicae,* 2 (1955), p. 40–59.

Full bibliographical descriptions of thirty-two 16th- and 17th-century prints of Italian secular music in branch libraries.

1749. British Museum (London) Department of Printed Books. Hand-list of music published in some British and foreign periodicals between 1787 and 1848, now in the British Museum. London, The Trustees of the British Museum, 1962. 80 p.

Indexes to music, chiefly songs, in 12 periodicals. 1,855 entries arranged by composer.

Review by Richard Schaal in *Die Musikforschung,* 17 (1964), p. 423.

1750. The British Union-Catalogue of Early Music Printed before the Year 1801. A record of the holdings of over 100 libraries throughout the British Isles. Edited by Edith B. Schnapper. London: Butterworths Scientific Publications, 1957. 2 v.

A major reference tool for work with early printed sources of music. These volumes provide the key to sources in British libraries. Brief bibliographical entries; locations established in more than 100 libraries in England, Scotland, and Ireland.

Review by A. Hyatt King in *Music and letters,* 39 (1958), p. 77–79; by Richard S. Hill in *Notes,* 15 (1958), p. 565–68; by Richard Schaal in *Die Musikforschung,* 12 (1959), p. 367–69.

1751. Brook, Barry S. La symphonie française dans la seconde moitie du XVIIIe siècle. Paris: Publications de l'Institut de Musicologie de l'Université de Paris, 1962. 3 v.

Vol. 1 is a study of the French symphony of the latter half of the 18th century, with important bibliographical supplements: Annexe IV: "Index thematique arrangé par tonalites et temps" (p. 511–73); Annexe V : "Index alphabetique des incipits transposés en do majeur ou do mineur et indiqués par les lettres" (p. 574–84); Annexe VI: "Inventaire sommaire de la symphonie et de la symphonie concertante françaises" (p. 585–633); Annexe VII: "Reeditions et enregistrements" (p. 634–39). Bibliography (p. 643–65); general index.

Vol. 2: "Catalogue thématique et bibliographique." Full descriptions of the works, location of sources, short biographies of each composer.

Vol. 3: Scores of 6 previously unedited symphonies.

The work treats some 1,200 symphonies by 150 composers.

Review by Marc Pincherle in *Revue de musicologie,* 49 (1963), p. 131–33; by H. C. Robbins Landon in *Die Musikforschung,* 17 (1964), p. 435–39; by Jan LaRue in *Musical quarterly* (1963), p. 384–88.

1752. Brown, Howard M. Instrumental music printed before 1600; a bibliography. Cambridge, Mass.: Harvard Univ. Press, 1965. 559 p.

A bibliography of the greatest importance for students of early instrumental music. Chronologically arranged beginning with Michel de Toulouze's *L'Art et instruction de bien dancer* (148?) and ending with works printed in 1599. Full bibliographical descriptions incorporating much valuable commentary. Includes references to works now lost.

P. 441–69: list of works cited. Indexes: (1) list of libraries and their holdings; (2) volumes described, arranged by type of notation; (3) volumes described, arranged by performing medium; (4) names; (5) first lines and titles.

Review by Claudio Sartori in *Notes,* 22 (1966), p. 1,209–1,212; by Jack A. Westrup in *Music and letters,* 47 (1966), p. 354–55; by Jeremy Noble in *JAMS,* 19 (1966), p. 415–17; by Ingrid Brainard in *Die Musikforschung,* 20 (1967), p. 465–70; by Martin Picker in *MQ,* 28 (1967), p. 136–39; by A. Hyatt King in *The Library,* ser. 5, 22 (June 1969), p. 154–58.

1753. Bryden, John R. and David G. Hughes. An index of Gregorian Chant. Cambridge, Mass.: Harvard Univ. Press, 1969. 2 v.

An index of chants found chiefly in modern service books. Vol. 1 gives text incipits; vol. 2, melodic incipits in number notation. A useful tool for identifying the chants used in polyphonic composition.

Review by Don M. Randel in *Notes,* 27 (1971), p. 477–78; by Andrew Hughes in *Music & letters,* 51 (1970), p. 317–19.

1754. Caldwell, John. "Sources of keyboard music to 1660," in *The New Grove Dictionary of Music and Musicians,* edited by Stanley Sadie, v. 17, p.717–33. London: Macmillan, 1980.

Includes "sources up to 1660, divided into broad geographical areas, and further divided within those areas into manuscript and printed sources arranged geographically." Sources are described and contents incompletely analyzed, modern editions and secondary literature are cited.

1755. Catalog of orchestral and choral compositions published and in manuscript between 1790 and 1840 from the library of the Musical Fund Society of Philadelphia. Philadelphia: Musical Fund Society, 1974. 81 p.

Listing of 299 scores now in the custody of the Music Department of the Free Library of Philadelphia.

1756. Chaillon, Paule. "Les fonds musicaux de quelques bibliothèques de province." In *Fontes artis musicae,* 2 (1955), p. 151–63.

A listing of libraries in 24 French provinces with descriptions of their catalogs, if any, followed by a list of *unica* or of rare or unusual works in their collections.

1757. Coover, James B. "Composite music manuscripts in facsimile" in *Notes,* 38 (1982), p. 275–95.

"This list comprises only complete manuscripts, mostly medieval and renaissance, reproduced in facsimile." Arranged by location, with cross references from names of manuscripts. Index to personal names. Identifies RISM items in the list. Index to items in series.

1758. Corbin, Solange. Répertoire de manuscrits médievaux contenant des notations musicales. Paris: Éditions du Centre National de la Recherche Scientifique, 1965– . V. 1– .

V. 1: Bibliothèque Sainte-Geneviève (1965).

V. 2: Bibliothèque Mazarine, par Madeleine Bernard (1966).

V. 3: Bibliothèque Parisiennes—Arsenal, Nationale (Musique), Universitaire, École des Beux-Arts, et Fonds Privés, par Madeleine Bernard (1974).

This series promises to provide descriptions and inventories of all the manuscripts containing medieval chant notation. Each volume includes bibliographies and facsimiles.

V. 1 includes tables of origins of notation (describing types of books and their notations), of the provenance of each manuscript, of the contents of the manuscripts by musico-liturgical genres, of neumes, and of pictorial images of instruments. Map of notational styles in northern France. Plates. Extensive tables in other volumes. V. 3 includes a table of text incipits.

Review by John A. Emerson in *JAMS,* 22 (1969), p. 119–22; by Ewald Jammers in *Die Musikforschung,* 21 (1968), p. 103–4.

1759. Crane, Frederick. Materials for the study of the 15th-century Basse danse. New York: Institute of Medieval Music, 1968. 131 p. (Wissenschaftliche Abhandlungen, 16)

Review by Peter Gülke in *Die Musikforschung,* 24 (1971), p. 339–40.

1760. Daniel, Ralph T. and Peter Le Huray. The sources of English church music 1549–1660. London: Published for the British Academy by Stainer and Bell, 1972. 2 v.

This is the first attempt to compile a complete inventory of sacred music in English covering the period from the early years of the Reformation to the mid-17th century. [*Preface*]

Part I is a listing of the sources, printed or in manuscript, a thematic catalog of all anonymous works, and a first-line index of anthems. Part II: services and anthems arranged in alphabetical order by composer, with all the data as to sources and locations of sources.

1761. Danner, Peter. "Bibliography of guitar tablatures, 1546–1764." In *Journal of the Lute Society of America,* 5 (1972), p. 40–51.
A bibliography of 165 printed and 50 manuscript sources. Brief descriptive annotations.

1762. Dart, Thurston. "A hand-list of English instrumental music printed before 1681," in *Galpin Society journal,* 1955, p. 13–26.

1763. Daschner, Hubert. Die gedruckten mehrstimmigen Chansons von 1500–1600. Bonn: Rheinische Friedrich-Wilhelms-Universität, 1962. 195 p.
A dissertation the greater part of which consists of a first-line index of polyphonic chansons from the printed collections of the 16th century. 4,273 chansons entered.
P. 175–82: "Verzeichnis der Musikdrucke;" p. 184–86: "Verzeichnis der anonymen Gedichtsammlungene;" p. 187–95; "Literaturverzeichnis."

1764. Davidsson, Åke. Catalogue critique et descriptif des imprimes de musique des XVIe et XVIIe siècles conservés dans les bibliothèques suédoises (excepté la Bibliothèque de l'Université Royale d'Upsala). Upsala: Almquist et Wiksells, 1952. 471 p. (Studia musicalogica upsaliensia, 1)
A union catalogue of early music in 18 Swedish libraries, excluding the University of Uppsala, which is treated elsewhere (see no. 2423). Full descriptions, contents, references; p. 455–71: bibliography of works cited.

1765. Deakin, Andrew. Outlines of musical bibliography: a catalogue of early music and musical works printed or otherwise produced in the British Isles; the whole chronologically arranged with descriptive and critical notes on the principal works. Birmingham: A. Deakin, 1899. 112 p.
Reprint of the 1899 edition by Olms, Hildesheim, c. 1971.
A work projected on a much larger scale, but not completed. P. 5–18: a listing of manuscript sources. P. 19–96: chiefly printed music of the 16th and 17th centuries, but with a few manuscripts included. The entries are not precise, and the locations given are indefinite. Indexed by composer and title.

1766. Dichter, Harry. Handbook of American sheet music ... first annual issue, 1947. Philadelphia: H. Dichter, 1947. 100 p.
Second series, with Bernice Larrabee. Philadelphia, 1953.
Catalogs of early American sheet music for sale by the author. Full of

useful bibliographical data. Classified under selected headings: topic, author, title. Prices given. No index. The 1947 volume lists over 2,000 items.

1767. Dichter, Harry and Elliott Shapiro. Early American sheet music, its lure and its lore, 1768–1889. . . . including a directory of early American music publishers. . . . New York: R. R. Bowker, 1941. 287 p.

A cross-section of early American sheet music, classified as to subject content. Composer, main title, publisher, and date included. The directory of publishers is an alphabetical listing of firms active from 1768 to 1899 and carries their histories to 1940. Additional lists of lithographers and artists active before 1870. Plates of illustrated title pages. Index.

1768. Draudius, Georg. Verzeichnisse deutscher musikalischer Bucher, 1611–1625. In originalgetreuem Nachdruck herausgegeben von Konrad Ameln. Bonn: Deutschen Musikverleger-Verband, 1957.

Facsimile reprint of the music sections from the 1611 and 1625 editions of Draudius's *Bibliotheca librorum germanicorum classica,* an early document in the history of music bibliography. ("Musikalische Bucher" here means "scores.") Classified according to type of composition. Primarily of historical interest.

1769. Duckles, Vincent H. "The music for the lyrics in early seventeenth-century English drama: a bibliography of the primary sources." In *Music in English renaissance drama. Ed. by* John H. Long. Lexington: Univ. of Kentucky Press, 1968. p. 117–60.

Directs the reader to manuscript and early printed sources for the songs introduced into English drama from 1603–1642. Modern editions of these songs are cited when available.

1770. Duyse, Florimond van. Het oude Nederlandsche lied; wereldlijke en geestelijke liederen uit vroegeren tijd, teksten en melodieën, verzameld en toegelicht door Fl. van Duyse. . . . 's-Gravenhage: M. Nijhoff, 1903–1908. 4 v.

First issued in parts, 1900–1908; unaltered reprint by Frits A. M. Knuf, Hilversum, 1965.

The standard reference book for the study of early Dutch song. Actually an edition of 714 melodies given with their variants and with an abundance of related information on texts and music. Sacred song is treated in vol. 3; vol. 4 contains indexes of names, of song titles, and of first lines of texts.

1771. Edwards, Warwick. "Sources of instrumental ensemble music to 1630," in *The New Grove Dictionary of Music and Musicians,* edited by Stanley Sadie, v. 17, p. 702–17. London: Macmillan, 1980.

"Concerned with . . . music for two or more instruments (excluding . . . keyboards, lutes and other chordal instruments) to play together without the voice. . . . An attempt has been made to identify music originally conceived for instruments." Organized goegraphically, entries give locations, manuscript numbers or titles (and if titles, then imprint information) and a description of contents, citing any modern editions or secondary literature.

1772. Eitner, Robert. Bibliographie der Musik-Sammelwerke des XVI. und XVII. Jahrhunderts. Im Vereine mit Frz. Xav. Haberl, A. Lagerberg und C. F. Pohl. Berlin: L. Liepmannssohn, 1877. 964 p.

Supplemented by additions and corrections published in Eitner's *Monatshefte für Musikgeschichte,* 14 (1882), p. 152–55, 161–64.

Reprint of the original edition by Olms, Hildesheim, 1963.

Chronological bibliography of some 795 collections of music published between 1501 and 1700, with full descriptions, summary of contents, lists of composers represented, and library locations of individual copies. The second part of the work, p. 297–938, is a first-line index of the vocal texts, arranged alphabetically by composer.

Eitner's *Sammelwerke* is one of the major bibliographical tools for historical research in music, although it has been superseded, in part, by the first volume to appear of the *International inventory of musical sources* (see no. 1819).

1773. Eitner, Robert. Biographisch-bibliographische Quellen-Lexikon der Musiker und Musikgelehrten der christlichen Zeitrechnung bis zur Mitte des 19. Jahrhunderts. . . . Leipzig: Breitkopf & Hartel, 1898–1904. 10 v.

Supplemented by the *Miscellanea musicae bio-bibliographica* (no. 1803), and by G. Radiciotti's "Aggiunte e correzioni ai dizionari biografici dei musicisti" (no. 1813).

Reprinted with the supplements by Musurgia, New York, 1947. Neuauflage published by Breitkopf & Hartel, Wiesbaden, 1959–60. "2. verbesserte Auflage," Graz, Akademische Druck- und Verlagsanstalt, 1959–60.

Eitner's *Quellen-Lexikon* was the basic tool for locating primary sources of music before 1800. Both printed music and manuscripts are included, with their locations in European libraries. The work is badly out of date; much of the information, particularly as regards locations, is no longer correct. The *International inventory of musical sources* has replaced Eitner as a key to the sources of early music. See nos. 1159–1162, 1817–1826, 1876, 1889. Eitner is still valuable, especially to identify works no longer extant as it precedes the two major multi-national conflagrations which resulted in so much damage to European library collections.

Stephen A. Wilier's article "The present location of libraries listed in Robert Eitner's Biographis-bibliographisches Quellen-Lexikon" in *Fontes artis musicae,* 28 (1981), p. 220–39, documents the present location of most of the collections mentioned in the *Verzeichnis der Bibliotheks-Abjürzungen* in the first volume of the *Quellen-Lexikon.*

1774. Fischer, Kurt von. Studien zur italienischen Musik des Trecento und fruhen Quattrocento. Bern: P. Haupt, 1956. 132 p. (Publikationen der Schweizerischen Musikforschenden Gesellschaft, ser. 2, v. 5.)

A bibliography of Italian secular music of the 14th and early 15th centuries. Text incipits, arranged alphabeticlly, for 177 madrigals, 25 caccie, and 423 ballate, with information as to sources and modern editions.

Review by Hans Tischler in *Notes,* 15 (1958), p. 405–6.

1775. Flurschütz, Kaspar. Die Kataloge des Augsburger Musikalien-Händlers Kaspar Flurschütz, 1613–1628. Mit einer Einleitung und Registern

zum ersten Mal herausgegeben von Richard Schaal. Mit einer Bibliographie zur Augsburger Musikgeschichte 1550–1660. Wilhelmshaven:
Heinrichshofen, 1974. 159 p. (Quellen Kataloge zur Musikgeschichte, 7)

A transcription with indexes by name and genre of the 7 extant catalogs of the early 17th century music dealer. Bibliography of writings on
the history of music in Augsburg, 1550–1650.

1776. Ford, Terence. "Index to the facsimiles of polyphonic music before
1600 published in *Die Musik in Geschichte und Gegenwart*" in *Notes,* 39
(1983), p. 283–315.

Providing access to c. 400 facsimiles by four indexes: informal name
of the manuscript; titles of prints; first line and/or title of compositions;
personal names. *MGG*—Early music facsimiles—Index

1777. Fortune, Nigel. "A handlist of printed Italian secular monody books,
1602–1635." In *R.M.A. Research Chronicle,* No. 3. Published for the Royal
Musical Association, 1963. p. 27–50.

A list of all publications containing at least one Italian secular monody
from the first in 1602 to 1635. Location symbols given for the scarcer
volumes. The notes indicate contemporary reprints and modern editions
where they exist. By far the most comprehensive listing of Italian monody books available.

1778. Friedlaender, Max. Das deutsche Lied im 18. Jahrhundert, Quellen
und Studien. . . . Stuttgart und Berlin: Cotta, 1902. 2 v. in 3.

Vol. 1:1, p. 1–62: a chronological listing of 798 German songbooks of the
18th century (1689–1799), followed by a detailed commentary on the most
important examples. Vol. 1:2, a collection of musical examples. Vol. 2:
discussion of the poets, with indexes of names, text incipits.

1779. Fuld, James J. and Mary Wallace Davidson. 18th-century American
secular music manuscripts: an inventory. Philadelphia: Music Library
Association, 1980. 225 p. (MLA index and bibliography series, 20)

> Included are eighty-five secular musical manuscripts held by twenty libraries
> and private individuals. The manuscripts vary from one piece to collections
> of about four hundred pieces, and include a variety of types: keyboard sona-
> tas, suites, variations, and other classical forms, military marches and bugle
> calls, ballroom dances, ballads, childrens's songs, folk songs, and theater mu-
> sic. [authors' *Preface*]

The manuscripts are fully described, analyzed, and indexed.

1780. Geck, Martin. Deutsche Oratorien, 1800 bis 1840. Verzeichnis der
Quellen und Auffuhrungen. Wilhelmshaven: Heinrichshofen's Verlag,
1971. 105 p. (Quellen-Kataloge zur Musikgeschichte, 4)

The bibliography has three major parts: (1) an alphabetical listing of
the oratorios under composer; (2) a listing of performances by place; and
(3) a listing by chronology. Some reviews and notices in contemporary
periodicals are indicated. Oratorios by some 100 composers are cited.

1781. Geering, Arnold. Die Organa und mehrstimmigen Conductus in den
handscriften des deutschen Sprachgebietes vom 13. bis 16. Jahrhundert.

Bern: P. Haupt, 1952. 99 p. (Publikationen der Schwiezerischen Musik-forschenden Gesellschaft, ser. 2:1)

A study concerned with the sources of early polyphony in the German-speaking countries, with a listing of the relevant manuscripts and an inventory of the organum and conductus settings they contain.

1782. Gennrich, Friedrich. Bibliographie der ältesten französischen und lateinischen Motetten. Darmstadt: Selbstverlag, 1957. 124 p. (Summa musicae medii aevi, 2)

A bibliography of the 13th-century motet, serving also as a guide to the manuscript sources and a record of scholarly work done in this field. Gennrich expands the work begun by Friedrich Ludwig in his *Repertorium* (see no. 1801). Motets are grouped under their respective tenors, with references to all known concordances and modern editions. Supplementary bibliographies of literature and of scripts, indexes of Latin and French tenors, and incipits to motettus and triplum parts.

Review by Hans Tischler in *Notes,* 16 (1959), p. 561–62.

1783. Gennrich, Friedrich. Der musikalische Nachlass der Troubadours. Kommentar. Darmstadt: Selbstverlag, 1960. 176 p. (Summa musicae medii aevi, 4)

A complete bibliography of the surviving musical settings of Troubadour song, 302 entries in all, with information as to source, editions of text and music, verse forms, use of the melody as a contrafactum. Songs are numbered consecutively but grouped under composer, with bibliographical references to work done on the individual musicians. 25 manuscript sources are described and discussed.

Vol. 3 of the series, Summa musicae medii aevi (1958), is a musical edition of the surviving Troubadour melodies.

1784. Göhler, Albert. Verzeichnis der in den Frankfurter und Leipziger Messkatalogen der Jahre 1564 bis 1759 angezeigten Musikalien.... Leipzig: C. F. Kahnt Nachf., 1902. 4 parts in 1 v.

Unaltered reprint by Frits A. M. Knuf, Hilversum, 1965.

A bibliography of the music listed in the Frankfurt and Leipzig trade catalogs from 1564 to 1759. Works separately listed by century, under composer. Works identified by type.

1785. Gröninger, Eduard. Repertoire-Untersuchungen zum mehrstimmigen Notre-Dame-Conductus. Regensburg: Bosse, 1939. 163 p. (Kolner Beitrage zur Musikforschung, 2)

An introductory essay of 59 pages, followed by tabulations, with concordances, of the polyphonic conductus compositions found in the four major Notre Dame sources.

1786. Gustafson, Bruce. French harpsichord music of the 17th century; a thematic catalog of the sources with commentary. Ann Arbor: UMI Research Press, 1979. 3 v.

Volume one presents descriptions and commentary on each manuscript arranged by present location. Volumes 2 and 3 provide detailed bibliographic description, thematic entries, and concordances to other manuscripts. The complex thematic catalog and the index to all three volumes are not well-explained, but once understood are quite useful. A monumental bibliographic feat.

1787. Haberkamp, Gertraut. "Text- und Musikincipit-Register zu den Anhängen 1 und 2 in RISM A/1 Band 9," zusammengestellt von Gertraut Haberkamp und Helmut Rösing. In *Fontes Artis Musicae*, 28 (1981), p.48ff and p. 259–306. *Einzeldrucke vor 1800*—Indexes *Einzeldrucke vor 1800*—Indexes

1788. Hagopian, Viola L. Italian ars nova music, a bibliographic guide to modern editions and related literature. Second edition, revised and expanded. Berkeley and Los Angeles: Univ. of California Press, 1973. 175 p.
First printed in 1964.
An organized, annotated bibliography treating the work done by scholars in the field of 14th-century Italian music.
Review of the first edition by Ursula Günther in *Die Musikforschung,* 20 (1967), p. 83–84.

1789. Hixon, Donald L. Music in early America: a bibliography of music in Evans. Metuchen: Scarecrow Press, 1970. 607 p.

This bibliography is an index to the music published in 17th- and 18th-century America as represented by Charles Evans' *American Bibliography* and the Readex Corporation's microprint edition of *Early American Imprints, 1639–1800.* ...

The first two parts consist of an alphabetical composer-editor-compiler arrangement. Part III is devoted to biographical sketches. Parts III-VI are indexes: composer-compiler, title, and numerical index. *Early American Imprints, 1639–1800*—Music entries—Indexes *American Bibliography*— Music entries—Indexes

1790. Hughes, Andrew. Medieval manuscripts for mass and office: a guide to their organization and terminology. Toronto; Buffalo: University of Toronto Press, 1982. 470 p.
Best exemplifies the concept of bibliography as a tool for learning. The 1980 revision consists of some alterations in the 1974 text with a supplemental section added at the end of the volume.
Review by Richard Crocker in *Cum notis variorum,* 66 (1982), p. 7–8.

1791. Huglo, Michel. Les tonaires; inventaire, analyse, comparison. Paris: Société française de musicologie, 1971. 487 p.
This is an extended bibliographic and historical work on the medieval tonaries. Huglo describes and discusses the significance of each manuscript, analyses its contents and compares it to others. The mansucripts are classed by date, by region, by musical and litergical characteristics. There is an index of books discussed arranged by city, library, and manuscript name and number. Bibliography of printed tonaries (facsimiles and originals). There is a bibliography of secondary literature. Table of incipits and mnemonic formulas. A magisterial work.

1792. Index to Early American Periodicals to 1850. E. SONGS. (Cards E1 to E11). New York: Readex Microfilm Corp., [1965]. (Bibliographic aids in microprint)

Microprint edition of the entries under "Songs" from an index of some 650,000 cards compiled by members of the English department of Washington Square College, New York University, with the aid of the WPA. Indexes some 340 early American magazines by authors, composers, anonymous titles, first lines.

1793. International Association of Music Libraries. Radio Commission. Catalogue of rare materials, and first supplement. Edited by Folke Lindberg. Stockholm: 1959. 185 leaves.

Supplement I: leaves 175–85.

A list designed for the use of radio librarians in locating copies of rare material that can be used for performance purposes.

International inventory of musical sources. See Répertoire International des Sources Musicales, no. 1159–1162, 1817–1826, 1876, 1889.

Internationales Quellenlexikon der Musik. See Répertoire International des Sources Musicales, no. 1159–1162, 1817–1826, 1876, 1889.

1794. Keller, Kate Van Winkle. Popular secular music in America through 1800: a preliminary checklist of manuscripts in North American collections. Philadelphia: Music Library Association, 1981. 140 p. (Music Library Association. MLA index and bibliography series, 21)

Explores a little known area of scholarship.

1795. Kreider, J. Evan. "A checklist of Spanish chant sources at the Hill Monastic Manuscript Library, St. John's Abbey and University" in *Notes,* 40 (1984), p. 7–29.

A tabulation of resources gathered from Spain and elsewhere at HMML.

1796. Kreider, J. Evan. "Austrian graduals, antiphoners, and noted missales on microfilm in the Hill Monastic Manuscript Library, St. John's Abbey and University" in *Notes,* 36 (1980), p. 849–63.

1797. De La Cuesta, Ismael Fernández. Manuscritos y fuentes musicales en España: Edad media. Madrid: Editorial Apluerto, 1980. 397 p.

An international inventory of medieval Spanish musical manuscripts and other sources arranged in order of collection. Annotations include physical description, notational style, contents analytics, references to related manuscripts, and bibliographical references. General bibliography. Indexes of first lines of visigothic and mozarabic chants, gregorian chants, latin monody, polyphony, and romances. Index of locations.

1798. Linker, Robert W. Music of the Minnesinger and early Meistersinger, a bibliography. Chapel Hill: University of North Carolina Press, [1961]. 79 p.

A bibliography of German medieval song arranged alphabetically under the composers' names. A preliminary list gives 40 manuscript sources and 41 modern publications of literary history, music, and text editions.

Review by Walter Salmen in *Die Musikforschung,* 17 (1964), p. 432.

Loewenberg, Alfred. Annals of opera, 1597–1940. . . . See no. 0491.

1799. Lowens, Irving. A bibliography of songsters printed in America before 1821. Worcester, Mass.: American Antiquarian Society, 1976. 229 p.

A bibliography of collections of secular poems or song lyrics intended to be sung. Introductory essay on the songster. Detailed bibliographical descriptions with extensive annotations in chronological order. Geographical directory of printers, publishers, booksellers, engravers, etc. Index of compilers, editors, proprietors, and editors. Index to titles of songsters.

1800. Ludwig, Friedrich. "Die Quellen der Motetten ältesten Stils." In *Archiv für Musikwissenschaft,* 5 (1923), p. 185–222, 273–315.

A basic source study of medieval polyphony, in which the author gives complete or partial inventories for some 50 manuscripts containing motets of the *ars antiqua* period.

This study has been reprinted as a supplement to Gennrich's edition of Ludwig's *Repertorium, Abteilung 2.* (see below, no. 1801).

1801. Ludwig, Friedrich. Repertorium organorum recentioris et motetorum vetustissimi stili. Band 1: Catalogue raisonne der Quellen. Abteilung 1: Handschriften in Quadrat-Notation. Halle: Niemeyer, 1910. 344 p.

Ludwig's *Repertorium,* although incomplete, is the starting point for all studies in the music of the ars antiqua period. It is essentially an inventory, with concordances, of the contents of the major manuscripts of the Notre Dame repertory.

Band 1, Abteilung 2: *Handschriften in Mensuralnotation.* Besorgt von Friedrich Gennrich. Langen bei Frankfurt, 1961. (Summa musicae medii aevi, 7.)

This portion of the *Repertorium* appeared in proof copy but was never published in Ludwig's lifetime. It consists chiefly of inventories of two major sources of the 13th-century motet, the *Montpellier Codex* and the *Clayette MS.* Included as a supplement to this volume is a reprint of Ludwig's study, "Die Quellen der Motetten altesten Stils," which appeared in the *Archiv für Musikwissenschaft,* 5 (1925). See no. 1800, above.

A "2. erwieterte Auflage" edited by Luther A. Dittmer, appeared 1964–78 as a joint publication of the Institute of Mediaeval Music, New York, and Georg Olms, Hildesheim. 2 v. in 3. Includes Band 1, Abteilung 1: *Handschriften in Quadrat-Notation.* (Wissenschaftliche Abhandlungen, Bd. 7, 17, 26)

Band 2: *Musikalisches Anfangs-Verzeichnis des nach Tenores geordneten Repertorium.* Besorgt von Friedrich Gennrich. Langen bei Frankfurt, 1962. 71 p. (Summa musicae medii aevi, 8.) Reprinted in a new edition by Luther A. Dittmer by the Institute of Mediaeval Music and Olms, Hildesheim, 1983.

A thematic catalog of 515 motets based on 50 tenors taken from the liturgy of the Mass. Reprinted, incomplete, from Ludwig's unpublished proof copy. *Ars antiqua* music—Bibliography

1802. Meyer, Ernst H. "Quellennachweise." In his *Die mehrstimmige Spielmusik des 17. Jahrhunderts in Nord- und Mittel-Europa.* . . . Kassel: Bärenreiter, 1934. p. 128–258.
A bibliography of the sources of 17th-century chamber music of the North-European school. Partially thematic for the English sources.

1803. Miscellanea Musicae Bio-Bibliographica. . . . Hrsg. von H. Springer, M. Schneider, und W. Wolffheim. 2., um einen Anhang vermehrte Auflage. New York: Musurgia, 1947. 435 p.
Originally published by Breitkopf & Hartel in quarterly issues, 1912–16, with annual index for each of the years covered. Provides corrections and additions to all the kinds of information in Eitner's *Quellen-Lexikon,* no. 1773.
Reprinted in vol. 11 of the Akademische Druck- und Verlagsanstalt 2. *verbesserte Auflage of the Quellen-Lexikon,* which also contains marginal numerical references to the *Miscellanea. Quellen-Lexikon*—Supplement

1804. Mischiati, Oscar. Bibliografia delle opere dei musicisti bresciani pubblicate a stampa dal 1497 al 1740. Editio minor. Brescia: Centro di studi musicali 'Luca Marenzio', 1982. 205 p. (Pubblicazioni del Centro di studi musicali "Luca Marenzio," presso la Civica biblioteca queriniana di Brescia)
Also known as the *Bibliografia dei musicisti bresciani.*

1805. Mischiati, Oscar. La prassi musicale presso i Canonici regolari del Ss. Salvatore: nei secoli XVI e XVII e i manoscritti polifonici della Biblioteca musicale "G.B. Martini" di Bologna. Roma: Edizioni Torre d'Orfeo, 1985. 157 p. (Documenti. Istituto di paleografia musicale; 1)
A study of musical practices with bibliographic references.

1806. Monumenta Monodica Medii Aevi. Band I- . Herausgegeben im Auftrag des Musikwissenschaftlichen Seminars der Univesität Erlangen-Nürnberg von Bruno Stäblein. Kassel: Barenreiter, 1956- .
Band I: Hymnen (1956), 724 p.
Band II: Die Gesange des altromischen Graduale. Vat. lat. 5319. (1970), 724 p.
Band III: Introitus-Tropen 1. Das Repertoire der südfranzösischen Tropare des 10. und 11. Jahrhunderts (1970), 470 p.
Band VII: Alleluia-Melodien I, bis 1100. (1968), 682 p.
A series devoted to the publication of medieval monody, chiefly sacred. The music is organized liturgically and given in neume notation, with copious documentation. A basic tool for research in medieval music.

1807. Musiker Handschriften . . . Composers' autographs; translated from the German with a new preface by Ernst Roth. London: Cassell, 1968. 2 v.
Translation of *Musikerhandschriften von Palestrina bis Beethoven,* edited by W. Gerstenberg, and *Musikhandschriften von Schubert bis*

Strawinsky, edited by M. Hurlimann, both of which are based on *Musikerhandschriften von Bach bis Schumann, by* G. Schunemann (1936).

Two handsome volumes of facsimiles made chiefly from composers' autographs in the Berlin State Library. Vol. 1 contains 159 plates; vol. 2, 140, with brief descriptive commentaries and identification of the sources.

Published in the U.S.A. under the imprint of Fairleigh Dickinson University Press.

Review by Werner Neumann in *Die Musikforschung,* 17 (1964), p. 454–55.

1808. Ness, Arthur J. "Sources of lute music," in *The New Grove Dictionary of Music and Musicians,* edited by Stanley Sadie, v. 17, p.733–53. London: Macmillan, 1980.

An introduction to the sources with descriptions and analysis of each source. Arranged by zones of origin and chronologically. Modern editions and secondary cited with each source.

1809. Newman, Joel. An index to capoversi and titles cited in Einstein's *The Italian madrigal.* New York: Publications of the Renaissance Society of America, 1967. 39 p. (Indexes and bibliographies, 3)

Incorporated in the 1971 edition of *The Italian Madrigal.*

Indexes more than 2,000 madrigal titles cited in Einstein's work. Composer and poet are cited where known. Those with musical settings in the Einstein book are identified. *The Italian Madrigal*—Indexes

1810. Nisser, Carl M. Svensk instrumentalkomposition, 1770–1830. Nominalkatalog. Stockholm: Bökforlaget Gothia, [1943]. 467 p.

Swedish instrumental music, native composers or composers living in Sweden. Alphabetical listing by composer, with detailed bibliographical and analytical descriptions, including key, movements, time signature, measure count. Bibliographical references, Index of names and places.

1811. Page, Christopher. "A catalogue and bibliography of English song from its beginnings to c. 1300" in *R.M.A. Research Chronicle,* 13 (197?), p. 67–83.

"This catalogue lists all the twelfth- and thirteenth-century songs with English words known to exist." Nineteen items arranged in chronological order, indicating first line and source, with extensive descriptions and listing modern editions.

1812. Pillet, Alfred. Bibliographie der Troubadours. Erg., weitergeführt und herausgegeben von Dr. Henry Carstens. Halle: Niemeyer, [1933]. 518 p. (Schriften der Konigsberger Gelehrten Gesellschaft. Sonderreihe, 2)

Reprinted by B. Franklin, N.Y., 1968.

Based on a bibliography of troubadour songs compiled by Karl Bartsch in 1872. Songs arranged alphabetically by first word of text, with inclusive numeration and subseries of numbers for works by individual authors. The emphasis is directed toward literary rather than musical scholarship.

1813. Radiciotti, Giuseppe. "Aggiunte e correzioni ai dizionari biografici dei musicisti." In *Sammelbande der Internationalen Musikgesellschaft,* 14 (1914), p. 551–67; 15 (1915), p. 566–86.

Corrections and additions to Eitner's *Quellen-Lexikon* (no. 1773) with special attention to Italian composers.

Reprinted in the Musurgia edition of the *Quellen-Lexikon,* and as vol. 11 of the Akademische Druck- und Verlagsanstalt, *2. verbesserte Auflage,* 1960. *Quellen-Lexikon*—Supplement

1814. Randel, Don M. An index to the chants of the Mozarabic rite. Princeton: Princeton Univ. Press, 1973. 670 p.

A comprehensive bibliography of the manuscript sources of Mozarabic chant, indicating the parts of the Office for which each chant would have been used.

1815. Raynaud, Gaston. Bibliographie des altfranzösischen Liedes. Neu bearbeitet und erganzt von Hans Spanke. Erster Teil. Leiden: E. J. Brill, 1955. 386 p.

Reprinted by Brill in 1980 with a discography and index to chansons by A. Bahat. 348 p.

The first part of a projected revision of Raynaud's *Bibliographie des chansonniers français des XIIIe et XIVe siècles.* Paris, 1884. 2 v. This work serves as a guide to trouvere songs, similar to that offered by the Pillet (no. 1812) or the Gennrich (no. 1783) for the troubadour repertory. Lists more than 2,130 songs, arranged according to the rhyme word of the first stanza, with references to the manuscript source and to literary and musical studies concerned with the item. P. 1–32: a bibliography of the manuscript sources and of modern editions and studies.

1816. Reich, Wolfgang. Threnodiae sacrae. Katalog der gedruckten Kompositionen des 16.-18. Jahrhunderts in Leichenpredigtsammlungen innerhalb der Deutschen Demokratischen Republik. Dresden: 1966. 75 p. (Veroffentlichungen der Sachsischen Landesbibliothek, 7)

A catalog of 434 funereal compositions of the 16th through the 18th centuries found in East German collections, chiefly, Gotha, Dresden, East Berlin, and Zwickau.

Review by Martin Geck in *Die Musikforschung,* 22 (1969), p. 389–90.

1817. Répertoire International des Sources Musicales. Einzeldrucke vor 1800. Redaktion Karlheinz Schlager. Kassel: Bärenreiter, 1971–81. v. 1–9. (RISM ser. A, pt. I, v. 1–9)

These volumes are the first part of the Series A of RISM which are intended to supersede the list of works in Eitner's *Quellenlexikon,* This part, A/I, is an alphabetical catalog covering individual editions of music printed between 1500 and 1800 under the name of a singel composer. The ninth volume includes an appendix devoted to printed editions with composers' attributions by initial and another appendix including anonymous printed editions. the *Anhängen exclude entries in the British Union Catalogue of Early Music* and *Das Deutsche Kirchenlied* (RISM B/VIII "DKL").

Each entry includes as much of the title as is needed to distinguish the edition, imprint, a unique RISM identifier, and the location of each surviving exemplar known. Each volume contains a list of contributing libraries ordered by country and city.

Karlheinz Schlager was responsible for v. 1–7 (Aarts—Schreyer). Otto Albrecht joined Schlager for v. 8 & 9 (Schrijer—Zwingmann).

Gertraut Haberkamp and Helmut Rösing were responsible for *Anhangen* 1 & 2. Rösing and Haberkamp prepared *"Text- und Musikincipit-Register zu den Anhängen 1 und 2 in RISM A/I Band 9," for Fontes artis musicae,* 28 (1981), 48 p. This is an index to the text incipits appearing as part of a title in either of the appendices and an index to the music incipites cited in the appendices. In the brief explanation of the two indexes, the use of asterisks is indentified as denotations of the existence of music incipits.

For documentation concerning Series A see *"RISM: zur Katalogisierung von Musikdrucken und Musikhandschriften der Serie A," by* Karlheinz Schlager, Jürgen Kindermann, and Helmut Rösing in *ActaM,* 51 (1979), p. 173–92.

V. 7 reviewed by Richard Schaal in *Die Musikforschung,* 32 (1979), p. 86–87; and by François Lesure in *Fontes artis musicae,* 26 (1979), p. 145.

1818. Répertoire International des Sources Musicales. Einzeldrucke vor 1800; Addenda et Corrigenda. Bd. 11. Redaktion Ilse Kindermann und Jürgen Kindermann. Kassel: Bärenreiter, 1986. 491 p. (RISM, ser. A, pt. I, v. 11)

Incorporating new rules for inclusion allowing entries for all editions by composers born before 1770, published before 1830; and by composers born after 1770 but who died before 1810. "Works by these composers published by 1830 and 1850 (the final terminus) are also included if no earlier editions of these works are recorded."

1819. Répertoire International des Sources Musicales. Handschriften mit mehrstimmiger Musik des 14., 15. und 16. Jahrhunderts. Mehrstimmige Musik in italienischen, polnischen, und tschechischen Quellen des 14. Jahrhunderts. Mehrstimmige Stücke in Handschriften aller Länder aus der Zeit um 1400–1425/30. Organale Sätze im älteren Stil und mehrstimmige Stücke in Choralhandschriften des 15. und 16. Jahrhunderts. Beschreiben und inventarisiert von Kurt von Fischer und herausgegeben in Zusammenarbeit mit Max Lutolf. München-Duisburg: G. Henle, 1972. 2 v. (RISM ser. B, vol. 4:3–4)

Group one, the manuscripts of polyphonic music of the 14th, 15th, and 16th centuries follows *RISM* volumes B/IV/1 and B/IV/2. It covers sources of the Italian trecento and Polish and Czech sources of the 14th century.

Group two, the sources of 14th century polyphonic music in manuscripts from all countries and dating from 1400 to 1425/30 links *RISM* volumes B/IV/2 to the present volume.

"Group 3 consists of sources of organ polyphony of the 15th and 16th centuries and of choral manuscripts of these centuries in which polyphonic pieces in black notation occur next to liturgical, monodic ones."

The manuscripts are arranged by country, city, and library in each of the groups described above. indexes of text incipits and composers.

1820. Répertoire International des Sources Musicales. Handschriftlich überlieferte Lauten- und Gitarrentabulaturen des 15. bis 18. Jahrhunderts: beschreibender Katalog von Wolfgang Boetticher. München: Henle,

1978. 82, 374 p. (RISM, ser. B, 7)

A descriptive catalog of 726 manuscripts containing lute and guitar music in tablature within the RISM time span (until c. 1820). Includes manuscripts containing music for other plectoral instruments (e.g. theorbo, chitarrone ...). Organized by country, city, and library. RISM issued a separate supplement by Christian Meyer, *Register der Tabulaturgattungen und Namen zusammengestellt,* a classified register of the tablatures and an index to names in the catalogs.

Supplemental information in *"Zur inhaltlichen Bestimmung des für Laute intavolierten Handschriftenbestands,"* by Wolfgang Boetticher in *ActaM,* 51 (1979), p. 193–203.

Review by Hans Lenneberg in *Notes,* 36 (1979), p. 108; by Jörg Wagner in *Musica,* 33 (1979), p. 74–75; and by Arthur Ness in *JAMS,* 34 (1981), p. 339–45.

1821. Répertoire International des Sources Musicales. Manuscripts of polyphonic music (c. 1320–1400). Edited by Gilbert Reaney. München-Duisburg, G. Henle, 1969. 427 p. (RISM ser. B, vol. 4:2)

Organized as in the preceding volume. Indexes of composers and text incipits. Includes *Supplement of manuscripts to RISM B/IV/1* in alphabetical order by country, town and library with its own indexes to composers and text incipits.

Review by Ernest Sanders in *Music and letters,* 51 (1970), p. 458–59.

1822. Répertoire International des Sources Musicales. Manuscripts of polyphonic music, 11th-early 14th century. Edited by Gilbert Reaney. München-Duisburg: G. Henle, 1969. 876 p. (RISM ser. B, vol. 4:1)

The manuscripts are grouped by nationality of location; described individually with detailed bibliographical references. Thematic incipits in square notation.

1823. Répertoire International des Sources Musicales. Musikhandschriften 1600–1800: Datenbank-Index. Music manuscripts 1600–1800: database index. Manuscrits musicaux 1600–1800: banque de données, index. [1986 ed.] Kassel: Bärenreiter, 1986. 2 microfiches & a 16 p.pamphlet. (RISM, ser. A, pt. II.)

First issued in 1983, also in microfiche.

> Series A/II ... could not be published in book form as originally planned, and indeed could never be published in its entirety as a self-contained catalogue, because of the enormous number of items in it. The Commission Mixte and The Advisory Research Committee accordingly decided on publication in a new form: that of indices only, on microfiche. [pamphlet, p. 5.]

RISM A/II is the part of the international union catalog of music devoted to music attributable to a single composer and preserved in manuscripts dating between 1580 and 1850. The bibliographic approach here is based on individual musical works, rather than bibliographic entities or documents; this means that there will be a principal entry describing each manuscript and then as many analytical entries as are needed to describe the individual works in each manuscript.

RISM A/II is a database and the microfiche indexes distributed by the RISM Sekretariat in Kassel are intended to provide the most commonly needed access points to fuller information in the data base. It is possible, however, to query the data base by other access points and to combine searches. Among the available possibilities are names (composer, librettist, former owners, dedicatee, copyist), musical information (instrumentation, key or mode, genre, musical incipits), text (title, text incipit, text language), physical attributes (type of manuscript, size, format, collation, watermark), provenance, dates, and opus or thematic catalog number. For example, it should be possible to extract entries for works involving a single librettist from a particular geographical region or location; it should be equally possible to discover what works there are written in the 18th century for flute in the key of b-minor. Indeed, it is the specific intention of the RISM Commission Mixte that national organizing bodies will produce catalogs of holdings based on the RISM data base. One such is *Die Musikhandschriften der Benediktiner-Abtei Ottobeuren: Thematischer Katalog* by Gertraut Haberkamp (see no. 2287).

So far, almost 300,000 European worksheets have been provided to the RISM Sekretariat, but only 48,000 of these have been entered into the data base. The U.S. Music Manuscript Inventory based in the Isham Memorial Library of the Loeb Music Library at Harvard University is midway in the cataloging and analysis of the nearly 12,000 American manuscripts qualifying for inclusion in RISM A/II. Queries are accepted by the staffs of the RISM Sekretariat in Kassel and the U.S. for interrogations of the files in their hands. Remote access by BITNET to the U.S. file is projected for the near future.

The microfiche index provides access by composers' names, uniform title, medium of performance, thematic catalog number, opus number, key, location and shelf mark, and RISM control number. Entries in the microfiche index do not include music or text incipits.

The following articles describe the development and principles of the RISM A/II enterprise:

"Computer-Einsatz bei der Serie A/II RISM: Möglichkeiten, Bedingungen, Vorschläge" by Norbert Böker-Heil in *Fontes artis musicae* 22 (1975), p. 86–89;

"The changing face of RISM" by Kurt Dorfmüller in *Fontes artis musicae,* 25 (1978), p. 285–89;

"RISM-Handschriftenkatalogisierung und elektronische Datenverarbeitung (EDV)" by Helmut Rösing in *Fontes artis musicae,* 26 (1979), p. 107–09;

"Zur Katalogisierung von Musikdrucken und Musikhandschriften der Serie A: Konzept und Realisation der Serie A/II des Internationales Quellenlexikon de Musik" by Helmut Rösing in *ActaM,* 51 (1979), p. 184;

"Sinn und Nutzen des Versuchs einer weltweiten Erfassung von Quellen zur Musik" by Helmut Rösing in *Quellenforschung in der Musikwissenschaft,* ed. by Georg Feder (no. 15 in the series *Wolfenbüttler Forschungen* published 1982.)

1824. Répertoire International des Sources Musicales Recueils impremés XVIe-XVIIe siècles. Ouvrage publié sous la direction de François Lesure. I. Liste chronologique. München-Duisburg: G. Henle, [1960–]. 639 p. (RISM ser. B, vol. 1)

This volume is Part I of the systematic-chronological section of a comprehensive bibliography of musical sources currently being compiled under the joint auspices of the International Musicological Society and the International Association of Music Libraries. The present volume supersedes Eitner's *Bibliographie der Musik-Sammelwerke* (no. 1772) and, when completed, the entire *RISM* project will replace his *Quellen-*

Lexikon (no. 1773) as a modern, comprehensive reference tool for locating primary source materials for musical research.

This volume lists collections of music published between 1501 and 1700, with a summary of their contents and with the locations of copies in major European and American libraries. Index of editors and printers, and of titles and authors.

Review by Vincent H. Duckles in *Notes,* 18 (1961), p. 225–27; by Jack A. Westrup in *Music and letters,* 42 (1961), p. 76; by Daniel Heartz in *JAMS,* 14 (1961), p. 268–73; by Gustave Reese in *Fontes artis musicae,* 8 (1961), p. 4–7.

For documentation on U.S. response to the International Inventory, see "RISM: a report on U.S. activities," by Wayne D. Shirley in *Notes,* 23 (1967), p. 477–97.

1825. Répertoire International des Sources Musicales Recueils imprimés XVIIIe siècle. Ouvrage publié sous la direction de François Lesure. München-Duisburg: G. Henle, [1964]. 461 p. (RISM ser. B, vol. 2)

Cites about 1,800 collections printed between 1701 and 1801, giving basic bibliographic descriptions, composers represented, and locations of copies throughout the world. This volume is organized alphabetically by title rather than chronologically as in the preceding entry. Indexes of publishers and printers, and composers' names.

1826. Répertoire International des Sources Musicales Tropen- und Sequenzenhandschriften. Von Heinrich Husmann. München-Duisburg: G. Henle, [1964]. 236 p. (RISM ser. B, vol. 5:1)

A volume of the Inventory set devoted to the manuscript sources of tropes and sequences. Sources grouped by country. Each entry gives information as to the signature, provenance, type of liturgical book, notation, structure of the source, contents, and related literature. Indexes of manuscripts arranged by libraries and by places of origin. Further indexes of places and subjects, names of saints, names of persons. Bibliography.

Review by Edward H. Roesner in *JAMS,* 21 (1968), p. 212–15.

1827. Riaño, Juan F. Critical and bibliographical notes on early Spanish music. . . . London: B. Quaritch, 1887. 154 p.

Reprint by the Da Capo Press, New York, 1971.

Manuscripts and printed music to 1600, classified, giving descriptions and library locations of manuscripts. Numerous facsimile plates.

1828. Riedel, Friedrich W. Quellenkundliche Beiträge zur Geschichte der Musik für Tasteninstrumente in der zweiten Halfte des 17. Jahrhunderts (vornehmlich in Deutschland). Kassel und Basel: Bärenreiter, 1960. 224 p. (Schriften des Landesinstituts für Musikforschung Kiel, 10)

A "source study" concerned with late 17th-century prints and manuscripts of keyboard music, with emphasis on the German school. Numerous useful lists and inventories incorporated into the work, e.g., "Verzeichnis der 1648–1700 im Druck veroffentlichten Musik für Tasteninstrumente" (p. 57–72); "Quellenregister" [Handschriften], p. 219–24.

1829. Rimbault, Edward F. Bibliotheca madrigaliana; a bibliographical account of the musical and poetical works published in England during the 16th and 17th centuries under the titles of madrigals, ballets, ayres, canzonets, etc. London: J. Smith, 1847. 88 p.

Reprint by B. Franklin, New York, (196-?).

An early, and rather faulty, chronological list of vocal music published in England, 1588–1638, giving bibliographical descriptions and contents, source references. First-line index of madrigals and songs. Composer index.

1830. Samuel, Harold E. "Sources, musical (pre-1500)" In the *New Harvard dictionary of music* edited by Don M. Randel. Cambridge, Harvard Univ. Press, 1986. p. 773–78.

A brief but useful listing of some of the major sources of Gregorian chant, secular monophonic and polyphonic music to 1500. Each entry includes citation of more recent literature about the source. Locations of the sources are given with references to modern editions, if any.

1831. Sartori, Claudio. "Finalmente svelati i misteri delle biblioteche italiane." In *Fontes artis musicae,* 2 (1955), p. 15–37; 3 (1956), p. 192–202.

A product of the work on *RISM* in Italy, this article contains a summary report of the holdings of 40 Italian libraries and an alphabetical listing of early printed music newly discovered in these collections.

1832. Sartori, Claudio. Bibliografia della musica strumentale italiana stampata in Italia fino al 1700. Firenze:, L. Olschki, 1952–68. 2 v. (Biblioteca di bibliografia italiana, 23)

Chronological list of instrumental music, collections of vocal music containing one or more instrumental pieces or vocal music with one or more instrumental parts, published in Italy to 1700. Includes a few works by Italian composers published outside Italy. Excludes lute music and dramatic music. Complete bibliographical data, including dedications, prefaces, tables of contents. Composer index.

Review by Dragan Plamenac in *Notes,* 10 (1953), p. 616–19; by Harvey Olnick in *MQ,* 40 (1954), p. 98–102; by Willi Apel in *JAMS,* 7 (1954), p. 84–86; by Richard Schaal in *Die Musikforschung,* 7 (1954), p. 342.

Vol. II. (Volume secondo di aggiunte e correzioni con indici.) Firenze: Leo S. Olschki, 1968. 216 p. (Biblioteca di bibliografia italiana, 56.)

Review by Owen Jander in *Notes,* 26 (1970), p. 738–39, and by Howard M. Brown in *JAMS,* 23 (1970), p. 531–33.

1833. Schanzlin, Hans Peter. "Musik-Sammeldrucke des 16. und 17. Jahrhunderts in schweizerischen Bibliotheken." In *Fontes artis musicae,* 4 (1957), p. 38–42.

1834. Schanzlin, Hans Peter. "Musik-Sammeldrucke des 18. Jahrhunderts in schweizerischen Bibliotheken (I)." In *Fontes artis musicae,* 6 (1959), p. 20–26; (II) ibid., 8 (1961), p. 26–29.

Preliminary reports prepared by the Swiss office of *RISM.*

1835. Scheurleer, Daniel F. Nederlandsche liedboeken; lijst der in Nederland tot het jaar 1800 uitgegevan liedboeken. . . . s'Gravenhage: M. Nijhoff, 1912. 321 p.

Erste supplement, 1923.

A bibliography of song books published in the Netherlands from 1487 to 1800, with or without music, arranged chronologically under main headings of sacred and secular music, with index by author, editor, publisher, main word of title. 3,887 titles in the main work, 660 in the supplement.

1836. Schierning, Lydia. Die Überlieferung der deutschen Orgel- und Klaviermusik aus der 1. Hälfte des 17. Jahrhunderts. Eine quellenkundliche Studie. Kassel: Bärenreiter, 1961. 147 p. (Schriften des Landesinstituts für Musikforschung Kiel, 12)

A source study devoted to the manuscripts of German organ and keyboard music of the first half of the 17th century. Each manuscript is described and the contents inventoried.

1837. Silbiger, Alexander. Italian manuscript sources of 17th-century keyboard music. Ann Arbor: UMI Research Press, 1980. 219 p. (Studies in musicology, 18)

Inter alia an annotated catalog of about 75 manuscripts. Each manuscript is described, but individual works are not listed. Extensive bibliography, an extended essay on the sources, and short studies on seven of the most important composers.

Review by Georgie Durosoir in *Fontes artis musicae,* 28 (1981), p. 330.

1838. Smith, Carleton. "Music manuscripts lost during World War II." In *The Book Collector,* 17 (1968), p. 26–36.

Deals with holographs by Bach, Beethoven, Haydn, Mozart et al. stored in Silesia and now presumably in Wroclaw (formerly Breslau), Poland.

1839. Sonneck, Oscar G. T. A bibliography of early secular American music (18th century). . . . rev. and enl. by W. T. Upton. [Washington, D.C.]: Library of Congress, Music Division, 1945. 617 p.

First published in 1905. Reprinted, with a new preface by Irving Lowens, by Da Capo Press, New York, 1964.

A title list, with full bibliographical descriptions, including first lines of texts. Completely indexed, with lists of composers, first lines, publishers, etc.

Review of the 1964 reprint by Harry Eskew in *Anuario, Inter-American Institute for Musical Research,* 1 (1965), p. 134.

1840. Stevenson, Robert. "Sixteenth and seventeenth century resources in Mexico." In *Fontes artis musicae,* 1 (1954), p. 69–78; 2 (1955), p. 10–15.

The first installment is concerned with the manuscript resources of the Puebla Cathedral music archive, comprising some 365 sacred works by 36 composers. Arranged alphabetically by composer. The second part is a description of a 16th-century manuscript of sacred music in the library of Canon Octaviano Valdes of Mexico City.

1841. Stevenson, Robert Murrell. Renaissance and Baroque musical sources in the Americas. Washington, D.C.: Organization of American States, 1970. 346 p.

Typescript catalog of printed and manuscript works seen in Bogotá, Cuzco, Guatemala City, La Paz, Lima, Mexico City, Montevideo, Morelia, Oaxaca, Puebla Sucre, Buenos Aires, Rio de Janeiro, and Santiago. Music cited from the last 3 locations exceeds the chronological limits into the 20th century. Almost completely lacking in description, although each source is analyzed and many individual works are described. Not indexed or cross referenced. Some of the commentary is idiosyncratic. Corrigenda provided on a separate page.

Review by Samuel Claro Valdédes in *Revista musical Chilena,* 31 (1977), p. 123–24.

1842. Das Tenorlied: mehrstimmige Lieder in deutschen Quellen 1450–1580. Hrsg. vom Deutschen Musikgeschichtlichen Archiv Kassel und vom Staatlichen Institut für Musikforschung Preussischer Kulturbesitz Berlin. Zusammelgestellt und bearbeitet von Norbert Böker-Heil, Harald Heckmann, und Ilse Kindermann. Kassel: Bärenreiter, 1979. 3 v. (Catalogus Musicus, 9 (RISM Sonderband))

A thematic catalog with incipits for each voice, arranged by source (both printed and manuscript) with indexes to text incipits and musical incipits. A most significant achievement made possible through the application of automated data processing techniques.

1843. Thibault, Genèvieve. and Louis Perceau. Bibliographie des poésies de P. de Ronsard mises en musique au XVIe siècle. Paris: E. Droz, 1941. 121 p. (Publications de la Societe Francaise de Musicologie, 2 ser. t. 8)

Chronological bibliography, 1552–1629, of some 148 collections containing musical settings of lyrics by Ronsard. Full bibliographical citations of the collections, with Ronsard settings listed for each. Index of text incipits and of collections and names.

1844. Walther, Hans. Initia carminum ac versuum medii aevi posterioris latinorum. Alphabetisches Verzeichnis der Versanfange mittellateinischer Dichtungen. . . . Göttingen: Vanderhoeck & Ruprecht, 1959. 1,186 p. (Carmina medii aevi posterioris latina, 1)

Not a music bibliography but a most valuable reference tool for musicologists working in the field of medieval studies. An alphabetical index of text incipits for more than 20,000 medieval Latin lyrics, with references to manuscript sources and modern editions. Bibliography of literature; index of names and subjects.

1845. Winternitz, Emanuel. Musical autographs from Monteverdi to Hindemith. Princeton: Princeton Univ. Press, 1955. 2 v.

Reissued by Dover Publications, New York, paperbound edition, 1965. 2 v.

Vol. 1 is devoted to commentary on the plates, with two introductory chapters: ':The written sign" and "The writing act." Vol. 2 contains 196 full-page plates of autographs.

1846. Wolf, Johannes. Handbuch der Notationskunde. I. Teil: Tonschriften des Altertums und des Mittelalters. II. Teil: Tonschriften der Neuzeit,

Tabulaturen, Partitur, Generalbass und Reformversuche. Leipzig: Breit-kopf & Hartel, 1913–19. 2 v. (Kleine Handbucher der Musikgeschichte, 7) Reprinted by Olms, Hildesheim, 1963.

The Wolf Handbuch is cited here on the strength of its useful listings of early manuscript sources connected with the author's discussion of notational practices. For example: "Quellen der *Ars antiqua*" (vol. 1, p. 258–63); "Die *Ars nova*" (vol. 1, p. 351–54); "Handschriftliche Quellen des 15. und 16. Jahrhunderts" (vol. 1, p. 444–65); "Verzeichnis einiger wichtiger deutscher Lautentabulaturen" (vol. 2, p. 47–59); "Italienische Lautentabulaturen" (vol. 2, p. 66–71); "Quellen franzosischer Lautentabulatur" (vol. 2, p. 95–106); "Guitarretabulaturen" (vol. 2, p. 209–18).

1847. Wolfe, Richard J. Secular music in America, 1801–1825. A bibliography. Introduction by Carleton Sprague Smith. New York: New York Public Library, Astor, Lenox and Tilden Foundations, 1964. 3 v.

A major work of bibliography in the field of early American music. Prepared as a continuation of the Sonneck-Upton *Bibliography* (no. 1839). The arrangement is alphabetical by composer. Brief biographies. Full bibliographical descriptions and locations of copies in American libraries and private collections.

Appendices: (1) "Unrecorded 18th-century imprints located during the course of this work." (2) "A list of works in the Sonneck-Upton Bibliography which have been redated into 19th-century." (3)"Locations of newly discovered copies of works in the Sonneck-Upton Bibligraphy." Index of titles; of first lines; of publishers, engravers, and printers; of numbering systems. General index.

Complemented by Fuld and Davidson *18th-century American Secular Music Manuscripts.* (see no. 1779).

Review by James C. Downey in *Anuario of the Inter-American Institute for Musical Research,* 1 (1965), p. 122–24.

1848. Wotquenne, Alfred. Table alphabétique des morceaux mesurés contenus dans les œuvres dramatiques de Zeno, Metastasio, et Goldoni. Leipzig: Breitkopf & Hartel, 1905. 77 p.

An alphabetical first-line index of aria and ensemble texts by Zeno, Metastasio, and Goldoni, citing volume and page numbers in the standard editions of their works and title of the work from which the incipit is derived. Table of librettos by the three authors.

FOLK SONG AND BALLAD

This section should be used in conjunction with the section "Bibliographies of Music Literature: Ethnomusicology," which lists studies and monographs pertaining to folk song and ballad. Here, the emphasis is on the music itself. The user should bear in mind, however, that a work such as Haywood's *Bibliography of North American folklore and folksong* (no. 912) contains numerous entries for music, both printed and on sound recordings. Also relevant in certain respects are such bibliographies as Sear's *Song index* (no. 1439), Fuld's *American popular music* (no. 1551) and the bibliographies by Sonneck-Upton (no. 1839) and by Wolfe (no. 1847) which serve to bridge the uncertain gap between folk and popular song.

1849. Bronson, Bertrand H. The traditional tunes of the Child ballads, with their texts, according to the extant records of Great Britain and Americ. Princeton: Princeton Univ. Press, 1959–1972. 4 v.

Vol. 1: ballads 1–53; vol. 2: ballads 54–113; vol. 3: ballads 114–243; vol. 4: with addenda to vols. 1–4.

A monumental work of scholarship in the field of English-Scottish ballads. Based on the work of Francis J. Child but far exceeding it in scope and authority. The literary and musical traditions of each ballad are discussed, together with a printing of all the known variants both literary and musical.

Review by Klaus Roth in *Jahrbuch für Volksliedforschung,* 13 (1968), p. 228–29. *English and Scottish Popular Ballads*

1850. Brunnings, Florence E. Folk song index; a comprehensive guide to the Florence E. Brunnings Collection. N.Y.: Garland Publishing, 1981. 357 p.

A title index to the 49,399 songs in the printed and recorded anthologies of folk songs in the Brunnings Collection with references from first lines to titles. There is a list of the 1,305 anthologies indexed.

1851. California. University. Department of Music. Check list of California songs. Archive of California folk music. Part I: texts in print. Berkeley: Univ. of California, 1940. 160 leaves (typescript).

Published in connection with a WPA project supervised by Sidney H. Robertson.

A list, alphabetical title, of more than 2,500 songs from texts either published or known to have circulated in California, with an index of first lines. P. 157–60: bibliography of songsters and broadsides.

1852. Chappell, William. Popular music of the olden time. A history of the ancient songs, ballads, and of the dance tunes of England. . . . Reprint by Dover Publictions, Inc., of the original London publication of 1855–59. New York: Dover, 1965. 2 v.

A revision of this work, by H. Ellis Wooldridge, appeared in 1893. This edition was, in turn, reprinted by Jack Brussel, New York, 1961.

Chappell is the classic work on English popular song. It is the basis for the expanded work by Claude Simpson on *The British broadside ballad* (see no. 1855).

1853. Dean-Smith, Margaret. A guide to English folksong collections. . . . Liverpool: University Press of Liverpool, in association with the English Folk Dance and Song Society, 1954. 120 p.

Foreword by Gerald Abraham.

Indexes approximately 62 collections of English folk song, 1822–1952. Main entry is by song title, with cross references from text incipit. Chronological list of collections. Detailed annotations.

Review by Bertrand H Bronson in *JAMS,* 8 (1955), p. 57–58.

1854. Sidel'nikov, Viktor M. Russkaia narodnaia pesnia: bibliograficheskii ukazatel' 1735–1945. Moskva: Izd. Akademii Nauk SSSR, 1962.

At head of title: Akademia Nauk SSSR, Institut mirovoi literatury im. A. M. Gor'kogo.

Part I: texts of folk poetry and folk songs, published in journals, newspapers, etc., with or without music. Part II: books, articles, etc., about Russian folk song. Index of names.

1855. Simpson, Claude M. The British broadside ballad and its music. New Brunswick, N.J.: Rutgers Univ. Press, 1966. 919 p.

An indispensable reference tool for students of English popular song from the 16th through the 18th centuries. Gives music for 540 broadside ballads and traces each melody from its earliest printed and manuscript sources. No ballad texts printed. The work takes its point of departure from William Chappell's *Popular music of the olden time* (1855–59, 2 v.; see no. 1852) but far exceeds Chappell in coverage.

Review by Bertrand H. Bronson in *MQ*, 52 (1966), p. 384–87; by John Ward in *JAMS*, 20 (1967), p. 131–34 (see also Ward's extended commentary "Apropos The British broadside ballad and its music" in the same issue of *JAMS*, p. 28–86); by Walter Woodfill in *Journal of research in music education*, 14 (1955), p. 238–39; by Walter Suppan in *Jahrbuch für Volksliedforschung*, 13 (1968), p. 229–31; by Charles Heywood in *Ethnomusicology*, 11 (1967), p. 133–34.

1856. Sonkin, Annabelle B. Jewish folk-song resources; an annotated bibliography. New York National Jewish Music Council, 1957. 24 *l.*

Somewhat dated, but still useful.

1857. Van der Merwe, F. Z. Suid-Afrikaanse musiekbibliografie 1787–1952. Pretoria, J. L. Van Schaik, 1958. 410 p.

Supplemented by *En 1953–1972 bygewerk vir die Raad vir Geesteswetenskaplike Navorsing deur* Jan van de Graaf. (Kaapstad: Tafelberguitgewers vir die Instituut vir Taal. Lettere en Kuns. Raad vir Geesteswetenskaplike Navorsing, 1974. 297 p.)

A comprehensive bibliography of music related to South Africa (by South African composers wherever published, writings on South African themes or subject matter). The largest part of the citations refer to songs, marches, dance music of a popular nature, although a few studies and monographs are interfiled. Entries are unclassified, arranged alphabetically by composer or author. Index of South African composers and musicians. The language is Afrikaans.

SACRED MUSIC

Many of the items entered in this section are actually editions of Protestant or Catholic liturgical music. At the same time, they qualify as reference books because of the scope and authority of their documentation.

1858. Baumker, Wilhelm. Das katholische deutsche Kirchenlied in seinen Singweisen, von den fruhesten Zeiten bis gegen Ende des 17. Jahrhunderts. Freiburg: Herder'sche Verlagshandlung, 1883–1911. 4 v.

Reprinted from the original by Georg Olms, Hildesheim, 1962.

Baumker's work is the basic study of the German Catholic church song. The main body of the work consists of quotations and discussion of the individual melodies, classified according to the church year or liturgical use. Each volume contains an extensive bibliography, arranged chronologically, of early printed song collections. Entries cover the period from 1470 to 1800. Transcriptions from the prefaces of early song collections are given.

1859. Becker, Carl F. Die Choralsammlungen der verschiedenen christlichen Kirchen. Hildesheim: H. A. Gerstenberg, 1972. 220 p.

Reprint of the edition of F. Fleischer, Leipzig, 1845 ed.

A bibliography of hymnbooks.

1860. Chevalier, Ulysse. Repertorium hymnologicum. Catalogue des chants, hymnes, proses, séquences, tropes en usage dans l'eglise latine depuis les origines jusqu'è nos jours. Louvain: 1892–1920. 6 v.

The standard bibliography of Latin rhymed poetic texts for liturgical use. A 315 p. volume of additions and emendations was prepared by Clemens Blume under the title *Repertorium Repertorii, Leipzig, 1901.*

The Repertorium has been reprinted by Bollandistes, 1959; the Blume supplement by Olms, Hildesheim, 1971.

1861. Cunningham, W. Patrick. The music locator. Saratoga: Resource Publications, 1976. 187 p.

A computer-generated index to over 12,800 songs usable in Christian worship by title and composer. The main list is classified and entries in it supply information on year of publication, format, style and publisher.

1862. Diehl, Katharine S. Hymns and tunes—an index. Metuchen: Scarecrow Press, 1966. 1,242 p.

A comprehensive finding tool for anyone interested in locating or identifying a Protestant hymn or hymn tune. Approach offered through first lines of text, authors, tune names, composers, and by melodies given in alphabetical notation. The texts are almost exclusively English. Appendices include a glossary and a chronological list of hymnals indexed.

1863. Ellinwood, Leonard W. Bibliography of American hymnals compiled from the files of the Dictionary of American hymnology a project of the Hymn Society of Americ. Elizabeth Lockwood, associate editor.

New York : University Music Editions, c1983. 27 microfiche.

Lists 7,500 entries for hymnals in all languages using the Roman alphabet; includes non-demoninational collections. Eye-readable contents-guides on sheets in pockets with microfiches in binder.

1864. Ellinwood, Leonard W. Dictionary of American hymnology; first line index. A project of the Hymn Society of Americ. New York: University Music Editions, 1984. 179 reels.

Accompanied by printed guide consisting of the front matter and pages 1–26 of the Introduction (Reel 001). These pages provide the useful detail neded in using first-line index. There are "Essays on hymns with confused authorship" on p. 27–118 on reel 001.

1865. Foster, Myles B. Anthems and anthem composers, an essay upon the development of the anthem from the time of the Reformation to the end of the 19th century; with a complete list of anthems (in alphabetical order) belonging to each of the four centuries. . . . London: Novello, 1901. 225 p.
Reprint by Da Capo Press, New York, 1970.

1866. Frost, Maurice. English and Scottish psalm and hymn tunes, c. 1543–1677. London: Oxford Univ. Press, 1953. 531 p.
P. 3–50: a bibliography of English-Scottish "Old Version" psalters from 1556 to 1677, with full descriptions and lists of contents. The main body of the work is an edition of 457 psalm tunes or harmonized versions thereof.
For an index to this work compiled by Kirby Rogers, see no. 3193.

1867. Higginson, J. Vincent. Handbook for American Catholic hymnals. New York: Hymn Society of America, 1976. 334 p.
A complex work presenting information (text, themes, sources, composers, authors and bibiliography) in several sections arranged by use in the church year. There are indexes to composers, authors, tune names, and first lines.

1868. Kirsch, Winfried. Die Quellen der mehrstimmigen Magnificat- und Te Deum-Vertonungen bis zur Mitte des 16. Jahrhunderts. Tutzing: Hans Schneider, 1966. 588 p.
Review by James Erb in *JAMS*, 22 (1969), p. 122–25; by Martin Just in *Die Musikforschung*, 21 (1968), p. 523–24.

1869. Laster, James H. Catalogue of choral music arranged in Biblical order. Metuchen: Scarecrow Press, 1983. 261 p.
Anthems arranged in order from Genesis to Revelation according to Biblical passage, including those with texts from the Apocrypha. Citations include information about performing forces necessary, publisher and date of publication. There is a short addendum and a composer index.

1870. Laster, James H . . . Catalogue of vocal solos and duets arranged in Biblical order. Metuchen: Scarecrow Press, 1984. 204 p.
Works arranged in order from Genesis to Revelation.

1871. Mason, Henry L. Hymn-tunes of Lowell Mason: a bibliography. New York: AMS Press, 1976. 118 p.
Reprint of the 1944 ed. published by University Press, Cambridge, Mass.
A bibliography of the hymn tunes of the prolific 19th century American composer.

1872. Metcalf, Frank Johnson. American psalmody; or titles of books containing tunes printed in America from 1721 to 1820. New introduction by Harry Eskew. New York: Da Capo Press, 1968.

An unabridged republication of the first edition published in New York in 1917.

Review by Richard A. Crawford in *Notes,* 26 (1969), p. 42–43.

1873. Parks, Edna D. Early English hymns: an index. Metuchen: Scarecrow Press, 1972. 168 p.

Lists 1,157 hymns from some 51 hymnals and psalters and other sources. No music is given, but the tune names are identified and metrical structure is given.

1874. Protestant Episcopal Church in the U.S.A. Joint Commission on Church Music. Service music and anthems for the nonprofessional choir. Greenwich, Connecticut: Seabury Press, 1955. 56 p.

Service music classified by liturgical use; anthems by the church year. Information includes degree of difficulty, number of parts, presence of solos, type of accompaniment, publisher, and number in series.

1875. Rado, Polykarpe. Repertoire hymnologique des manuscrits liturgiques dans les bibliothèques publiques de Hongrie. Budapest: Stephaneum Nyomda, 1945. 59 p. (Az országos széchenyi könyvtár kiadványai, 20)

Alphabetical listing of 727 hymns found in 146 liturgical manuscripts in libraries in Hungary.

1876. Répertoire International des Sources Musicales. Das Deutsche Kirchenlied, DKL: kritische Gesamtausgabe der Melodien herausgegeben von Konrad Ameln, Markus Jenny und Walther Lipphardt. Kassel: Bärenreiter, 1975–80. 2 v. (RISM, ser B., pt. VIII, 1–2)

Contents: Bd. 1, T. 1. Verzeichnis der Drucke.—Bd. 1, T. 2. Register.

"This volume comprises the catalog of traceable printed sources of German hymns, of all denominations, that contain at least one melody in musical notation." The entries are arranged in chronological order and consist of title page transcriptions including imprint, format and dimensions, and bibliographical references when necessary. The second part includes indexes to titles, names of persons, place names, printers and publishers, and the *DKL* symbols. There is also an afterword and corrigenda.

Review in *Die Musikforschung,* 30 (1977), p. 83–84.

1877. Rogal, Samuel J. "A bibliographical survey of American hymnody, 1640–1800" in *Bulletin of the New York Public Library,* (Winter 1975), p. 231–252.

1878. Rogal, Samuel J. Sisters of sacred song: a selected listing of women hymnodists in Great Britain and Americ. N.Y.; London: Garland, 1981. 162 p.

Lists women hymnodists and their hymns, classifying them by nationality and denominations. Cites collections of hymns. Title index to hymns cited.

1879. Schreiber, Max. Kirchenmusik von 1500–1600, Originaldrucke und Manuskripte chronologisch zusammengestellt. . . . [Regensburg]: Druckerei St. Georgsheim Birkeneck, 1932. 88 p.

Chronological list of 16th-century sacred music, printed and manuscript sources. Entered alphabetically by composer under year of issue. Brief titles, and locations in British and continental libraries. Index of composers and classified index of forms.

1880. Schreiber, Max. Kirchenmusik von 1600–1700, Originaldrucke und Manuskripte chronologisch zusammengestellt. . . . [Regensburg]: Druckerei St. Georgsheim Birkeneck, 1934. 184 p.

Treats 17th-century sacred music as in the entry above.

1881. Spencer, Donald Amos. Hymn and Scripture selection guide: a cross-reference of scripture and hymns with over 12,000 references for 380 hymns and gospel songs. Valley Forge: Judson Press, 1977. 176 p.

An index relating biblical text to hymns.

1882. Stellhorn, Martin H. Index to hymn preludes . . . and other organ compositions, based on hymns, chorales, and carols. A listing of 2,200 selections of various publishers according to key, difficulty, and length. St. Louis: Concordia Publishing House, [1948]. 151 p.

1883. Szövérffy, Joseph. Repertorium hymnologicum novum. Berlin: Classical Folia Editions, 1983– . (Publications of the Archives for medieval poetry ; v. 1, etc.)

"Das Repertorium novum will Chevaliers altes Werk (Repertorium hymnologicum) ersetzen und mit neuem Material bereichern" (from the introduction). (This work corrects and supplements Chevalier's *Rpertorium hymnologicum* and Blume's *Repertorium.*)

Contents: T. 1, Bd. 1. Einführung und alphabetisches Verzeichnis. Religiöse Dichtung als Kulturphänomen und Kulturleistung.

1884. Thuner, O. E. Dansk Salme-Leksikon: Haandbog i dansk Salmesang. En hymnologisk Sammenstilling af Ord og Toner med historiske og bibliografiske Oplysninger. København: O. Lohse, 1930. 592 p.

Lists 1,108 Danish psalm settings, with detailed information as to sources of texts and music. Index of melody groups, personal names, first lines of texts.

1885. Wackernagel, Philipp. Bibliographie zur Geschichte des deutschen Kirchenliedes im XVI. Jahrhundert. Frankfurt am Main: 1855. 718 p.

Unaltered reprint of the original edition by Georg Olms, Hildesheim, 1961.

A chronological listing of 1,050 editions of German sacred song published during the 16th century. Detailed bibliographical descriptions, with annotations. Transcriptions given of the introductions to 110 of the collections.

1886. Wackernagel, Philipp. Das deutsche Kirchenlied von der ältesten Zeit bis zu Anfang des 17. Jahrhunderts. Mit Berücksichtigung der deutschen kirchlichen Liederdichtung im weiteren Sinne und der lateinischen von Hilarius bis Georg Fabricius und Wolfgang Ammonius. Leipzig: Teubner, 1864–1877. 5 v.

Reprinted by Olms, Hildesheim 1964.
Includes bibliographical references.

1887. Zahn, Johannes. Die Melodien der deutschen evangelischen Kirchenlieder aus den Quellen geschopft und mitgeteilt. . . . Gutersloh: Bertelsmann, 1889–93. 6 v.

Reprint of the original edition by Olms, Hildesheim, 1963.

Zahn is primarily an edition presenting 8,806 melodies, derived from the earliest sources, for the German Protestant liturgy. Classified according to metrical form.

Vol. 5, p. 307–494: biographical notices of 463 chorale composers or editors of chorale collections. Index of composers; first-line index of texts.

Vol. 6: a bibliography of 1,408 items listing the sources of the melodies and arranged chronologically from 1507 to 1892, with locations of copies in the principal European libraries. Further supplements give non-German sources and manuscript sources.

Catalogs of Music Libraries
and Collections

A knowledge of the published catalogs of the major music libraries and collections is essential for locating source materials for study or research. Access to this information has been made immeasurably easier by the *Directory of music research libraries,* published under the auspices of the International Association of Music Libraries (see no. 1889 below) as *Series C of RISM.* This work supplies international coverage for music libraries in Europe, North America and other parts of the world. Substantial lists of libraries are found in *MGG* (by Alfons Ott) and in *The New Grove,* although the former is out of date. The German music libraries are separately described and their catalogs cited in Richard Schaal's *Führer durch deutsche Musikbibliotheken,* 1971 (see no. 2067), and Claudio Sartori has done likewise for the Italian institutions in a 1971 issue of *Fontes artis musicae* (see no. 2117).

The following section covers the catalogs of the principal music libraries of the world and also includes a number of important exhibition catalogs, although we have made no effort to be comprehensive in the latter category. Excluded are the auction or sale catalogs of music collections that have been dispersed—with a few exceptions such as the famous Wolffheim catalog (no. 2524), which is itself a bibliographical tool of first importance.

It goes without saying that a great many musical source materials have never been cited in special music catalogs. Information must be sought in general library catalogs of early printed books and manuscripts. Descriptions of the music manuscripts in the Bodleian Library at Oxford, for example, must be extracted from the seven volumes of Madan's *Summary catalogue of Western manuscripts in the Bodleian library . . .* (1895–1953). Likewise, Cambridge University music manuscripts are fully described in the series of college library catalogs compiled by Montague Rhodes James. No attempt has been made here to cite general catalogues of this kind, but the reader's attention may be called to the invaluable guide to Latin manuscript books before 1600, a list of the printed catalogues and unpublished inventories of extant collections by Paul Kristeller (rev. ed., Fordham Univ. Press, 1960). The search for sources has, of course, been greatly facilitated by the continuing appearance of volumes in the series *Répertoire International des Sources Musicales* and related volumes deriving from the large store of information in the offices of the RISM-Sekretariat in Frankfurt.

In the present list the catalogs have been grouped, as far as is possible, by place. Place is ordinarily designated as a city followed by the appropriate country (or state in the case of the United States). Certain national union catalogs or descriptions of the holdings of several libraries within a country are entered under the name of the country in small capital letters (GERMANY, GREAT BRITAIN, SWEDEN, etc.).

There are a few catalogs of important collections that remain in private hands or that have been dispersed or changed their locations in recent years: the Hirsch, Cortot, and Wolffheim collections are examples. These catalogs are grouped in a special category at the end of this section; see nos. 2500–2524.

The first two entries of this chapter, nos. 1888 and 1889 provide substantial information about research music libraries, their holdings, and their catalogs. The second entry is for an international directory of music research libraries issued under the auspices of the Internation Association of Music Libraries and issued as Series C of *RISM*. The first entry supplements the second.

1888. **"Libraries"** in *The New Grove Dictionary of Music and Musicians,* edited by Stanley Sadie, v. 10, p. 719–821, by Rita Benton, Mary Wallace Davidson, Samuel Claro, Catherine Dower, José Ignacio Perdomo Escobar, Norma González, Francesco Curt Lange, Mercedes Resi Pequeno, Robert Stevenson, Pola Suárez Urturbey, Dorothy Freed, Werner Gallusser, Don Harran, Katharine A. Haslam, James Siddons. London: Macmillan, 1980.

After a discussion of the history and various functions and types of music libraries, there follows a geographically organized survey of music libraries. There is a introductory paragraph on each country's music libraries which occasionally cites the principal means of access to music bibliographic records for that country. Each entry in the survey describes the library's history and holdings as well as citing any literature about the library, including catalogs. This survey supplements the *RISM* series C *Directories* and provides information to libraries in countries not yet covered by those directories. The article covers only institutional libraries.

Includes a directory of national music information centers.

1889. **Répertoire International des Sources Musicales.** Directory of music research libraries. Rita Benton, general editor. Kassel; New York: Bärenreiter, 1983– . (RISM, ser. C)

The continuation and re-editions of the International Association of Music Libraries, Commission on Research Libraries *Directory.*

Contents:

v. 1: *Canada* [edited by] Marian Kahn and Helmut Kallmann. *United States [edited by]* Charles Lindahl. 2nd rev. ed.

v. 4: *Australia* [edited by] Cecil Hill. *Israel* [edited by] Katya Manor. *Japan* [edited by] James Siddons. *New Zealand* [edited by] Dorothy Freed.

v. 5: *Czechoslovakia; Hungary; Poland* [edited by] James B. Moldovan. *Yugoslavia* [edited by] Lillian Pruett.

As did their predecessors, these Directories provide very full information on the collections, services, and literature about libraries holding significant holdings for musical research. The bibliographies of catalogues, articles, and other descriptive pieces have been found again and again to be uniquely useful.

See Maurice Esses *"New information concerning some music research libraries in Spain,"* in *Fontes artis musciae,* 26 (1979), p. 189–91, which serves as a supplement to the volume including Spain.
V. 4 reviewed by Harold J. Diamond in *Notes,* 36 (1980), p. 660–61.

AARHUS, DENMARK

1890. Clausen, Per Groth. Dansk Musik; Katalog over Statsbibliothek samling af trykte musikalier. Danish music; a catalog of printed music in the State and University Library, Aarhus. Aarhus: Universitetsforlaget, 1977. 316 p.
A classified catalog of the Danish printed music in the Aarhus collections as of 1975. Entries give publisher, opus number, and number of pages. Index to names cited in the classified catalog. There is an alphabetical list of composers and titles not listed in the classified catalog but available at the University in an "unbound" collection.

1891. Statsbibliotek. Musikalier. Udenlandsk musik. 2. udg. Aarhus: Aarhus Statsbiblioteketsforlaget, 1951–1970. 4 v.
Volume 1 covers collections and music for one instrument. Volume 2 covers chamber music and orchestral music. Volume 3 covers vocal music, dramatic music, and folk music. Volume 4 is a supplement to the first three and contains an index to composers.

1892. Statsbilioteket. Fagkataloger (redigeret af Erling Winkel og Ingeborg Heilmann). 2. forogede udg. Aarhus: Aarhus Stiftsbogtrykkerie, 1946–57. 4 v.
Three volumes cover scores; one, music literature. Entries for scores include collections and separate publications, with contents given for collections.

ABERDEEN, SCOTLAND

1893. Cooper, B. A. R. "Catalogue of early printed music in Aberdeen libraries" in *R.M.A. Research Chronicle,* 14 (1978), p. 2–138.
Covers holdings of the University Library, the Library of the University Music Department, and the Aberdeen City Public Library. Updates the *British Union Catalogue of Early Music* and *RISH*; provides 800 entries, of which 100 seem to be unique. Arranged alphabetically by main entry (author or title). Entries occasionally provide annotations. Appendices: writings on music; volumes containing plainsong; private collections; chronological index. Index to genres. index of publishers.

ADRIA, ITALY

1894. Cattedrale, Archivio, Fondo Musicale. "Il fondo musicale dell'Archivio della Chiesa Cattedrale di Adria: Elenco" by Ivano Cavallini in *Fontes artis musicae,* 27 (1980), p. 84–91.
An inventory of early printed editions and manuscripts, most of the 19th century.

AGEN, FRANCE

1895. Archives Communales. Inventaire sommaire des Archives communales antérieures à 1790. Lot-et-Garonne. Supplement à la série II: Bibliothèque d'ouvrages de musique provenant du château des ducs d'Aiguillon. [Rédigé par MM. M. Bosvieux et G. Tholin]. PAris: P. Dupont, 1884. 26 p. (Collection des inventaires sommaire des archives départementales antérieures à 1790)

Aldrich, Richard. A catalogue of books. . . . See No. 1991.

AMSTERDAM, HOLLAND

1896. Toonkunst-Bibliotheek. Catalogus van de uitleen-afdeling. Amsterdam-Zuid: Toonkunst-Bibliotheek, 1968. 43 p.
Catalog of a loan collection of music for performance in the Amsterdam municipal library. Classified by performance forces. Index of names.

1897. Vereniging Voor Nederlandse Muziekgeschiedenis. Bibliotheek. Catalogus van de bibliotheek der Vereniging voor Nederlandse Muziekgeschiedenis. Amsterdam: G. Alsbach, 1919. 274 p.
Classified catalog, including both early and recent works. Contains a special section of manuscripts. Index of names and titles.

ANN ARBOR, MICHIGAN

1898. University of Michigan. "The University of Michigan's purchase of the Stellfeld music library." By Louise E. Cuyler, Gordon A. Sutherland, and Hans T. David. In *Notes*, , 12 (1954), p. 41–57.
Describes Michigan's acquisition of the collection of the jurist, musicologist, and collector Dr. J. A. Stellfeld of Antwerp. Hans David gives a brief summary of some of the important holdings of the library. Eight facsimile plates.

AOSTA, ITALY

1899. Cattedrale. Biblioteca Capitolare. Il fondo musicale della Biblioteca Capitolare di Aosta [di] Giogio Chatrian. Torino: Centro Studi Piemontesi, Fondo "Carlo Felice Bona," 1985. 252 p.
A classified catalog of manuscripts and printed works. Dedications are transcribed in full and anthologies are analyzed. Extensive introductory essay on the cathedral and the collection. Name index.

ARLINGTON, TEXAS

1900. University of Texas. Garrett Library. "Sheet music related to the United States war with Mexico (1846–1848) in the Jenkins Garrett Library, University of Texas at Arlington" by Elise K. Kirk in *Notes,* 37 (1981), p. 15–30.
An inventory arranged by composer, providing information on other

copies at the Beinecke Library of Yale University, the Lilly Library of Indiana University, and the Library of Congress.

ASSISI, ITALY

1901. La Cappella della Basilica di S. Francesco. Biblioteca. Catalogo del fondo musicale nella Biblioteca Comunale di Assisi, a cura di Claudio Sartori. Milano: Istituto Editoriale Italiano, 1962. 449 p. (Bibliotheca musicae, 1.)

Expands the work of Francesco Pennacchi published in the series *Associazione dei musicologi italiani* (see no. 2112). Lists early printed music, books, and manuscripts separately. Most of the material is pre-1800, but a few 19th-century manuscripts are included. Entries give contents of early items, locations for rarities. Descriptive annotations.

Review by Walther Durr in *Die Musikforschung,* 18 (1965), p. 83–84.

ATLANTA, GEORGIA

1902. Emory University. Woodruff Library. "Confederate sheet music at Robert W. Woodruff Library, Emory University" by Frank W. Hoogerwerf in *Notes,* 34 (1978), p. 7–26.

A check-list of Emory's collection of Confederate sheet music arranged by title.

AUGSBURG, GERMANY

1903. Schaal, Richard. Das Inventar der Kantoriei St. Anna in Augsburg. Ein Beitrag zur protestantischen Musikpflege im 16. und beginnenden 17. Jahrhundert. Kassel: Barenreiter, 1965. 107 p. (Catalogus Musicus, 3)

Transcription of an inventory compiled in the early 17th century of the music collection of the Lutheran church and school of St. Anna in Augsburg. The collection itself is no longer intact.

1904. Schletterer, Hans M. Katalog der in der Kreis- und Stadtbibliothek dem Städtischen Archive und der Bibliothek des Historischen Vereins zu Augsburg befindlichen Musikwerke. Augsburg: Fidelis Butsch Sohn, 1879. 138 p. (Monatsheft fur Musikgeschichte, Beilage, Jahrgang 10–11, 1878–79.)

1905. Staats- und Stadtbibliothek. Handschriften der Staats- und Stadtbibliothek Augsburg. Band I: Die Musikhandschriften der Staats- und Stadtbibliothek Augsburg (einschliesslich der Litürgica mit Notation). Beschreiben von Clytus Gottwald. Wiesbaden: Otto Harassowitz, 1974. 328 p.

A catalog providing extensive descriptions and full analytical entries of musical manuscripts in the state and city library of Augsburg. Index to names, places, and things. Index of first lines and titles. List of prior owners. Facsimile pages.

BAD TÖLZ.

1906. PfarrKirchen Indersdorf. Thematischer Katalog der Musikhandschriften der Benediktinerinnenabtei Frauenwörth und der Pfarrkirchen Indersdorf, Wasserburg am Inn und Bad Tölz. Unter d. Leitung von Robert Münster, bearb. von Ursula Bockholdt, Robert Machold u. Lisbet Thew. München: G. Henle, 1975. 211 p. (Kataloge bayerischer Musiksammlungen)

BADAJOZ, SPAIN

1907. Monasterio de Guadalupe. Catalogo del archivo musical del Monasterio de Guadalupe, por El. P. Dr. Archangel Barrado, O.F.M., Bibliotecario y maestro de capilla. Badajoz: 1945. 181 p.
Catalog of a collection of accompanied sacred vocal music, chiefly late 18th century. 947 items, preceded by an historical study of the archive. Index of composers, and of musical forms.

BALTIMORE, MARYLAND

1908. Milton S. Eisenhower Library. Guide to the Lester S. Levy collection of sheet music. Baltimore: Milton S. Eisenhower Library, Johns Hopkins University, 1984. 40 p.
An introduction to one of the most extensive collections of sheet music in the United States.

BARCELONA, SPAIN

1909. Diputación Provincial. Biblioteca Central. Catàlech de la Biblioteca Musical . . . per en Filipe Pedrell. Barcelona: Palau de la Diputació, 1908–1909. 2 v.
Classified catalog of 1,271 entries, including theory, history, practical music. Full bibliographical entries, collations, extensive notes, facsimiles, and musical quotations. Items listed by signature number, with an alphabetical index in vol. 2.

1910. Diputación Provincial. Biblioteca Central. La música española desde la edad media hasta nuestros días; catálogo de la exposición histórica . . . por Higinio Anglés. Barcelona: Diputación Provincial de Barcelona, Biblioteca Central, 1941. 82 p.
Exhibition catalog commemorating the centennial of the birth of Filipe Pedrell. 171 items, manuscripts and printed books, associated with the history of Spanish music, assembled from a number of collections. Chronological arrangement, full entries, 52 facsimiles.

BASEL, SWITZERLAND

1911. Kunstmuseum. Strawinsky: Sein Nachlass. Sein Bild. Kunstmuseum Basel in zusammenarbeit mit der Paul Sacher Stiftung Basel. Basel: Kunstmuesum, 1984. 386 p.
Publication on the occasion of the 1st exhibition of the Stravinsky collection after it was acquired by the Paul Sacher Stiftung in 1983.

Includes a list of manuscripts by Igor Stravinsky in the Sacher Stiftung (p. 33–42) and facsimiles & photographs. Essays by Hans Jörg Jans, Albi Rosenthal, Jacques Handschin, Leo Schrade, Hans Oesch, Christian Geelhaar, Hugo Wagner, and James Lord.

Some copies have tipped in: *Strawinsky: Sein Nachlass. Sein Bild.— Katalog der ausgestellten Bildnisse un Entwürfe für die Ausstattung seiner Bühnenwerke* (which cites the 272 items displayed in the exhibit); and *Programm und Ansprachen des Eröffnungsaktes in Stadttheater Basel 5. June 1984, 17.00 Uhr* (which includes the remarks of Christian Geelhaar, Theodore Stravinsky, Albi Rosenthal, and Paul Sacher).

Albi Rosenthal's essay in this volume, "Der Strawinsky-Nachlass in der Paul Sacher Stiftung," is complemented by an excellent article by John Shepard, "The Stravinsky *Nachlass*: a provisional checklist of music manuscripts," which appeared in *Notes*, 40 (1984), p. 719–50. Shepard provides a brief introduction to the collection of sketches, scores, clippings, letters, and many other documents as well as a very useful checklist of music manuscripts in the Stravinsky *Nachlass*. Each entry in the checklist provides reasonably full description of the various versions of the work in the collection.

1912. Öffentliche Kunstsammlung. Musikhandschriften in Basel : aus verschiedenen Sammlungen: Ausstellung im Kunstmuseum Basel vom 31. Mai bis zum 13. Juli 1975. Veranstaltet vom Kunstmuseum Basel in Verbindung mit einer ad hoc gebildeten Ausstellungskommission ; Katalog, Tilman Seebass; Ausstellung, Yvonne Boerlin-Brodbeck und Tilman Seebass]. Basel: Kunstmuseum, 1975. 99 p.

193 items from Praetorius to Stockhausen with informative descriptions. Numerous facsimiles.

1913. Paul Sacher Stiftung. Komponisten des 20. Jahrhunderts in der Paul Sacher Stiftung. Basel: Paul Sacher Stiftung, 1986. 462 p.

Diese Publikation erscheint aus Anlass der Eröffnung der damit verbundenen Austellung *"Die Musik des 20. Jahrhunderts in der Paul Sacher Stiftung" im Kunstmuseum Basel, 25. April bis 20. Juli 1986*

"Vorrede" by Paul Sacher. "Die Paul Sacher Stiftung in der Öffentlichkeit zu Ausstellung und Publikation" by Hans Jörg Jans. "Enstehung und Zicle der Paul Sacher Stiftung" by Albi Rosenthal.

The exhibition included not only 20th-century manuscripts, but also Bach and Handel autographs.

The book consists of 47 essays on composers and works displayed; there are English summaries of each article. Includes Die Genere des Webern-Archivs" by Hans Moldenhauer, "Komponisten des 20. Jahrhunderts in der Paul Sacher Stiftung; Katalog in alphabetischer Reihenfolge" by Felix Myer and Sabine Stumpfl, which includes entries for individual manuscripts and for entire collections. The collection of the Sacher Stiftung includes autograph compositions, sketches, photographs, letters, essays, and other documentation. There are important collections of the following composers: Conrad Beck, Luciano Berio, Pierre Boulez, Bruno Maderna, Frank Martin, Igor Stravinsky, and Anton Webern.

1914. Paul Sacher Stiftung. Musikhandschriften aus der Sammlung Paul Sacher; Festschrift zu Paul Sachers siebsigstem Geburtstag. In Verbinding mit Ernst Lichtenhahn und Tilman Seebass von F. Hoffmann-La Roche & Co. Basel: Éditions Roche, 1976. 197 p.

In addition to a number of facsimiles of manuscripts in the Sammlung Sacher, there is a "Katalog sämtlicher Musikhandschriften der Sammlung Paul Sacher", p. 47–79.

1915. Universität. Bibliothek. Katalog der Musik-Sammlung auf der Universitäts-Bibliothek in Basel (Schweiz) ... von Julius Richter. Leipzig: Breitkopf & Härtel, 1892. 104 p. (Beilage. Monatshefte für Musikgeschichte. Jahrgang 23–24.)

Full descriptions, contents, musical quotations for manuscripts and early printed music in the university library.

1916. Universität. Bibliothek. Katalog der Musikabteilung der Öffentlichen Bibliothek der Universität Basel und in ihr enthaltenen Schweizerischen Musikbibliothek. Band I: Musikalische Kompositionen. Hrsg. von Edgar Refardt. Basel: Universitäts-Bibliothek, 1925. 141 p.

Works listed in alphabetical order by composer; important collections analyzed. Separate listing of collections, followed by a summary of the contents of several manuscript collections of music by Swiss composers. Index of editors, arrangers, librettists.

1917. Universität. Bibliothek. Thematischer Katalog der Instrumentalmusik des 18. Jahrhunderts in den Handschriften der Universitätsbibliothek Basel. Von Edgar Refardt. Bern: P. Haupt, 1957. 59 p. (Publikationen der Schweizerischen Musikforschenden Gesellschaft, ser. 2, v. 6.)

The major part of this collection was assembled by the Basel silk manufacturer Lucas Sarasin (1730–1802). Some 473 of the works cited were once part of his library. With these are incorporated the collection of the Basel *Collegium musicum* and that of the de Pury family. References are made to 18th-century printings of the works here found in manuscript.

1918. Universität. Bibliothek. Catalog der Schweizerischen Musikbibliothek. Hrsg. von der Öffentlichen Bibliothek der Universität Basel. I. Musikgeschichtliche und theoretische Werke. Basel: E. Birkhauser, 1906. 39 p.

A collection of music literature. The catalog of music which was to form vol. 2 was issued as vol. 1 of the library's *Katalog der Musikabteilung der Offentlichen Bibliothek* ... (see no. 1916).

BATH, ENGLAND

1919. Holburne of Menstrie Museum Science and music in eighteenth century Bath: an exhibition in the Holburne of Menstrie Museum, Bath, 22 September 1977–29 December 1977; catalogue by Anthony J. Turner, with the assistance of I. D. Woodfield (section III) and contributions by H. S. Torrens. Bath: University of Bath, 1977. 131 p.

Covering 212 items relating to the 18th-century astronomer and musician Sir William Herschel. Bibliography.

BAVARIA

1920. Kataloge Bayerischer Musiksammlungen. Hrsg. von der Generaldirektion der Bayerischen staatlichen Bibliotheken. Thematischer Katalog der Musikhandschriften der ehemaligen Klosterkirchen Weyarn, Tegernsee, und Benediktburn. Hrsg. von Robert Munster und Robert Machald. München: Henle, 1971. 196 p.

Records the holdings of Bavarian cloisters and abbeys, catalogs of which are maintained in the Bavarian State Library in Munich.

1921. Musik in Bayern. I. Bayerische Musikgeschichte, Überblick und Einzeldarstellungen. Hrsg. von Robert Münster und Hans Schmid. II. Ausstellungskatalog Augsburg, Juli bis Oktober 1972. Hrsg. von Folker Göthel. Tutzing: Hans Schneider, 1972. 2 v.

Vol. I is a collection of essays on various aspects of Bavarian music history; vol. II is an exhibition catalog of 850 items illustrative of Bavarian musical history and culture. Numerous facsimile plates.

1922. Münster, Robert. "Die Erfassung von Musikhandschriften aus nichtstaatlichem Besitz in Bayern," in *Mitteilungen für die Archivpflege in Bayern,* 12 (1966) Heft 2, p. 45ff.

Describes the seizing of private collections of privately owned collections of musical autographs.

BELGIUM

Borren, Charles van den. "Inventaire des manuscrits de musique polyphonique qui se trouve en Belgique." See no. 1744.

BEREA, OHIO

1923. Balwin-Wallace College. Riemenschneider Memorial Bach Library. Catalog of the Emilie and Karl Riemenschneider Memorial Bach Library. Ed. by Sylvia W. Kenney. New York; Columbia Univ. Press, 1960. 295 p.

A numbered catalog of 2,537 items, of which the first 520 are writings on Bach and his time. No. 521–31: music of Bach's sons and contemporaries. No. 532 to end: music of J. S. Bach. The principal grouping is by musical forms; manuscripts listed separately. Index of cantatas, and general index.

Two *Supplemental catalogs,* compiled by J. B. Winzenburger, have been issued to members of the Riemenschneider Bach Institute (Dec. 1970 and Jan. 1972). Current acquisitions reported in the periodical *Bach,* 1970– .

Review by Walter Emery in *Music and letters,* 42 (1961), p. 376–77.

BERGAMO, ITALY

1924. Biblioteca Civica. Il fondo musicale Mayr della Biblioteca Civica di Bergamo, nel secondo centenario della nascita di Giovanni Simone Mayr (1763–1963). Ed. Arrigo Gazzaniga. Bergamo: Edizioni "Monumenta Bergomensia," 1963. 149 p. (Monumenta bergomensia, 11)

A classified catalog of works by Simone Mayr and his contemporaries in the Biblioteca Civica in Bergamo. Chiefly manuscripts, including many autographs. 24 p. of facsimiles.

1925. Il Museo Donizettiano. Catalogo. Bergamo: Centro di Studi Donizettiani, 1970. 273 p.

First published in 1936.

The present edition gives a brief historical introduction, followed by a tabulation of important Donizetti performances between 1946 and 1969.

The *Catalogo* (p. 53–273) is subdivided into six sections: (1) autographs and manuscripts, (2) musical publications, (3) theatrical publications, (4) letters and documents, (5) iconography, and (6) artifacts.

BERKELEY, CALIFORNIA

1926. California. University. Catalog of the opera collections in the Music Libraries: University of California, Berkeley [and] University of California, Los Angeles. Boston: G. K. Hall, 1983. 697 p.

Photo-offset duplication of the main entry cards in each library representing substantial collections of opera scores. Divided into sections for each library; the Berkeley portion is further sub-divided into operas and dramatic music for children. Cataloging for the Berkeley collection was subsequently entirely revised to meet contemporary cataloging standards and entered into the scores file of the Research Libraries Information Network (RLIN) of the Research Libraries Group (RLG) in the period 1984–1986.

1927. University of California. Music Library. "Musique classique française à Berkeley: pièces inédites de Louis Couperin, Lebègue, La Barre, etc." By Alan Curtis. In *Revue de musicologie*, 55 (1969), p. 123–64.

Describes and inventories 14 manuscripts of French music, chiefly keyboard, of the late 17th and early 18th centuries in the Music Library of the University of California at Berkeley.

1928. University of California. Music Library. Autograph manuscripts of Ernest Bloch at the University of California. Berkeley: Univ. of California, 1962. 20 p.

Describes 35 autograph manuscripts bequeathed to the University of California Music Library from the estate of Ernest Bloch. The catalog was compiled by Minnie Elmer.

1929. University of California. Music Library. "Ernest Bloch manuscripts at the University of California" by David L. Sills in *Notes,* 42 (1986), p. 7–21.

A new catalog which corrects and expands the one prepared by Minnie Elmer (see no. 1928) and which is supplemented by the one the author prepared on the Bloch holdings of the Library of Congress (see no. 2473).

1930. University of California, Music Library. Early music printing in the Music Library of the University of California, Berkeley. An exhibition in honor of the 12th Congress of the International Musicological Society. Compiled by Mary Kay Duggan. Forward by Vincent H. Duckles. Berkeley: The General Library of the University of California, 1977. 32 p. 78 numbered items; 9 facsimile plates.

1931. University of California. Music Library. Thematic catalog of a manuscript collection of 18th-century Italian instrumental music in the University of California, Berkeley, Music Library. By Vincent Duckles and Minnie Elmer. Berkeley and Los Angeles: Univ. of California Press, 1963. 403 p.

A collection comprising some 990 manuscripts containing works by 82 composers of the Tartini school at Padua. The central figures are Giuseppe Tartini and Michele Stratico. Preliminary chapters discuss the historical background of the collection, and tabulate the handwritings and the watermarks represented. A revision of the catalog has been completed by Gloria Eive to accompany a microfiche edition of the manuscripts in the collection which has not yet appeared.

Review by Charles Cudworth in *Galpin Society journal*, 18 (March 1965), p. 140–41; by Denis Stevens in *Musical times*, 105 (July 1964), p. 513–14; by Donald Krummel in *Notes*, 22 (1966), p. 1025–26.

BERLIN, GERMANY

1932. Die Amalien-Bibliothek. Musikbibliothek der Prinzessin Anna Amalia von Preussen (1732–1787). Historische Einordnung und Katalog mit Hinweisen auf die Schreiber der Handschriften. Von Eva Renate Blechschmidt. Berlin: Merseburger, 1965. 346 p. (Berliner Studien zur Musikwissenschaft, 8)

Reconstruction of the catalog of an important 18th-century music collection formed by the youngest sister of Friedrich the Great. The bulk of the collection was acquired by the Joachimsthalsche Gymnasium in the late 18th century. The collection was dispersed for safe-keeping in World War II, and since then parts of it have found their way to libraries in Tubingen, Marburg, and the Deutsche Staatsbibliothek in Berlin. Blechschmidt's study treats the history of the collection and describes each item in detail, including both printed music and manuscripts. Special attention is given to the identification of the scribes responsible for the manuscript copies.

1933. Deutsche Staatsbibliothek. "Die Musikabteilung," von Karl-Heinz Köhler. In *Deutsche Staatsbibliothek*, 1661–1961. Band I: Geschichte und Gegenwart, p. 241–74.

A narrative account of the founding of the music division of the Berlin State Library, the work of its successive directors, and the growth of its collections up to the restoration of the music room after its destruction in World War II. The riches of the collection are summarized, particularly the Bach, Mozart, and Beethoven holdings. The author is director of the Music Division.

1934. Deutsche Staatsbibliothek. "Return of treasures to the Deutsche Staatsbibliothek" by Karl-Heinz Köhler in *Fontes artis musicae*, 26 (1979), p. 86–87.

A report on the location of manuscripts moved from Berlin in the closing days of the Second World War.

1935. Deutsche Staatsbibliothek. Die Bach-Handschriften der Berliner Staatsbibliothek, von Paul Kast. Trossingen: Hohner-Verlag, 1958. 150 p. (Tübinger Bach-Studien, 2/3)

A catalog of manuscripts of music by members of the Bach family, once a part of the collection of the Prussian State Library, now distributed between the two Deutsche Staatsbibliotheken (West and East) and the University Library at Tübingen. Essentially a finding list for one of the world's great collections of Bach sources now dispersed. Brief; indexes of composers, scribes, and former owners of the manuscripts.

1936. Deutsche Staatsbibliothek. Die Beethoven-Sammlung in der Musikabteilung der Deutschen Staatsbibliothek. Verzeichnis: Autographe, Abschriften, Dokumente, Briefe. Aufgenommen und zusammengestellt von Eveline Bartlitz. Berlin: Deutsche Staatsbibliothek, 1970. 229 p.

A well-organized bibliography of all types of materials in the extensive Beethoven collections of the German State Library (East). Includes manuscripts, sketches, first editions, letters, items from Beethoven's library, etc. Numerous bibliographical references.

Review by William Drabkin in *Notes,* 28 (1972), p. 692–94.

1937. Internationale Musikleihbibliothek. Katalog. Berlin: 1952. 276 p.

Classified catalog of an international lending library of instrumental, vocal, and choral works. Includes parts for orchestral music. Strong in works by Soviet composers, but other countries are also well represented. Composer index.

1938. Joachimsthalsches Gymnasium. Bibliothek. Katalog der Musikaliensammlung des Joachimsthalschen Gymnasium zu Berlin. Verfasst von Robert Eitner. Berlin: T. Trautwein, 1884. 106 p. (Beilage, Monatshefte für Musikgeschichte. Jahrgang 16)

This collection incorporates the library of Princess Anna Amalie, sister of Friedrich the Great (see also no. 1932). Strong in 18th-century music of the North-German school. 627 numbered items. Author-composer index. The collection was partially dispersed and destroyed in World War II.

1939. Joachimsthalsches Gymnasium. Bibliothek. Thematischer Katalog der Von Thulemeir'schen Musikalien-Sammlung in der Bibliothek des Joachimsthal'schen Gymnasiums zu Berlin. Hrsg. von Robert Eitner. Leipzig: Breitkopf & Härtel, 1899. 110 p. (Beilage, Monatshefte für Musikgeschichte. Jahrgang 30–31)

The collection covers the period 1700–1800.

1940. Königliche Hausbibliothek. Katalog der Musiksammlung aus der Königlichen Hausbibliothek im Schlosse zu Berlin. Verfasst und erlautert von Georg Thouret. ... Leipzig: Breitkopf & Härtel, 1895. 356 p.

Supplemented by *Neue Erwerbungen der Königliche Hausbibliothek zu Berlin (Beilage, Monatshefte ... Jahrgang 35, 1903).*

Brief entries, alphabetical by composer. 6,836 items, printed and manuscript, with a special section of works dedicated to members of the royal family and a supplementary section for military music.

1941. Staatsbibliothek der Stiftung Preussischer Kulturbesitz Die Handschrift Johann Sebastian Bachs : Musikautographe aus der Musikabteilung der Staatsbibliothek Preussischer Kulturbesitz Berlin, Ausstellung zum 300. Geburtstag von J. S. Bach 22. März bis 13. Juli 1985; [Hrsg. von Rudolf Elvers ... et al.]. Wiesbaden: Reichert, 1985. 148 p.

Catalog of an exhibition of autographs from one of the largest collections of Bach sources.

1942. Staatsbibliothek der Stiftung Preussischer Kulturbesitz. Katalog der Sammlung Bokemeyer, [von] Harald Kümmerling. Kassel: Bärenreiter, 1970. 423 p. (Kieler Schriften zur Musikwissenschaft, 18)

Reconstruction of an 18th-century private music library of more than 3,000 manuscripts, printed music, and theoretical works. Partially dispersed. Parts of the collection surviving in the West Berlin State Library have been identified by Kümmerling.

Review by Richard H. Hunter in *Notes,* 28 (1971), p. 57–58.

1943. Staatsbibliothek der Stiftung Preussischer Kulturbesitz Ludwig van Beethoven, Autographe und Abschriften: Katalog bearbeitet von Hans-Günter Klein. Berlin: Merseburger, 1975. 344 p. (Kataloge der Musikabteilung. Erste Reihe, Handschriften. Staatsbibliothek Preussischer Kulturbesitz, 2)

1944. Staatsbibliothek der Stiftung Preussischer Kulturbesitz. Ludwig van Beethoven 1770–1970. Autographe aus der Musikabteilung der Staatsbibliothek Preussischer Kulturbesitz. [Ausstellung 1.-30. Dez. 1970 im Mendelssohn-Archiv der Staatsbibliothek. Bearbeiter von Rudolf Elvers und Hans-Günter Klein]. Berlin-Dahlem: Staatsbibliothek Preussischer Kulturbesitz 1970. 32 p.

Exhibition catalog of one of the most important collections of Beethoven sources, by the curator of the collection and one of the outstanding Beethoven scholars.

1945. Staatsbibliothek der Stiftung Preussischer Kulturbesitz. Mendelssohn-Archiv. Felix Mendelssohn-Bartholdy. Dokumente s. Lebens. Ausstellg. zum 125. Todestag im Mendelssohn-Archiv d. Staatsbibliothek Preuss. Kulturbesitz, Berlin-Dahlem. 1.-30. Nov. 1972. [Bearb. von Rudolf Elvers.] Berlin: Staatsbibliothek Preussischer Kulturbesitz, 1972. 23 p.

An exhibition of important Mendelssohn holdings.

1946. Staatsbibliothek der Stiftung Preussischer Kulturbesitz. Wolfgang Amadeus Mozart Autographe und Abschriften: Katalog; bearbeitet von Hans-Günter Klein. Kassel: Merseburger, 1982. 542 p. (Kataloge der Musikabteilung. Erste Reihe, Handscriften. Staatsbibliothek Preussischer Kulturbesitz, 6)

Catalog of the rich holdings of Mozart manuscripts and correspondence.

BERN, SWITZERLAND

1947. Schweizerische Landesbibliothek. Katalog der Schweizerischen Landesbibliothek. Musik-Werke der Mitglieder des Schweizerischen Tonkünstlervereins veröffentlicht von 1848–1925. ... Hrsg. von K. Joss. Bern-Bumpliz: Buchdruckerei Benteli, 1927. 152 p.

About 5,000 titles, abridged to essential information, in a classified arrangement.

BETHLEHEM, PENNSYLVANIA

1948. Archives of the Moravian Church. A catalogue of music by American Moravians, 1724–1842, from the Archives of the Moravian Church at Bethlehem, Pa. Bethlehem, Pa.: The Moravian Seminary and College for Women, 1938. 118 p.

Reprint by AMS Press, New York, 1970.

Short biographies and lists of compositions by 17 Moravian-American composers. Appendix of 24 plates of selected compositions and sample pages from the original manuscripts.

BIRMINGHAM, ENGLAND

1949. University of Birmingham. Barber Institute of Fine Arts. Catalogue of the printed music and music manuscripts before 1801 in the Music Library of the University of Birmingham, Barber Institute of Fine Arts. Edited by Ian Fenlon. London: Mansell, 1976. (also München: Verlag Dokumentation, 1976) 140 p. plus 7 microfiche.

Catalog of printed music provides complete title page transcription and physical description. Catalog of manuscript music describes and analyzes more fully each manuscript. Facsimiles of interesting pages. Indexes to booksellers, printers and publishers, to artists, designers, and engravers, and to previous owners. Microfiche of Barber MS 5001: Autograph anthems by English composers c. 1665–1685.

BLOOMINGTON, INDIANA

1950. Indiana University. School of Music. Latin-American Music Center. Latin American music available at Indiana University: score library, tape archive (art music), folk and primitive music. Bloomington: Indiana University, 1964. 101 leaves (typescript).

1951. Indiana University. Lilly Library. The Fritz Busch collection. Bloomington: Indiana University Libaries, 1972.

1952. Indiana University, Bloomington. Archives of Traditional Music. Catalog of the Terence R. Bech Nepal Music Research Collection compiled by Anne Helen Ross supported by a Research Collections Grant from the National Endowment for the Humanities; project coordinator, Terence R. Bech; project librarian, Anne H. Ross; project director, Frank J. Gillis. Bloomington: Archives of Traditional Music, Folklore Institute, Indiana University, 1978. 435 p.

Catalog of a collection of materials, including musical instruments, on musical culture in Nepal.

BOGOTA, COLOMBIA

1953. Catedral de Bogota. El Archivio Musical de la Catedral de Bogota. [By]Jose Ignacio Perdomo Escobar. Bogota: Instituto Caro y Cuervo, 1976. 818 p.

Includes a dictionary catalog of the archive and a bibliography.

Review by Catherine Massip in *Fontes artis musicae,* 26 (1979), p. 61.

BOLOGNA, ITALY

Accademia Filarmonic. Archivio. See no. 2100.

Archivio di S. Petronio. See no. 2100.

Biblioteca Ambrosini. See no. 2100.

1954. Accademia Filarmonica. Catalogo descrittivo degli autografi e ritratti di musicisti lasciati alla Reale Accademia Filarmonica di Bologna dall-'Abb. Dott. Masseangelo Masseangeli. Compilato a cura degli Accademici Prof. Cav. Federico Parisini e Maestro Ernesto Colombani. Bologna: Regia Tipografia, 1896. 435 p.

This catalog first appeared, under a slightly different title, in 1881. Reprint of the 1881 edition by Forni, Bologna, 1969.

1955. Accademia Filarmonica. Mostra internazionale di musica in Bologna 1888. Catalogo con brevi cenni biografici e succinte discrizioni degli autografi e documenti de' celebri o distinti musicisti posseduti da Emilia Succi. Accademia Filarmonica di Bologna. Bologna: Società Tipografica già Compositori, 1888. 179 p.

A collection of 886 items, chiefly letters of musicians of the 18th and 19th centuries, mostly autograph. Arranged alphabetically, with brief biographical notices and descriptions of the items.

1956. Biblioteca Universitaria. "Codici musicali della R. Biblioteca Universitaria di Bologna," by Lodovico Frati. In *Rivista musicale italiana,* 23 (1916), p. 219–42.

A general description of the resources of the music collection in the library of the University of Bologna, drawing attention to major holdings in plainchant, early theory, and polyphony.

1957. Civico Museo Bibliografico Musicale. (Formerly Conservatorio di Musica "G. B. Martini.") Catalogo della biblioteca del Liceo Musicale di Bologna, compilato da Gaetano Gaspari, compiuto e pubblicato da Federico Parisini per cura del municipio. ... Bologna: Libreria Romagnoli dall'Acqua, 1890–1943. 5 v.

Vols. 1–4 reissued in photo-offset by Arnaldo Forni (Bologna, 1961) with corrections by Napoleone Fanti, Oscar Mischiati, and Luigi Ferdinando Tagliavini.

Vol. 1: music theory. Vol. 2: sacred vocual music (ed. Luigi Torchi). Vol. 3: secular vocal music and opera (ed. Luigi Torchi). Vol. 4: instrumental music and pedagogy (ed. Raffaele Caldolini). Vol. 5: Libretti (ed. Ugo Sesini).

This catalog provides access to one of the richest collections of early music in the world, incorporating the library of the 18th-century scholar Padre Giambattista Martini. Full bibliographical descriptions; contents given for collections, transcriptions of numerous prefaces and dedications. Entries are alphabetical within each category. General index of names.

1958. Civico museo bibliografico musicale. Padre Martini's collection of letters in the Civico museo bibliografico musicale in Bologna: an annotated index by Anne Schnoebelen. New York: Pendragon Press, 1979. 721 p. (Annotated reference tools in music, 2)

Covers 5,876 letters written by or to 670 correspondents of Giovanni Battista Martini during his 45 years at the monastery of San Francesco, 1730–84. For each letter, the incipit in the original language is supplied along with names of persons and pieces of music cited in the letter. The content of each letter is summarized. Index to names and subjects.

Review by John W. Hill in *Notes,* 36 (1980), p. 893–94; and by Vincent H. Duckles in *Music and letters,* 61 (1980), p. 376–77.

1959. Il Convento di S. Francesco. Catalogo del fondo musicale. By Gino Zanotti. Bologna: Forni, 1970. 2 v. (Bibliotheca musica bononiensis, VI, 3)

Vol. I: "Le edizioni." 324 p. Vol. II: 'I manoscritti." 393 p.

Catalogs the music collection of the Franciscan church where Padre Martini lived and worked during the 18th century. The collection includes a considerable amount of his music.

1960. Enrico, Eugene. The orchestra at San Petronio in the Baroque era. Washington, D.C.: Smithsonian Institution Press, 1976. 64 p. (Smithsonian studies in history and technology, 35)

P. 45–60: "A catalogue of manuscripts at San Petronio, the sources of Torelli's festival compositions with trumpet."

BOLZANO, ITALY

1961. Palazzo Toggenburg. La raccolta di manoscritti e stampe musicali "Toggenburg" di Bolzano (secc. XVIII-XIX) [di] Tarcisio Chini, Giuliano Tonini. Torino: EDT/Musica, 1986. 307 p. (Cataloghi di fondi musicali italiani, 5)

Catalog of a colection gathered by a merchant from Menz, containing prints and manuscripts from the last quarter of the 18th century and through the first half of the 19th. The libretto collection is cataloged as well.

BONN, GERMANY

1962. Beethoven-Haus. "Die Beethovenhandschriften des Beethovenhauses in Bonn," by Hans Schmidt. In *Beethoven-Jahrbuch.* Jahrgang 1969/70. Bonn: Beethovenhaus, 1971. p. 1–443.

A catalog of 776 items. Major section are letters (489 items), documents partially or wholly in Beethoven's hand (29 items), works (76 items), copies by Beethoven of other composers' works (9 items), sketches (106 items), copyist's work (31 items), and early printed music with annotations by the composer (11 items). Detailed indexes.

1963. Beethoven-Haus. Eine Schweizer Beethovensammlung. Von Max Unger. Zurich: Verlag der Corona, 1939. 235 p. (Schriften der Corona, 24)

Catalog of the Bodmer collection, perhaps the world's greatest accumulation of Beethoven documents, once in private hands but now part of the archive of the Beethoven House in Bonn. The catalog is organized in 12 categories, the most important of which are 389 letters, including those of the composer's contemporaries, 108 manuscripts of music; 43 early or first editions; 17 pictures; 16 facsimile plates; index of names.

1964. Friedrich-Wilhelms-Universität. Bibliothek. "Die musikalischen Autographen der Universitats-Bibliothek Bonn." By Theo Clasen. In *Festschrift Joseph Schmidt-Görg zum 60. Geburtstag.* Bonn: Beethoven-Haus, 1957. p. 26–65.

567 autographs by 245 musicians, extracted from bequests or autograph books. Wide representation of musicians and musical scholars of the early 19th century.

1965. Friedrich-Wilhelms-Universität. Musikwissenschaftliche Seminar. Katalog der Musikhandschriften im Besitz des Musikwissenschaftlichen Seminars der Rheinischen Friedrich-Wilhelms-Universität zu Bonn. By Magda Marx-Weber. Köln: Arno Volk-Verlag, 1971. 138 p. (Beitrage zur Rheinischen Musikgeschichte, 89)

A collection of 595 manuscripts, some 550 of which were assembled by the organist-cantor Christian Benjamin Klein (1754–1825). Prominent among the composers represented are Benda, Bernabei, Homilius, Reichardt, Weinlig, Wirbach, and Zumsteeg.

BORDEAUX, FRANCE

1966. Galerie des Beaux-Arts. L'art et la musique dix-neuvième. Exposition du Mai organisée à l'initiative de Monsieur Jacques Chaban-Delmas, Maire de Bordeaux. . . . Bordeaux: Galerie des Beaux-Arts, 1969. 119 p.

Catalog for an exhibition held in Bordeaux from 30 May to 30 September, 1969.

206 items, including 30 instruments. 81 plates. Brief descriptions including bibliographies and some information as to provenance.

BOSTON, MASSACHUSETTS

1967. Boston Public Library. Catalogue of the Allen A. Brown collection of music. Boston, Mass., 1910–16. 4 v.

A dictionary catalog of composers, titles, subjects, with explicit contents and analytics given for all collections. One of the first, and one of the few printed catalogs for a major American music collection. Rich in opera and in orchestral scores, primarily 19th-century editions.

1968. Boston Public Library. Dictionary catalog of the music collection of the Boston Public Library. Boston, Mass.: G. K. Hall and Co., 1972. 20 v.

Photo-offset publication of the card file for a collection of some 80,000 volumes covering music, biography, history and criticism, theory and composition, music education, collected editions and monuments, bibliographical works, libretti, and periodicals. This catalog incorporates the Allen A. Brown music collection, but excludes sheet music, clippings and programs, and recordings.

BRANDENBURG, GERMANY

1969. St. Katharinenkirche. Bibliothek. Die musikalischen Schätze der St. Katherinenkirche zu Brandenburg a.d. Havel. Ein Beitrag zur musikalischen Literatur des 16. und 17. Jahrhunderts. Von Johann F. Täglichsbeck. Brandenburg: A. Müller, 1857. 50 p.

Manuscripts and printed works, 1564–1671, chronologically arranged, with full bibliographical information and descriptive notes.

BRASOV, RUMANIA

1970. Honterusgymnasium. Bibliothek. Die Musiksammlung der Bibliothek zu Kronstadt, von Erich H. Müller. Kronstadt: J. Gött's Sohn, 1930. 176 p.

Manuscripts, printed music and books. Brief biographical sketches of authors or composers. Publication dates, plate numbers.

BRESCIA, ITALY

1971. Archivio Capitolare del Duomo. Catalogo del fondo musicale dell'Archivio Capitolare del Duomo di Brescia. Compiled by Mariella Sala. Torino: E.D.T./Musica, 1984. 288 p. (Cataloghi di Fondi Musicali Italiani, no. 3)

A catalogue of printed and manuscript music, mostly from the 16th-18th centuries, including anthologies. Indexed by composer, text incipits, and by musical genre. Useful histories of the Cappella and the Archivio.

BRESLAU, GERMANY AND BRIEG, GERMANY

See WROCLAW, POLAND

BRNO, CZECHOSLOVAKIA

1972. Moravskř Muzeum. Průuvodce po archívních fondech Ústavu dějin hudby Moravského musea v Brně. Zprac. Theodora Straková, *et al.* 1. vyd. Brno, Ustav dějin hudby: Mor. musea, rozmn., 1971. 256 p. 22 plates.

Summary in Russian, German, and English.

Catalog of the music holdings of the Moravian Museum in Brno (Brunn).

1973. Universitätsbibliothek. Alte Drucke der Werke von tschechischen Komponisten des 18. Jahrhunderts in der Universitätsbibliothek in Brno. Von Vladimír Telec. Praha: Státní Pedagogické Nakladatelství, 1969. 163

p.

Cites 1,278 works by 42 Czech composers; a total of 522 bibliographical units. 278 of the items are on microfilm. Full bibliographical descriptions, including tempo and metrical indications for the movements of composite works. Introduction in German and Czech. Eight plates.

BRUSSELS, BELGIUM

1974. Bibliothèque royale Albert Ier. "De Afdeling Muziek (van de Koninklijke Bibliotheek van België)" [by] Bernard Huys in *Koninklijke Bibliotheek. Liber memorialis 1559–1969, p. 311–34.* Brussels: 1969.

A history of the music collection of the Royal Library at Brussels, including the establishment of a new Music Divison in that library.

1975. Bibliothèque royale Albert Ier. Catalogue des partitions musicales éditées en Belgique et acquises par la Bibliothèque royale Albert Ier; fascicule spécial de la Bibliographie de Belgique [par] Bernard Huys [chef de la Section de la musique]. Bruxelles: La Bibliothèque, 1976– . 2 v.

Published with an added title page: *Catalogus van de muziekpartituren in Belgié uitgegeven en verworven door de Koninklijke Bibliotheek Albert I. Speciale aflevering van de Belgische bibliografie.*

Serves as a catalog of music published in Belgium and acquired by the library; contents: [1] 1966–1975; [2] 1976–1980. *Bibliographie de Belgique Belgische bibliografie*

1976. Bibliothèque royale Albert Ier. Trésors musicaux de la Bibliothèque royale Albert Ier, 1220–1800; [exposition, Bibliothèque royale Albert Ier du 6 au 27 septembre 1975] catalogue de l'exposition rédigé par Bernard Huys. Bruxelles: Bibliothèque royale Albert Ier, 1975. 49 p.

Simultaneously published as *Muzikale Schatten uit de koninklijke Bibliotheek Albert I, 1220–1800.*

A splendid catalog of an exposition of some of the early sources in this important collection.

1977. Bibliothèque Royale de Belgique. Catalogue de la bibliothèque de F. J. Fétis, acquise par l'Etat belge. Bruxelles: C. Muquardt, 1877. 946 p.

The Fétis library was acquired by the Bibliothèque Royale in 1872 and contains many rarities. 7,325 items classified under two main headings: (1) "Bibliothèque générale" and (2) "Bibliothèque musicale."

1978. Bibliothèque Royale de Belgique. Catalogue des imprimés musicaux des XVe, XVIe et XVIIe siècles. Fonds général. Par Bernard Huys. Bruxelles: Bibliothèque Royale de Belgique, 1965. 422 p.

446 numbered items. The catalog lists those works not part of the Fétis collection (above), although if another copy or a more complete copy is found in *Fétis,* this information is given. Contents listed for each item. Of particular interest is the listing of music excerpted from theoretical works such as Kircher, Glareanus, Zarlino, etc.

Fonds Général Supplement published in 1974, by Bernard Huys.

Review by François Lesure in *Revue de musicologie,* 51 (1965), p. 102; by Ute Schwab in *Die Musikforschung,* 21 (1968), p. 104–5.

1979. Bibliothèque Royale de Belgique. Catalogue des imprimés musicaux du XVIIIe siècle. Fonds général. Catalogus van de muziek drukken van de XVIIIde eeuw. Algemene verzameling Bernard Huys. Bruxelles: Bibliothèque Royale Albert Ier, 1974. 519 p.

The catalog presents all the musical works and writings about music printed in the 18th century possessed by the Bibliothèque Royale *not* in the Fètis collection (see no. 1977). Complete title page transcriptions, physical descriptions, provenance, references in other catalogs, cross references, and analysis of collections are provided. There are indexes to authors, composers and translators, to printers an book sellers, to persons and institutions formerly owning the works, to engravers of music and to musical genres. A masterful catalog.

1980. Bibliothèque Royale de Belgique. De Grégoire le Grand à Stockhausen. Douze siècles de notation musicale. Catalogue de l'exposition rédigé par Bernard Huys. Bruxelles: Bibliothèque Royale, 1966. 169 p.

Catalog of a well-organized exposition of 100 items tracing the history of musical notation. 16 facsimile plates and 48 illustrations in the text. Each entry is fully described, with bibliographical references.

1981. Bibliothèque Royale de Belgique. François-Joseph Fétis et la vie musicale de son temps, 1784–1871. Bruxelles: Bibliothèque Royale, 1972. 254 p. 64 plates.

"Exposition organisée à l'occasion du centième anniversaire de l'achat de la collection Fétis." May 27 to August 26, 1972.

An admirably documented exhibition catalog treating the multiple interests and activities of Fétis as a musicologist, historian, composer and collector.

1982. Conservatoire Royal de Musique. Bibliothèque. Catalogue de la bibliotheque. . . . par A. Wotquenne. Bruxelles: Coosemans, 1898–1912. 4 v.

Annexe I: Libretti d'opéras et d'oratorios italiens du XVIIe siècle. Bruxelles, O. Schepens, 1901.

An unaltered reprint was published in 1980 by Éditions Culture et Civilization, Brussels.

A classified catalog to one of the richest European music collections. Printed scores and manuscripts interfiled.

BUDAPEST, HUNGARY

1983. Országos Széchényi Könyvtár. "Catalogue raisonné der Esterházy Opernsammlung, in chronologischer Ordnung der Premièren." In *Haydn als Opernkapellmeister; die Haydn-Dokumente der Esterházy Opernsammlung.* Bearbeitet von Dénes Bartha und László Somfai. Budapest: Verlag der Ungarischen Akademie der Wissenschaften, 1960. p. 179–403.

Chronological listing of the operatic works preserved in the Esterházy archive in the National Széchényi Library. Each work is fully described, with special attention given to Haydn's annotations on works performed under his direction. An important new approach to Haydn research.

1984. Országos Széchényi Könyvtár. "Die Musikalien der Pfarrkirche zu St. Aegidi in Bartfa." By Otto Gombosi. In *Festschrift für Johannes Wolf.* Berlin, 1929. p. 38–47.

The collection described here is now in the National Széchényi Library at Budapest. Gombosi discusses some 20 music prints of the 16th century and a number of important 16th- and 17th-century manuscripts.

1985. Országos Széchényi Könyvtár. Haydn compositions in the music collection of the National Széchényi Library, Budapest. Published on the occasion of the 150th anniversary of Haydn's death (1809–1959). Edited by Jeno Vecsey. Budapest: Publishing House of the Hungarian Academy of Sciences, 1960. 167 p.

Also published in Hungarian and German.

A classified listing of 372 items, 72 of which are Haydn Autographs. 42 facsimiles of manuscripts, prints, and other documents related to the composer's career.

1986. Országos Széchényi Könyvtár. Zenei kéziratok jégyzeke. Budapest: Kiadja a Magyar Nemzeti Múzeum Országos Széchényi Könyvtár, 1921–40. 2 v. (Catalogus bibliothecae musaei nat. hungarici. Musica, I, II)

Vol. 1 (391 p.): editor, Isoz Kalman. Catalog of 1,449 autograph letters of musicians, including some of Haydn and Liszt. Vol. 2 (237 p.): editor, Lavotta Rezso. Catalog of music manuscripts.

CAMBRAI, FRANCE

1987. Coussemaker, Edmond de. Notice sur les collections musicales de la Bibliothèque de Cambrai et des autres villes du Department du Nord. . . . Paris: Techener, 1843. 180, 40 p.

Concerned chiefly with 16 manuscripts and 4 printed collections in the Cambrai library. The descriptions are brief, faulty, and outdated.

CAMBRIDGE, ENGLAND

1988. University. Peterhouse College. Catalogue of the musical manuscripts at Peterhouse, Cambridge, compiled by Anselm Hughes. Cambridge: Cambridge Univ. Press, 1953. 75 p.

Important source materials for the study of English church music of the 16th and 17th centuries comprising four Latin partbooks of c. 1540 and two sets of English partbooks c. 1630–40.

1989. University. Fitzwilliam Museum. Catalogue of the music in the Fitzwilliam Museum, Cambridge, by A. J. Fuller-Maitland and A. H. Mann. London: C. J. Clay and Sons, 1893. 298 p.

209 manuscripts, 196 printed books, and an important collection of Handel materials.

1990. Cambridge University Library. Cambridge music manuscripts, 900–1700, edited by Iain Fenlon. Cambridge: Cambridge University Press, 1982. 174 p.

A catalog of music manuscripts in the various libraries at Cambridge.

Published to coincide with an exhibition in the Fitzwilliam Museum, July-August 1982. Bibliographical references.

CAMBRIDGE, MASSACHUSETTS

1991. Harvard University. Music Library. A catalogue of books relating to music in the library of Richard Aldrich. New York (printed at the Plimpton Press, Norwood, Mass.), 1931. 435 p.

A classified catalog of music literature, primarily of the 19th and 20th centuries, with a small collection of books printed before 1800 (p. 35–55). This library has been incorporated into the Harvard University music collection.

1992. Harvard University. Houghton Library. Loeb Music Library. Music in Harvard libraries; a catalogue of early printed music and books on music in the Houghton Library and the Eda Kuhn Loeb Music Library. By David F. Wood. Cambridge, Massachusetts: Houghton Library of the Harvard College Library and Harvard University Department of Music, 1980. 306 p.

> The catalogue describes the music and books on music [1,628 titles] printed before 1801, which had been added to the Harvard Libraries by 1967.

Arrangment by author and composer. References to principal bibliographic tools. Index to names, including names of printers, book sellers and editors. Bibliography. Additions and corrections cited on p. 282.

1993. Harvard University. Isham Memorial Library. "The collection of photographic reproductions at the Isham memorial Library, Harvard University" by Willi Apel in *Musica disciplina,* 1 (1946), p. 68–73.

Describes the first stages of the Isham collection of microfilms of musical source materials and other holdings.

1994. Harvard University. Isham Memorial Library. "The Isham Memorial Library of Harvard University" by Archibald T. Davison in *Organ Institute Quarterly,* 3 (1953), p. 13–16.

Describes the holdings of the Isham collection particularly of interest to historians of keyboard music.

1995. Harvard University. Loeb Music Library. The Eda Kuhn Loeb Music Library" by Nino Pirotta in *Harvard Library Bulletin* 12 (1958), p. 410–17.

Describes the development and holdings of the library.

1996. Harvard University. University Library. "Rare music manuscripts at Harvard" by Craig Wright in *Current Musicology* (1970), p. 25–33.

Describes the holdings of the Loeb Library, the Houghton Library, and the Isham Library at Harvard.

CARPENTRAS, FRANCE

1997. Bibliothèque d'Inguimbert. Catalogue de la collection musicale J. B. Laurens donnée a la ville de Carpentras pour la Bibliothèque d'Inguimbert. Carpentra: J. Seguin, 1901. 151 p.

Classified catalog of music books and scores; a 19th-century scholar's library. Preceded by a biography of the donor, J. B. Laurens, archeologist, painter, writer, organist, composer, and musicologist.

CARRIBBEAN ISLANDS

1998. "Libraries with music collections in the Carribbean Islands" by Catherine A. Dower in *Notes,* 34 (1978), p. 27–38.

Descriptions of music collections in Aruba, Barbados, Bermuda, Cuba, Curaçao, Haiti, Jamaica, Martinique, Puerto Rico, Trinidad, and the Virgin Islands.

CESENA, ITALY

1999. Biblioteca Comunale. "Catalogo delle opere musicali a stampa dal '500 al '700 conservate presso la Biblioteca Comunale di Cesena." By Sergio Paganelli. In *Collectanea historiae musicae,* 2 (1957), p. 311–38.

95 early prints of vocal and instrumental music; 6 theory works.

CHARLOTTESVILLE, VIRGINIA

2000. University of Virginia. Alderman Library. Computer catalog of nineteenth-century American-imprint sheet music; compiled by Lynn T. McRae. Charlottesville: University of Virginia, 1977. 12 p. 8 microfiche

Catalog of a collection in the Rare Book Room, Alderman Library, University of Virginia. Indexes about 7,700 pieces of American sheet music.

CHICAGO, ILLINOIS

2001. The Newberry Library. "The Newberry Library, Chicago." By Donald W. Krummel. In *Fontes artis musicae* (July-December 1969), p. 119–24.

A narrative account of the music resources of the Newberry Library in the areas of medieval music, Renaissance and Baroque music, music of the 18th and 19th centuries, music of master composers, and Americana.

2002. Newberry Library. Bibliographical inventory to the early music in the Newberry Library, Chicago, Illinois. Edited by D. W. Krummel. Boston: G. K. Hall, 1977. 587 p.

Photo-offset duplication of cards from the Newberry Library representing musical items published before 1860 and manuscripts dating from before 1860. These cards had been arranged in a classified order for the catalog.

"The Newberry Library has what is considered to be one of the most important music collections in the United States, particularly rich in the fields of Renaissance music, early theory, and Americana." [from the forward]

Comprehending the introduction is of crucial importance to the efficient use of this work. Addenda and corrigenda p. 527–532. Index to composers, editors, and musical subjects. Index to printers, engravers, artists, copyists, and publishers.

2003. Newberry Library. The Newberry Library catalog of early American printed sheet music. Compiled by Bernard E. Wilson. Boston: G. K. Hall, 1983. 3 v.

Photo-offset duplication of cards representing c. 6,300 pieces of early American sheet music, including the James Francis Driscoll collection. The catalog covers works printed before 1871. There are sections devoted to main entries, added entries, chronological entries, places, and titles. Aproximately 90,000 pieces of American sheet music held by the Newberry are not included in this catalog.

COIMBRA, PORTUGAL

2004. Universidade. Biblioteca. Inventário dos inéditos e impressos musicais (subsidios par um catálogo). Fasc. I. Prefaciado por Santiago Kastner. Coimbra: Impresso nas oficinas da "Atlântida," 1937. 47, 55 p.

Separate alphabets and pagination for manuscripts and early printed works. Full descriptions.

2005. Universidade. Biblioteca. Os manuscritos musicasi nos. 6 e 12 da Biblioteca Geral da Universidade de Coimbra (Contribuïçãao para um catálogo definitivo). Por Mário de Sampayo Ribeiro. Coimbra: 1941. 112 p.

A detailed study of two manuscripts of polyphonic music in the university library at Coimbra.

COLLEGE PARK, MARYLAND

2006. University of Maryland at College Park. Music Library. A guide to the Jacob Coopersmith Collection of Handeliana: at the University of Maryland College Park; compiled by Richard Brundage and Neil Ratliff. College Park, Md.: Music Library, University of Maryland, 1986. 18 p.

COLLEGEVILLE, MINNESOTA

2007. St. John's Abbey and University. Hill Monastic Microfilm Library. "Music manuscripts on microfilm in the Hill Monastic Manuscript Library at St. John's Abbey and University" by Peter Jeffrey in *Notes*, 35 (1978), p. 7–30.

A survey of the entire collection of microfilms gathered from a large number of Roman Catholic repositories in Europe.

2008. St. John's University. Alcuin Library. "The monastic manuscript microfilm library," by Julian G. Plante, in *Notes*, 25 (1968), p. 12–14.

The article describes a microfilm library of nearly 11,000 codices filmed from the monastic libraries in Europe (Göttwieg, Heiligenkreuz, Herzogenburg, Klosterneuburg, Kremsmünster, Lambach, Lilienfeld, Melk, etc.). The author cites 27 manuscripts of early music theory available for study in the collection at Collegeville.

2009. St. John's University. Alcuin Library and Hill Monastic Manuscript Library. A bibliography for medieval and renaissance musical manuscript research; secondary materials at the Alcuin Library and the Hill Monastic Manuscript Library . . . by Peter Jeffrey. Collegeville: St. John's University Press for the Hill Monastic Manuscript Library, 1980. 68 p.

A very handy, pocket-size, annotated bibliography with sections on musical paleography, musical iconography, catalogs, music texts and studies, and reference materials. Index to names and titles.

COLOGNE, GERMANY

2010. Domcapelle. Die Leiblsche Sammlung. Katalog der Musikalien der Kölner Domcapelle. Von Gottfried Göller. Köln: Arno Volk-Verlag, 1964. 133 p. (Beiträge zur rheinischen Musikgeschichte, 57)

Thematic catalog of 291 sacred choral works, chiefly early 19th century, formerly in the chapel of Cologne Cathedral. The collection is now in the Diözesanbibliothek of the Archbishopric of Cologne. Former owner—Carl Leibl, Kapellmeister.

Review by Winfried Kirsch in *Die Musikforschung*, 20 (1967), p. 95.

2011. Universitäts- und Stadtbibliothek. Katalog der in der Universitäts- und Stadtbibliothek Köln vorhandenen Musikdrucke des 16., 17., und 18. Jahrhunderts By Willi Kahl. Köln: 1958. 20 p.

118 items. Bibliographical references.

CONSTANCE, SWITZERLAND

2012. Kollegiat- und Pfarrkirche St. Stephan. "Das Noteninventar der Kollegiat- und Pfarrkirche St. Stephan," -von- Manfred Schuler in *Kirchenmusikalisches Jahrbuch*, 58/59 (1974/75) p. 85–103.

COPENHAGEN, DENMARK

2013. Kommunebiblioteker. Katalog over dansk og udenlandsk musik og musiklitteratur. 2. udgave. København: B. Lunos Bogtrykkeri, 1932. 157 p.

First published in 1921.

Tilvaext (supplement), 1932–39. København, B. Lunos, 1939.

2014. Kommunebiblioteker. Katalog over musik og musiklitteratur. København, Nordlunde, 1954–58. 4 v.

Vol. 1: orkestermusik, kammermusik, enkelte instrumenter, 1956, 72 p.

Vol. 2: klaver, orgel, harmonium, 1954, 65 p.

Vol. 3: vokalmusik, 1958, 118 p.

Vol. 4: operaer, operetter, balletter, 1955, 46 p.

A fifth volume devoted to books on music was never published.

2015. Kongelige Bibliothek. Catalogue of Giedde's music collection in the Royal Library of Copenhagen. Compiled by Inge Bittmann. Copenhagen: Edition Egtved, 1976. 198 p.

A catalog of "a fairly comprehensive collection, mostly of flute music from the second half of the 18th century." [from the Preface]

Arranged alphabetically by composer with thematic incipits. There is a classified list of titles, a list of publishers, and a bibliography.

CREMONA, ITALY

2016. Biblioteca Governativa e Libreria Civica. Mostra bibliografica dei musicisti cremonesi: catalogo storico-critico degli autori e catalogo bibliografico. Cremona: Biblioteca Governativa e Libreria Civica, 1951. 149 p.
Catalog of an exhibition held in 1949. P. 1–106: biographical notices of Cremonese musicians; p. 107–45: exhibition catalog, arranged chronologically; about 140 items related to the history of music in Cremona.

CRESPANO VENETO, ITALY

2017. Biblioteca Musicale del Prof. Pietro Canal in Crespano Veneto. Bassano: Prem. Stabilimento Tipogr. Sante Pezzato, 1885. 104 p.
A scholar's library of 1,152 items, of which the first 1,034 are books on music. Contains many rarities. The owner was a professor at the University of Padua and wrote studies of music in Mantua and Venice.

CUENCA, SPAIN

2018. Catedral. Archivo. Catálogo musical del Archivo de la Santa Iglesia Catedral Basilica de Cuenca. Recogido por Restituto Navarro-Gonzalo. Revisado por Jesús López-Cobos. Dirigido por Antonio Iglesias. 2nd ed. revised and corrected. Cuenca: Ediciones del Instituto de Música Religiosa, 1973. 376 p. (Instituto de musica religiosa, Publicaciones, 9)
First edition published as v. 1 of the series in 1965, 372 p.
Contains extensive holdings of sacred and secular music. Indexes by composer and by century.

CZECHOSLOVAKIA

2019. Fischer, Kurt von. "Repertorium der Quellen tschechischer Mehrstimmigkeit des 14. bis 16. Jahrhunderts." In *Essays in musicology in honor of Dragan Plamenac on his 70th birthday.* Pittsburgh: Univ. of Pittsburgh Press, 1969. p. 49–60.
Identifies 73 manuscript sources of early Czech polyphony in 23 institutions, chiefly in Czechoslovakia but including the Austrian National Library at Vienna.

2020. Plamenac, Dragan. "Music libraries in Eastern Europe, a visit in the summer of 1961." In *Notes,* 19 (1962), p. 217–34; 411–20; 584–98.
An illuminating account of present conditions in some of the major East-European music libraries, including those in Czechoslovakia. Locations of important bodies of source materials are indicated.

2021. Průvodce po pramenech k dějinám Hudby. Fondy a sbirky uložené v. Čechach. (Music collections and archives in the CSSR.) Zpracovali: Jaroslav Bužga, Jan Kouba, Eva Mikanová a Tomislav Volek. Redigoval: Jan Kouba. Praha: Ceskoslovenská Akademie Ved, 1969. 323 p.

General descriptions of the music resources of Czech museums, libraries, and archives. Name index.

2022. Svobodová, Maria. "Musikbücherein, Archive und Museen in der CSSR." In *AIBM, Ländergruppe Deutsche Demokratische Republik. Internationaler Sommerkurs für Musikbibliothekare,* 1964. Berlin, 1965. p. 48–69.
A descriptive account of the major music archives, libraries, and museums in Czechoslovakia.

2023. Terrayová, Maria J. "Súpis archívnych hudobných fondov na Slovensku." In *Hudobnovedné studie.* VI. Bratislava: Vydavatel'stvo Slovenskej Akadémie, Vied, 1960. p. 197–328.
Thematic catalog of the music manuscripts in two hitherto undescribed Czech archives: the archive of the Pfarrkirche of Púchov (on deposit in the Musicological Institute of the Slovakian Academy of Sciences) and the archive of the Príleský Ostrolucky family (on deposit in the Slovakian National Museum in Martin). The manuscripts are chiefly of late 18th-century instrumental and vocal music by Italianate Czech composers of the period.

DAGENHAM, ENGLAND

2024. Public Libraries. Catalogue of music; a complete catalogue of the scores, miniature scores, recorded music and books . . . in the Dagenham Public Libraries. Compiled by W. C. Pugsley and G. Atkinson. Dagenham (Essex): 1958. 299 p.

DANZIG

See GDANSK, POLAND.

DARMSTADT, GERMANY

2025. Hofbibliothek. "Musik-Handschriften der Darmstädter Hofbibliothek." Beschrieben von F. W. E. Roth. In *Monatshefte für Musikgeschichte,* 20 (1888), p. 64–73; 82–92.
117 items, 10th to 19th centuries. Brief descriptions.

2026. Hofbibliothek. "Zur Bibliographie der Musikdrucke des XV. bis XVII. Jahrhunderts in der Darmstädter Hofbibliothek." Von F. W. E. Roth. In *Monatshefte für Musikgeschichte,* 20 (1888), p. 118–25; 134–41; 154–61.
75 items, fully described.

2027. Internationales Musikinstitut Darmstadt. Informationszentrum für zeitgenossische Musik. Katalog der Abteilung Noten. Darmstadt: Internationales Musikinstitut, 1966. 293 p.
Title varies, began as *Kranichsteiner Musikinstitut.*
Supplements published for 1967, 1968, 1969/70, 1971/73, 1974/75 and

1976/77. In 1970, a supplement covering books and periodicals was published.

An international lending library established in 1948 to further the study and performance of contemporary music. Classified catalog, chiefly scores, but a small collection of books.

Review by Karl Kroeger in *Notes,* 23 (1967), p. 531–32.

DENTON, TEXAS

2028. North Texas State College. Music Library. A bibliography of contemporary music in the Music Library of North Texas State College, March 1955. Compiled by Anna Harriet Heyer. Denton, Texas, 1955. 128 leaves (typescript).

Alphabetical listing by composer, and by title under composer. Chiefly scores and chamber music with parts. No index.

Review by Dorothy A. Linder in *Notes,* 13 (1956), p. 656–57.

2029. North Texas State University. Hans Nachod Collection. The Arnold Schoenberg-Hans Nachod Collection. Detroit: Information Coordinators, 1979. 119 p. (Detroit Studies in Music Bibliography, 41)

Annotated catalog of the collection of correspondence, proof sheets and holographs in the Music Library of North Texas State University, Denton, Texas.

DETROIT, MICHIGAN

2030. Detroit Public Library. Hackley Collection. Catalog of the E. Azalia Hackley Memorial Collection of Negro music, dance and drama [in the] Detroit Public Library]. Boston: G. K. Hall, 1979. 510 p.

Photo-offset duplication of cards representing books, scores, sheet music, broadsides, posters, and photographs in the Hackley Collection.

DRESDEN, GERMANY

2031. Sächische Landesbibliothek. Die Musiksammelhandschriften des 16. und 17. Jahrhunderts in der Sächsischen Landesbibliothek zu Dresden. Unter Verwendung von Vorarbeiten Harald Kümmerling in Auftrag der Sächsischen Landesbibliothek beschreiben von Wolfgang Steude. Wilhelmshaven: Heinrichshofen, 1974. 315 p. (Quellenkataloge zur Musikgeschichte, 6.)

Fully describes and analyzes 112 manuscripts. Indexes of persons, Latin titles and first lines, and German titles and first lines.

2032. Sächsische Landesbibliothek. Katalog der Musiksammlung der Kgl. öffentlichen Bibliothek zu Dresden (im Japanischen Palais). Robert Eitner und Otto Kade, bearb. Leipzig, Breitkopf & Härtel, 1890. (Monatshefte für Musikgeschichte. Beilage. Jahrgang 21–22.) 150 p.

Music manuscripts to the date of compilation; printed music and books on music to 1700.

2033. Sächsische Landesbibliothek. Klaviermusik der sozialistischen Länder aus der Sächsischen Landesbibliothek. Bestandsverzeichnis zusammengestellt von Wolfgang Reich. Dresden: Sächsische Landesbibliothek, 1962. 79 p.

A list, grouped alphabetically by country, of keyboard music by East-European composers. Date, publisher, and pagination given for each entry.

DUBLIN, IRELAND

2034. Charteris, Richard. A catalogue of the printed books on music, printed music, and music manuscripts in Archbishop Marsh's Library, Dublin. Clifden, Ireland: Boethius Press, 1982. 142 p.

2035. Trinity College Library. "The lute books of Trinity College, Dublin."By John Ward. In *The Lute Society journal,* 9 (1967), p. 17–40; 10 (1968), p. 15–32.

DURANGO, MEXICO

2036. Catedral. Capilla de música. La capilla de música de la Catedral de Durango, México, siglos XVII y XVIII. [Por Francisco Antúnez] Aguascalientes: 1970. 47 p.

Includes a short catalog of the music manuscript holdings of the cathedral.

DURHAM, ENGLAND

2037. Durham Cathedral. A catalogue of Durham Cathedral music manuscripts, compiled by Brian Crosby. Oxford: Oxford University Press for the Dean and Chapter of Durham Cathedral, 1986. 271 p.

Includes descriptions of manuscripts from the monastery, the Cathedral and Bamburgh Castle. Indexes of composers, dates, dated signatures (for liturgical manuscripts only), copyists, musical genres, titles and first lines (for Bamburgh Castle manuscripts). The manuscripts are described, but no title analytics are included in the descriptions. The indexes provide the analysis of contents.

2038. Durham Cathedral. Library. A catalogue of the printed music and books on music in Durham Cathedral Library. By Alec Harman. London —New York—Toronto: Oxford Univ. Press, 1968. 136 p.

Review by Imogen Fellinger in *Die Musikforschung,* 25 (1972), p. 99–100; by Henry Leland Clarke in *Notes,* 25 (1969), p. 501–2.

EDINBURGH, SCOTLAND

2039. L'Institut Français d'Ecosse. Hector Berlioz (1803–1869), an exhibition at l'Institut Français d'Ecosse on the occasion of the 1963 Edinburgh International Festival. Edinburgh: Institut Français d'Ecosse, 1963. 40 p.

An exhibition catalog compiled by Richard Macnutt. 127 items, arranged chronologically with respect to the composer's career. Fully annotated with connecting commentary.

2040.   University. Reid Library. Catalogue of manuscripts, printed music, and books on music up to 1850 in the library of the Music Department of the University of Edinburgh. . . . Edited by Hans Gal. Edinburgh: Oliver and Boyd, 1941. 78 p.

Important for its holdings in 18th-century music, printed and in manuscript, from the private collection of John Reid, 1721–1807. Brief entries.

EISENACH, GERMANY

2041.   Richard Wagner-Museum. Katalog einer Richard Wagner Bibliothek; nach den vorliegenden Originalien systematisch-chronologisch geordnetes und mit Citaten und Anmerkungen versehenes authentisches Nachschlagebuch durch die gesammte Wagner-Literatur. Von Nikolaus Oesterlein. Leipzig: Breitkopf & Härtel, 1882–95. 4 v.

Apart from the bibliography of Wagner literature (vols. 1–2), this work provides a catalog of a collection of Wagner documents, formerly in Vienna but purchased by the city of Eisenach in 1895 (vols. 3–4).

ENGLAND

See under GREAT BRITAIN.

ESCORIAL, SPAIN

2042.   Monasterio de San Lorenzo El Real. Catálogo del Archivio Música del Monasterio de San Lorenzo El Real de El Escorial. [By] Samuel Rubio. Préambulo de Antonio Iglesias. Cuenca: Instituto de Musica Religiosa, 1976–82. 2 v. ((Instituto de Música Religiosa. Ediciones, 12 & 18)

V. 2 gives the incipits of the works listed in v. 1 and has title: *Catálogo del archivo de música de San Lorenzo El Real de El Escorial, [por Samuel Rubio y* J. Sierra; presentación Pablo López de Osaba].

A catalog of manuscript choirbooks, scores, part books, and unbound sets of parts from the 16th to the 19th century, with descriptions and analyzed contents. There is an appendix of brief biographies of the principal composers and an index of names.

ESSEN, GERMANY

2043.   Essen Stadtbibliothek. Systematischer Katalog der Musikbibliothek. Verzeichnis des Gesamtbestandes 1973. Bearbeitet von Manfred Willfort. Essen: Stadtbibliothek, 1974. 372 p.

Teil 1: Bücher.

A classified catalog of books on music.

FERRARA, ITALY

Biblioteca Comunale. See no. 2109.

FLORENCE, ITALY

2044. Biblioteca Nazionale Centrale. Catalogo dei manoscritti musicali della Biblioteca Nazionale di Firenze di Bianca Becherini. Kassel, Bärenreiter, 1959. 178 p.

144 numbered items; detailed descriptions, contents of collections. Indexes of text incipits, musicians, poets, and names mentioned in the descriptive notes.

Review by Frank L. Harrison in *Music and letters,* 42 (1961), p. 281; by Nanie Bridgman in *Fontes artis musicae,* 8 (1961), p. 31–33; by Walther Durr in *Die Musikforschung,* 14 (1961), p. 234–35.

2045. Biblioteca Nazionale Centrale. Mostra bibliografica di musica italiana dalle origini alla fine del secolo XVIII. Firenze: L. S. Olschki, 1937. 102 p.

An exhibition catalog. Preface signed: Anita Mondolfo.

Conservatorio di Musica "Luigi Cherubini" (formerly cited as R. Istituto Musicale). See also no. 2102.

2046. Conservatorio di Musica "Luigi Cherubini." "I manoscritti e le stampe rare della Biblioteca del Conservatorio 'L. Cherubini' di Firenze" di Bianca Becherini. In *La bibliofilia,* 66 (1964), p. 255–99.

20 manuscripts and 21 early printed books "nuova catalogazione e reintegrazione."

A catalog compiled for the purpose of giving full descriptions of those items in the collection that are most rare and most interesting to foreign scholars.

2047. Conservatorio di Musica "Luigi Cherubini". Catalogo delle opere musicali teoriche e pratiche di autori vissuti sino ai primi decenni del secolo XIX [nella] Biblioteca del Conservatorio di Musica di Firenze, per R. Gondolfi, C. Cordara, ed A. Bonaventura. Bologna: Forni, 1977. 321 p. (Bibliotheca musica bononiensis, I, 11)

A reprint of the edition 1929, published in Parma, which was itself a slightly altered version of the corresponding volume (IV, 1) in the Associazione dei Musicologi Italiani *Catalogo generale ...* (see no. 2102)

2048. Conservatorio di Musica "Luigi Cherubini." Esposizione nazionale dei Conservatori Musicali e delle Bibliotheche. Palazzo Devanzati, 27 ottobre 1949–8 gennaio 1950. Firenze: G. Barbera, 1950. 121 p.

Exposition catalog celebrating the 100th anniversary of the founding of the conservatory. Includes manuscripts, printed music, and some musical instruments.

2049. Conservatorio di Musica "Luigi Cherubini." Indice di alcuni cimeli esposti appartenenti alla Biblioteca del R. Istituto di Riccardo Gandolfi. Firenze: Tipografia Galletti e Cocci, 1911. 32 p.

At head of title: "Nella commemorazione cinquantenaria dalla fondazione del R. Istituto Musicale 'Luigi Cherubini' di Firenze."

Brief descriptive entries for 30 manuscripts and 37 early printed books, 32 theory works, and 4 "Curiosita diversi."

2050. Conservatorio di Musica "Luigi Cherubini." Basevi Collection. "The 'Basevi' collection in the Library of Cherubini Conservatory, Florence" by Anna Maria Trivisonno in *Fontes artis musicae,* 32 (1985), p. 114–16.

A very brief introduction to the collection of Abramo Basevi who was a composer, musicologist, editor (for the publishing house of Guidi and of the journals *L'Armonia* (1856–59) and *Il Boccherini.* A book-length catalog is anticipated.

2051. Galleria degli Uffizi. Gli strumenti musicali nei dipinti della Galleria degli Uffizi di Marziano Bernardi e Andrea Della Corte. Torino: Edizioni Radio Italiana, 1952. 177 p. 51 plates.

A handsome volume devoted to representations of musical activity in paintings in the Uffizi gallery. Index of artists and of instruments depicted.

2052. Galleria degli Uffizi. I disegni musicali del Gabinetto degli "Uffizi" e delle minori collezioni pubbliche a Firenze di Luigi Parigi. Firenze: L. S. Olschki, 1951. 233 p.

A catalog of prints and drawings with musical content or subject matter: musicians, musical instruments, performance practice, etc. Indexed by instruments and by subjects.

2053. Galleria degli Uffizi. Mostra di strumenti musicali in disegni degli "Uffizi." Catalogo a cura di Luisa Marcucci con prefazione di Luigi Parigi. Firenze: L. S. Olschki, 1952. 47 p.

An exhibition of 65 items from the Uffizi print collection; 25 plates.

2054. Gandolfi, Riccardo. Illustrazioni di Alcuni Cimeli Concernenti l'Arte Musicale in Firenze ... di Riccardo Gandolfi. In Firenze, a cura della Commissione per la Esposizione di Vienna, 1892.

A lavish, illustrated catalog prepared for the Vienna exposition of 1892. Limited edition, elephant folio, 39 facsimile plates of Italian musical documents from the 11th to the 19th centuries. Historical introduction and notes on the plates.

FRANCE

2055. Bridgman, Nanie. "Musique profane italienne des 16e et 17e siècles dans les bibliothèques françaises." In *Fontes artis musicae* (1955:1), p. 40–59.

Precise description of 32 rarities of the 16th and 17th centuries found in 5 public or private libraries in France.

2056. Chaillon, Paule. "Les fonds musicaux de quelques bibliothèques de province." In *Fontes artis musicae* (1955:2), p. 151–63.

Describes a group of source materials found in 24 French provincial libraries, sources that came to light in connection with work done in preparation for the RISM volumes.

FRANKFURT AM MAIN, GERMANY

2057. Deutsches Rundfunkarchiv. Die ersten vier Jahrsehnte unseres Jahrhunderts im Psiegel einer Berliner Schallplaatensammlung. Verzeichnis von Musik- und Sprechschallplatten aus der Sammlung des Berliner Theaterwissenschaftlers Martin Günther Sarneck. Frankfurt am Main: Deutsches Rundfunkarchiv, 1966. 2 v.
Preface signed by Hans-Joachim Weinbrenner.
Bd 1: Sänger und Sängerinnen A-S. Nr. 1–1278.
Bd 2: Sänger und Sängerinnen T-Z; Instrumentalmusik. Wortaufnahmen. Nr. 1279–2312.
A catalog of the Sarneck Collection in the Deutsches Rundfunkarchiv. Vol. 2 contains indexes of persons by profession. Separate composer index.

2058. International Exhibition "Music in the Life of the People." Katalog der Internationalen Austellung "Musik im Leben der Völker" von Kathi Meyer. Frankfurt am Main: Hauserpresse Werner U. Winter, 1927. 340 p.
Catalog of the large international music exhibition held June 11 to August 28, 1927. Organized according to the systematic arrangement of the exhibition halls. Includes printed books, manuscripts, instruments, pictures and other artifacts. 49 plates.
A separate catalog of the Italian section was printed in Rome, 1927. 161 p.

2059. Lessing-Gymnasium. bibliothek. Die musikalischen Schatze der Gymnasialbibliothek und der Peterskirch zu Frankfurt a. M. von Carl Isräel. Frankfurt a. M.: Mahlau und Waldschmidt, 1872. 118 p.
Covers the period to about 1800; full bibliographical data.

2060. Stadt- und Universitätsbibliothek. Thematischer Katalog der kirchlichen Musikhandschriften des 17. und 18. Jahrhunderts in der Stadt- und Universitätsbibliothek Frankfurt am Main: (Signaturengruppe Ms. Ff. Mus.); bearb. u. beschrieben von Joachim Schlichte; [hrsg. von d. Stadt- u. Univ.-Bibliothek Frankfurt am Main]. Frankfurt am Main: Klostermann, 1979. 500 p. (Kataloge der Stadt- und Universitätsbibliothek Frankfurt am Main, 8)

2061. Stadtbibliothek. Kirchliche Musikhandschriften des XVII. und XVIII. Jahrhunderts; Katalog von Carl Süss, im Auftrage der Gesellschaft der Freunde der Stadtbibliothek, bearb. und hrsg. von Peter Epstein. Berlin: Frankfurter Verlags-Anstalt, 1926. 224 p.
Chiefly cantatas arranged alphabetically under composer, with a separate section of 834 works by G. P. Telemann. Entries give date if known, title, instrumentation.

FREIBURG, GERMANY

2062. Gamber, Klaus. Codices liturgici latini antiquiores. Freiburg: Universitätsverlag, 1963. (Spicilegii friburgensis subsidia, 1.)
Liturgical music manuscripts in the library of the University at Freiburg.

2063. Kade, Otto. Die älteren Musikalien der Stadt Freiburg in Sachsen. Leipzig: Breitkopf & Härtel, 1888. (Beilage. Monatshefte für Musikgeschichte. Jahrgang 20.) 32 p.

FREIBURG IM BREISGAU, GERMANY

2063.1. Universität Freiburg im Breisgau. Bibliothek. Die Musikhandschriften der Universitätsbibliothek und anderer öffentlicher Sammlungen in Freiburg im Breisgau und Umgebung. Beschreiben von Clytus Gottwald. Wiesbaden: Otto Harrassowitz, 1979. 224 p.

Covers music manuscripts in seven institutions. Each manuscript is described and analyzed fully. Some descriptions include thematic incipits. Indexes to text incipits and to persons, places, and things.

GDANSK, POLAND (FORMERLY DANZIG)

2064. Stadtbibliothek. Die musikalischen Handschriften der Stadtbibliothek und in ihrer Verwaltung befindlichen Kirchenbibliotheken von St. Katharinen und St. Johann in Danzig von Otto Günther. Danzig, 1911. (Katalog der Handschriften der Danziger stadtbibliothek, Bd. 4: Handschriften, Teil 4.)

The surviving music manuscripts and early printed books of the Danzig Stadtbibliothek have been filmed and are listed in the catalog of music sources published by the Polish National Library in Warsaw (see no. 2464). Professor Plamenac in his articles on East European music libraries (no. 2020) has given a summary listing of the major holdings of this collection.

GENOA, ITALY

2065. Biblioteca dell'Istituto Musicale "Nicolo Paganini." Catalogo del fondo antico a cura di Salvatore Pintacuda. Milano: Istituto Editoriale Italiano, 1966. (Bibliotheca musicae, 4.) 489 p.

Review by Frank A. D'Accone in *Notes,* 23 (1967), p. 530–31.

Biblioteca Universitaria. See no. 2107.

GERMANY

2066. Kahl, Willi und Wilhelm-Martin Luther. Repertorium der Musikwissenschaft. . . .

For complete citation and annotation, see no. 2066.

2067. Schaal, Richard. Führer durch deutsche Musikbibliotheken. Wilhelmshaven: Heinrichshofen's Verlag, 1971. (Taschenbücher zur Musikwissenschaft, 7.) 163 p.

German libraries are listed alphabetically by place, covering both West and East Germany. For the major libraries there are descriptions given of the collection, with some historical information. Bibliographies include catalogs and other publications related to the libraries under consideration.

GERMANY (DEUTSCHE DEMOKRATISCHE REPUBLIK)

2068. Deutscher Bibliotheksverband. Sektion Musikbibliotheken. Musikbibliotheken und Musikaliensammlungen in der Deutschen Demokratischen Republik. Red. Peter Thuringer. Mitarb. Jutta Theurich und Rose Hebenstreit. Halle: Internat. Vereinigung d. Musikbibliotheken, Landergruppe DDR, 1969. 62 p.

A publication sponsored by the East German section of the International Association of Music Libraries.

91 institutions are described, with pertinent data concerning their resources and servieces. Catalogs and other publications cited.

GLASGOW, SCOTLAND

2069. Anderson's College. Library. Euing Collection. The Euing musical library. Catalogue of the musical library of the late Wm. Euing, Esq., bequeathed to Anderson's University, Glasgow. . . . Glasgow: Printed by W. M. Ferguson, 1878. 256 p.

Classified catalog. The collection is strong in theoretical works from 1487 and liturgical music of the Church of England, 16th to 19th centuries.

GOTTINGEN, GERMANY

2070. Niedersächsische Staats- und Universitäts-Bibliothek. Die Musikwerke der Kg. Universitäts-Bibliothek in Gottingen. Verzeichnet von Albert Quantz. Berlin: T. Trautwein, 1883. (Monatshefte für Musikgeschichte. Beilage, Jahrgang 15.) 45 p.

45 theoretical works and some 100 music prints of the 16th and 17th centuries. Good representation of German composers of the period.

2071. Niedersächsische Staats- und Universitäts-Bibliothek. Johann Sebastian Bach Documenta. Hrsg. von Wilhelm-Martin Luther zum Bachfest 1950 in Göttingen. Kassel, Bärenreiter, 1950. 148 p.

545 numbered items from an exhibition illustrating J. S. Bach's influence from his own time to the present day. Covers a wide area of documentation. 54 plates.

GOTTWEIG (BENEDICTINE ABBEY), AUSTRIA

2072. Göttweig. Graphisches Kabinett. Musik, Theater, Tanz vom 16. Jahrhundert bis zum 19. Jahrhundert in ihrem Beziehungen zur Gesellschaft. Ausstellung Stift Göttweig, Niederösterreich, 28. Mai-23. Okt. 1966. 86 p.

This library has been enriched by materials from the collection of the Viennese collector Aloys Fuchs.

2073. Wondratsch, Heinrich. Der Göttweiger thematische Katalog von 1830 hrsg., kommentiert und mit Registern versehen von Friedrich W. Riedel. München: E. Katzbichler, 1979. 2 v. (Studien zur Landes- und Sozialgeschichte der Musik, Bd. 2–3)

Edition of a thematic catalog originating in 1830 of a collection of music in the Benedictine Abbey of Göttweig in Austria.

Original manuscript title page reads: *Katalogus operum musicalium in choro musicali monasterii O.S.P.B. Gottwicensis, R.R.D.D. Altmanno abbate, per R.D. Henricum Wondratsch, p.t. chori regentem, conscriptus. Anno MDCCCXXX. Tom. 1.*
Contents: 1. Faksimile der Originalhandschrift; 2. Historisch-quellen-kundliche Bemerkungen, Kommentar und Register.

GRANADA, SPAIN

2074. Capilla Real. Archivo. "El Archivo de música de la Capilla Real de Grenada," por José Caló Calo. In *Anuario musical,* 13 (1958), p. 103–28.
A small collection of manuscripts, early printed books, and documents. Lists full contents for polyphonic sources.

GRAZ, AUSTRIA

2075. Neue Galerie. Bilder aus Beethovens Leben, aus der Beethoven Sammlung G. L. de Baranyai. Ausstellung des Landes Steiermark und der Stadt Graz. Graz, 1962. 77 p.

GREAT BRITAIN

2076. Bibliotheca Musico-Liturgica. A descriptive handlist of the musical and Latin-liturgical mss. of the Middle ages preserved in the libraries of Great Britain and Ireland. Drawn up by W. H. Frere ... and printed for the members of the Plainsong and Mediaeval Music Society. London: B. Quaritch, 1901–1932. 2 v.
Reprint by Georg Olms, Hildesheim, 1967.
See no. 1739 for complete annotation.

2077. British Museum. Printed music in the British Museum: an account of the collections, the catalogues, and their formation, up to 1920; by Alexander Hyatt King. London: C. Bingley; Munich, etc.:K. G. Saur, etc., 1979. 210 p.
A descriptive, historical work of particular use to those making intense use of the collections of printed music in the British Museum.

2078. Penney, Barbara. Music in British libraries: a directory of resources. 3rd ed. London: Library Association, 1981. 452 p.
Published in 1971, 1974 & 1978 in editions by Maureen W. Long.

2079. Schnapper, Edith B., ed. The British Union-Catalogue of Early Music Printed Before the Year 1801. A record of the holdings of over 100 libraries throughout the British Isles. London: Butterworths Scientific Publications, 1957. 2 v.
See no. 1750 for complete annotation.

GREENSBORO, NORTH CAROLINA

2080. University. Walter Clinton Jackson Library. Cello music collections in the Jackson Library, University of North Carolina at Greensboro. Part I:

The Luigi Silva Collection. Compiled by Barbara B. Cassell and Clifton
E. Karnes III. Greensboro: Walter Clinton Jackson Library, 1978. 20 p.
  Photocopies of catalog cards. The library is made of chiefly of 20th
century compositions and editions.

GRIMMA, GERMANY

2081. Königliche Landesschule. Bibliothek. Verzeichniss der in der Bibliothek
der Königl. Landesschule zu Grimma vorhandenen Musikalien aus dem
16. und 17. Jahrhundert, von N. M. Petersen. Grimma: G. Gensel, 1861. 24
p.
  The greater part of this collection is now in the Säcsischen Landesbibliothek in Dresden.

GROTTAFERRATA, ITALY

2082. Biblioteca della Badia di Grottaferrata. "La musica bizantina e i codici
di melurgia della biblioteca di Grottaferrata." In *Academie e biblioteche
d'Italia,* 1930–31.
  Library of the principal center of Byzantine musical studies in Italy.

THE HAGUE, THE NETHERLANDS

2083. Gemeentemuseum. Nederslansche muziekleven 1600–1800. 's-Gravenhage: Gemeentemuseum, 6 Juni-6 September, 1936. 124 p.
  Catalog of an exhibition on Dutch musical life of the 17th and 18th
centuries. Includes printed books, manuscripts, musical instruments,
and paintings with musical subjects. Illustrated. Introduction by D. J.
Balfoort.

2084. Gemeentemuseum Catalogus van de musiekbibliotheek. Amsterdam:
F. Knuf, 1969– . 2 v. (Catalogi van de muziekbibliotheek en de collectie
muziekinstrumenten)
  Deel I: *Historische en theoretische werken tot 1800, door* Marie H.
Charbon.
  Deel II: *Vocale muziek van 1512 tot ca 1650, door Marie H. Charbon.*
  The first two volumes in a series of catalogs projected to cover the
resources, printed and in manuscript of the Music Library of the Gemeentemuseum at The Hague. These catalogs will incorporate the holdings of the Scheurleer collection. A parallel series is devoted to the
musical instruments in the Gemeentemuseum (see no. 2553).
  Deel II covers a cappella and accompanied works. Provides entries for
new acquisitions and analyzes contents more extensively than the
Scheurleer *Catalogus* (see no. 2085, below) and this supplements it. Index
of text incipits, names and publishers.

2085. Muziekhistorisch Museum van Dr. D. F. Scheurleer. Catalogus van de
muziek-werken en de boeken oven muziek. 's-Gravenhage: M. Nijhoff,
1923–25. 3 v.
  The catalog was preceded by two earlier compilations, one in two
volumes in 1885–87 and one in three volumes, 1893–1910.

A classified catalog; volume 3 is a general index. Numerous facsimiles of early title pages. The Scheurleer collection is an outstanding working library of musicology as well as containing many rarities. It is now the property of the city of The Hague.

HALLE, GERMANY

2086. Händel-Haus. Katalog zu den Sammlungen des Händel-Hauses in Halle. Halle and der Saale: Händel-Haus, 1961– . v. 1– .
Teil 1: Handschriftensammlung (1961). Teil 2: Bildsammlung, Porträts (1962). Teil 3: Bildsammlung, Städte- und Gebäudedarstellung (1964). Teil 5: Musikinstrumentensammlung, Besaitete Tasteninstrumente (1966). See no. 2557.
A growing series of catalogs concerned not only with Handel documents but with material on early-19th-century German song, iconography. Numerous plates.

HAMBURG, GERMANY

2087. Gesellschaft der Freunde des vaterländischen Schul- und Erziehungswesens, Hamburg. Ausschuss für Musik. Musikalisches Schaffen und Wirken aus drei Jahrhunderten. Sein fortleben in der Gegenwart. Ausstellung musikgeschichtlicher Drucke, Handschriften und alter Musikinstrumente. Staats- und Universitätsbibliothek. Museum für hamburgische Geschichte. Hamburg: Staats- und Universitätsbibliothek. Museum für hamburgische Geschichte, 1925. 89 p.
An exhibition catalog covering manuscripts, early prints, and instruments in the Hamburg City and University Library and the Museum für hamburgische Geschichte.
Contents: Aufsätze 1. *Kurzer Abrias der Musikgeschichte Hamburgs,* von dr. Hans Schröder; 2. *Alte Musikinstrumente im Museum für hamburgische Geschichte,* von dr. Hans Schröder.
Katalog I. T. *Musikalisches Schaffen aus drei Jahrhunderten.* Einführung von Philip Thorn. II. T. *Alte quellen neuer Musikübung.* Einführung von Armin Ciasen.

2088. Hamburger Musikbücherei. Oper, Operette, Singspiel. Ein Katalog der Hamburger Musikbücherei, 1965. Hrsg von Annemarie Eckhoff. Hamburg: Hamburger Öffentlichen Bücherhallen, 1965. 207 p.
A catalog of the theater holdings of the Hamburg Musikbücherei comprising some 3,198 volumes, 1,590 titles. Full scores and vocal scores are indicated, with publishers and plate numbers. Chiefly 19th and 20th century works, but with some early items. Arranged alphabetically by composer, with indexes of Singspiele, of full scores, of titles.
Review by Klaus Hortschansky in *Die Musikforschung,* 22 (1969), p. 521–22.

HARBURG, GERMANY

2089. Wallerstein'schen Bibliothek. Thematischer Katalog der Musikhandschriften der Fürstlich Oettingen-Wallerstein'schen Bibliothek Scholss Harburg [von] Gertraut Haberkamp; mit einer Geschichte des Musika-

lienbestandes, von Volker von Volckamer. München: G. Henle, 1976. 298 p. Kataloge bayerischer Musiksammlungen
Review by Stephen M. Fry in *Notes,* 34 (1977), p. 89.

HEILBRONN, GERMANY

2090. Gymnasium. Bibliothek. Alter Musikschatz, geordnet und beschreiben von Edwin Mayers. Heilbronn: C. F. Schmidt, 1893. 82 p. (Mitteilungen aus der Bibliothek des Heilbronner Gymnasiums, 2)

2091. Stadtarchiv. Die Musiksammlung der Stadtarchiv Heilbronn. Katalog mit Beitragen zur Geschichte der Sammlung und zur Quellenkunde des XVI. Jahrhunderts. Von Ulrich Siegele. Heilbronn: Stadtarchiv, 1967. 323 p. (Veroff. des Archivs der Stadt Heilbronn, 13)
Gives full bibliographical descriptions with contents of collections. RISM items are identified. 16 plates of early manuscripts, bindings, and editions. First line index; index of names and subjects.

HRADEC KRÁLOVÉ (KÖNIGGRÄTZ), CZECHOSLOVAKIA

2092. Cerný, Jaromir. Soupis hudeních rukopisů muzea v. Hraci Kralové Catalog of music manuscripts in the Museum at Hradec Kralove). Praha: Universita Karlova, 1966. 240 p. (Miscellanea musicologica, 19)
Catalog of 56 items, chiefly manuscripts of liturgical music. Copiously indexed by form, texts by language, with a bibliography of relevant literature; 16 facsimile plates.

HUNGARY

Rado, Polykarpe. Répertoire hymnologique. . . .

See no. 1875.

2093. Pethas, Iván. "Musikbibliotheken in Ungarn." In *Fontes artis musicae* (May-December 1968), p. 114–18.
Describes 15 current Hungarian music libraries, with a table giving comparative statistics on their holdings and services.

IOWA CITY, IOWA

2094. University Library. An annotated catalog of rare musical items in the libraries of the University of Iowa. Additions: 1963–1972. Compiled by Gordon S. Rowley, with a preface by Rita Benton. Iowa City: 1973. 121 p.
A catalog of 278 items, articulating with the volume entered below. Extended annotations, descriptive and biographical. RISM items identified. Bibliography (p. 107–16). Index of names.

2095. University Library. An exhibit of music and materials on music, early and rare. Preface by Albert T. Luper. Iowa City: The Graduate College and The University Libraries, State University of Iowa, April 1953. 39 p.

An annotated exhibition catalog of materials on loan from the Library of Congress, The Newberry Library, The University of Illinois, The Sibley Musical Library, and private sources. Part I: autograph scores (13 items). Part II: early music editions and manuscripts. Part III: books on music (45 items).

2096. University Library. Rare musical items in the libraries of Iowa. By Frederick K. Gable. Foreword by Albert T. Luper. Iowa City: 1963. 130 p.

A carefully annotated catalog of 275 items. Part I: books on music. Part II: music scores. Index of names and of selected subjects. Selected bibliography.

For an account of the history, resources, and services of this rapidly growing music library, see Rita Benton, " The music library of the University of Iowa," in *Fontes artis musicae* (July-December 1969), p. 124–29.

ITALY

2097. Associazione dei Musicologi Italiani. Catalogo generale delle opere musicali, teoriche o pratiche, manoscritti o stampate, di autori vissuti fino ai primi decenni del XIX secolo, esistenti nelle biblioteche e negli archivi d'Italia. . . . Parma: Freschig, 1911–1938. 14 v.

The *Associazione* catalogs are of mixed quality and completeness, but in many cases they represented the best available listings of the holdings of important Italian libraries. Their coverage is confined to music and theoretical works written or published before 1810. RISM should be consulted before these catalogs are approached.

2098. Associazione dei Musicologi Italiani. Catalogo generale delle opere musicali. . . . Vol. 1/1. Citta di Parma. (Compilatori: Guido Gasperini e Nestore Pellicelli). 1909–11. 295 p.

Reprint by Forni, Bologna, 1970.

2099. Associazione dei Musicologi Italiani. Catalogo generale delle opere musicali. . . . Vol. 1/2. Citta di Reggio-Emilia. (Compilatori: Guido Gasperini e Nestore Pellicelli). 1911. 24 p.

Reprint by Forni, Bologna, 1970.

2100. Associazione dei Musicologi Italiani. Catalogo generale delle opere musicali. . . . Vol. 2/1. Citta di Bologna. (Compilatori: Alfredo Bonora e Emilio Giani). 1910–11–38. 159 p.

Archivio della R. Accademia Filarmonica (p. 1–43).
Biblioteca dell'Avv. Raimondo Ambrosini (p. 47–66).
Archivio di S. Petronio (p. 71–159).

2101. Associazione dei Musicologi Italiani. Catalogo generale delle opere musicali. . . . Vol. 3. Citta di Milano. Biblioteca Ambrosiana. (Compilatore: Gaetano Cesari). 1910–11. 20 p. (incomplete)

2102. Associazione dei Musicologi Italiani. Catalogo generale delle opere musicali. . . . Vol. 4/1. Citta di Firenze. Biblioteca del R. Istituto Musicale.

(Compilatori: Riccardo Gandolfi, Carlo Cordara). 1910–11. 321 p.

2103. Associazione dei Musicologi Italiani. Catalogo generale delle opere musicali. ... Vol. 4/2. Citta di Pistoia. Archivio capitolare della cattedrale. (Compilatore: Umberto de Laughier). 1936–37. 106 p.

2104. Associazione dei Musicologi Italiani. Catalogo generale delle opere musicali. ... Vol. 5. Citta di Roma. Biblioteca della R. Accademia di S. Cecilia. (Compilatore: Otello Andolfi). 1912–13. (incomplete)

2105. Associazione dei Musicologi Italiani. Catalogo generale delle opere musicali. ... Vol. 6/1. Citta di Venezia. (Compiltore: Giovanni Concina). 1913–13. 382 p.
    Biblioteca Querini Stampalia (p. 1–25).
    Museo Correr (p. 29–113).
    Pia Casa di Ricovero (p. 117–61).
    R. Biblioteca di S. Marco (compilatori: Taddeo Wiel, A. d'Este, R. Faustini) (p. 169–382).

2106. Associazione dei Musicologi Italiani. Catalogo generale delle opere musicali. ... Vol. 6/2. Citta di Vicenza. Biblioteca bertoliana ... ; Archivio della cattedrale. (Compilatore: Primo Zanini). 1923. 48 p.

2107. Associazione dei Musicologi Italiani. Catalogo generale delle opere musicali. ... Vol. 7. Citta di Genova. R. Biblioteca Universitaria. (Schedatore: Raffaele Bresciano). n.d. 21 p.

2108. Associazione dei Musicologi Italiani. Catalogo generale delle opere musicali. ... Vol. 8. Citta di Modena. R. Biblioteca Estense. (Compilatore: Pio Lodi). 1916–24. 561 p.
    Reprint by Forni, Bologna, 1967.

2109. Associazione dei Musicologi Italiani. Catalogo generale delle opere musicali. ... Vol. 9. Citta di Ferrara. Biblioteca Comunale. (Compilatori: Emmannuele Davia e Alessandro Lombardi). 1917. 40 p.

2110. Associazione dei Musicologi Italiani. Catalogo generale delle opere musicali. ... Vol. 10/1. Citta di Napoli. Archivio dell'Oratorio dei Filippini. (Compilatore: Salvatore di Giacomo). 1918. 108 p.

2111. Associazione dei Musicologi Italiani. Catalogo generale delle opere musicali. ... Vol. 10/2. Citta di Napoli. Biblioteca del R. Conservatorio di S. Pietro a Majella. (Compilatori: Guido Gasperini e Franca Gallo). 1918–34. 696 p.

2112. Associazione dei Musicologi Italiani. Catalogo generale delle opere musicali. ... Vol. 11. Citta di Assisi. Biblioteca Comunale. (Compilatore: Francesco Pennacchi). 1921. 45 p.

2113. Associazione dei Musicologi Italiani. Catalogo generale delle opere musicali. ... Vol. 12. Citta di Torino. R. Biblioteca Nazionale. (Compilatori: Attilo Cimbro e Alberto Gentili). 1928. 38 p.

2114. Associazione dei Musicologi Italiani. Catalogo generale delle opere musicali. ... Vol. 13. Biblioteche e archivi della citta di Pisa. (Compilatore: Pietro Pecchiai). 1932–35. 90 p.

2115. Associazione dei Musicologi Italiani. Catalogo generale delle opere musicali. ... Vol 14. Citta di Verona. Biblioteca della Soc. Accademica Filarmonica di Verona. Fondo musicale antico. (Compilatore: Giuseppe Turrini). 1935–36. 54 p.

2116. Rubsamen, Walter H. "Music research in Italian libraries." In *Notes*, 6 (1948–49), p. 220–33, 543–69; 8 (1950–51), p. 70–89, 513.
A narrative account of the author's experiences working in Italian libraries shortly after World War II. Contains useful inventories, partially thematic, of manuscripts of early music in Italian libraries. Many of the difficulties described in this article have long since disappeared.

2117. Sartori, Claudio. "Italian music libraries." In *Fontes artis musicae*, 18 (1971), p. 93–157.
An issue of *Fontes* devoted primarily to the description of Italian music libraries and their resources; preceded by an illuminating discussion, in Italian, English, and German, of the general situation.

2118. Smijers, Albert. "Vijftiende en zestiende eeuwsche muziek handschriften in Italie met werken van Nederlandsche componisten." In *Tijdschrift der Vereeniging voor Nederlandse Muziekgeschiedenis*, 14 (1935), p. 165–81.
Describes a card file of compositions by Netherland composers of the 15th and 16th centuries in 50 manuscripts in Italian libraries. By means of collation, the author has been able to clarify numerous misattributions and identify anonymous works in these sources. Compositions by non-Netherlands composers in the mss. are not listed.

JENA, GERMANY

2119. Universitätsbibliothek. Die geistlichen Musikhandschriften der Universitätsbibliothek Jena, von Karl Erich Roediger. Jena: Frommansche Buchhandlung Walter Biedermann, 1935. 2 v.
Vol. 1: *Textband.* Vol. 2: *Notenverzeichnis.*
Reprinted by Olms, Hildesheim, 1985.
Primarily a source study with inventories of 18 choirbooks containing music of the Burgundian-Netherland repertory in the University Library at Jena. Vol. 1 treats the sources and their contents, with indexes of liturgical settings, of cantus firmi, of composers. Vol. 2 is a thematic catalog of the choirbooks. Vol. 1, p. 111–14: a listing of sixty-three 16th-century prints in the Jena library.

JERUSALEM, ISRAEL

2120. Jewish National and University Library, A. Z. Idelsohn Archives. A. Z. Idelsohn archives at the Jewish National and University Libary, Catalogue. Jerusalem: The Magnes Press, The Hebrew University, 1976. 134 p. (Yuval monograph series, 4)

A guide to the *Nachlass* of one of the founder of historical and ethnic studies on Jewish music.

Reviewed by Simha Arom in *Fontes artis musicae,* 24 (1977), p. 103.

JONKÖPING, SWEDEN

2121. Ruuth, Gustaf. Katalog over aldere musikalier i Per Brahegymnasiet i Jonkoping (Catalog of the music collection in Per Brahegymnasiet, Jonkoping). Stockholm: Svenskt Musikhistoriskt Arkov, 1971. 131 p. (Musik i Sverige, 2)

A collection of 18th- and 19th century music reflecting the repertoires of local musicians.

KALININGRAD, U.S.S.R. (FORMERLY KÖNIGSBERG, GERMANY)

2122. Staats- und Universitäts-Bibliothek. Bibliotheca Gottholdiana. Die musikalischen Schätze der Königlichen- und Universitäts-Bibliothek zu Königsberg in Preussen. Aus dem Nachlasse Friedrich August Gottholds. Ein Beitrag zur Geschichte und Theorie der Tonkunst, von Joseph Muller. Im Anhang: Joseph Muller-Blattau, "Die musikalischen Schätze der Staats- und Universitäts-Bibliothek zu Königsberg in Preussen". Hildesheim and New York: Georg Olms, 1971. 731 p.

Reprint of the edition originally published by Adolph Marcus, Bonn, 1870. The article by Muller-Blattau was published in the *Zeitschrift für Musikwissenschaft,* 6 (1924), p. 215–39.

An important collection of 55,000 volumes, strong in 17th-century church music, in print and in manuscript; also vocal music from the 16th to the 19th centuries. Works by various Königsberger Kapellmeister such as Eccard, Stobaeus, Sebastini. Also numerous first editions of Beethoven, Haydn, Mozart. *see* Kaliningrad

KASSEL, GERMANY

2123. Deutsches Musikgeschichtliches Archiv. Katalog der Filmsammlung. Zusammengestellt und bearbeitet von Harald Heckmann [und Jurgen Kindermann]. Kassel: Barenreiter, 1955– . Band I, Nr. 1– .

Title varies: Nr. 1, Mitteilungen und Katalog. ...

A series of lists documenting the holdings of a microfilm archive of primary source materials for the study of German music history. Includes manuscripts and early printed books. For a description of this project and its catalogs, see Harald Heckmann, "Archive of German music history", in *Notes,* 16 (1958), p. 35–39.

Brief review by Stephen M. Fry in *Notes,* 32 (1976), p. 781.

2124. Landesbibliothek. Katalog der Musikalien der Landesbibliothek, Kassel. Durchgearbeitet und abgeschrieben von Wilhelm Lange. Kassel: 1920. 1 v. (various pagings)

An unpublished catalog, available on microfilm from the *Deutsches Musikgeschichtliches Archiv,* which supplements the printed catalog by Carl Israël, below, extending the coverage to 18th- and 19th-century materials. The Lange catalog describes 438 folio volumes, 247 quartos, 53 octavos, and a supplement of 32 items.

2125. Landesbibliothek. Übersichtlicher Katalog der ständischen Landes-bibliothek zu Cassel. Bearbeitet von Carl Israel. Cassel: A. Freyschmidt, 1881. 78 p.

Works from the 16th and 17th centuries, both manuscripts and printed books. Rich in German and Italian church and chamber music. An un-published catalog by Wilhelm Lange, available in Kassel, supplements the coverage supplied by Israel's work.

KIEL, GERMANY

2126. Hortschansky, Klaus. Katalog der Kieler Musiksammlungen: die Notendrucke, Handschriften, Libretti und Bücher über Musik aus der Zeit bis 1830. Kassel: Barenreiter, 1963. 270 p. (Kieler Schriften zur Musikwissenschaft, 14)

A catalog of the music in three libraries in Kiel: the Schleswig-Hol-steinische Landesbibliothek; Bibliothek des Musikwissenschaftlichen Instituts der Universität; Universitätsbibliothek.

KNOXVILLE, TENNESSEE

2127. University of Tennessee Library. The Gottfried Galston Music Collec-tion and the Galston-Busoni Archive. By Pauline Shaw Bayne. Knoxville: University of Tennessee Library, 1978. 297 p.

1,490 numbered items. Multiple indexes: class index, title index, index of arrangers, editors, transcribers. Describes a small collection of minia-ture scores, books on music, and archival materials.

KÖNIGSBERG, GERMANY

See KALININGRAD, U.S.S.R.

KRAKOW, POLAND

2128. Uniwersytet Jagielloński. Bibljoteka. Ksiazki o muzyce w Bibljotece Jagielloński. Krakow: 1924–38. 3 v.

At head of the title: Jósef Reiss.

KREMSMÜNSTER, AUSTRIA

2129. Benediktiner-Stift Kremsmünster. Bibliothek. Die Lautentabulaturen des Stiftes Kremsmünster. Thematischer Katalog. Wien: Hermann Bohlaus, 1965. 274 p. (Tabulae musicae austriacae, 2)

Describes and inventories a group of 9 manuscripts and two early prints of lute music in the library of the Benedictine Abbey at Krems-munster.

Review by Hans Radke in *Die Musikforschung,* 21 (1968), p. 242–44.

LANCASTER, GREAT BRITAIN

2130. University. Library. Catalogue of the Hans Ferdinand Redlich Collection of musical books and scores, including material on the Second Viennese School; cataloging by Graham Royds. Lancaster: The University, 1976. 117 p.

LAŃCUT, POLAND

2131. Biblioteka Muzyczna Zamku w Lancucie. Katalog. By Krzyztof Bieganski. Kraków: Polske Wydawnictwo Muzyczne, 1968. 430 p.
A library of some 2,637 items, strong in late-18th- and early-19th-century music. Broadly classified as to vocal and instrumental music, theory and didactic works, with very specific subdivisions. Index of composers, of arrangers, of publishers (listed by place), ballets, operas, first-line index of texts.

LANGENBURG, GERMANY

2132. Fürstlich Hohenlohe-Langenburg'sche Schlossbibliothek. "Fürstlich Hohenlohe-Langenburg'sche Schlossbibliothek. Katalog der Musikhandschriften'. [Hrsg. von] Norbert Böker-Heil, Ursula Böker-Heil, Gertraut Haberkamp, und Helmut Rösing. In *Fontes artis musicae,* 25 (1978) p. 205–411.
An experimental printed form of part of the RISM A/II data base covering 249 manuscripts with thematic incipits and brief descriptions. Indexes to text incipits, to titles, to genres, to names, and to the musical incipits.

LAUSANNE, SWITZERLAND

2133. Vaud. Bibliothèque Cantonale et Universitaire. Département de la musique. Inventaire du fonds musical François Olivier, par Jean-Louis Matthey. Lausanne: 1971. 69 p. (Inventaire des fonds manuscrits, 2.)

2134. Vaud. Bibliothèque cantonale et universitaire. Département de la musique. Catalogue de l'ouvre de Hans Haug par Jean-Louis Matthey et Louis-Daniel Perret. Lausanne: Bibliothèque cantonale et universitaire, 1971. 83 p. (Inventaire des fonds manuscrits, 1)

2135. Vaud. Bibliothèque cantonale et universitaire. Département de la musique. Inventaire du fonds Adrien Bovy par Micheline Demont. Lausanne: Bibliothèque cantonale et universitaire, 1980. 63 *l.* (Inventaire des fonds manuscrits, 11)

2136. Vaud. Bibliothèque cantonale et universitaire. Département de la musique. Inventaire du Fonds musical Alfred Pochon par Jean-Louis Matthey. Lausanne: Bibliothèque cantonale et universitaire, 1979. 51 p. (Inventaire des fonds manuscrits, 9)

2137. Vaud. Bibliothèque cantonale et universitaire. Département de la musique.
Inventaire du fonds musical, Auguste Sérieyx par Jean-Louis Matthey.
Lausanne: Biblioth'eque cantonale et universitaire, 1974. 124 p. (Inventaire des fonds manuscrits, 4)

2138. Vaud. Bibliothèque cantonale et universitaire. Département de la musique.
Inventaire du fonds musical Bernard Reichel par Jean-Louis Matthey.
Lausanne: Bibliothèque cantonale et universitaire, 1974. 101 p. (Inventaire des fonds manuscripts, 5)

2139. Vaud. Bibliothèque cantonale et universitaire. Département de la musique.
Inventaire du fonds musical Carlo Hemmerling par Jean-Louis Matthey,
avec la collaboration de Rose Hemmerling-Dumur. Lausanne: Bibliothèque cantonale et universitaire, 1976. 77 p. (Inventaire des fonds manuscrits, 7)

2140. Vaud. Bibliothèque cantonale et universitaire. Département de la musique.
Inventaire du fonds musical Émile-Robert Blanchet par Jean-Louis Matthey, avec la collaboration de Germaine Schmidt. Lausanne: Bibliothèque cantonale et universitaire, Département de la musique, 1975. 71
p. (Inventaire des fonds manuscrits 6)

2141. Vaud. Bibliothèque cantonale et universitaire. Département de la musique.
Inventaire du fonds musical Ferenc Farkas: catalogue des ouvres Jean-Louis Matthey et András Farkas; avec la collab. de Ferenc Farkas. Lausanne: Bibliothèque cantonale et universitaire, 1979. 49 p.

2142. Vaud. Bibliothèque cantonale et universitaire. Département de la musique.
Inventaire du fonds musical George Templeton Strong, par Jean-Louis
Matthey. Lausanne: Bibliothèque cantonale et universitaire, Département de la musique, 1973. 134 p. (Inventaire des fonds manuscrits, 3)

2143. Vaud. Bibliothèque cantonale et universitaire. Département de la musique.
Inventaire du fonds musical Jean Apothéloz par Jean-Louis Matthey.
Lausanne Bibliothèque cantonale et universitaire, 1977. 35 p. (Inventaire des fonds manuscrits, 8)

2144. Vaud. Bibliothèque cantonale et universitaire. Département de la musique.
Inventaire du fonds Paul Budry (1883–1949) par Marianne Perrenoud.
Lausanne: Bibliothèque cantonale et universitaire, 1970. 36 *l.* (Inventaire des fonds manuscrits, 8)

LEGNICA, POLAND (FORMERLY LIEGNITZ, GERMANY)

2145. Ritter-Akademie. "Katalog der in der Kgl. Ritter-Akademie zu Liegnitz gedruckten und handschriftlichen Musikalien nebst den hymnologischen und musikalisch-theoretischen Werken," by Robert Eitner.

In *Monatshefte für Musikgeschichte,* 1 (1869), p. 25–39, 50–56, 70–76 (incomplete). *See* Legnica

2146. Ritter-Akademie. Die Musik-Handschriften der Konigl. Ritter-Akademie zu Liegnitz. Verzeichnet von Ernst Pfudel. Leipzig: Breitkopf & Hartel, 1886–89. 74 p. (Monatshefte für Musikgeschichte. Beilage. Jahrgang 18 u. 21)

LEIPZIG, GERMANY

2147. Breitkopf & Härtel. Catalogo delle sinfonie, partite, overture, soli, trii, quattri e concerti per il violino, flauto traverso, cembalo ed altri stromenti, che si trovano in manuscritto nella officina musica di Giovanni Gottlob Breitkopf in Lipsia. Leipzig: 1762–65. 6 parts.
Supplemento I-XVI (1766–87).
Reprint by Dover Publications, New York, with an introduction by Barry S. Brook (1966).
An 18th-century thematic catalog of great importance. Chiefly instrumental music, but some vocal, from the archives of Breitkopf & Härtel. Useful in tracing or identifying works of the period.

2148. Breitkopf & Härtel. Katalog des Archive von Breitkopf & Härtel, Leipzig, im Auftrag der Firma. Hrsg. von Wilhelm Hitzig. Leipzig: Breitkopf & Hartel, 1925–26. 2 v. in 1.
1. Musik-Autographe. 2. Briefe.
348 autograph score from Handel to Hindemith, fully described, with a composer index. Autograph letters are limited to persons born before 1780. Separate index to letters.

2149. Musikbibliothek der Stadt Leipzig. Erst- und Frühdrucke von Robert Schumann in der Musikbibliothek Leipzig. Leipzig: 1960. 64 p. (Bibliographische Veroffentlichungen der Musikbibliothek der Stadt Leipzig.)
The exhibition also included pictures, autographs, and literature on Robert Schumann.

2150. Musikbibliothek der Stadt Leipzig. Handschriften der Werke Johann Sebastian Bachs in der Musikbibliothek der Stadt Leipzig. Bearb. von Peter Krause. Leipzig: 1964. 62 p.

2151. Musikbibliothek der Stadt Leipzig. Katalog der vor 1800 gedrukten Opernlibretti der Musikbibliothek der Stadt Leipzig bearbeitet von Cornelia Krumbiegel und Peter Krause. Leipzig: Musikbibliothek der Stadt Leipzig, 1981–82. 2 v.
Catalog of an extensive collection, brought together in part from the collection of Carl Ferdinand Becker and the music library of the publishing firm Peters.
Review by Claudio Sartori in *Fontes artis musicae,* 30 (1983), p. 225.

2152. Musikbibliothek der Stadt Leipzig. Quellenwerke zur Händelforschung: Katalog. Hrsg. anlässlich der wissenschaftlichen Konferenz zur

Händel-Ehrung der D.D.R., 11–19 April, 1959, in Halle. Leipzig: 1959. 29 p.

2153. Musikbibliothek Peters. Katalog der Musikbibliothek Peters, neu bearb. von Rudolf Schwartz. Band I: Bucher und Schriften. Leipzig: C. F. Peters, 1910. 227 p.

An earlier edition by Emil Vogel (1894) included both books and music.

Classified catalog of a large reference library of music literature maintained by C. F. Peters before the war. All publishers represented. Many early works, although the chief strength is in 19th-century literature. Entries give place and date of publication but not publisher. Major classes: dictionaries, periodicals, music history, biographies and monographs, instruction, instruments, aesthetics, etc.

LENINGRAD, U.S.S.R.

2154. Golubovskii, I. V. Muzykal'nyii Leningrad. Leningrad: Gosudarstvennoe Muzykalnoe Izdatel'stvo, 1958.

"Bibliotek i muzei," p. 351–411.

Describes in general terms the musical content of 14 libraries, 2 record libraries, and 12 museums. Lists manuscripts of Russian composers and mentions a few examples of western manuscripts and early books in various collections. Details as to organization, cataloging, circulation, etc.

LEXINGTON, KENTUCKY

2155. University of Kentucky. Library. "The Alfred Cortot collection at the University of Kentucky Libraries," by Frank Traficante in University of Kentucky Library *Library Notes,* 1 p. 1–18.

An account of that portion of the Cortot collection now resident at the University of Kentucky. Well illustrated with facsimiles. An alphabetical listing of all the Cortot materials.

LIÈGE, BELGIUM

2156. Conservatoire Royal de Musique. Fonds Terry. Catalogue de la Bibliothèque du Conservatoire Royal de Musique de Liège. Fonds Terry: Musique dramatique. Liege, Conservatoire Royal, 1960. 75 p.

A second volume covers 'Musique instrumentale." 51 p.

The Terry collection was acquired by the Liege Conservatory in 1882. The dramatic works stem chiefly from the period 1780 to 1880. Broadly classified as to full or vocal scores and by language of the libretto: French or foreign. The instrumental music is late 18th- or early 19th-century material, both printed and in manuscript.

2157. Conservatoire royal de musique. Bibliothèque. Inventaire général des manuscrits anciens du Conservatoire royal de musique de Liège [par] Maurice Barthélemy, bibliothécaire. Liège: DUP, 1977. 128 leaves

Lists manuscripts in the general collection, the Debroux collection and the Terry collection. Addenda on p. 119. Index.

LIEGNITZ, GERMANY

See LEGNICA, POLAND.

LILLE, FRANCE

2158. Bibliothèque de Lille. Catalogue des ouvrages sur la musique et des compositions musicales de la Bibliothèque de Lille. Lille: Imprimerie de Lefebvre-Ducrocq, 1879. 752 p.

2,721 items. The collection is particularly rich in late 18th- and early 19th-century French operas, which exist here in complete sets of performance materials. Also a large collection of symphonies, overtures, chamber music.

LINZ, AUSTRIA

2159. Bundesstaatliche Studienbibliothek. "An inventory of pre-1600 manuscripts pertaining to music, in the Bundesstaatliche Studienbibliothek (Linz, Austria)" by William Liddel Smith in *Fontes artis musicae,* 27 (1980), p. 162–71.

Includes a list of liturgical documents. Based on the microfilm holdings of the Hill Monastic Microfilm Library at St. John's Abbey and University, Collegeville, Minnesota.

LISBON, PORTUGAL

2160. Biblioteca da Ajuda. Catalogo de música manuscrita ... Elaborado sob a direcçao de Mariana Amelia Machado-Santos, directora da bibliotec. Lisboa: 1958–63. 6 v.

A collection of manuscripts, 3,617 items, entered alphabetically by composer and running consecutively through the six volumes. The collection is strong in 18th- and early 19th-century music, particularly opera.

2161. Biblioteca da Ajuda. Flores de música da Ajuda: exposição de raridades musicais manuscritas e impressas dos séculos XI a XX. Lisboa: Ministério da Educaçáo Nacional, Biblioteca da Ajuda, 1973. 63 p.

Catalog of an exhibition of 390 rare and unusual items from the collection.

2162. Library of João IV, King of Portugal. Primeira parte do index de livraria de musica do muyto alto, e poderoso Rey Dom João o IV ... Por ordem de sua Mag. por Paulo Crasbeck. Anno 1649. (Edited by J. de Vasconcellos). Porto: 1874–76. 525 p.

Reprinting of a catalog, compiled in 1649 by Paul Crasbeck, for the royal library in Lisbon, which was destroyed in the earthquake of 1755. The catalog, although of a collection now destroyed, remains an important bibliographical tool for the study of early Spanish and Portuguese music.

LIVERPOOL, ENGLAND

2163. Public Library. Catalogue of the music library. Liverpool: Central Public Libraries, 1954. 572 p.
Supersedes an earlier catalog of the same type, 1933.
About 45,000 entries for books and music published for the most part after 1800.

LONDON, ENGLAND

British Broadcasting Corporation. Central Music Library.

See no. 1212.

2164. British Library. Printed music before 1800, collection one of the Music Collection of the British Library, London. Series I: British printed music; Period A: Music before 1650; Part one: Individual composers; [and] Part two: Anthologies and tract volumes. Introduction by William Pidduck. General editor Roger Bray, Consultant editor Oliver Neighbor. Brighton: Harvester Press Microform Publications, 1983–86. 108 p.
As in the other Harvester guides, there is a list on the contents of each reel in each part and a listing of the manuscripts in each part followed by an index to names and composers in anthologies.

2165. British Library. The British Library Music Manuscript Collection; a listing and guide to [parts one through ten] of the Harvester microfilm collection; compiled by Professor Roger Bray. Brighton: Harvester Press Microform Publications, 1983–86. 4 v.
As in the other Harvester guides, there is a list on the contents of each reel in each part and a listing of the manuscripts in each part followed by a unifed index of names and composers for each volume. Vol. 3 includes a separate index of works by Handel.

2166. British Library. Dept. of Printed Books. The catalogue of printed music in the British Library to 1980; [editor Laureen Baillie]. Preface to v. 1 by Oliver W. Neighbor. London; New York: K.G. Saur, 1981– . 59 v. to date
"The collection of printed music up to 1980 listed in the present catalogue forms part of the Department of Printed Books ..."
Editor: v. 21–59, Robert Balchin.
A bibliographical tool of the first rank. Completion in approximately 60 volumes. Estimated at more than 1 million entries.

2167. British Library. Reference Division. "The music collections of the British Library Reference Division" by Malcolm Turner and Arthur Searle.
An historical resume of the situation with a description of the services and catalogs of the British Library, followed by descriptions of the Royal Music Library, The Hirsch Library, the general collections of printed music, music in the Department of Manuscripts, and The Music Library in the Department of Printed Books. There is a chronoogical survey of music manuscripts in the collections and a bibiliography of works about the music holdings in the British Library. A most helpful summary.

2168. British Museum. "Early Dutch librettos and plays with music in the British Museum." by Alfred Loewenberg. In *The journal of documentation,* 2 (March 1947). 30 p.

Subsequently published as a separate pamphlet by Aslib, London, 1947.

Catalog of 97 Dutch librettos of the 17th and 18th centuries. The list was projected as the first installment of a complete bibliography of librettos in the Museum, a project never carried out. *see* London, British Museum

2169. British Museum. Beethoven and England: an account of sources in the British Museum. By Pamela J. Willetts. London: The Trustees of the British Museum, 1970. 76 p. 16 plates.

Review by William Drabkin in *Notes,* 28 (1972), p. 692–94.

2170. British Museum. Four hundred years of music printing. By A. Hyatt King. London: Trustees of the British Museum, 1964. 48 p.

2nd edition 1968, incorporating a few changes in the text and additions to the bibliography

An exhibition catalog.

A fine outline with, particularly good examples, of the history of music printing.

2171. British Museum. Henry Purcell, 1659–1695; George Fredric Handel, 1685–1759; catalogue of a commemorative exhibition, May-August 1959. London: Published by the Trustees,1959. 47 p.

66 items related to Purcell, 180 to Handel. Introduction; annotations; eight full-page plates.

2172. British Museum. Mozart in the British Museum. London: Published for the Trustees, 1956. 27 p. 12 plates.

Catalog of an exhibition of 196 prints, autographs, early editions, etc., drawn from various collections in the British Museum, including the Department of Prints and Drawings, the Burney collection, Maps, Hirsch, and Zweig collections.

2173. British Museum. Department of Manuscripts. Catalogue of manuscript music in the British Museum, by A. Hughes-Hughes. London: 1906–9. 3 v.

Reprint of the first edition, London, 1964.

Vol. 1: sacred vocal music. Vol. 2: secular vocal music. Vol. 3: instrumental music, treatises, etc.

Entries are classified by genre or form, which means that the contents of the manuscripts are often separated and distributed through the three volumes. Author indexes; title, first-line index of songs.

2174. British Museum. Department of Manuscripts. Handlist of music manuscripts acquired 1908–67. By Pamela J. Willetts, Assistant Keeper, Department of Manuscripts. London: Published by the Trustees of the British Museum, 1970. 112 p.

This handlist supplements the Hughes-Hughes *Catalogue of manuscript music* (above).

Covers Additional manuscripts, Egerton manuscripts, music manuscripts on loan to the Department of Manuscripts, and music manuscripts preserved with printed collections in the Department of Printed Books. Index of names.

Review by Gordon Dodd in *Chelys, journal of the Viola da Gamba Society,* 2 (1970), p. 41–42; by Jack A. Westrup in *Music & letters,* 52 (1971), p. 184–85.

2175. British Museum. Department of Printed Books. Catalogue of music. Accessions. London:, British Museum, 1884– . Vol. 1– .

An annual publication compiled from the printing catalog slips. It is ordinarily reserved for departmental use in the British Museum, but there are copies in the New York Public Library and the Library of Congress. Occasional volumes of special bibliographical interest, like the Paul Hirsch collection, have been given wider distribution. See nos. 2178, 2179.

2176. British Museum. Department of Printed Books. Catalogue of printed music published between 1487 and 1800 now in the British Museum, by W. Barclay Squire. London: Printed by order of the Trustees, 1912. 2 v.

Reprint by Kraus, 1969.

First supplement, 34 p., bound in. *Second supplement,* by W. C. Smith. Cambridge Univ. Press, 1940. 85 p.

Includes early music of all countries, but particularly rich in British sources. Early theory and some literary works on music included. Brief entries with dates, or estimated dates, of publication.

2177. British Museum. Department of Printed Books. Hand-list of music published in some British and foreign periodicals between 1787 and 1848, now in the British Museum. London, Trustees of the British Museum, 1962. 80 p.

Indexes the music, chiefly songs, in 12 periodicals. 1,855 entries arranged by composer. Printed from slips prepared for entry in the British Museum catalog.

Review by Richard Schaal in *Die Musikforschung,* 17 (1964), p. 423.

2178. British Museum. Department of Printed Books. Hirsch Music Library. Books in the Hirsch Library, with supplementary list of music. London: Trustees of the British Museum, 1959. 542 p. (Catalogue of printed books in the British Museum. Accessions, 3rd ser., Pt. 291B.)

A catalog of over 11,500 books on music, acquired by the British Museum in 1946 as part of the Paul Hirsch library. Brief entries printed from slips prepared for the Museum catalog.

Review by Richard S. Hill in *Notes,* 17 (1960), p. 225–27.

See also no. 2508 under "Catalogs of Private Collections."

2179. British Museum. Department of Printed Books. Hirsch Music Library. Music in the Hirsch Library. London: Trustees of the British Museum, 1951. 438 p. (Catalogue of printed music in the British Museum. Accessions, Pt. 53.)

About 9,000 entries listed in two sections: "Music printed before 1800," p. 1–112; "Music printed since 1800," p. 113 to end.

See also the "Supplementary list of music" printed in the catalog of

Books in the Hirsch Library, above.
Review by Vincent H. Duckles in *Notes,* 10 (1952), p. 281–82.
See also no. 2508 under "Catalogs of Private Collections."

2180. British Museum. King's Music Library. Catalogue of an exhibition of music held in the King's Library, October 1953. London: 1953.

2181. British Museum. King's Music Library. Catalogue of the King's Music Library, by WIlliam Barclay Squire and Hilda Andrews. London: Printed by order of the Trustees, 1927–29. 3 v.
Part I: the Handel manuscripts, by William Barclay Squire, 143 p., five facsimile plates. Part II: the miscellaneous manuscripts, by Hilda Andrews, 277 p. Part III: printed music and musical literature, by William Barclay Squire, 383 p.
The King's Music Library, once on loan, is now part of the permanent collection of the British Museum. It is now generally referred to as the Royal Music Library.

2182. British Museum. Royal Music Library. A list of manuscript and printed music available on positive microfilm. London: British Museum Photographic Service, 1968. 17 p.
A useful listing of primary source material on positive microfilm. Lengths of film strips are noted so that estimates can be made.

2183. Guildhall Library. Gresham Music Library. A catalogue of the printed books and manuscripts deposited in Guildhall Library. London: The Corporation of London. Printed by authority of the Library Committee, 1965. 93 p.
A collection made up chiefly of late 18th-century materials reflecting the collecting activity of Edward Taylor, Gresham Professor from 1837 to 1883.
The section on manuscripts was prepared by Margery Anthea Baird. Index of names.

2184. Historical Music Loan Exhibition, 1885 ... A descriptive catalogue of rare manuscripts and printed books, chiefly liturgical. . . . by W. H. James Weale. London: B. Quaritch, 1886. 191 p.
An exhibition held at Albert Hall, London, June-October 1885.
Full bibliographical citations, with descriptive annotations, for 23 liturgical manuscripts, 73 liturgical books, 46 theory works, and some 56 items of early music. 14 plates.

2185. Musicians' Company. An illustrated catalogue of the music loan exhibition held. . . . by the Worshipful Company of Musicians at Fishmongers' Hall, June and July 1904. London: Novello, 1909. 353 p.
Includes early printed music, manuscripts, instruments, portraits, concert and theater bills, etc. Descriptive annotations; numerous plates and facsimiles.

2186. Plainsong and Mediaeval Music Society. Catalogue of the Society's library. Nashdom Abbey, Burnham, Bucks.: 1928. 39 p.

A short-title catalog. Four facsimile plates. The collection is now on deposit in the Music Library of the University of London.

2187. Royal College of Music. Catalogue of the manuscripts in the Royal College of Music, by William Barclay Squire, with additions by Rupert Erlebach. . . . London: 1931. 568, 216 leaves (typescript).

This catalog was never published. Typewritten copies are available in the major British libraries, and the catalog may be obtained on microfilm.

2188. Royal College of Music. Catalogue of the printed music in the library of the Royal College of Music by William Barclay Squire. . . . London: Printed by order of the Council . . ., 1909. 368 p.

This collection, rich in sources of early English music, incorporates the holdings of the Sacred Harmonic Society, below, and the library of Sir George Grove.

2189. Royal College of Music. The music collection of the Royal College of Music, London; a listing and guide to parts [one through nine] of the Harvester microfilm collection. Compiled by Roger Bray. Brighton: Harvester Press Microform Publications, 1983–85. 3 v.

As in the other Harvester guides, there is a list on the contents of each reel in each part and a listing of the manuscripts in each part followed by a unifed index of names and composers for each volume.

2190. Sacred Harmonic Society. Catalogue of the library . . . new edition, revised and augmented. London: Published by the Society, 1872. 399 p.

First printed in 1862, with a Supplement in 1882.

Classified catalog of printed music, manuscript music, and musical literature. 2,923 numbered items. General index.

2191. Westminster Abbey. Musik-Katalog der Bibliothek der Westminster-Abtei in London. Angefertigt von William Barclay Squire. Leipzig: Breitkopf & Hartel, 1903. 45 p. (Monatshefte für Musikgeschichte, Beilage. Jahrgang 35.)

Broadly classified catalog, including both printed and manuscript music, sacred and secular.

2192. English Folk Dance and Song Society, Cecil Sharpe House. Vaughan Williams Memorial Library. The Vaughan Williams Memorial Library catalog of the English Folk Dance and Song Society; acquisitions to the Library of books, pamphlets, periodicals, sheet music, and manuscripts, from its inception to 1971. London: Mansell, 1973. 769 p.

Located at Cecil Sharpe House, the collection focuses primarily, but not exclusively, on folk song and dance of the British Isles. There is an author catalog, a classified subject catalog, and an index to subjects.

LORETO, ITALY

2193. Santa Casa di Loreto. Archivio Musicale. L'Archivio musicale della Cappella Lauretana. Catalogo storico-critico. By Giovanni Tebaldini. Loreto: A cura dell'Amminstrazione di S. Casa, 1921. 198 p.

Printed music, 16th-18th centuries; manuscripts of the same period; an archive of manuscript scores by the Maestri della Cappella, anonymous works, etc. Full descriptions. Detailed history of the chapel. Index of composers.

LOS ANGELES, CALIFORNIA

2194. University of California, Los Angeles. Music Library. European folk music: a century of systematic scholarship. Catalog of the exhibition at the Music Library and the Foyer of Schoenberg Hall. Los Angeles: The UCLA Music Library, 1978. 31 p.

Exhibit coordinated by Stephen M. Fry.

95 items, each copiously annotated.

2195. University of California, Los Angeles. Music Library. The George Pullen Jackson collection of southern hymnody: a bibliography by Paul Joseph Revitt. Los Angeles, University of California Library, 1964. 26 p.

Review by Harry Eskew in *Anuario* of the Inter-American Institute for Musical Research, 1 (1965), p. 135.

LÜBECK, GERMANY

2196. Stadtbibliothek. Die Musikabteilung der Lubecker Stadtbibliothek in ihren älteren Bestanden: Noten und Bücher aus der Zeit von 12. bis zum Anfang des 19. Jahrhunderts, verzechnet von Wilhelm Stahl. Lübeck: 1931. 61 p.

2197. Stadtbibliothek. Katalog der Musik-Sammlung auf der Stadtbibliothek zu Lübeck. Verzeichnet von Carl Stiehl. Lübeck: Druck von Gebruder Borchers, [1893]. 59 p.

2198. Stadtbibliothek. Musik-Bücher der Lübecker Stadtbibliothek, verzeichnet von Prof. Wilhelm Stahl. Lübeck: Verlag der Lübecker Stadtbibliothek, 1927. 42 p.

Classified catalog of 19th- and 20th-century music literature.

LUCCA, ITALY

2199. Biblioteca del Seminario. "Il fondo di musiche a stampa della Biblioteca del Seminario di Lucca." By Claudio Sartori. In *Fontes artis musicae* (1955:2), p. 134–47.

A listing, alphabetically by composer, of the early music prints in the Seminary library, including, at the end of the list, five anthologies and three manuscripts.

2200. Biblioteca del Seminario. Catalogo delle musiche stampate e manoscritte del fondo antico. Ed. by Emilio Maggini. Milano: Istituto Editoriale Italiano, 1965. 405 p. (Bibliotheca musicae, 3)
Early printed music and manuscripts from the 16th to the early 19th centuries, with a small collection of writings on music. Contents of collections and locations of other copies listed. The collection is rich in early 17th-century prints of sacred music.

2201. Bonaccorsi, Alfredo. "Catalogo con notizie biografiche delle musiche dei maestri lucchesi esistenti nelle biblioteche di Lucc." In *Collectanea historiae musicae,* 2 (1957), p. 73–95.
Sources listed from three libraries in Lucca: the Seminario Arcivescovile; the Istituto Musicale "L. Boccherini;" and the Biblioteca Governativa.

2202. Lucca all'Esposizione della Musica e del Teatro in Vienna nel 1892. Lucca: Dalla Tipografia Giusti, 1892. 50 p.
A rare exposition catalog of music from Lucca displayed at the exposition in Vienna in 1892. 37 facsimile plates, with detailed discussions, and a brief introduction on the history of music in Lucc.

2203. Paoli, Marco. I corali della biblioteca statale di Lucca. Firenze: L. S. Olschki, 1977. 143 p. (Biblioteca di bibliografia italiana, 83)
Catalog of choir books and other manuscripts of choral music in the city library at Lucc. Includes bibliographical references and indexes.

LUND, SWEDEN

2204. Universitets Bibliotek. Die Handschriften und Varia der Schubertiana-Sammlung Taussig in der Universitätsbibliothek Lund [von] Siegfried Mühlhäuser. Wilhelmshaven: Heinrichshofen, 1981. 203 p. (Quellenkataloge zur Musikgeschichte, 17)
A richly illustrated catalog with facsimile pages of the Taussig collection of Schubertiana in Lund, Sweden. Includes bibliographical references and index.

LÜNEBURG, GERMANY

2205. Ratsbücherei. Katalog der Musikalien der Ratsbücherei Lüneburg, von Friedrich Welter. Lippstadt: Kistner & Siegel, 1950. 332 p.
Music prints and manuscripts, theory and practical music to 1850, holdings in 17th- and 18th-century instrumental music, particularly in the manuscript collections, which are listed separately. Numerous thematic incipits given.

LUZERN, SWITZERLAND

2206. Theater- und Musik-Liebhabergesellschaft. Die Haydndrucke aus dem archiv der "Theater- und Musik-Liebhabergesellschaft zu Luzern," nebst Materialien zum Musikleben in Luzern um 1800. Von Wilhelm Jerger. Freiburg in der Schweiz: Universitatsverlag, 1959. 45 p. (Frei-

burger Studien zur Musikwissenschaft, 7)
Entries for 64 early Haydn editions, with a table of concordances with
the Hoboken *Thematisch-bibliographisches Werkverzeichnis* of Haydn's
compositions.

MACERATA, ITALY

2207. Biblioteca Comunale. Studi sulla Biblioteca Comunale e sui tipografi
di Macerata. Miscellanea a cura di Aldo Adversi. Casa di Risparmio della
Provincia di Macerata, 1966.
P. 63–77: "La raccolta musicale ed in particolare gli spartiti autografi
della Cappella del Duomo di Macerata nella Biblioteca Comunale Mozzi-
Borgetti," by Lepanto de Angelis.
P. 79–122: "Catalogo del fondo musicale fino all'anno 1800 della Bibli-
oteca Comunale di Macerata," by Antoni Garbelatto.
A small collection comprising 22 items of early printed music, 24 of
music literature, and 23 music manuscripts.

MADRID, SPAIN

2208. Ayuntamiento. Biblioteca Musical Circulante. Catálogo. Ed. ilus. Madrid:
Ayuntamiento, Seccion de Cultura e Informacion, 1946. 610 p.
Apéndice 1, 1954. 213 p.
Music arranged in 16 classes, by instrument and form. Class T, "Bibliografia," contains books on music almost exclusively in Spanish. No publishers or dates given for entries. Many light and popular works. No
index.

2209. Biblioteca Medinaceli. "Catalogue of the music in the Biblioteca
Medinaceli, Madrid." By J. B. Trend. In *Revue hispanique,* 71 (1927), p.
485–554.
"The Medinaceli library is notable for possessing almost the entire
corpus of Spanish (Castilian) madrigals." 34 items fully described, with
inventories of contents and biographical sketches of the composers. Appendix: musical settings of famous poets.

2210. Biblioteca Municipal. Catálogo de la sección de música de la Biblioteca Municipal de Madrid. By José Subirá. Tomo primero: Teatro Menor
tonadillas y sainetes. Madrid: Sección de Cultura Artes Gráficas Munici-
pales, 1965. 394 p.
A collection of Spanish popular drama. Works are identified by text
incipits.

2211. Biblioteca Nacional. Catálogo músical de la Biblioteca Nacional de
Madrid, por Higinio Anglés y José Subirá. Barcelona: Consejo Superior de
Investigaciones Científicas, Instituto Español de Musicología, 1946–51. 3
v.
Vol. 1: Manuscritos (490 p., 27 facsimile plates). Vol. 2: Impresos: Libros
litúrgicos y teóricos musicales (292 p., 12 facsimile plates). Vol. 3: Impresos: Música práctica (410 p., 13 facsimile plates).
Entries for 234 manuscripts, 285 liturgical and theoretical prints, 337
music prints. Full descriptions with bibliographical references, lists of

contents.

2212. Biblioteca Nacional. Esposicion de música sagrada española. Catalog de los codices, manuscritos y libros musicales expuestos por Jaime Moll-Requeta. Madrid: 1954. 41 p.
120 items. 12 facsimile plates.

2213. La Casa de Alba. "La musique de chambre espagnole et française du XVIIIe siècle dans la bibliothèque du Duc d'Alba," par José Subirá. In *Revue de musicologie,* 7 (1926), p. 78–82.

2214. La Casa de Alba. La música en la Casa de Alba; estudios históricos y biográficos, por José Subirá. Madrid: [Establecimiento tipográfico "Sucesores de Rivadeneyra"], 1927. 374 p.
Not a catalog, but a mine of bibliographical information concerning the early music and books on music in the library of the Casa de Alba. Numerous early prints and manuscripts cited and described; 60 plates, chiefly facsimiles of bibliographical interest.

2215. Palacio Nacional. Capilla. Archivo de Música. Catálogo del Archivo de Música de la Real Capilla del Palacio, por Jose Garcia Marcellan. Madrid: Editorial del Patrimonio Nacional, [1938]. 361 p.
P. 13–142: listing of works by composer. P. 151–247: brief biographies of the composers represented. P. 249–361: classified listing of works.

MAINZ, GERMANY

2216. Gutenberg-Museum. Tausend Jahre Mainzer Musik; Katalog der Ausstellung, 1957 [Text: Adam Gottron]. Mainz: 1957. 32 p. (Kleiner Druck der Gutenberg-Gesellschaft, 63)
An illustrated exhibition catalog of 138 items related to the history of music in Mainz.

2217. Stadtbibliothek. "Zur Bibliographie der Musikdrucke des XV.-XVIII. Jahrhunderts der Mainzer Stadtbibliothek." By F. W. E. Roth. In *Monatshefte für Musikgeschichte,* 21 (1889), p. 25–33.
A catalog of 45 early music prints, including both theory works and practical music. Full bibliographical citations for some items, otherwise reference to citations in the catalogs of other collections.

MANCHESTER, ENGLAND

2218. Henry Watson Music Library. George Frideric Handel. The Newman Flower collection in the Henry Watson Music Library. A catalogue compiled by Arthur D. Walker, with a foreword by Winton Dean. Manchester: The Manchester Public Libraries, 1972. 134 p.

2219. Henry Watson Music Library. List of glees, madrigals, part-songs, etc. in the Henry Watson Music Library. Compiled by J. A. Cartledge. New York: B. Franklin, 1970. 197 p.

Reprint of the original edition of 1913.

MANNHEIM, GERMANY

2220. Hof- und Nationaltheater. Archiv und Bibliothek des Grossh. Hof- und Nationaltheaters in Mannheim, 1779–1839. . . . von Dr. Friedrich Walter. Leipzig: S. Hirzel, 1899. 2 v.

Band I: Das Theater-Archiv . . . Repertorium mit vielen Auszügen aus den Akten und Briefen, Inhalts-Ausgaben, usw.

Band II: Die Theater-Bibliothek . . . Katalog der gedruckten Bücher, Manuskripte und Musikalien der älteren Periode nebst einem Repertoire der Dalbergschen Zeit.

An important collection of theater history, in which music is well represented.

MECKLENBURG-SCHWERIN

See SCHWERIN, GERMANY.

MEXICO, D.F.

2221. Spiess, Lincoln and Thomas Stanford. An introduction to certain Mexican musical archives. Detroit: Information Coordinators, 1969. 185 p. (Detroit studies in music bibliography, 15)

Review by Henry Cobos in *Notes,* , 27 (1971), p. 491–92.

MILAN, ITALY

Biblioteca Ambrosiana. See no. 2101.

2222. Biblioteca Nazionale Braidense. "Musiche a stampa nella Biblioteca Braidense di Milano." By Mariangela Donà. In *Fontes artis musicae,* 7 (1960), p. 66–69.

Although it does not have a music collection as such, the National Library at Milan has a number of important items catalogue under "music." This article describes some 30 such items.

2223. Biblioteca Nazionale Braidense. La musica nelle biblioteche milanesi. Mostra di libri e documenti, Milano, 28 maggio-8 giugno 1963. . . . Milano: U. Allegretto di Campi, 1963. 55 p.

An exhibition catalog compiled by Mariangela Donà.

2224. Biblioteca Trivulziana. Civica Raccolta delle Stampe. Ritratti di musicisti ed artisti di teatro conservati nella raccolta delle stampe e dei disegni. Catalogo descrittivo. By Paolo Arrigoni e Achille Bertarelli. Milano: Tipografia del "Popolo d'Italia," 1934. 454 p., 30 plates.

Catalog of the Bertarelli collection of portraits of musicians, singers, comedians, dancers, and persons connected with the theater. Separate sections for acrobats, extemporaneous poets, child prodigies, etc. Entries give full names of subjects, descriptions of pictures, biographical information. Numerous indexes: names, places, theatrical performances, etc.

2225. Cappella del Duomo. Archivio. La Cappella del Duomo di Milano. Catalogo delle musiche dell'archivio. By Claudio Sartori. Milano: a cura della Ven. Fabbrica del Duomo, 1957. 366 p.

The archive, established in 1394, contains important manuscript holdings of the 15th century and sacred vocal works to the 19th. Separate section for manuscripts and printed music. Brief entries; contents for anthologies.

2226. Conservatorio di Musica "Giuseppe Verdi." Catalogo della biblioteca. Letteratura musicale e opere teoriche. Parte prima: Manoscritti e stampe fino al 1899. Milan: (Distributed by Casa Editrice Leo S. Olschki, Florence), 1969. 151 p.

This and the following entry are part of a series of catalogs devoted to the holdings of the library of the Milan conservatory, edited under the supervision of Guglielmo Barblan. This volume lists 2,458 writings on music published before 1900. Index of subjects, of editors, compilers, translators.

Review by Susan Sommer in *Notes,* 27 (1971), p. 730–31.

2227. Conservatorio di Musica "Giuseppe Verdi." Catalogo della biblioteca . . . Fondi speciali I: Musiche della Cappella di Santa Barbara in Mantova. Schede compilate da Gilda Grigolato. Prefazione di Guglielmo Barblan. Indici a cura di Agostina Zecca-Laterza. Milan: 1972. 530 p.

The collection of the Cappella di Santa Barbara in Mantua has been incorporated into the collection of the Milan conservatory.

2228. Conservatorio di Musica "Giuseppe Verdi." Indice generale dell'Archivio Musicale Noseda; compilato dal Prof. Eugenio de' Guarinoni . . . con una breve biografia del fondatore e con alcuni cenni intorno all'archivio stesso ed alla Biblioteca del R. Conservatorio di musica di Milano. Milano: E. Reggiani, 1898. 419 p.

First published in the *Anuario* of the Milan conservatory. 1889–96. 10,253 titles.

The strength of the collection is centered in late 18th- and early 19th-century music. Preceded by a brief historical introduction. Index of composers represented in autographs, and of operas in full score.

2229. Museo Teatrale alla Scala. Catalogo del Museo teatrale alla Scala. Edito a cura del consiglio direttivo; compilato da Stefano Vittadini. . . . Milano: E. Bestetti, 1940. 401 p.

An illustrated catalog of the musical-theatrical collection at La Scala. Bibliography: p. 375–93.

2230. Parigi, Luigi. La musica nelle gallerie di Milano. Con 21 illustrazioni in tavole fuori testo. Milano: Perrella, 1935. 71 p.

Paintings with musical subjects in the art galleries of Milan. Descriptions of each work and its subject matter. 21 plates.

MODENA, ITALY

Biblioteca Estense. See also no. 2108.

2231. Archivio di Stato. "Repertorio dei libri musicali di S. A. S. Francesco II d'Este nell'Archivio di Stato di Modena." By E. J. Luin. In *La Bibliofilia,* 38 (1936), p. 419–45.

A catalog compiled in the late 17th century of the holdings of the music library of Francesco II d'Este. Much of the material has been incorporated into the collection of the Biblioteca Estense in Modena. Rich in late 17th-century opera, oratorios, cantatas, etc. Both manuscripts and prints.

2232. Biblioteca Estense. "Bibliografia delle stampe musicali della R. Biblioteca Estense." By Vittorio Finzi. In *Rivista delle biblioteche* (1892–95): v. 3, p. 77–89, 107–14, 162–76; v. 4, p. 16–28, 174–85; v. 5, p. 48–64, 89–142. Full descriptions of 321 works. Index.

MONTECASSINO, ITALY

2233. Archivio Musicale. "I manoscritti musicali gregoriani dell'archivio di Montecassino." By Paolo M. Ferretti. In *Casinensia*: miscellanea di studi Cassinesi. ... V. 1 (1929), p. 187–203.

Detailed descriptions of 11 manuscripts of Gregorian chant in the Montecassino archive. The 11th consists of a group of fragments from various sources. Two facsimile plates.

2234. Archivio Musicale. "L'Archivio musicale di Montecassino." By Eduardo Dagnino. In *Casinensia*: miscellanea di studi Cassinesi pubblicati in occasione del XIV centenario della fondazione della Badia di Montecassino. V. 1 (1929), p. 273–96.

A summary account of the music holdings of the Montecassino archive, a collection of some 1,100 items, including more than 100 full scores of 18th-century operas, oratorios, etc. Four plates illustrating rarities from the collection.

MONTECATINI-TERME, ITALY

Biblioteca Antonio Venturi. ... See no. 2330.

MONTSERRAT, SPAIN

2235. Lenaerts, Rene B. "Niederlandische polyphone Musik in der Bibliothek von Montserrat." In *Festschrift Joseph Schmidt-Gorg zum 60. Geburtstag.* Bonn:, Beethoven-Haus, 1957. P. 196–201.

Describes six manuscripts containing Netherlands polyphony: manuscript numbers 765, 766, 769, 771, 772, 778.

MONZA, ITALY

2236. Duomo. Catalogo musicale del Duomo di Monza, per Rossana Dalmonte. Bologna: Forni, 1969. 219 p. (Bibliotheca musica Bononiensis, 6:2)

MOSCOW, U.S.S.R.

2237. Publichnaia Biblioteka. Otdel Rukopsei. Sobraniia D. V. Razumovskogo i V. F. Odoevskogo. Arkhiv D. V. Razumovskogo. Opisaniia pod radaktsiei I. M. Kudriavtseva. Moskva: 1960. 261 p.

Catalog of manuscripts, 15th-19th centuries, primarily of church music in various notations. The Razumovskii collection contains 135 manuscripts, the Odoevskii, 35. Description of biographical material, papers, letters, etc. in the Razumovskii archive. Chronological index; index of names and titles.

MOUNT ATHOS, GREECE

2238. Stathēs, Grēgorios Th. Ta cheirographa vyzantinēs mousikēs. Hagion Oros: Katalogos perigraphikos tōn cheirographōn Kōdikōn vyzantinēs mousikēs tōn apokeimenon en tais vivliothēkais tōn hierōn monōn Kai sketon tou Hagiou Orous. [The byzantine musical manuscripts of the Athos monasteries] Athēnai: Hidryma Byzantines Mousikologias, 1975-76. 2 v.

Added title page in French: *Les manuscrits de musique byzantine. Projected to 7 v.*

Covers manuscripts in the monasteries Eisagōgē, Xeropotamou, Docheiariou, Kōnstamonitou, Xenophōntos, Panteleēmonos, Simōnos Petras, Grēgoriou, Dionysiou.

MUNICH, GERMANY

2239. Bayerische Staatsbibliothek. "Die Augsburger Bibliothek Herwart und ihre Lautentabulaturen. Ein Musikbestand der Bayerischen Staatsbibliothek aus dem 16. Jahrhundert," by Marie Louise Martinez-Göllner. In *Fontes artis musicae* (January-Juni, 1969) p. 29-48.

A study focused primarily on 15 manuscripts of lute tablature acquired in 1586 by the Bavarian State Library with the purchase of the private library of Johann Heinrich Herwart of Augsburg. The article includes publication of a 16th-century catalog of printed instrumental music in the Herwart collection.

2240. Bayerische Staatsbibliothek. Carl Orff. Das Bühnenwerk. Mit einem Vorwort von Wolfgang Schadewaldt und einem chronologischen Werkverzeichnis. Ausstellung anlässlich des 75. Geburtstags, 10. Juni bis 31. Juli 1970. [Ausstellung und Katalog von Robert Münster]. München: Bayerische Staatsbibliothek, 1970. 58 p.

An exhibition on Orff's operatic works in honor of the composer's 75th birthday. Includes bibliography and index.

2241. Bayerische Staatsbibliothek. Das Orff-Schulwerk: Ausstellung, Bayerische Staatsbibliothek, 27. Oktober 1978 bis 20. Januar 1979. [Ausstellung und Katalog, Robert Münster und Renata Wagner]. Tutzing: H. Schneider, 1978. 139 p.

An exhibition on the Orff-Schulwerk materials and method. Includes bibliography and index.

2242. Bayerische Staatsbibliothek. Die musikalischen Handschriften der K. Hof- und Staatsbibliothek in München beschreiben von Jul. Jos. Maier. Erster Theil: Die Handschriften bis zum Ende des XVII. Jahrhunderts. München, in Commission der Palm'schen Hofbuchhandlung, 1879. 176 p.

278 items, chiefly anthologies, containing about 6,380 pieces of music. One of the richest collections of 16th-century music. A notable collection of 74 choirbooks belonging to the original Bavarian court chapel. "Inhalts-Verzeichnis" of anonymous and attributed works.

2243. Bayerische Staatsbibliothek Katalog der Musikhandschriften; Bayerische Staatsbibliothek. München: G. Henle, 1979– . 2 v. (Kataloge bayerischer Musiksammlungen, 5)

Contents:

V. 2: Marie Louise Göllner. *Tabulaturen und Stimmbücher bis zur Mitte des 17. Jahrhunderts.*

B. 3: Bettina Wackernagel. *Collectio Musicalis Maximilianea.*

2244. Bayerische Staatsbibliothek. La finta giardiniera; Mozarts Münchener Aufenthalt, 1774/75: Bayerische Staatsbibliothek, 13. Januar bis 28. Februar 1975. [Text und Ausstellung, Robert Münster]. München: Bayerische Staatsbibliothek, 1975. 45 p.

Catalog of an exhibition of 119 items relating to Mozart's stay in Munich. Includes bibliography and index.

2245. Bayerische Staatsbibliothek. Volksmusik in Bayern: ausgewählte Quellen und Dokumente aus sechs Jahrhunderten. Ausstellung, München 8.5–31.7. 1985. [Ausstellung und Katalogredaktion, Robert Münster; Mitarbeit, Margot Attenkofer]. München: Ehrenwirth, 1985. 207 p.

Catalog of an exhibition on folk music in Bavaria. Includes bibliography and index.

2246. Bayerische Staatsbibliothek. Wolfgang Amadeus Mozart, Idomeneo: 1781–1981: Essays, Forschungsberichte, Katalog mit der Rede zur Eröffnung der Ausstellung von Wolfgang Hildesheimer. Ausstellung, 27. Mai bis 31. Juli 1981. Bayerische Staatsbibliothek; [Ausstellung und Katalog, Robert Münster, Mitarbeit, Margot Attenkofer]. München; Zürich: Piper, 1981. 328 p.

Catalog of an exhibition on Mozart's *Idomeneo.* Includes bibliography and index.

2247. Hofkapelle Musikhandschriftensammlungen. Die ehemaligen Musikhandschriftensammlungen der Königlichen Hofkapelle und der Kurfürstin Maria Anna in München thematischer Katalog [von] Gertraut Haberkamp [und] Robert Münster. München: G. Henle, 1982. 251 p. (Kataloge bayerischer Musiksammlungen, 9)

2248. St. Michaelskirche Die Musikhandschriften der St. Michaelskirche in München: thematischer Katalog. [Von] Hildegard Herrmann-Schneider. München: G. Henle, 1985. 392 p. (Kataloge bayerischer Musiksammlungen, 7)

2249. Städtische Musikbücherei. Kataloge der städtischen Musikbücherei München . . . Erster Band: Klavier. Bearbeitet von Bibliotheksrat Dr. Willy Krienitz. München: 1931. 407 p.

Catalog of the holdings in keyboard music of one of the major public music libraries in Germany. Some 40,000 items, classified. Includes works for piano solo, duet, and two pianos. Index of names.

2250. Theatermuseum. "Die vor 1801 gedruckten Libretti des Theatermuseums München." By Richard Schaal. In *Die Musikforschung,* 10 (1957), p. 388–96, 487–94; 11 (1958), p. 54–69, 168–77, 321–36, 462–77; 12 (1959), p. 60–75, 161–77, 299–306, 454–61; 13 (1960), p. 38–46, 164–72, 299–306, 441–48; 14 (1961), p. 36–43, 166–83.

Also published separately by Bärenreiter, Kassel, 1962.

983 librettos listed alphabetically by title, with date and place of first performance, name of composer, etc.

2251. Theatinerkirche Sankt Kajetan. Die Musikhandschriften in der Theatinerkirche St. Kajetan in München, thematischer Katalog. [Von] Siegfried Gmeinwieser. München: Henle, 1979. 208 p. (Kataloge bayerischer Musiksammlungen, 4)

2252. Universitätsbibliothek. Die Musikhandschriften der Univesitätsbibliothek München. Beschrieben von Clytus Gottwald. Wiesbaden: Harrassowitz, 1968. 127 p. (Die Handschriften der Universitatsbibliothek Munchen, 2)

MÜNSTER, GERMANY

2253. Bischöfflichen Priesterseminars. Santini Bibliothek. "Verzeichnis der italienischen Messkompositionen aus der Bibliothek des Abbate Fortunato Santini, 18. Jahrhundert", p. 45–58 in Studien über Gebrauch der Instrumente in dem italienischen Kirchenorchester des 18. Jahrhunderts. Ein Beitrag zur Geschichte der instrumental begleiteten Messe in Italien. (Auf Grund des Materials in der Santini-Bibliothek zu Münster i. W.). Quakenbrück: Robert Kleinert, 1929.

Lists 450 18th-century masses in the Santini library, alphabetically by composer, with descriptions of their instrumentation.

2254. Bischöflichen Priesterseminars. Santini Bibliothek. "Verzeichnis der kirchenmusikalischen Werke der Santinischen Sammlung." In *Kirchenmusikalisches Jahrbuch,* p. 26–33 (1931–38).

An incomplete inventory of the sacred music in the Santini collection.

2255. Bischöflichen Priesterseminars. Santini Bibliothek. Kirchenmusikalische Schätze der Bibliothek des Abbate Fortunato Santini, ein Beitrag zur Geschichte des katholischen Kirchenmusik in Italien. By Joseph Killing. Dusseldorf: L. Schwann, 1910. 516 p.

A study based on the material in the Santini collection, a library of early music scored from the original partbooks by Fortunato Santini (1778–1862) and acquired about 1856 by the University Library at Munster.

P. 455–67: "Verzeichnis der in der Bibliothek Santini enthaltenen Druckwerke." P. 469–516: "Verzeichnis von Musikwerken die in der Santinischen Bibliothek als Handschriften enthalten sind."

2256. Universitätsbibliothek. Die musikalischen Schätze der Santinischen Sammlung. Führer durch di Ausstellung der Universitäts-Bibliothek. ...
Munster: Westfälische Vereinsdruckerei, 1929. 32 p.
Exhibition catalog prepared by K. G. Fellerer.

NAPLES, ITALY

2257. Biblioteca Nazionale. "Il fondo musicale cinquecentesco della Biblioteca Nazionale di Napoli." By Anna Mondolfo. In *Collectanea historiae musicae*, 2 (1957), p. 277–90.
Describes fifty-one 16th-century works.

2258. Biblioteca Nazionale. I codici notati della Biblioteca Nazionale di Napoli. By Raffaele Arnese. Firenze: Leo S. Olschki, 1967. 257 p. (Biblioteca di bibliografia italiano, 47)
Concerned chiefly with liturgical manuscripts in which musical notation is present, but also including a few sources in mensural notation. Indexes of types of notation, types of script, chronological arrangement, titles, and names. Bibliography, p. 127–47.
Review by Ewald Jammers in *Die Musikforschung*, 21 (1968), p. 504–6.

Conservatorio di Musica S. Pietro a Majella. See also no. 2111.

2259. Conservatorio di Musica "San Pietro a Majella." Biblioteca. Catalogo dei libretti d'opera in musica dei secoli XVII e XVIII, a cura di Francesco Melisi. Naples: Conservatorio di Musica "San Pietro a Majella.", 1985. 295 p.
Covers about 1,500 libretti in the Conservatory.

2260. Conservatorio di Musica S. Pietro a Majella. "La biblioteca del Conservatorio di Napoli." In *Accademie e biblioteche d'Italia*, 38 (1970), p. 286–92.
A brief narrative account stressing the important holdings of the library, particularly works related to the opera and cantata and documents of the Bellini-Donizetti period.

2261. Conservatorio di Musica S. Pietro a Majella. "Mozart alla Biblioteca del Conservatorio di Napoli." By Francesco Bossarelli. In *Analecta musicologica*, 5 (1968), p. 248–66; 7 (1969), p. 190–212.
A bibliography of the Mozart holdings of the Naples conservatory.

2262. Conservatorio di Musica S. Pietro a Majella. Il Museo storico musicale di S. Pietro a Majella. Napoli: R. Stabilimento Tipografico Francesco Giannini e Figli, 1930. 153 p.
A collection of musicians' portraits, busts, autographs, musical instruments, medals, and photographs. 734 items. Special archives of materials

related to Vincenzo Bellini and Giuseppe Martucci.

2263. Conservatorio di Musica S. Pietro a Majella. Mostra autografi musicali della scuola napoletana. . . . settembre-ottobre 1936. Napoli: Confederazione Fascista dei Professionisti e degli Artisti, 1936. 58 p.

An exhibition catalog of musical autographs and portraits of musicians of the Neapolitan school.

Oratorio dei Filippini. Archivio. See no. 2110.

THE NETHERLANDS

2264. Nederlands Bibliotheek- en Lektuurcentrum. Sektie Muziekbibliotheken en Fonotheken. Standaardkatalogus van boeken over muziek samengesteld in opdracht van de Sektie Muziekbibliotheken en Fonotheken. 2e, herz. dr. 's-Gravenhage:Nederlands Bibliotheek en Lektuur Centrum, 1977. 43 p.

NEW HAVEN, CONNECTICUT

2265. Yale University. Beinecke Rare Book and Manuscript Library. Music, printed and manuscript, in the James Weldon Johnson Memorial Collection of Negro Arts and Letters: an annotated catalog by Rae Linda Brown. New York: Garland Pub., 1982. 322 p.

A catalog of the 1,057 musical works in the collection established by Carl van Vechten.

2266. Yale University. Jackson Music Library. "The Filmer manuscripts: a handlist" by Robert Ford in *Notes,* 40, (1978), p. 814–25.

An inventory of 37 manuscripts of English music from the late 16th through the early 18th centuries.

2267. Yale University Music Library. A temporary mimeographed catalog of the music manuscripts and related materials of Charles Edward Ives. . . . Compiled by John Kirkpatrick in 1954–60. New Haven: Yale School of Music, 1960. 279 p. (typescript)

2268. Yale University, Music Library, Horatio Parker Archives. "The Horatio Parker Archives in the Yale University Music Library" by William C. Rorick in *Fontes artis musicae,* 26 (1979), p. 298–304.

A description of the papers left by the prominent member of the the "Second New England School."

NEW YORK, NEW YORK

2269. American Music Center Library. Catalog of the American Music Center Library. N.Y.: American Music Center, 1975–1982. 3 v.

Volume 1, edited by Judith Greenberg Finnell, covers choral and vocal works and is arranged by composer and title.

Volume 2, edited by Karen McNerney Famera, covers chamber music and is classified; there is a composer index.

Volume 3 covers music for orchestra. band, and large ensembles and is composed of biblioraphic entries drawn from the New York Public Library's data base; the catalog is in a single alphabetical sequence with composer, title, and subject entries as well as cross references.

The American Music Center Library collects printed and manuscript works of contemporary American composers and disseminates information about those works.

2270. American Music Center. Library. The National Endowment for the Arts: Composer/librettist program collection at the American Music Center. New York: American Music Center 1979. 304 p.

"In the spring of 1978 a brochure was distributed by AMC under the title: *Compositions, libretto and translations; supported by the National Endowment for the Arts: Composer/librettist program.*"

2271. Bartók Archives. The Béla Bartók Archives, history and catalogue. By Victor Bator. New York: Bartók Archives Publication, 1963. 39 p.

Description of the Archives and of their founding, with summary inventories of materials in such categories as letters, books, articles, clippings, concert programs, printed music, photgraphs, and recordings as well as autograph manuscripts.

This collection has been virtually inaccessible in recent years because of legal compilications involving its ownership. Two reports by Fritz A. Kuttner, published in *Die Musikforschung,* will help to clarify its present status: (1) "Der Katalog des Bartók-Archives in New York City," 21 (1969), p. 61–63, and (2) "Das Bartók-Archiv in New York City, ein Nachtrag," 22 (1969), p. 75–76.

2272. New York Public Library. Music Division. Elliott Carter: sketches and scores in manuscript; a selection of manuscripts and other pertinent material from the Americana Collection of the Music Division, the New York Public Library, on exhibition December 1973 through February 1974 in the Vincent Astor Gallery, Library & Museum of the Performing Arts, the New York Public Library at Lincoln Center. New York: New York Public Library, Astor, Lenox and Tilden Foundations, 1973. 64 p.

Includes an extensive bibliography on Elliott Carter.

2273. New York Public Library. Music Division. "Musicalia in der New York Public Library, mitgeteilt von Hugo Botstiber." In *Sammelbande der Internationalen Musikgesellschaft,* 4 (1902–3), p. 738–50.

A summary account of some of the more interesting and important items in the Drexel collection. Gives a full inventory of the "Sambrook MS," with brief entries for other manuscripts and early printed books. Includes a listing of musicians' autographs.

2274. New York Public Library. Music Division. "The Music Division of the New York Public Library," [by Frank C. Campbell] in *Fontes artis musicae* (Juli-Dezember 1969), p. 112–19.

General account of the history, holdings, special indexes, and collections of one of America's richest music libraries.

2275. New York Public Library. Music Division. Catalogue of Jos. W. Drexel's musical library. Part I: Musical writings. Philadelphia: King and Baird, 1869. 48 p.

This catalog contains only 1,536 of the more than 6,000 items in the Drexel collection. Especially rich in English printed music and manuscripts in the 16th, 17th, and 18th centuries. The collection contains numerous items from the library of Edward F. Rimbault, English antiquarian and collector.

2276. New York Public Library. Music Division. Dictionary catalog of the music collection, New York Public Library. 2nd ed. Boston, G. K. Hall, 1982. 44 v.

First published in 1965 in 33 v. Supplemented 1973 and 1976.

Duplication by photo-offset of a catalog of the holdings of the Music Division of the New York Public Library. Books, pamphlets, and musical scores in one alphabet. The catalog includes numerous analytics for articles in Festschriften, periodicals, etc. A comprehensive reference tool based on the resources of one of the great music libraries of the United States.

Kept current by the *Bibliographic guide to music,* an annual supplement published by the G. K. Hall Company beginning in 1976. These volumes include all publications cataloged by the New York Public Library and entries from the Library of Congress MARC tapes.

2277. New York Public Library. Vincent Astor Gallery. Musical treasures in American libraries. An exhibition in the Vincent Astor Gallery. Reprinted from the *Bulletin* of the New York Public Library, vol. 72 (Spring 1968). 16 p.

33 items fully described, illustrated in four full-page plates.

2278. The Pierpont Morgan Library. The Mary Flager Cary music collection: printed books and music, manuscripts, autograph letters, documents, portraits. New York: The Pierpont Morgan Library, 1970. 108 p., 49 plates.

Introduction signed by Charles Ryskamp, Director.

Collection comprises 64 printed books and 216 manuscripts as well as a large list of autograph letters and 18 items under "portraits and miscellany."

Compiled by Otto E. Albrecht (manuscripts), Herbert Cahoon (autograph letters and documents), and Douglas C. Ewing (printed books, portraits, and memorabilia).

Review by Susan T. Sommer in *Notes,* 28 (1972), p. 681–82.

2279. Pierpont Morgan Library. "Musical treasures in the Morgan Library," by Otto E. Albrecht in *Notes,* 28 (1972), p. 643–51.

A tantalizing introduction to the music collections of the Morgan Library.

2280. Pierpont Morgan Library. "ROLF", by Robert O. Lehman in *Notes,* 21 (1963), p. 83–93.

Describes the development of the Robert Owen Lehman Collection on deposit in the Morgan Library. Appended list of manuscripts no longer accurate as some have been removed from the collection and many others added.

2281. Pierpont Morgan Library. Nineteenth-Century autograph music manuscripts in the Pierpont Morgan Library a checklist [by] J. Rigbie Turner. N.Y.: Pierpont Morgan Library, 1982. 53 p, with 17 facsimile plates.

First appeared as an article in *19th-century music*, 2 (1980).

Brief descriptive entries on manuscripts dating from 1791 to 1911 given to the the Morgan Library including the Heineman Collection, and the Mary Cary Flagler Collection, deposited in the Morgan Library by Robert Owen Lehman and Margaret G. Cobb, or purchased by the Morgan Library. Describes briefly the large number of autograph letters in the Morgan collection. Entries include references to sources of further information on the collections and collectors.

2282. Pierpont Morgan Library. Sir Arthur Sullivan; composer and personage by Reginald Allen in collaboration with Gale R. D'Luhy. New York: The Pierpont Morgan Library, 1975. 215 p.

This volume presents the life of Sir Arthur Sullivan as seen in the archive formed first of all by his mother, and then by Sir Arthur himself. The original archive has been supplemented with dozens of autograph manuscripts and letters, printed scores, librettos, posters, drawings, prints, photographs, and memorabilia which came to the Pierpont Morgan Library before the acquisition of the papers of Sir Arthur Sullivan, and afterword, and which today form the Gilbert and Sullivan Collection in the Library. [from the *Introduction*]

An exhibition catalog of heroic scope. Includes items associated with Sir William Gilbert and Richard D'Oyly Carte.

2283. Pierpont Morgan Library. The Dannie and Hettie Heineman Collection. Compiled by Herbert Cahoon and others. New York: Pierpont Morgan Library, 1978.

A description of the entire Heineman collection, of which music manuscripts are only a part.

NUREMBERG, GERMANY

2284. Stadtbibliothek. Das Schrifttum zur Musikgeschichte der Stadt Nürnberg. Hrsg. im Auftrag der Stadt Nürnberg Schul- und Kulturreferat von der Stadtbibliothek [von] Franz Krautwurst. Nürnberg: Stadtbibliothek, 1964. 68 p. (Veröffentlichungen der Stadtbibliothek Nürnberg, 7)

A prose bibliography of writings about the music history of the city of Nuremberg.

OBERLIN, OHIO

2285. Oberlin College. Conservatory of Music. Mary M. Vial Music Library. Mr. and Mrs. C. W. Best collection of autographs in the Mary M. Vial Music Library of the Oberlin College Conservatory of Music. Oberlin: Oberlin College Library, 1967. 55 p.

A collection of 110 autograph letters, signed photographs, etc., chefly related to 19th- and early 20th-century musicians. Partial translations given for many of the documents. 10 facsimile plates.

OSTIGLIA, ITALY

2286. Biblioteca Greggiati. "Nascita, letargo e risveglio della Biblioteca Greggiati" by Claudio Sartori in *Fontes artis musicae,* 24 (1977), p. 126–38.

Describes a large and rich collection of music, including much by Mantuan composers, gathered by Giuseppe Greggiati in the mid-19th century.

OTTOBEUREN, GERMANY

2287. Benediktiner-Abtei. Die Musikhandschriften der Benediktiner-Abtei Ottobeuren: thematischer Katalog [von] Gertraut Haberkamp. München: G. Henle, 1986. 299 p. (Kataloge bayerischer Musiksammlungen, 12)

OXFORD, ENGLAND

2288. University. Bodleian Library. "Seventeenth-century Italian instrumental music in the Bodleian Library," by Denis Stevens. In *ActaM,* 26 (1954), p. 67–74.

The author lists some 85 sets of parts of early Italian instrumental music in the Bodleian, by composer in alphabetical order, with essential bibliographical information. In an article in *Collectanea historiae musicae,* 2 (1957), p. 401–12, he discusses nine unica from the above collection.

2289. University. Bodleian Library. [Catalog, in manuscript, of the music manuscripts in the Bodleian Library, with a list of books given to the University by Dr. Heather.] 1 v., unpaged.

An unpublished, handwritten catalog made in the early 19th century, available for study in the Bodleian Library. Gives contents for some 303 "Music School" manuscripts dating from the early 17th century.

2290. University. Bodleian Library. English music, guide to an exhibition held in 1955. Oxford: Bodleian Library, 1955. 40 p.

An exhibition catalog of 101 items, well annotated. 8 full page plates. Informative introduction, unsigned. The exhibition covers English music from the 11th to the 20th century, although early music is stressed.

2291. University. Bodleian Library. Manuscripts of Byzantine chant in Oxford by N. G. Wilson and D. I. Stefanovic. Oxford: Bodleian Library, 1963. 56 p.

An exhibition catalog. Facsimiles. Bibliography, p. 5–6.

2292. University. Bodleian Library. Medieval polyphony in the Bodleian Library, by Dom Anselm Hughes. Oxford: Bodleian Library, 1951. 63 p.

Descriptions and inventories of contents for 51 manuscripts and fragments in the Bodleian. Index of text incipits and of composers and places

of origin.
Review by Manfred Bukofzer in JAMS, 5 (1952), p. 53–65. *see* Oxford, Bodleian Library

2293. University. Christ Church. Catalogue of music [manuscripts] in the Library of Christ Church, Oxford, by G. E. E. Arkwright. London: Oxford University Press, 1915–23.

Part I: works of ascertained authorship, 1915. 128 p. Reprint of the 1915 volume by S. R. Publishers, East Ardsley, England, 1971, with a preface by T. B. Strong. Part II:1: manuscript works of unknown authorship. Vocal. 1923. 182 p. Part II:2: [manuscripts of instrumental music of unknown authorship.] An unpublished catalog, completed in 1935, available for examination in the Christ Church College library.

2294. University. Christ Church. Catalogue of printed music published prior to 1801, now in the Library of Christ Church, Oxford. Edited by Aloys Hiff. London: Oxford Univ. Press, 1919. 76 p.

A collection rich in Italian and English music of the 16th and 17th centuries. Alphabetical arrangement by composer, with analytics for collections.

2295. University. Bodleian Library. "American sheet music in the Walter N. H. Harding Collection at the Bodleian Library, Oxford University" by Jean Geil in *Notes,* 34 (1978), p. 805–13.

A description of the collection of 60,000 to 70,000 pieces of American sheet music donated to the Bodleian Library.

2296. University. Bodleian Library. The Bodleian Library Music Collection; a listing and guide to part two, part three, part four, and part five [and part six] of the Harvester Microfilm Collection. Compiled by Professor Roger Bray. Brighton: Harvester Press Microform Publications, 1984–86. 2 v.

Each volume lists the contents of the reels in each part of the collection and then lists the manuscripts in each part. There is a unified index of names and composers in each volume.

2297. University. Bodleian Library. The Oxford Music School collection at the Bodleian Library, Oxford; a guide and index to the Harvester microfilm collection. With an introduction by Margaret Crum. Brighton: Harvester Press Microform Publications, 1979. 41 p.

Contains a guide to the contents of the 19 reels in the collection, an excellent introduction, and an index of composers and their works. This is a finding aid to a commercial microfilm collection and forms in effect part one of the Harvester Bodleian Library Music Collection.

2298. University. Christ Church College. The music collection of Christ Church, Oxford; a listing and guide to [parts one through three] of the Harvester microfilm collection. Compiled by Professor Roger Bray and [the guide for part three] by Professor Tim Carter. Brighton: Harvester Press Microform Publications, 1981–82. 3 v.

As in the other Harvester guides, there is a list on the contents of each reel in each part and a listing of the manuscripts in each part.

2299. Basilica di San'Antonio. Archivio Musicale. L'Archivio musicale della Cappella Antoniana in Padova; illustrazione storico-critico, con cinque eliotipie. Padova: Tiografia e Libreria Antoniana, 1895. 175 p.
Compiled by Giovanni Tebaldini.
P. 1–92: Historical essay on the chapel of St. Anthony. P. 93–149: Partial catalog of manuscripts and prints. Complete lists of works for Vallotti, Sabbatini; thematic incipits for Tartini concertos.

2300. Biblioteca Capitolare. "Codici musici della Biblioteca Capitolare di Padova." [By Antonio Garbelotti.] In *Revista musicale italiana,* 53 (1951), p. 289–314; 54 (1952), p. 218–30.
A summary description of the manuscript holdings of the Biblioteca Capitolare in Padua. Sources discussed chronologically by centuries. Both plainchant and polyphonic manuscripts considered.

2301. Archives Nationales. Archives du Théâtre nationale de l'Opéra (AJ13 a à 1466), Inventaire par Brigitte Labat-Poussin. Paris: Archives Nationales, 1977. 677 p.
In addition to the archives of the Opéra, the archives of the Théâtre Italien, the Opéra Comique, and the Théâtre Lyrique are described.
Review by François Lesure in *Fontes artis musicae,* 25 (1978), p. 195–96.

2302. Archives Nationales. Minutier Central. Documents du Minutier Central concernant l'histoire de la musique (1600–1650). Comp. by Madelaine Jurgens. Préface de François Lesure. Paris: S.E.V.P.E.N., 1966–74. 2 v. (Ministère des Affaires Culturelles. Direction des Archives de France. Archives Nationales.)
An organized presentation of documents related to musicians of the first half of the 17th century in the French national archives. Musicians are grouped according to their occupations: musicians of the court, of the city, instrument makers, music printers, etc. Tome I, general index, p. 895–1038.
Tome II presents records of contracts and depositions, giving names and monetary values. The material is arranged chronologically within social categories, as in Tome I, dealing with the Parisian cultural milieu of the first half of the 17th century. Lists instrument collections. Useful introduction of 90 p. Extensive index, p. 911–1,085.
Review of Tome I by Albert Cohen in *JAMS,* 22 (1969), p. 126–29; by James R. Anthony in *Notes,* , 26 (1970), p. 511–13.
Review of Tome II by Margaret Murata in *Notes,* 35 (1978), p. 310.

2303. Bibliothèque de l'Arsenal. Catalogue des livres de musique (manuscrits et imprimés) de la Bibliothèque de l'Arsenal à Paris, par L. de La Laurencie. . . . et A. Gastoué. Paris: E. Droz, 1936. 184 p. (Publications de la Societe francaise de musicologie, 2. ser., t. 7.)
Manuscripts and printed music arranged alphabetically by composer,

or catchword of title if anonymous, under main divisions of sacred and secular. Manuscripts from the 10th century; printed works of the 16th-18th centuries. Exceptionally rich in editions of little-known French composers of the 18th century.

2304. Bibliothèque Nationale. Claude Debussy. Paris: Bibliothèque Nationale, 1962. 73 p.

An exposition catalog of 335 items celebrating the centennial of Debussy's birth. Arranged chronologically. Eight plates.

2305. Bibliothèque Nationale. Frédéric Chopin. Exposition du centenaire. Paris: [Bibliothèque Nationale], 1949. 82 p.

234 items, eight plates; documents arranged to parallel the chronology of the composer's life.

2306. Bibliothèque Nationale. Gabriel Fauré. Paris: [Bibliothèque Nationale], 1963. 16 p.

An exhibition catalog of 100 items, with a chronology of the composer's life and work.

2307. Bibliothèque Nationale. Introduction à la paléographie musicale byzantine; catalogue des manuscrits de musique byzantine de la Bibliothèque Nationale de Paris et des bibliothèques publiques de France. [Paris: Impressions artistiques L. M. Fortin, 1928.] 99 p. (Publications de la Societe internationale de musique. Section de Paris.)

Compiled by Amédée Gastoué.

2308. Bibliothèque Nationale. Jean-Philippe Rameau, 1683–1764. Paris: [Bibliothèque National], 1964. 100 p.

Illustrated exhibition catalog celebrating the 200th anniversary of the death of Rameau.

2309. Bibliothèque Nationale. La musique française du moyen âge à la revolution, catalogue rédigé par Amédée Gastoué, Abbé V. Leroquais, André Pirro, Henry Expert, Henry Prunières, et Emile Dacie. Paris:, Édition des Bibliothèques Nationales de France, 1934. 196 p.

Illustrated catalog of 660 manuscripts, books, and works of art from major French public and private collections, displayed at the "Exposition de la musique francaise," 1933, in the Galerie Mazarine of the Bibliothèque Nationale.

2310. Bibliothèque Nationale. Mozart en France. Paris: [Bibliothèque Nationale], 1956. 76 p.

Illustrated exhibition catalog of 234 items related to Mozart's life in France. P. 67–76: a bibliography of early French editions of Mozart's music.

2311. Bibliothèque Nationale. Department des Imprimés. Catalogue du fonds de musique ancienne de la Bibliothèque Nationale. [By Jules Ecorcheville.] Paris: 1910–14. 8 v.

Reprint by Da Capo Press, New York, 1972.

Manuscripts, printed music, and theoretical and literary works on music not included in the general catalog of the library, to 1750. Partially thematic. Arranged alphabetically by composer, with collections analyzed. Brief bibliographical descriptions.

2312. Bibliothèque Nationale. Collection Toulouse-Philidor. "La collection musicale Toulouse-Philidor à la Bibliothèque nationale" by Catherine Massip in *Fontes artis musicae,* 30 (1983), p. 184–207.

Following the sale of the bulk of the collection by St. Michael's College, Tenbury, in 1978, this article provides an inventory of the collection and a concordance to earlier catalogs.

2313. Bibliothèque Nationale. Département de la musique. Lettres autographes conservées au Département de la musique: catalogue sommaire par Antoine Bloch-Michel. Paris: Bibliothèque nationale, 1984. 404 p.

2314. Bibliothèque Sainte-Geneviève. Catalogue du fonds musical de la Bibliothèque Sainte-Geneviève de Paris. Manuscrits et imprimes. Par Madeleine Garros and Simone Wallon. Kassel: Internationale Vereinigung der Musikbiliotheken; Internationale Gesellschaft für Musikwissenschaft, 1967. 156 p. (Catalogus musicus, 4.)

2315. Bibljoteka Polska. Frédéric Chopin, George Sand et leurs amis. Exposition à la Bibliothèque Polonaise. Paris: 1937. 63 p.

An exposition of 638 items related to Chopin, George Sand, and their circle. Includes manuscripts, letters, portraits. Illustrated.

2316. Catalogue de la musique imprimée avant 1800 conservée dans les Bibliothègues publique de Paris. Edited by François Lesure. Paris: Bibliothèque Nationale, 1981. 708 p.

The majority of works catalogued in this source are contained in the Département de la musique (créé en 1942) and in the collections of the Bibliothèques du Conservatoire brought into the Bibliothèque Nationale in 1964.

A catalog by composer generally showing genre or performing forces, imprint, and location, including shelf-marks. Unattributed works appear in a separate listing by title at the end of the catalog. RISM numbers, when appropriate, are supplied. First lines are provided for vocal works. When known, bibliographic announcements in contemporaneous French publications are cited.

2317. Conservatoire National de Musique et de Déclamation. Catalogue bibliographique par J. B. Weckerlin, bibliothécaire. Paris: Firmin-Didot et Cie., 1885. 512 p.

Covers the period to about 1800. Includes only part of the early materials in the collection. Following a prefatory history of the library, three sections are given: early treatises, vocal music, early instrumental music of the French school.

2318. Conservatoire National de Musique et de Déclamation. Fonds Blancheton. Inventaire critique du Fonds Blancheton. Paris, E. Droz, 1930–31. 2 v. (Publications de la Societe francaise de musicologie. 2. ser., 2:1–2.)

Compiled by Lionel de La Laurencie.

The Blancheton collection consists of 27 volumes containing some 330 instrumental compositions by 104 composers. It was assembled before 1750. Important source materials for the history of the symphony. Full descriptions, with critical and biographical notes, on the composers.

2319. Opéra. Bibliothèque, Archives et Musee. Bibliothèque musicale du Theatre de l'Opéra. Catalogue historique, chronologique, anecdotique... rédigé par Théodore De Lajarte. Paris: Librairie des Bibliophiles, 1878. 2 v.

Reprint by Olms, Hildesheim, 1969.

A descriptive list of 594 stage works arranged in order of their first production at the Paris Opera, 1671–1876. Classified by periods. Each period is included with a biographical section which lists composers and librettists alphabetically. Composer and title index to works in the repertoire.

PARMA, ITALY

Citta di Parma. See no. 2098.

2320. Conservatorio di Musica "Arrigo Boito." "Biblioteche musicali in Italia: La Biblioteca del Conservatorio di Parma e un fondo di edizioni dei sec. XVI e XVII non comprese nel catalogo a stampa." [By Riccardo Allorto.] In *Fontes artis musicae,* (1955: 2), p. 147–51.

Describes a collection of 31 sets of 16th- and 17th-century partbooks acquired by the library in 1925.

2321. Conservatorio di Musica "Arrigo Boito." "Osservazioni sulla Biblioteca Musicale di Parma." [By Mario Medici.] In *Avrea Parma,* 48 (May-August 1964), p. 3–49.

Provides copious data on the library of the Conservatorio. Many of the rare manuscripts and printed books are cited in full, along with an account of the history of the institution and its administrative structure.

PHILADELPHIA, PENNSYLVANIA

2322. Curtis Institute of Music. Catalogue of the Burrell Collection of Wagner documents, letters, and bibliographical material. London: The Nonpareil Press, 1929. 99 p.

2323. Free Library. Drinker Library of Choral Music. Catalog. [By Henry R. Drinker.] Philadelphia: 1957. 116 p.

First published in 1947 by the Association of American Choruses, Princeton, New Jersey, with a *Supplement,* July 1948.

Catalog of a lending library of choral materials, made available to members of the Association of American Choruses.

2324. Free Library. Edwin A. Fleisher Collection of Orchestral Music. The Edwin A. Fleisher orchestral music collection in the Free Library of Philadelphia; a cumulative catalogue, 1929–1977. The Fleisher Collection in the Free Library of Philadelphia. Boston: G. K. Hall, 1979. 956 p.

First published in 1933–45, two volumes, with a *Supplementary List,* 1945–55. (1956), 33 p. Revised edition published 1965.

Catalog of a loan collection of orchestral music, much of the material unpublished. Classified; information includes dates of composer, title of each work in the original language, with English translation, publisher, instrumentation, timing, date of composition, and information relating to first performance. Occasional thematic incipits provided. Indexed by performing forces.

Review by Joseph N. Boonin in *Notes,* 36 (1979), p. 92–3.

2325. Library Company. American song sheets, slip ballads and poetical broadsides, 1850–1970; a catalogue of the collection of the Library Company of Philadelphia, by Edwin Wolf 2nd. Philadelphia: 1963. 205 p.

A listing, alphabetical by title, of 2,722 American song sheets, ballads, and broadsides, with information as to author, composer, format, cover design, etc. Separate listing of 194 Confederate songs. Index of printers and publishers, of authors and composers, of singers. Reproduction of pictorial covers.

2326. The Musical Fund Society. Catalog of orchestral and choral compositions published and in manuscript between 1790 and 1840 from the library of the Musical Fund Society of Philadelphia. Philadelphia: Musical Fund Society, 1974. 81 p.

Listing of 299 scores now in the custody of the Music Department of the Free Library of Philadelphia.

PIACENZA, ITALY

2327. Archivio del Duomo. "L'Archivio del Duomo di Piacenza e il Liber XIII di Costanzo Antegnati." [By Claudio Sartori.] In *Fontes artis musicae,* (1957: 4), p. 28–37.

Description of the collection and catalog of its early printed music. Special attention given to a unique copy of the *Liber XIII,* a collection of sacred and secular vocal music by C. Antegnati. *Liber XIII*

2328. Archivio del Duomo. Catalogo del fondo musicale a cura di Francesco Bussi. Milano: Istituto editoriale italiano, 1967. 209 p.

A catalog in four parts: (1) printed music, chiefly of the 16th and 17th centuries; (2) music manuscripts, including anthologies; (3) manuscript and printed liturgical books; and (4) a small collection of books on music. Index of names.

PIRNA, GERMANY

2329. Hoffmann-Erbrecht, Lothar. "Die Chorbücher der Stadtkirche zu Pirna." In *ActaM,* 27 (1955), p. 121–37.

Detailed description of eight choirbooks of polyphonic music of the mid-16th century. Partially thematic; summary inventories; two facsimile plates. These manuscripts are now in the Sachsische Landesbibliothek in Dresden.

PISA, ITALY

Biblioteche e Archivi. . . . See no. 2114.

PISTOIA, ITALY

Archivio Capitolare della Cattedrale. See no. 2103.

2330. Biblioteca Antonio Venturi. "La collection Antonio Venturi, Montecatini-Terme (Pistoia), Italie." [By Raymond Meylan.] In *Fontes artis musicae,* (1958: 1), p. 21–44.
A private collection of late 18th-century vocal and instrumental music.

PITTSBURGH, PENNSYLVANIA

2331. Finney, Theodore M. "A group of English manuscript volumes at the University of Pittsburgh," in *Essays in musicology in honor of Dragon Plamenac on his 70th birthday.* Pittsburgh: Univ. of Pittsburgh Press, 1969. p. 21–48.
Describes the contents of a collection of twelve 17th- and 18th-century manuscripts of English provenance, formerly privately owned but now owned by the Music Library of the University of Pittsburgh. The study incorporates two indexes, one of composers and the other of initial words and titles.

2332. Finney, Theodore M. A union catalogue of music and books on music printed before 1801 in Pittsburgh libraries. 2nd ed. Pittsburgh: Univ. of Pittsburgh, 1963. 106 leaves (typescript).
First published in 1959. Second edition supplement, 1964. 42 leaves.
Lists the holdings in early music in four Pittsburgh libraries: the Carnegie Library, the University of Pittsburgh, St. Vincent's College, and the private library of the compiler. There is a strong emphasis on early English music.
Review by Donald W. Krummel in *Notes,* 21 (1963–64), p. 129–31.

PLASENCIA, SPAIN

2333. Catedral. Archivo. "El Archivo de musica en la catedral de Plasencia." By Samuel Rubio. In *Anuario musical,* 5 (1950), p. 147–68.
A small collection of early manuscripts and printed music, fully described and contents listed.

POLAND

2334. Music libraries of the Polish People's Republic. "Traditions and achievements of music libraries and library science in the Polish People's Republic" by Maria Prokopowicz in *Fontes artis musicae,* 26 (1979), p.

36–43.

A brief resume of activities in Poland since the Second World War, including a bibliography of pertinent articles on libraries, catalogs of collections, works on music publishing and printing, and works on music bibliography and librarianship.

2335. Musicalia vetera: Katalog tematyczny rekopismiennych zabytkow dawnej muzyki w Polsce redakcja Zygmunt M. Szweykowski; Thematic Catalogue of Early Musical Manuscripts in Poland. Warsaw: Polskie Wydawnictwo Muzyczne, 1969– .

> The edition will consist of a number of volumes constituting thematic cata-logues of individual early manuscripts or their groups. . . . The first volumes will be devoted to the collections copied for use at Wawel, the following to the collections from Sandomierz and Lowicz regions and from the surroundings of Cracow. [Editor's description]

T. 1 zesz. 6. Zbiory muzyczne proweniencji wawelskiej [Collections of music copied for use at Wawel.] Edited by Elzbieta Gluszcz-Zwolińska. 1969.

T. 2, zesz. 1. Zbiory muzyczne proweniencji podkrakowskiej [Collec-tions of music from the surroundings of Cracow.] Edited by Zofia Suro-wiak. 1972.

See also WARSAW, POLAND. Biblioteka Narodowa. No. 2464.

See also Dragan Plamenac's article in *Notes,* 19 (1962), no. 2020.

PORTUGAL

For information about Portuguese music libraries, see no. 2383.

PRAGUE, CZECHOSLOVAKIA

2336. Cathedral. Catalogus collectionis operum artis musicae quae in bibliotheca capituli metropolitani pragensis asservantur. Composuit DR. Antonius Podlaha. Prague: Metropolitan Capitulary of Prague, 1926. 87 p.

2337. National Museum. Hudební sbírka Emiliána Troldy (The music li-brary of Emilián Trolda). By Alexander Buchner. Prague: Národní Mu-seum, 1954. 132 p.

Thematic catalog of the Trolda music collection deposited in the Music Department of the National Museum. The collection contains music from c. 1550–1820 scored by Trolda from numerous archives, native and foreign.

2338. University Library. Catalogus codicum notis musicis instructorum qui in bibliotheca publica rei publicae bohemiae socialisticae—in Biblio-theca Universitatis Pragensis servantur. (Catalog of Latin musical man-uscripts in the state Library of the CSSR.) Prague: University Library, 1971. 830 p. in 2 v.

Edited by Vaclav Plocek.

PUEBLA, MEXICO

2339. Catedral. "Sixteenth- through eighteenth-century resources in Mexico: part III" by Robert M. Stevenson in *Fontes artis musicae*, 25 (1978), p. 156–87.

A continuation of Stevenson's earlier articles on sources in Mexico, no. 1840 & 1841.

A catalog of 130 sources, arranged by composer.

PULLMAN, WASHINGTON

2340. Washington State University. Rosbaud Library. "The Hans Rosbaud Library at Washington State University, Pullman, Washington, U.S.A." by Joan Evans in *Notes*, 41 (1985), p. 26–40.

A description of an extensive collection of correspondence between Rosbaud, a conductor who championed the cause of new music, and composers, performers, conductors, and other persons significant in the history of 20th-century music.

QUÉBEC, CANADA

2341. Hôtel-Dieu and the Ursuline Convent. "The motet in New France: some 17th- and 18th-century manuscripts in Quebec" by Erich Schwandt in *Fontes artis musicae*, 28 (1981), p. 194–219.

Presents thematic entries for 128 pieces found in 6 manuscript anthologies in the two convents. Index to titles.

REGENSBURG, GERMANY

2342. Fürst Thurn und Taxis Zentralarchiv und Hofbibliothek Die Musikhandschriften der Fürst Thurn und Taxis Hofbibliothek Regensburg: thematischer Katalog. [Von] Gertraut Haberkamp; mit einer Geschichte des Musikalienbestandes von Hugo Angerer. München: Henle, 1981. 500 p. (Kataloge bayerischer Musiksammlungen, 6)

2343. Fürstlich Thurn und Taxissche Hofbibliothek. "Verzeichnis der vollständigen opern, melodramen und ballette, wie auch der operntextbücher der Fürstlich Thurn und Taxisschen hofbibliothek, Regensburg," von dr. Sigfrid Färber, in *Verhandlungen des Historischen vereins von Oberpfalz und Regensburg*, 86 (1936). 30 p.

Part of the author's inaugural dissertation, Munich, issued under title: *Das Regensburger Fürstlich Thurn und Taxissche hoftheater und seine oper, 1760–1786* (Regensburg, 1936).

"Opern, melodramen und ballette aus dem 18. jahrhundert." [from the *Vorbemerkung*].

REGGIO-EMILIA, ITALY

Citta di Reggio-Emilia. See no. 2099.

RIO DE JANEIRO, BRAZIL

2344. Biblioteca Nacional. "Estudio Brasilenos I. Manuscritos musicales en la Biblioteca Nacional de Rio de Janeiro." By Francesco Curt Lange. In *Revista de estudios musicales,* 1 (April 1950), p. 98–194.
Chiefly 19th-century composers. A: works by European composers. B: works by Brazilian composers or Europeans active in Brazil.

2345. Biblioteca Nacional. Música no Rio de Janeiro imperial 1822–1870. Rio de Janeiro: Biblioteca Nacional, 1962. 100 p.
At head of title: "Exposiçio comemorativa do primeiro decênio da seçao de música e arquivo sonore."
391 items, chiefly Brazilian imprints of the period.

2346. Biblioteca Nacional. Rio musical; crônica de uma cidade. Rio de Janeiro: Biblioteca Nacional, 1965. 51 p.
At head of title: "Exposiçao comemorativa do IV centenário da cidade do Rio de Janeiro."

RIVER FOREST, ILLINOIS

2347. Concordia Teachers College. Klinck Memorial Library. Hymnals and chorale books of the Klinck Memorial Library, compiled by Carl Schalk. River Forest: Concordia Teachers College, 1975. 89 p.

2348. Schalk, Carl, comp. Hymnals and chorale books of the Klinck Memorial Library. River Forest, Il.: Concordia Teachers College, 1975. 89 p.
A catalog of the holdings of the Concordia Teachers College Library.

RÖ, SWEDEN

2348.1. "The Silverstolpe music collection in Rö, Uppland, Sweden: a preliminary catalogue" in *Fontes artis musicae,* 29 (1982), p. 93–103.
Introducing an extensive collection of 19th century music in manuscript and printed editions gathered by a family of Swedish noblepersons and diplomats.

ROME, ITALY

For catalogs of music collections in the Vatican, see under VATICAN CITY.

2349. Accademia di Santa Cecilia. Biblioteca. "Cantata and aria manuscripts in the Santa Cecilia Library," by John Glenn Paton in *Notes,* 36 (1980), p. 563–74.
An inventory of 36 manuscripts of the 17th and 18th centuries. Not

indexed, but analyzed. Cites modern editions.

2350. Basilica of Santa Maria in Trastevere. "Music in the archives of the Basilica of Santa Maria in Trastevere." By Beekman C. Cannon. In *Ac-taM,* 41 (1969), p. 199–212.

Description and inventory of the music in one of the most renowned Roman churches. Most of the material comes from the latter half of the 17th century. The collection is rich in music by Angelo Berardi, who became Maestro di Cappella in 1693.

2351. Biblioteca Casanatense. "Cantata manuscripts in the Casanatense Library" by John Glenn Paton in *Notes,* 40 (1988), p. 826–35.

An analyzed inventory to 32 manuscripts for the most part consisting of Italian cantatas of the 17th century.

2352. Biblioteca Corsiniana. "La collezione Corsini di antichi codici musicali e Girolamo Chiti." By Vito Reali. In *Rivista musicale italiana,* 25 (1918–20).

Describes the founding of the Corsini library and the role played by the early 18th-century church musician, Girolamo Chiti, friend of Padre Martini.

2353. Biblioteca Corsiniana. Biblioteca corsiniana e dell'Accademia Nazionale dei Lincei; catalogo dei fondi musicali Chiti e Corsiniano. Ed. Argia Bertini. Milano: Istituto editoriale italiano, 1964. 109 p. (Bibliotheca musicae, 2.)

Catalog covering printed music, theoretical works, and manuscripts. 17th- and early 18th-century vocal and instrumental music.

Biblioteca della R. Accademia di S. Cecilia. See no. 2104.

2354. Biblioteca Doria-Pamphilj. "Die Musiksammlung der Fürsten Doria-Pamphilj in Rom." By Andreas Holschneider. In *Archiv fur Musikwissenschaft,* 18 (1961), p. 248–64.

Description of the collection and inventory of its contents, classified under five main headings: (1) collections, 16th and 17th centuries; (2) sacred music; (3) oratorios (early manuscripts); (4) operas, early manuscripts; (5) German instrumental music, chiefly 18th century.

2355. Biblioteca Doria-Pamphilj. "Die Sinfonien-Manuskripte der Bibliothek Doria-Pamphilj in Rom." By Friedrich Lippmann. In *Analecta musicologica,* 5 91968), p. 201–47.

Thematic catalog of some 119 symphonies by 36 composers. Many of the works are not known from other sources.

2356. Biblioteca Doria-Pamphilj. "Die Streichquartettmanuskripte der Bibliothek Doria-Pamphilj in Rom." By Friedrich Lippmann with Ludwig Finscher. In *Analecta musicologica,* 7 (1969), p. 120–44.

Thematic catalog of the string quartet repertory in the library.

2357. Biblioteca Doria-Pamphilj. "Die Streichtriomanuskripte der Bibliothek Doria-Pamphilj in Rom." By Friedrich Lippmann with Hubert Unverricht. In *Analecta musicologica,* 9 (1970), p. 299–335.
Thematic catalog of string trios in the Doria-Pamphilj collection.

2358. Congregazione dell'Oratorio di Roma. Inventario del fondo musicale dell'Oratorio. A cura di Argia Bertini. Roma: 1968–71. 4 fascicles.

2359. Conservatorio di Musica "S. Cecilia." Biblioteca. "Cantata and aria manuscripts in the Saint Cecilia Library" by John Glenn Paton in *Notes,* 36 (1980), p. 563–74.
An analyzed inventory of manuscripts dating between 1600 and c. 1760.

2360. Deutsches Historische Institut in Rom. "Die Musikgeschichtliche Abteilung des Deutschen Historischen Instituts in Rom." By Karl Gustav Fellerer. In *Die Musikforschung,* 20 (1967), p. 410–13.
Brief description of the leading musicological reference library in Italy, calling attention to its major areas of interest, special files, and indexes.

2361. Doria Phamphili Archivio Musicale. "L'Archivio musicale Doria Pamphilj: saggio sulla cultura aristocratica a Roma fra il 16o e 19o secolo", by Claudio Annibaldi. In *Studi musicali,* 11 (1982), p. 91–120.
Discusses the origin and organization of the archive. Cites and describes the catalogs of manuscripts and printed materials, the subject catalog and the author catalog.

2362. Kast, Paul. "Romische Handschriften." In *MGG,* 11 (1963), col. 750–61.
A narrative account citing and describing the principal manuscripts, chiefly polyphonic, in Rome. Much attention given to sources in the Vatican Library. Bibliography of writings on Roman libraries and their manuscript sources.

2363. San Pantaleo, Archivio dei Padri Scolopi. Fondo musicale: (manoscritti, stampe, copie fotostatiche e dattiloscritte). Ed. by Argia Bertini. Roma: Archivio dei padri Scolopi a San Pantaleo, [1981?]

Vatican Library See under VATICAN CITY, ROME

SALAMANCA, SPAIN

2364. Catedral. Archivo de Música Catálogo archivo de música de la catedral de Salamanca. Por Dámaso García Fraile. Cuenca: Instituto Música Religiosa de la Diputación Provincial, D.L. 1981. (Instituto de Música Religiosa. Ediciones)

SALEM, NORTH CAROLINA

2365. Collegium Musicum. "Repertory and resources of the Salem Collegium Musicum, 1780–1790" by Jeannine S. Ingram in *Fontes artis musicae,* 26 (1979), p. 267–81.

A survey of the 100 pieces in printed editions and manuscript remaining in the Moravian community's musical establishment.

SALT LAKE CITY, UTAH

2366. University of Utah. Library. A catalogue of books and music acquired from the library of Hugo Leichtentritt. Edited by Carol E. Selby. Salt Lake City: Univ. of Utah, 1954. 106 p. (Bulletin of the University of Utah, 45:10.)

A scholar's working library of music books and scores; a few early editions, but centered in the 19th and 20th centuries. The catalog is divided in two sections: books (p. 9–46) and music (p. 49–106).

SALZBURG, AUSTRIA

2367. Mozart-Museum. Katalog des Mozart-Museums im Geburts- und Wohnzimmer Mozarts zu Salzburg ... 4. Aufl. Salzburg: Im Selbstverlage des obengenannten Stiftung, 1906. 62 p.

Describes a collection of Mozart memorabilia maintained in the composer's birthplace. The collection includes portraits, medals, letters, and music.

2368. Museum Carolino Augusteum. Die Musikaliensammlung im Salzburger Museum Carolino Augusteum. By Josef Gassner. Salzburg: 1962. 247 p.

Originally published in the Museum's *Jahresschrift,* 1961. Salzburg, 1962, p. 119–325.

The collection, founded in 1834, is rich in 19th-century editions. Manuscripts and printed music interfiled. Full bibliographical citations, with publishers' plate numbers given. Facsimile plates.

2369. Die Musikaliensammlung der Erzabtei St. Peter in Salzburg. Katalog. Erster Teil. Leopold und Wolfgang Amadeus Mozart, Joseph und Michael Haydn. Mit einer Einfuhrung in die Geschichte der Sammlung vorgelegt von Manfred Hermann Schmid. Salzburg: 1970. 300 p. (Schriftenreihe der Internationalen Stiftung Mozarteum, Band 3/4. Zugleich Band I der Publikationen des Instituts fur Musikwissenschaft der Universitäts Salzburg.)

Review by Susan T. Sommer in *Notes,* 29 (1972), p. 258.

SAN FRANCISCO, CALIFORNIA

2370. San Francisco State University. Frank V. De Bellis Collection. Orchestra scores and parts in the Frank V. De Bellis Collection of the California State Colleges. San Francisco State College: 1964. 24 unnumbered leaves (typescript).

A preliminary catalog of the orchestral portion of the De Bellis collection, a collection devoted exclusively to Italian music. Entries listed alphabetically by composer, with early and modern editions interfiled.

Parts specified.

2371. San Francisco State University. Frank V. De Bellis Collection. The Frank V. De Bellis Collection: San Francisco State University (RISM siglum, US-SFsc), bound music manuscript miscellanies, preliminary survey of contents with index of names. [San Francisco: San Francisco State University, 1975. 92 leaves

Typescript (photocopy), "Introductory note" signed by James L. Jackman.

SAN MARINO, CALIFORNIA

2372. Henry E. Huntington Library and Art Gallery. Catalogue of music in the Huntington Library printed before 1801. Compiled by E. N. Backus. San Marino, Calif.: The Library, 1949. 773 p.

"Music publications and publications without music notation but of distinct interest to musicians and musicologists. . . ." Excluded are manuscripts, song texts, opera librettos. Includes music published in periodicals. Entry is under composer, with anonymous works under title. Index to composers and editors, chronological index, first-line index of songs. The collection is strong in 17th- and 18th-century English music.

Review by Cyrus L. Day in *Notes,* 6 (1949), p. 609–10; by Harold Spivacke in *MQ,* 35 91949), p. 640–42.

SANTIAGO, CHILE

2373. Catedral. Archivo de Musica. Catalogo del Archivo musical de la Catedral de Santiago de Chile [por] Samuel Claro. Santiago de Chile: Editorial del Instituto de Extensión Musical, Universidad de Chile, 1974. 67 p.

SANTIAGO, CUBA

2374. Hernandez Balaguer, Pablo. Catalogo de musica de los archivos de la catedral de Santiago de Cuba y del Museo Bacardi. La Habana: Biblioteca Nacional "Jose Marti," 1961. 59 p.

Catalog of works by Cuban composers in the archives of the cathedral at Santiago and in the Bacardi Museum in the same city.

SANTIAGO, SPAIN

2375. Catedral. Archivo. Catalogo musical del Archivo de Santa Iglesia Catedral de Santiago, edited by José López-Calo. Cuenca: Ediciones del Instituto de Musica Religiosa, 1972. 386 p. (Instituto de musica religiosa, Publicaciones, 8)

Catalog of 2,292 items from one of the richest musical traditions of Spanish cathedrals. Arranged by century and then by composer. Appendix of documents. Index and bibliography.

SCHOTTEN, GERMANY

2376. Liebfrauenkirche. Thematischer Katalog der kirchlichen Musik-handschriften in der Liebfrauenkirche zu Schotten; von Joachim Schlichte; mit einer Geschichte der Kirchenmusik und ihren Notenbes-tänden von Peter Albrecht. Tutzing: H. Schneider, 1985. 375 p. (Frank-furter Beiträge zur Musikwissenschaft, 19)

SCHWERIN, GERMANY

2377. Grossherzogliche Regierungsbibliothek. Der musikalische Nachlass der Frau Erbgrossherzogin Auguste von Mecklenburg-Schwerin. ... von Otto Kade. Schwerin: Druck der Sandmeyerschen Hofbuchdruckerei, 1899. 142 p.

2378. Grossherzogliche Regierungsbibliothek. Die Musikalien-Sammlung des grossherzoglich Mecklenburg-Schweriner Furstenhauses aus den letzten zwei Jahrhunderten. Schwerin: Druck der Sandmeyerschen Hof-buchdruckerei, 1893. 2 v.

Reprinted by Olms, Hildesheim, 1974.

Compiled by Otto Kade.

Primarily 18th- and 19th-century manuscripts and printed music. Part I is a thematic catalog, alphabetical by composer, with a classified sec-tion under "Anonyma." Part II: librettos. Part III: index of dedications, autographs, etc.

SEVILLE, SPAIN

2379. Biblioteca Colombina. "La musica conservada en la Biblioteca Colom-bina y en la Catedral de Sevilla." By Higinio Anglés. In *Anuario musical,* 2 (1947), p. 3–39.

88 manuscripts and prints from the Colombina library; 9 manuscripts and 22 prints from the cathedral archives. Bibliographical references and notes on all the items.

2380. Biblioteca Colombina. "Printed collections of polyphonic music owned by Ferdinand Columbus." By Catherine Weeks Chapman. In *JAMS,* 21 (1968), p. 34–84.

Reconstruction of the 16th-century library of the son of Christopher Columbus, based on a manuscript catalog preserved in that library. The catalog makes reference to a number of editions now lost.

SITTEN, SWITZERLAND (VALAIS)

2381. Stenzl, Jurg. Repertorium der liturgischen Musikhandschriften der Diozesen Sitten, Lausanne und Genf. Band I: Diozese Sitten. Frieburg:, Universitatsverlag, 1972– . (Veroffentlichungen der Geregorianischen Akademie zu Freiburg in der Schweiz. Neue Folge, Band I.)

The first volume of a series devoted to the liturgical music manuscripts in the dioceses of Sitten, Lausanne, and Geneva. Band I has 383 pages, 100 illustrations, 60 facsimiles, and 72 pages of edition.

SORAU, GERMANY

See ZARY, POLAND

SPAIN

2382. Aubry, Pierre. "Iter Hispanicum: notices et extraits de manuscrits ancienne conserves dans les bibliotheques d'Espagne." In *Sammelbande der Internationalen Musikgesellschaft,* v. 8 and 9 (1907–8). Also issued as a separate.

A series of essays treating early Spanish sources of polyphony, Mozarabic chant, the "Cantigas de Santa Maria," and folk music.

2383. "New information concerning some music research libraries and archives in Spain and Portugal" by Eugene Casjen Cramer in *Notes,* 40 (1984), p. 30–40.

A second update to the *Directory of Music Research Libraries, Part III: Spain, France, Italy, Portugal.*

2384. "New information concerning some music research libraries in Spain." by Maurice Esses in *Fontes artis musicae,* 26 (1979), p. 189–91.

A list of corrections and additions to the *Directory of Music Research Libraries* (RISM, C/III).

2385. Riano, Juan F. Critical and bibliographical notes on early Spanish music. London: B. Quaritch, 1887. 154 p.

Reprint by the Da Capo Press, New York, 1971.

Manuscripts and printed music to 1600, classified, giving descriptions and library locations of manuscripts. Numerous facsimile plates.

SPRINGFIELD, OHIO

2386. Wittenberg University. Hamma School of Theology. School of Music. Hymnbooks at Wittenberg: a classified catalog of the collections of Hamma School of Theology, Wittenberg School of Music, Thomas Library by Louis Voigt with the collaboration of Darlene Kalke ... [et al.]. Springfield, Ohio: Chantry Music Press, 1975. unnumbered [96 p.]

Lists 1084 hynmnbooks, principally Lutheran. Index of names.

STANFORD, CALIFORNIA

2387. Stanford University. Library. Catalogue of the Memorial Library of Music, Stanford University, by Nathan van Patten. Stanford, Calif.: Stanford Univ. Press, 1950. 310 p.

A collection of manuscripts, prints, inscribed copies of books and scores; the emphasis is on "association items." 1,226 entries.

Review by Otto E. Albrecht in *Notes,* 8 (1951), p. 706–9.

STOCKHOLM, SWEDEN

2388. J. H. Roman-samling i Kungl. Musikaliska Adademien. Handstilar och notpikturer i Kungl. Musikaliska akademiens Roman-samling. Hand-

writing and musical calligraphy in the J.H. Roman-collection of the
Swedish Royal Academy of Music. Av Ingmar Bengtsson och Ruben Dan-
ielson. With an English summary. Uppsala: Almqvist & Wiksells boktr.,
1955. 74 p. (Studia musicologica Upsaliensia, 3)

A brief guide to the collection with some facsimiles.

2389. Musikaliska Akademiens Bibliotek. Mr. Roman's spuriosity shop; a
thematic catalogue of 503 works from c. 1680 to 1750 by more than sixty
composers. Compiled and presented by Ingmar Bengtsson. Stockholm:
Swedish Music History Archive, 1976.

A catalog of more than 1,200 works composed and gathered by Johann
Helmich Roman of which only 250 have supportable attributions.

**2390. Stiftelsen Musikkulturens Framjande [Foundation for Furthering Musical
Culture].** Fortechning over musikhandskrifter: musikalier, brev och bio-
grafica [Catalog of music manuscripts, letters and biographical docu-
ments]. Stockholm: Svenskt Musikhistoriskt Arkiv, 1972. 51 p. (Bulletin,
8)

A preliminary catalog, or checklist, of the manuscript collection of
Rudolf Nydahl, Stockholm, now owned by the Foundation for Furthering
Musical Culture. About 4,500 items in all, including some 1,200 autographs, correspondence, and other documents. The catalog is in two
parts: (1) music manuscripts, (2) letters and other documents. The collection is strong in the work of 19th-century musicians.

STRASBOURG, FRANCE

2391. Archives de la Ville. "Aperçu général sur les sources dans les Archives de la Ville de Strasbourg" by René Kopff in *Fontes artis musicae,*
26 (1979), p. 47–54.

An inventory, of musical documents in the city archives as well as the
archives of St. Thomas Church, the Cathedral, and the musicologist Eu-
gène Wagner.

STUTTGART, GERMANY

2392. Württembergische Landesbibliothek. Die Handschriften der Wurttem-
bergischen Landesbibliothek Stuttgart. Erste Reihe, erster Band: Codices
musici (Cod. Mus. fol. I 1–71). Beschrieben von Clytus Gottwald. Wiesbad-
en: Otto Harrassowitz, 1964. 184 p.

Describes 53 manuscripts in mensural notation and 18 plainchant
sources, giving concordances for texts and music, index of text incipits,
thematic catalog for anonymous works, with full bibliographical apparatus. An exemplary catalog.

Review by Franz Krautwurst in *Die Musikforschung,* 21 (1968), p. 233–
37.

2393. Württembergische Landesbibliothek. Die Handschriften der Württem-
bergischen Landesbibliothek Stuttgart. Zweite Reihe: Die Handschriften
der ehemaligen koniglichen Hofbibliothek. Sechster Band: Codices
musici. Erster Teil . . . Beschrieben von Clytus Gottwald. Wiesbaden: Otto
Harrassowitz, 1965. 66 p.

Continues the cataloguing begun in the preceding volume, covering a different series of manuscripts.
Review by Ute Schwab in *Die Musikforschung*, 24 (1971), p. 210–12.

2394. Württembergische Landesbibliothek. Katalog uber die Musik-Codices des 16. und 17. Jahrhunderts auf der K. Landesbibliothek in Stuttgart. Angefertigt von A. Halm. Langensalza: Beyer, 1902–3. 58 p. (Monatshefte fur Musikgeschichte. Beilage. Jahrgang 34–35.)
Cites 70 manuscripts with listings of contents for each. Index to text incipits under individual composers.

SUCRE, BOLIVIA

2395. Catedral Platense. Un archivo musical americano. [By] Carmen García Muñoz and Waldemar Axel Roldán. Buenos Aires: Editorial Universitaria de Buenos Aires, 1972. 166 p.
Catálogo de los manuscritos p. 51–96.
183 numbered items.

SWEDEN

The Swedish bibliographer Ake Davidsson has prepared union catalogs of early printed music and of music theory works in Swedish libraries. See his *Catalogue critique et descriptif des ouvrages théoriques sur la musique imprimes au XVIe et au XVIIe siècles et conserves dans les bibliothèques suédoises* (no. 1155), and his *Catalogue critique et descriptif des imprimés de musique des XVIe et XVIIe siècles conservés dans les bibliothèques suédoises . . .* (no. 2417).

SYDNEY, AUSTRALIA

2396. Australia Music Centre. Military and brass band music [in the] Australia Music Centre. Sydney: Australia Music Centre, 1977. 28 p. Catalogues of Australian compositions, 6
A catalog of the holdings of the Australia Music Centre in this genre.

SYRACUSE, NEW YORK

2397. University Libraries. Sources for the study of 19th-century opera in the Syracuse University Libraries; an annotated libretti list by Aubry S. Garlington. Syracuse: Syracuse University Libraries, 1976. 563 p.
A catalogue of libretti indexed by composer, librettist, choreographers, etc. Addenda, p. 445–70.

TENBURY WELLS, ENGLAND

2398. St. Michael's College (Tenbury. Library. The music collection of St Michael's College, Tenbury; a listing and guide to parts one to five. Compiled by Professor Roger Bray. Brighton: Harvester Press Microform Publications, 1983–86. 98 p.

The *Catalog of manuscripts in the Library of St. Michael's College compiled by* E. H. Fellowes " has been completely revised" and has been reproduced in full on the first reel.

As in the other Harvester guides, there is a list on the contents of each reel in each part and a listing of the manuscripts in each part followed by a unifed index of names and composers in the volume. There is also a numerical index to the manuscript volumes in the collection.

2399. St. Michael's College (Tenbury). Library. A summary catalogue of the printed books and music in the library of St. Michael's College, Tenbury. Compiled by E. H. Fellowes, 1934. 143 leaves (unpublished manuscript).

An unpublished catalog of the printed books and music in the library of St. Michael's College. Intended as a companion volume to the manuscript catalog above, but never printed.

2400. St. Michael's College (Tenbury). Library. The catalog of manuscripts in the library of St. Michael's College, Tenbury. Compiled by E. H. Fellowes. Paris: Éditions de l'Oisea-Lyre, 1934. 319 p.

Manuscripts in the library bequeathed to the College by Sir Frederick Ousely. 1,386 items; rich in early English music. The library also holds a large portion of the "Toulouse-Philidor collection," consisting of 290 volumes of manuscripts and 67 printed books devoted to the repertory of early 18th-century French opera. Composer index.

2401. St. Michael's College (Tenbury). Library. Auction catalogues of the Toulouse-Philidor collection, the late property of St. Michael's College, Tenbury, Eng.; sold by auction by Sotheby Parke Bernet & Co., London 26 June 1978 and Pierre Ber'es, Paris 30 Nov. 1978. London; Paris: Sotheby Parke Bernet, 1978. 2 v.

Pre-auction catalog of a sale which resulted in the dissolution of one of England's most distinguished collections. Materials from St. Michael's College found new homes in the British Library and the Bibliothèque Nationale, Paris.

TOKYO, JAPAN

2402. Musashino Academia Musicae. Biblioteca. List of acquisitions. Tokyo: Musashino Academia Musicae, 1957– . No. 1– .

Text in Japanese and English.

An annual volume listing materials acquired from April of one year to March of the next. Classified listing of both books and scores. The first section of each issue is devoted to rare materials. No. 15 by March 1972.

2403. Musashino Academia Musicae. Biblioteca. Litterae rarae. Tokyo: Musashino Academia Musicae, 1962– . Liber primus– .

A catalog of rare music materials added to the collection. Published irregularly; *Liber secundus* appeared in 1969. A library rich in first or early editions of music and music literature from the 16th through the 19th centuries. The librarian is Dr. Yoshio Ito.

Liber primus (1962), 141 p. *Liber secundus* (1969), 276 p.

2404. Nanki Music Library. Catalogue of rare books and notes: the Ohki Collection, Nanki Music Library. Tokyo: 1970.

2405. Nanki Music Library. Catalogue of the Nanki Music Library. Part I: Musicology. Tokyo: 1929. 372 p.
A reference library for the historical study of Western music. Much of the material came from the collection of W. H. Cummings, English collector whose library was sold at auction in 1918.

2406. Nanki Music Library. Catalogue of the W. H. Cummings collection in the Nanki Music Library. Tokyo: 1925. 70 p.
A catalog focused on the rare materials acquired in the Cummings sale. About 450 items, including much important early English music.

TOLEDO, OHIO

2407. Museum of Art. The printed note, 500 years of music printing and engraving, January 1957. Toledo: Museum of Art, 1957. 144 p.
Foreword by A. Beverly Barksdale.
Catalog of an exhibition devoted to the history of music printing and engraving. Splendidly illustrated, 188 items, on loan from major public and private collections throughout the country. Informative annotations; bibliography of 67 items.

TOLEDO, SPAIN

2408. Biblioteca Capitolar. "Les manuscrits polyphoniques de la Bibliotheque Capitulaire de Tolede." By René Lenaerts. In *International Society for Musical Research, Fifth Congress, Utrecht, 1952,* p. 267–81.
Brief descriptions and discussion of about 30 sources of early polyphonic music in the Toledo library.

TORONTO, CANADA

2409. University of Toronto. Thomas Fisher Rarebook Library. "A collection of oratorio libretti, 1700–1800 in the Thomas Fisher Rarebook Library, University of Toronto" by Robert Elliott and Harry M. White in *Fontes artis musicae,* 32 (1985) p. 102–13.
The collection includes opera libretti which are not included in this inventory, but are included in Beatrice Corrigan's *Catalogue of Italian Plays, 1500–1700, in the University of Toronto* (Toronto: University of Toronto Press, 1961). Arranged in chronological order in chart form with indexes to librettists and composers.

TREVISO, ITALY

2410. Archivio Musicale del Duomo. La Cappella Musicale del Duomo di Treviso (1300–1633). By Giovanni d'Alessi. Vedelago: Tipografia "Ars et Religio," 1954. 272 p.
Historical study of the musical establishment of the cathedral at Treviso. Chapter 15, p. 169–218, deals with the musical archive and its re-

sources. Manuscripts are listed briefly; printed works in greater detail.

2411. Pfarrkirche St. Stephan. Das alte Musikarchiv der Pfarrkirche St. Stephan in Tulln. By Karl Schnürl. Wien: Bohlau, 1964. 88 p. (Tabulae musicae austriacae, 1.)

The catalog is chiefly concerned with manuscripts, although a short section of prints is included. Partially thematic. The principal composers represented are Albrechtsberger, Diabelli, Eybler, Joseph and Michael Haydn, Krottendorfer, Mozart, Schneider, Schubert, Winter, etc.

Review by Imogene Horsley in *Notes,* 24 (1967), p. 52–53.

2412. Biblioteca Nazionale. "L'Intavolatura d'organo tedesca della Biblioteca Nazionale di Torino. Catalogo ragionato." By Oscar Mischiati. In *L'Organo, rivista di cultura organaria e organistica,* 4 (1963), p. 1–154.

An inventory of the contents of 16 volumes of German organ tablature in the National Library in Turin, the largest body of source material for German organ music known. The manuscripts contain 1,770 compositions on 2,703 written folios, compiled between 1637 and 1640. Appendices include paleographical descriptions of the volumes, author lists added by later hands, watermarks, concordant prints, manuscripts and modern editions, and an index of composers.

2413. Biblioteca Nazionale. "La raccolta di rarità musicali "Mauro Foa" alla Biblioteca Nazionale di Torino." By Alberto Gentili. In *Accademie e biblioteche d'Italia,* 1 (1927), p. 36–50.

Descriptive account of a collection of 95 volumes, manuscripts, and prints founded by Count Giacomo Durazzo, Genoan Ambassador to Venice in 1765. Includes autographs of Vivaldi and Stradella, as well as the organ tablatures mentioned above.

2414. Biblioteca Nazionale. Manoscritti e libri a stampa musicali esposti dalla Biblioteca Nazionale di Torino. Firenze: L. Franceschini, 1898. 24 p.

Exposition catalog of 20 manuscripts and 36 prints of the 16th-18th centuries.

Biblioteca Nazionale. See also no. 2113.

2415. Albrecht, Otto E. A census of autograph music manuscripts of European composers in American libraries. Philadelphia: Univ. of Pennsylvania Press, 1953. 331 p.

Lists 2,017 manuscripts now in America by 571 European composers, giving title, pagination, dimensions, and descriptive notes. Current and former owners indicated. Organized alphabetically by composer. Index of owners.

Review by Jack A. Westrup in Music Review, 16 (1955), p. 84–85.

2416. Seaton, Douglas, ed. "Important library holdings at forty-one North American universities" in *Current musicology*, 17 (1974), p. 7–68.

Brief accounts by domestic corresponding editors of the musical rarities in the university libraries of the following institutions:

Boston University
Bryn Mawr College
Catholic University of America
City University of New York
CUNY Hunter College
CUNY Queens College
Columbia University
Cornell University
Harvard Univrsity
Indiana University
Julliard School
Memphis State University
New York University
Northwestern University
Princeton University
Rutgers University
Stanford University
University of California, Berkeley
University of California, Los Angeles
University of California, Riverside

University of California, Santa Barbara
University of Chicago
University of Colorado
University of Illinois
University of Iowa
University of Kansas
University of Maryland
University of Miami
University of Michigan
University of Minnesota
University of North Carolina
University of Oregon
University of Pennsylvania
University of Pittsburgh
University of Rochester (Eastman)
University of Texas
University of Washington
University of Western Ontario
University of Wyoming
West Virginia University
Yale University

UPPSALA, SWEDEN

2417. Universitetsbiblioteket. Catalogue critique et descriptif des imprimés de musique des XVIe et XVIIe siècles, conservés à la Bibliothèque de l'Université Royale d'Upsala; par Rafael Mitjana avec une introduction bibliographique par Isak Collijn. . . . Upsala: Almqvist et Wiksell, 1911–1951. 3 v.

Vol. 1: Musique religieuse, I, par Rafael Mitjana (1911). Vol. 2: Musique religieuse, II; musique profane; musique dramatique, musique instrumentale; additions au Tome I par Åke Davidsson (1951). Vol. 3: Recueils de musique religieuse et profane, par Åke Davidsson (1951).

Entries in vols. 1 and 2 are arranged alphabetically within each category; vol. 3 is chronological, with an index of the contents of the collections under composer. Index of printers and publishers and a bibliography of works cited. Full bibliographical entries, with locations of copies in other libraries.

2418. Universitetsbiblioteket. Catalogue of the Gimo collection of Italian manuscript music in the University Library of Uppsala. By Åke Davidsson. Uppsala: 1963. 101 p. (Acta Bibliothecae R. Universitatis Upsaliensis, 14.)

A catalog of 360 items, comprising both vocal and instrumental music of the 18th century. An introduction relates the history of the collection. Useful bibliography of sources and related literature.

Review by Minnie Elmer in *Notes,* 22 (1965), p. 715–16; by R. Thurston Dart in *The Library,* 5th ser., 20 (June 1965), p. 166–67.

2419. Universitetsbiblioteket. Sammlung Düben. "Die Dübensammlung. Ein Versuch ihrer chronologischen Ordnung." Von Bruno Grusnick In *Svensk tidskrift för musikforskning,* 46 (1964), p. 27–82; 48 (1966), p. 63–186.

VALENCIA (REGION), SPAIN

2420. Fondos musicale de la región Valenciana. Por José Climent. Valencia: Istituto de musicología; Institución Alfonso el Magnánimo; Diputación Prvincial de Valencia, 1979– . 2 v.

Vol. 1 covers the holdings of the Catedral Metropolitana de Valencia (1979, 471 p.). It is a catalog of the manuscript and printed works in this very large collection. Biographical notes on composers are provided, but only brief bibliographical descriptions of the sources. Index to names.

Vol. 2 covers the holdings of the Archivio musical of the Real Colegio de Corpus Christi Patriarca (1984, 849 p.). It is a catalog of manuscripts and printed works in what was an extraordinary musical establishment. Index to names.

VALLADOLID, SPAIN

2421. Catedral. Archivo Musical. "El Archivo Musical de la Catedral de Valladolid." By Higinio Anglés. In *Anuario musical,* 3 (1948), p. 59–108.

20 manuscripts and 97 early printed books. Inventories given for the contents of the manuscripts and full bibliographical citations for the prints, with references to Eitner and other bibliographies.

VATICAN CITY, ROME

2422. Biblioteca Apostolica Vaticana. Libretti di melodrammi e balli del secolo XVIII [nella] Fondo Ferraioli della Biblioteca Apostolica Vaticana [per]Elisabetta Mori. Firenze: L. Olschki, 1984.

A catalog of the libretti in the Ferraioli collection. Indexes.

2423. Biblioteca Apostolica Vaticana. "Die Sammlungen der Oratorienlibretti (1679–1725) und den restlichen Musikbestand der Fondo San Marcello der Biblioteca Vaticano in Rom." By Andreas Liess. In *ActaM,* 31 (1959), p. 63–80.

Cites 106 oratorio libretti in the Fondo San Marcello of the Biblioteca Vaticano. References to whether or not the works are known to Eitner.

2424. Biblioteca Apostolica Vaticana. Monumenti vaticani di paleografia musicale latina. By. H. M. Bannister. Lipsia: O. Harrassowitz, 1913. 2 v. 130 plates. (Codices e vaticanis selecti, 12.)

Reprint by the Gregg Press, 1969.

A volume of commentary and a volume of plates containing excerpts from Vatican manuscripts, assembled for the purposes of paleographical study. Contains a vast amount of information on the manuscript sources of plainchant in the Vatican Library.

2425. Biblioteca Apostolica Vaticana. Cappella Giulia. Le opere musicali della Cappella Giulia. I. Manoscritti e edizioni fino al '700. By José M. Llorens. Citta del Vaticana: Biblioteca Apostolica Vaticana, 1971. 412 p. (Studi e testi, 265.)

Review by Samuel F. Pogue in *Notes,* 29 (1973), p. 445–48.

2426. Biblioteca Apostolica Vaticana. Cappella Sistina. Bibliographischer und thematischer Musikkatalog des Päpstlichen Kapellarchives im Vatikan zu Rom. . . . von Fr. X. Haberl. Leipzig: Breitkopf & Hartel, 1888. 183 p. (Monatshefte fur Musikgeschichte. Beilage. Jahrgang 19/20.)

Descriptions of 269 items, manuscripts and early printed works, with a thematic catalog, by composer, of the early polyphonic sources. Considerable documentation on the Cappella Sistina and the musicians employed there. The Haberl catalog represents only a small part of the Cappella Sistina collection. See no. 2427 below.

2427. Biblioteca Apostolica Vaticana. Cappella Sistina. Capellae Sixtinae codices musicis notis instructi sive manuscripti sive praelo excussi. Rec. José M. Llorens. Citta del Vaticana: Biblioteca Apostolica Vaticana, 1960. 555 p. 10 facsimile plates.

A catalog of the collection treated by F. X. Haberl, above, but much more thoroughly, since Haberl covered only 269 of the 660 manuscripts and printed volumes present. Volumes listed by number, with detailed inventories of contents. Descriptive annotations in Latin. Thematic catalog of anonymous works.

Review by Dragan Plamenac in *Notes,* 19 (1961), p. 251–52; by Peter Peacock in *Music and letters,* 42 (1961), p. 168–69; by Glen Haydon in *MQ,* 48 (1962), p. 127–29.

VENICE, ITALY

2428. Biblioteca del Palazzo Giustinian Lolin. Stampe e manoscritti preziosi e rari della Biblioteca del Palazzo Giustinian Lolin a San Vidal. By Siro Cisilino. Venezia: A cura del fondatore Dott. Ugo Levi sotto gli auspici dell'Ateneo Veneto, 1966. 55 p.

At head of title: Fondazione Ugo e Olga Levi, Centro di Cultura Musicale Superiore.

Catalog of the library of a recently established musical foundation in Venice. 70 items listed, including printed books and manuscripts from the 16th to the early 19th centuries. Many of the manuscripts are composite in content. The collection contains important source materials for the study of 18th-century instrumental music.

2429. Biblioteca Nazionale Marciana. I codici musicali contariniani del secolo XVII nella R. Biblioteca di San Marco in Venezia. Illustrati dal Dr. Taddeo Wiel. Venenzia: F. Ongania, 1888. 121 p.

Reprinted by Forni, Bologna, 1969.

The Contarini collection is a special library of manuscript scores of 17th-century Venetian opera, by such composers as Cesti, Cavalli, Pallavicino, Ziani, etc. 120 numbered items. Entries give information as to date of first performance, librettist, cast, general description of the work. Composer index.

Biblioteca Nazionale Marciana. See also no. 2105.

Biblioteca Querini Stampalia. See no. 2105.

2430. Conservatorio di Musica Benedetto Marcello. Il Conservatorio di musica Benedetto Marcello di Venezia, 1876–1976: centenario della fondazione: Palazzo Pisani, Venezia [un'exposizione a cura di] Pietro Verardo. Venezia: Stamperia di Venezia, 1977. 299 p.

A catalog of the exposition including a description of the conservatory's holdings of research materials. Almost 50 pages of "documenti" are included.

2431. Conservatorio di musica Benedetto Marcello. Biblioteca. I manoscritti del Fondo Torrefranca del Conservatorio Benedetto Marcello: catalogo per autori [di] Franco Rossi. Firenze: Leo S. Olschki, 1986. 357 p. (Biblioteca "Historiae musicae cultores," 45)(Catalogo dei fonti storici della biblioteca del Conservatorio di musica Benedetto Marcello, Venezia, I,)

This is an alphabetically ordered catalog of manuscripts in the Torrefranca collection, but the catalog also includes anthologies, libretti, treatises, and non-musical manuscripts. Includes some thematic incipits.

2432. Fondazione Cini. La raccolta di libretti d'opera. Catalogo e indici a cura di Anna Laura Bellina, Bruno Brizi, e Maria Grazia Pensa. Roma: Istituto della Enciclopedia Italiana fondata da Giovanni Treccani, 1986. 185 p.

There are approximately 40,000 libretti in the Rolandi collection. This volume provides numerous indexes to the multi-volume catalog of the collection which has been in preparation for some time.

Museo Correr. See no. 2105.

Pia Casa di Ricovero. See no. 2105.

VERCELLI, ITALY

2433. Archivio della Cattedrale. "Il fondo musicale dell'archivio della Cattedrale di Vercelli." By Claudio Sartori. In *Fontes artis musicae,*, 5 (1958), p. 24–31.

VERONA, ITALY

2434. Accademia Filarmonica. L'Accademia Filarmonica di Verona, dalla fondazione (Maggio 1543) al 1600 e il suo patrimonio musicale antico. By Giuseppe Turrini. Verona: "La Tipografica Veronese," 1941. 345 p.

A detailed history of the Accademia Filarmonica from its beginnings to 1600. Chapter 16 discusses the holdings of the library on the basis of early inventories. Chapter 17 continues the discussion to the first half of the 19th century. Chapter 18 includes a catalog of the existing materials in the "Fondo musicale antico," some 217 prints and 21 manuscripts.

Accademia Filarmonic. See also no. 2115.

2435. Biblioteca Capitolare. Il patrimonio musicale della Biblioteca Capitolare di Verona dal sec. XV al XIX. By Giuseppe Turrini. Verona: "La Tipografica Veronese," 1953. 83 p. (Estratto dagli Atti dell'Academia di Agricoltura, Scienze e Lettere di Verona, ser. 6:2, p. 95–176.)

VICENZA, ITALY

2436. Archivio Capitolare del Duomo. Il fondo musicale dell'Archivio Capitolare del Duomo di Vicenza [di] Vittorio Bolcato, Alberto Zanotelli. Torino: E.D.T. Edizioni di Torino, 1986. 514 p. (Cataloghi di fondi musicali Italiani, 4)

A result of collaboration between The Società Italiana di Musicologia and RISM, this catalog treats a corpus of manuscripts and prints from the 18th century, 15th- and 16th-century prints, choir and liturgical books, and a few theoretical works. Includes an index.

Archivio della Cattedrale. See no. 2106.

Biblioteca Bertoliana. See no. 2106.

VIENNA, AUSTRIA

2437. Beethoven-Zentenarausstellung. Fuhrer durch die Beethoven-Zentenarausstellung der Stadt Wien: "Beethoven und die Wiener Kultur seiner Zeit." Wien: Selbstverlag der Gemeinde Wien, 1927. 248 p.

An exhibition catalog of 1,070 items, including letters, documents, pictures, musical instruments, scores, and prints related to Beethoven and his circle.

2438. Gesellschaft der Musikfreunde. "Sources of Brahms's manuscript copies of early music in the Archiv der Gellschaft der Musikfreunde in Wien" by Virginia L. Hancock in *Fontes artis musicae,* 24 (1977), p. 113–21. *Abschriften Abschriften Abschriften*

2439. Gesellschaft der Musikfreunde. Die Volksmusiksammlung der Gesellschaft der Musikfreunde in Wien (Sonnleithner-Sammlung). 1. Teil, bearbeitet von Walther Deutsch und Gerlinde Hofer, mit einem Beitrag von Leopold Schmidt. Wien: A. Schendl, 1969. 186 p. (Schriften zur Volksmusik, 2.)

Catalog of a collection of folk music, chiefly Austrian, begun in 1818. Entries are grouped by genre and by region. First-line index of songs; indexes of places and names. 29 plates duplicating pages from the collection.

Review by Hartmut Braun in *Jahrbuch fur Volksliedforschung,* 15 (1970), p. 159–60.

2440. Gesellschaft der Musikfreunde. Geschichte der Gesellschaft der Musikfreunde in Wien, 1912–1927. (Fortsetzung der Festschrift zur Jahrhundertfeier vom Jahre 1912.) Wien: Gesellschaft der Musikfreunde, 1937.

Continues the documentation given in the preceding volume. Of particular interest is the account by Hedwig Kraus of 'Die Sammlungen der Gesellschaft der Musikfreunde, 1912–1937," p. 1–42.

2441. Gesellschaft der Musikfreunde. Geschichte der K.K. Gesellschaft der Musikfreunde in Wien. . . . In einem Zusatzbande: "Die Sammlungen und Statuten," von Dr. Eusebius Mandyczewski. Wien: Adolf Holzhausen, 1912. 2 v.

Vol. 1 is a history of the Gesellschaft from 1812–1870 and from 1870–1912. Vol. 2, "Zusatz-Band," is not a true catalog but a summary listing of the holdings of the archive, library, and museum. Of particular value is Mandyczewski's listing of "Bucher und Schriften uber Musik. Druckwerke und Handschriften aus der Zeit bis zum Jahre 1800," p. 55–84. Also "Musik-Autographe," p. 85–123.

2442. Hoftheater. Katalog der Portrait-Sammlung der K.V.K. Generalintendanz der K.K. Hoftheater. Zugleich ein biographisches Hilfsbuch auf dem Gebiet von Theater und Musik. Wien: Adolph W. Kunast, 1892–94. 3 v.

Catalogs a large collection of portraits and other graphic materials related to the theater; classified according to type of theater or kind of entertainment. Gruppe III, Vol. 1, p. 119–264, is concerned with pictorial documents on musicians: composers, librettists, concert singers, writers on music, etc.

2443. Internationale Ausstellung für Musik- und Theaterwesen. Fach-Katalog der Musikhistorischen Abteilung von Deutschland und Österreich-Ungarn. . . . Wien: 1892. 591 p.

Catalog for a large and varied music exhibition held in Vienna in 1892. Includes prints, manuscripts, instruments, portraits, letters, and other documents arranged roughly in chronological order from ancient times to the end of the 19th century.

2444. Kunstlerhaus. Katalog der Ausstellung anlässlich der Centenarfeier Domenico Cimarosas. Wien: Verlag des Comites, 1901. 163 p.

Exhibition catalog of 524 items related to Cimarosa and his contemporaries; includes scores, portraits, medals, etc.

2445. Minoritenkonvent. Das Musikarchiv im Minoritenkonvent zu Wien (Katalog des alteren Bestandes vor 1784). By Friedrich Wilhelm Riedel. Kassel: Bärenreiter, 1963. 139 p. (Catalogus musicus, 1.)

Broadly classified catalog of manuscripts and printed music, chiefly 17th and 18th centuries. Strong in early keyboard music. Indexes of composers, copyists, and former owners.

Review by Othmar Wessely in *Die Musikforschung,* 18 (1965), p. 204–6.

2446. Museum des 20. Jahrhunderts. Schönberg—Webern—Berg: Bilder—Partituren—Dokumente. (Catalog of an exhibition at the Museum des 20. Jahrhunderts, Vienna, 17 May–20 July, 1969.) Wien: Museum des 20. Jahr-

hunderts, 1969. 118 p.
Review by Dika Newlin in *Notes,* 27 (1971), p. 488–89.

2447. Österreichische Nationalbibliothek. Die Lautentabulaturhandschriften der Österreichischen Nationalbibliothek (17. und 18. Jahrhundert). Von Elizabeth Maier. Wien: Verlag der Österreichischen Akademie der Wissenschaften, 1974. 131 p. (Tabulae musicae Austriacae, 8)
A thematic catalog to the contents of 9 manuscripts with references to modern editions and an extensive introduction. Index of names and titles or captions.

2448. Österreichische Nationalbibliothek. Die Estensische Musikalien; thematisches Verzeichnis mit Einleitung von Robert Haas. Regensburg: G. Bosse, 1927. 232 p.
Reissued in 1957 as Bd. VII of *Forschungsbeitrage zur Musikwissenschaft.* Regensburg, G. Bosse.
Catalog, largely thematic, of an important collection of 18th-century instrumental music originating in northern Italy. Includes a small group of cantatas and othe vocal works. Classified with major sections of prints and manuscripts. Index of names, text incipits.

2449. Österreichische Nationalbibliothek. "Die Musikbibliothek von Raimund Fugger d.J.: ein Beitrag zur Musikuberlieferung des 16. Jahrhunderts." By Richard Schaal. In *ActaM,* 29 (1957), p. 126–37.
Catalog of the Fugger library, from a 16th-century manuscript in the Staatsbibliothek, Munich. The bulk of the Fugger family music collection is now in the Vienna Library.

2450. Österreichische Nationalbibliothek. "Die Musiksammlung." By Leopold Nowak. In *Die Österreichische Nationalbibliothek. Festschrift herausgegeben zum 25. Jährigen Dienstjubiläum des Generaldirektors Prof. Dr. Josef Bick.* Wien: H. Bauer-Verlag, 1948. p. 119–38.

2451. Österreichische Nationalbibliothek. "Die Musiksammlung der Nationalbibliothek." By Robert Haas. In *Jahrbuch der Musikbibliothek Peters,* 37 (1930), p. 48–62.

2452. Österreichische Nationalbibliothek. Richard Strauss Ausstellung zum 100. Geburtstag. Bearbeitet von Franz Grasberger und Franz Hadamowsky. Wien: Österreichische Nationalbibliothek, 1964. 360 p.
Exhibition catalog of a rich collection of documents related to Richard Strauss. Illustrated.

2453. Österreichische Nationalbibliothek. Tabulae codicum manuscriptorum praeter graecos et orientales in Bibliotheca Palatina Vindobonensi asservatorum ... x. IX-X: Codicum musicorum, Pars I-II. Vindobonae: venum dat. Geroldi filius, 1897–99. 2 v. in 1.
Catalog, compiled by Joseph Mantuani, of the manuscripts numbered 15,501–19,500 comprising the music holdings of the Austrian National Library. Introduction and descriptive notes in Latin. Each volume has an index of names, of subjects, and of text incipits.

2454. Österreichische Nationalbibliothek. Photogrammarchiv. Katalog des Archiv für Photogramme musikalischer Meisterhandschriften, Widmung Anthony van Hoboken. Bearb. von Agnes Ziffer. Wien: Prachner, 1967 – . 482 p. (Museion; Veröffentlichungen der Österreichischen Nationalbibliothek, neue Folge. 3. Reihe, 3)
An archive of photocopies of the autographs of a selected group of great composers, chiefly Viennese, founded in 1927 by Anthony van Hoboken and Heinrich Schenker. 2,684 entries, many references to related literature.

2455. Österreichische Nationalbibliothek. Musiksammlung. Der Franz-Schreker-Fonds in der Musiksammlung der Österreichischen Nationalbibliothek: Katalog bearb. v. Friedrich C. Heller, unter Mitarb. v. Hans Jancik und Lucia Vogel. Wien: Hollinek in Komm., 1975. 70 p. (Museion; Veröffentlichungen der österreichischen Nationalbibliothek, Neue Folge, Reihe 3, 4)
A description of the Schreker collection with a brief bibliography of his works.

2456. Österreichische Nationalbibliothek. Musiksammlung. Die Musiksammlung der Österreichischen Nationalbibliothek, funktion und benützung von Franz Grasberger. Wien: Österreichische Nationalbibliothek, 1980. 100 p.
Includes bibliographical references and index.

2457. Österreichische Nationalbibliothek. Musiksammlung. Die österreichische Nachfolge der Wiener Schule. Musiksammlung d. Österr. Nationalbibliothek, Inst. f. Österr. Musikdokumentation. Sonderausstellung, 2.-21. Mai 1974. (Ausarb. des Ausstellungskataloges: Lieselotte Theiner [und] Lucia Vogel.) Wien: Musiksammlung d. Österr. Nationalbibliothek, 1974. 44 p.
Catalog of an exhibition of holdings of the Viennese School.

2458. Österreichische Nationalbibliothek. Musiksammlung. Katalog der Handschriften Österreichische Nationalbibliothek, Wien, Musiksammlung. Vienna: Olms Microform, 1983. 106 microfiches with 29 p. booklet (Die Europäische Musik. I, Kataloge, 1)
Booklet *Die Musiksammlung der Österreichischen Nationalbibliothek und ihr Handschriftenkatalog* by Günther Brosche.
Photographic reproduction of the music manuscript catalog.

2459. Österreichische Nationalbibliothek. Musiksammlung. Österreichische Spätromantiker: Studien zu Emil Nikolaus von Reznicek, Joseph Marx, Franz Schmidt und Egon Kornauth: mit einer Dokumentation der handschriftlichen Quellen in der Musiksammlung der Österreichischen Nationalbibliothek [von] Thomas Leibnitz. Tutzing: H. Schneider, 1986. 182 p. (Instituts für Österreichische Musikdokumentation, 11)
Monograph on some early 20th-century Viennese composers with a catalog of the manuscript sources.

2460. Österreichische Nationalbibliothek. Musiksammlung. Richard-Strauss-Bibliographie bearb. von Oswald Ortner. Aus dem Nachlass hrsg. von

Franz Grasberger. Wien: G. Prachner, 1964–73. 2 v. (Museion; Veröffentlichungen der Österreichischen Nationalbibliothek, neue Folge, 3. Reihe, 2)

V. 2 published by Kommission bei Verlag Brüder Hollinek. V. 2 compiled by Günther Brosche.

Contents: v. 1. 1882–1944; v. 2. 1944–1964.

2461. Österreichische Nationalbibliothek. Musiksammlung. Sammlung Eleonore Vondenhoff. Gustav Mahler Dokumentation, Sammlung Eleonore Vondenhoff: Materialien zu seinem Leben und Werk; hrsg. von Bruno Vondenhoff und Eleonore Vondenhoff. Tutzing: Schneider, 1978. 676 p. (Institut für Österreichische Musikdokumentation, 4)

2462. Österreichische Nationalbibliothek. Musiksammlung. The music collection of the Austrian National Library by Franz Grasberger. (Transl: Hans Suesserott.) Vienna: Federal Chancellery, Federal Press and Information Dept., 1972. 32 p.

Translation of the 1970 version of *Die Musiksammlung der Österreichischen Nationalbibliothek.*

2463. Österreichische Nationalbibliothek. Sammlung Anthony van Hoboken. Katalog der Sammlung Anthony van Hoboken in der Musiksammlung der Österreichischen Nationalbibliothek: musikalische Erst- und Frühdrucke. Herausgegeben vom Institut für österreichische Musikdokumentation, unter der Leitung von Günther Brosche. Tutzing: H. Schneider, 1982–1986. 5 v.

A catalog of the first and early imprints in the Hoboken collection. Contents:

Bd. 1. *Johann Sebastian Bach und seine Söhne, bearbeitet von* Thomas Leibnitz.

Bd. 2. *Ludwig van Beethoven, bearbeitet von* Karin Breitner und Thomas Leibnitz.

Bd. 3. *Ludwig van Beethoven, Werke ohne Opuszahl und Sammelausgaben bearbeitet von Thomas Leibnitz.*

Bd. 4. *Johannes Brahms, Frederic Chopin bearbeitet von Karin Breitner und Thomas Leibnitz.*

Bd. 5. *Christoph Willibald Gluck, Georg Friedrich Händel bearbeitet von Karin Breitner.*

Catalogs of the contents of the collection of manuscripts, first and early editions of Anthony van Hoboken.

WARSAW, POLAND

2464. Biblioteka Narodowa. Katalog mikrofilmów muzycznych (Catalog of musical microfilms). Warszawa: Biblioteka Narodowa, 1956– . Vol. 1 – .

A series of catalogs originating in the microfilm archive of the National Library at Warsaw. Three volumes—volumes 8, 9, and 10—of a larger series (Katalog mikrofilmow) are concerned with music. The holdings of numerous Polish libraries are represented.

Vol. 1 (1956): chiefly manuscripts and printed materials of the 19th century. Vol. 2 (1962): musical documents of the 17th and 18th centuries.

Vol. 3 (1965): historical source materials related to Polish music.

2465. University Library. Katalog druków muzycznych XVI, XVII e XVIII w. Biblioteki Uniwersytetu warszawskiego. Tom I: Wiek XVI. Warszawa: Wydawn. Uniwers. warszawsk, 1970. 380 p. (Acta bibliothecae universitatis varsoviensis, 7.)

Catalog of printed music of the 16th-18th centuries in the University Library at Warsaw.

This work is highly praised in a brief description in *Fontes artis musicae,* 19 (1972), p. 46.

WASHINGTON, DISTRICT OF COLUMBIA

2466. Library of Congress. Gertrude Clarke Whittall Foundation. Autograph musical scores and autograph letters in the Whittall Foundation collection, prepared by Edward N. Waters. Washington, D.C.: Gertrude Clarke Whittall Foundation, 1953. 18 p.

2467. Library of Congress. M, ML & MT shelflist. Ann Arbor: University Microfilms International, 1979.

A microfiche edition of the shelflists of classified materials in the Music Division of the Library of Congress; thus a classified catalog.

A study of the L.C. shelflist was prepared by Michael A. Keller and Holly Rowe and published as "An analysis of the L.C. music shelflist on microfiche" in *Cum notis variorum,* 78 (December 1983), p. 11–18. Additional information on the L.C. shelflist and its relationship to the actual content of the shelves at L.C. was provided by Robert J. Palian in "Discrepancies between the Keller shelflist count and the contents of the shelves in the Music Division of the Library of Congress" in *Cum notis variorum,* no. 83 (June 1984), p. 43–46.

2468. U. S. Library of Congress. Music Division. "Bloch manuscripts at the Library of Congress" by by David L. Sills in *Notes,* 42 (1986), p. 727–53.

A survey of the collection of music manuscripts, complementing the author's catalog of the Bloch music manuscripts at the Berkeley Music Library (see no. 1929).

2469. Library of Congress. Music Division. The music manuscripts, first editions, and correspondence of Franz Liszt (1811–1886) in the collections of the Music Division, Library of Congress compiled by Elizabeth H. Auman, Gail L. Freunsch, and Robert J. Palian. Washington, D.C.: Library of Congress, 1986.

2470. Library of Congress. Music Division. The musical manuscripts and letters of Johannes Brahms (1833–1897) in the collections of the Music Division, Library of Congress prepared by George S. Bozarth with the assistance of Elizabeth H. Auman and William C. Parsons. Washington, D.C.: Library of Congress, 1983. 22 p.

2471. U.S. Copyright Office. Dramatic compositions copyrighted in the United States, 1870–1916. Washington: Govt. Printing Office, 1918. 2 v.
Unaltered reprint by Johnson Reprint Corp., New York, 1968.
Review by Lenore Coral in *Notes,* 26 (1969), p. 52–53.

2472. U.S. Library of Congress. Music Division. Catalogue of early books on music (before 1800) by Julia Gregory. Washington: Govt. Printing Office, 1913. 312 p.
Supplement (Books acquired by the Library, 1913–42) by Hazel Bartlett ... with a list of books on music in Chinese and Japanese. 1944. 143 p.
Republication in one volume of the original catalog and its supplement by the Da Capo Press, New York, 1969.
The Library of Congress has one of the richest collections of early music theory in the world. The entries conform to the Library's printed catalog cards.
Review by Ruth Watanabe in *Notes,* 26 (1970), p. 521–24.
Music literature—To 1800—Bibliography

2473. U.S. Library of Congress. Music Division. Catalogue of first editions of Edward MacDowell (1861–1908) by O. G. Sonneck. Washington: Govt. Printing Office, 1917. 89 p.
Includes works with and without opus numbers, compositions written under pseudonyms, and works edited by the composer. Index of titles, first line of texts, authors and translators, publishers.

2474. U.S. Library of Congress. Music Division. Catalogue of first editions of Stephen C. Foster (1826–1864) by Walter R. Whittlesey and O. G. Sonneck. Washington: Govt. Printing Office, 1915. 79 p.
Works arranged by title; indexed by authors of text, publishers, first lines. Detailed annotations.

2475. U.S. Library of Congress. Music Division. Catalogue of opera librettos printed before 1800 prepared by O. G. T. Sonneck. Washington: Govt. Printing Office, 1914. 2 v.
Reprint by Johnson Reprint Corp., New York, 1970; and by Burt Franklin, New York, 1967.
The Library's collection of librettos began in 1909 with the purchase of the Schatz collection. By 1914 it contained 17,000 items and was particularly strong in first editions of 17th- and 18th-century works. Vol. 1 is a title listing, with notes giving date of first performance, place, name of composer if known. Vol. 2 is an index by composers, by librettists, and of titles of specific arias mentioned.

2476. U.S. Library of Congress. Music Division. Dramatic music. Catalogue of full scores, compiled by O. G. T. Sonneck. Washington: Govt. Printing Office, 1908. 170 p.
Reprint by Da Capo Press, New York, 1969.
Full scores of operas in original editions, some manuscript copies included, and some photocopies. Arranged alphabetically by composer.
Review by Ruth Watanabe in *Notes,* 26 (1970), p. 521–24.

2477. U.S. Library of Congress. Music Division. Orchestral music ... catalogue. Scores. Prepared under the direction of O. G. T. Sonneck. Washington: Govt. Printing Office, 1912. 663 p.
Reprint by Da Capo Press, New York, 1969.
Orchestra scores from about 1830 to 1912.
Review by Ruth Watanabe in *Notes,* 26 (1970), p. 521–24.

2478. U.S. Library of Congress. Music Division. The Music Division, a guide to its collections and services. Washington: Govt. Printing Office, 1972. 22 p.
Published in 1960 under the title: The Music Division in the Library of Congress.
A brief descriptive account of the work and resources of the Music Division, with illustrations.

2479. U.S. Library of Congress. Music Division. Elizabeth Sprague Coolidge Foundation. Coolidge Foundation program for contemporary chamber music; preliminary checklist of works available for loan (November 1961). Compiled by Frances G. Gewehr. Washington: Library of Congress, 1961. 38 p. (typescript)
Supplement, April 1963.
A classified list of contemporary chamber music scores and parts which may be borrowed by qualified ensembles for study purposes. Entries give publisher and price; recordings if available are also cited.

2480. Washington Cathedral. Library. "The Douglas collection in the Washington Cathedral Library." In *The life and work of Charles Winfred Douglas,* by Leonard Ellinwood and Anne Woodward. New York: Hymn Society of America, 1958. p. 36–72. (Hymn Society of America, Papers, no. 23.)
A library of hymnology and liturgical music formed by one of the leading authorities in the field.

WASSERBURG AM INN, GERMANY

2481. Benediktinerinnenabtei Frauenwörth. Thematischer Katalog der Musikhandschriften der Benediktinerinnenabtei Frauenwörth und der Pfarrkirchen Indersdorf, Wasserburg am Inn und Bad Tölz. Unter d. Leitung von Robert Münster, bearb. von Ursula Bockholdt, Robert Machold u. Lisbet Thew. München: G. Henle, 1975. 211 p. (Kataloge bayerischer Musiksammlungen)

WINDSOR, GREAT BRITAIN

2482. Windsor Castle. St. George's Chapel. The musical manuscripts of St. George's Chapel, Windsor Castle: a descriptive catalogue, by Clifford Mould. Windsor: Oxley and Son (Windsor) Ltd for the Dean and Canons of St. George's Chapel in Windsor Castle, 1973. 76 p. (Historical monographs relating to St. George's Chapel, Windsor Castle, 14)
An index to composers in the 93 manuscripts followed by a table of descriptions and then descriptions of individual manuscripts and groups of manuscripts. Thematic incipits for anonymous music. Appendix list-

ing additional early printed music in the collection.

WINSTON-SALEM, NORTH CAROLINA

2483. Moravian Church. Catalog of the Salem congregation music edited by Frances Cumnock. Chapel Hill: University of North Carolina Press, 1980. 682 p.

2484. Moravian Music Foundation. Catalog of the Johannes Herbst collection. Ed. by Marilyn Gombosi. Chapel Hill: Univ. of North Carolina Press, 1970. 255 p.

A thematic catalog of some 500 manuscripts of sacred music for use in the Moravian service. There are about 1,000 anthems and arias in the collection. The catalog is preceded by a historical introduction describing the musical practices of the 18th-century Moravian church. Index of composers and titles.

Review by Susan T. Sommer in *Notes,* 29 (1972), p. 258–59.

WOLFENBUTTEL, GERMANY

2485. Herzog-August-Bibliothek. Die Handschriften nebst den älteren Druckwerken der Musikabteilung . . . Beschrieben von Emil Vogel. Wolfenbuttel: J. Zwissler, 1890. 280 p. (Die Handschriften der Herzoglichen Bibliothek zu Wolfenbuttel . . . 8.)

2486. Herzog-August-Bibliothek. Libretti: Verzeichnis der bis 1800 erschienenen Textbücher. Hrsg. von Eberhard Theil und Gisela Rohr. Frankfurt am Main: Klostermann, 1970. 395 p. (Katalog der Herzog-August-Bibliothek Wolfenbuttel, 14.)

The entire collection, 1,742 listings, of pre-1800 libretti of operas, interludes, operettas, musical comedies, burlesques, and ballets was available for purchase on microfiche from Kraus-Thomson, Nendeln, Liechtenstein.

Review by Susan T. Sommer in *Notes,* 29 (1972), p. 259.

2487. Herzog-August-Bibliothek. Musik: alte Drucke bis etwa 1750. Beschrieben von Wolfgang Schmieder. Mitarbeit von Gisela Hartwieg. Text- und Registerband. Frankfurt am Main: V. Klostermann, 1967. 2 v. (Kataloge der Herzog-August-Bibliothek Wolfenbuttel, 12 u. 13.)

Vol. I: Textband. 764 p. Vol. II: Registerband. 310 p.

A splendid catalog of 1,334 entries, representing the resources of one of the great German libraries. Early printed music and theoretical treatises.

Review by Harald Heckmann in *Die Musikforschung,* 23 (1970), p. 207–9; by Donald W. Krummel in *Notes,* 26 (1969), p. 39–40.

WROCLAW, POLAND (FORMERLY BRESLAU, GERMANY)

2488. Bohn, Emil. Bibliographie der Musik-Druckwerke bis 1700 welche in der Stadtbibliothek, der Bibliothek des Acad. Inst. für Kirchenmusik, und der K. und Universitäts-Bibliothek zu Breslau aufbewahrt werden. . . .

Berlin: A. Cohn, 1883. 450 p.

Reprint by Georg Olms, Hildesheim, 1969.

The three collections cataloged here are outstanding for their 16th- and 17th-century manuscripts and prints, particularly of liturgical and vocal music. P. 1–31: theoretical works; p. 32–351: practical works (music); p. 371–74: collections in chronological order; p. 374–400: continuation of practical works. Full bibliographical descriptions.

2489. Staats- und Universitats-Bibliothek. Beschreibendes Verzeichnis der alten Musikalien-Handschriften und Druckwerke des Koniglichen Gymnasiums zu Brieg. Bearbeitet von Friedrich Kuhn. Leipzig: Breitkopf & Härtel, 1897. 98 p. (Monatshefte für Musikgeschichte. Beilage, Jahrgang 29.)

A collection placed in the library of Breslau University in 1890. 54 manuscripts and some 110 printed books, chiefly 16th century. Contents given for manuscript anthologies; full bibliographical description for prints. Index.

2490. Stadtbibliothek. Die musikalischen Handschriften des XVI. und XVII. Jahrhunderts in der Stadtbibliothek zu Breslau.... von Emil Bohn. Breslau: Commissions-Verlag von J. Hainauer, 1890. 423 p.

Reprint by Georg Olms, Hildesheim, 1970.

356 items, with full inventories of contents. Numerous indexes and supplementary lists; first-line incipits of vocal texts, anonymous compositions, composer index, etc.

2491. Uniwersytet Wroclawski. Katalog muzycznych dziel teoretycynych XVI i XVII wieku. [Catalog of music theory works of the 16th and 17th centuries]. Compiled by Aniela Kolbuszewska. Wroclaw: Biblioteka Uniwersytecka, 1973. 67 p.

A catalog of 102 numbered theoretical works. Precise bibliographical descriptions with references to descriptive literature. Information as to provenance. Call numbers given. Index of printers and publishers, by place. Index of names.

WUPPERTAL, GERMANY

2492. Stadtbibliothek. Musikalien-Bestand der Stadtbibliothek. Wuppertal: 1960. 117 p.

YORK, GREAT BRITAIN

2493. York Minster. Library. A catalogue of the music manuscripts in York Minster Library compiled by David Griffiths. [York: University of York Library, 1981. 266 p.

A catalog of 218 manuscripts in the collection, each described and analyzed. Indexes to composers, first lines and titles, copyists, previous owners, genres and performing forces, and to other names and places.

2494. York Minster. Library. A catalogue of the printed music published before 1850 in York Minster Library compiled by David Griffiths. York:

The Library, 1977. 118 p.,

2495. Glasbeni Rokopisi in Tiski na Slovenskem do Leta 1800. Music manuscripts and printed music in Slovenia before 1800. Catalogue. [Compiled
by J. Höfler and I. Klemencic.] Ljubljani: Narodna in Univerzitetna knjiz-
nica v Ljubljani, 1967. 105 p.

> The present catalogue is an attempt to catalogue all surviving early musical
> material in libraries and archives throughout Slovenia. [From the introduc-
> tion by the editors]

The material comprises 32 chant manuscripts, 343 general manuscripts, chiefly 18th and early 19th century, and an unnumbered section
devoted to printed music. Items are located in 17 Slovenian libraries or
collections.

2496. Hauptkirche. Musikalienkatalog der Hauptkirche zu Sorau N. L.
Hergestellt von G. Tischler und K. Burchard. [Langensalza: H. Beyer &
Söhne, 1902.] 24 p. (Monatshefte für Musikgeschichte. Beilage. Jahrgang
34.)
The collection contains 33 prints, chiefly 17th-century, and a small
group of manuscripts in which Telemann, Petri, and C. G. Tag are well
represented.

2497. Allgemeine Musikgesellschaft. Katalog der gedruckten und handschriftlichen Musikalien des 17. bis 19. Jahrhunderts im Besitze der All-
gemeinen Musikgesellschaft Zürich. Red. von Georg Walter. Zurich:
Hug, 1960. 145 p.
A collection rich in 17th- and 18th-century instrumental music. Thematic incipits for works in manuscript.
Review by Donald W. Krummel in *Notes,* 19 (1961), p. 77; by Willi Kahl
in *Die Musikforschung,* 16 (1963), p. 284.

2498. Zentralbibliothek. "Die Osterreichische Musiküberlieferung der Züricher Zentralbibliothek." [By Erich Schenk.] In *Die Österreichische Nationalbibliothek. Festschrift hrsg. zum 25. Jährigen Dienstjubiläum des
Generaldirektors Prof. Dr. Josef Bick.* Wien: H. Bauer-Verlag, 1948. p.
576–81.
Consists chiefly of a listing of works by Austrian composers in the
Zurich library, giving place, publisher and library signature. Special
attention given to works not mentioned in Eitner.

2499. Ratsschulbibliothek. Bibliographie der Musikwerke in der Ratsschulbibliothek zu Zwickau, bearb. . . . von Reinhard Vollhardt. Leipzig: Breitkopf & Härtel, 1893–96. 299 p. (Monatshefte für Musikgeschichte.

Beilage. Jahrgang 25–28.)

764 numbered items, manuscripts and printed books, including liturgical works, theoretical works, instrumental and vocal music. Chiefly 16th- and 17th-century materials.

CATALOGS OF PRIVATE COLLECTIONS

In this section some of the catalogs of major private music collections are cited. Few of these remain intact. Some, like the Cortot or the Wolffheim collections, have been dispersed; others have changed location in recent years. No attempt has been made here to list the numerous catalogs issued in connection with auction sales, although some of these are of great bibliographical interest. Some indication of the information to be gained from the study of early music auction catalogs, a field very little explored as yet, can be found in A. Hyatt King's book *Some British collectors of music, c. 1600–1960,* Cambridge University Press, 1963. James B. Coovers' *Provisional checklist of priced antiquarians' catalogues containing musical materials* (see no. 702) and the bibliography of literature about private collections of books and scores he announced as forthcoming in his *Musical instrument collections; catalogues and cognate literature* will be of use to those interested in private collections. Lenore Coral's work on British book sale catalogs (her thesis, *Music in English auction sales, 1676–1750* (University of London, 1974) and with A. N. L. Munby, *British book sale catalogues, 1676–1800; a union list* [London: Mansell, 1977]) will shed some light on this subject as well.

Frits Knuf, Amsterdam, has published a series of reprints of important auction catalogs of music from the collections of Selhof, Burney, Turk, Coussemaker, Novello, and Rimbault. Numerous entries in the preceding section refer to private collections now in institutional custody; there are entries in the subject index in the names of the previous, private owners of these collections.

Aldrich, Richard. A catalogue of books. . . . See no. 1991.

2500. Bokemeyer, Heinrich. Collection.

An important 18th-century music library assembled by the theorist Heinrich Bokemeyer (1679–1751). Harald Kümmerling has reconstructed the collection and identified its surviving elements now in the Stiftung Preussischer Kulturbesitz in Berlin.

See under BERLIN, GERMANY, no. 1942.

2501. Burney, Charles. Catalogue of the music library of Charles Burney, sold in London, 8 August 1814. With an introduction by A. Hyatt King. Amsterdam: Frits Knuf, 1973. (Auction catalogues of music, no. 2)

A facsimile list of the music collection Burney gathered on his travels and in response to his need for sources while writing *A General History of Music* (see no. 544).

2502. Burrell, Mary. The Richard Wagner collection formed by ... Mary Burrell. The property of The Curtis Institute of Music, Philadelphia; which will be sold on Friday, October 27, 1978. New York: Christie, Manson & Woods, International, 1978. 172 p.

One of the most distinguished collection of Wagneriana ever in private hands, the collection was sold and largely dispersed. See the earlier catalog of the collection, no. 2322

2503. Cortot, Alfred. Bibliothèque Alfred Cortot. ... v. 1. Catalogue établi par Alfred Cortot et rédigé par Frederik Goldbeck, avec la collaboration de A. Fehr. Préface de Henry Prunieres. [Argentueil: Sur les presses de R. Coulouma, 1936.] 221 p.

Premiere partie (all published): Traités et autres ouvrages théoriques des XVe, XVIe, XVIIe, & XVIIIe siècles.

The music holdings in the library of Alfred Cortot. Cortot's interests as a collector extended over a wide area of musical practice. The collection passed into the hands of a dealer at the owner's death in 1962.

Portions of the Cortot library have since been acquired by the British Museum, the Newberry Library in Chicago, the University of California Music Library at Berkeley, and the University of Kentucky at Lexington. For an account of this dispersal, and a complete lists of Kentucky's acquisition of 290 treatises, see Frank Traficante, 'The Alfred Cortot collection at the University of Kentucky Libraries," in *University of Kentucky Library Notes,* 1:3 (Spring 1970), 19 p. A shorter version of the same paper is printed in *Notes,* 26 (1970), p. 713–17. The Cortot materials in the British Museum are described by A. Hyatt King and O. W. Neighbor in *The British Museum Quarterly,* 31 (1966), p. 8–16.

2504. Coussemaker, Charles Edmond Henri de. Catalogue of the music library of Charles Edmond Henri de Coussemaker, sold at Brussels 1877. With an introduction by A. Hyatt King. Buren: Frits Knuf, 1977. (Auction catalogues in music, no. 4)

A facsimile of the classified catalogue of the holdings of the pioneering musicologist. Portions of the Coussemakr collection were acquired by Van der Straeten, Weckerlin, the Bibliothèque Royale of Brussels, and the Bibliothèque de Douai.

2505. The Dickinson Collection. "New Schumann materials in upstate New York: a first report on the Dickinson Collection, with catalogues of its manuscript holdings" by Ralph P. Locke and Jurgen Thym in *Fontes artis musicae,* 27 (1980), p. 137–61.

An inventory of manuscripts, letters, printed music, books, and miscellaneous items in the collection gathered by Edward and June Dickinson and kept in Livona, New York.

2506. Feininger, Laurence. Repertorium cantus plani. Tridenti: Societas Universalis Sanctae Ceciliae, 1969. 2 v.

Catalog of a private collection of liturgical manuscripts. Vol. I: Antiphonaria. Vol. II: Gradualia.

Each volume treats 24 manuscripts. Descriptions are followed by complete inventories of the contents of each source. Indexes of liturgical incipits conclude each volume.

2507. Fuchs, Aloys. "The autographs of the Viennese music collections of Aloys Fuchs, using the original catalogues." Edited by Richard Schaal, in *Haydn Yearbook,* Vol. VI (1969), p. 3–191.

The autographs are listed alphabetically by composer, with information as to provenance and destination if known. Introduction in German and English.

Fuchs (1799–1853) was the first great collector of musical autographs. His collection was dispersed, but portions of it can be found in the Berlin Staatsbibliothek, the Staatsbibliothek der Stiftung Preussischer Kulturbesitz, and the Benedictine Abbey at Gottweig.

See also no. 2508.

2508. Fuchs, Aloys. Quellen und Forschungen zur Wiener Musiksammlung von Aloys Fuchs von Richard Schaal. Wien: H. Böhlaus Nachf., 1966. 151 p. (Veröffentlichungen der Kommission für Musikforschung, 5)

A report on the contents of the Fuchs Collection. Bibliography: p. 135–151.

2509. Heyer, Wilhelm. Musikhistorisches Museum von Wilhelm Heyer in Köln, Katalog, Katalog von George Kinsky. Band 4: Musik-Autographen. Leipzig: Breitkopf & Hartel, 1916. 870 p.

1,673 items, one of the finest collection of musical autographs ever assembled. Dispersed and sold at auction in 1926 by the firm of Henrici and Liepmannssohn. Kinsky's catalogs of the Heyer collecion are models of music bibliography, full of biographical and descriptive detail. 64 facsimile plates.

For other volumes of the Heyer Katalog, see no. 2561.

2510. Hirsch, Paul. Katalog der Musikbibliothek Paul Hirsch . . . Frankfurt am Main, hrsg. von K. Meyer und P. Hirsch. Berlin: M. Breslauer, 1928–47. 4 v. (V. 4 has imprint: Cambridge Univ. Press.)

Vol. 1: Theoretische Drucke bis 1800. Vol. 2: Opera-Partituren. Vol. 3: Instrumental- und Vokalmusik bis etwa 1830. Vol. 4: Erstausgaben, Chrowerke in Partitur, Gesamtausgaben, Nachschlagewerke, etc. Erganzungen zu Bd. I-III.

The Paul Hirsch Library, one of the great private music collections of the world, was removed from Frankfurt to Cambridge, England, just prior to World War II and was acquired by the British Museum in 1946.

See the brief article, "The Hirsch catalog," by P. H. Muir in *Music review,* 9 (1948), p. 102–07.

See also nos. 2178, 2179.

2511. Jacobi, Erwin R. Musikbibliothek Erwin R. Jacobi. Seltene Ausgaben und Manuskripte. Katalog. The music library of Erwin R. Jacobi. Rare editions and manuscripts. Zusgest. von Regula Puskás. [Hrsg.:] Allgemeine Musikgesellschaft Zürich. 3., erg. und rev. Aufl. Zürich: Hug, 1973. 84 p.

Second ed. published in 1970 titled: *Seltene Originalausgaben von Musica Practica und Musica Theoretica aus dem 15.-20. Jahrhundert.*

A private collection of 514 items. 11 plates. Preface in English and German. Errata slip inserted.

2512. Koch, Louis. Collection. Katalog der Musikautographen Sammlung Koch. . . . Manuskripte, Briefe, Dokumente, von Scarlatti bis Stravinsky. Beschrieben und erläutert von Gerog Kinsky. Stuttgart: Hoffmannsche Buchdruckerei F. Krais, 1953. 360 p.

An important collection of musical autographs. Strong in German music of the classic and romantic periods. 21 facsimile plates.

Review by Richard S. Hill in *Notes,* 11 (1953), p. 119–20.

Levy, Lester S., Collection, See No. 1908.

2513. Meyer, André. Music Collection. Collection musicale André Meyer: manuscrits, autographes, musique imprimée et manuscrite, ouvrages théoriques, historiques et pédagogiques, livrets, iconographie, instruments de musique. Abbeville: F. Paillart, [1960]. 118 p.

Catalog compiled by Francois Lesure and Nanie Bridgman.

A collection of manuscripts and early printed music, particularly noteworthy for its holdings in iconography. Beautifully illustrated by 292 plates.

Review by Hans Halm in *Die Musikforschung,* 17 (1964), p. 83–84.

2514. Die Musikalien der Grafen von Schönborn-Wiesentheid. Thematisch-bibliographischer Katalog. Bearbeitet von Fritz Zobeley. I. Theil: Das Repertoire des Grafen Rudolf Franz Erwein von Schönborn (1677–1754). Tutzing: Hans Schneider, 1967–82. 2 v. (Veroffentlichungen der Gesellschaft für bayerische Musikgeschichte e.V.)

Band I: Drucke aus den Jahren 1676 bis 1738; Band II: Handschriften.

Thematic catalog of a private collection of early vocal and instrumental music assembled by the Counts von Schönborn-Wiesentheid in Schloss Weiler bei Aschaffenburg. 149 items, with full bibliographical descriptions and inventories of contents. Informative introductory chapters on the history of the collection and its composition. Further catalogs of the MSS and archive materials projected.

Review by W. Gordon Marigold in *Notes,* 24 (1968), p. 715–16.

2515. Novello, Vincent. Catalogue of the music library of Vincent Novello, sold in London 25 June 1852 and 3 September 1862. With an introduction by A. Hyatt King. Buren: Frits Knuf, 1975. (Auction catalogues in music, no. 5)

A facsimile of the listing of the collection of one with "a remarkable grasp of the functions of a music librarian."

2516. Pretlack, Ludwig, Freiherr von Die Musikbibliothek des Ludwig Freiherrn von Pretlack (1716–1781). [Hrsg. von] Joachim Jaenecke. Wiesbaden: Breitkopf & Härtel, 1973. 330 p. Neue musikgeschichtliche Forschungen, 8

The Pretlack collection is now in the Staatsbibliothek der Stiftung Preussischer Kulturbesitz Berlin.

2517. Rimbault, Edward Francis. Catalogue of the music library of Edward Francis Rimbault, sold at London 31 July - 7 August 1877. With the Library of Dr. Rainbeau. With an introduction by A. Hyatt King. Buren:

Frits Knuf, 1975. (Auction catalogues of music, no. 6)

A facsimile of the list of music and books which supported various of Rimbault's musical studies, such as *Bibliotheca madrigaliana* (see no. 1829). Many of the more valuable titles went to Joseph Drexel and thereafter to the New York Public Library (see no. 2275).

With the actual sale catalog is published the satirical *Catalogue of the extensive library of Doctor Rainbeau which was previously published as a separate facsimile with an introduction by* James B. Coover (n.p.: Distant Press, 1962).

2518. Scheide, William. Selections from the library of William H. Scheide. New York: Grolier Club, 1967. 11 p.

Catalog of the exhibition of selections from Mr. Scheide's collection, known to be rich in manuscripts and early prints. The exhibit occured in March 1967.

2519. Selhof, Nicolas. Catalogue of the music library, instruments and other property of Nicholas Selhof, sold in The Hague; 1759. With an introduction by A. Hyatt King. Amsterdam: Frits Knuf, 1973. (Auction catalogues of music, no. 1)

A facsimile listing about 2,940 works, published and in manuscript.

2520. Stainer, John, Sir, Library. Catalogue of English song books: forming a portion of the library of Sir John Stainer. Boston: Longwood Press, 1977. 107 p.

Reprint of the Novello, Ewer edition of 1889.

A catalog prepared by Stainer's children on not only song books, but books about bells in Stainer's library.

2521. Türk, Daniel Gottlob. Catalogue of the music library of Daniel Gottlob Türk, sold in Halle, 13 January 1817. With an introduction by A. Hyatt King. Amsterdam: Frits Knnuf, 1973. (Auction catalogues in music, no. 3)

A facimile of the catalogue of music and books about music auctioned posthumously. Includes references to works not sold but in Türk's collection.

2522. Weckerlin, Jean Baptiste Théodore, Library. Katalog der Musikbibliothek des Herrn J. B. Weckerlin. Music—Tanz—Theater. Versteigerung, 10. bis 12. März 1910. Leipzig: C. G. Boerner, 1910. 172 p.

Auction catalog of the private library of Weckerlin, distinguished French music librarian and musicologist of the 19th century. Illustrated with facsimiles pages. Extensive holdings of vocal music. Foreword in French and German by C. G. Boerner. Catalog has descriptive notes mainly in French.

2523. Wittgenstein Collection. "Ursrung und Geschichte der Sammlung Wittgenstein im 19. Jahrhundert," by E. Fred Flindell, in *Die Musikforschung,* 22 (1969), p. 298–314.

A 19th century collection of musical autographs including works of Mendelssohn, Brahms, Joachim, Grillparzer, Beethoven, Schubert, etc. Now largely dispersed, a part is in the Library of Congress.

2524. Wolffheim, Werner J. Library. Versteigerung der Musikbibliothek des Herrn Dr. Werner Wolffheim ... durch die Firmen: M. Breslauer & L. Liepmannssohn. ... Berlin, 1928–29. 2 v. in 4.

One of the finest collections ever brought together by a private person ... the 2-volume catalog compiled at the time of its sale will always rank as an indispensable work of reference." [*Grove's*, 5th ed.]

Classified catalog of a library that included not only rarities but the standard reference books and editions as well. Full descriptions with copious notes. Numerous facsimile plates.

Catalogs of Musical
Instrument Collections

Collections of musical instruments are frequently annexed to music libraries. The reader will note that a number of the catalogs in the preceding section are concerned, in part, with Western or Asian instruments. In the section that follows, the catalogs of some of the major specialized collections of musical instruments are listed along with a number of exhibition catalogs emphasizing this area of collecting activity.

For a comprehensive and historical view of instrument collections, see Alfred Berner's article, "Instrumentensammlungen," in *MGG*, 6, col. 1295–1310. There is also an illuminating paper by Georg Kinsky entitled "Musikinstrumentensammlungen in Vergangenheit und Gegenwart," in the *Jahrbuch Peters*, 27 (1920), p. 47–60.

Two surveys provide a broad, if somewhat dated, overview of the potential sources for literature in this chapter. One is that of the Music Library Association, *A survey of musical instrument collections in the United States and Canada* (see no. 2526) and the other is the International Council of Museums' *International directory of musical instrument collections* (see no. 2963) . James B. Coover's *Musical instrument collections; catalogues and cognate literature* (see no. 2525) cites 2,418 catalogs published up to the late 1970's. In the main, new entries to this chapter have been important titles published after Coover's bibliography appeared.

2525. Coover, James B. Musical instrument collections; catalogues and cognate literature. Detroit: Information Coodinators, 1981. 464 p. (Detroit Studies in Music Bibliography, 47)

An annotated bibliography of 2,418 titles arranged in section one by names of institutions or exposition and in section two by names of private collectors. Appendices list chronologically some early inventories, expositions, and exhibitions. General index and index to auctioneers, antiquarians, and firms.

Review by Paula Morgan in *Notes*, 39 (1982), p. 198. Review by Jeremy Montagu in *Early Music*, 11 (1983), p.100–102.

2526. A survey of musical instrument collections in the United States and Canada. Conducted by a committee of the Music Library Association: William Lichtenwanger, chairman & compiler; Dale Higbee, Cynthia Adams Hoover, Phillip T. Young. Ann Arbor: Music Library Association, 1974. 137 p.

Details on 572 collections in institutions. Information on collections of historical instruments, modern replicas, ethnic instruments, toy instru-

ments, etc. Directory with addresses, personnel, hours of service, catalogs and bibliography. Index of instruments and classes of instruments; of cultural, geographical, and historical origins.
Review by Laurence Libin in *Notes,* 33 (1976), p. 57–59.

2526.1. Young, Philip T. 2,500 historical woodwind instruments; an inventory of major collections. N.Y.: Pendragon Press, 1982. 155 p.
Organized alphabetically by makers' last name. Instruments listed in orchestral score order: flutes, oboes, clarinets, bassoons, etc. Bibliography. Appendices of museums and collections represented and bibliography of sources of illustrations.

ANN ARBOR, MICHIGAN

2527. University of Michigan. Stearns Collection of Musical Instruments. Catalog of the Stearns collection of musical instruments, by Albert A. Stanley. 2nd ed. Ann Arbor: University of Michigan, 1921. 276 p.
First published in 1918. A supplement, *Stearns collection of musical instruments—1965, by* Robert Austin Warner was published in 1965. 10 p.
A catalogue of 1,464 instruments, Western and Asian. 13 plates, descriptive annotations. Bibliography and indexes of makers, geographical distribution, names of instruments.
A brief, informative survey of the history of the collection, its character and present condition. Three plates.

ANTWERP, BELGIUM

2528. Museum Vleeshuis. Catalogus van de muziekinstrumenten uit de verzameling van het Museum Vleeshuis. Antwerpen: Ruckers Genootschap, 1981. 189 p.

BASEL, SWITZERLAND

2529. Historisches Museum. Katalog der Musikinstrumente im Historischen Museum zu Basel. Von Dr. Karl Nef. Basel: Universitäts-Büchdruckerei von Friedrich Reinhardt, 1906. 74 p.
Bound with *Festschrift zum zweiten Kongress der Internationalen Musikgesellschaft*, Basel, 1906. 294 instruments listed and described. 12 plates.

BERKELEY, CALIFORNIA

2530. University of California. Department of Music. Catalogue of the collection of musical instruments in the Department of Music, University of California, Berkeley. Part I. Edited by David Boyden. . . . Berkeley, Calif.: 1972. 104 p.
An unpublished catalog.
A collection of 88 instruments, including early originals and modern replicas. Short essays on the principal instrument forms. Each instrument is introduced historically followed by its precise dimensions. A

second part is projected.

2531. Institut für Musikforschung. Die Berliner Musikinstrumentensammlung; Einführung mit historischen und technischen Erläuterungen von Alfred Berner. Berlin: 1952. 58 p.

Not strictly a catalog, but a guide to the principal types of instruments with reference to examples in the Berlin collection. 11 plates.

2532. Staatliche Akademische Hochschule für Musik. Führer durch die Sammlung alter Musik-Instrumente, von Dr. Oskar Fleischer. Berlin: A. Haack, 1892. 145 p.

Classified catalog, chiefly early Western instruments, with a few Asian.

2533. Staatliche Akademische Hochschule für Musik. Sammlung alter Musikinstrumente bei der Staatlichen Hochschule für Musik zur Berlin; beschreibender Katalog von Curt Sachs. Berlin: J. Bard, 1922. 384 cols., 30 plates.

The collection contains some 3,200 items, of which about 250 are non-European instruments. Classified catalog. Entries give descriptions of instrument, maker, date and place of manufacture. Index of instruments, places, makers, etc.

2534. Staatliches Institut für Musikforschung. Das Musikinstrumenten Museum Berlin. Eine Einfuhrung in Wort und Bild. Berlin: 1968. 70 p.

Historical essay: "75 Jahre Musikinstrumenten-Sammlung' by Irmgard Otto; 56 photo plates of instruments.

2535. Staatliches Institut für Musikforschung. Musikinstrumenten Museum Berlin. Ausstellungsverzeichnis mit Personen- und Sachregistern. Bearbeitet von Irmgard Otto. Berlin: 1965. 144 p.

A guide to the Berlin musical instrument collection as currently displayed, with a diagram of the exposition halls, index of donors, a list of catalog numbers, and 12 pages of photo plates of instruments.

2536. Tagliavini Collezione. Clavicembali e spinette dal XVI al XIX secolo: collezione L. F. Tagliavini a cura di Luigi Ferdinando Tagliavini e John Henry van der Meer; con i contributi di Wanda Bergamini e Friedemann Hellwig. Casalecchio di Reno; Bologna: Grafis, 1986. 243 p.

At head of title: Cassa di risparmio in Bologna. (Collezioni d'arte e di documentazione storica) . Catalog of an exhibition held at Chiesa di San Giorgio in Poggiale, Nov. 1-Dec. 21, 1986.

Catalog of a remarkable private collection gathered by the distinguished musicologist, organologist, and organist. The collection was exhibited while the 1987 Congress of the International Musicological Society was held in Bologna.

BOSTON, MASSACHUSETTS

2537.   Museum of Fine Arts. Leslie Lindsey Mason Collection. Ancient European musical instruments. . . . by N. Bessaraboff. Cambridge: Pub. for the Museum . . . by the Harvard Univ. Press, 1941. 503 p.

An authoritative catalog, well-illustrated, 213 items. Provides a wealth of background information for the historical study of instruments. Bibliography, p. 453–69. Indexes of names and subjects. 16 plates and 72 illustrations in text. The collection of Canon Francis W. Galpin forms the basis of the Mason collection.

Review by Curt Sachs in *MQ,* (July 1942), p. 380–83.

For an evaluation of the book, and a tribute to its author, see David Boyden's article "Nicholas Bessaraboff's Ancient European musical instruments," in *Notes,* 28 (1971), p. 21–27.

BRAUNSCHWEIG, GERMANY

2538.   Städtisches Museum. Verzeichnis der Sammlung alter Musikinstrumente im Städtischen Museum Braunschweig . . . Instrumente, Instrumentenmacher und Instrumentisten in Braunschweig. . . . Braunschwieg: E. Appelhans, 1928. 124 p. (Werkstucke aus Museum, Archiv und Bibliothek der Stadt Braunschweig, 3.)

The catalog occupies p. 5–34; lists 113 items, all European. The remainder of the volume is devoted to studies of local instrument makers and performers.

BRUGES, BELGIUM

2539.   Gruuthusemuseum. Catalogus van de muziekinstrumenten. [Prepared by] M. Awouters, I. De Keyser, [and] S. Vandenberghe. Brugge: Brugge Gruuthusemuseum, 1985. 120 p.

BRUSSELS, BELGIUM

2540.   Conservatoire Royal de Musique. Musée Instrumental. Catalogue descriptif et analytique du Muséepar Victor-Charles Mahillon, conservateur . . . 2e ed. Gand: A. Hoste, 1893–1922. 5 v.

One of the great instrument collections of the world. More than 3,000 instruments of all cultures. Classified catalog. The descriptions include precise indications of each instrument's pitch, tuning, and range.

BUSSUM, HOLLAND

2541.   Leeuwen Boomkamp, C. van. and J. H. Van der Meer. The Carel van Leeuwen Boomkamp collection of musical instruments. Amsterdam: Frits Knuf, 1971. 188 p. 80 plates.

A private collection of 112 items, expertly described and illustrated in photographs. The collection is strongest in its stringed instruments (57) and its bows (32).

Review by Anthony Baines in *Galpin Society Journal,* 25 (1972), p. 123–35.

CAIRO, EGYPT

2542. Museum of Egyptian Antiquities. Catalogue général des antiquites égyptiennes du Musée du Caire. Nos. 69201–69852: Instruments de musique, par Hans Hickmann. Le Caire: Imprimerie de l'Insitut français d'archéologie orientale, 1949. 216 p. 116 plates.

Classified catalog of 651 ancient Egyptian instruments, or fragments thereof, with detailed descriptions and photo reproductions.

CAMBRIDGE, MASSACHUSETTS

2643. Eddy Collection. The Eddy Collection of Musical Instruments: a checklist, by Edwin M. Good. Berkeley: Fallen Leaf Press, 1985. 91 p. (Fallen Leaf reference books in music)

CINCINNATI, OHIO

2544. Art Museum. Musical instruments. [Collection of the Cincinnati Art Museum.] Cincinnati: 1949.

An illustrated brochure listing 110 instruments, 60 European, 50 non-European.

COPENHAGEN, DENMARK

2545. Carl Claudius Collection. Carl Claudius' Samling af gamle musikinstrumenter. København: Levin og Munskgaard, 1931. 423 p.

A rich private collection of musical instruments, now administered by the University of Copenhagen. The catalog describes 757 items.

2546. Musikhistorisk Museum. Das Musikhistorische Museum zu Kopenhagen: beschreibender Katalog von Angul Hammerich; deutsch von Erna Bobe. Mit 179 illustrationen. Kopenhagen: G. E. C. Gad; Leipzig: Kommissionsverlag von Breitkopf & Härtel, 1911. 172 p.

The Danish edition appeared in 1909.

Classified catalog of 631 items, 582 of which are instruments, Western and Asian, followed by a short listing of liturgical manuscripts, prints, and miscellany.

EDINBURGH, SCOTLAND

2547. University. Dept. of Early Keyboard Instruments. The Russell collection and other early keyboard instruments in Saint Cecilia's Hall, Edinburgh. [Compiled by Sidney Newman and Peter Williams.] Edinburgh: Edinburgh Univ. Press, 1968. 79 p.

2548. University. Galpin Society Exhibition. An exhibition of European musical instruments. Edinburgh International Festival, Aug. 18th-Sept. 7th, 1968, Reid School of Music, Edinburgh University. Edinburgh: 1968. 99 p. 40 plates.

The 21st anniversary exhibition of the Galpin Society.

An exhibition catalog of 716 items, including bibliography. Instruments described, dimensions given. The introductory paragraphs for each group of instruments are supplied by specialists. The editor of the catalog is Graham Melville-Mason.

See also the Galpin Society exhibition catalog, London 1951 (no. 2568).

EISENACH, GERMANY

2549. Bachmuseum. Verzeichnis der Sammlung alter Musikinstrumente im Bachhaus zu Eisenach, hrsg. von der Neuen Bach Gesellschaft. 4., erweiterte Aufl. Leipzig: Breitkopf & Härtel, 1964. 97 p. (Veröffentlichungen der Neuen Bachgesellschaft. Vereinsjahr 50, 1962.)

First issued in 1913.

Classified catalog of more than 230 items. Illustrated with line drawings.

FLORENCE, ITALY

2550. Conservatorio di Musica "Luigi Cherubini." Gli strumenti musicali raccolti nel Museo del R. Istituto L. Cherubini a Firenze. [By Leto Bargagna.] [Firenze: G. Ceccherini, 1911.] 70 p.

A catalog of 146 instruments; 12 plates.

2551. Museo del Conservatorio "Luigi Cherubini." Gli strumenti musicali della corte medicea e il Museo del Conservatorio "Luigi Cherubini" di Firenze. Cenni storici e catalogo descrittivo. [By] Vincio Gai. Firenze: LICOSA, 1969. 286 p.

The instruments are illustrated by line drawings with precise measurements. P. 255–71: "Bibliografia." Preceded by an introduction relating the history of the collection.

GIJÓN, SPAIN

2552. Museo Internacional de la Gaita. Catalogo. Gijón:, Asturias (España), 1970. 152 p.

Catalog of a museum devoted to the bagpipe, its history and distribution. Organized by country, with numerous color plates and black-and-white illustrations.

THE HAGUE, THE NETHERLANDS

2553. Gemeentemuseum. Catalogi van de muziekbibliotheek en de collectie muziekinstrumenten onder redactie van dr. C. C. J. von Gleich.Catalogus van de muziekinstrumenten. Deel I: Hoorn- en trompetachtige blaasinstrumenten door Leo J. Plenckers. Amsterdam: Frits Knuf, 1970. 85 p.

The first of a series of catalogs projected to cover the musical instrument collections at the Gemeentemuseum. Describes 136 instruments of the horn and trumpet type. Eight plates; a classified grouping of instrument types, and a glossary. Index of names.

This series is paralleled by another devoted to the holdings of the Museum's music library (see no. 2084).

2554. Gemeentemuseum. Europese muziekinstrumenten in het Haagse Gemeentemuseum. [By A. W. Ligtvoet and W. Lievense.] 's-Gravenhage: Gemeentemuseum, 1965. 160 p.

With 64 full-page illustrations.

2555. Gemeentemuseum. Exotische en oude Europese muziekinstrumenten, in de muziekafdeling van het Haagse Gemeentemuseum; 25 afbeeldingen toegelicht. [By A. W. Ligtvoet.] s'-Gravenhage: Nijgh & Van Ditmar, [1955]. 51 p.

A general, popular introduction to the collection. 25 plates. Text in Dutch and English.

2556. Haags Gemeentemuseum. Pianofortes from the Low Countries. Pianofortes uit de Lage Landen. [Text, Dr. Clemens von Gleich; translation: Delboy & Behnsen; photographs: B. Frequin *et al.*] Buren: Haags Gemeentemuseum; F. Knuf, 1980. 55 p.

Pianofortes from the 18th and 19th centuries by Dutch makers from the instrument collection of the Haags Gemeentemuseum. In English and Dutch.

HALLE, GERMANY

2557. Händel-Haus. Katalog zu den Sammlungen des Händel-Hauses in Halle. 5. Teil: Musikinstrumentensammlung. Besaitete Tasteninstrumente. By Konrad Sasse. Halle: Händel-Haus, 1966. 292 p. 115 illustrations.

One of the largest collections of keyboard instruments in Europe, comprising some 115 items. Founded on the collection of J. C. Neupert of Nuremberg, acquired in the 1930s.

Review by Friedrich Ernst in *Die Musikforschung,* 21 (1968), p. 506–07.

For a catalog of the complete holdings of the Handel House in Halle, see nos. 2086.

HOLYOKE, MASSACHUSETTS

2558. Mount Holyoke College. The Belle Skinner collection of old musical instruments. . . . A descriptive catalogue compiled under the direction of William Skinner. [Philadelphia; New York; etc.: Printed by the Beck Engraving Co.], 1933. 210 p.

Illustrated catalog of 89 instruments, including some particularly fine examples of keyboard instruments. Colored plates.

Since 1959 this collection has been on loan to Yale University.

JOHANNESBURG, SOUTH AFRICA

2559. Kirby, Percival Robson. Catalogue of the musical instruments in the collection of Percival R. Kirby, compiled by Margareet M. de Lange. Johannesburg: Africana Museum, 1967. 155 p.

LEIPZIG, GERMANY

2560. Heyer Collection. Kleiner Katalog der Sammlung alter Musikinstrumente, verfasst von Georg Kinsky. Köln: 1913. 250 p.

An abridgement of the material in the following catalog; valuable because it contains entries for the wind instruments in the Heyer collection, not included in the larger catalog.

2561. Heyer Collection. Musikhistorisches Museum von Wilhelm Heyer in Köln. Katalog von Georg Kinsky. Leipzig: Breitkopf & Härtel, 1910–16. 2 v.

The two volumes of the catalog are concerned with the instrument collection. Vol. 1: Besaitete Tasteninstrumente. Orgel und orgelartige Instrumente. Vol. 2: Zupf- und Streichinstrumente. Vol. 3 (not published) was intended to cover the wind instruments. The Heyer instrument collection, one of the finest in the world, was transferred to Leipzig in 1926, where it was destroyed in World War II.

Kinsky's catalog is a mine of information for the student of early instruments; copiously illstrated, rich in detail.

See also nos. 2560, 2561.

2562. Karl-Marx-Universität. Führer durch das Musikinstrumentenmuseum der Karl-Marx-Universität Leipzig. Von Paul Rubardt. Leipzig: Breitkopf & Härtel, 1955. 84 p. 16 plates.

2563. Leipzig. Universität. Musikinstrumenten-Museum. Kataloge des Musikinstrumenten-Museums der Karl-Marx-Universität zu Leipzig. Leipzig: Deutscher Verlag für Musik, 1978– . 6 v. to date.

Contents:

v.1. *Flöten [von]* Herbert Heyde.
v.2. *Kielinstrumente [von]* Hubert Henkel.
v.3. *Trompeten, Posaunen, Tuben [von]* Herbert Heyde.
v.4. *Clavichorde [von] Hubert Henkel.*
v.5. *Hörner und Zinken [von]* Herbert Heyde.
v.6. *Orgelinstrumente, Harmoniums [von]* Klaus Gernhardt, Hubert Henkel [und] Winfried Schrammek.

Scientific studies of instruments in the Karl-Marx-University in Leipzig. Precise measurements provided.

2564. Universität. Musikwissenschaftliches Instrumentenmuseum. Führer durch das Musikwissenschaftliche Instrumentenmuseum der Universität Leipzig. Hrsg. von Helmut Schultz. Leipzig: Breitkopf & Härtel, 1929. 85 p. 19 plates.

A classified catalog organized according to the ground plan of the display.

LINZ, AUSTRIA

2565. Landesmuseum. Die Musikinstrumentensammlung des Oberösterreichischen Landesmuseums. Bearbeitet von Othmar Wessely. Linz: Demokratische Druck- und Verlags-Gesellschaft, [n.d.] 47 p. (Kataloge des Oberösterreichischen Landesmuseums, 9.)

A collection of 188 items, classified and described briefly.

LONDON, ENGLAND

2566. British Museum. Department of Western Asiatic Antiquities. Ancient musical instruments of Western Asia in the Department of Western Asiatic Antiquities, the British Museum. By Joan Rimmer. London: British Museum, 1969. 51 p. 26 plates.

Actual instruments as well as depictions are described. Treats the use of string, wind, and percussion instruments in Sumerian, Babylonian, Anatolian, Assyrian, and Hellenistic Asiatic societies. Corrects several inaccurate reassemblies. Appendix gives a classified list of instruments and a table of musical references in the Old Testament.

2567. Fenton House. Benton Fletcher Collection. Catalogue of the Benton Fletcher collection of early keyboard instruments at Fenton House, Hampstead. London: Country Life, Ltd., for the National Trust, 1957. 26 p.

A descriptive brochure by Raymond Russell for a collection of early keyboard instruments maintained in playing condition in a late 17th-century house in Hampstead, London.

2568. Galpin Society. British musical instruments. August 7–30, 1951. [London: The Galpin Society, 1951.] 35 p.

A classified exhibition catalog of instruments, chiefly of British make or use. Includes 151 woodwind, 61 brass, 27 keyboard, 62 of the viol family, 16 of the viol family, and 16 miscellaneous. Brief descriptions, with short introductions for each class of instruments.

See also the Galpin Society exhibition catalog, Edinburgh, 1968.

2569. Horniman Museum. The Adam Carse collection of old musical wind instruments [now in the Horniman Museum, London]. London: Staple Press for the London County Council, 1951. 88 p.

A collection of 320 instruments, briefly described, with historical notes for each family. Illustrated by drawings.

2570. Horniman Museum and Library. Musical instruments: handbook to the Museum's collection, by Jean L. Jenkins. 2nd ed. London: Inner London Education Authority, 1970. 104 p.

First edition published in 1958.

A catalog which is at the same time a handbook for the study of musical instruments, chiefly non-Western. 32 plates; bibliography, discography, and index.

2571. Royal College of Music. Catalog of historical musical instruments, paintings, sculpture, and drawings. [London: Royal College, 1952.] 16 p.

Foreword by George Dyson.

Contains the Donaldson collection of musical instruments. Brief inventory with minimum description.

2572. Royal Military Exhibition, 1890. A descriptive catalogue of the musical instruments recently exhibited at the Royal Military Exhibition, London, 1890. Compiled by Charles Russell Day. London: Eyre & Spottiswoode, 1891. 253 p.

An exhibition confined to wind and percussion instruments. 457 wind instruments (percussion not inventoried). Plates.

2573. South Kensington Museum. A descriptive catalogue of the musical instruments of the South Kensington Museum..By Carl Engel.... London: Printed by G. E. Eyre and W. Spottiswoode for H. M. Stationery Office, 1874. 402 p.

Preceded by an essay on the history of musical instruments.

2574. Victoria and Albert Museum. Catalogue of musical instruments. London: Her Majesty's Stationery Office, 1978–85. 2 v.

First published in 1968.

Vol. 1: Keyboard instruments, by Raymond Russell. 94 p. and 47 plates. Detailed descriptions of 52 keyboard instruments, including pianos and organs described by Austin Niland. Appendix B: The decoration of keyboard instruments by Peter Thornton; biographical notes on the makers, bibliography and index.

Vol. 2: Non-keyboard instruments, by Anthony Baines. 121 p., 138 plates. The instruments are grouped as stringed instruments and wind instuments, with 16 subgroups of the former, 8 of the latter. Full technical descriptions, clear plates of details; bibliography and index.

Review of the 1968 edition by Don L. Smithers in *Notes,* 26 (1969), p. 47–48.

2575. Victoria and Albert Museum. Musical instruments as works of art. London: Victoria and Albert Museum, 1968. 50 unnumbered leaves.

Illustrated with more than 100 plates showing details of early musical instruments characterized by fine workmanship. All from the instrument collection of the Victoria and Albert.

LOS ANGELES, CALIFORNIA

2576. Lachmann Collection. Erich Lachmann collection of historical stringed musical instruments, by Erich Lachmann. Los Angeles: Allan Hancock Foundation, Univ. of Southern California, 1950. 53 p.

A handsome catalog of 42 items; noteworthy for its photographic illustrations by Irvin Kershner.

LUCERNE, SWITZERLAND

2577. Richard Wagner Museum. Katalog der städtischen Sammlung alter Musikinstrumente im Richard-Wagner-Museum, Tribschen, Luzern. Erstellt im Auftrag der Museum-Kommission von René Vannes.... Luzern: Otto Dreyer, 1956. 40 p.

A catalog of 95 stringed instruments, 46 wind, 11 idiophones, 37 exotic instruments. 16 plates.

LUTON, ENGLAND

2578. Museum and Art Gallery. The Ridley collection of musical wind instruments in the Luton Museum. [Luton: the Corp. of Luton, Museum and Art Gallery, 1957.] 32 p.

65 wind instruments. Historical note, p. 1–21. Plates.

MILAN, ITALY

2579. Conservatorio di Musica "Giuseppe Verdi." Gli strumenti musicali nel Museo del Conservatorio di Milano. Ed. E. Guarinoni. Milano: Hoepli, 1908. 109 p.

A collection of 278 instruments, 177 European and 91 non-European. Index of donors and of instruments.

2580. Museo degli Strumenti Musicali. Catalogo, a cura di Natale Gallini e Franco Gallini. [Milano]: Castello Sforzesco, [1963]. 448 p.

An earlier catalog of the same collection issued in 1958 under the title: *Civico Museo di antichi strumenti musicali. The 1963 catalog, completely reorganized, lists 641 items, well described and illustrated in 141 plates.*

2581. Museo degli Strumenti Musicali. Mostra di antichi strumenti musicali della Collezione N. Gallini (Maggio, 1953). Milano: Villa Comunale (Ex Reale), [1955]. 43 p.

An exhibition catalog of 200 items dating from the time when the Gallini collection was in private hands. It has since become the property of the city of Milan, and its complete catalog appears above. Preface signed by Natale Gallini; 32 plates.

MUNICH, GERMANY

2582. Bayerisches Nationalmuseum. Ausstellung alter Musik, Instrumente, Noten und Dokumente aus drei Jahrhunderten. Veranstaltet durch die Stadt München im Bayerischen Nationalmuseum, November-Dezember, 1951. Katalog. München: Musikverlag Max Hieber, 1951. 71 p. 23 plates.

An exhibition devoted to music in cultural history. 636 items, of which the majority are early instruments.

NEW HAVEN, CONNECTICUT

2583. Yale University. Checklist, Yale collection of musical instruments. New Haven: Yale University, 1968. 43 p.

Preface signed by Richard Rephann, Curator, 1968.

Check-list of 310 instruments comprising items from the Morris Steinert, the Belle Skinner, and the Emil Herrmann collections as well as gifts from private donors and Friends of Music at Yale. Brief descriptions, no bibliography, chiefly Western instruments.

2584. Yale University. Art Gallery. Musical instruments at Yale, a selection of Western instruments from the 15th to 20th centuries. Catalog by Sibyl Marcuse. . . . [New Haven]: Yale University Art Gallery, [1960]. 32 p.

An exhibition, Feb. 19-March 27, 1960, of 26 instruments as well as paintings, drawings, prints, and manuscripts. Illustrated.

2585. Yale University. Morris Steinert Collection. The Morris Steinert collection of keyed and stringed instruments. New York: Tretbar [1893].

NEW YORK, NEW YORK

2586. Metropolitan Museum of Art. Catalog of keyboard instruments. New York: Metropolitan Museum of Art, 1903. 313 p.

2587. Metropolitan Museum of Art. Keyboard instruments in the Metropolitan Museum of Art, a picture book by Emanuel Winternitz. New York: The Metropolitan Museum of Art, 1961. 48 p.

Not a catalog, but a book of photo reproductions of keyboard instruments from the Metropolitan's collection, including details, with commentary by the Curator.

2588. Metropolitan Museum of Art. Crosby Brown collection. Catalog of the Crosby Brown collection of musical instruments of all nations. . . . New York: Metropolitan Museum of Art, 1903–1907. 3 v. in 4.

Vol. 1: Europe (1904). Vol. 2: Asia (1903). Vol. 3: Instruments of savage tribes and semi-civilized peoples: Pt. 1, Africa (1907); Pt. 2: Oceania (1907); Pt. 3: Historical groups (1905).

See the article by Emanuel Winternitz, "The Crosby Brown collection of musical instruments: its origin and development," in *Metropolitan Museum Journal,* 3 (1970). Also printed as a separate, 20 p.

NUREMBURG, GERMANY

2589. Nuremberg. Germanisches Nationalmuseum. Musikinstrumente: von der Antike bis zur Gegenwart [von] John Henry van der Meer. München: Prestel-Verlag, 1983. 301 p. (Bibliothek des Germanischen Nationalmuseums Nürnberg zur deutschen Kunst- und Kulturgeschichte, 2)

A history of musical instruments based, in large measure, upon the collections of the Germanisches Nationalmuseum, Nuremburg.

2590. Nuremberg. Germanisches Nationalmuseum. Verzeichnis der europäischen Musikinstrumente im Germanischen Nationalmuseum Nürnberg; [Hrsg. von] John Henry van der Meer. Wilhelmshaven; Hamburg; Locarno; Amsterdam: Heinrichshofen, 1979– . 1 v. (to date) (Instrumentenkataloge des Germanischen Nationalmuseums, Nürnberg, 1)(Quellenkataloge zur Musikgeschichte, 16)

Bd. 1: *Hörner und Trompeten, Membranophone, Idiophone, 1979. 220 p., 195 pl.*

A classified index. Bibliography and index to makers.

2591. Nuremberg. Germanisches Nationalmuseum. Wegweiser durch die Sammlung historischer Musikinstrumente, Germanisches National-museum Nürnberg; 2. Aufl. [Hrsg. von] John Henry van der Meer. Nürn-berg: Germanisches Nationalmuseum, 1976. 96 p.
First published 1971.
A guide to the collections.

OXFORD, ENGLAND

2592. Ashmolean Museum. Catalogue of the Hill collection of musical in-struments in the Ashmolean Museum, Oxford, by David D. Boyden. Lon-don: Oxford Univ. Press, 1969. 54 p. 57 plates.
Review by Joan Rimmer in *Notes,* 26 (1970), p. 741–44.

PARIS, FRANCE

2593. Conservatoire National. Le Musée du Conservatoire National de musique. Catalogue descriptif et raisonné, par Gustave Chouquet. Nou-velle edition. Paris: Firmin-Didot, 1884. 276 p.
First published in 1875. Supplement by Léon Pillaut, in 1894, 1899, and 1903.
A catalog of 1,006 instruments, subdivided into European and non-European sections. Index of instruments and of names. Catalogers of musical instruments owe much to the classification established by Chou-quet in this catalog.

ROME, ITALY

2594. Museo nazionale strumenti musicali. Antichi strumenti musicali in un moderno museo: Museo nazionale strumenti musicali, Roma [a cura di] Luisa Cervelli. 2a ed. Roma: Gela, 1986. 75 p.
A catalog of the older instruments in the museum. Includes index and bibliography.

SALZBURG, AUSTRIA

2595. Museum Carolino-Augusteum. Alte Musik-Instrumente im Museum Carolino-Augusteum Salzburg. Führer und beschreibendes Verzeichnis von Karl Geiringer. Leipzig: Breitkopf und Hartel, 1932. 46 p.
A catalog of 288 instruments, with an index of makers and four photo-graphic plates showing 48 different instruments.

TOKYO, JAPAN

2596. Musashino Academia Musicae. Catalogue, museum of musical instru-ments. On the 40th anniversary of the Institute. Tokyo: 1969. 108 p. 4 p. of illustrations.
Text in Japanese and English.
The collection was established in 1953. The catalog is classified by national origins of the instruments, with a taxonomy according to meth-od of sound production. Part 2 is a catalog of accessories; part 3 a catalog

of mechanical devices.

2597. Ueno Gakuen College. Institute for the Study of Musical Instruments. Catalogue of the European musical instruments of the XVIIth, XVIIIth and XIXth centuries in the Ueno Gakuen collection. Tokyo: Ueno Gakuen Educational Foundation, 1980. 243 p.

Text in Japanese and English. 82 pages of photographs incorporating 3 to 6 views of each of 71 instruments. Text references to photographs by number.

TORONTO, CANADA

2598. Royal Ontario Museum. Musical instruments in the Royal Ontario Museum, by Ladislav Dselenyi. Toronto: Royal Ontario Museum, 1971. 96 p.

A well-illustrated catalog of more than 100 instruments. The instruments come from the bequest of R. S. Williams, beginning in 1913.

VERONA, ITALY

2599. Accademia filarmonica di Verona. Catalogo degli strumenti musicali dell'Accademia filarmonica di Verona [per] John Henry van der Meer [e] Rainer Weber. Verona: Accademia filarmonica di Verona, 1982. 146 p.

Catalog of the instrument collections of one of the oldest continuously operating musical organizations in Italy.

VIENNA, AUSTRIA

2600. Gesellschaft der Musikfreunde. "Musikinstrumente," in *Zusatz-Band zur Geschichte der K.K. Gesellschaft der Musikfreunde in Wien. Sammlung und Statuten..* von Dr. Eusebius Mandyczewski. Wien: 1912. p. 154–85.

Catalog of a collection of 355 instruments, of which 221 are of Western origin. The remaining are of ehtnic interest: Turkey, Africa, Arabia, Persia, Siam, India, China, Japan, etc.

2601. Kunsthistorisches Museum. Alte Musikinstrumente; die Sammlung des Kunsthistorischen Museums in der neuen Burg zu Wien. [By Victor Luithlen.] Wien: H. Bauer, 1954. 28 p.

A brief visitor's guide to the collection described below.

2602. Kunsthistorisches Museum. Die Sammlung alter Musikinstrumente. Beschreibendes Verzeichnis von Julius Schlosser. Wien: Anton Schroll, 1920. 138 p.

The catalog describes 361 instruments, most of which are illustrated in 57 plates. 31 Asian and folk instruments. Western instruments are entered in chronological order, grouped according to type, with full descriptions and an informative introduction to each major section: i.e., "Das Orchester des 16. und 17. Jahrhunderts;' 'Die Entwicklung des Instrumentenbaus seit dem 18. Jahrhundert." Much useful historical information given, as, for example, a supplement quoting the descriptions of

20 early instruments from Mattheson's *Neu-eröffnetes Orchester* (1713).

2603. Kunsthistorisches Museum. Katalog der Sammlung alter Musikinstrumente. I. Teil. Saitenklaviere. Wien: Kunsthistorisches Museum, 1966. 95 p. 32 plates.

Classified catalog and description of 76 keyboard instruments. Full of detailed information respecting instrument makers, dimensions of the instruments, bibliographical references. The catalog is the work of the music instrument collection's director Victor Luithlen and his assistant Kurt Wegerer. This volume is the first of three that will eventually cover all of the museum's holdings.

Review by Friedrich Ernst in *Die Musikforschung,* 21 (1968), p. 506-7.

2604. Museum für Völkerkunde. Aussereuropäische Musikinstrumente. Wien: Museum für Völkerkunde, [1961]. 89 p.

Foreword by Alfred Janata.

Illustrated, classified catalog of 654 non-European instruments.

WASHINGTON, DISTRICT OF COLUMBIA

2605. Library of Congress. Gertrude Clarke Whittall Foundation. The Stradivari memorial at Washington, the national capital, by William Dana Orcutt. Washington: Library of Congress, Gertrude Clarke Whittall Foundation, [1938]. 49 p.

Description of the matched set of Stradivarius instruments donated to the Library of Congress.

2606. Library of Congress. Music Division. Musical instruments in the Dayton C. Miller flute collection at the Library of Congress, a catalog. Washington, D.C.: Library of Congress, 1982– .

V.1: *Recorders, fifes, and simple system transverse flutes of one key; compiled by* Michael Seyfrit.

This catalog, when complete, will cover the 6,000 instruments in the collection in 7 v. The catalog was preceded by a checklist: *Dayton C. Miller FLute Collection, a checklist of the instruments by* Laura E. Gilliam and William Lichtenwanger, 1961.

V. 1 treats 273 instruments. 56 photographs. Indexes of instrument makers, cities, symbols and sources.

Review by Jane P. Ambrose in *Notes,* 39 (1983), p. 853.

2607. Library of Congress. Music Division. Three masters: the stringed instrument collection in the Library of Congress. Text by Rembert Herbert; additional research by Paula Forrest; photographs by Paula Forrest, Michael Seyfrit and Dane Penland. Washington, D.C.: The Library of Congress, 1983. 28 p.

A brief guide to the collection.

2608. Smithsonian Institution. Harpsichords and clavichords, by Cynthia A. Hoover. Washington: Smithsonian Institution Press, 1969. 43 p.

A guide to the instruments in the Smithsonian Institution.

2609. Smithsonian Institution. Division of Musical Instruments. A checklist of keyboard instruments at the Smithsonian Institution. Washington: Smithsonian Institution, 1967. 79 p.

Full description lacking, but remarkably rich in information: maker, place of origin, date, type, compass, etc. Five plates.

For another publication based on the Smithsonian's collection of keyboard instruments, see no. 2609.

2610. Smithsonian Institution. Handbook of the collection of musical instruments in the United States National Museum, by Frances Densmore. Washington: Govt. Printing Office, 1927. 164 p. 49 plates. (Smithsonian Institution U. S. National Museum. Bulletin 136.)

Histories and Bibliographies
of Music Printing and
Publishing

Included here are bibliographies of the output of some of the major early music printers and publishers, such as Petrucci, Playford, Walsh, Ballard, etc.; studies of music publishing in particular regions or countries (England, Italy, Paris, Vienna, etc.); and a few works concerned with the technical processes of music printing or engraving. An extensive, but now dated bibliography on the history of music printing has been compiled by Ake Davidsson: see no. 2624, below.

2611. Bergmans, Paul. "La typographie musicale en Belgique au XVIe siècle." In *Histoire du livre et de l'imprimerie en Belgique des origines à nos jours,* 5 (Bruxelles, 1929), p. 47–75.
An illustrated account of 16th-century Belgian music printers and printing.

2612. Bernstein, Jane A. "The burning salamander: assigning a printer to some sixteenth-century music prints" in *Notes,* 42 (1986), p. 483–501.
Concerning the attribution of a number of prints to the Venetian music publisher Girolamo Scotto.

2613. Berz, Ernst-Ludwig. Die Notendrucker und ihre Verleger in Frankfurt am Main von den Anfängen bis etwa 1630. Eine bibliographische und drucktechnische Studie zur Musikpublikation. Kassel: International Association of Music Libraries and International Musicological Society, 1970. 336 p. (Catalogus musicus, 5.)
A thoroughly documented study of music printing in Frankfurt to 1630. with a bibliography of 258 printed works by some 43 printers.

2614. Bobillier, Marie. "La librairie musicale en France de 1653 à 1790, d'après les Registres de privilèges." [Par Michel Brenet, pseud.] In *Sammelbande der Internationalen Musikgesellschaft,* 8 (1906–1907), p. 401–66.
An examination with extensive transcriptions from the archives in the Bibliotheque Nationale pertaining to licenses granted for the publication of music and books on music in Paris from 1652 to 1790. Thorough discussion of the inception of the royal *privilège,* with transcriptions of sample 17th-century *privileges.* Supplemented by Cucuel, no. 2623 below.

The Breitkopf Thematic Catalogue ... See no. 1746.

2615. Calderisi, Maria. Music publishing in the Canadas, 1800–1867. L'Edition musicale au Canada, 1800–1867. Ottawa: National Library of Canada, 1981. 128 p.
A bibliographic study with a list of imprints beginning about 1800.
Reviewed by Donald W. Krummel in *Fontes artis musicae,* 29 (1982), p. 90.

2616. Castelain, Raoul. Histoire de l'édition musicale; ou, du droit d'éditeur au droit d'auteur, 1501–1793. Pref. de Andre Siegfried. Paris: H. Lemoine, 1957. 92 p.
Brief history of music publishing, with emphasis on legal aspects.

2617. Il Catalogo numerico Ricordi 1857 con date e indici; [per] Agostina Zecca-Laterza; prefazione di Philip Gossett. Roma: Nuovo istituto editoriale italiano, 1984– . v. 1– (Bibliotheca musicae; 8)
Originally published in Florence by Presso Ricordi e Jouhaud, 1857.
A plate number catalog for the most important Italian publishing firm, covering the first 50 years of Ricordi's output, annotated with approximate dates of publication. Introduction in English.

2618. Chrysander, Frederick. "A sketch of the history of music—printing, from the fifteenth to the nineteenth century" in *The Musical Times,* 18 (1877), p. 265–68, 324–26, 375–78, 470–75, 524–27, 584–87.
Also published in German as "Abriss einer Geschichte des Musikdruckes vom fünfsehnten bis zum neunsehnten Jahrhundert" in *Allgemeine musikalishe Zeitung,* 14 (1879), cols. 161–67, 177–83, 193–200, 209–14, 225–32, 241–48.

2619. Cinq catalogues d'éditeurs de musique à Paris (1824–34): Dufaut et Dubois, Petit, Frère, Delahante-Erard, Pleyel. Avec une introduction de François Lesure. Genève: Minkoff Reprint, 1976. (Archives de l'édition musicale française, 2)
Reprints of the catalogs of the five publishers, each classified, some with tables of contents. The introduction provides information on each firm's history. The Pleyel catalogs provide plate numbers.
Review by Rita Benton in *Fontes artis musicae,* 25 (1978), p. 198–99.

2620. Cipolla, Wilma Reid. A Catalog of the works of Arthur Foote, 1853–1937. Detroit: Information Coordinators, 1980. 214 p. (Bibliographies in American Music, 6)
A thorough bibliography of the published and unpublished compositions documenting quite well some of the work of the publisher A. P. Schmidt.

2621. Cohen, Paul. Musikdruck und Drucker zu Nürnberg im 16. Jahrhundert erschienenen Noten- und Musikbücher. ... Nürnberg: H. Zierfuss, 1927. 63 p.
Also issued as a dissertation (Erlangen) under the title, *Die Nürnberger Musikdrucker im sechzehnten Jahrhundert,* 1927. Historical study with

brief accounts of the individual printers, followed by a chronological listing of 443 works published in Nürnberg from 1501 to 1600.

2622. Cucuel, Georges. "Notes sur quelques musiciens, luthiers, éditeurs et graveurs de musique au XVIIIe siècle" in *Sammelbände der Internationalen Musikgesellschaft,* 14 (1912–13), p. 243–52.

2623. Cucuel, Georges. "Quelques documents sur la librairie musicale au XVIIIe siècle." In *Sammelbande der Internationalen Musikgesellschaft,* 13 (1911–1912), p. 385–92.
A further study of the archives related to the licensing of music publications in France supplementing the article by Bobillier, no. 2614, above.

2624. Davidsson, Åke. Bibliographie zur Geschichte des Musikdrucks. Uppsala: Almquist & Wiksell, 1965. 86 p. (Studia musicologica Upsaliensia, Nova Ser. 1.)
A bibliography of 598 items related to the history of music printing and publishing, with a brief introductory survey of the literature. The expansion of a bibliography first issued as a part of the author's *Musikbibliographische Beiträge.* See no. 2625, below.

2625. Davidsson, Åke. "Die Literatur zur Geschichte des Notendrucks." In his *Musikbibliographische Beiträge.* Uppsala: A. B. Lundequistkska Bokhandeln, 1954. P. 91–115. (Uppsala Universitets Arsskrift, 1954:9.)
A survey of writings on the history of music printing, with a bibliography of 268 items.
Superseded by the author's *Bibliographie zur Geschichte des Musikdrucks,* no. 2624, above.
Review by Edward N. Waters in *Notes,* 12 (1955), p. 604; by Vincent H. Duckles in *The Library Quarterly,* 26 (1956), p. 73–74.

2626. Davidsson, Åke. Danskt musiktryck intill 1700-talets mitt. Dänischer Musikdruck bis zur Mitte des 18. Jahrhunderts. Uppsala: [Almquist & Wiksell], 1962. 100 p. (Studia musicologica upsaliensia, 7.)
An historical study of early Danish music printing, with a chronological listing of Danish prints issued during the period under consideration. Bibliography and index of names.
Review by Martin Geck in *Die Musikforschung,* 18 (1965), p. 346–47.

2627. Davidsson, Åke. Studier rörande svenskt musiktryck före ar 1750. Studien über schwedischen Musikdruck vor 1750. Uppsala: [Almquist & Wiksell], 1957. 167 p. (Studia musicologica upsaliensia, 5.)
Part I (Allmän del) is a general survey of early Swedish music printing. Part II (Speciell del) is a bibliography of 124 Swedish imprints issued between 1585 and 1750, in chronological order. Text in Swedish, summary in German. General bibliography and index of persons.
Review by Rudolph Gjelsness in *Notes,* 15 (1958), p. 569–70.

2628. Day, Cyrus L. and E. B. Murrie. English song-books, 1651–1702; a bibliography with a first-line index of songs. London: Bibliographical Society, 1940 [for 1937]. 439 p.

Lists and describes the contents of 252 secular song books published in England and Scotland. Arrangement is chronological, nonextant works included. First-line index of 4,150 songs by about 250 composers. Also indexed by composer, author of text, performer, tunes and airs, sources, titles of collections, printers, publishers, and booksellers. A model of descriptive bibliography, particularly valuable for its coverage of the publishing activity of John and Henry Playford and their contemporaries.

2629. Deaville, James. "The C. F. Kahnt archive in Leipzig: a preliminary report" in *Notes,* 42 (1986), p. 502–17.
Concerning the survival and contents of the papers of one of the lesser Leipzig publishing houses.

2630. Deutsch, Otto E. Musikverlags-Nummern. Eine Auswahl von 40 datierten Listen. Zweite, verbesserte und erste deutsche Ausgabe. Berlin: Merseburger, 1961. 32 p.
Revision and expansion of a list originally published in the *Journal of Documentation,* 1 (1946), under the title: "Music publishers' numbers, a selection of 40 dated lists, 1710–1900."
Treats 20 German, 14 Austrian, 3 Dutch, 1 English, 1 French, and 1 Swiss firm. Index of places and individual publishers. Supplemented by the author's "Musikverlags-Nummern, ein Nachtrag," in *Die Musikforschung,* 15 (1962), p. 155.
Review by Donald W. Krummel in *Notes,* 19 (1961), p. 76–77; by Richard Schaal in *Die Musikforschung,* 16 (1963), p. 389.

2631. Devriès, Anik. "Les Éditions musicales Sieber," in *Revue de musicologie,* 55 (1969), p. 20–46.

2632. Devriès, Anik. "Un éditeur de musique 'à la tête ardente' Maurice Schlesinger" in *Fontes artis musicae,* 27 (1980), p. 125–36.
A brief recounting of the publishing career of the person responsible for the *Revue et Gazette musicale.*

2633. Devriès, Anik. Édition et commerce de la musique gravée à Paris dans la première moitié du XVIIIe siècle: Les Boivin, Les Leclerc. Genève: Minkoff, 1976. 274 p. (Archives de l'édition musical française, 1)
A study of Parisian music engraving in the early 18th century with particular regard for one of the principal engravers.
"Catalogue général de la production des Leclerc": p. [127]-272, an extensive catalog of the production of the Leclercs.
Review by Neal Zaslaw in *Notes,* 33 (1977), p.825–6.

2634. Devriès, Anik and François Lesure. Dictionnaire des éditions de musique française des origines à environ 1820. Genève: Minkoff, 1979. 2 v. (Archives de l'édition musicale françise, 4)
V. 1 contains the dictionary of music publishers and dealers in France from the 16th century to 1820, including in each a biography, lists of successive addresses, lists of published catalogs, citations of privileges received, and a bibliography. The second volume presents facsimiles of

more than 200 catalogs by 50 publishers and forms a supplement to Cari Johansson's *French Music Publishers Catalogs* (see no. 2663). There is an index to insignia. Indexes to composers and titles in the reproduced catalogs. Source for each catalog and the rationale for attribution of date is given in a list proceding the reproductions.

Review by Eugene K. Wolf in *JAMS,* 33 (1980), p. 592–96, and by Lenore Coral in *Notes,* 37 (1980), p. 61–2.

2635. Donà, Mariangela. La stampa musicale a Milano fino all'anno 1700. Firenze: Olschki, 1961. 167 p. (Biblioteca di bibliografia italiana, 39.)

Milanese music publishers given in alphabetical order, with chronological listings of their publications. Copies of rare works located in major European libraries. Index of composers and works, index of persons to whom works are dedicated.

Review by Richard Schaal in *Die Musikforschung,* 17 (1964), p. 183.

2636. Dunning, Albert. De muziekuitgever Gerhard Fredrik Witvogel en zijn fonds. Ein bijdrage tot de geschiedenis van de Nederlandse muziekuitgeverij in de achttiende eeuw. Utrecht: A. Oosthoek's Uitgevermaatschappij N.V., 1966. 64 p. (Muziekhistorische Monografieen, 2.)

"Uitgegeven door de Vereniging voor Nederlandse Muziekgeschiedenis."

Discussion of the life and works of Witvogel, with an annotated bibliography of 95 music publications by the firm. Locations of copies given, list of composers whose works were published, bibliography and index of names.

2637. Eitner, Robert. Buch- und Musikalienhändler, Buch- und Musikaliendrucker nebst Notenstecher, nur die Musik betreffend nach den Originaldrucken verzeichnet.... Leipzig: Breitkopf & Hartel, 1904. 248 p. (Monatshefte für Musikgeschichte, Beilage.)

Compiled as a by-product of the *Quellen-Lexikon*; limited to material before 1850. Alphabetical listing of publishers, printers, and dealers, their dates of location at various addresses, changes in name, branches if any. International coverage.

2638. Elvers, Rudolf. "Musikdrucker, Musikalienhändler und Musikverleger in Berlin 1750–1850." In *Festschrift Walter Gerstenberg zum 60. Geburtstag.* Wolfenbüttel: Möseler Verlag, 1964. p. 37–44.

Lists 155 Berlin music printers, dealers, and publishers active during the century under consideration.

2639. Epstein, Dena J. Music publishing in Chicago before 1871; the firm of Root and Cady, 1858–1871. Detroit: Information Coordinators, 1969. 243 p. (Detroit studies in music bibliography, 14.)

This is an especially careful study illuminating the work of a firm of central importance in the history of American music publishing.

Review by Klaus Hortschansky in *Die Musikforschung,* 24 (1971), p. 464–65.

2640. Fisher, William A. 150 years of music publishing in the U.S.; an historical sketch with special reference to the pioneer publisher Oliver Ditson Co., 1783–1933. Boston: Oliver Ditson, [1934]. 156 p.

A revision and extension of portions of the author's *Notes on music in old Boston. Boston: 1918.*

2641. Fog, Dan. "Random thoughts on music dating and terminology" in *Fontes artis musicae,* 24 (1977), p. 141–44.

"My main purpose in voicing these observations is to suggest that the two principal preoccupations of our present work, dating and terminology, call for a new and different way of thinking. We must break free from the conventional, book-infected concepts that are often transferred to music bibliography."

2642. Fog, Dan. Dänische Musikverlage und Notendruckereien. Beiträge zur Musikaliendatierung. Kopenhagen: 1972. 27 p.

Basic factual information concerning 60 Danish music printers and publishers. Important events in the history of these firms are given chronologically.

2643. Fog, Dan. Notendruck und Musikhandel im 19. Jahrhundert in Dänemark. Ein Beitrag zur Musikaliendatierung und zur Geschichte der Musikvermittung. Copenhagen: Dan Fog Musikverlag, 1986. 336 p.

A revised and shortened edition of the first edition (1984) in Danish of the 2 v.: *Musikhandel og Nodetryk I Danmark efter 1750: I: Musik handel 1700–1754; II: Nodetryk efter 1750.*

A guide to music publishing and music trades in Denmark after 1750 until roughly 1899, incorporating a brief section on dating music of the period by plate numbers and other characteristics. Includes a dictionary of music dealers and publishers citing plate numbers. Bibliography and indexes.

2644. Fog, Dan and Kari Michelsen. Norwegian music publication since 1800. A preliminary guide to music publishers, printers, and dealers. Copenhagen: Dan Fog Musikforlag, 1976. 30 p.

Brief sketches of the activity of 38 Norwegian music publishers, printers and dealers. Plate numbers given where known. Cites music hire libraries. In English, with an informative introduction.

2645. Fraenkel, Gottfried S. Decorative music title pages; 201 examples from 1500 to 1800. Selected, introduced, and annotated by Gottfried S. Fraenkel. New York: Dover, 1968. 230 p.

Introduction, p. 1–15, an historical survey of the items in the collection. 201 plates with historical and descriptive annotations.

2646. Fuld, James J. and Frances Barulich. "Harmonizing the arts: orignal graphic designs for printed music by world-famous artists" in *Notes,* 43 (1987), p. 259–71.

A bibliography of the works of well-known artists created as illustrations to printed music. Arranged in alphabetical order by artist.

2647. Gamble, William. Music engraving and printing; historical and technical treatise. . . . London; New York: Pitman, 1923 [1922]. 266 p.

Reprinted by Arno Press, New York, 1979.

Discusses the technical processes of music printing and engraving, with emphasis on contemporary practices. Illustrated.

2648. Gericke, Hannelore. Der Wiener Musikalienhandel von 1700 bis 1778. Graz: H. Bohlaus Nachf., 1960. 150 p. (Wiener musikwissenschaftliche Beitrage, 5.)

Contents: Wiener Buchhändler als Verkaufer von Musikalien; Privatverkäufer; Kopisten; Kupferstecher; Verzeichnis der Wiener Musikdrucke von 1700–1778; Liste der verbotenen Musikbücher; Zusammenfassung; Literaturverzeichnis.

Review by Donald W. Krummel in *Notes,* 18 (1961), p. 229–30.

2649. Göhler, Albert. Verzeichnis der in den Frankfurter und Leipziger Messkatalogen der Jahre 1564 bis 1759 angezeigten Musikalien. . . . Leipzig: C. F. Kahns Nachf., 1902. 4 parts in 1 v.

Reprint by Frits Knuf, Hilversum, 1965.

A major source of information on the activities of early music dealers, printers, and publishers. It lists music entered in the Frankfurt and Leipzig trade catalogs from 1564 to 1759.

This work is also entered as no. 1784.

2650. Goovaerts, Alphonse J. M. A. Histoire et bibliographie de la typographie musicale dans les Pays-Bas. Anvers: P. Kockx, 1880. 608 p. (Extrait des Memoires de l'Academie Royale de Belgique, Collection in-8; tome XXIX.)

Reprint issued by Frits Knuf, Hilversum, 1963.

Part I (historical): a chronological discussion of music publishing in the Netherlands from 1539. Part II (bibliographical): chronological list of 1,415 music publications from 1539 to 1841. Full descriptions. Index of personal names, titles, and places.

2651. Grand-Carteret, John. Les titres illustrés et l'image au service de la musique. Turin: Bocca, 1904. 269 p.

Premiere partie (p. 3–120): Le titre de musique sous la Révolution, le Consulat et le premier Empire (1500–1800). Deuxième partie: Le titre de musique et la lithographie; 1. 1817–30, 2. 1830–50.

Abundantly illustrated with facsimiles of title pages, printers' devices, and pages of music.

2652. Hase, Oskar von. Breitkopf & Härtel. Gedenkschrift und Arbeitsbericht. 5. Aufl. Wiesbaden: Breitkopf & Härtel, 1968. 2 v. in 3.

Bd. 1: 1542–1827. Bd. 2: 1828–1918. Bd. 3: 1918–1968.

Thorough documentation of the activities of the great Leipzig publishing house of Breitkopf & Härtel. Reviews the history of the firm, its business relationships, its dealings with the great composers of the late 18th and 19th centuries; editorial work on the *Denkmäler* and *Gesamtausgaben.* Bd. 3, by Hellmuth von Hase, reviews the history of the firm through World War II to its establishment in Wiesbaden.

2653. Heartz, Daniel. "La chronologie des recueils imprimes par Pierre Attaingnant." In *Revue de musicologie,* 44 (1959), p. 178–92.

Brief survey of Attaingnant's activity as a music printer, followed by a chronological tabulation of all collections published by him from 1528 to 1537. Superseded by Heartz's magisterial study, no. 2654, below.

2654. Heartz, Daniel. Pierre Attaingnant, royal printer of music: a historical study and bibliographical catalogue. Berkeley and Los Angeles: Univ. of California Press, 1969. 451 p.

P. 1–204: Historical study treating the founding of the Attaingnant press, new techniques of music printing, commercial and artistic relationships, together with selected documents, dedications, and privileges.

P. 207–377: Bibliographical catalog of 174 works issued by the press, with precise bibliographical descriptions, listings of contents, and location of surviving copies. 16 black-and-white plates, with a frontispiece in color. An outstanding work in book design and subject coverage. Chronological and alphabetical short-title lists. Index of Latin and French first lines, and of composers.

Review by Nicolas Barker in *The Book Collector* (Summer 1971), p. 261–70; by Samuel Pogue in *Notes,* 27 (1970), p. 258–60; by G. Dottin in *Revue de musicologie,* 57 (1971), p. 87–88; by Howard M. Brown in *JAMS,* 24 (1971), p. 125–26; by Frank Dobbins in *Music & letters,* 51 (1970), p. 447–49.

2655. Henle, Günter. 25 Jahre G. Henle Musikverlag 1948–1973. München: G. Henle, 1973. 75 p.

A history of the firm, chiefly a reprint from part of the author's autobiograpy: *Weggenosse des Jahrhunderts,* published in 1968.

2656. Hill, Richard S. "The plate numbers of C. F. Peters' predecessors." In *Papers . . . of the American Musicological Society . . .* Dec. 29 and 30, 1938 [c. 1940], p. 113–34.

Surveys the publishing activities of F. A. Hofmeister and A. Kuhnel, 1784–1814, with a detailed analysis of their production in 1801–1802, plate numbers 1–102.

2657. Hoffmann-Erbrecht, Lothar. "Der Nürnberger Musikverlager Johann Ulrich Haffner." In *ActaM,* 27 (1955), p 141–41.

2658. Hoogerwerf, Frank W. Confederate sheet-music imprints. Brooklyn: Institute for Studies in American Music, Conservatory of Music, College of the City University of New York, 1984. 158 p. (I.S.A.M. monographs, 21)

A study on music printing in the Confederate States of America during the American Civil War.

2659. Hopkinson, Cecil. A dictionary of Parisian music publishers, 1700–1950. London: printed for the author, 1954. 131 p.

Reprinted in 1979 by DaCapo, New York.

Describes some 550 printers, tabulating their name forms and addresses where they were active during specific periods. A useful tool for determining date of undated French publications.

Review by Inger M. Christensen in *Notes,* 11 (1954), p. 550–51; by Vincent H. Duckles in *JAMS,* 8 (1955), p. 62–64.

See nos. 2663 and 2634 for another approach to the dating of 18th-century French music publications. The IAML *Guide for dating early published music* provides more references and techniques. See no. 2679.

2660. Hopkinson, Cecil. Notes on Russian music publishers. Printed for the author for private distribution to the Members of the I.A.M.L. at the Fifth International Congress, Cambridge, June 29th-July 4th, 1959. 10 p.

"This edition limited to 125 numbered copies."

2661. Humphries, Charles and William C. Smith. Music publishing in the British Isles, from the beginning until the middle of the nineteenth century; a dictionary of engravers, printers, publishers, and music sellers, with a historical introduction. 2nd ed. with suppl. New York: Barnes and Noble; Oxford: B. Blackwell, 1970. 392 p.

First published in 1954 by Cassell and Co., London. The 2nd edition differs only in the addition of a 36-page supplement.

This work supersedes the Kidson volume (no. 2667). It covers more than 2,000 persons and firms associated with British music printing and publishing. An introductory essay gives an excellent survey of the field. Indexes of firms outside London and of makers and repairers of musical instruments. 25 plates.

Review of the first edition by J. M. Coopersmith in *Notes,* 11 (1954), p. 549–50; of the second edition by William Lichtenwanger in *Notes,* 27 (1971), p. 489–90.

2662. Imbault, Jéan-Jerôme. Catalogue thématique des ouvrages de musique. Avec un index des compositeurs cités. [Réimpression de l'édition de Paris, c. 1792.] Geneve: Minkoff Reprint, 1972. 284 p.

Classified thematic catalog of works published by Imbault. Each section has its own pagination.

2663. Johansson, Cari. French music publishers' catalogues of the second half of the eighteenth century. Uppsala: Almquist & Wiksell, 1955. 2 v.

Vol. 1 (octavo): Textband. 228 p. Vol. 2 (folio): Tafeln. 145 facsimiles from catalogs by French music publishing houses.

The first volume analyzes and describes the contents of the catalogs and their use for dating purposes. Compare Johansson's method with that of Hopkinson, no. 2659 above. Index of names, of titles, and of catalogs chronologically under name of firm.

Review by Donald W. Krummel in *Notes,* 17 (1960), p. 234–35; by A. Hyatt King in *Music and letters,* 37 (1956), p. 376–77; by Wolfgang Schmieder in *Die Musikforschung,* 10 (1957), p. 180–82.

2664. Johansson, Cari. J. J. & B. Hummel. Music-publishing and thematic catalogues. Stockholm: Almqvist & Wiksell, 1972. 3 v. (Publications of the Library of the Royal Swedish Academy of Music, 3.)

Vol. 1: Text, containing essays on the life and work of the brothers J. J. and B. Hummel; "Aids to the dating of Hummel prints," transcription of the Hummel catalogs 1762–1814; list of plate numbers; index of names and titles; index of catalogs. Vol. 2: music publishing catalogs in facsimile; vol. 3: thematic catalog 1768–74 in facsimile.

2665. Journal général d'annonces des ouvres de musique, gravures, lithographies, publié en France et à l'étranger. Avec un index des noms cités. Genève: Minkoff Reprint, 1976. 1 v. (Archives de l'édition musicale française, 3)

Reprint of weekly editions of a trade paper published in 1825. Most heavily weighted to French publications.

2666. Kast, Paul. "Die Musikdrucke des Kataloges Giunta von 1604." In *Analecta musicologica,* 2 (1965), p. 41–47.

Transcribes the music portion of a general catalog issued by the Florentine music dealer and publisher Giunta in 1604. Contains masses, motets, and secular works of the late 16th century as well as a small selection of instrumental and theory works.

2667. Kidson, Frank. British music publishers, printers and engravers ... from Queen Elizabeth's reign to George IV, with select bibliographical lists of musical works printed and published within that period. London: W. E. Hill & sons, 1900. 231 p.

Unaltered reprint by Benjamin Blom, Inc., New York, 1967.

The pioneer work on English music publishing. Not as comprehensive as Humphries and Smith, no. 2661 above, but many of Kidson's entries are fuller and are accompanied by lists of publications. Entries arranged alphabetically by place. No index.

2668. King, A. Hyatt. "English pictorial music title-pages, 1820–1885, their style, evolution and importance." In *The Library,* ser. 5:4 (1949–50), p. 262–72.

2669. King, A. Hyatt. Four hundred years of music printing. 2nd ed. London: published by the Trustees of the British Museum, 1979. 48 p.

First ed. 1964. 48 p.

A short, well-written account of the history of music printing, with a selected bibliography of 29 items on the subject. Illustrated with facsimile pages of early music printing.

2nd edition, 1968, incorporating a few changes in the text and additions to the bibliography.

Review of the first edition by Harry Carter in *The Library,* ser 5:20 (June 1965), p. 154–57; by Donald W. Krummel in *Notes,* 22 (1965–66), p. 902–3.

2670. Kinkeldey, Otto. "Music and music printing in incunabula." In *Bibliographic Society of America, Papers,* 26 (1932), p. 89–118.

For other discussions of music incunabula, see nos. 2696 & 2768.

2671. Kinsky, Georg. "Beethoven-Erstdrucke bis zum Jahre 1800." In *Philobiblon,* 3 (1930), p. 329–36.

2672. Kinsky, Georg. "Erstlingsdrucke der deutschen Tonmeister der Klassik und Romantik." In *Philobiblon,* 7 (1934), p. 347–64.

Also printed separately by H. Reichner, Vienna, 1934.

2673. Kinsky, Georg. Die Originalausgaben der Werke Johann Sebastian Bachs; ein Beitrag zur Musikbibliographie. Wien: H. Reichner, [1937]. 134 p.
This and the two preceding items are contributions by one of the leading specialists in music printing of the 18th and 19th centuries.

2674. Krohn, Ernst Christopher. Music publishing in the Middle Western States before the Civil War. Detroit: Information Coordinators, 1972. 44 p. (Detroit studies in music bibliography, 23.)

2675. Krummel, Donald W. "Graphic analysis, its application to early American engraved music." In *Notes,* 16 (1959), p. 213–33.
Discussion of the history of early American music publishing in terms of the printing processes used, with special reference to the work of Blake and Willig. Seven plates.

2676. Krummel, Donald W. "Late 18th century French music publishers' catalogs in the Library of Congress," in *Fontes artis musicae,* 7 (1960), p. 61–64.

2677. Krummel, Donald W. "Musical functions and bibliographical forms" in *The Library, Transactions of the Bibliographical Society, London,* (1976), p. 327–50.
A most important concept, that of grouping editions into "bibliographical forms" is presented.

2678. Krummel, Donald W. English music printing, 1553–1700. London: Bibliographical Society, 1975. 188 p. (Bibliographical Society publication, 1971)
This book is a history, a typographical study, and a bibliographical study. It is *not* a bibliography, although it is filled with useful bibliographic references. It is included here as a model of bibliographic investigation. Uses the concept of "bibliographical forms." Appends "A chronological synopsis of music type faces." A successor to Steele (see no. 2727).
Review by Lenore Coral and Stanley Boorman in *Notes,* 34 (1977), p. 65–67.

2679. Krummel, Donald W. Guide for dating early published music: a manual of bibliographical practices. Hackensack: Joseph Boonin; Kassel: Bärenreiter, 1974. 267 p.
"Supplement to the Guide for Dating Early Published Music" in *Fontes artis musicae,* 24 (1977), p. 175–84 by Donald W. Krummel adds and corrects information in the *Guide.*
Krummel was the chair of the IAML Commission for Bibliographical Research which created this very important compilation of information on the dating of early editions of music bearing no date of publication. There is a synopsis, or systematic outline, of the methodology. Plate numbers, publishers' and dealers' addresses, publishing practices, and other

kinds of evidence are discussed. There is a section organized by country discussing specifics of music publishing: studies; directories; important publishers, printers and engravers; plate number files; catalogs. Also considered in each national report are copyright, announcements of music publications, design and printing practices, paper, units of currency and pricing practices, important collections, and other evidence. The first section is followed by footnotes and a bibliography, which the second section incorporates by references in each of the national reports. Index of composers.

The contents of the IAML *Guide* is made more accessible by Linda I. Solow's "An index to publishers, engravers, and lithographers and a bibliography of the literature cited in the IAML *Guide for Dating Early Published Music*" in *Fontes artis musicae*, 24 (1977), p. 81–95. Solow's work is, in effect, an appendix to the IAML *Guide*.

2680. Layer, Adolf. Katalog des Augsburger Verlegers Lotter von 1753. Kassel: Bärenreiter, 1964. 44 p. (Catalogus musicus, 2.)

Facsimile edition of the 1753 catalog of the music publications of the firm of Johann Jacob Lotter in Augsburg. Lists some 370 titles by 170 composers of the late 17th and early 18th centuries. Index and "Nachwort" provided by the editor.

2681. Lenneberg, Hans. "The haunted bibliographer" in *Notes,* 41 (1985), p. 239–48.

Concerning lack of understanding of the importance of stereotypography and lithography in music printing in the 19th century.

2682. Lenz, Hans U. Der Berliner Musikdruck von seinen Anfängen bis zur Mitte des 18. Jahrhunderts. Lippstadt: Westf., Buchdruckerei Thiele, 1932. 116 p.

Also issued as a dissertation, Rostock, 1932.

Discussion of the Berlin music printers, their output, their techniques. P. 27–35: chronological listing of 126 prints.

2683. Lesure, François. Bibliographie des éditions musicales publiées par Estienne Roger et Michel-Charles Le Cène (Amsterdam, 1696–1743). Paris: Heugel, 1969. 173 p. (Publications de la Société Française de Musicologie. Sér. 2, Tome 12.)

Documents the production of one of the most active music publishers of the early 18th century, some 700 volumes of vocal and instrumental music for French and Italian musicians.

Contains a transcription of the catalog by Roger published in 1716 and a facsimile of a Le Cène catalog printed in Amsterdam in 1737.

2684. Lesure, François et G. Thibault. "Bibliographie des éditions musicales publiées par Nicolas Du Chemin (1549–1576)." In *Annales musicologiques,* 1 (1953), p. 269–373.

Bibliography similar in scope and format to the preceding work. Covers 100 editions published by Du Chemin, with full descriptions, listings of contents, and locations of copies. Numerous facsimiles of title pages. First-line index of Latin and of French texts, and of titles and names.

2685. Lesure, François et G. Thibault. Bibliographie des editions d'Adrian le Roy et Robert Ballard (1551–98). Paris: Société française de musicologie, Heugel et Cie., 1955. 304 p. (Publications de la Société française de musicologie. 2 sér., Tome 9.)

An exemplary bibliography of 319 musical editions issued by the Le Roy-Ballard press, cited chronologically with full bibliographical descriptions, lists of contents, and locations in public and private collections. Brief historical introduction, and an anthology of the most important prefaces, dedications, and other documents. First-line index of texts, index of titles and personal names. Nine facsimile plates.

Review by Kenneth Levy in *JAMS*, 8 (1955), p. 221–23; by Vincent H. Duckles in *Notes*, 15 (1957), p. 102–03.

2686. Lesure, François. "Cotages d'éditeurs antérieurs à c. 1850: Liste prèliminaire," In *Fontes artis musicae*, 14 (1967), p.22–37.

A list by country of late 18th- and 19th-century music publishers who used plate numbers.

2687. Littleton, Alfred H. A catalog of one hundred works illustrating the history of music printing from the 15th to the end of the 17th century, in the library of Alfred H. Littleton. ... London: Novello, 1911. 38 p., 12 facsimile plates.

Includes both musical and theoretical works grouped by nationality, with annotations directing attention to their interest as examples of music printing.

2688. Macmillan, Barclay. "Tune-book imprints in Canada to 1867: a descriptive bibliography" in the *Papers of the Bibliographical Society of Canada*, 16 (1977), p. 31–57.

Complements the Calderisi study, no. 2615, and covers imprints of Canada up to the Confederacy, thus omitting any publications from the Maritime Provinces.

2689. Mailliot, Sylvette. "Un couple de marchands de musique au XVIIIe siècle: Les Boivin," in *Revue de musicologie*, 54 (1968), p. 106–13.

2690. Marco, Guy A. The earliest music printers of continental Europe, a checklist of facsimiles illustrating their work. [Charlottesville]: The Bibliographical Society of the University of Virginia, 1962. 20 p.

An index of facsimile plates of the work of early music printers to be found in a variety of music histories, monographs, and other reference works. 101 printers from the late 15th century to 1599 are included.

2691. Matthäus, Wolfgang. "Quellen und Fehlerquellen zur Datierung von Musikdrucken aus der zeit nach 1750," in *Fontes artis musicae*, 15 (1967), p. 37–42.

A discussion of the three criteria which should be used to ascertain the date of a print.

2692. Matthäus, Wolfgang. Johann André Musikverlag zu Offenbach am Main; Verlagsgeschichte und Bibliographie, 1772–1800. [Nach dem Tode

des Verfassers hrsg. von Hans Schneider]. Tutzing: H. Schneider, 1973.
401 p.

A history and description of the publishing house of Johann André
including a chronological survey of the publications listing plate numbers. There follows an extensive annotated bibliography of the publications in chronological order. Index to composers in the bibliography.

2693. Meissner, Ute. Der antwerpener Notendrucker Tylman Susato. Eine
bibliographische Studie zur niederländischen Chansonpublikation in
der ersten Hälfte des 16. Jahrhunderts. Berlin: Merseburger, 1967. 2 v.
(Berliner Studien zur Musikwissenschaft, 11.)

Vol. 1 contains biographical information and an analysis of Susato's
activity as a music printer. Vol. 2 is a chronological bibliography of all
of Susato's publications, with indexes of composers and a first-line index
of compositions.

Review by Winfried Kirsch in *Die Musikforschung,* 22 (1969), p. 237–38;
by Donald W. Krummel in *Notes,* 25 (1969), p. 500–501.

2694. Meyer, Kathi and Eva J. O'Meara. "The printing of music, 1473–1934."
In *The Dolphin,* 2 (1935), p. 171–207.

A well-illustrated sketch of the history of music printing. Includes a
bibliography of works on the subject.

2795. Meyer, Kathi and Inger M. Christensen. "Artaria plate numbers." In
Notes, 15 (1942), p. 1–22.

2696. Meyer-Baer, Kathi. Liturgical music incunabula, a descriptive catalog. London: The Bibliographical Society, 1962. 63 p.

257 entries, arranged alphabetically by title, treating of some 800 items.
References made to the standard bibliographies of incunabula and to
locations of copies in major libraries. 12 plates illustrating types of notation. Chronological index, and index of printers and places.

See also the author's preliminary study, "Liturgical music incunabula
in the British Museum," in *The Library,* 4th ser., 20 (1939), p. 272–94.

Review, anon., in *Times Literary Supplement,* Nov. 16, 1962, p. 880; and
by Donald W. Krummel in *Notes,* 21 (1964), p. 366–68.

2697. Mischiati, Oscar. Indici, cataloghi e avvisi degli editori e librai
musicali italiani dal 1591 al 1798. Firenze: Leo S. Olschki Editore, 1984.
553 p. (Studi e testi per la storia della musica, 2)

Transcriptions of lists of published Italian music from contemporaneous sources with descriptions of the sources, a composer-title index to the
transcriptions, an index to names cited in the text, and a list of libraries
cited in the text with page references.

2698. Molitor, Raphael. "Italienische Choralnotendrucke." In his *Die
nach-tridentischen Choral-Reform zu Rom, v. 1, p. 94–119.* Leipzig: 1901.
Reprinted by Olms, Hildesheim, 1982.

A general discussion of Italian printers of liturgical books of the later
15th and 16th centuries.

2699. Müller, Hans Christian. Bernhard Schott, Hofmusikstecher in Mainz: die Frühgeschichte seines Musikverlages bis 1797. Mit einem Verzeichnis der Verlagswerke 1779–1898. Mainz: Schott, 1977. 219 p. (Beiträge zur mittelrheinischen Musikgeschichte, 16)

An historical sketch of the the publishing house of Schott until 1797 followed by a bibliographic study of musical works published until that time.

Review by Rita Benton in *Fontes artis musicae,* 25 (1978), p. 194–95.

2700. Music publishing, copyright, and piracy in Victorian England: a twenty-five year chronicle, 1881–1906, from the pages of the *Musical Opinion & Music Trade Review* and other English music journals of the period. Gathered by James B. Coover. London & N.Y.: Mansell, 1985. 169 p.

Includes bibliography and index.

2701. Neighbor, Oliver W. and Alan Tyson. English music publishers' plate numbers in the first half of the 19th century. London: Faber, 1965. 48 p.

Review by Klaus Hortschansky in *Die Musikforschung,* 21 (1968), p. 102.

2702. Novello. A century and a half in Soho; a short history of the firm of Novello, publishers and printers of music, 1811–1961. London: Novello, [1961]. 85 p.

A popular history of the music publishing house that has exercised a wide influence on pulbic taste in England through the printing of inexpensive editions of the classics.

Review by Donald W. Krummel in *Notes,* 19 (1961), p. 60–61; by Richard Schaal in *Die Musikforschung,* 17 (1964), p. 183–84.

2703. Oldman, Cecil B. Collecting musical first editions. London: Constable, 1938. 29 p. (Aspects of book collecting.)

Reprinted from *New paths in book collecting, ed.* John Carter, London, 1934, p. 95–124.

An informal and inviting discussion of the pleasures of collecting early music. Bibliography, p. 120–24.

2704. Pattison, Bruce. "Notes on early music printing." In *The library,* ser. 4, 19:4 (1939), p. 239–421.

2705. Plesske, Hans-Martin. "Bibliographie des Schrifttums zur Geschichte deutscher und österreichischer Musikverlage." In *Beiträge zur Geschichte des Buchwesens,* Band III (1968), p. 135–222.

A bibliography of 755 items listed alphabetically under the names of the firms. The first section is devoted to information in general reference works, the second to histories of music publishing.

2706. Pogue, Samuel F. Jacques Moderne, Lyons music printer of the sixteenth century. Genève: Librairie Droz, 1969. 412 p. (Travaux d'humanisme et renaissance, 101.)

The book includes an extensive biobligraphy of all of Moderne's output, with full bibliographical descriptions of the non-musical books, and contents with concordances of the music books—a total of 149 entries, of which 59 are for books of music.

Includes music.

Review by Albert Dunning in *Notes,* 29 (1972), p. 46–47; by Frank Dobbins in *JAMS,* 24 (1971), p. 126–31; by Charles Cudworth in *Music & letters,* 51 (1970), p. 85–86.

2707. Poole, Edmund. "New music types: invention in the eighteenth century." In *Journal of the printing historical society,* 1 (1965), p. 21–38.

Reviews the history of music printing, with special emphasis on the contribution of Breitkopf.

2708. Poole, H. Edmund and Donald W. Krummel. "Printing and publishing of music," in *The New Grove Dictionary of Music and Musicians,* edited by Stanley Sadie, v. 15, p. 232–74. London: Macmillan, 1980.

A review of the history of printing from the early stages to modern practices and a survey of publishing practices from 1501 to the present. Followed by an excellent classified bibliography on the subject.

2709. Pougin, Arthur. "Notes sur la presse musicale en France," in *Encyclopédie de la musique et dictionnaire du Conservatoire,* pt. 2, v. 6 (1931), p. 3,841–3,859. Paris: Librarie Delagrave, 1931.

2710. Przywecke-Samecka, Maria. Drukarstwo muzyczne w Polsce do kónca XVIII wieku. Kraków: Polskie Wydawnictwo Muzyczne, 1968. 263 p., 40 plates.

A study of music printing and publishing in Poland from the 16th through the 18th centuries.

Bibliography of early printers' works, arranged under location (p. 181–240). Bibliography of literature on music printing.

2711. Redway, Virginia L. Music directory of early New York City; a file of musicians, music publishers and musical instrument makers listed in N. Y. directories from 1786 through 1835, together with the most important New York music publishers from 1836 through 1875. . . . New York: The New York Public Library, 1941. 102 p.

Three main sections: (1) musicians and teachers; (2) publishers, printers, lithographers, and dealers, with names and addresses as they appeared in successive years; (3) instrument makers and dealers. Appendices include chronological list of firms and individuals, 1786–1811, and a list of musical societies, 1789–99.

2712. Reese, Gustave 'Printing and engraving of music," in *The International Cyclopedia of music and musicians,* 9th ed., originally edited by Oscar Thompson, this ed. by Robert Sabin, p. 1,441–43.

2713. Rheinfurth, Hans. Der Musikverlag Lotter in Augsburg (c. 1719–1845). Tutzing: Schneider, 1977. 344 p. Musikbibliographische Arbeiten, 3

2714. Ricordi (Firm, Music Publishers, Milan). Casa Ricordi, 1808–1958; profilo storico a cura di Claudio Sartori. ... Milano: G. Ricordi, 1958. 116 p., 48 plates.

16 of the plates are facsimile pages of composers' autographs; the remainder are chiefly reproductions, in color, of cover designs for noteworthy Ricordi music publications.

Review by Donald W. Krummel in *Notes,* 17 (1960), p. 400–401.

2715. Robert, Henri. Traité de gravure de musique sur planches d'étain et des divers procédés de simili gravùre de musique ... precédé de l'historique du signe, de l'impression et de la gravure de musique. 2e ed. Paris: Chez l'auteur, 1926. 151 p.

First published in 1902.

A rather sketchy historical survey of music writing, printing, and engraving, followed by a description of the technical processes involved in preparing engraved plates.

2716. Rochester Museum and Science Center. Music publishing in Rochester, 1859–1930: a checklist of the sheet music printed in Rochester in the collection of the Rochester Museum and Science Center compiled by Stuart A. Kohler. Rochester, N.Y.: Rochester Museum and Science Center, 1975. 75 leaves in various foliations

2717. Ross, Ted. The art of music engraving and processing; a complete manual, reference and text book on preparing music for reproduction and print. Miami: Hansen Books, 1970. 278 p.

Full of historical and technical information. Well-illustrated.

2718. Sartori, Claudio. Bibliografia delle opere musicali stampate da Ottaviano Petrucci. Firenze: Olschki, 1948. 217 p. (Biblioteca di bibliografia italiana, 18.)

Chronological bibliography of Petrucci's work, with full descriptions, contents of each publication. Index of titles, lists of libraries and their holdings of Petrucci prints. Bibliography.

2719. Sartori, Claudio. Dizionario degli editori musicali italiani (tipografi, incisori, librai-editori). Firenze: Olschki, 1958. 215 p. (Biblioteca di bibliografia italiana, 32.)

Italian music printers, editors, and publishers from the 16th century to the present. Some bibliographical references given. The principal issues of the publishers are noted but no complete catalogs given. Index of names, but no chronology. Eight plates of early title pages.

Review by Dragan Plamenac in *Notes,* 16 (1959), p. 242–43; by Gerhard Croll in *Die Musikforschung,* 12 (1959), p. 255–56.

2720. Schaal, Richard. Die Kataloge des Augsburger Musikalien-Händlers Kaspar Flurschütz, 1613–1628. Mit einer Einleitung und Registern zum ersten Mal hrsg. von Richard Schaal. Mit einer Bibliographie zur Augsburger Musikgeschichte 1550–1650. Wilhelmshaven: Heinrichshefen's Verlag, 1974. 159 p. (Quellen-Kataloge zur Musikgeschichte, 7)

A catalog with introduction and index to the publisher/music seller

Flurschütz. Includes a bibliography of the history of music in Augsburg from 1550–1650.

2721. Schaefer, Hartmut. Die Notendrucker und Musikverleger in Frankfurt am Main von 1630 bis um 1720: eine bibliographisch-drucktechnische Untersuchung. Kassel: Bärenreiter, 1975. 2 v. (711 p.) (Catalogus musicus, 7)
Bibliography: p. 663–687.

2722. Schmid, Anton. Ottaviano dei Petrucci da Fossombrone, erste Erfinder des Musiknotendruckes mit beweglichen Metalltypen, und seine Nachfolger im sechzehnten Jahrhunderte.... Wien: P. Rohrmann, 1845. 342 p.
Reprint by B. R. Gruner, Amsterdam, 1968. 356 p. with 4 fold. l.
One of the first scholarly studies of early music printing. Contains important information about Petrucci's contemporaries in other European centers of music printing.

2723. Smith, William C. A bibliography of the musical works published by John Walsh during the years 1695–1720. London: The Bibliographical Society, 1948. 215 p., 38 plates.
622 Walsh publications cited for the period under consideration, with numerous descriptive annotations. Index of titles and works and general index.
Review by J. Coopersmith in *Notes,* 7 (1949), p. 104–6; by A. Hyatt King in *Music and letters,* 30 (1949), p. 273–76.

2724. Smith, William C. and Charles Humphries. A bibliography of the musical works published by the firm of John Walsh during the years 1721–1766. London: The Bibliographical Society, 1968. 351 p.
Review by J. Merrill Knapp in *Notes,* 26 (1969), p. 274–75; by Lenore Coral in *JAMS,* 23 (1970), p. 141–43; by Charles Cudworth in *Music & letters,* 50 (1969), p. 416–17.

2725. Squire, William Barclay. "Publishers' numbers" in *Sammelbände der Internationalen Musikgesellschaft,* 15 (1913–14), p. 420–27.
Refers to music publishers' plate numbers.

2726. Steele, Robert. "Early music printing, 1601–1640," in the *Transactions of the Bibliographical Society, 11 (1909) p. 13–15.*
Describes a project of extending his *Earliest English music printing.*

2727. Steele, Robert. The earliest English music printing; a description and bibliography of English printed music to the close of the 16th century. London: printed for The Bibliographical Society, 1903. 102 p. (Illustrated monographs, 11.)
Brief introduction covers methods of printing, and the book includes a chapter on early English printers of music. The bibliography of 197 items is arranged chronologically from 1495 to 1600, giving full title and collation, library locations, and notes on typography. Bibliography of 34 items on music printing.

Reprinted London, 1965, with a new appendix of *addenda* and *corrigenda*.

2728. Stellfeld, J. A. Bibliographie des éditions musicales plantiniennes. [Bruxelles: Palais des Academies, 1949.] 248 p. (Academie royale de Belgique. Classe des beaux-arts. Memoires, T. 5, fasc. 3.)

Brief historical account of the Plantin press, with detailed bibliographical description and discussion of the 21 music items printed by the press at Antwerp and at Leiden. 21 plates.

Toledo (Ohio). Museum of Art. The printed note. . . . See no. 2407.

2729. Tyson, Alan. The authentic English editions of Beethoven. London: Faber and Faber, 1963. 152 p.

An important work, one of the first to apply detailed bibliographical analysis to early 19th-century music printing. The author is able to make significant revisions in the chronology of Beethoven's works.

Review by Dagmar von Busch-Weise in *Die Musikforschung,* 17 (1964), p. 443–44; by Albi Rosenthal in *Music and letters,* 45 (1964), p. 256–58; by Donald W. MacArdle in *Notes,* 22 (1965–66), p. 920.

2730. Valentin, Erich. 50 Jahre Gustav Bosse Verlag: Streiflichter aus der Verlagsarbeit, statt einer Festschrift. Regensburg: G. Bosse, 1963. 161 p.

"Verzeichnis der im Gustav Bosse Verlag erschienenen Werke:" p. 149–161.

2731. Vernarecci, D. Augusto. Ottaviano dei Petrucci da Fossombrone, inventore dei tipi mobili metalli fusi della musica nel secolo XV. Seconda edizione. Bologna: Romagnoli, 1882. 288 p.

2732. Vol'man, B. Russkie pechatnye noty XVIII veka. Leningrad: Gosudarstvennoe muzykal'noe izdatel'stvo, 1957. 293 p.

Russian printed music of the 18th century.

2733. Weinhold, Liesbeth. "Musiktitle und Datierung," in *Fontis artis musicae,* 13 (1966), p. 136–40.

2734. Weinmann, Alexander. Beiträge zur Geschichte des Alt-Wiener Musikverlages. 1948– .

A series of studies related to Viennese music publishing of the late 18th and early 19th centuries. They appear under varied imprints and in two subseries: Reihe 1, *Komponisten*; Reihe 2, *Verleger.* The volumes are listed below in series order.

2735. Weinmann, Alexander. Beiträge zur Geschichte des Alt-Wiener Musikverlages. Reihe 1, Folge 1: Verzeichnis der im Druck erschienen Werke von Joseph Lanner, sowie Listen der Plattennummern der Originalausgaben für alle Besetzungen. . . . Wien: Leuen, [1948]. 31 p.

Tables listing the work of Lanner (1801–43) in opus number order, with plate numbers of the first editions. Alphabetical index of works by title.

2736. Weinmann, Alexander. Beiträge zur Geschichte des Alt-Wiener Musikverlages. Reihe 1, Folge 2. Verzeichnis sämtlicher Werke von Johann Strauss, Vater und Sohn. Wien: Musikverlag L. Krenn, 1956. 171 p.

2737. Weinmann, Alexander. Beiträge zur Geschichte des Alt-Wiener Musikverlages. Reihe 1, Folge 3: Verzeichnis sämtlicher Werke von Josef und Eduard Strauss. Wien: Ludwig Krenn, 1967. 104 p.

2738. Weinmann, Alexander. Beiträge zur Geschichte des Alt-Wiener Musikverlages. Reihe 2, Folge 1a. Verzeichnis der Verlagswerke des Musikalischen Magazins in Wien, 1784–1802, Leopold (und Anton) Kozeluch. 2., erg. und vollständig umgearb. Aufl. Wien: L. Krenn, 1979. 53 p.
First published in 1950 by Össterreichisher Bundesverlag, Vienna. 31 p.
Works without plate numbers, and with questionable plate numbers, in chronological order; works with plate number in numerical order, followed by an alphabetical list by composer, of Kozeluch's catalog, 1800.

2739. Weinmann, Alexander. Beiträge zur Geschichte des Alt-Wiener Musikverlages. Reihe 2, Folge 2. Vollständiges Verlagsverzeichnis Artaria & Comp. 2. erg. Aufl. Wien: L. Krenn, 1978. 201 p.
First edition published 1952.
A history of the Artaria firm, with a classified list, chronological within classifications, of its publications, giving in most cases exact dates of publication. Index by composers.
Review of the first ed. by Richard S. Hill in *Notes,* 10 (1953), p. 449–50.

2740. Weinmann, Alexander. Beiträge zur Geschichte des Alt-Wiener Musikverlages. Reihe 2, Folge 3: "Vollständiges Verlagsverzeichnis der Musikalien des Kunst- und Industrie-Comptoirs in Wien, 1801–1819." In *Studien zur Musikwissenschaft; Beihefte der DTOe,* 22 (1955), p. 217–52.
Contains a listing of 802 plate numbers in numerical order, with composer, title, and date of publication of the corresponding works. Composer index.
Review by William Klenz in *Notes,* 14 (1956), p. 117.

2741. Weinmann, Alexander. Beiträge zur Geschichte des Alt-Wiener Musikverlages. Reihe 2, Folge 4: "Verzeichnis der Musikalien des Verlages Johann Traeg in Wien, 1794–1818." In *Studien zur Musikwissenschaft; Beihefte der DTÖ,* 23 (1956), p. 135–83.
Lists all works published by the firm, in chronological order.

2742. Weinmann, Alexander. Beiträge zur Geschichte des Alt-Wiener Musikverlages. Reihe 2, Folge 5: Wiener Musikverleger und Musikalienhandler von Mozarts Zeit bis gegen 1860; ein firmengeschichtlicher und topographischer Behelf. Wien: Rohrer, 1956. 72 p. (Österreichische Akademie der Wissenschaft ... Veröff. der Kommission für Musikforschung, 2.)
Lists and discusses 38 music dealers and publishers and 19 related

general book dealers and publishers. Tables showing early and existing addresses of the firms. Useful in dating Viennese musical imprints.
Review by Richard S. Hill in *Notes*, 15 (1958), p. 396–97.

2743. Weinmann, Alexander. Beiträge zur Geschichte des Alt-Wiener Musikverlages. Reihe 2, Folge 6: Verzeichnis der Musikalien aus dem K.K. Hoftheater-Musik-Verlag. Wien: Universal, [1961]. 130 p. (Wiener Urtext Ausgabe.)
Brief history of the firm and biographical notes on the men associated with it. List of publications from 1796 to c. 1820, with plate numbers and dates of issue if known.
Review by Donald W. Krummel in *Notes*, 19 (1961), p. 76.

2744. Weinmann, Alexander. Beiträge zur Geschichte des Alt-Wiener Musikverlages. Reihe 2, Folge 7: Kataloge Anton Huberty (Wien) und Christoph Torricella. Wien: Universal, 1962. 135 p.
Brief histories of the firms, followed by detailed listings of their publications, giving composer, title, date of publication if known, location of copies in European libraries.
Review by Richard Schaal in *Die Musikforschung*, 18 (1965), p. 83.

2745. Weinmann, Alexander. Beiträge zur Geschichte des Alt-Wiener Musikverlages. Reihe 2, Folge 8: Die wiener Verlagswerke von Franz Anton Hofmeister. Wien: Universal, 1964. 252 p.
Contains a biography of Hofmeister; a dated list of plate numbers; entries, largely thematic, for all of the firm's publications; brief historical discussions of aspects of the firm's history.

2746. Weinmann, Alexander. Beiträge zur Geschichte des Alt-Wiener Musikverlages. Reihe 2, Folge 8a. Addenda und Corrigenda zum Verlagsverzeichnis Franz Anton Hoffmeister. Wien: L. Krenn, 1982. 46 p.

2747. Weinmann, Alexander. Beiträge zur Geschichte des Alt-Wiener Musikverlages. Reihe 2, Folge 9: Verlagsverzeichnis Tranquillo Mollo (mit und ohne Co.). Wien: Universal, 1964. 111 p.
Biography of the Mollo family and history of the firm. Transcriptions of catalogs, with plate numbers. Alphabetical indexes by composers. The firm was a successor to Artaria.

2748. Weinmann, Alexander. Beiträge zur Geschichte des Alt-Wiener Musikverlages. Reihe 2, Folge 9a. Ergänzungen zum Verlags-Verzeichnis Tranquillo Mello. Wien: Universal Edition, 1972.

2749. Weinmann, Alexander. Beiträge zur Geschichte des Alt-Wiener Musikverlages. Reihe 2, Folge 10: Verlagsverzeichnis Pietro Mechetti quondam Carlo (mit Portraits). Wien: Universal Edition, 1966. 205 p.
Review by Harald Heckmann in *Die Musikforschung*, 21 (1968), p. 507–8.

2750. Weinmann, Alexander. Beiträge zur Geschichte des Alt-Wiener Musikverlages. Reihe 2, Folge 11: Verlagsverzeichnis Giovanni Cappi bis A. O. Witzendorf. Wien: Universal Edition, 1967. 210 p.
Review by Imogen Fellinger in *Die Musikforschung,* 25 (1972), p. 371.

2751. Weinmann, Alexander. Beiträge zur Geschichte des Alt-Wiener Musikverlages. Reihe 2, Folge 12: Verzeichnis der Musikalien des Verlages Joseph Eder-Jeremias Bermann. Wien: Universal Edition, 1968. 78 p.

2752. Weinmann, Alexander. Beiträge zur Geschichte des Alt-Wiener Musikverlages. Reihe 2, Folge 13: Wiener Musikverlag "Am Rande." Ein lückenfüllender Beitrag zur Geschichte des Alt-Wiener Musikverlages. Wien: Universal Edition, 1970. 155 p.

2753. Weinmann, Alexander. Beiträge zur Geschichte des Alt-Wiener Musikverlages. Reihe 2, Folge 14: Verzeichnis der Musikalien des Verlages Maisch-Sprenger-Artaria. Mit 2 Supplementen: I. Die Firma Mattias Artarias Witwe u. Compagnie. II. Supplement zum Verlagsverzeichnis des Musikalischen Magazins in Wien (Kozeluch). Wien: Universal Edition, 1970. 95 p.

2754. Weinmann, Alexander. Beiträge zur Geschichte des Alt-Wiener Musikverlages. Reihe 2, Folge 15. Verlagsverzeichnis Ignaz Sauer (Kunstverlag zu den Sieben Schwestern), Sauer und Leidesdorf und Anton Berka & Comp. Wien: Universal Edition, 1972. 100 p.

2755. Weinmann, Alexander. Beiträge zur Geschichte des Alt-Wiener Musikverlages. Reihe 2, Folge 16. Verlagsverzeichnis Johann Traeg (und Sohn). 2. verm. und verb. Aufl. Wien: Universal Edition 1973. 89 p.

2756. Weinmann, Alexander. Beiträge zur Geschichte des Alt-Wiener Musikverlages. Reihe 2, Folge 17. Johann Traeg; die Musikalienverzeichnisse von 1799 und 1804 (Handschriften und Sortiment). Wien: Universal Edition, 1973. 133 p.
Facsimiles of the two lists: *Verzeichniss alter und neuer sowohl geschriebener als gestochener Musikalien and Erster Nachtrag zu dem Verzeichniss alter und neuer sowohl geschriebener als gestochener Musikalien.*

2757. Weinmann, Alexander. Beiträge zur Geschichte des Alt-Wiener Musikverlages. Reihe 2, Folge 19. Vollständiges Verlagsverzeichnis Senefelder, Steiner, Haslinger. München; Salzburg: Musikverlag Katzbichler, 1979–1983. v. 1 & 3. (Musikwissenschaftliche Schriften, 14 & 16)
Contents: Bd. 1. A. Senefelder, Chemische Druckerey, S.A. Steiner, S.A. Steiner & Comp., (Wien 1803–1826); Bd. 3. Tobias Haslingers Witwe und Sohn und Carl Haslinger qdm. Tobias, (Wien 1843–1875).

2758. Weinmann, Alexander. Beiträge zur Geschichte des Alt-Wiener Musikverlages. Reihe 2, Folge 20. Verzeichnis der Musikalien des Verlages Anton Pennauer. Wien: Krenn, 1981. 58 p.

2759. Weinmann, Alexander. Beiträge zur Geschichte des Alt-Wiener Musikverlages. Reihe 2, Folge 21. Verzeichnis der Verlagswerke J.P. Gotthard. Wien: L. Krenn, 1981. 55 p.

2760. Weinmann, Alexander. Beiträge zur Geschichte des Alt-Wiener Musikverlages. Reihe 2, Folge 22. Verzeichnis der Musikalien des Verlages Thadé Weigl. Wien: L. Krenn, 1982. 178 p.

2761. Weinmann, Alexander. Beiträge zur Geschichte des Alt-Wiener Musikverlages. Reihe 2, Folge 23. Verlagsverzeichnis Peter Cappi und Cappi & Diabelli (1816 bis 1824). Wien: Krenn, 1983. 150 p.

2762. Weinmann, Alexander. Beiträge zur Geschichte des Alt-Wiener Musikverlages. Reihe 2, Folge 24. Verlagsverzeichnis Anton Diabelli & Co. (1824 bis 1840). Wien: L. Krenn, 1985. 494 p.

2763. Weinmann, Alexander. Der Alt-Wiener Musikverlag im Spiegel der *Wiener Zeitung.* Tutzing: Schneider, 1976. 71 p. (Institut für Österreichische Musikdokumentation. Publikation, 2) *Wiener Zeitung* (Printer)

2764. Weinmann, Alexander. Die Anzeigen des Kopiaturbetriebes Johann Traeg in der Wiener Zeitung zwischen 1782 und 1805: Bd. 2 zu seinen Musikalienverzeichnissen von 1799 und 1804 aus der Reihe *Beiträge zur Geschichte des Alt-Wiener Musikverlags.* Wien: L. Krenn, 1981. 109 p. (Wiener Archivstudien, 6)

2765. Wolf, Johannes. "Verzeichnis der musiktheoretischen Inkunabeln mit Fundorten." In Francesco Caza, *Tractato vulgare de canto figurato.* ... Berlin: M. Breslauer, 1922. p. 64–92. (Veröffentlichungen der Musikbibliothek Paul Hirsch, 1.)
Wolf lists 104 incunabula in the field of music theory, with locations where copies are preserved, as a supplement to his edition of Caza's treatise.

2766. Zur Westen, Walter von. Musiktitel aus vier Jahrhunderten; Festschrift anlässlich der 57 jährigen Bestehens der Firma C. G. Räder. Leipzig: [1921]. 116 p.
A study of musical title pages from the Renaissance to the end of the 19th century, with 96 facsimile illustrations.

Discographies

Within the last few decades the field of recorded sound has given rise to an abundance of documentation of interest to librarians, teachers, research scholars, and private collectors. One effort to bring these diverse interests together has resulted in an Association for Recorded Sound Collections, which issued in 1967 *A preliminary directory of sound recordings collections in the U.S. and Canada* (see no. 2937). More recently, the International Association of Sound Archives has issued a directory of member archives covering the holdings, services, and staffs of institutions globally (see no. 2771).

Recorded music has a particular attraction for the collector, whether his interests lie in early vocal discs or cylinders or in jazz recordings. There has been a proliferation of record reviews, listeners' guides, manufacturers' catalogs and numerical lists, and journals devoted almost exclusively to discography. Some indication of the scope and variety of the bibliographical coverage is suggested by the *Bibliography of discographies* edited by Michael Gray and Gerald D. Gibson (see no. 2768) in 3 volumes. No effort has been made here to list more than a few recent representative examples of the major types of reference tools available to the specialist in recorded sound. Some outmoded works are included to suggest the distance travelled by specialists in the course of this century.

Gordon Stevenson in an article, "Discography: scientific, analytical, historical and systematic," in *Trends in archival and reference collections of recorded sound [Library Trends, 21, 1]* (1972, p. 101–35) has provided some of the basic theoretical principles of discography. There have been a number of articles in the *Journal of Jazz Studies* which have discussed some of these same philosophical and methodological points in the course of careful examinations of discographic questions concerning jazz recordings. The *Journal* is well worth perusal even for those not engaged in jazz studies.

In the organization following, "Encyclopedias of recorded music" have been distinguished from "Collectors' guides." The distinction is perhaps an arbitrary one, but it is intended to separate the few comprehensive discographies from those directed toward the interests of collectors of classical music, jazz or early discs.

BIBLIOGRAPHIES OF DISCOGRAPHIES

2767. Association for recorded sound collections. Journal. v. 1– (1968–)
In addition to the regular appearance of discographies as articles in the
Journal, there are reviews of discographies and citations of discographies not reviewed in every issue. The journal of the professional discog-
rapher.

2768. Bibliography of discographies. N.Y.: Bowker, 1977–83. 3 v. to date.
V. 1: *Classical music, 1925–1975, by* Michael H. Gray and Gerald D.
Gibson.
V. 2: *Jazz, by* Daniel Allen.
V. 3: *Popular music, by* Michael H. Gray.
Not yet issued are v. 4, which will treat discographies of ethnic and folk
music, and v. 5, which will cover general discographies of music, lable
lists, speech recordings, and natural sounds.
These bibliographies are the most complete and scholarly in the field
of discography. They include entries for monographs as well as for discographies appearing as articles or appended to articles. Each volume
separately indexed.
V. 1 contains 3,307 entries arranged in subject order. Each citation
includes complete bibliographic information and annotations.
V. 2 cites discographies of jazz, blues, ragtime, gospel, and rhythm and
blues music published between 1935 and 1980. It excludes record company catalogs, works primarily of a critical nature, and lists of records,
whether to support an accompanying text or for popular consumption.
Entries are ordered by subject. A list of subject headings other than
personal names or names of groups is provided. There is a list of periodicals cited and an index.
V. 3 cites discographies of pop music, rock and country, hillbilly and
blue grass, motion picture and stage show music. Excludes record company catalogs, but includes pricing guides to out-of-print records and
lists of charted popular music. There is a list of periodical titles cited and
an index.
V. 1 reviewed by Jean-Michel Nectoux in *Fontes artis musicae,* 25
(1978), p. 418–19.

2769. Cooper, David Edwin. International bibliography of discographies:
classical music and jazz & blues, 1962–1972; a reference book for record
collectors, dealers and libraries. Preface by Guy A. Marco. Littleton: Libraries Unlimited, 1975. 272 p.
Brief review by Stephen M. Fry in *Notes,* 32 (1976), p. 554–55.

2770. Dearling, Robert and Celia Dearling with Brian Rust. The Guinness book
of recorded sound. London: Guinness, 1984. 225 p.
A vast assemblage of facts about the history of recorded sound.

2771. International Association of Sound Archives. Directory of member ar-
chives compiled by Grace Koch. London: The Association, c1982. 174 p.
(Special publication, 3)
First edition edited by Ann Briegleb and Don Niles and published 1978.
94 p.
Extensive entries modeled on the *RISM* Series C directories to music

collections.

2772. Ritchie, Verna Ford. "A burgeoning in the world of discography," in *RQ,* 21 (1982), p. 254–67.
An annotated, classified bibliography of some 70 discographies, most published in the late 1970s. Includes art music, jazz, and popular music. Lists journals and other publications which carry reviews of recorded music.

2773. Robbins, Donald C. "Current resources for the bibliographic control of sound recordings," in *Trends in archival and reference collections of recorded sound, (Library trends,* 21, no. 1 (July 1972) edited by Gordon Stevenson, p. 136–46.
Incorporates a review of then current discographies.

2774. Rust, Brian A. L. Brian Rust's guide to discography. Westport: Greenwood Press, 1980. 133 p. (Discographies, 4)
Contents: purposes and functions of discography; short history of the science of discography; creation of a discography; securing information about discographies; labels; bibliography of book length discographies.

2775. Stevenson, Gordon. Trends in archival and reference collections of recorded sound. V. 21, no. 1 of *Library Trends.* Edited by Gordon Stevenson. Urbana, Illinois: University of Illinois Press, 1972. 155 p.
Contents: Introduction by Gordon Stevenson;
Sound scholarship: scope, purpose, function and potential of phonorecord archives by Edward E. Colby;
The struggle of sound archives in the United States by Carlos B. Hagen;
Recorded sound in the Library of Congress by Donald L. Leavitt;
Oral history by Norman Hoyle;
Preservation and restoration of authenticity in sound recordings by William L. Welch;
Discography: scientific, analytical, historical and systematic by Gordon Stevenson;
Current resources for the bibliographic control of sound recordings by Donald C. Robbins;
Copyright and archival collections of sound recordings by Abraham A. Goldman.

ENCYCLOPEDIAS OF RECORDED MUSIC

2776. Clough, Francis F. and G. J. Cuming. The world's encyclopedia of recorded music. London: Sidgwick & Jackson, 1952. 890 p.
First supplement (April 1950 to May-June 1951) bound with the main volume.
Second supplement (1951–52) London, 1952. 262 p.
Third supplement (1953–55) London, 1957. 564 p. Reprint by Greenwood Press, Westport, Ct., 1970.
The world's encyclopedia is a useful reference tool for record specialists. Arrangement is alphabetical by composer, with a subclassfication of

works under prolific composers. Full information given as to content and labels. Special section for anthologies.

Review by Philip Miller in *Notes,* 10 (1952), p. 94–95; of the *Third supplement* by Richard S. Hill in *Notes,* 14 (1957), p. 357–59.

2777. Eastman School of Music, Rochester. Sibley Music Library. Catalog of sound recordings. Boston: G.K.Hall, 1977. 14 v.

Photo reproduction of the dictionary catalog of an extensive LP collection. Until the time of publication, the Sibley Music Library had a collection development policy to collect all currently issued L.P.s. This catalog provides excellent coverage with numerous cross references and added entries.

2778. Gramophone Shop, Inc., New York. The Gramophone Shop encyclopedia of recorded music. New York: The Gramophone Shop, Inc., 1936. 574 p.

Reprint of the 3rd edition (1948) by Greenwood: Westport, 1970.

Compiled by R. D. Darrell. 2nd ed., New York, Simon & Schuster, 1942; George C. Leslie, supervising editor. 558 p. 3rd ed., rev. and enl., New York, Crown, 1948; Robert H. Reid, supervising editor. 639 p.

The prototype for all encyclopedias of recorded music in its organization and coverage. Works arranged alphabetically under composer and partially classified. Brief biographical accounts of composers. All three volumes must be consulted, since the later editions are not fully cumulative. Coverage restricted to 78 rpm discs.

2779. Johnson, William W. The gramophone book, a complete guide for all lovers of recorded music. London: Hinrichsen, [1954]. 169 p.

A compendium of miscellaneous information useful to record collectors. British emphasis. Lacks an index.

2780. New York Public Library. Rodgers and Hammerstein Archives of Recorded Sound. Dictionary catalog of the Rodgers and Hammerstein Archives of Recorded Sound. Boston: G. K. Hall, 1981. 15 v.

Photo-reproduction of the card catalog of the enormous collection at Lincoln Center. Entries under composer, important performers, titles and subjects.

2781. The Penguin stereo record guide [by] Edward Greenfield, Robert Layton, Ivan March; edited by Ivan March. 2nd ed. Harmondsworth; New York: Penguin, 1977. 1,168 p.

First edition 1975.

A successor to the *Stereo record guide* (see no. 2803)

The authors are reviewers for *Gramophone.* This is a catalog of about 4,000 recordings in order by composer (or title for collective recordings). Each entry supplies copious discographical and performance information and the authors' opinions of the recording. focused principally on recordings marketed in Great Britain; virtually ignores modern American composers.

COLLECTORS' GUIDES TO CLASSICAL MUSIC

As the number of homes equipped with high fidelity sound reproduction equipment, there has been a concomitant rise in the number of publications featuring reviews of recorded music. Journals such as *High fidelity,* the *American Record Guide,* and *Opus* provide numerous reviews of current releases. A large number of books intended to guide the amateur collector in the purchase of recordings for home use have been published. Few of these titles will be found listed here as they offer minimal and dubious information to the scholar. We have listed here books which are compilations of brief record reviews in which observations on the technical quality of the recordings are combined with musically informed comments on the work recorded and on its performance. The listings below are confined to the more comprehensive English-language works in this category.

2782. Basart, Ann Phillips. The sound of the fortepiano: a discography of recordings on early pianos. Berkeley: Fallen Leaf Press, 1985. 472 p. (Fallen Leaf reference books in music)

2783. Bloch, Francine. Francis Poulenc, 1928–1982. Paris: Bibliothèque Nationale, Département de la Phonothèque Nationale et de l'Audiovisuel, 1984. 255 p. (Phonographies, 2)

An extensive discography arranged by opus. Index to names of performers. Includes a discography of Poulenc as performer.

2784. Bontinck-Küffel, Irmgard, Kurt Blaukopf, and Manfred Wagner. Opern und Schallplatten (1900–1962); ein historischer Katalog vollständiger oder nahezu vollständiger Aufnahmen. Wien: Universal; Karlsruhe: Braun, 1974. 184 p.

A comprehensive list of recordings of about 500 of the most important operas, mostly on L.P.s, but with some 78 rpm recordings. Includes information about cast and dates of recording. No index!

2785. Cohn, Arthur. Recorded classical music; a critical guide to compositions and performances. N.Y.: Schirmer Books, 1981. 2,164 p.

Entries arranged by composer, then title.

Review by Cohn of recordings of thousands of compositions. Record label index enables the reader to discover which works appear on the same disc.

2786. Coover, James B. and Richard Colvig. Medieval and Renaissance music on long-playing records. [Detroit: Information Service, Inc.], 1964. 122 p. (Detroit studies in music bibliography, 6.)

Supplement, 1962–71 (1973) 258 p. Issued as *Detroit studies in music bibliography, 26.*

A well-organized guide to the recorded resources in Medieval and Renaissance music. Part I of the *Supplement* analyzes 901 anthologies, as compared with the 322 analyzed in the 1964 edition. Part II: index to anthologies and individual discographies by composer. Part III: performer index.

The journal *Early music* (1973–) features listings and reviews of recordings of early music and is the current complement to this work.

Review of the 1964 edition by George F. DeVine in *Journal of research in music education,* 13 (1965), p. 260; by Ludwig Finscher in *Die Musikforschung,* 20 (1967), p. 84–85.

2787. Croucher, Trevor. Early music discography: from plainsong to the sons of Bach. Phoenix: Oryx Press, 1982. 2 v.

First published by the Library Association, London.

Lists over 3,000 recordings in arrangements by period, location, and form. Indexes to names, plainsong melodies, and titles (of anonymous works).

2788. Deays, Carl. La discothèque idéale. Rev. éd. Paris: Éditions Universitaires, 1973. 443 p.

First published in 1970.

Categorized entries of recommended recordings with evaluative comments. Of interest because of the inclusion of recordings marketed principally in Europe. Indexes to names of performers and composers.

2789. Discography Series Utica, N.Y.: J. F. Weber, 1970– . Nos. 1– .
Editors: no. 1–4, 8–10, 12– , J. F. Weber; no. 5–7, 11, Peter Morse.
Contents:

1. Schubert Lieder. 49 p.
2. Hugo Wolf complete works. 2nd ed. 85 p.
3. Schumann Lieder. 20 p.
4. Brahms Lieder. 20 p.
5. Schubert, Schumann, Brahms, choral music. 26 p.
6. Mendelssohn vocal music. 2nd ed. 30 p.
7. Strauss Lieder. 2nd ed. 46 p.
8. Loewe and Franz. 20 p.
9. Mahler. 2nd ed. 48 p.
10. Bruckner. 34 p.
11. Debussy and Ravel vocal music. 38 p.
12. Edgard Varese. 13 p.
13. Leonard Bernstein. 16 p.
14. Alban Berg. 16 p.
15. Pfitzner and Marx. 18 p.
16. Benjamin Britten. 58 p.
17. Richard Strauss opera. 51 p. By Alan Jefferson.
18. Leos Janacek. 65 p. By William D. Curtis.
19. Carter and Schuman. 20 p.

Each number is preceded by an informative introduction, including reference to bibliographical sources.

2790. Gilbert, Richard. The clarinetists' solo repertoire: a discography. New York: Grenadilla Society, 1972. 100 p.

A supplement, The clarinetists' discography II was published in 1975. 150 p.

These are more than discographies. They include reviews and critiques, portraits of leading clarinetists, bibliographies, and lists of record publishers and their addresses.

2791. The Guide to Long Playing Records. New York: Knopf, 1955. 3 v.
Reprinted by Greenwood Press, Westport, 1978.
Vol. 1: Irving Kolodin, *Orchestral music.* 268 p. Vol. 2: Philip L. Miller, *Vocal music.* 381 p. Vol. 3: Harold C. Schonberg, *Chamber and solo instrument music.* 280 p.

2792. Hall, David. Records: 1950 edition. New York: Knopf. 524 p.
Hall's books are addressed to the private collector with an interest in serious music. In the earlier editions the material is classified by medium. Beginning with the *International edition* (above) the arrangement is alphabetical by composer. Much general information for the record collector is included. The 1950 edition is the first to direct attention to long-playing discs.

2793. Hall, David. The record book. International edition. New York: Durrell, 1948. 1,394 p.

2794. Hall, David. The record book, a music lover's guide to the world of the phonograph. New York: Smith & Durrell, 1940. 771 p.
Suppplement. 1941. (Continuing pagination, 777–886).
Second supplement. 1943. (Continuing pagination, 887–1013).
Complete edition. New York: Citadel Press, 1946. 1,063 p. Incorporates the two preceding supplements.

2795. Halsey, Richard Sweeney. Classical music recordings for home and library. Chicago: American Library Association, 1976. 340 p.
Intended to provide guidance to librarians and amateur collectors in building a basic collection of classical music. Arranged by genre and within genre by composer. Indexes to title and manufacturers' names and numbers. Readers should ignore the ratings provided by the compiler.

2796. Hermil, Hélène. Musique: 10,000 compositeurs du XIIe au XXe siècle, répertoire chrono-ethnique. Saint-Mandè, France: Production et distribution Groupe de Recherche et d'Etudes Musicales, 1983. 842 p.
An alphabetical list of composers with dates and places of birth and death, followed by a chronological list of composers by country, showing ethnic origin. Lists of women composers. Lists of composers related by familial, marital or other significant ties. A product of the Bibliothêque Internationale de Musique Contemporaine.

2797. Jackson, Paul T. Collector's contact guide, 1975. 2nd ed. Peoria: author, 1975. 58 p.
Brief review by Stephen M. Fry, in *Notes,* 32 (1975), p. 302.

2798. Kolodin, Irving. A guide to recorded music. Garden City, N.Y.: Doubleday, 1941. 495 p.

2799. Kolodin, Irving. A new guide to recorded music. International edition. Garden City, N.Y.: Doubleday, 1950. 524 p.

Kolodin adhered to an alphabetical arrangement by composer, with classification by form and medium under composer. Index of performers and performing groups.

2800. Kolodin, Irving. New guide to recorded music. Rev. ed. Garden City, N.Y.: Doubleday, 1947. 512 p.

2801. Lory, Jacques. Guide des disques; l'aventure de la musique occidentale, du chant grégorien à la musique électronique. 3eme éd. Paris: Buchet-Chastel, 1971. 416 p.
First published in 1967.
Arranges entries in historical order with comments on each historical period as well as upon the recordings. Recordings by European and American manufacturers.

2802. Opern auf Schallplatten, 1900–1962: ein historischer Katalog vollständiger oder nahezu vollständiger Aufnahmen als Beitrag zur Geschichte der Aufführungspraxis. Red. Irmgard Bontinck-Küffel, Mitarb., Kurt Blaukopf, Manfred Wagner. Wien: Universal Edition, 1974. 184 p.
One of the first attempts to apply discography to historical research. The editors identify the first recording of each opera with information as to cast, orchestra, and label. Discography arranged by composer and title. Alternative titles given as well as complete discographical information. Bibliography.

2803. The Penguin stereo record guide by Edward Greenfield, Robert Layton, Ivan March; edited by Ivan March. 2d ed. Harmondsworth, England; New York: Penguin, 1977. 1,168 p.
The authors are reviewers for *Gramophone.* This is a catalog of about 4,000 recordings in order by composer (or title for collective recordings). Each entry supplies copious discographical and performance information and the authors' opinions of the recording. Focused principally on recordings marketed in Great Britain; virtually ignores modern American composers.

2804. Pirie, Peter J. 20th century British music: a collector's guide. Beverly Hills, California: Theodore Front Musical Literature, 1980. 20 p. (Front musical publications, 2)
A discography covering "The English musical renaissance" of the 20th century.

2805. Purcell, Ronald C. Classic guitar, lute and vihuela dicography. Melville, N.Y.: Belwin-Mills, 1976. 116 p.

2805.1. "Recordings" in *Early music,* v. 1– (1973–).
A quarterly checklist of commercial recordings of early music. Organized by composers name if a single composer collection, otherwise listed under name of performer or ensemble.

2806. Records in Review. Great Barrington, Mass.: The Wyeth Press, 1955
– . v. 1– .
The set through volume 12 (1972) has been reprinted by the AMS Press,
Inc., 1972– .
Reviews from *High fidelity,* generally authoritative and signed by the
reviewer. The main listing is by composer, followed by nine categories
of collections: vocal, piano, organ and harpsichord, strings, woodwinds
and brass, guitar, orchestra, medieval and Renaissance, miscellaneous.
Index of performers.

2807. Rowell, Lois. American organ music on records. Braintree, Mass.:
Organ Literature Foundation, 1976. 105 p.
415 entries of recorded organ music by American composers.
Brief review by Stephen M. Fry in *Notes,* 33 (1976), p. 306.

2808. Russcol, Herbert. Guide to low-priced classical records. New York:
Hart, (1969). 831 p.
"Over 300 composers covered; over 1,500 works appraised; over 3,000
records evaluated; a wealth of solid information." [from the book jacket]

2809. Sackville-West, Edward and D. Shawe-Taylor. The record guide. London: Collins, 1951. 763 p.

2810. Sackville-West, Edward and D. Shawe-Taylor. The record guide . . . with
Andrew Porter and William Mann. Rev. ed. London: Collins, [1955]. 957
p.
Supplement [1956], 191 p.

2811. Sackville-West, Edward and D. Shawe-Taylor. The record year, a guide
to the year's gramophone records, including a complete guide to long
playing records. Assisted by Andrew Porter. London: Collins, [1952]. 383
p.
The Sackville-West guides are designed for British record collectors.
The commentary is literate and well informed. The discs are arranged
by composer, with special sections devoted to collections and a performer
index.

2812. Shoaf, R. Wayne. The Schoenberg discography. Berkeley: Fallen
Leaf Press, c1986. 200 p. (Fallen Leaf reference books in music)

2813. Stahl, Dorothy. A selected discography of solo song: cumulation
through 1971. Detroit: Information Coordinators, 1972. 137 p. (Detroit
Studies in Music Bibliography, 24)
Supplement, 1975–1982, 236 p. Detroit, 1984 (no. 52)
Supplement, 1971–1974, 99 p. Detroit, 1976 (no. 34)
First published in 1968 and supplemented in 1970.

2814. The Stereo Record Guide. By Edward Greenfield, Ivan March, and
Denis Stevens. London: The Long Playing Record Library, Ltd., 1960– 72.
8 v.

The main arrangement for each volume is by composer, followed by special sections devoted to concerts, recitals, light music, etc. Vol. 1 contains a selection of 50 outstanding records for 1958/59; vol. 2, a selection of 100 outstanding records for 1960/61. The third volume supplements the two preceding, but it relists the important recordings from the earlier books, with page references to earlier commentary. The guide is distinguished by its intelligent, highly readable annotations.

2815. Turner, Patricia. Afro-American singers: an index and preliminary discography of long-playing recordings of opera, choral, music, and song. Minneapolis: Challenge, 1977. 255 p.

A 44 p. supplement was issued by the author in 1980.

2816. Wilson, William John. The stereo index: a complete catalogue of every recommended stereo disc. 5th ed. Westport: Greenwood, 1978. 192 p.

3rd ed. 1967. 4th ed. 1969.

COLLECTORS' GUIDES TO EARLY RECORDINGS

The field of discs and cylinder recordings of the period from 1898 to 1925 has long been the province of private collectors. Emphasis is usually placed on the performer, particularly the vocalist, rather than on the composer. The importance of collecting in this area has been recognized on a large scale by libraries and research institutions throughout the world, as, for example, at the New York Public Library, the Library of Congress, the British Institute of Recorded Sound, the Stanford University Archive of Recorded Sound, the Yale University Collection of Historical Sound Recordings, and Syracuse University. Lately there have been increasing numbers of musicological studies based on early recordings. To pursue this research most effectively, discographers are discovering the value of research in the catalogs issued by recording manufacturers and in their archives of contracts and logs of studio work.

2817. Bauer, Robert. The new catalogue of historical records, 1898–1908/09. London: Sidgwick and Jackson, [1947]. 494 p.

Reprinted, 1970.

Recordings listed under performer, grouped under label and year of pressing. Serial numbers given. Brief entries for composer and title of work.

2818. Bescoby-Chambers, John. The archives of sound, including a selective catalogue of historical violin, piano, spoken, documentary, orchestral, and composer's own recordings. Lingfield, Surrey: Oakwood Press, 1964. 153 p.

Vocal recordings are fairly well documented today. ... Violin, piano, and orchestral recordings are rarely written about, and there is a vast, almost uncharted sea of piano roll recordings that are almost forgotten today.

A valuable contribution to the discography and player piano resources for instrumental music. Brief biographies of performers, and listings of their recordings. Some chapter headings: "The violin on record," "Historical piano recordings," "Orchestral recordings," and "The composer's own interpretation."

2819. Deakins, Duane D. Cylinder records; a description of the numbering systems, physical appearance, and other aspects of cylinder records made by the major American companies, with brief remarks about the earliest American companies and the foreign record manufacturers. [2nd ed.] Stockton, Calif., [1958]. 35 p.

2820. Deakins, Duane D., Elizabeth Deakins, and Thomas Grattelo. Comprehensive cylinder record index. Stockton, Calif., 1966– .

Pt. 1. Edison amberol records.
Pt. 2. Edison standard records.
Pt. 3. Edison blue amberol records.
Pt. 4. Indestructible records.
Pt. 5. U.S. everlasting records.

2821. Girard, Victor and Harold M. Barnes. Vertical-cut cylinders and discs; a catalogue of all "hill-and-dale" recordings of serious worth made and issued between 1897–1932 *circa*. London: British Institute of Recorded Sound, 1971. 196 p.
Facsimile reprint (corrected) of the original 1964 edition.
A major contribution to the discography of early recordings. Arranged in three major categories: (1) vocal recordings; (2) speech recordings; (3) instrumental and orchestral recordings; with appendices devoted to complete operas and to anonymous Pathé discs. The approach is mainly by performer.

2822. Hurst, P. G. The golden age recorded. New and revised edition. The Oakwood Press, 1963. 187 p.
First published by Sidgwick and Jackson, London, 1946.
A manual for private collectors. General discussions of record collecting followed by biographical notices of the major artists classified by voice. Appendix, p. 147–87: a selected list, by performer, of important early recordings.

2823. Karlin, Fred J. Edison Diamond Discs 50001–52651. Santa Monica, Calif.: Bona Fide Publishing Co., [n.d.] 160 p.
A numerical listing of every Edison Diamond Disc issued in the 50,000 series from 1912–1929. Cites 5,200 titles as well as the performing artists, composers, and lyricists.

2824. Koenigsberg, Allen. Edison cylinder records, 1889–1912, with an illustrated history of the phonograph. New York: Stellar Productions, 1969. 159 p.
Review by Edward Colby in *Notes*, 27 (1971), p. 499–500.

2825. Moogk, Edward B. Roll back the years: history of Canadian recorded sound and its legacy: genesis to 1930. Ottawa: National Library of Canada, 1975. 443 p. & 7 inch disc

Issued also in French as *En remontant les années*, 1975.

A history, but includes discographies of Canadian performers, composers, and early recordings.

2826. Moses, Julian M. Collector's guide to American recordings, 1895–1925; foreword by Giuseppe di Luc. New York: American Record Collectors' Exchange, [1949]. 199 p.

Reprinted by Dover, N.Y., 1977. First ed. Concert Bureau, 1936. 44 p.

Discs arranged under performers by serial or matrix number. P. 172–95: numerical guide, Columbia and other labels. Index of operas and instrumental index.

2827. Moses, Julian M. Price guide to collectors' records, with new value chart. New York: American Record Collectors' Exchange, 1976. 31 p.

First published in 1952.

Discs identified by matrix number under performer, with estimates of value on the current market. Designed to accompany the author's *Collector's guide,* above.

2828. RAI-Radiotelevisione Italiana. Direzione Programmi Radio. Discoteca centrale. Catalogo della discoteca storica. Rome: RAI, Servizio archivi, 1969. 3 v.

A catalog of the 78 rpm recordings in the collection arranged by genre. Includes popular and folk music recordings. The collection is particularly strong, of course, in Italian recordings.

2829. Rigler and Deutsch Record Index. Washington, D.C.: Association for Recorded Sound Collections, 1981–83. 977 microfiche.

Originally issued on 36 reels of microfilm.

This is an index to the 78 rpm recordings held by five of the largest recorded sound collections in the United States: New York Public Library, Rodgers and Hammerstein Archives of Recorded Sound; Yale University Collection of Historical Sound Recordings; Syracuse University Belfer Audio Laboratory and Archives; Stanford University Archive of Recorded Sound; Library of Congress, Motion Picture, Broadcasting, and Recorded Sound Division. A total of 615,000 recordings held among these institutions are reflected in the *Rigler and Deutsch Index.*

The index is in several parts: an author-composer section, a title section, a performer section, a label name and issue number section, a label name and matric number section, and a section in which label name and issue numbers are arranged by institution. There is an introduction to the *Index* on the first microfiche explaining the innovative methodology used to gather the data from the discs. No attempt has been made to bring the names and titles into consistency or under authority control. Many scholars who have used the *Index* have been rewarded for the extra effort needed to assure oneself that all possible forms of names and titles have been seached. Inevitably numerous previously unknown or unlisted recordings have come to light thanks to the *Rigler and Deutsch Index.*

Only a dozen copies of the *Index* have been distributed.

The Associaton of Recorded Sound Collections and the Associated Audio Archives, the name of the group of five contributing collections, are attempting to convert the *Index* to machine-readable form, thereby vastly improving the ease of use, even if no attempt is made to bring the forms of names and titles into consistency.

There is an excellent, if brief, article on the *Index* by David Hamilton, entitled "A new way to find old records", in *Opus* (December 1985), p. 12–13.

2830. Rust, Brian A. L. Discography of historical records on cylinders and 78s. Westport: Greenwood Press, 1979. 327 p.

In fact a history of the earliest period of sound storage. Includes index.

2831. Voices of the Past. [Lingfield, Surrey: The Oakwood Press, 1955–] v. 1– .

Vol. 1: A catalogue of vocal recordings from the English catalogues of the Gramophone Company, 1898–1899; the Gramophone Company Limited, 1899–1900; the Gramophone & Typewriter Company Limited, 1901–1907; and the Gramophone Company Limited, 1907–1925; by John R. Bennet. [1955] Reprinted 1978 by Greenwood Press, Westport.

Vol. 2: A catalogue of the vocal recordings from the Italian catalogues of the Gramophone Company Limited, 1899–1900; the Gramophone Company (Italy) Limited, 1899–1909; the Gramophone Company Limited, 1909; Compagnia del Gammofono 1912–1925; by John R. Bennett. [1957]

Vol. 3: Dischi Fonotipia, including supplement (1958) and addenda (1964), by John R. Bennett. [1964?]

Vol. 4: The international red label catalogue of "DB" & "DA" His Master's Voice recordings, 1924–1956; book 1: "DB" (12-inch), by John R. Bennett and Eric Hughes. [1961]

Vol. 5: The catalogue of "D" & "E" His Master's Voice recordings, by Michael Smith. [1961]

Vol. 6: The international red label catalogue of "DB" & "DA" His Master's Voice recordings, 1924–1956; book 2: "DA", by John R. Bennett and Eric Hughes. [1967?]

Vol. 7: A catalogue of vocal recordings from the 1898–1925 German catalogues of the Gramophone Company Limited, Deutsche Grammophon A.-G., by John R. Bennett and Wilhelm Wimmer. [1967]. Reprinted 1978 by Greenwood Press, Westport.

Vol. 8: Columbia Gramophone Company, Ltd.; English celebrity issues: D and LB series, L and LX series. (By Michael Smith.) [1968?]

Vol. 9: A catalogue of vocal recordings from the 1898–1925 French catalogues of the Gramophone Company Limited, Compagnie française du gramophone, by John R. Bennett. [1971?]

Vol 10: Plum label 'C' series (12 inch) by Michael Smith and Frank Andrews.

Vol. 11: A catalogue of vocal recordings from the Russian Catalogues of the Gramophone Company Limited: Obshchestvo Grammofon c Ogr. Otv. 1899–1915, by John R. Bennett. [1977]

Vol. LP1: Columbia (blue and green labels) Oct. 1952-Dec. 1962, compiled by Alan J. Poulton. [1975]

Vol. LP2: H.M.V. (Red label) Oct. 1952-Dec. 1962 [1975]

Vol. LP3: H.M.V. (Plum label) Oct. 1952-Dec. 1962 [1975]

Re-issue supplement: HMV/Columbia Great recordings of the century (Oct. 1957-Dec. 1966); HMV Golden treasury of immortal performances

(Sept. 1956-June 1957) [1975]

These catalogs list the early recordings, chiefly vocal, in numerical order under their respective labels. Most of the volumes also provide an artist index. These are invaluable tools for organizing and identifying early vocal discs.

COLLECTORS' GUIDES TO JAZZ RECORDINGS

The jazz record collector lives in a world of his own and is well equipped with reference tools designed to meet his needs. The impetus toward doucmentation has come from European rather than American enthusiasts: see Delaunay and Panassie, below. Danial Allen's *Jazz* volume in the Gibson and Gray *Bibliography of discographies* provides entries for almost 4,000 discographies. Only some of the most important ones are cited in this section.

2832. Allen, Walter C. Studies in jazz discography I- . Intro. by William M. Weinberg. New Brunswick, N.J.: Institute of Jazz Studies, Rutgers University, 1971.

A periodical consistently presenting serious and important jazz discographic work. Lists of recordings and actual discographic investigations are featured as well as reviews of similar works published elsewhere.

Review by James Patrick in *Notes,* 29 (1972), p. 236–39.

2833. Bruynincx, Walter. Jazz: modern jazz, be-bop, hard bop, West Coast. Mechelen: 60 Years of Recorded Jazz Team, 1985– . 1– v.

5 volumes issued to date.

2834. Bruynincx, Walter. Modern jazz: modern big band. Mechelen: 60 Years of Recorded Jazz Team, 1986?– . 1– v.

Apparently to be issued in several volumes.

2835. Bruynincx, Walter. Progressive jazz: free—third stream fusion. Mechelen: 60 Years of Recorded Jazz Team, 1984– . 1– v.

Three volumes issued to date covering A - S.

2836. Bruynincx, Walter. 60 years of recorded jazz, 1917–1977. Mechelen: author, 1980. 16 v. (various pagings, issued unbound)

Originally issued between 1967 and 1975 as *50 Years of Recorded Jazz.* Supplement volume issued 1980.

Update M-P issued 1986.

Focused primarily on LPs, entries, arranged by name of performer or group, includes brief biographical or historical information. Discographies cite all recordings with personnel and individual titles, including dates and places of recording sessions. Gives unissued and alternate takes when known. A few major artists (e.g. Louis Armstrong and Duke Ellington) have comprehensive discographies which include 78 rpm disks as well as LPs. There is a separate artist index, not subjected to authority control, which treats every musician listed anywhere in the set. Although intended for the avid amateur, Bruynincx's work is an substantial asset to the jazz scholar.

2837. Carey, David A. and Albert M. McCarthy. The directory of recorded jazz and swing music. London: Cassel, 1950– .

Cover title: *Jazz directory*. Vols. 2–4 have appeared in 2nd editions, 1955–57.

An alphabetical listing of performers and ensembles, with detailed information as to their recorded output. Informative annotations.

The work has progressed through six volumes (as of 1957), paged continuously through p. 1112, as far as the entry "Longshaw."

Vols. 1–4 published by the Delphic Press, Fordingbridge, Hants. The 2nd editions of vols. 2–4 and vols. 5 and 6 are published by Cassel, London.

Continued in Jepsen (no. 2841) and McCarthy (no. 2840).

2838. Delaunay, Charles. New hot discography, the standard dictionary of recorded jazz. Edited by Walter E. Schaap and George Avakian. New York: Criterion, 1948. 608 p.

First published in France in 1936. Reprinted 1982.

Separates the "pioneers of jazz" from "post-1930 jazz." Subdivided by region. An elaborate classification system groups recordings by major jazz personalities. Complete index of names.

2839. Harris, Rex and Brian Rust. Recorded jazz. [Harmondsworth, Middlesex]: Penguin Books, 1958. 256 p.

It must not be regarded as a comprehensive discography, but nevertheless the authors have presented a reasonable cross-section of real jazz, together with biographical notes of performers and a critical assessment of the records listed." [*Preface*]

2840. Jazz on Record: A Critical Guide to the First 50 Years: 1917–1967. By Albert McCarthy, Alun Morgun, Paul Oliver, and Max Harrison. London: Hanover Books; New York: Oak Publications, 1968. 416 p.

Jazz on record is not a gramophone catalogue but a reference book to the best, the most significant, or occasionally simply the most typical recorded works of the leading jazz and blues artists to come to prominence during the last half century' [Authors' *Introduction*]

Much biographical and critical commentary. Arranged mainly by jazz artists, with additional sections devoted to styles and traditions.

Supersedes a work published under the same title by C. Fox, P. Gammond, and A. Morgan, London: Hutchinson, 1960.

Review by Frank Tirro in *Notes,* 26 (1970), p. 756–58.

2841. Jepsen, J. G. Jazz records: A-Z, 1942–1969; a discography. Holte, Denmark: Knudsen, 1963–70. 11 v. in 8.

A major reference work covering recorded jazz from 1942 to 1969. Vols. 5 and 6 published by Nordisk Tidskrift Forlag, Copenhagen.

2842. Lange, Horst H. Die deutsche Jazz-Discographie. Eine Geschichte des Jazz auf Schallplatten von 1902 bis 1955. Berlin: Bote & Bock, 1955.

652 p.

One of several recent European compilations of jazz records. Includes a number of English and Continental performers.

2843. McCarthy, Albert J. Jazz discography 1: an international discography of recorded jazz, including blues, gospel, and rhythm-and-blues for the year January-December 1958. London: Cassell, 1960. 271 p.

The first volume of a projected yearbook to cover all jazz recordings issued throughout the world. New releases are listed alphabetically by country. Full contents of each disc listed, with personnel, place, and date of recording if known.

This volume was an attempt to carry on the work stated by Carey and McCarthy in their Directory of recorded jazz (no. 2837). Only one volume was published but supplements appeared in McCarthy's periodical Jazz monthly.

2844. Panassié, Hughes. Discographie critique des meilleurs disques de jazz. Paris: Robert Laffont, [1958]. 621 p.

An earlier edition, Paris, Corrêa, 1951. 371 p.

The author is a prolific writer on jazz and one of the first important discographers in the field. Arrangement is by performer, with an analytical index by medium and an index of names.

2845. Rust, Brian. Jazz records, 1897–1942. London: Storyville Publications, 1970. 2 v.

Vol. 1: A-Kar. Vol. 2: Kar-Z.

This work supersedes an earlier edition issued under the title *Jazz records A-Z (1961–65)*.

This set of two books covers in the fullest possible detail all known records made in the years between 1897 and 1942 in the ragtime, jazz and swing idioms.... Only records made by American and British musicians are listed. [Compiler's *Introduction*]

Performers and groups are listed alphabetically with their records identified by matrix numbers and titles. Introduction and index of abbreviations for musical terms and record labels. Artists' index compiled by Mary Rust. A rich source of information on jazz history and recording activity for the period specified.

2846. Smith, Charles E. The jazz record book .... with Frederic RamseChy Jr., Charles Payne Rogers and William Russell. New York: Smith and Durrell, 1942. 515 p.

P. 1–125: a survey of the history of jazz in its various regional styles. P. 130–508: record listings by major performers and ensembles, with critical and descriptive commentary. Selected bibliography of jazz; index of bands.

2847. Tudor, Dean and Nancy Tudor. Jazz. Littleton, Colo.: Libraries Unlimited, 1979. 302 p. (American popular music on Elpee)

A discography of American jazz on long-playing records for the amateur aficionado.

2848. Tulane University. William Ransom Hogan Jazz Archive. Catalog of the William Ransom Hogan Jazz Archive: the collection of seventy-eight rpm phonograph recordings, Howard-Tilton Memorial Library, Tulane University. Boston: G. K. Hall, 1984. 2 v.

Photoreproduction of the card catalog for older recordings of one of the most significant jazz archives in the U.S.

COLLECTORS' GUIDES TO POPULAR RECORDINGS

2849. Albris, Jon and Anders Laurson. "Zydeco & cajun" in *Fontes artis musicae,* 31 (1984), p. 108–12.

A brief discography with references to two periodical articles on the subjects.

2850. Bennetzen, Jørgen "Reggae" in *Fontes artis musicae,* 29 (1982), p. 182–86.

A brief discography with bibliographies of literature and music.

2851. George, Nelson. Top of the charts, the most complete listing ever. Piscataway: New Century, 1983. 470 p.

Lists of the top 10 best-selling records in various genres. Arranged chronologically for the 1970s and early 1980s, as listed in *Record World* weekly.

2852. Godrich, J. and R. M. M. Dixon. Blues and gospel records, 1902–1942. 2nd ed., revised. London: Storyville Publications, 1969.

First published by Brian Rust.

Review by Frank J. Gillis in *Ethnomusicology,* 14 (1970), p. 499–500.

2853. Helander, Brock. Rock 'n' Roll to Rock: a discography. Sacramento: Brock Helander, 1978. 328 p.

2854. Hounsome, Terry and Tim Chambre. Rock record. New York: Facts on File, 1981. 526 p.

First published in a limited edition (Rockmaster, 1978) and revised, expanded edition (Rock record, 1979) published and produced in the United Kingdom by Terry Hounsome. This edition published in the United Kingdom in 1981 by Blandford Books Ltd., as *New rock record.*

Listings of rock records with names of groups and individual musicians.

2855. Hummel, David. The collector's guide to the American musical theatre. [New rev. & enl. ed.] Metuchen: Scarecrow Press, 1984. 2 v.

First published by the author in Grawn, Michigan, 1978 and 1979.

An extensive discography of recordings arranged by the title of the show. Each entry gives performance dates and titles of the principal members. Extensive notes.

Preceded by four essays:

Rexton S. Bunnet. *"The British musical."*

Peter Pinne. *"Australian theatre on disc."*
Glenn Atchison. *"The musical theatre in Canada—on-stage and on record."*
Larry Warner. *"Researching the pre-LP original cast recording."*
Appendix of sources of excerpts. V. 2 is an index of all personal names cited.

2856. Jay, Dave, *pseud.* The Irving Berlin songography; 1907–1966. New Rochelle, N.Y.: Arlington House, [1969]. 172 p.

2857. Leadbitter, Mike and Neil Slaven. Blues records, January 1943 to December 1966. London: Hanover Books, Ltd., 1968. 381 p.
A listing by artist and ensembles with discographies as complete as the compilers could make them. Gives instrumentation for the groups and dates of recordings where known.
Review by Frank Tirro in *Notes,* 26 (1970), p. 756–58.

2858. Marsh, Dave and John Swenson. The new Rolling Stone record guide. Rev., updated ed. New York: Random House/Rolling Stone Press, 1983. 648 p.
Rev. ed. of *The Rolling stone record guide, 1979. 631 p.*
"Reviews and rates over 12,000 rock, pop, soul, country, blues, folk, and gospel albums." [from the *Preface*] Citations, with critical ratings.

2859. Marsh, Dave and John Swenson. The *Rolling Stone* record guide: reviews and ratings of almost 10,000 currently available rock, pop, soul, country, blues, jazz, and gospel albums. N.Y.: Random House, 1979. 631 p.
A discography with ratings and reviews of recordings appearing up to 1976. It is, in effect, a survey of a large swath of recorded popular music.
Review by William H. Tallmadge in *American music,* 1 (1983), p. 92–94.

2860. Raymond, Jack. Show music on record from the 1890s to the 1980s; a comprehensive list of original cast and studio cast performances issued on commercial phonograph records, covering music of the American stage, screen and television, with composer performances and other collateral recordings. N.Y.: Frederick Munger, 1982. 253 p.
Shows arranged chronologically. Lists 784 source recordings. "Artist albums" and anthologies separately listed. Artist index.

2861. Rohde, H. Kandy, ed. The gold of rock & roll, 1955–1967. New York: Arbor House, 1970. 352 p.
A discography listing the ten most popular rock and roll recordings for each week during the years covered. "The top fifty" for each individual year are extracted, Brief commentary for each year's activity. Indexed by song titles and artists.

2862. Rust, Brian A. L. The American dance band discography 1917–1942. New Rochelle: Arlington House, 1975. 2 v.
Contents: v. 1 Irving Aaronson to Arthur Lange; v. 2. Arthur Lange to

Bob Zurke.

Covering 2,300 dance orchestras and listing their 78 rpm recordings with matrix and label numbers, dates of recording, personnel, arrangers, vocalists, etc. 50,000 records cited, artist index of about 8,000 names. Black ensembles, Glenn Miller and Benny Goodman are omitted. No title index.

Brief review by Stephen M. Fry in *Notes,* 32 (1976), p. 782.

2863. Smolian, Steven. A handbook of film, theater, and television music on record, 1948–1969. New York: The Record Undertaker, 1970. 64 p. alphabetical listing and 64 p. index.

A handbook for collectors of show and soundtrack recordings.

> This book should assist the reader in two basic ways—to outline what has been issued: what can be bought through regular record shops, and when he will either have to do some "bin hunting" or call on the services of a specialist dealer in cut-outs, and also to identify the records in his collection and tell him something about them. [Compiler's *Introduction*]

2864. Tudor, Dean. Popular music; an annotated guide to recordings. Littleton, Colorado: Libraries Unlimited, 1983. 647 p.

> ... a thorough updating and revision of the four separate volumes published by Libraries Unlimited in 1979 as *Jazz, Black Music, Grass Roots Music, and Contmeporary Popular Music. [Preface]*

Arranged by categories as indicated by the predecessor volumes, but includes also popular religious music. Index of artists.

2865. Tudor, Dean and Nancy Tudor. Contemporary popular music. Littleton, Colo.: Libraries Unlimited, 1979. 313 p. (American popular music on Elpee)

A discography of American popular music.

2866. Whitburn, Joel. Top pop records, 1955–1970. Facts about 9,800 recordings listed in Billboard's "Hot 100" charts grouped under the names of the 2,500 recording artists. Detroit: Gale Research Company, 1972.

> This publication is a complete factual record of the most successful popular music in the United States for the past 16 years. [Editor's note]

2867. Whitburn, Joel. Top rhythm & blues (soul) records, 1972–1973. Menomonee Falls, Wisc.: Record Research, c1973. 184 p.

Supplement published 1974, 48 p.

"Facts about 4000 recordings listed in *Billboard*'s 'Best selling rhythm & blues (soul) singles' charts, grouped under the names of the 1200 recording artists."

Soul music—United States—Discography

ETHNIC AND FOLK MUSIC ON RECORDS

The use of recorded materials is basic to the techniques of modern eth-nomusicology. Here the scholar is concerned less with commercially recorded discs and tapes than he is with recordings made in the field by research institutions and by individual collectors. The problem of bring-ing these diverse materials under "bibliographical control" is a difficult one. A good start has been made with the cooperation of UNESCO in two series published under the general title Archives of recorded music. Se-ries B is concerned with Oriental music; Series C, with ethnographical and folk music. (Series A, not under consideration here, is devoted to Occidental music and has produced a general discography of the works of Frederic Chopin.)

2868. Archives of Recorded Music (Archives de la Musique Enregistrée). Series B: Oriental Music. A catalogue of recorded classical and tradition-al Indian music. General discography and introduction by Alain Danie-lou. Paris: UNESCO, [1952]. 236 p.

The main organization is by region, subdivided by instrumental and vocal music, and listed under the performing artists. Chapter V is devot-ed to the songs of Rabindranath Tagore. Index of names. Bilingual (En-glish-French).

2869. Archives of Recorded Music. . . . Series C: Ethnographical and Folk Music. 2. Collection Musée de l'Homme (Paris). Catalogue prepared by the Inter-national Commission on Folk Arts and Folklore. Paris: UNESCO, [1952]. 74 p.

Catalog of a collection of 1,007 recordings, chiefly made in the field in various parts of Asia and Afric. Grouped under the name of the collector or expedition.

2870. Archives of Recorded Music. . . . Series C: Ethnographical and Folk Music. 1. Collection Phonothèque Nationale (Paris). Catalogue prepared by the International Commission on Folk Arts and Folklore. Paris: UNESCO, [1952]. 254 p.

Lists 4,564 discs in groups as acquired by the Phonothèque. Recordings for any particular national group are scattered throughout the volume. There is an index of countries, however. Bilingual (French-English).

2871. Archives of Recorded Music. . . . Series C: Ethnographical and Folk Music. 4. International catalogue of recorded folk music. . . . Edited by Norman Fraser, with a preface by R. Vaughan Williams and introduction by Maud Karpeles. Prepared and published for UNESCO by the Internation-al Folk Music Council in association with Oxford Univ. Press, 1954. 201 p.

Part I: "Commercial records," a listing of the commercially recorded discs of ethnic and folk music, arranged by continent and by country. Part II: "Recordings held by institutions," a survey of the major collec-tions of ethnic and folk music in libraries and research institutions throughout the world. Statistical summary of their holdings; addresses, names of chief administrators.

**2872. Archives of Recorded Music. .... Series C: Ethnographical and Folk Music.
3.** Katalog der europäischen Volksmusik im Schallarchiv des Instituts
für Musikforschung Regensburg. Bearbeitet von Felix Hoerburger. Regensburg: Gustav Bosse, [1952]. 189 p.
Material grouped by country and province.

2873. Barnett, Elise B. A discography of the art music of India. Ann Arbor:
The Society for Ethnomusicology, 1975. 54 p.
315 numbered items arranged alphabetically by record label, Indexed
by sacred chants, art music (sacred and secular), Hindustāni rāg, Tāl,
performers, performing forces, dance music, folk music, and composers.

2874. Briegleb, Ann, ed. Directory of ethnomusicological sound recording
collections in the U.S. and Canada. Ann Arbor, Mich.: Society for Ethnomusicology, 1971. 46 p. (Special series, 2.)
Not a discography, but a surveys of the resources of 124 collections,
public and private. Arranged alphabetically by state. Includes a list of
institutions with "no holdings in ethnomusicology."

**2875. Etnomusica. Catalogo della musica di tradizione orale nel reistrazioni dell-
'Archivio Etnico Linguistico-Musicale della Discoteca di Stato. A cura di** Sandro
Biagiola. Roma: Discoteca di Stato, 1986. 886 p.
Succeeds the first catalog, published in 1970.
Covers over 11,000 recordings, of which perhaps 9,000 are of Italian
music "of the oral tradition,"and liturgical music of Judaism and Chris-
tianity in Italy. Indexes genres, occasions, regions and localities.
Review by Giovanni Giuriati in *Musica/Realtà,* 23 (Agosto 1987), p.
155–56.

2876. Gillis, Frank. "The incunabula of instantaneous ethnomusicological
sound recordings, 1890–1910: a preliminary list." In *Problems and solutions; occasional essays in musicology presented to Alice D. Moyle, p.
322–355. Edited by* Jamie C. Kassler and Jill Stubington. Sydney: Hale
and Iremonger, 1984.
Includes a list organized by Murdoch's *Outline of World Cultures* of
the earliest known ethnomusicological recordings and their present locations.

2877. Hickmann, Hans et Charles Grégoire, Duc de Mecklenbourg. Catalogue
d'enregistrements de musique folklorique égyptienne. Strasbourg: Heitz,
1958. 78 p. (Collection d'études musicologiques, 37.)
Description and analysis of the contents of a recorded collection of
Egyptian folk music assembled in 1955. 211 items. Preceded by a discussion of the music and instruments employed.

2878. Indiana. University. Archives of Traditional Music. A catalog of phonore-
cordings of music and oral data held by the Archives of Traditional
Music. Boston: G. K. Hall, 1975. 541 p.
Photoreproduction of the card catalog of this extensive collection. The
reduction ratio is so great that reading is difficult. Indexes recording
companies, collectors, depositors, performers and "informers."

2879. Indiana. University. Archives of Traditional Music. Native North American music and oral data: a catalogue of sound recordings, 1893–1976; by Dorothy Sara Lee, foreword by Willard Rhodes. Bloomington: Indiana University Press, 1979. 463 p.

A guide to native North American music and oral data holdings at the Indiana University Archives of Traditional Music. Includes indexes.

2880. International Institute for Comparative Music Studies and Documentation, Berlin, compiler. Oriental music: a selected discography. New York: Foreign Material Center, University of the State of New York, State Education Department and National Council of Associations for International Studies, 1971. 100 p. (Foreign Area Material Center: Occasional Publication, 16)

2881. Library of Congress. Music Division. Archive of American Folk Song. Checklist of recorded songs in the English language in the Archive . . . to July 1940. Washington: Library of Congress, Division of Music, 1942. 3 v. in 1.

A guide to the holdings of one of the world's great folk song collections. Songs listed by title, with name of singer, collector, and date of recording. The third volume is a geographical index.

2882. Library of Congress. Music Division. Recording Laboratory. Folk music: a catalog of folk songs, ballads, dances, instrumental pieces, and folk tales of the United States and Latin-America on phonograph records. Washington: Library of Congress, [1964]. 107 p.

Earlier listings of the same nature appeared in 1948, 1953, and 1959.

A catalog of recordings available for purchase from the Archive of American Folk Song at the Library of Congress. Presents a sampling of American folk music and tales recorded for the most part of their native environment.

2883. Lumpkin, Ben G. and N. L. McNeil. Folksongs on records. . . . Issue three, cumulative, including essential material in issues one and two. Boulder, Col.: Folksongs on Records, 1950. 98 p.

Lists 700 commercially recorded discs and albums of folksong and folk music, chiefly American. Contents of discs given, with informal annotations. Useful indexes to English and Scottish ballads, spirituals, work songs, Irish songs, Mexican and Latin-American songs; numerical list of albums.

2884. Merriam, Alan P. African music on L.P. An annotated discography. Evanston, Ill.: Northwestern University Press, 1970. 200 p.

Describes and inventories the contents of some 389 recordings of African music, excluding the Hugh Tracy "Sound of Africa" series since it has been documented elsewhere. Entries are grouped by record labels. 18 indexes permit a wide variety of approaches to the information.

2885. Museum für Volkerkunde. Katalog der Tonbandaufnahmen M1-M2000 der Musikethnologischen Abteilung des Museums für Völkerkunde Berlin. Hrsg. von Dieter Christensen unter Mitarbeit von Hans-

Jurgen Jordan. Berlin: Museum für Völkerkunde, 1970. 355 p.

2886. Musics of the world: a selective discography edited by Nancy Dols; compiled under the auspices of the Ethnomusicology Archive, University of California, Los Angeles. Los Angeles: UCLA Music Library, 1977 – . 4 vols. to date. (UCLA Music Library Discography Series, 1- .)

Volumes 2 - 4 are entitled *Musics of the world.*

V. 1 covers Sub-saharan Africa, Bulgaria, Ethiopia, Guatemala, Japan, Romania, Tibet, U.S.S.R., United States, Yugoslavia.

V. 2 edited by Don Niles covers Indonesia, Korea, Oceania, Taiwan, and Thailand.

V. 3 edited by Nora Yeh covers the United States: Afro-American, European-American, Hispanic-American, and Native American musics.

V. 4 edited by Kenneth Culley includes an index.

2887. La musique traditionnelle. Établie par Chantal Nourrit et William Pruitt. Paris: Radio-France Internationale, 1979–83. 20 v. in 2 series.

Each volume provides introductory essays on aspects of music in the area in question, followed by annotated discographies of 78 rpm and 33 1/3 rpm disks arranged by record manufacturer. There are indexes to ethnic groups, instruments, performers and authors, location, to historic and legendary people, to subjects, and to record titles. Each volume includes a bibliography. The volumes range from c. 60 p. to 260 p. There are two series:

La musique traditionnelle de l'Ocean Indien: v. 1—Ile Maurice; v. 2.— Seychelles; v. 3: Madagascar.

La musique traditionnelle de Afrique Noire: v. 1—Mali; v. 2—Haute-Volta; v. 3—Mauritanie; v. 4—Senegal/Gambia; v. 5—Niger; v. 6—Côte D'Ivoire; v. 7—Benin; v. 8—Togo; v. 9—Cameroun; v. 10—Tchad; v. 11— Centrafrique; v. 12—Gabon; v. 13—Congo; v. 14—Zaire; v. 15—Burundi; v. 16—Rwanda; v. 17—Djibouti.

2888. Quinn, Jennifer Post. An index to the field recordings in the Flanders Ballad Collection at Middlebury College, Middlebury, Vermont. Middlebury: Middlebury College, 1983. 242 p.

An index to a collection focused on New England folk song which was gathered by Helen Hartness Flanders and others during the period 1930–58. There is a history of the collection and a bibliography of sources. Entries include title as given by the performer, uniform title (or the commonly known title), name and location of the performer and location of the recording in the collection. Indexes to titles, uniform titles, performers and locations.

See the article "The Helen Hartness Flanders Ballad Collection, Middlebury College" by Dale Cockrell in *Notes,* 39 (1983), p. 31–42, for description of the collection.

2889. Stone, Ruth and Frank J. Gillis. African music and oral data: a catalog of field recordings, 1902–1975. Bloomington: Indiana University Press, 1976. 412 p.

Includes a catalog of collectors. Indexes to countries, cult repositories, and subjects.

2890. Tracey, Hugh. Catalogue of the Sound of Africa series; 210 long playing records of music and songs from Central, Eastern, and Southern Afric. Roodepoort, South Africa: International Library of African Music, 1973. 2 v.

Volume one is an extensive introduction to the recordings in the *Sound of Africa* series and thus to the musical cultures; it includes data on instruments, language zones, and scales. Volume 2 is the catalog. Recordings were made in the field 1929-c. 1963.

2891. Tudor, Dean and Nancy Tudor. Grass roots music. Littleton, Colo.: Libraries Unlimited, 1979. 367 p. (American popular music on Elpee)

A discography of American folk music and folk songs, including country music and bluegrass music.

2892. Tudor, Dean, Nancy Tudor. Black music. Littleton, Colo.: Libraries Unlimited, 1979. 262 p. (American popular music on Elpe)

A discography of Afro-American music.

2893. Waterhouse, David. "Hogaku preserved: a select list of long-playing records issued by Japanese record companies of the national music of Japan." In *Recorded sound,* no. 33 (Jan. 1969), p. 383–402.

CURRENT OR ANNUAL DISCOGRAPHIES

Current listings and record reviews are in abundant supply. There are periodicals, such as *High Fidelity,* the *American Record Guide,* and *The Gramophone,* devoted exclusively to the interests of record collectors. For a description of some 30 foreign periodicals devoted to recordings, see no. 829.

2894. Bielefelder Katalog; Katalog der Schallplatten klassischer Musik. Bielefelder Katalog Jazz; Verzeichnis der Jazz-schallplatten. Bielefeld: Bielefelder Verlagsanstalt, 1962– .

The German equivalent to *The Schwann,* with superior analytics and indexing.

2895. Deutsche Bibliographie: Musiktonträger-Verzeichnis. Frankfurt am Main: Buchhändler-Vereinigung, 1978– .

Successsor to the Deutsche Bibliographie: *Schallplatten-Verzeichnis, the Musiktonträger-Verzeichnis* is a monthly publication with with an annual composer/title index.

The premiere national discography, recording not only sound recordings published in the Bundes Republik Deutschland, but distributed there. The depth and accuracy of indexing is impressive. *Musiktonträger-Verzeichnis Musiktonträger-Verzeichnis*

2896. Diapason: Catalogue général. Paris: Diapason-microsillon, 1956– .

Title varies: *Catalogue disques et cassettes Diapason; Catalogue génér-*

al de musique classique et de diction.
The French equivalent to *The Schwann.*

2897. Gramophone classical catalogue. Gramophone popular record catalogue. Harrow, Middlesex, England: General Gramophone Publications,
1953– .
Title varies: *Gramophone long playing classical record catalogue.*
The British version of *The Schwann,* with substantially better analysis
of anthologies and more extensive indexing.

2898. Gramophone Shop, Inc., Record Supplement. V. 1:1 (Jan. 1938)-17:2 (Feb.
1954).
Title varies: 1939, *Record reviews.* (Cover title: *Record supplement.*)
Extensively annotated listing of the major releases in the field of serious music. Confined chiefly to 78 rpm discs. A monthly publication.

2899. High Fidelity Record Annual. Edited by Roland Gelatt. Philadelphia: J.
B. Lippincott, 1955– .
Title varies: from 1957, *Records in review. Great Barrington, Mass.,
Wyeth Press. Editor, 1957:* Joan Griffiths. Editor, 1958–60: Frances New-
bury.
A yearly compilation of reviews from *High fidelity* magazine. Record-
ings arranged alphabetically by composer, with a section on "Collections
and miscellany." Signed reviews by *High fidelity* contributors.

**2900. "Index of Record Reviews, with symbols indicating opinions of reviewers."
In** *Notes,* 5 (March 1948)- .
Since its inception, this index has been a regular feature. Compiled
chiefly by Kurtz Myers until recently with the assistance of various specialists from time to time. A valuable guide to record selection for libraries and for private collectors. The quarterly appearances of this column
have been cumulated; see no. 2901.
The current compiler for the column in *Notes* is Richard Le Sueur. He
has included compact discs in the column.

2901. Myers, Kurtz. Index to record reviews; based on material originally
published in *Notes, the journal of the Music Library Association* between 1949 and 1977. Boston: G. K. Hall, 1978. 5 v.
Supersedes the edition of Crown Publishers by Myers and Richard S.
Hill issued in 1956. Continued by *Index to record reviews, 1978–1983,*
compiled and edited by Kurtz Myers and issued by G. K. Hall, 1985. 873
p. and by the monthly column in *Notes.*
Index to Record Reviews is a guidebook to a huge body of critical
writing about recordings. Reviews from about 50 periodicals and other
sources, specialized in music and general, have been indexed.

> The index has two sections. The first and longer is primarily a listing by
> composer. The second section, "composite releases," is necessary for handling
> records containing works by more than one composer. The entries here are
> arranged alphabetically under the name of the manufacturer, and then seri-
> ally by the manufacturer's number. The names of composers appearing in
> this second list are indexed in volume five which also affords access to the first
> four volumes by manufacturer's label and number, and by performer. [from

the *Introduction*]

The compiler has taken great pains to clarify and verify information about discs and their contents. This is a major reference work in the field of discography.

2902. Polart Index to Record Reviews. Detroit: Polart, 1960– .
An annual publication indexing all record and tape reviews published in the major journals. No evaluations, but the length of the review is indicated. Main entries under composer, with separate sections for collections and for "pop and jazz" recordings.

2903. The Schwann [record and tape guide]. Boston: ABC Schwann Publications, c1949– .
A publication with several variant titles: *New Schwann record & tape guide; Schwann-1, record & tape guide; Schwann-2, record & tape guide.*
A monthly guide to currently available musical sound recordings in North Americ. The main section is arranged by composer. There are sections for anthologies, jazz and popular music. The triennial *Schwann Artist Issue* provides access by performer; names occur in sections by performing specialty. All forms of recorded sound are included.

SPECIALIZED DISCOGRAPHIES

2904. American Music on Records. A catalogue of recorded American music currently available. Prepared in cooperation with the Committee on Recordings of American Music of the National Music Council. New York: American Music Center, [1956]. 39 p.
A composer listing in alphabetical order, with references to published scores and parts if available.

2905. American Society of Composers, Authors and Publishers. 30 years of motion picture music, the big Hollywood hits from 1928–1958. New York: ASCAP, (1959?). 122 p.

2906. American Society of Composers, Authors and Publishers. 40 years of show tunes, the big Broadway hits from 1917–57. New York: ASCAP, [1958]. 149 p.
Chronological list of recorded show tunes arranged alphabetically under year of production. Composer, publisher, performing artist, and record number given. Title index.

2907. Band Record Guide. Alphabetical listing of band records by title of composition, composer, performing group, and record title. 1969 edition. Evanston, Ill.: The Instrumentalist Co., (c. 1969). 102 p.
Indexes 1,480 works by title; 574 composers, 170 bands. There is also a listing of record manufacturers and distributors.

2908. Celletti, Rodolfo. Il teatro d'opera in disco. Milano: Rizzoli, 1976. 614 p.

"The first catalog of all complete opera recordings with commentary on execution and interpretation." [from the forward]

Each citation provides original and re-issue numbers. Anthologies of recorded excerpts are included.

2909. Cohn, Arthur. The collector's twentieth-century music in the Western Hemisphere. Philadelphia: Lippincott, [1961]. 256 p.

One of the best discographies of contemporary music. Well annotated; full coverage for American composers.

2910. Cohn, Arthur. Twentieth-century music in Western Europe, the compositions and the recordings. Philadelphia and New York: J. B. Lippincott, [1956]. 510 p.

Part I, p. 3–345: discussion of the compositions of 30 contemporary European composers. Part II, p. 349–510: entries for the recordings of the works discussed in the preceding section. The records are graded from "poor" to "exceptional" in performance quality. The annotations in this section are devoted almost entirely to observations on performance.

2911. Creighton, James. Discopaedia of the violin, 1889–1971. Toronto: University of Toronto Press, 1974. 987 p.

A discography of the recordings of nearly 1,800 violinists. Main entries by artist, with recorded works listed alphabetically by composer. Indexed by composer and by popular names of the compositions.

2912. Davies, Hugh. "A discography of electronic music and musique concrète." In *Recorded sound, journal of the British Institute of Recorded Sound,* no. 14 (April 1964), p. 205–24.

Fully annotated listings of records and tapes; addresses of distributors and index of compositions.

2913. Davis, Eizabeth A. Index to the *New World Recorded Anthology of American Music*; a user's guide to the initial one hundred records. N.Y.: Norton, 1981. 235 p.

A guide to the contents of a series of recordings of concert music by American composers supported by the Rockefeller Foundation as part of the American Bicentennial celebration. There is a master index providing a description of each record in numerical order and four indexes: names and titles of all recorded works; subjects and authors in the liner notes; genres and performing forces; dates of composition. *New World Recorded Anthology of American Music*—Index

2914. Frasier, Jane. Women composers; a discography. Detroit: Information Coordinators, 1983. 308 p. (Detroit Studies in Music Bibliography, 50)

Covering 337 composers or art music. Indexes to recording company, genres, titles. Bibliography.

2915. International Roman Catholic Association for Radiodiffusion and Television. Catalogue du disque de musique religieuse. Préf. de J. Schneuwly; introd. de Jean-Michel Hayoz. Edité par UNDA, Association catholique internationale pour la radiodiffusion et la télévision. Fribourg, [1956]. 300 p.

2916. Kondracki, Miroslaw, Marta Stankiewicz, and Frits C. Weiland. International Diskographie elektronischer Musik. International electronic music discography. Discographie internationale de la musique électronique. Mainz, etc.: Schott, 1979. 174 p.

Arranged by composer. Includes information about dates of recording and names of studios. Index to names.

2917. Kratzenstein, Marilou and Jerald Hamilton. Four centuries of organ music; an annotated discography. Detroit: Information Coordinators, 1984. 308 p. (Detroit Studies in Music Bibliography, 51)

Analyzing recordings of organ music from the Robertsbridge Codex through J.S.Bach. Indexes of organs, performers, and composers.

2918. Kroó, György. "New Hungarian music" in *Notes,* 39 (1983), p. 43–71.

An annotated discography of the works of contemporary Hungarian composers in the period 1969–82.

2919. Laster, James H. A discography of treble voice recordings. Metuchen: Scarecrow Press, 1985. 147 p.

2920. Maleady, Antoinette, O.. Record and tape reviews index 1971–74. Metuchen, N.J.: Scarecrow Press, 1972–75. 4 v.

16 periodicals indexed. Section I: a listing of reviews by composer. Section II: reviews of music in collections, listed under record labels. Section III: spoken recordings.

Succeeded by her *Index to record and tape reviews,* a classical music buying guide, published by Chulain press in San Anselmo, California, 1976–.

2921. Schweizer Musik auf Schallplatten. Musique suisse sur disques. Swiss music on records. Zürich: Schweizerishes Musik-Archiv, 1979. 79 p.

2922. Smart, James R. The Sousa band: a discography. Washington: Library of Congress, 1970. 123 p.

COMPOSER DISCOGRAPHIES

2923. Bloch, Francine. Francis Poulenc, 1928–1982. Paris: Bibliothèque nationale, Département de la phonothèque nationale et de l'audiovisuel, 1984. 255 p. (Phonographies, 2)

Includes a discography of Poulenc as performer.

2924. Nectoux, Jean Michel. Gabriel Fauré: 1900–1977. Paris: Bibliothèque nationale, Département de la phonothèque nationale et de l'audiovisuel, 1979. 262 p. (Phonographies, 1)

DEBUSSY, CLAUDE

2925. Cobb, Margaret G. Discographie de l'œuvre de Claude Debussy (1902
–1950). Geneva: Editions Minkoff, 1975. 120 p. (Publications du Centre de
Documentation Claude Debussy, 1)
   Brief review by Stephen M. Fry in *Notes,* 32 (1975), p. 301. Review by
James R. Briscoe in *Notes,* 34 (1978), p. 862–65.

STRAVINSKY, IGOR

2926. Igor Strawinsky (1882–1971) Phonographie. Seine Eigeninterpre-
tation auf Schallplatten und in den euopäischen Rundfunkanstalten,
zusammen mit einem Verzeichnis der in den deutschen Rundfunkanstalten und im Deutschen Rundfunkarchiv vorhandenen Rundfunk-
produktionen und historischen Schallplattenaufnahmen von
Strawinsky-Werken. Frankfurt am Main: Deutsches Rundfunkarchiv,
1972. 216 p.

Yearbooks and Directories

Publications appearing under the title "Yearbook" can take a variety of forms. They may be annual volumes issued by learned societies, as, for example, the Spanish *Annuario musical*, the British *Proceedings of the Royal Musical Association*, the Swiss *Schweizerisches Jahrbuch für Musikwissenschaft*, or the *Jahrbuch für Liturgik und Hymnologie*. They may be annual volumes issued by music publishing houses such as C. F. Peters, Simrock, or Breitkopf & Härtel; or they may be publications of societies devoted to the work of a particular composer, as, for example, *Bach Jahrbuch, Handel Jahrbuch, Mozart Jahrbuch,* or *Haydn Jahrbuch*. Finally, they may be directories or compilations of factual information covering a specific year. Works of this latter kind have been emphasized in the following, highly selective list. Yearbooks in this sense are often useful for reference purposes, since they provide data on current musical activities and personalities difficult to find otherwise. It should be remembered That the titles listed in this chapter are exemplars of their types; conscientious bibliographic sleuthing should reveal the presence of works of this genre on many subjects, societies, regions, and persons not found here.

2927. Adelmann, Marianne. Musical Europe; an illustrated guide to musical life in 18 European countries. N.Y.: Paddington Pres, 1974. 447 p.

2928. The American musical directory, 1861 with a new introduction by Barbara Owen. New York: Da Capo Press, 1980. 260 p.
Reprint of the original published in New York by Hutchinson, 1861.

2929. American Musicological Society. Directory of members and subscribers. Philadelphia: American Musicological Society, 1983– . pagination varies.
Annual publication listing members and subscribers separately.

2930. L'Année musicale; publiée par mm. Michel Brenet [pseud. used by Marie Bobillier], J. Chantavoine, L. Laloy, L. de La Laurencie. . . . 1.-3. année; 1911–13. Genève: Minkoff Reprints, 1972. 3 v.
Réimpression des éditions de Paris, 1912–1914. No more published.
Includes section "Bibliographie" and "Bibliographie des bibliographies musicales": v. 3, p. [1]-152.

2931. Annuaire du Spectacle, cinéma, théâtre, télévision & radio, musique, va-riétés. [1.]-27. année; 1942/43–1973 Paris: Editions Roault, 1942–73. 27 v.
With numerous pages of photos and indexes.
A yearbook of the French world of entertainment, emphasizing the commercial aspects. All areas are treated, including theater, cinema, music, radio, and television.

2932. Annuaire National de la Musique, 1967–68. Paris: Annuaire National de la Musique, (1970). 677 p.
Classified listings of names, with addresses, of people associated with musical activities, including performers of all kinds, editors, printers, societies and associations.

2933. Annuaire OGM, 1970. Industries et commerces de radio, télévision, elec-tronique, electroacoustique, musique. Paris: Horizons de France. 61e année, 1970. 532, 880 p.
An annual directory of the French audio-television industries. Includes listings of dealers and manufacturers of musical instruments.

2934. Annuario del Teatro Lirico Italiano, 1940– . Pubblicazione ufficiale della Federazione Nazionale Fascista dei Lavoratori dello Spettacolo. Milano: Edizioni Corbaccio, 1940– . 737 p.
A compendium of facts related to the Italian lyric theater, including opera companies, legal aspects, theaters, artists (with portraits), index of interpreters for the standard repertory, instrumentalists, statistics on performances.

2935. Annuario Generale della Musica Italiana. Rassegna delle attivita lirico-concertistiche in Italia. Prima edizione 1968–69. Tito Chelazzi, direttore. ALber-to Calcagno, condirettore. Roma, 1970– . 174 p.

2936. Annuario musicale italiano, 1981– . Rome: Centro Italiano di Iniziativa Musicale (CIDIM), 1981– .
1981—353 p. 1982/83—590 p.
Divided into 9 sections, the annual cites events of importance in the Italian musical scene. There are short essays on matters of current inter-est (e.g. "Rock e jazz in Italia," Ethnomusicologia in Italia").
The 9 sections are: Produzione e distribuzione (citing programs at op-era theaters, concert halls, and the like); stato e regioni (covering laws and governmental matters); sindacati e associazioni; didattica e aggi-oramento (including a directory of music libraries and archives); autori e interpreti (directories arranged by specialty); editoria e stampa (direc-tories including musicologists, periodicals, and publishers); negozie e fabbriche (directories); Europa musica (including a very useful list of national and international musical associations of all sorts); *Italia: altre espressioni musicali* (a section of essays).
The second year (1982/83) featured more sections including a list of books on music published since 1981 and a list of periodicals on music with extensive descriptions.

2937. Association for Recorded Sound Collections. A preliminary directory of sound recordings collections in the United States and Canada. Prepared by a committee of the Association for Recorded Sound Collections. New York: New York Public Library, 1967. 157 p.

Preface written "for the Committee" by Jean Bowen.

Collections listed alphabetically by state. Addresses given; brief information as to content of collections. Many private collectors listed.

2938. Australian Directory of Music Research. Edited by Philip J. Drummond. With a foreword by Barry S. Brook. Sydney: Australia Music Centres, 1978. 399 p.

A publication celebrating the birth of interest in music research in Australia. The *Directory* consists of three parts: a section of biographies of Australian scholars; abstracts of current literature; and a subject/author index.

2939. Bowles, Garrett H. Directory of music library automation projects. 2nd edition. Philadelphia: Music Library Association, 1979. 23 p. (MLA Technical Reports, 2)

A listing of automated information storage and retrieval systems projects underway in North American music libraries.

2940. British music yearbook. London [etc.]: Bowker, 1975– .

Continues *The Music yearbook.*

Arthur Jacobs, ed. "A survey and directory with statistics and reference articles." Covers most aspects of musical life in Great Britain, including radio and television performances. Directories of performers, associations, concert and rehearsal halls, music publishers, critics, festivals, and competitions.

2941. Brody, Elaine and Claire Brook. The music guide to Austria and Germany. N.Y.: Dodd Mead, 1975. 271 p.

This guide and the three following titles describe concert halls, conservatories, libraries, museums, musical organizations, and musical businesses of the major cities of each country. Included also is information about festivals, competitions, societies, journals, and available services. Addresses, telephone numbers, schedules, hours of opening are provided. For the musical tourist, scholar, and reference librarian.

Review by Stephen M. Fry in *Notes,* 34 (1978), p. 619.

2942. Brody, Elaine and Claire Brook. The music guide to Belgium, Luxembourg, Holland and Switzerland. N.Y.: Dodd Mead, 1977. 156 p.

See annotation to no. 2941, above.

2943. Brody, Elaine and Claire Brook. The music guide to Great Britain: England, Scotland, Wales, Ireland. N.Y.: Dodd Mead, 1975. 240 p.

See annotation to no. 2941, above.

2944. Brody, Elaine and Claire Brook. The music guide to Italy. N.Y.: Dodd Mead, 1978. 233 p.

See annotation for no. 2941, above.

2945. Contemporary Music Almanac 1980/81. Edited by Ronald Zalkind. N.Y.: Schirmer Books, 1980. 947 p.

"The *Contemporary music almanac* is about rock music and the people who make it."

Rock events of 1979, monthly lists of rock albums, directories of record companies, producers, studios, managers, agents, awards. Bibliography of books on the subject by R. Serge Denisoff. Projected on an annual basis, only this volume issued. Contains a variety of facts, biographical notices, and the like about rock, popular, and other commercial music.

Review by Victor Cardell in *Notes,* 37 (1980), p. 329–30.

2946. Directory of American and foreign contemporary operas and American opera premieres, 1967–1975. N.Y.: Central Opera Service, 1975. 66 p.

An issue of the *Central Opera Service Bulletin,* v. 17, no. 2 (Winter, 1975).

Brief review by Stephen M. Fry in *Notes,* 32 (1976), p. 555.

2947. Directory of music faculties in colleges and universities, U. S. and Canada. 1967/68– ; 1st ed.- . Boulder, Colorado: College Music Society, 1968– .

A biennial. Originally compiled and edited as *Directory of music faculties in American colleges and universities* by Harry B. Lincoln, began publication with the volume for 1967–1968. Craig R. Short subsequently edited the *Directory.*

A directory of 11,800 teachers of music in 1,100 instions. Part I: departmental listing by state and school. Part II: Listings by areas of specialization. Part III: national alphabetical listings.

Review of the 1967–68 edition by Rey. M. Longyear in *Journal of research in music education,* 16 (1968), p. 220–21.

2948. Directory of music librarians in the United States and Canada; a preliminary edition compiled by the Membership Committee of the Music Library Association. Edited by Don Phillips. Ann Arbor: Music Library Association, 1976. 46 p.

An alphabetical list identifying each librarian's area(s) of special responsibility.

2949. "Directory of National Music Centers." Compiled by Keith MacMillan. In *Notes,* 27 (1971), p. 680–693.

Describes the history, organization, and services of 19 music information centers: Australia, Austria, Belgium, Canada, Czechoslovakia, Denmark, Finland, France, Federal Republic of Germany, Iceland, Israel, The Netherlands, Norway, Poland, Portugal, Sweden, Switzerland, United Kingdom, and United States.

2950. Douglas, John R. "Musician and composer societies: a world directory" in *Notes,* 34 (1978), p. 39–51.

An updated version of the 1974 directory. Arranged alphabetically by names of composers and musicians.

Supplemented in "Societies devoted to individual musicians and composers: a world directory" in *Cum notis variorum,* no. 83 (June 1984), p. 5–12, by Douglas.

2951. Farrell, Susan Caust. Directory of contemporary musical intrument makers. Colombia: University of Missouri Press, 1981. 216 p.

Alphabetical directory, list of makers by instrument, and state appendices list schools and societies. Bibliography.

2952. Felton, Gary S. Record collector's international directory. N.Y.: Crown, 1980. 365 p.

An international directory of record dealers, but with a focus on those in English-speaking countries. Lists journals and newsletters. List of directories and guides. Index of dealers by specialties.

2953. Finell, Judith Greenberg. The contemporary music performance directory; a listing of American performing ensembles, sponsoring organizations, performing facilities, concert series and festivals of 20th-century music. N.Y.: American Music Center, 1975. 238 p.

A useful contact guide produced under the auspices of the American Music Center.

Brief review by Stephen M. Fry in *Notes,* 32, (1976), p. 780–81.

2954. Flemming, Bill. Directory of Australian music organisations. 3rd ed. Sydney: Australia Music Centre, 1985. 67 p.

Previously published in 1978 and 1980.

Indexed.

2955. Gardeton, César. Annales de la musique: ou, Almanach musical pour l'an 1819 et 1820. Genève: Minkoff Reprint, 1978. 322, 318 columns (Archives de L'Édition musicale française, 5)

Reprint of the edition of Paris, 1819–20.

An almanac of musical events, including the publishing of music in Paris.

2956. Gids van muziekbibliotheken en fonotheken in Nederland. Samengesteld onder auspicién van de sektie muziekbibliotheken en fonotheken. 2e herz. druk. 's-Gravenhage: Nederlands Bibliotheek en Lektuurcentrum, 1976. 1 v. (unpaged)

First edition issued in 1975. Also known as *Muziekbibliotheken en fonotheken.*

A directory of Dutch music libraries and phonorecord collections. Describes collections in basic terms, relates services, hours of opening, addresses and telephone numbers.

2957. Goertz, Harald. Musikhandbuch für Österreich; Struktur und Organisation in 2,500 Stichworten Namen, Addresses, Information. Eine Publikation des Österreichischen Musikraten. Wien; München: Doblinger, 1983. 157 p.

Previously published in 1971 by Jugend und Volk Verlag, Munich. 349 p.

A classified directory. Entries provide brief descriptions of organizational function. Index to designated historical sites by composers' names. Index to names of organizations.

2958. Guía de la música argentina. 1971/72– . Buenos Aires: Instituto Luccheli Bonadeo, .
An annual which serves as a directory of music and musicians in the Argentine Republic.

2959. Gusikoff, Lynne. Guide to musical Americ. N.Y.: Facts on file, 1984. 347 p.
> ... Historic highlights of different styles of music as they developed in particular regions of the United States at various times; and to certain geographical locations where one may hear different styles of music today ... [*Introduction*]

Entries displayed by geographic area, each section beginning with an explanatory essay. Directories of performing arts centers, festivals and other public musical locations.

2960. Hewlett, Walter B., and Eleanor Selfridge-Field. Directory of computer assisted research in musicology. Menlo Park: Center for Computer Assisted Research in the Humanities, 1986. 86 p.
Originally issued in 1985 in 56 p.
Includes a review article "Printing music by computer" and numerous illustrations of the state of the art. There is a section devoted to brief notices on activities and studies pertaining to computer-assisted musicology. Current applications are categorized and described in some detail. There is a short bibliography of recent literature and a list of names and addresses cited in the directory.

2961. Hinrichsen's Musical Year Book, 1944–61. London: Hinrichsen Edition, Ltd., 1944–61. 11 v.
A series of volumes edited by Max Hinrichsen, issued at irregular intervals, remarkably varied in content. The articles range from trivia to substantial contributions by recognized authorities. Most of the volumes contain bibliographies of current music publications as well as numerous lists, illustrations, chronologies. More recent volumes have been organized about some central theme, i.e., vol. 8, "The organ of Bach and matters related to this subject" (1956); vol. 9, "John Gay and the Ballad Opera" (1956); vol. 10, "Organ and choral aspects and prospects" (1958). Vol. 11 (1961) contains the papers read at the Joint Congress of the International Association of Music Libraries and the Galpin Society, Cambridge, 1959.

2962. International Association of Sound Archives. Directory of member archives compiled by Grace Koch. London: The Association, c1982. 174 p. (Special publication, 3)
First edition edited by Ann Briegleb and Don Niles and published 1978. 94 p.
Extensive entries modeled on the *RISM* Series C directories to music collections.

2963. International Council of Museums. International directory of musical instrument collections; edited by Jean Jenkins [for the International Council of Museums]. Buren: F. Knuf for [the] International Council of

Museums, 1977. 166 p.

2964. International Directory of Music Education Institutions. Paris: UNESCO, 1968. 115 p.

A source book of information compiled by the International Society for Music Education for UNESCO. Covers 10 categories:

1. Conservatories and academies of music.
2. Music and music education schools or faculties in universities.
3. Other music institutions.
4. International music and music education workshops, summer courses, teacher-training courses.
5. International competitions.
6. International music festivals.
7. Music libraries, archives and documentation centers of international standing.
8. Collections of musical instruments.
9. Organizations, societies and institutions of music and music education.
10. National and international music periodicals.

2965. International Folk Music Council. The International folk directory of ethnic music and related traditions: a world listing of regional archives, institutes, and organizations, together with individual collectors, concerned wholly, or in part, with recording, documenting, and disseminating information about authentic local folk music and related tradtional arts, crafts, and customs, etc. Totnes, England: Published for the International Folk Music Council, with the assistance of the Calouste Gulbenkian Foundation by the Dartington Institute of Traditional Arts, 1973. c. 200 p.

First publ. in 1964 under title: *Directory of institutions and organisations concerned wholly or in part with folk music.*

2966. International music guide, 1977– . Edited by Derek Elley. London: Tantivy Press; South Brunswick, New Jersey and New York: A. S. Barnes, 1976– .

Publisher varies.

Intended to be "a readable annual surveying internationally all points of interest to the modern concert goer and general music-lover." Edited successively by Elley (through 1981), Jane Dudman (1981–85), and Hugh Canning (1986–).

Several sections: musicians of the year; world survey (arranged by country); music festivals; musical necrology; non-classified reports (by genre); recorded music scene; audio reports; music shops; music schools; book reviews; music in print; music magazines.

No section attempts comprehensive or systematic coverage. Sections have been added and deleted through the course of this annual publication. Usually includes a guide to music festivals.

2967. Jackson, Paul T. Collectors' contact guide, 1975. Peoria: Recorded Sound Research, 1975. 58 p. (Record collectors' source book, 3)

Bibliography: p. 46–58.

Brief review by Stephen M. Fry in *Notes,* 32 (1975), p. 302.

2968. Jackson, Paul T. Sound search: recording occasional papers. Peoria: Recorded Sound Research, 1976. 35 p. (Record collectors source book, 5)

"How to find out if something has been recorded, and if so, who has done it. For radio broadcasts, Watergate recordings, the women's movement, organ music, etc." [from the *Preface*

2969. Jahrbuch der Musikwelt. The yearbook of the music world. Annuaire du monde musical. 1. Jahrgang, 1949–50. Bayreuth: Verlag Julius Steeger, 1949. 696 p.

Only one volume published. Contains a vast amount of information regarding musicians and musical institutions throughout the world. Contents include a classified listing of German music dissertations, 1885–1948; a chronology of music dictionaries and encyclopedias; a list of European music periodicals, 1945–48; a bibliography of German music and writings on music, etc.

2970. Kajanef, Marc. L'Année de la musique. Paris: Éditions Stock, 1979. 560 p.

An almanac beginning with a very large directory of persons and events important in the French, and particularly Parisian, musical scene. Other sections cover special topics (e.g. Musique à lire, Profil de France-musique). Index to names.

2971. Kemp's international music & recording industry year book; a comprehensive reference and marketing guide to the music and recording industry in Great Britain and overseas. v.1– 1965– London: Kemps Group, 1965– .

Title varies: 1965–197?, *Kemp's music & recording industry yearbook.* Known also as the *International music & recording industry year book* and the *Music & recording industry year book.*

Brief review by Stephen M. Fry in *Notes,* 32 (1975), p. 302–03.

2972. MacMillan, Keith. "Directory of national music centers," with a foreword by Andre Jurres, in *Notes,* 27 (1971), p. 680–93.

Describes the work of 19 national music centers, giving their histories and discussing their services and publications.

2973. Mapp, Edward. Directory of blacks in the performing arts. Metuchen: Scarecrow Press, 1978. 428 p.

A classified directory with entries including brief biographical and career information for about 800 performers. Most of these persons are American and contemporary, but persons from other countries and historical figures are listed. Much of the information about living persons was gathered by questionnaire.

2974. Music industry directory. 7th ed., 1983. Chicago: Marquis, 1983. 678p. Formerly the Musician's guide, issued 1954–80.

... provides comprehensive coverage of the music industry. It contains descriptive listings for service and professional organizations, schools and colleges, competitions, periodicals, festivals, libraries, and foundations, as well as addresses and 'phone numbers for hundreds of music businesses. [from the *Preface*]

Index to music publishers and general index.

2975. Music Library Association. New England Chapter. Directory of music libraries and collections in New England [compiled and edited by the Publications Committee of the Music Library Association, New England Chapter. 7th ed. New London: Greer Music Library, Connecticut College, 1985. 100 p.

A guide to the holdings, services,and facilities of music libraries in New England.

2976. Music Library Association. Southern California Chapter. A directory of special music collections in Southern California libraries and in the libraries of the University of California and the California State Universities and Colleges. Compiled by the Music Library Survey Committee. Edited by Don L. Hixon. Rev. ed. *s.l.*: Music Library Association, Southern California Chapter, 1976. 36 p.

2977. The Music Magazine/Musical Courier. The annual directory of the concert world. Evanston, Ill.: Summy-Birchard Co., 1963– .

Editions for 1957–61 published as the mid-January issue of *Musical courier,* with title: *Directory issue of the musical arts and artists.*

The 1963 issue, edited by Max D. Jones, contains pertinent information on American and foreign music organizations, artist and concert managers, artist availability, current series and associations, orchestras, opera booking organizations, festivals, foundations, schools of music, publishers, periodicals, recording firms, and music dealers.

2978. The music yearbook; a survey and directory with statistics and reference articles. Edited by Arthur Jacobs. 1972/3– . London: Macmillan; St. Martin's Press, 1972– .

Publisher varies.

Principal focus is on London and the rest of Great Britain. Directories of overseas musical scene organized by country. Occasional practical essays ("The musicians and income tax").

Marianne Barton succeeded Jacobs as editor in 1981.

2979. Musical America. [Annual directory or Annual booking edition.] New York: Music Publications, Ltd.

A special annual issue devoted chiefly to advertising performing artists, but editions in recent years contain many special articles and lists.

2980. Musical America International directory of the performing arts. Great Barrington, Mass: ABC Leisure Magazines, 1974– .

Continues *Musical America directory of performing arts* and was first issued as a special issue of *Musical America.*

International in scope, but focused most heavily on North America. Intended for use by agents, impresarios, and concert hall managers, the directory lists orchestras, dance and opera companies, choral groups, festivals, music schools, contests, foundations and awards, publishers, professional organizations, managers, and magazines and trade papers amid a welter of advertisements. Index of advertisers.

2981. The Musician's Guide: the directory of the world of music. 1972 ed. Gladys S. Field, editor-in-chief. New York: Music Information Service, Inc., 1972. 1,013 p.

First issued in 1955. 3rd ed., 1957; 4th ed., 1968.

A classified directory of names connected with all phases of commercial music activity. Contains more than 50 rosters of persons, organizations, activities, and businesses concerned with the musical profession.

Review of the 1957 edition by Richard S. Hill in *Notes,* 14 (1957), p. 111–13; of the 1968 edition by Thor Wood and Neil Ratliff in *Notes,* 25 (1969), p. 736–37; also reviewed in *The Booklist and subscription books bulletin,* Dec. 1, 1972, p. 307–8.

2982.   Musiol, Karol. "Bibliothèques des conservatoires, académies, et écoles de musique" in *Fontes artis musicae,* 22 (1975), p. 97–154.

A compendium of information on such libraries. International in scope.

2983.   The National directory for the performing arts and civic centers. Beatrice Handel, editor; Janet W. Spencer, associate editor ... [et al.]. 3d ed. New York: J. Wiley, 1978. 1,049 p.

First edition published in Dallas by Handel, 1973. 604 p.

Covers the United States. Organized by state and then by locality. Data on facilities, organizations devoted to instrumental music, vocal music, theater, dance, etc. Key management personnel listed.

2984.   Neue Musik in der Bundesrepublik Deutschland. Dokumentation. 1953– . Köln: Gesellschaft für Neue Musik, Sektion Bundesrepublik Deutschland der Internationalen Gesellschaft für Neue Musik, 1953– .

A biennial source book of information about the performance of new music in Germany. Preliminary group of essays; the accomplishments and the programs of regional radio centers are described. New music festivals and activities supporting or featuring new music are listed by cities.

2985.   Norris, Gerald. A musical gazeteer of Great Britain and Ireland. Newton Abbot, England; North Pomfret, Vermont: David and Charles, 1981. 352 p.

Like a literary gazeteer, but dealing entirely with the homes and haunts of composers and other musicians. Arranged concentrically by region, county, and place.

2986.   Opera Annual. Edited by Harold Rosenthal. London: John Calder, 1953–54– . No. 1– .

Articles on aspects of the opera world during the current year. Attention focused on developments in Great Britain.

2987.   Pavlakis, Christopher. The American music handbook, a guide to organized musical activity in the United States. An inventory of musical resources: the people, places, and organizations. New York: Free Press, 1974. 836 p.

A directory focused on professional musicianship in the United States:

organizations, vocal and instrumental ensembles, performers, composers, festivals and awards, education, radio and television, music industries, periodicals, and management. A foreign supplement treats
international festivals·and contests, music publishers.

2988. Penney, Barbara. Music in British libraries: a directory of resources.
3rd ed. London: Library Association, 1981. 452 p.
Maureen W. Long edited the first and second editions (1971 and 1974).
The results of a broad survey of music holdings in Great Britain. Includes information about services, personnel, and hours of opening. Collections are described in some detail. Index to locations and names of
libraries. Index to composers, names of collections, and nature of collections.

2989. Pierre Key's Music Year Book, the standard music annual, 1924–38. New
York: Pierre Key, Inc., 1925–38. 6 v.
A directory of musical organizations and musicians, chiefly performers; issued irregularly over a period of 13 years. The earlier volumes are
international in scope, the later are restricted to U.S. coverage.

2990. The Purchaser's Guide to the Music Industries. Annual edition, 1897– . New
York: The Music Trades, 1897– .
Title varies: after 1958, *Directory issue. . . .*
Annual classified directory of instrument manufacturers, music pub-
lishers, engravers and printers, retail music stores, dealers in music mer-
chandise, etc. Excludes performers and performing groups.

2991. Rabin, Carol Price. A guide to music festivals in America. Revised
and enlarged edition. Stockbridge, Mass.: Berkshire Traveller, 1983. 286
p.
Covers over 150 classical and popular music festivals, providing some
history on each, names of current directors, and the focus of each. Addresses provided for tickets and for accomodations near each festival.
Rock music events are not included. Index to names of festivals.

2992. Rabin, Carol Price. Music festivals in Europe and Britain. Stock-
brisge, Mass.: Berkshire Traveller, 1984. 191 p.
Similar to the preceding title.

2993. "Register of early music" in *Early music,* v. 1– (1973–).
An annual "list of names, addresses, phone numbers and instruments
. . ." of persons engaged in playing early music, as amateurs or professional musicians. Intended to stimulate performance of early music.

2994. Ross, Anne. The opera directory. London: John Calder; New York:
Sterling Pub. Co., [1961]. 566 p.
A source book of current opera facts and figures. Introductions and
headings in six languages (English, French, German, Italian, Spanish,
Russian). Material organized under 13 headings, the most important of
which are opera singers, conductors, producers and designers, technical
staff, theaters and producing organizations, festivals, living composers,

works by living composers, librettist, colleges and schools of music, casting index, glossary.

The identical volume is issued with various foreign title pages under the imprints of publishers in Paris, Geneva, Berlin, London, New York, etc.

2995. Shteinpress, Boris S. Opernye premiery XX veka 1901–1940: slovar. Moskva: Sovetskii Kompozitor, 1983. 469 p. ; 22 cm.

A listing of first performances of 20th century operas in the Soviet Union. Includes index.

2996. Steinbeck, Hans. "Directory of Music Information Centres" in *Fontes artis musicae,* 26 (1979), p. 147–59.

Provides information on each organization including support, publications, agencies, services, and projects.

2997. Steinbeck, Hans. Schweizer Musik-Handbuch: Informationen über Struktur und Organisation des Schweizer Musiklebens. Guide musical suisse: informations sur la structure et l'organisation de la vie musicale suisse. Guide musicale svizzera: informazioni sulla struttura e l'organizzazione della vita svizzera. Zürich: Schweizerischen Musik-Archiv, 1985. 222 p.

Previously published in 1979 and 1983.

2998. A survey of musical instrument collections in the United States and Canada. Conducted by a committee of the Music Library Association: William Lichtenwanger, chairman & compiler; Dale Higbee, Cynthia Adams Hoover, Phillip T. Young. Ann Arbor: Music Library Association, 1974. 137 p.

Details on 572 collections in institutions. Information on collections of historical instruments, modern replicas, ethnic instruments, toy instruments, etc. Directory with addresses, personnel, hours of service, catalogs and bibliography. Index of instruments and classes of instruments; of cultural, geographical, and historical origins.

Review by Laurence Libin in *Notes,* 33 (1976), p. 57–59.

2999. Who's new wave in music: an illustrated encyclopedia, 1976–1982 (the first wave) compiled and edited by David Bianco. Ann Arbor: Pierian Press, 1985. 430 p.

Bibliography: p. 333–338. Includes discographies and indexes.

3000. The Year in American Music, 1946/47–1947/48. New York: Allen, Towne & Heath, [1947–48]. 2 v.

1946/47 edited by Julius Bloom; 1947/48 by David Ewen.

The first part of each volume is a chronological survey of the important musical events of the year; this is followed by a miscellany of factual information, biographical and bibliographical.

3001. The Year's Work in Music, 1947/48–1950/51. Edited by Alan Frank. London; New York: published for the British coucil by Longmans, Green & Co., 1948–51. 3 v.

Each volume contains a series of essays by various specialists on aspects of British musical life during the year: musical research, the making and playing of instruments, the British Broadcasing Corporation and contemporary music, etc. Contains an annual bibliography of published music and musical literature compiled by A. Hyatt King.

Women in Music

James B. Coover's work on music dictionaries has shown that the first of this genre devoted entirely to women was the Michaelis *Frauen als schaffende Tonkünstler: ein biographisches Lexikon* (Stettin; Leipzig, 1888). In the recent few years, there has been substantial new work on the subject and while many of the works cited in this chapter are relevant to other sections of this book, they are brought together here as well to demonstrate the extent and rapidity that scholarship on women in music has developed.

3002. Block, Adrienne Fried and Carol Neuls-Bates. Women in American music; a bibliography of music and literature. Westport: Greenwood, 1979, 302 p.

A classified bibliography of 5,024 entries organized as the RILM model with abstracts. Author-subject index to the literature. Composer-Author index to music. Index to recordings. Very thorough indexing and annotating.

3003. Claghorn, Charles Eugene. Women composers and hymnists. Metuchen: Scarecrow, 1984. 272 p.

A "comprehensive biographical dictionary of women hymnists and composers of church and sacred music covering all leading Protestant denominations, many Roman Catholics and a few Jewish hymnists." Covers 755 persons. Bibliography.

3004. Cohen, Aaron I. International encyclopedia of women composers. N.Y. & London: R. R. Bowker, 1981. 597 p.

Provides brief biographical coverage with lists of compositions for almost 5,000 women composers. Appendix of composers listed by country and century. Extensive bibliography of works about women composers.

3005. Frasier, Jane. Women composers; a discography. Detroit: Information Coordinators, 1983. 308 p. (Detroit Studies in Music Bibliography, 50)

Covering 337 composers or art music. Indexes to recording company, genres, titles. Bibliography.

3006. Handy, D. Antoinette. Black women in American bands & orchestras. Metuchen: Scarecrow Press, 1981. 319 p.

Includes an extensive bibliography, p. 254–273.

3007. Hixon, Donald L. and Don Hennessee. Women in music: a biobibliography. Metuchen: Scarecrow Press, 1975.

Indexes articles in 48 standard references works about women involved in classical music. Classified list of women musians provided.

3008. Meggett, Joan M. Keyboard music by women composers: a catalog and bibliography; foreword by Nancy Fierro. Westport: Greenwood Press, 1981. 210 p.

A catalog of the work of 290 composers including brief biographies and lists of sources. Discography. Extensive, annotated bibliography of sources referring to more than one woman composer.

3009. Rogal, Samuel J. Sisters of sacred song: a selected listing of women hymnodists in Great Britain and Americ. N.Y.; London: Garland, 1981. 162 p.

Lists women hymnodists and their hymns, classifying them by nationality and denominations. Cites collections of hymns. Title index to hymns cited.

3010. Skowronski, JoAnn. Women in American music: a bibliography. Metuchen: Scarecrow Press, 1978. 183 p.

Arranged in four sections covering periods of American history, and two genre bibliographies: general history and reference works. Some entries are annotated. Name index.

Review by Carol Neuls-Bates in *Notes,* 35 (1979), p. 635–36.

3011. Smith, Julia, ed. Directory of American women composers, with selected music for senior and junior clubs. First edition. Chicago: National Federation of Music Clubs, 1970. 51 p.

Here is a first *Directory of American Women Composers.* ... The *Directory* contains the names of over 600 composers who have written, or are now writing music that ranges from very easy to the most difficult and experimental, including electronic music. [Editor's *Foreword*]

No work lists, but type of music composed is indicated for each composer as well as for the publishers who have issued their works. Key to music publishers and distributors (p. 48–51).

3012. Stewart-Green, Miriam. Women composers: a checklist of works for the solo voice. Boston: G. K. Hall, 1980. 296 p.

In the general section, lists 3,746 women composers who have composed "classical" music. Cites song titles and publishers or locations when known. Separate lists for: operas, cantatas, oratorios, masses, cycles and collections, works for voice with instruments, dramatic scenes. Bibliography and index of names.

3013. Women in music: an anthology of source readings from the Middle Ages to the present; edited by Carol Neuls-Bates. New York: Harper & Row, c1982. 351 p.

Bibliography: p. 333–338.

3014. Zaimont, Judith Lang and Karen McNerney Famera. Contemporary concert music by women; a directory of the composers and their works. A project of the International League of Women Composers. Westport: Greenwood, 1981. 355 p.

Half-page biographies including photographic portraits and manuscript samples of over 60 composers and 6 other musicians. Classified lists of music. Addresses of composers and publishers. Discography and index.

Miscellaneous and Bibliographical Tools

This section has grown to twice its previous size, partly by the fact that we list here in numerical order the publications appearing in the few series of music bibliographies such as the *MLA Index Series,* the series *Music Indexes and Bibliographies,* and *Detroit Studies in Music Bibliography.* That these series have proliferated so mightily may be seen as a sign of health of our craft. Also cited here are bibliographies of music bibliography, together with a selected group of statements concerning the nature and current state of music bibliography. The principal codes for cataloging music have been included, as well as the major guides to music library practice. Among the remaining miscellany will be found several works concerned with music copyright. Judicious use of the subject catalog will direct the reader to the less obvious reaches of this concluding chapter.

3015. Allen, Warren D. "Bibliography of literature concerning the general history of music in chronological order." In his *Philosophies of music history.* New York: American Book Co., 1939. P. 343–65.

Reprinted New York, Dover, 1962.

317 titles arranged chronologically from 1600 to 1939. Not all can be described as histories in the modern sense, but they have bearing on the development of music historiography.

3016. Basart, Ann P. "Copyright" in *Cum notis variorum,* 56 (October 1981), p. 25–26.

A brief, but valuable bibliography on the subject of copyright in the United States.

3017. Bayne, Pauline Shaw. A basic music library: essential scores and books. 2nd edition. Compiled by the Music Library Association, subcommittee on the basic music collection, under the direction of Pauline Bayne Shaw. Edited by Robert Michael Fling. Chicago: American Library Association, 1983. 357 p.

First published in 1978, 173 p.

Review by Margaret F. Lospinuso in *Notes,* 36 (1979, p. 94–95).

3018. Berner, A., J. H. van der Meer, and G. Thibault. Preservation and restoration of musical instruments. Provisional recommendations. The International Council of Museums, 1967. 76 p.

Not a full-scale treatise on its subject, but suggests the problems to be encountered in the restoration and preservation of instruments. Illustrated with plates from early treatises on musical instruments. p. 23–29: bibliography.

3019. Besterman, Theodore. Music and drama, a bibliography of bibliographies. Totowa: Rowman and Litlefield, 1971. 365 p.
Compiled from the 4th edition of the author's *World Bibliography of Bibliographies.*

3020. Bibliographies in American Music. Published for the College Music Society. No 1– . Detroit: Information Coordinators, 1974– .

3021. Bibliographies in American Music. (1) George Gershwin; a selective bibliography and discography by Charles Schwartz. Detroit: Published for the College Music Society by Information Coordinators, 1974. 118 p.

3022. Bibliographies in American Music. (2) William Billings, data and documents by Hans Nathan. Detroit: Published for the College Music Society by Information Coordinators, 1976. 69 p.

3023. Bibliographies in American Music. (3) Charles T. Griffes; an annotated bibliography-discography by Donna K. Anderson. Detroit: Published for the College Music Society by Information Coordinators, 1977. 255 p.

3024. Bibliographies in American Music. (4) First performances in America to 1900: works with orchestra by Harold Earle Johnson. Detroit: Published for the College Music Society by Information Coordinators, 1979. 446 p.

3025. Bibliographies in American Music. (5) Haydn autographs in the United States by Irving Lowens with Otto Albrecht. Detroit: Published for the College Music Society by Information Coordinators, 1979. 134 p.

3026. Bibliographies in American Music. (6) A catalog of the works of Arthur Foote, 1853–1937 by Wilma Reid Cipolla. Detroit: Published for the College Music Society by Information Coordinators, 1980. 193 p.

3027. Bibliographies in American Music. (7) Louis Moreau Gottschalk, 1829–1869; a bibliographical study and catalog of works by John G. Doyle. Detroit: Published for the College Music Society by Information Coordinators, 1982. 386 p.

3028. Bibliographies in American Music. (8) American music studies; a classified bibliography of master's theses by James R. Heintze. Detroit: Published for the College Music Society by Information Coordinators, 1984. 312 p.

3029. Bibliographies in American Music. (9) American piano concertos; a bibliography by William Phemister. Detroit: Published for the College Music Society by Information Coordinators, 1985. 323 p.

3030. Bloesch, Ethel. "Music autographs and first editions on postage stamps" in *Fontes artis musicae,* 25 (1978), p. 250–63.
A check-list of 50 stamps from 24 countries.

3031. Bobillier, Marie (Michel Brenet, pseud.) "Bibliographie des bibliographies musicales," in *L'Année musicale,* 3 (1913), p. 1–152.
Reprint by Da Capo Press, New York, 1971. 152 p.
One of the first, and still one of the few specialized bibliographies of music bibliography. Outdated but still useful. Lists general works, including periodical articles, by author; individual bibliographies; catalogs of libraries; catalogs of dealers and publishers.

3032. Bradley, Carol J. The Dickinson classification; a cataloguing and classfication manual for music. Including a reprint of the George Sherman Dickinson, *Classification of musical compositions.* Carlisle, Pa.: Carlisle Books, 1968. 176 p.
A classification system developed by George Sherman Dickinson, music librarian at Vassar College, 1927–1953. This volume contains a reprint of the Dickinson Classification, originally published in 1938, together with a manual of cataloging procedures based on it.
For a description of the classification and a demonstration of its applications, see Carol Bradley's article *"The Dickinson classification for music"in Fontes artis musicae,* 19 (1972), p. 13–22.

3033. Bradley, Carol June. Music collections in American libraries: a chronology. Detroit: Detroit Information Coordinators, 1981. 249 p. (Detroit studies in music bibliography, 46)
A chronological approach to the history of music librarianship in Americ.
Review by Paula Morgan in *Notes,* 39 (1983), p. 357–8.
Review by Vincent H. Duckles in *Fontis Artis Musicae,* 29 (1982), p. 147–48.

3034. The British Catalogue of Music Classification. Compiled for the Council of the British National Bibliography, Ltd., by E. J. Coates. London: Council of the British National Bibliography, Ltd., British Museum, 1960. 56 p.
The classification scheme developed for use in the British Catalogue of Music (no. 1233).

3035. Brook, Barry S. Thematic catalogues in music, an annotated bibliography, including printed, manuscript, and in-preparation catalogues; related literature and reviews; an essay on the definitions, history, functions, historiography, and future of the thematic catalogue. Hillsdale, N.Y.: Pendragon Press, 1972. 347 p.
Published under the joint sponsorship of the Music Library Association and RILM *abstracts of music literature.* This work supersedes A

check-list of thematic catalogues edited by an MLA Committee on Thematic Indexes (1954) and its *Supplement* issued by Queens College (1966).

Indexes some 1,500 entries, including a number of 18th-century manuscript catalogs, a great many unpublished catalogs, and some large-scale national projects currently in progress.

A new edition of this bibliography is underway and publication is expected shortly.

3036.   Brown, Howard Mayer and Joan Lascelle. Musical iconography; a manual for cataloguing musical subjects in Western art before 1800. Cambridge: Harvard University Press, 1972. 220 p.

Includes bibliographical references.

3037.   Bryant, Eric Thomas. Music librarianship; a practical guide. London: James Clarke, [1959]. 503 p.

Reprint by Stechert-Hafner, 1963.

Part I, p. 3–285: discussion of the administration, services, and technical processes of music libraries. Part II, p. 289–450: a series of annotated bibliographies of basic materials, chiefly scores, for a public library collection. The emphasis is on British practices.

Review by Alfons Ott in *Fontes artis musicae,* 7 (1960), p. 72–73; by Rita Benton in *Notes,* 17 (1960), p. 397–98.

3038.   Carlsen, James C. and David Brian Williams. A computer annotated bibliography: music research in programmed instruction, 1952–1972. Reston, Virginia: Music Educators National Conference, 1978. 71 p.

3039.   Central Opera Service. Directory of selected opera films available from American distributors. N.Y.: Central Opera Service, 1976. 42 p. (Central Opera Service Bulletin, v. 19 , no. 2 (Winter, 1976/77))

Eleventh annual Directory issue.

3040.   Code International de Catalogage de la Musique. II. Code restreint. Rédigé par Yvette Féderoff. .... Kurzgefasste Anleitung - Limited Code. Übersetzung von Simone Wallon. Trans. by Virginia Cunningham. Frankfurt/London: C. F. Peters, 1961. 53 p.

Review by Minnie Elmer in *Notes,* 19 (1961), p. 247–49; by Richard Schaal in *Die Musikforschung,* 17 (1964), p. 295–96.

3041.   Code International de Catalogage de la Musique. I. Der Autorenkatalog der Musikdrucke. The author catalog of published music. By Franz Grasberger; translated by Virginia Cunningham. Frankfurt/London: C. F. Peters, 1961. 53 p.

This and the two following volumes are the result of the work of the Commission on Music Cataloguing of the International Association of Music Libraries. Later volumes projected include a code for the cataloging of music manuscripts and sound recordings.

Review by Richard S. Angell in *Notes,* 15 (1957), p. 110–11.

3042. Code international de catalogage de la musique. V. Le catalogage des enregistrements sonores. The cataloging of sound recordings. Rédigé par Simone Wallon, Kurt Dorfmüller, avec la collaboration [de] Yvette Fëdoroff, et Virginia Cunningham. Frankfurt; New York: C.F. Peters, 1983. 105 p. (Code international de catalogage de la musique, 5)

Parallel text in English, French, and German.

3043. Code international de catalogage de la musique. Rules for cataloging music manuscripts. Compiled by Marie Louise Göllner. Translation [French] by Yvette Federoff, [German] by Horst Leuchtmann. Frankfurt & London: C. F. Peters, 1975. 56 p.

A result of the work of a committee of the International Association of Music Libraries.

3044. Code International de Catalogage de la Musique. III. Rules for full cataloging—Réles de catalogage detaille—Regeln für die vollstandige Titelaufnahme, compiled by Virginia Cunningham. . . . Frankfurt: C. F. Peters, 1971. 116 p.

3045. Cooper, B. Lee. The popular music handbook, a resource guide for teachers, librarians, and media specialists. Littleton: Libraries Unlimited, 1984. 415 p.

In four parts:

Part 1: Recommended teaching topics;

Part 2: Print resources on popular music, a classified bibliography, occasionally annotated;

Part 3: Discographies of popular music;

Part 4: A basic popular music collection for libraries.

The introductory sections to parts 2 and 3 are heavily annotated guides to the fundamental literature on the subject. Selective general bibliography. Index to artists and performers, and to subjects.

3046. Coover, James B. "The current status of music bibliography," in *Notes,* 13 (1956), p. 581–93.

A survey of the accomplishments, progress, and lacunae in the field of music bibliography as of 1956. The paper takes its point of departure from A. Hyatt King's statement in *The library* (1945); see no. 3129, below.

3047. Coover, James B. Music lexicography, including a study of lacunae in music lexicography and a bibliography of music dictionaries. Third edition, revised and enlarged. Carlisle, Pa.: Carlisle Books, 1971. 175 p.

First published as A *bibliography of music dictionaries,* Denver: Bibliographical Center for Research, 1952. Second edition, Denver, 1958.

The most comprehensive bibliography available of music dictionaries. 1,801 items arranged alphabetically, including all known editions of the works cited. Preceded by a general discussion of the history of music lexicography and of existing lacunae. Index to personal names, index to topics and types, and an index, by date of publication, to dictionaries before 1900.

Nyal Williams and Peg Daub substantially increased the number of dictionaries cited in "Coover's *Music Lexicography*: two supplements" in *Notes,* 30 (1974), p. 492 ff.

Review of the 2nd edition by Irene Millen in *Notes,* 16 (1959), p. 383–84.

3048. Crawford, Richard. The American Musicological Society 1934–84; an anniversary essay with lists of officers, winners of awards, editors of the *Journal,* and honorary and corresponding members. Philadelphia: American Musicological Society, 1984. 46 p.

A publication marking the 50th anniversary the founding of the AMS.

3049. Currall, Henry F. J. Gramophone record libraries, their organization and practice. . . . With a preface by A. Hyatt King. 2d ed. Published for the International Association of Music Libraries, United Kingdom Branch. London: Crosby Lockwood and Son, 1970. 303 p.

The work was first published in 1963.

A manual for the administration of record library, with contributions by British librarians and sound recording experts. P. 131–46: "A basic stock list'; p. 171–76: "Gramophone librarianship: a bibliography." Illustrated.

3050. Dadelsen, Georg von. Editionsrichlinien musikalischer Denkmäler und Gesamtausgaben. Im Auftrag der Gesellschaft für Musikforschung. . . . Kassel; Basel: Bärenreiter, 1967. 143 p. (Musikwissenschaftliche Arbeiten, 22.)

Presents standards and techniques for editorial practice as employed in the German critical editions.

Review by Robert L. Marshall in *Notes,* 25 (1969), p. 733–35.

3051. Davies, John H. Musicalia: sources of information in music. Second edition, revised and enlarged. Oxford: Pergamon Press, 1969. 184 p. 48 facsim.

First published in 1966.

A practical guide to music reference materials, illustrated with facsimile pages of the major reference works.

Review by François Lesure in *Fontes artis musicae,* 17 (Jan.-Aug. 1970), p. 55.

3052. Dearling, Robert and Celia Dearling. The Guinness book of music facts and feats. 3rd ed. [Compiled with the assistance of Brian Rust. Enfield, Middlesex : Guinness Superlatives, 1986. 288 p.

First edition, 1976. Published in a Dutch translation by Charles Fabius in Haarlem by De Haan, 1978. 2nd ed., 1981.

A list of curious and wondrous musical feats and feats in music. Well arranged for reference use. Includes a bibliography of 50 titles and a good, index.

3053. Detroit Studies in Music Bibliography. Detroit, Information Coordinators, Inc., 1961– . () No. 1– .

A series of manuals, diverse in character and content, but each concerned with some aspect or area of music bibliography.

3054. Detroit Studies in Music Bibliography. (1) Reference materials in ethnomusicology by Bruno Nettl. Second edition, revised, 1967.

First published in 1961. Also entered as no. 932.

3055. Detroit Studies in Music Bibliography. (2) Sir Arthur Sullivan: an index to the texts of his vocal works by Sirvart Poladian. 1961.

3056. Detroit Studies in Music Bibliography. (3) An index to Beethoven's conversation books by Donald W. MacArdle. 1961. 46 p.
Review by Fred Blum in *Notes,* 20 (1963), p. 225–27.

3057. Detroit Studies in Music Bibliography. (4) General bibliography for music research by Keith E. Mixter. 1962. 38 p.
Surveys the nonmusical aids to musical research, with emphasis on such reference works as general bibliographies of bibliography, national and trade bibliographies, general dictionaries, encyclopedias, union lists, and library catalogs.
Superseded by no. 33 in this series, see no. 3086.
Review by Fred Blum in *Notes,* 20 (1963), p. 225–27.

3058. Detroit Studies in Music Bibliography. (5) A handbook of American operatic premieres, 1731–1963 by Julius Mattfeld. 1963. 142 p.
Also entered as no. 3141.

3059. Detroit Studies in Music Bibliography. (6) Medieval and Renaissance music on long-playing recordsby James B. Coover and Richard Colvig. 1964. 122 p.
Also entered as no. 2786. *Supplement* issued 1972 as no. 26 in this series, see no. 3079.

3060. Detroit Studies in Music Bibliography. (7) Rhode Island music and musicians, 1733–1850 by Joyce Ellen Mangler. 1965. 90 p.
Also entered as no. 215.

3061. Detroit Studies in Music Bibliography. (8) Jean Sibelius, an international bibliography on the occasion of the centennial celebrations, 1965 by Fred Blum. 1965. 114 p.
P. 1–11: Books and dissertations devoted to Sibelius; p. 13–45: books partially devoted to Sibelius; p. 47–71: music journals; p. 73–94: non-music journals. Index of names.
Also entered as no. 1199.

3062. Detroit Studies in Music Bibliography. (9) Bibliography of theses and dissertations in sacred music by Kenneth R. Hartley. 1967. 127 p.

3063. Detroit Studies in Music Bibliography. (10) Checklist of vocal chamber works by Benedetto Marcello by Carolin S. Fruchtman. 1967. 37 p.
Also entered under no. 1658.

3064. Detroit Studies in Music Bibliography. (11) An annotated bibliography of woodwind instruction books, 1600–1830 by Thomas E. Warner. 1967.

138 p.
Also entered under no. 1165.

3065. Detroit Studies in Music Bibliography. (12) Works for solo voice of Johann Adolf Hasse (1699–1783) by Sven Hostrup Hansell. 1968. 110 p.
Also entered as no. 1643.

3066. Detroit Studies in Music Bibliography. (13) A selected discography of solo song by Dorothy Stahl. 1968. 95 p.
Supplement, 1968–1969. (1970). 95 p.
Also entered under no. 2813.

3067. Detroit Studies in Music Bibliography. (14) Music publishing in Chicago before 1871: the firm of Root and Cady, 1858–1871 by Dena J. Epstein. 1969. 243 p.
Also entered under no. 2639.

3068. Detroit Studies in Music Bibliography. (15) An introduction to certain Mexican musical archives by Lincoln Spiess and Thomas Stanford. 1969. 184 p.
Also entered under no. 2221.

3069. Detroit Studies in Music Bibliography. (16) A checklist of American music periodicals, 1850–1900 by William J. Weichlein. 1970. 103 p.
Also entered as no. 860.

3070. Detroit Studies in Music Bibliography. (17) A checklist of 20th-century choral music for male voices by Kenneth Roberts. 1970. 32 p.
Also entered as no. 1404.

3071. Detroit Studies in Music Bibliography. (18) Published music for the viola da gamba and other viols by Robin De Smet. 1971. 105 p.
Also entered as no. 1464.

3072. Detroit Studies in Music Bibliography. (19) The works of Christoph Nichelmann: a thematic index by Douglas A. Lee. 1971. 100 p.

3073. Detroit Studies in Music Bibliography. (20) The reed trio: an annotated bibliography of original published works by James E. Gillespie Jr. 1971. 84 p.
Also entered as no. 1467.

3074. Detroit Studies in Music Bibliography. (21) An index to the vocal works of Thomas Augustine Arne and Michael Arne by John A. Parkinson. 1972. 82 p.
Also entered under no. 1597.

3075. Detroit Studies in Music Bibliography. (22) Bibliotheca Bouduaniana: a Renaissance music bibliography by Donald W. Krummel. 1972. 191 p.

3076. Detroit Studies in Music Bibliography. (23) Music publishing in the Middle Western States before the Civil War by Ernst C. Krohn. 1972. 44 p.
Also entered under no. 2674

3077. Detroit Studies in Music Bibliography, (24) A selected discography of solo song; cumulation through 1971 by Dorothy Stahl. (1972) 137 p.
A revision and expansion of no. 3066, above. See also no. 3087.

3078. Detroit Studies in Music Bibliography, (25) Violin and violoncello in duo without accompaniment. ... based on the work of Alex Feinland, by Oscar Lotti Raoul. (1972) 122 p.
See also no. 1340.

3079. Detroit Studies in Music Bibliography, (26) Medieval and Renaissance music on long-playing records, Supplement 1962–71, by James B. Coover and Richard Colvig. (1973) 258 p.
Supplement to no. 6 (1964) in the Detroit series (above no. 3059). Also entered as no. 2798.

3080. Detroit Studies in Music Bibliography (27) Bibliography of literature concerning Yemenite-Jewish Music by Paul F. Marks. (1973) 50 p.

3081. Detroit Studies in Music Bibliography, (28) Solos for unaccompanied clarinet; an annotated bibliography of published works by James E. Gillespie. (1973) 79 p.

3082. Detroit Studies in Music Bibliography (29) Claude Debussy; a bibliography by Claude Abravanel. (1974) 214 p.

3083. Detroit Studies in Music Bibliography (30) String class publications in the United States, 1851–1951 by Charles Sollinger. (1974) 71 p.

3084. Detroit Studies in Music Bibliography (31) Bibliography of cello ensemble music by Claude Kenneson. (1974) 59 p.
Also entered as no. 1458.

3085. Detroit Studies in Music Bibliography (32) Karel Boleslav Jirak; a catalog of his works by Alice Tischler. (1975) 85 p.

3086. Detroit Studies in Music Bibliography (33) General bibliography for music research, 2nd edition, by Keith E. Mixter. (1975) 135 p.
A bibliographic study of general reference works pertinent to advanced musical scholarship.
First edition published in this series as no. 4, see above.

3087. **Detroit Studies in Music Bibliography (34)** A selected discography of solo songs: supplement 1971–1974 by Dorothy Stahl. (1976) 99 p.

3088. **Detroit Studies in Music Bibliography (35)** Thematic catalog of the works of Jeremiah Clarke by Thomas Taylor. (1977) 134 p.

3089. **Detroit Studies in Music Bibliography (36)** Music and dance research of southwestern United States; past trends, present activities, and suggestions for further research by Charlotte J. Frisbie. (1977) 109 p.

3090. **Detroit Studies in Music Bibliography (37)** Italian Baroque solo sonatas for the recorder and the flute by Richard A. McCowan. (1978) 70 p.

3091. **Detroit Studies in Music Bibliography (38)** A chronology of music in the Florentine theater, 1590–1750; operas, prologues, finales, intermezzos, and plays with incidental music by Robert L. Weaver and Norma W. Weaver. (1978) 421 p.
Also entered as no. 1006.

3092. **Detroit Studies in Music Bibliography (39)** Carlo d'Ordoñez, 1734–1786; a thematic catalog by A. Peter Brown. (1978) 234 p.

3093. **Detroit Studies in Music Bibliography (40)** Lute, vihuela, guitar to 1800; a bibliography by David B. Lyons. (1978) 214 p.
Also entered as 961.

3094. **Detroit Studies in Music Bibliography (41)** The Arnold Schoenberg-Hans Nachod Collection [in the] Music Library [of] North Texas State University [in] Denton, Texas [by] John A. Kimmey. (1979) 119 p.
Also entered as no. 2029.

3095. **Detroit Studies in Music Bibliography (42)** Music for viola by Michael D. Williams. (1979) 362 p.
Also entered as no. 1456.

3096. **Detroit Studies in Music Bibliography (43)** Music in the Paris Academy of Sciences, 1666–1793; a source archive in photocopy at Stanford University by Albert Cohen and Leta E. Miller. (1979) 69 p.

3097. **Detroit Studies in Music Bibliography (44)** The extant music of Rodrigo de Ceballos and its sources by Robert J. Snow. (1980) 155 p.

3098. **Detroit Studies in Music Bibliography (45)** Fifteen black American composers; a bibliography of their works by Alice Tischler. (1981) 328 p.

3099. **Detroit Studies in Music Bibliography (46)** Music collections in American libraries: a chronology by Carol June Bradley. (1981) 249 p.
Also entered as no. 3054.

3100. Detroit Studies in Music Bibliography (47) Musical instrument collections; catalogues and cognate literature by James B. Coover. (1981) 464 p.
Also entered as no. 2525.

3101. Detroit Studies in Music Bibliography (48) Anton Webern; an annotated bibliography by Zoltan Roman. (1983) 219 p.

3102. Detroit Studies in Music Bibliography (49) Fuguing Tunes in the eighteenth century by Nicholas Temperley and Charles G.Manns. (1983) 504 p.

3103. Detroit Studies in Music Bibliography (50) Women composers; a discography by Jane Frasier. (1983) 308 p.

3104. Detroit Studies in Music Bibliography (51) Four centuries of organ music; an annotated discography by Marilou Kratzenstein and Jerald Hamilton. (1984) 308 p.

3105. Detroit Studies in Music Bibliography (52) Discography of solo song: supplement 1975–1982 by Dorothy Stahl. (1984) 236 p.

3106. Detroit Studies in Music Bibliography (53) Index to composer bibliographies by Richard D. Green. (1985) 86 p.

3107. Detroit Studies in Music Bibliography (54) A comprehensive bibliography of music for film and television compiled by Steven D. Wescott. (1986) 435 p.
Also entered as no. 743.

3108. Deutsch, Otto Erich. "Music bibliography and catalogues," in *The Library,* 23 (1943), p. 151–70.

3109. The Diagram Group. Musical instruments of the world; an illustrated encyclopedia by the Diagram Group. *s.l.*: Paddington Press, 1986. 320 p.
Drawings of instruments, some with diagrams showing details of construction or methods of sound production and music-making. Drawings are accompanied by brief prose explications. Index and bibliography.

3110. Directory of music library automation projects. Compiled by Garrett H. Bowles. 2nd ed. Philadelphia: Music Library Association, 1979. 23 p. (MLA technical reports, 2)
First edition published 1973.
A guide to the application of automated data processing techniques and processes to various music library functions in American and Canadian music libraries.

3111. Duckles, Vincent H. "Music literature, music, and sound recordings," in *Bibliography, current state and future trends,* ed. Robert B. Downs

and Frances B. Jenkins. Urbana: University of Illinois Press, 1967. p.
158–183.
First published in *Library trends,* January 1967.

3112. Duckles, Vincent H. Music libraries and librarianship. *Library
trends,* 8 (April 1960), p. 495–617. [Published by the University of Illinois,
School of Librarianship.] Edited by Vincent H. Duckles.
15 specialists discuss various aspects of music librarianship, covering
the areas of training for the profession, bibliography and selection, cataloging, services, and administration.
Review by Vladimir Fedorov in *Fontes artis musicae,* 8 (1961), p. 30–31.

3113. Duckles, Vincent H. Music reference and research materials, an an-
notated bibliography. 3rd ed. New York: Schirmer Books; London: Collier
Macmillan, 1974. 526 p.
First published in 1964. 2nd ed. New York, Free Press; London, Collier-
Macmillan, 1967, 385 p.
Review of the 1st ed. by Jan LaRue in *JAMS,* 19 (1966), p. 257–61; by
Klaus Speer in *Notes,* 21 (1964), p. 375; of the 2d ed. by William S. New-
man in *Notes,* 24 (1967), p. 265–66; review of the 3rd edition in *ALA
reference and subscription book reviews* (1 December 1974), p. 83–84.

3114. Encyclopedia of quotations about music, compiled and edited by Nat
Shapiro. Garden City: Doubleday, 1978. 418 p.
Over 2,000 quotations, all originally in or translated to English, arrayed
in subject categories. Indexes to persons and sources, and to keywords.

3115. Erickson, J. Gunnar, Edward R. Hearn, and Mark E. Halloran. Musician's
guide to copyright. San Francisco: Bay Area Lawyers for the Arts, 1979.
86 p.
A brief review intended for the layman of the laws and regulations
governing copyright of printed and recorded music.

3116. Fischer, Wilhelm. "Verzeichnis von bibliographischen Hilfswerken
für musikhistorischen Arbeiten." In Guido Adler, *Methode der Musikgeschichte.* Leipzig: Breitkopf & Hartel, 1919. p. 200–222.
Classified list, including general bibliographical works, general musical works, and bibliographies of single aspects of music history. Some
inaccurate dates and incomplete titles for French and English works,
which are less well covered.

3117. Folter, Siegrun F. "Library restrictions on the use of microfilm copies" in *Fontes artis musicae,* 24 (1977), p. 207–243.
A codification of information on restrictions placed on the use of microfilm copies of sources by the libraries holding the originals. A very
useful and compact delineation of various practices. The IAML Research
Libraries Commission issued a "Report on the supply and use of microfilms" in *Fontes artis musicae,* 27 (1980), p. 207–09.

3118. Fuchs, Albert. Taxe der Streichinstrumente; Anleitung zur Ein-
schätzung von Geiger, Violen, Violoncelli, Kontrabässen usw. nach Her-

kunft und Wert. 12. Auflage.
eubearbeitet von Rudolf E. Pliverics. Hofheim am Taurus: Friedrich
Hofmeister, 1985. 206 p.
First published in 1906.
A handbook for appraising the origins and values of string instruments. Brief entries on luthiers. Index to places.

3119. Gaeddert, Barbara Knisley. The classification and cataloging of sound recordings, 1933–1980; an annotated bibliography. 2nd ed. Philadelphia: Music Library Association, 1981. (Music Library Association Technical Reports, 4)
First published in 1977.
First edition reviewed by Kären Nagy in *Notes,* 34 (1977), p. 88.

3120. Grimsey, A. H. R. Checklist of postage stamps about music. London: National Philatelic Society, 1977.
A check-list of over 4,000 stamps portraying music instruments, composers, and other musical subjects.

3121. Harrison, David B. Computer applications to music and musicology: a bibliography. Waterloo, Ontario: University of Waterloo, 1977. 116 p.

3122. Hoboken, Anthony van. "Probleme der musikbibliographischen Terminologie." In *Fontes artis musicae,* 1958:1. p. 6–15.
A discussion centered on the dificulties of establishing music bibliography as an "exact science" in view of the variety and complexity of the materials with which it is concerned.

3123. Hopkinson, Cecil. "The fundamentals of music bibliography." In *Fontes artis musicae,* 1955:2. p. 122–31.
An attempt to stimulate discussion of some basic points as to the nature, content, and procedures of music bibliography as it serves the needs of collectors, musicians, and historians.

3124. Iampolski, I. M. "Muzykalnoi bibliografii," in *Muzykalnaia entsyklopedia,* (see no. 47.1).
A survey of music bibliographical works without chronological or geopolitical boundaries, but with substantial coverage of works done in socialist countries, particularly the U.S.S.R.

3125. International Association of Music Libraries. Deutsche Gruppe. Systematik der Musikliteratur und der Musikalien für öffentliche Musikbüchereien. Erarbeitet von der Kommission für Musiksystematik bei der Arbeitsgemeinschaft für Musikbüchereien in der Deutschen Gruppe der Association Internationale des Bibliotheques Musicales (AIBM). [Reutlingen]: Bücherei und Bildung, 1963. 39 p.
A system of music classification devised for German public library practice.

3126. International Music Centre. Music in film and television: an international selective catalogue, 1964–1974: opera, concert, documentation compiled and edited by the International Music Centre, Vienna. Paris: Unesco Press, 1975. 197 p.

Provides information on 223 films that employ music. Indexed by titles, composers, librettists, authors, translators, producers and directors, conductors, performing artists, orchestras and ensembles, organizations and companies.

3127. Karchoschka, Erhard Notation in new music; a critical guide to interpretation and realization. Translated from the German by Ruth Koenig. N.Y.ö Praeger, 1972.

First published as *Das Schriftbild der Neuen Musik* by Moeck in 1966. Also published in London by Universal Edition in 1972.

A summary of notational problems and solutions with a method for looking up specific notational symbols. Extensive section of examples of new notations with annotations. Indexes to subjects and to names and works.

3128. Keys to Music Bibliography. Kent, Ohio, Kent State Univ. Press, 1970. v. 1– .

1. Anna Tipton Voorhees. Index to symphonic program notes in books. 1970.

3129. King, A. Hyatt. "Recent work in music bibliography." In *The library*, 26:2 (Sept.-Dec. 1945), p. 99–148.

Surveys the accomplishments in music bibliography during the period just prior to and during World War II.

3130. King, A. Hyatt. Some British collectors of music. Cambridge: Cambridge Univ. Press, 1963. 178 p. (The Sandars Lectures for 1961.)

A pioneer study of the activity of private collectors of music in England, with an appendix containing classified lists of collectors from the mid-17th century to the present.

3131. Koltypina, Galina Borisovna, ed. Bibliografia muzykalnoi bibliografii. [Bibliography of musical bibliography.] Moscow: 1963. 226 p.

An annotated bibliography of Russian music bibliographies. The work cites bibliographies of literature on music separately published, lists books, articles, and reviews. Designed for bibliographers and scholars.

3132. Koltypina, Galina Borisovna, ed. Spravochnaia literatura po muzyke. [Reference literature on music ... 1773–1962.] Moscow: 1964. 249 p.

A publication of the Moscow State Library.

Annotated bibliography of Russian reference literature on music, including dictionaries, collected biography, calendars, etc., published in Russia from 1773 to 1962. Cites reviews in Russian periodical literature.

3133. Krohn, Ernest C. "The bibliography of music." In *MQ*, 5 (1919), p. 231–54.

One of the first surveys of the state of music bibliography by an American scholar. Useful as a statement of the accomplishments in the field at the time of writing. Incomplete cititations. Narrative style.

3134. Krummel, Donald W. "Bibliography of music," in *The New Grove Dictionary of Music and Musicians,* edited by Stanley Sadie, v. 2, p. 682–92. London: Macmillan, 1980.

Divided into three sections: analytical and descriptive bibliography; reference bibliography; history of Music Bibliography. This article provides an overview of the subject and mentions some of the principal sources. It is particularly helpful in placing music bibliography in the context of general bibliography and in an historical perspective. Excellent classified bibliography and numerous references to related articles.

3135. Krummel, Donald W. and James B. Coover. "Current national bibliographies, their music coverage." In *Notes,* 17 (1960), p. 375–88.

Surveys the music coverage in the national bibliographies in the Western Hemisphere, Western and Eastern Europe, Africa, Asia, and Oceania.

3136. Kupferberg, Herbert. The book of classical music lists. New York: Facts on File, 1985. 240 p.

A collection of statistics and other information, serious and trivial, unlikely to be found easily elsewhere.

3137. Laforte, Conrad. Le catalogue de la chanson folklorique francaise. Québec: Les Presses Universitaires Laval, 1958. 397 p. (Publications des archives de folklore, Universite Laval.)

Demonstrates a method for establishing an alphabetical catalog, by title, of French folk songs, with appropriate cross references to permit the grouping of variants under a common title. Based on material in Canadian archives and collections.

3138. Luther, Wilhelm-Martin. "Bibliographie . . . Literatur." In *MGG.* Kassel: Bärenreiter, 1949– . V. 1, col. 1837–39.

Recounts the history and surveys the concepts of music bibliography, with an extensive listing of titles pertaining to the field.

3139. Macken, Bob, Peter Fornatale, and Bill Ayres. The rock music source book. Garden City, N.Y.: Anchor Books, 1980. 644 p.

Bibliography p. 641–644.

3140. Mathiesen, Thomas J. "Towards a corpus of ancient Greek music theory: a new catalogue raisonné planned for RISM," in *Fontes artis musicae,* 25 (1978) p. 119–134.

Prospectus for a new *RISM* catalog. Includes bibliographical references.

3141. Mattfeld, Julius. A handbook of American operatic premieres, 1731–1962. Detroit: Information Service, Inc., 1963. (Detroit studies in music bibliography, 5.) 142 p.

This guide to operatic performances in the United States attempts to present a record of the premieres of nearly 2,000 operas and related works from 1731 to the end of 1962. . . . Included are operas by native and naturalized composers, which have been performed outside the country. [*Preface*]

Works listed alphabetically by title, with a composer index.

3142. McColvin, Lionel R. and Harold Reeves. Music libraries, including a comprehensive bibliography of music literature and a select bibliography of music scores published since 1957. . . . Completely rewritten, revised, and extended by Jack Dove. London: Andre Deutsch, 1965. 2 v.

First published in 1937–38.

Vol. 1 is made up of a series of chapters on various aspects of music library administration and practice: staff, binding, classification, cataloguing, etc. There are chapters devoted to British public libraries, British university and special libraries, overseas libraries, etc.

Vol. 2 consists of bibliographies and indexes of music literature and scores which are cited elsewhere.

Reviews by Harold Spivacke and by K. H. Anderson in *Notes,* 22 (1965–66), p. 872–77.

3143. Miller, Philip L. comp. and tr. The ring of words; an anthology of song texts. The original texts selected and translated, with an introd. by Philip L. Miller. New York: W. W. Norton, 1973. 518 p.

Reprint of the 1963 and 1966 editions of Doubleday.

German, French, Italian, Spanish, Russian, Norwegian, and Swedish, with English translations of song texts most likely to be heard in recitals.

3144. Mixter, Keith E. An introduction to library resources for music research. Columbus: School of Music, College of Education, Ohio State University, 1963. 61 p.

A practical list of music books and editions for use in courses in music bibliography at the college or university level. Selective. A minimum of annotations.

Review by Richard Schaal in *Die Musikforschung,* 17 (1964), p. 295.

3145. Mixter, Keith E. General bibliography for music research. 2d ed. Detroit: Information Coordinators, 1975. 135 p. (Detroit studies in music bibliography, 33)

"The purpose of this study is to present in an organized manner references to general bibliographical tools that may be of aid to those engaged in research in music. . . . The emphasis . . . is on titles from North America and Europe. Coverage includes books, but is not extended to articles." [from the *Introduction*]

This is an excellent introduction to non-musical reference works, albeit somewhat dated. Organized in chapters according to reference genres, there are indexes to names and to titles.

Brief review by Stephen M. Fry in *Notes,* 32 (1976), p. 781–82.

3146. Modern musical scholarship; edited by Edward Ollison. Stocksfield, England: Oriel Press, 1980. 246 p.

Proceedings of the Oxford International Symposia, held at Christ

Church, Oxford, 1977, under the title: *Modern musicology and the historical tradition of musical scholarship.*

3147. Music and bibliography: essays in honour of Alec Hyatt King. Edited by Oliver W. Neighbor. New York: K.G. Saur, C. Bingley, 1980. 256 p.

Contents:

"Venetian Baroque music in a London bookshop: the Robert Martin catalogues, 1633–50" by Donald W. Krummel.

"The Chapel Royal part-books" by Margaret Laurie.

"The harpsichord music of John Blow: a first catalogue" by Watkins Shaw.

"A Dresden opera-goer in 1756: Johann Christian Trömer, called 'Der Deutsch-Franzos'" by David Paisey.

"Henric Fougt, typographer extraordinary" by John A. Parkinson.

"Music engraving practice in eighteenth-century London: a study of some Forster editions of Haydn and their manuscript sources" by H. Edmund Poole.

"The origins of Mozart's 'Hunt' quartet, K. 458" by Alan Tyson.

"Some aspects of music publishing in nineteenth-century Berlin" by Rudolf Elvers.

"The early Novello octavo editions" by Miriam Miller.

"Meyerbeer's Italian operas" by Winton Dean.

"Chélard's Palladium des artistes: a project for a music periodical" by Richard Macnutt.

"Musical periodicals in 'Bourgeois Russia'" by Gerald Abraham.

"Alfred Cortot as collector of music" by Albi Rosenthal.

"The past, present, and future of the music library thematic catalogue" by Barry S. Brook.

"Problems in teaching the bibliography of music" by Brian Redfern.

3148. Music Indexes and Bibliographies. George R. Hill, general editor. No. 1– . Hackensack, N.J., Joseph Boonin, 1970– .

3149. Music Indexes and Bibliographies. (1) A thematic locator for Mozart's works, as listed in Koechel's Chronologisch-thematisches Verzeichnis. 6th ed. By George R. Hill, *et al.* 1970. 76 p.

3150. Music Indexes and Bibliographies. (2) A preliminary checklist of research on the classic symphony and concerto to the time of Beethoven (excluding Haydn and Mozart). By George R. Hill. 1970. 58 p.

3151. Music Indexes and Bibliographies. (3) A checklist of writings on 18th-century French and Italian opera (excluding Mozart). By Elvidio Surian. 1970. 121 p.

3152. Music Indexes and Bibliographies. (4) An index to the solo songs of Robert Franz. By Joseph M. Boonin. 1970. 19 p.

3153. Music Indexes and Bibliographies. (5) A catalog of Verdi's operas, by Martin Chusid. 1974. 201 p.

3154.   Music Indexes and Bibliographies. (6) A thematic index to the works of Salamon Rossi. Hackensack: J. Boonin, 1972. 143 p.

3155.   Music Indexes and Bibliographies. (7) A bibliography of computer applications in music, by Stefan M. Kostka. 1974. 58 p.

3156.   Music Indexes and Bibliographies. (8) Twentieth-century harpsichord music; a classified catalog, by Frances Bedford and Robert Conant. 1974. 95 p.

3157.   Music Indexes and Bibliographies. (9) The instrument catalogs of Leopoldo Franciolini, by Edwin M. Ripin. 1974. 201 p.

3158.   Music Indexes and Bibliographies. (10) A bibliography of sources for the study of ancient Greek music, [by] Thomas J. Mathiesen. 1974. 59 p.

3159.   Music Indexes and Bibliographies. (11) A thematic index to the works of Benedetto Pallavicino, by Peter Flanders. 1974. 85 p.

3160.   Music Indexes and Bibliographies. (14) A new catalog of music for small orchestra, by Cecilia Drinker Saltonstall and Henry Saltonstall. Clifton, N.J.: European American Music Corporation, 1978. 323 p.

3161.   Music Indexes and Bibliographies. (15) A thematic catalog of the sacred works of Giacomo Carissimi, by Iva M. Buff. Clifton, N.J.: European American Corp., 1979. 159 p.

3162.   Music Librarianship and Documentation. Report of the Adelaide Seminar, May 1970. Published by the Department of Adult Education, University of Adelaide, Adelaide, S. A. 145 p.
   A stimulating series of papers reporting on various aspects and problems of music librarianship and documentation in a part of the world where these disciplines have recently become established.

3163.   Music Library Association. Code for cataloging music and phonorecords. Prepared by a Joint Committee of the Music Library Association and the American Library Association, Division of Cataloging and Classification. Chicago: American Library Association, 1958. 88 p.
   The five major divisions of the now considerably dated code are entry, description, phonorecords, simplified rules, and filing rules for conventional titles. Glossary and index.

3164.   Music Library Association. MLA index series. No. 1– . Ann Arbor: Music Library Association, 1963– . No. 1– .
   A series of short, self-contained bibliographies or indexes prepared under the supervision of the Publications Committee of the Music Library Association. The volumes published to date are as follows:

3165. Music Library Association. MLA index series. (1) An alphabetical index to Claudio Monteverdi, *Tutte le opere.* Edited bythe Bibliography Committee of the New York Chapter MLA. 1963.

3166. Music Library Association. MLA index series. (2) An alphabetical index to Hector Berlioz, *Werke.* Edited by the Bibliography Committee of the New York Chapter MLA. 1963.

3167. Music Library Association. MLA index series. (3) A checklist of music bibliographies (in progress and unpublished). 2d, revised ed. by James Pruett. 1969.
1st ed, compiled by the Publications Committee MLA, [n.d.]

3168. Music Library Association. MLA index series. (4) A concordance of the thematic indexes to the instrumental works of Antonio Vivaldi. By Lenore Coral. 1965.

3169. Music Library Association. MLA index series. (5) An alphabetical index to Tomas Luis de Victoria, *Opera omnia.* Edited by the Bibliography Committee of the New York Chapter MLA. 1966.

3170. Music Library Association. MLA index series. (6) Schumann index, part I. An alphabetical index to Robert Schumann: *Werke.* Comp. by Michael Ochs. 1967.

3171. Music Library Association. MLA index series. (7) Schumann index, part II. An alphabetical index to the solo songs of Robert Schumann, comp. by William Weichlein. 1967.

3172. Music Library Association. MLA index series. (8) An index to Maurice Frost's English and Scottish psalm and hymn tunes, comp. by Kirby Rogers. 1967. *English and Scottish psalm and hymns tunes*—Indexes

3173. Music Library Association. MLA index series. (9) *Speculum*: an index of musically related articles and book reviews, compiled by Arthur S. Wolf. 1970.

3174. Music Library Association. MLA index series. (10) An index to *Das Chorwerk*, vols. 1–110, comp. by Michael Ochs. 1970. *Das Chorwerk*—Indexes

3175. Music Library Association. MLA index series. (11) Bach aria index, compiled by Miriam K. Wharples. 1970.

3176. Music Library Association. MLA index series. (12) An annotated bibliography of writings about music in Puertor Rico, compiled by Annie Figueroa Thompson. 1975.

3177. Music Library Association. MLA index series. (13) Analyses of twentieth-century music: 1940–1970, compiled by Arthur Wenk. 1975.

3178. Music Library Association. MLA index series. (14) Analyses of twentieth-century music, Supplement: 1970–1975, compiled by Arthur Wenk. 1975.

3179. Music Library Association. MLA index series. (15) Analyses of nineteenth-century music: 1940–1980, 2nd ed., compiled by Arthur Wenk.

3180. Music Library Association. MLA index series. (16) Writings on contemporary music notation, compiled by Gerald Warfield. 1976.

3181. Music Library Association. MLA index series. (17) Literature for voices in combination with electronic and tape music: an annotated bibliography, compiled by J. Michele Edwards. 1977.

3182. Music Library Association. MLA index series. (18) Johannes Brahms: a guide to his autograph in facsimile, by Peter Dedel. 1978.

3183. Music Library Association. MLA index series. (19) *Source: music of the avant-garde*: annotated list of contents amd cumulated indices, by Michale D. Williams. 1978.

3184. Music Library Association. MLA index series. (20) 18th-century American secular music manuscripts: an inventory, compiled by Mary Wallace Davidson and James J. Fuld. 1981.

3185. Music Library Association. MLA index series. (21) Popular secular music in America through 1800: a checklist of manuscripts in North American collections, compiled by Kate Van Winkle Keller. 1981.

3186. Music Library Association. MLA index series. (22) Palestrina: an index to the Casimiri, Kalmus, and Haberl editions, compiled by Alison Hall. 1980.

3187. Music Library Association. MLA index series. (23) E. H. Fellowes: an index to *The English Madrigalists* and the *The English School of Lutenist Song Writers*, compiled by Alison Hall. 1985.

3188. Music Library Association. Committee on Information and Organization. Manual of music librarianship. Ed. by Carol June Bradley. Ann Arbor: Music Library Association Executive Office, 1966. 150 p.

3189. Musica e filologia: contributi in occasione del festival "Musica e filologia" Verona, 30 settembre - 18 ottobre 1982, a cura di Marco Di Pasquale con la collaborazione di Richard Pierce. Verona: Edizioni della Società Letteraria, 1983. 212 p. (Quaderni della società letteraria, 1)

Contents:

"La filologia musicale e la tradizione musicologica italiana", di Giorgio Pestelli.

"Gli attuali indirizzi della storiografia e degli studi musicali in Italia", di Enrico Fubini.

"Il luogo della musica", di Giovanni Calendoli.

"The editing and publication of Baroque music in Hungary: principles and practice", di István Máriássy.

"Concordanze letterarie e divergenze musicali intorno ai Madrigali a cinque voci [...] Libro primo di Claudio Monteverdi", di Paolo Fabbri.

"Altro non è 'l mio cor: canzonetta del Seicento", di Ivano Cavallini.

"Due quadri musicali di scuola caravaggesca", di Franca Trinchieri Camiz.

"La Cappella musicale del Duomo di Verona, 1620–1685: qualche integrazione", di Marco Materassi.

"The application and usefulness of 'rastrology', with particular reference to early eighteenth-century Italian manuscripts", di Paul Everett.

"Le 'Liste de' musici e sonatori': fonti d'archivio sulla prassi esecutiva della musica strumentale romana del primo Settecento", di Franco Piperno.

"Antonio Vivaldi e la cantata profana", di Piero Mioli.

"Il copista raggiratore : un apocrifo durantiano conservato presso la British Library", di Carlo Vitali e Pinuccia Carrer.

"Estetica e prassi della musica sacra nei documenti di Benedetto XIV", di Osvaldo Gambassi.

"'Prend ton Metastase et travaille!': per una indagine melodrammaturgica di Julie ou la Nouvelle Hüélroïse", di Giovanni Morelli.

3190. New York Public Library. Reference Department. Music subject headings, authorized for use in the catalogs of the Music Division. Boston: G. K. Hall, 1959. 512 p.

Reproduced from cards in the subject heading file of the New York Public Library. An important tool for music catalogers, since it represents the practice of one of the great American music libraries.

3191. Orobko, William. The musician's handbook: a practical guide to the law and business of music. Vancouver: International Self-Counsel Press Ltd.; Seattle: Self-Counsel Press, 1985. 189 p.

A popular introduction to practice in the music business and to Canadian and American laws relating to that music.

3192. Ott, Alfons. "Die Musikbibliotheken." In Fritz Milkau's *Handbuch der Bibliothekswissenschaft, 2nd ed.* Vol. 2, p. 222–42.

Also printed separately by Harrassowitz, Wiesbaden, 1959.

Review by Cecil B. Oldman in *Fontes artis musicae*, 7 (1960), p. 71–72.

3193. Pethes, Iván. A flexible classification system of music and literature on music. Translated by Mihaly Sandory. Budapest: Centre of Library Science and Methodology, 1968. 49 p.

In Hungarian and English.

3194. Pohlmann, Hansjöorg. Die Frühgeschichte des musikalischen Urheberrechts (c. 1400–1800). Neue Materialen zur Entwicklung des Urheberrechtsbewusstseins der Komponisten. Kassel: Bärenreiter, 1962. 315 p. (Musikwissenschaftliche Arbeiten, 20.)

One of the few studies in the history of music copyright practice treating the sociological and psychological aspects of composers' rights, plagiarism, the history of honoraria for composers. An appendix gives 31 original documents in transcription.

Review by Werner Braun in *Die Musikforschung,* 17 (1964), p. 298–99.

3195. Read, Gardner. Music notation: a manual of modern practice. 2d ed. New York: Taplinger Pub. Co., 1979, c1969. 482 p.

First published in 1964.

A practitioner's guide to contemporary conventions of musical notation. Includes some discussion of advanced, radical solutions. See also Risatti, no. 533.

3196. Reader in music librarianship. Edited by Carol June Bradley. Washington, D.C.: Microcard editions books, 1973. 340 p.

A selection of articles on various aspects of music librarianship. Concluding section is a bibliography.

3197. Regeln zur Katalogisierung der in der deutschen Bücherei eingehenden Musikalien. Entwurf. Leipzig: Deutsche Bücherei, 1959. 35 p.

Cataloging rules developed for German libraries.

Review by Virginia Cunningham in *Notes,* 16 (1959), p. 567.

3198. Rothenburg, Stanley. Copyright and public performance of music. The Hague: Martinus Nijhoff, 1954. 188 p.

A survey of the current status of music copyright and performers' rights in the United States and Europe.

3199. Samuel, Harold E. "Societies, musical" In the *New Harvard dictionary of music* edited by Don M. Randel. Cambridge, Harvard Univ. Press, 1986. p. 773–78.

A list of current professional societies citing titles and dates of principal publications.

3200. Schaal, Richard. Musiker-Monogramme: ein Verzeichnis mit einem Quellen-Anhang, Kataloge und Literatur. Wilhelmshaven: Heinrichshofen, 1976. 122 p. (Taschenbücher zur Musikwissenschaft, 27)

In two parts: an index of monograms with their explanations; an index of persons with the monograms associated with them. Appendix lists library catalogs, national and international, dictionaries of anonymous and pseudonymous works, and representative source studies.

3201. Schulze, Erich. Urheberrecht in der Musik. Dritte, neubearbeitete Auflage. Berlin: Walter De Gruyter, 1965. 474 p.

First published in 1951, 4th revised edition, 1972.

A source book of information on music copyright practice. European orientation. 37 appendices of codes and other documents related to copyright. The bibliography, p. xii-xxiv, provides an international listing of performers' rights organizations.

3202. Sharp, Harold S. and Marjorie Z. Sharp, comp. Index to characters in the performing arts. Metuchen: Scarecrow Press, 1966– .
Contents: pt. 2. Operas, and musical productions; pt. 3. Ballets A-Z and symbols.

3203. Sheehy, Eugene P. "Music" in *Guide to Reference Books.* 10th ed. Chicago and London: American Library Association, 1986. 1,560 p.
An annotated bibliography of 353 titles most likely to be found in general libraries.

3204. Siddons, James. "A librarian's guide to musical Japan" in *Fontes artis musicae,* 24 (1977), p. 59–68.
A brief introduction with sections on Japanese musical life and its relation to the West, an historical survey of music collections in Japan, and useful information about Japanese books and related matters.

3205. Smiraglia, Richard P. Cataloging music: a manual for use with AACR 2 by Richard P. Smiraglia ; [edited by Edward Swanson]. 2nd ed. Lake Crystal, Minn.: Soldier Creek Press, 1986. 181 p.
An excellent guide to the cataloging of music under the new terms of Anglo American Cataloging Rules, 2nd ed. and MARC. Bibliography p. 153–160.

3206. Smiraglia, Richard P. Shelflisting music: guidelines for use with the Library of Congress Classification, M. Philadelphia: Music Library Association, 1981. 21 p. (MLA technical reports, 9)
A brief, but excellent guide to the mysteries of classification.

3207. Sopeüna Ibú́nez, Federico and Antonio Gallego Gallego. La música en el Museo del Prado. Madrid: Dirección General de Bellas Artes. Ministerio de Educación y Ciencia. Patronato Nacional de Museos, 1972. 308 p.
A splendidly illustrated book devoted to works of art in the Prado with musical symbols or interest. Bibliography.

3208. U.S. Library of Congress. Subject Cataloging Division. Classification. Class M: music and books on music. 2nd ed., with supplementary pages. Washington: 1963. 157, 101 p.
First issued in 1904, revised 1917.
Largely the work of Oscar Sonneck, this classification schedule has been accepted, with various modifications, in a great many American music libraries, chiefly in colleges and universities.
"Additions and changes to July 1962" occupy the last 101 pages.

3209. U.S. Library of Congress. Subject Cataloging Division. Music subject headings used on printed catalog cards of the Library of Congress. Washington: Govt. Printing Office, 1952. 133 p.

3210. Wallon, Simone. "Musicologie." In L. N. Malclés, *Les sources du travail bibliographique. Tome II: Bibliographies spécialisées (Sciences humaines).* Genève: E. Droz, 1952. p. 536–52.

Basic but highly selective list of music reference works, classified and well annotated.

3211. Wallon, Simone. L'allemand musicologique. Paris: Beauchesne, 1980. 161 p. (Guides musicologiques, 2)

A phrase book devoted solely to musicological terms, translating German to French.

3212. Whitfield, Jane Shaw. Songwriters' rhyming dictionary. Edited by Frances Stillman. North Hollywood: Melvin Powers, Wilshire Book Company, 1975. 283 p.

First pubished as *The improved rhyming dictionary, 1951.*

"Entries are gouped phonetically in orders of increasing syllabic complexity" [from the review by D. Martin Jenni in *Fontes artis musicae,* 23 (1976), p. 149–50. Includes many non-English words. Includes a *Brief guide to English versification.*

Index of Authors, Editors, and Reviewers

Only names of persons are indexed here; institutional names will be found in the *Index of Titles*. Citation numbers in *italics* refer to reviewers.

Index of Subjects

Libraries and collections can be located by searching under the name of their cities or towns. Institutions, including libraries, are also entered directly under their names.

Aarhus, Statsbiblioteket—Catalogs, 1890, 1892
Abbreviations—Dictionary, 403
Abel, Karl Friedrich—Catalogs, 1596
Aberdeen libraries—Catalogs, 1893
Académie Royale des Sciences, Paris —Proceedings—Index, 1152
Accademia di S. Cecilia, Biblioteca, Rome—Catalogs, 2104
Accademia Filarmonica, Bologna—Catalog, 1954–1955
Accademia Filarmonica di Verona—Catalogs, 2434, 2599
Acculturation—Bibliography, 1077
Acoustics and physics, 1470
Acoustics and physics—Dictionaries, 532
Adria, Cattedrale, Archivio, Fondo Musicale—Catalog, 1894
Aesthetics, 636
Aesthetics of music, 643
Aesthetics—Bibliography, 699
African dance—Bibliography, 900
African music—Bibliography, 900, 905, 909, 920, 930, 936, 941–942, 1170
African music—Discographies, 2884
African music—Discography, 2887, 2889
African music—Discography—Catalogs, 2890
African musicians—Bio-Bibliography, 121
African musics—Discographies, 2869
Afro-American choral music—Catalog, 1410
Afro-American composers—Bibliography, 1323
Afro-American music literature—Bibliography, 723
Afro-American music—Bibliography, 707, 723–724, 905, 1077, 1099, 1314
Afro-American music—Catalog, 2030
Afro-American music—Discography, 2892

2892
Afro-American music—Discography—Bibliography, 723
Afro-American music—Dissertations —Bibliography, 887
Afro-American musicians—Bibliography, 1077, 1123
Afro-American musicians—Bio-bibliography, 121
Afro-American musicians—Biography, 239
Afro-American sacred music—Bibliography, 1170
Afro-American singers—Discography, 2815
Afro-Americans—Music—Bibliography—Catalogs, 2265
Afro-Americans—Music—History and criticism—Bibliography, 1123
Agen, Achives Communales—Catalogs, 1895
Aiguillon, ducs d', Bibliothèque Musicale—Catalog, 1895
Alba, Casa de, 2213
Alba, Casa de, Library—Description, 2214
Alcuin Library, St. John's University, Collegeville, 2008–2009
Alcuni Cimeli Concernenti l'Arte Musicale in Firenze, 2054
D'Alessandro, Raffaele—Bio-bibliography, 1310
Allen A. Brown collection of music, Boston—Catalog, 1967
Allgemeine Musikgesellschaft (Zurich)—Catalogs, 2497
Almanacs and yearbooks, 2930, 2940, 2970
Alte Oper (Frankfurt am Main, Germany), 1649
Die Amalien-Bibliothek, Berlin—Catalog, 1932
America—History—Opera—Bibliography, 487

Saxophone music—Bibliography, 1508–1509
Schatz Collection—Catalog, 2475
Scheide, William Hinsdale—Library—Exhibitions, 2518
Schenker, Heinrich, 2454
Schenker, Heinrich—Indexes, 722
Scheurleer, D. F., Collection—Catalog, 2085
Schlager, Karl-Heinz, *Einzeldrucke vor 1800*—Indexes, 1787
Schlesinger, Maurice (publisher), 2632
Schleswig-Holstein Landesbibliothek, Kiel—Catalog, 2126
Schmidt, A. P. (firm), 2620
Schmidt, Franz, 2459
Schoeck, Othmar—Bio-bibliography, 1310
Schoenberg, Arnold—Bibliography, 1196
Schoenberg, Arnold—Catalogs, 1195, 2029
Schoenberg, Arnold—Discography, 2812
Schoenberg, Arnold—Exhibition catalogs, 2446
Schönborn-Wiesentheid, Grafen von, Collections—Catalogs, 2514
School music—Bibliography, 1008
School music—Exhibitions, 2241
Schott, Bernhard, 2699
Schott's (B.) Söhne, Mainz, 2699
Schotten (Hesse), Liebfrauenkirche—Catalogs, 2376
Schreker, Franz—Bibliography, 2455
Schubert, Franz, Lieder—Discography, 2789
Schubert, Franz Peter— Choral music—Discography, 2789
Schubert, Franz—Goethe Lieder, 1678
Schubert, Franz—Manuscripts—Catalogs, 1680, 2204
Schubert, Franz—Thematic catalogs, 1679
Schuman, William Howard—Discography, 2789
Schumann, Clara—Bibliography, 1197
Schumann, Robert—Bibliography, 1197
Schumann, Robert—Bibliography—First editions, 1681
Schumann, Robert—Catalogs, 1682–1683
Schumann, Robert—Choral Music—Discography, 2789
Schumann, Robert—Exhibition catalogs, 2149
Schumann, Robert—Lieder—Discography, 2789
Schumann, Robert—Manuscripts, etc.

—Catalog, 2505
Schütz, Heinrich—Bibliography, 1198
Schütz, Heinrich—Modern editions—Indexes, 1684
Schweizerische Landesbibliothek, Bern—Catalog, 1947
Schweizerischen Tonkünstlerverein, 1947
Schwerin, Grossherzogliche Regierungsbibliothek—Catalogs, 2377–2378
Scolopian Fathers, Archive, San Pantaleo, Rome—Catalog, 2363
Scotland—Directories, 2943
Scottish music—Bibliography, 1306
Scotto, Girolamo (firm), 2612
Sea chanties—Indexes, 1418, 1431, 1554
Selhof, Nicolas, 2519
Senefelder, Alois (Printer)—Catalogs, 2757
Senegal—Discography, 2887
Sequences—Sources—Bibliography, 1826
Serbian music literature, 1079
Serial composers, 80
Serial music—Bibliography, 863, 868
Sérieyx, Auguste—Bibliography, 2137
17th-century music, 572, 582, 3189
17th-century music—Bibliography, 669, 1737, 1772, 2320, 2394
17th-century music—Catalogs, 1764
17th-century music—Germany—Bibliography, 1741, 1768, 1836
17th-century music—Great Britain—Bibliography, 1742
17th-century music—History and criticism, 812
17th-century music—Italy—Catalogs, 1748
17th-century—Manuscripts—Catalogs, 2031
17th-century music, Italian—Bibliography, 2288
17th-century music—France—Documents, 2302
17th-century opera—Venice—Bibliography, 2429
78 rpm recordings—Catalog, 2829
Seville, Biblioteca Colombina—Catalogs, 2379–2380
Seychelles—Discography, 2887
Shakespeare, William—Musical settings—Bibliography, 1211, 1213, 1427
Shakespeare, William—Songs—Bibliography, 1427
Shakespeare—Incidental music, 1211, 1213
Sheet music, American, 2295
Sheet music, American—Catalogs,

Stanford University, Archive of Recorded Sound—Catalog, 2829

Stanford, University, Memorial Library—Catalog, 2387

Stearns Collection of Musical Instruments—Catalog, 2527

Steiner, S. A. (Printer)—Catalog, 2757

Steinert, Morris, Collection—Musical instruments—Catalog, 2583, 2585

Stellfeld, J. A., Collection—Catalog, 1898

Stereotypography, 2681

Stockholm, Musikaliska Akademien, 2388

Stockholm, Musikaliska Akademiens Bibliotek, Roman Collection—Thematic catalog, 2389

Stockholm, Musikhistorika museet, 306

Stockholm, Stiftelsen Musikkulturens Framjande—Catalogs, 2390

Stradella, Alessandro—Catalog, 1685

Stradivarius instruments—Catalog, 2605

Strasbourg, Archives de la Ville, 2391

Stratico, Michele—Catalog, 1931

Strauss, Eduard—Bibliography, 2737

Strauss, Johann, 1804-1849—Bibliography, 2736

Strauss, Johann, 1825-1899—Bibliography, 2736

Strauss, Josef—Bibliography, 2737

Strauss, Richard, Lieder—Discography, 2789

Strauss, Richard, Opera—Discography, 2789

Strauss, Richard—Bibliography, 1200, 1687, 2460

Strauss, Richard—Exhibition catalog, 2452

Strauss, Richard—Thematic catalog, 1686

Stravinsky, Igor, 1688

Stravinsky, Igor—Catalogs, 1690, 1911, 1913

Stravinsky, Igor—Discography, 2926

Stravinsky, Igor—Exhibition catalog, 1911

Stravinsky, Igor—Manuscripts—Inventory, 1689

String ensemble music—Bibliography, 1444-1445, 1447, 1452

String ensembles with winds—Bibliography, 1333

String instruments, Bowed—Appraising, 3118

String instruments—Bibliography, 972

String instruments—Catalogs, 2561, 2574

String instruments—Pedagogy, 1017, 3083

String music—Bibliography, 1444, 1446

String octets—Bibliography, 1333

String orchestra music—Great Britain —20th century—Bibliography, 1272

String quartets—Bibliography, 1333, 1443

String quartets—Thematic catalogs, 2356

String quintets—Bibliography, 1333

String sextets—Bibliography, 1333

String trios—Bibliography, 1333

String trios—Thematic catalogs, 2357

Stringed instrument makers—Germany, West, 947

Stringed instruments, 334

Stringed instruments, Bowed, 2607

Stringed instruments, Bowed—History, 355

Stringed instruments, Bowed—Terminology, 388

Stringed instruments—Construction, 315

Strong, George Templeton—Bibliography, 2142

Sturzenegger, Richard—Bio-bibliography, 1310

Stuttgart, Württembergische Landesbibliothek—Catalogs, 2392-2394

Subject headings, 3190

Succi, Emilia, Collection, 1955

Sucre, Catedral Platense, Archivo musica—Catalog, 2495

Suite, 568

Sullivan, Arthur, 1692

Sullivan, Arthur—Catalog, 1691

Sullivan, Sir Arthur—Exhibitions—Catalog, 2282

Suomalaista musiikkia, 1263

Susato, Tylman (firm)—Bibliography, 2693

Suter, Robert—Bio-bibliography, 1310

Swedish libraries—Catalogs, 1764

Swedish music literature—Bibliography, 1075

Swedish music—Bibliography, 1308-1309, 1361, 1537

Swedish music—1770-1830—Catalog, 1810

Swiss folk music—Bibliography, 901

Swiss libraries—Early music—Bibliography, 1833

Swiss libraries—18th-century music—Bibliography, 1834

Swiss music, 1310

Swiss music literature—Bibliography, 1108

Swiss music—Bibliography, 1237

Swiss music—Directories, 2997

Switzerland—Directories, 2942

Index of Titles

Including names of institutions.

Coimbra Universidade. Biblioteca, 2004–2005

Collecting musical first editions, 2703

Collectio musica: Musikbibliographie in Deutschland bis 1625, 712

Collectio Musicalis Maximilianea, 2243

"La collection Antonio Venturi, Montecatini-Terme (Pistoia), Italie, 2330

Collection Musée de l'Homme *(Paris)*, 2869

Collection musicale André Meyer, 2513

"La collection musicale Toulouse-Philidor à la Bibliothèque nationale", 2312

"A collection of oratorio libretti, 1700-1800 in the Thomas Fisher Rarebook Library, University of Toronto", 2409

"The collection of photographic reproductions at the Isham memorial Library, Harvard University", 1993

Collection Phonothèque Nationale *(Paris)*, 2870

Collections of music copied for use at Wawel, 2335

Collections of music from the surroundings of Cracow, 2335

Collector's guide to American recordings, 1895-1925, 2826

The collector's guide to the American musical theatre, 2855

The collector's twentieth-century music in the Western Hemisphere, 2909

Collectors' contact guide, 1975, 2797, 2967

Collegium Musicum *(Salem, North Carolina)*, 2365

"La collezione Corsini di antichi codici musicali e Girolamo Chiti", 2352

Collins music encyclopedia, 73

The combination violin and violoncello without accompaniment, 1336, 1449

Companion to Congregational Praise, 440

Companion to the hymnal, 451

The companion to twentieth century opera, 493

Compendium of liturgical music terms, 418

Complément à l'histoire de la musique, 541

Complete catalog of sheet music and musical works, 1209

A complete dictionary of music, 387, 401

Complete encyclopaedia of music,, 42

The complete encyclopedia of popular music and jazz, 1900-1950, 262

Componistenlexicon, 124

Composer/librettist program collection at the American Music Center, 2270

Composers in America, 225

Composers of the Americas, 182

Composers of today, 88

Composers of yesterday, 87

Composers since 1900, 88

Composers' autographs, 1807

Composers' collected editions from Europe, 1595

The Composers' Guild of Great Britain, 1272–1276

"Composite music manuscripts in facsimile", 1214, 1715, 1757

Compositeurs Canadiens Contemporains, 1073

Compositeurs contemporains: œuvres d'orchestre, 1347

Compositions, libretto and translations; supported by the National Endowment for the Arts: Composer/librettist program, 2270

Compositores argentinos, 128

Composium, a quarterly index of contemporary compositions, 1236

Composium Directory of New Music, 1236

A comprehensive bibliography of music for film and television, 743, 3107

Comprehensive catalogue of available literature for the double bass, 1461

Comprehensive cylinder record index, 2820

Comprehensive dissertation index, 1861-1972. Vol. 31 : Communications and the arts, 878

Computer applications to music and musicology: a bibliography, 3121

Computer catalog of nineteenth-century American-imprint sheet music, 2000

Computer music compositions of the United States, 1976, 1521

"Computer-Einsatz bei der Serie A/II RISM: Möglichkeiten, Bedingungen, Vorschläge", 1823

Concert and opera singers; a bibliography of biographical materials, 1138

Concert music (1630-1750), 579

Concerto themes, 521

"The concertos for clarinet", 1362

Concertos for violin and viola, a comprehensive encyclopedia, 1451

A concise biographical dictionary of singers, 102

Concise encyclopedia of Jewish music, 433